MACROECONOMICS

Understanding
the Wealth
of Nations

David Miles

Professor of Finance

The Management School

Imperial College

London

Andrew Scott

Professor of Economics

The London Business School

London

JOHN WILEY & SONS, INC.

New York / Chichester

Weinheim / Brisbane

Singapore / Toronto

ACQUISITIONS EDITOR: Leslie Kraham / Steve Hardman
ASSOCIATE DIRECTOR OF DEVELOPMENT: Johnna Barto
ASSOCIATE EDITOR: Cindy Rhoads
MARKETING MANAGER: Charity Robey
SENIOR PRODUCTION EDITOR: Valerie A. Vargas
TEXT AND COVER DESIGNER: Madelyn Lesure
PRODUCTION MANAGEMENT SERVICES: UG / GGS Information Services, Inc.
COVER PHOTO: Abacus: Taka Yamaki / Photonica
                 Globes: Wides & Holl / FPG

This book was set in 9.5/12 Ten Roman by UG / GGS Information Services, Inc. and printed and bound by Ashford Colour Press Ltd. Gosport.

This book is printed on acid-free paper. ∞

Table on inside cover: "Equity Market Capitalization (Billion U.S. $)," compiled by the Global Economic Research Team at Merrill Lynch and published by Merrill Lynch in Global Economic Trends in February 2000.

Printed in Great Britain

Reprinted July 2002, May 2003

UK ISBN 0-470-84288-1 (paperback)

BRIEF CONTENTS

CONTENTS

Why study macroeconomics? Economics is a fascinating and useful subject, dealing with issues that affect the welfare of every one of us. Why is the standard of living higher in some countries than in others? Why does unemployment sometimes rise sharply, and what can governments do about it? Why do stock market prices sometimes increase by 50% in a year, and then crash in the space of a week? Does it matter if governments run large fiscal deficits? Are countries better off fixing their foreign exchange rates, or should they let market forces determine their value? Understanding the answers to these questions is not only intellectually rewarding, but it also helps us make better commercial and financial decisions and participate more fully in democratic life.

WHY ANOTHER MACROECONOMICS TEXTBOOK?

One measure of the importance of macroeconomics is the large number of textbooks available. Writing another textbook requires some justification. Like most other texts, ours tries to help students think about economic issues like economists. *However, we differ in that we do not see this text as one stepping stone towards training the reader to be a professional economist. Instead, our aim is to deal with important issues using sophisticated economic theory, but in a manner that is accessible to someone who wishes to do only one course in macroeconomics.* We believe the best way to do this is to take real world economic issues and first describe why they matter. As a result, one of the distinguishing features of this text is an exhaustive focus on the data and the detail of the world economy—we use these facts as our entry point into the world of theory.

We want people to have a good understanding of the global economy and the way economists think about it. This text will enable the reader to think more clearly about the economy and be better able to spot the difference between good and bad arguments.[1]

Our target audience is the student who is enrolled in a self-contained one-semester course in macroeconomics and who wants to understand economic issues and debates. We assume no advanced level of maths or statistics, just a reasonable level of intelligence and an ability to follow the logic of arguments. Our teaching experience is mainly with MBA students, making the text particularly suited for such students. However, it is also suitable for undergraduates not majoring in economics but taking only a few courses in it. Our orientation recognizes how economic decisions impact the world of business.

---

[1]P.J. O'Rourke is probably not often quoted in textbooks, but we want to avoid the situation he notes in his book about economies, *Eat The Rich*, in which he says, "they [business majors] took econ and forgot everything in the textbook so they could get a job from somebody else who took econ and forgot everything in the textbook."

FEATURES OF THIS BOOK

To help reach our goals, we have planned and incorporated several features that distinguish our book from others.

LINKS THE ECONOMY TO FINANCIAL MARKETS   From our teaching experience we have found that students have a varied range of interests and are dissatisfied if they feel they do not understand the "big picture"; they want to see how different parts of the economy fit together. Therefore we deliberately tried to make this a comprehensive book about the world economy. We see it as particularly important to emphasize the links between financial markets and the rest of the economy. Understanding the links between fluctuations in bond, equity, and property markets and the wider economy is important and interesting. Often such links are neglected altogether. Macroeconomics courses sometimes avoid analyzing financial markets because students, particularly MBAs, also do another course called "Finance." But understanding the links between the wider economy and financial market is hugely important and something that too often gets lost down the cracks between courses.

HISTORICAL DATA   This text is a self-contained attempt to make students aware of how economists think, how the global economy operates, and which sets out to teach students the main results of established and recent economic theory. We do not want to train students to become professional economists, but instead enable them to understand and talk intelligently with one. To achieve this we examine lots of data and the experience of many different countries and many different time periods and utilize a variety of intellectual arguments—from formal logic to parables—which provide the intuition behind important results.

Understanding how the economy operates requires not only theory, but also knowledge about facts and data. Economic theories are not created in a vacuum but develop in response to events. As noted above, we examine data and the experience of many different countries and time periods. In fact, our textbook is packed with massive amounts of economic data covering a huge historical period (back to a million years B.C.!) and a huge range of countries (from the United States to Sierra Leone). This focus on international data from different eras is a unique feature of this text and one that reviewers have responded to very positively.

INTERNATIONAL PERSPECTIVE   As the world becomes more integrated, "globalization" is a fact of business. In macroeconomics this process is so advanced that a modern text must focus on a wide range of international experience and analyze how different countries interact within this system. More than any other textbook this one is truly about the international economy. Obviously what happens in the Untied States, Japan, and Europe is very important for the global economy, and we emphasize these countries. But the global economy is more than just these large economic nations, so we also focus much more widely. To give just a few examples from many, we consider poor growth in Africa, currency crises in Asia, and hyperinflation in Latin America and Eastern Europe.

CUTTING EDGE RESEARCH   Providing a good theoretical framework to help students understand the economic forces at work in the world is immensely valuable. Economists agree about many aspects of this framework. But this theoretical framework is evolving. And our understanding of the many complex issues that macroeconomists wrestle with is improving continuously as the result of active research. Conveying the results of this sophisticated, state of the art research is just as important as providing the basic building blocks that most textbooks focus on.

LEARNING TOOLS   Our carefully planned pedagogical structure is simple and effective. We have incorporated the following learning tools:

- Extensive use of real world data helps to motivate the use of theory, and to help understand the related models. It is crucial to know what real economies look like.
- The development of the theory is made interesting by inextricably linking the interesting examples and the models used to understand economics within the narrative (not in boxed-off applications).
- *Conceptual Questions* at the end of each chapter enable students to extend their understanding of the key concepts by trying to apply them to the real world.
- *Analytical Questions* at the end of each chapter test understanding of theories and models by posing numerical problems for students to solve and give additional scenarios to explore with the models provided.
- Web site support. The macroeconomic environment is a fast-moving one. Through our associated Web site (http://www.wiley.com/college/miles) we offer continual updates of all the charts in this textbook as well as additional material on new events that crop up between this and future editions. This makes both the textbook and students' understanding of the world economy a truly dynamic experience. The Web site also contains many links to useful macroeconomic and finance sites for students to explore.

OUR APPROACH TO TEACHING ECONOMICS

Students come to economics with high expectations. Appreciating the subject as relevant, they hope they will find answers to important questions. But wanting answers can stand in the way of understanding. The most useful thing that any economics course can do is to help students work out *how to analyze* an issue rather than just give the answer to any one particular question.

LOGICAL FRAMEWORK   Economists are good at thinking logically and consistently about real-world issues because they follow good rules. By adopting these rules of thinking we are more likely to understand the forces at work in the economy—and less likely to believe erroneous commonplaces that are often quoted in political or business discussions. It is worth investing in learning these rules.

But here we run into a problem between the expectations of students, particularly those who are not economics majors, and the goals of faculty. For very good reasons instructors often want to teach students the tools of the trade. This can mean setting up formal (often mathematical) models as the first and most natural way of analyzing any economic issue. Formal models are very useful because they encourage the good rules of thinking that economists value—rules like "be consistent" and "make explicit the assumptions that underpin an argument." But students—particularly MBA students—can be put off by what they see as abstract, mathematical reasoning that seems to take them away from the important issues rather than help them understand the world in which they live.

Our aim in this book is to teach the logical framework of macroeconomics—the rules of the game or the tools of the trade—but in a way that is accessible to a large number of students who want to understand the important, real-world forces that drew them to the subject.

Unfortunately, the teaching of these rules often becomes the foremost part of many textbooks and the important real-world questions get pushed to the background. A lot of time is spent developing models, and then a lot of time is spent doing exercises with models. This approach has two problems—first, it delays students grappling with real issues since they need to master the models first; second, sophisticated issues require complex and subtle models. The first set of models students are taught are not rich enough to deal with these complex issues. The second set of models, for example, those introduced in an intermediate text, can deal with these topics but only at the cost of rather incredible assumptions. It is often only at the graduate or doctoral level that the modeling framework students are given is rich enough to deal with demanding economic topics. But many students—and *most* MBA students—will do just one course in economics. They do not want to be fully trained as an economist before they can analyze intelligently economic issues.

THEORY MATTERS   Our strategy in this book is to use whatever tools of reasoning best help understand an economic issue. Sometimes the best tool is a graph; sometimes it is an analogy; sometimes it is a few simple equations. Often a good strategy is the *reductio ad absurdum*: we take what sounds like a perfectly sensible explanation of some phenomenon and show that if it were valid its consistent application in similar circumstances would generate outcomes that are obviously absurd.

In explaining why certain economic events occurred in the past, or in analyzing contemporary economic issues, we utilize logical economic thinking and modeling. Using this approach helps teach the reader how economists develop and test an idea. By taking real-world factual examples we also offer a detailed analysis of how actual economies operate. In other words, we use data and facts to provide the flesh and blood of our textbook but the skeleton of the book is constructed around economic theories. The real-world examples we focus on are chosen to illustrate an important idea—such as the diminishing marginal product of capital or the possibility of self-fulfilling banking panics.

Models are often introduced at first implicitly and only after the real-world problem of interest has been discussed. A combination of verbal, graphical and sometimes algebraic development of the model is then used to make sense of the issue and the data.

As an example, consider a very powerful idea in economics: the fallacy of composition. This is the idea that what is true at the individual level is no longer valid once everyone else's response is taken account of. The idea is easy to get across—standing on one's seat at the football game gets you a better view so long as no-one else does.

But once everyone is standing on his or her seat the outcome is much worse. No one sees any better and everyone is uncomfortable. But such a situation might persist because once everyone is standing up no one has an incentive to sit down. Through simple examples like this we can introduce the notion of an equilibrium and also show that we can have equilibria where everyone loses out; standing up can be a bad equilibrium. (Some people will recognize that standing up at the football game is a Nash equilibrium.)

THE ROLE OF MODELS   While modeling is not at the forefront of our approach, we do not avoid formal modeling. In fact we introduce more models—and more modeling concepts and tools—than is usual in a book suitable for MBA students. What we frequently do is to introduce some subtle concepts that have been developed by economists over the past few decades and which we believe are essential to a real understanding of macroeconomic and financial issues. So in this book we will often use the concept of rational expectations; we will illustrate important ideas in dynamic programming; we explain and illustrate the law of iterated expectations; we explore notions of time consistency and of incentive compatibility; we show how multiple equilibria can arise in many markets; we analyze unstable equilibria and show how small initial shocks can sometimes generate huge long-run effects.

Often the key ideas can be explained with relatively simple examples. "Backward induction applied to solving dynamic programs" could be a chapter heading from a graduate textbook on mathematical techniques of optimization. For us it a useful idea in working out how stock markets might work or in explaining the level of saving or consumption or in working out the impact of a government borrowing money to finance a tax cut. And it is an idea that can be explained in an intuitive way.

Consider the paradox of the surprise test . . .

The Surprise Test . . .

In the first lecture of "Macroeconomics and Finance," a course that lasts 13 weeks, the professor announces that he will spring a surprise test in one of the remaining 12 lectures before the end of the semester. The students look suitably depressed until one announces that no such test is possible. The lecturer is annoyed by such arrogance and asks the student to justify her assertion. Here is what she said:

> *Suppose you had not sprung the test by the end of the penultimate lecture (in week 12); then the test would have to come in week 13. But the test would then not be a surprise when it was announced at the start of the last lecture. So if it is to be a surprise the test has to come before the end of the penultimate lecture. But if the test has to come before the end of lecture 12, then in order for it be a surprise it cannot be left until lecture 12. If it were, then by the end of lecture 11 it would be no surprise when the test was coming. So now the test has to be before the end of lecture 11. But then the same argument applies again and the test has to come before the end of lecture 10. But then. . . . So you see that it is already too late to have a surprise test.*

The professor immediately wrote a reference to his ex-colleague who had defected from the academic world to an investment bank some years earlier and the smart student was offered a job at an illustrious Wall Street firm. The student went on to become chief executive and lived in unimaginable splendor, thus illustrating the advantages of solving dynamic programming problems from the end backwards using inductive arguments.

STRUCTURE OF THE BOOK

We think the text is comprehensive and organized in a way that makes it flexible for a range of different courses.

INTRODUCTION (CHAPTERS 1–3)   This introductory part describes what macroeconomics is about and why students should study it. It introduces key concepts—equilibrium, aggregate output, total demand, national income identities, and the production function—and explains why they are important and how they are measured in the real world. The final chapter of this section provides a condensed theoretical overview of the entire book.

ECONOMIC GROWTH AND THE SUPPLY SIDE (CHAPTERS 4–9)   In this part of the book we focus on the long-run forces that shape the evolution of economies over decades. We seek to understand why most countries have become wealthier over time and also why some countries are richer than others. Here we focus on the ability of society to produce output—the *supply* side of the economy. As well as considering long-run growth, we also consider what type of output a society produces through examining international trade.

MONEY AND TAXES (CHAPTERS 10–12)   This part considers the long-run framework though which governments affect the economy. We consider the reasons for government involvement in the economy and examine how governments work in practice. We examine the long-run relationships that determine the evolution of public finances and examine how taxes and expenditure should be set. We also consider the nominal side of the economy—the part of the economy that determines the level of prices—and how this is influenced by government policy.

BUSINESS CYCLES AND ECONOMIC POLICY (CHAPTERS 13–17)   Having examined the long-run determinants of economic behavior we change our focus in this part by analyzing medium-term business cycle fluctuations. We document the nature of these fluctuations, what causes them, and whether they are costly for society. We examine how business cycles are influenced by fluctuations in consumption and investment and consider in detail what drives these important variables. Finally, we consider in detail whether the government can help stabilize business cycles and review current practice in fiscal and monetary policy.

EXCHANGE RATES AND GLOBAL CAPITAL MARKETS (CHAPTERS 18–20)   The increasingly integrated nature of the world economy makes exchange rates crucial. Changes in exchange rates can severely affect the profitability of firms and can completely derail government policy. We provide in extensive detail a comprehensive analysis of what determines exchange rates and how exchange rates affect the economy. This analysis also involves examining how global capital markets work and whether the vast flows of finance from one country to another are a good or a bad thing.

ASSET MARKETS AND THE FINANCIAL SECTOR (CHAPTERS 21–24)   One of the main media interests in macroeconomics is in understanding why financial markets show such pronounced fluctuations and why in turn these shifts cause business cycle fluctuations. In the final part of the book we consider the operation of real estate, equities, bonds, and banking markets and their importance in influencing macroeconomic behavior.

TEACHING FROM THIS BOOK

Different schools tend to teach rather different types of macroeconomics course. We think this is a flexible and comprehensive book and that it can be used to teach a range of different courses. Instructors can choose whatever sequence of topics they prefer, but below we outline 3 different 10-topic courses that could be taught.

MACROECONOMICS—UNDERSTANDING THE GLOBAL ECONOMY   A comprehensive course covering growth, business cycles, exchange rates, stabilization policy, and trade.

> Lecture 1—Data and Definitions, Chapters 1–3
> Lecture 2—Capital Accumulation and Endogenous Growth, Chapters 4, 5, and 7
> Lecture 3—Technological Progress, Chapter 6
> Lecture 4—Labor Markets, Chapter 8
> Lecture 5—Trade, Chapter 9
> Lecture 6—Fiscal Policy, Chapter 11
> Lecture 7—Money and Inflation, Chapter 12
> Lecture 8—Exchange Rates, Chapters 18–20
> Lecture 9—Business Cycles, Chapter 15
> Lecture 10—Stabilization Policy, Chapters 16–17

MACROECONOMICS: BUSINESS CYCLES AND INTERNATIONAL MACROECONOMICS   A course focusing on business cycles and the international economy but excluding the supply side issues of growth, labor markets, and trade

> Lecture 1—Data and Definitions, Chapters 1–3
> Lecture 2—Fiscal Policy, Chapter 11
> Lecture 3—Money and Inflation, Chapter 12
> Lecture 4—Consumption and Investment, Chapters 13 and 14
> Lecture 5—Business Cycles, Chapter 15
> Lecture 6—Stabilization Policy, Chapter 16
> Lecture 7—Monetary Policy, Chapter 17
> Lecture 8—Exchange Rates: Prices and Real Exchange Rates, Chapter 18
> Lecture 9—Exchange Rates: Asset Markets, Chapter 19
> Lecture 10—Global Capital Markets, Chapter 20

MACROECONOMICS AND FINANCE   A course designed to help students understand relationships between financial markets and the wider economy.

Lecture 1—Data and Definitions, Chapters 1–3
Lecture 2—Fiscal Policy and Debt, Chapter 11
Lecture 3—Money and Inflation, Chapter 12
Lecture 4—Business Cycles and Stabilization Policy, Chapters 16–17
Lecture 5—Exchange Rates, Chapters 18–19
Lecture 6—Equity Markets, Chapter 21
Lecture 7—Bond Markets, Chapter 22
Lecture 8—Real Estate, Chapter 23
Lecture 9—Banking Sector, Chapter 24
Lecture 10—Global Capital Markets, Chapter 20

(A 12-lecture course could be taught by adding Economic Growth and teaching Chapters 4–7.)

SUPPLEMENTARY MATERIALS

• STUDY GUIDE   Includes some modeling questions based around the models developed in each chapter. But unlike the Study Guides for other texts, this one includes more about manipulating existing data and it discusses real-world issues as they apply to the content of the text. The modeling questions are supplemented with various data (and Web links), and students are asked to calculate or analyze various things that relate to the text using this data.

• INSTRUCTORS MANUAL   Provides guidance to instructors on how best to use the textbook, through its chapter summaries, learning objectives, teaching suggestions, additional examples, answers to end-of-chapter exercises, and additional problems and solutions.

• TESTBANK   An extensive set of multiple choice questions relating to the practice topics and concepts within the text.

• ELECTRONIC POWERPOINT SLIDES   A set of over a 1,000 PowerPoint slides is available for use by instructors, containing all charts, figures, and tables in this textbook as well as some additional material, such as key topics and concepts for each chapter. These slides are updated frequently so that the instructor and student always have access to the most recent data.

• WEB SITE   (http://www.wiley.com/college/miles) A robust Web site provides support for students and instructors. Students are able to take practice tests on-line and assess their understanding of core concepts within the text. Articles with discussion questions are also available from several of the most widely read financial news sources. And all of the instructor's teaching aids are provided by chapter electronically within a password-protected environment.

ACKNOWLEDGMENTS

When we embarked on writing this textbook we envisaged a lonely task with many hours spent in front of a computer screen. We were wrong on both counts—we didn't spend many hours but many, many, many hours writing the book and we were not lonely but had the input and wisdom of a huge range of talented individuals who offered much support, advice, and encouragement. A very large number of people at John Wiley deserve our thanks. We are much indebted to Steve Hardman, who originated discussions with us about producing the book and who stood by and helped us through a very long development process. Leslie Kraham and Cindy Rhoads politely reminded us of the importance of deadlines and provided us with an insight into the U.S. market and coordinated a large and demanding manuscript. Gerald Lombardi edited the text, patiently amended our Queen's English, and improved beyond measure the flow of the text. Johnna Barto was a source of advice and wisdom on many development matters. Susan Elbe and Joe Heider combined great enthusiasm for the project with their great experience of making books that work.

We owe a particular debt to our colleagues at Imperial College and the London Business School who have helped us develop our ideas of how to teach macroeconomics and finance to non-economists. We thank in particular Jean Imbs, Morten Ravn and Oren Sussman who instigated some of the themes and figures that appear in this text. We have also been fortunate to benefit within our institutions from first-rate administrative support—to Bernadette Courtney and Roma van Dam, we offer heartfelt thanks.

We have also benefited from extensive comments on successive drafts from the following individuals. We can only hope that the time they kindly spent away from their own research and teaching in aiding us to improve the manuscript is well rewarded by the end product.

Krishna Akkina, *Kansas State University*
Samuel Andoh, *Southern Connecticut University*
Ivo Arnold, *Nijenrode University*
Charles Bean, *London School of Economics*
Raford Boddy, *San Diego University*
Phil Bowers, *University of Edinburgh*
Thomas Cate, *Northern Kentucky University*
Grabriele Camera, *Purdue University*
Steven Cunningham, *University of Connecticut*
David N. DeJong, *University of Pittsburgh*
Raphael DiTella, *Harvard Business School*
Joseph Eisenhauer, *Canisius College-Buffalo*
Lynne Evans, *University of Durham*
Jean Fan, *Xavier University, Cincinnati*
Antonio Fatas, *INSEAD*
Adrien Fleiddig, *California State University-Fullerton*

Jim Fralick, *Syracuse University*
Lynn Geiger, *Eastern College*
Fred R. Glahe, *University of Colorado*
John Glen, *Cranfield School of Management*
Gregory Hess, *Oberlin College*
Owen Irvine, *Michigan State University*
Sherry L. Jarrell, *Wake Forest University, Babcock Graduate School of Management*
Peter Jonsson, *Fayetteville State University*
Judith Jordan, *University of the West of England*
Tim D. Kane, *University of Texas-Tyler*
Ben Knight, *University of Warwick*
Jim Knudsen, *Creighton University*
William E. Laird, *Florida State University*
Stefanie Lenway, *University of Minnesota, Carlson School of Management*
Thomas Lubik, *The Johns Hopkins University*

Kent Matthews, *University of Wales, Cardiff*

B. Starr McMullen, *Oregon State University*

Patrick McMurry, *Missouri Western State College*

Mico Mrkaic, *Duke University*

Akurlie Nyctcpc-Coo, *University of Wisconsin-La Crosse*

Allen Parkman, *University of New Mexico*

Daniel Pavsek, *Shenandoah University*

Chung Pham, *Professor Emeritus of Economics at University of New Mexico*

Mark Pingle, *University of Nevada*

Stephen Regan, *Cranfield School of Management*

Mary S. Schranz, *University of Wisconsin-Madison*

Carole Scott, *State University of West Georgia*

Harry Singh, *Grand Valley State University*

Case Sprenkle, *University of Illinois-Champaign-Urbana*

Raymond Strangways, *Old Dominion University*

Mark Strazicich, *University of Central Florida*

Oren Sussman, *University of Oxford*

Dominic Swords, *Henley Management College*

Randolph Tan, *Nanyang Technological University*

Peter Taylor, *University of the West of England*

Paul Wachtel, *New York University, Stern School of Business*

William Weirick, *University of Louisiana*

Chunchi Wu, *Syracuse University*

Chi-Wa Yuen, *University of Hong Kong*

Eric Zivot, *University of Washington*

It is commonplace to end a preface by thanking loved ones who put up with a lot while the book was being written and without whom etc. But cliches often reflect reality and without the support and love of Faye and Lorraine—well you know the rest. To Oscar and Georgia, and Helena, Louis and Kit go thanks for their continued reminders that there are more important things than even macroeconomics.

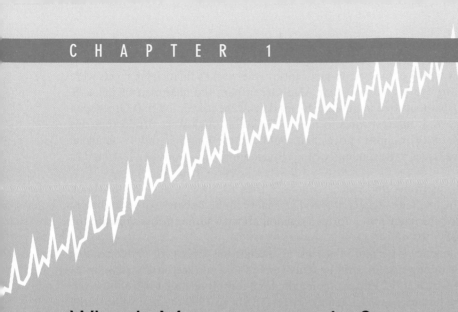

What Is Macroeconomics?

Overview

In this chapter we show you what macroeconomics is about by looking at some of the big questions that macroeconomists ask: Why do some countries enjoy a standard of living many times greater than others? What impact do changes in interest rates have upon the economy? How does growth in productivity evolve over time? We draw out what is distinctive about macroeconomics and contrast it with microeconomics, and illustrate this distinction by focusing on the types of risk that affect companies.

1.1 What Is Macroeconomics About?

Most books begin by defining their subject. But definitions are tricky and often are not the best way to introduce a subject. Imagine trying to interest people in tennis by defining what tennis is and describing how it is played. A better solution would be to let them watch a match or try to play themselves. This approach also applies to macroeconomics. Understanding how the economy works helps us interpret the past; it makes our world more comprehensible; and it helps us to think intelligently about the future. Because of this a knowledge of macroeconomics has clear commercial implications. However, we think offering a sophisticated definition of macroeconomics is a poor way to convince you of these things. To demonstrate its relevance, we prefer to illustrate the types of issues macroeconomics deals with.

In the first few weeks of the twenty-first century, the world's financial markets were anxiously examining every comment that Alan Greenspan, the chairman of the U.S. Federal Reserve Board, uttered in public. The markets were concerned that Greenspan was going to raise U.S. interest rates to prevent inflation; they were afraid that this would be bad for stock (or equity) prices and could end the long rise in U.S. financial asset values. These issues raise a number of macroeconomic questions as illustrated in Figure 1.1.

These are all questions that macroeconomics tries to answer, and this textbook should give you the intellectual apparatus to participate in the debate. After reading it, you will be able to offer your own informed opinion about whether Greenspan did the right thing in 2000.[1]

But macroeconomics is far more than just an intellectual toolkit for understanding the business pages of newspapers and the daily rumors that surface on TV news wires or the Internet. It is also about understanding the long-term forces that drive the economy and shape the business environment. Between 1870 and 1999 the real value of the output of goods and services produced *per person* in the United States increased more than ninefold. Over this same period, the U.S. population increased more than six-fold, and the total amount of goods and services produced in the United States increased by nearly 6000%. Not all countries have grown so swiftly. For example, over the same period, output per person in the Australian economy increased only slightly more than fourfold. Had Australia grown at the same rate as the United States over this period, it would have produced enough extra output to roughly double the standard of living for *every* man, woman, and child in the country. Politicians out for votes can only dream of that kind of largesse.

Compared to many other countries, Australia's performance was good. In 1913 the output produced per person in the Bangladesh economy was worth roughly $617

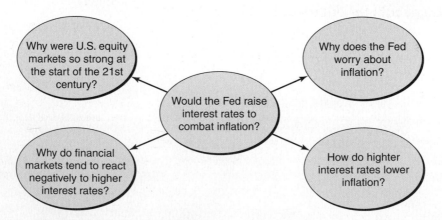

FIGURE 1.1 **Macroeconomic questions.**

[1]The Fed increased interest rates gradually over the course of 2000 by just over 1%. At the start of 2001 this process was dramatically reversed.

and by 1992 this total had risen to only $720.[2] By contrast, over this period the value of the output produced per person in Japan had increased from $1,334 (around three times the Bangladeshi level) to $19,425 (almost 30 times Bangladeshi output) (Figure 1.2). These calculations show why a leading macroeconomist and Nobel prizewinner says that, "Once one starts to think [about questions of economic growth] it is hard to think about anything else."[3]

Why have some countries grown so fast while others have stagnated? Can government policy boost a country's growth rate? These questions force us to examine key economic issues—the role of investment in machines and infrastructure (e.g., roads) in fostering growth, the importance of education and skills, and the critical role of technological progress (e.g., inventions). These are important issues, both for individual firms and for society. These issues are as relevant to households and businesses as the short-term considerations about what the U.S. Federal Reserve Board will do with interest rates; in fact they are probably much more important.

The above examples (the conduct of monetary policy and the sources of overall economic growth) suggest that macroeconomics is about the economy as a whole. In part this is correct: macroeconomics does focus on how the whole economy evolves over time rather than on any one sector, region, or firm. Yet macroeconomics also considers the important issues from the perspective of the firm and/or the individual consumer. It is the overall, or *aggregate*, implications of tens of thousands of *individual* decisions that companies and households make that generates the macroeconomic outcomes.

Throughout this book we shall consider many such macroeconomic issues from the perspective of firms, governments, and society. We will approach issues by analyzing

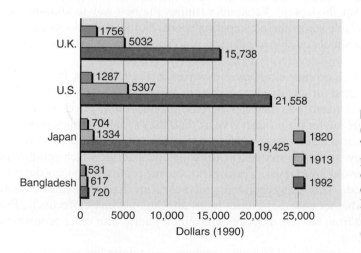

FIGURE 1.2 **Output difference over the long term.** The average level of output per person differs dramatically across countries. *Source*: Maddison, *Monitoring the World Economy 1820–1992* (OECD, Paris, 1995).

---

[2]These figures are quoted in terms of what are called "constant prices." We shall go into more detail about this in the next chapter, but essentially it means that everything is measured in terms of what a dollar could buy in the United States in 1985. We should also stress that cross-country comparisons of historical data are not among the most reliable aspects of economic measurement.

[3]Lucas, "On the Mechanics of Economic Development," *Journal of Monetary Economics* (1988).

the aggregate implications of the decisions many firms and consumers make, decisions that are generally interdependent.

1.2 But What about That Definition?

These examples have given you some ideas about the issues macroeconomics addresses, and they may even have aroused your interest in the subject. We hope so, because at this point we need to give you a more detailed insight into macroeconomics and its relationship with its sister discipline, microeconomics. In other words, it is time to turn to definitions.

> **DEFINITION**
>
> **Economics** is the study of the allocation of scarce resources.

The basic idea is simple: each of us has an almost inexhaustible list of desires, but most of us have a finite amount of money (or, more generally, resources) with which to satisfy these desires. The British economist Adam Smith, whose "Wealth of Nations" was arguably the first seminal treatise on economics (published in 1776), famously phrased this discussion in terms of whether a country should produce guns or butter. Today the choice is between more esoteric items—we all might like to buy a new top of the line laptop *and* regularly eat steak or lobster for lunch, but household finances dictate one or the other (and you had better get used to the crummy sandwich from the snack bar if you go for the laptop). Economics studies the best way to allocate the resources that are available across these competing needs. Not all these needs can be satisfied, but economics should be able to help you (and society) meet as many of them as possible.

A key way in which economies allocate resources is through prices. Prices tell producers what the demand for a particular product is—if prices are high, then producers know the good is in demand, and they can increase production. If prices are low, producers know that demand for the product is weak, and they should cut back production. Thus the market ensures that society produces more of the goods that people want and less of those that they do not. By studying prices consumers decide which goods to purchase and which to avoid; by examining prices and chasing profits, producers determine which goods to provide. This is why economics focuses so much on the determination of market prices and whether how they are set helps allocate resources effectively. Prices are not just dropped from heaven; they are determined jointly with other economic decisions at the firm level.

But what is *macro*economics? Broadly speaking, economics has two components: microeconomics and macroeconomics (Figure 1.3). Essentially microeconomics examines how individual units, whether they be consumers or firms, decide how to allocate resources and whether those decisions are desirable. Macroeconomics studies the economy as a whole; it looks at the aggregate outcomes of all the decisions that consumers,

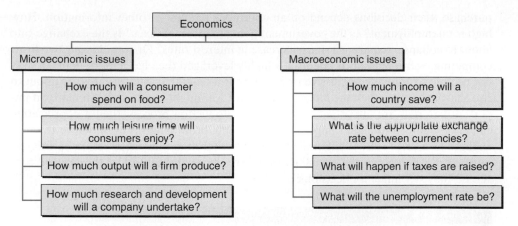

FIGURE 1.3 **Macroeconomic and microeconomic issues.** Macroeconomics focuses on aggregate outcome; microeconomics looks at individual markets, firms, or households.

firms, and the government make in an economy. Microeconomics is about how consumers and firms allocate resources. By contrast macroeconomics is about the aggregate variables—for example, the overall levels of output, consumption, employment, and prices—and how they move over time and between countries.

In terms of prices, microeconomics focuses on, for instance, the price of a particular firm's product, whereas macroeconomics focuses on the exchange rate (the price of one country's money in terms of that of another country) or the interest rate (the price of spending today rather than tomorrow).

1.3 The Difference between Macro and Microeconomics

These distinctions show that a gray area exists between micro and macroeconomics that relates to aggregation—at what point do the actions of a number of firms cease to be a microeconomic issue and become a macroeconomic issue? To answer that question, let's think of another way of outlining the differences between microeconomics and macroeconomics. In microeconomics the focus is on a small group of agents, say a group of consumers or two firms battling over a particular market. In this case economists pay a great deal of attention to the behavior of the agents the model is focusing on. They make assumptions about what consumers want or how much they have to spend, or about whether the two firms are competing over prices or market share, and whether one firm is playing an aggressive strategy, and so on. The result is a detailed analysis of what particular firms or consumers should do in a given situation.

However, this microeconomic analysis does *not* explain what is happening in the wider economic environment. Think about consumers' choice of what goods to consume. In addition to consumers' own income and the price of the goods they wish to purchase, their decisions depend on an enormous amount of other information. How high is unemployment? Is the government going to increase taxes? Is the exchange rate about to collapse, requiring a sharp increase in interest rates? Or consider our two firms competing over a market. If one firm is highly leveraged (i.e., has a lot of debt), it may not be able to adopt an aggressive price stance if it fears that interest rates are about to rise sharply because then the losses from a price war might bankrupt it. Similarly, if imported materials are important for the firm's production process, then a depreciating currency will lead to higher import costs, reducing profit margins even before the firm engages in a price war. While none of these background influences—shifts in interest rates or movements in the exchange rate—are under the control of the firm or consumer, they still influence decisions.

KEY POINT
Macroeconomics analyzes the backdrop of economic conditions against which companies and households make decisions.

Microeconomics tends to focus on variables that an individual or firm can influence—for example, how much labor to offer, what prices to set, and how much to produce; macroeconomics focuses on employment, prices, and output in the whole economy. However, the whole economy represents the outcome of millions of individual decisions that millions of firms and consumers make. Therefore, while each particular firm does not significantly affect inflation or the growth of output in the whole economy, the economic performance of an economy does reflect the overall decisions firms make. For instance, the chairman of the U.S. Federal Reserve will be concerned about rising inflation and consider the need to raise interest rates. No doubt many highly leveraged firms would rather the Federal Reserve did not raise rates. But the inflation rate determines whether interest rates increase, and the inflation rate reflects the number of firms that are increasing prices and the amount by which each firm is raising prices. In other words, all the individual pricing decisions that millions of firms make determines the macroeconomic environment. While microeconomics is mainly concerned with studying in detail the decisions of a few agents, taking as given the basic economic backdrop, macroeconomics is about studying how the decisions of all the agents who make up the economy create this backdrop.

Consider, for instance, the issue of whether a firm should adopt the latest developments in information technology (IT), which promise to increase labor productivity by, say, 20%. A microeconomic analysis of this topic would focus mainly on the costs the firm faces in adopting this technology and the likely productivity and profit gains that it would create. Macroeconomics would consider this IT innovation in the context of the whole economy. In particular, it would examine how if *many* firms were adopting this technology, then costs in the whole economy would fall, and the demand for skilled labor would rise. Combined with the resulting increase in labor productivity, this would lead to an increase in wages and the firm's wage bill. It might also shift demand away from unskilled towards skilled workers, causing the composition of unemployment and relative wages to change. This example reveals the differences between the two approaches. The microeconomic analysis is one where the firm *alone* is contemplating adopting a new technology, and the emphasis is on the firm's pricing and employment decisions, probably holding wages fixed. In other words, the analysis assumes that the firm's decisions do not influence the background economic environment. In contrast, the macroeconomic analysis examines the consequences when *many* firms implement the new technology and investigates how this affects economy-wide output, wages, and unemployment. Both forms of analysis have a role to play, and which is more appropriate depends on the issue to be analyzed and the question that needs answering.

1.4 Why Should People Interested in Business Study Macroeconomics?

When one of us first agreed to teach at a business school, an eminent microeconomic theorist told him that macroeconomics should not be taught to MBA students. Of course, the theorist argued that microeconomics, with its detailed focus on the behavior of individual firms, should be compulsory for students. But the only macroeconomic issue business people needed to know, he argued, was what the economy would be doing over the next few years. They could best find this out by buying a macroeconomic forecast. Taking a course in macroeconomics was a waste of time.

The excellent wines at dinner no doubt fueled such bold statements, but it seems too good a challenge to refuse, so here is why we think students interested in business need to understand macroeconomics.

UNDERSTANDING ECONOMIC POLICY ISSUES BETTER

The one argument the critical microeconomist would accept for teaching macroeconomics to students interested in business was that it enabled them to sound knowledgeable about current affairs at social events—the intellectual equivalent of not sounding dumb when being interviewed on CNN. But going to college—and certainly studying for an MBA or other degree—seems an expensive way to gain such an ability; it would be much cheaper to buy *The Economist*.

But macroeconomics is much more than just an analysis of what the chairman of the Federal Reserve says each day. And educating business people to talk knowledgeably about macroeconomics is not as trivial as this discussion makes it appear. Chief executives of large companies, politicians, or top government workers are expected to participate in the debate about economic policy (often on CNN!). Careless or poorly thought out comments can have unfortunate repercussions for a firm or a government and can damage people's reputations. When people become successful in a company, they show that they have good knowledge about their own market and are then expected to show similar knowledge about other markets and the whole economy. It can be unfortunate if they demonstrate that they know little beyond their own niche.

Aside from contributing to the policy debate, senior management in any international company also needs to understand the institutional structure of the global economy. Government policy and the structure of government provide the framework of rules within which firms operate. Any firm that wants to succeed must understand the behavior of other organizations that affect its market. Viewed in this light, firms are involved in a game in which the prizes are profits. The other players in the game include governments (whether it be a national government or an international organization like the International Monetary Fund) and other firms. In Chapter 9 we will discuss free trade and the battle between Airbus of Europe and Boeing of the United States. For each firm, success in the marketplace requires not just understanding the products and strategy of the opposition but also the policy stance of European and American governments as well as the attitude of international organizations like the World Trade Organization. Understanding the interests and behavior of the government and its policies is therefore an important part of corporate strategy, and this requires a good understanding of macroeconomics.

THE RELATIVE SIGNIFICANCE OF AGGREGATE AND FIRM-SPECIFIC UNCERTAINTY

Understanding macroeconomics is not simply a useful aspect of the PR role of the business person; nor is it solely related to better understanding government policy. The health of a company depends on the macroeconomy. Macroeconomic events like changes in interest rates, fluctuations in exchange rates, and shifts in the overall level of stock market prices affect individual companies. More local events—like a rise in the wages of the company's workforce or the bankruptcy of a competitor—are also important. Both types of factors—the localized and the general—are uncertain. Economists distinguish between two types of uncertainty: aggregate and idiosyncratic. Aggregate uncertainty affects all firms and sectors in the economy; idiosyncratic uncertainty affects only a few firms or industries. Macroeconomics is essentially about the aggregate sources of uncertainty that affect firms.

But which source of uncertainty is more important for corporate health—idiosyncratic or aggregate? Evidence (covering firms and consumers) shows that the biggest source of uncertainty in the short term for most firms is the idiosyncratic component. All firms should worry about loss through illness of key personnel, major clients can-

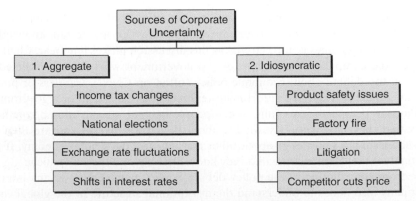

F I G U R E 1 . 4 **Macroeconomic and microeconomic uncertainty.** Risks can be idiosyncratic, specific to the individual, or aggregate, common to everyone.

celling contracts, loss through litigation or fire and theft, and so forth. However, while idiosyncratic shocks are a dominant influence on the typical firm, the evidence also suggests that on average around 10% of the short-term risk that a company faces is of an aggregate nature. For households, or individuals, idiosyncratic risk is also generally more important than systematic (or aggregate) uncertainty. Whether you pass an exam; how well you get along with your first boss; whether you avoid serious illness in your forties and fifties—for most people these things are likely to be more important for their standard of living over their lifetime than fluctuations in aggregate output or in inflation.

Consider the case of unemployment. In recessions unemployment rises, but not everyone becomes unemployed—many people also find jobs and many firms are hiring. Most people carry on with their regular job even through the worst recessions. Figure 1.5 shows employment trends in U.S. manufacturing over a volatile 13-year period (1973–1986). It shows that every year U.S. manufacturing had large inflows into work (job creation) and into unemployment (job destruction). For instance, 1975 was a recession year in the United States and 17% of manufacturing jobs were lost. However, even during these enormous layoffs, around 7% more new jobs were being created. Exactly what happens to unemployment depends on whether the flow into work is larger than the flow of people moving out of work. For instance, in 1975 unemployment increased sharply because the job destruction rate was more than twice the job creation rate.

Therefore, the aggregate measure of unemployment, while important, gives an incomplete picture of what is happening to individuals in the labor market. Idiosyncratic factors are significant—even during the worst recession some firms will be doing well (bankruptcy administrators?) and hiring workers; it is just that more firms are doing badly. In other words, business cycle peaks and troughs represent what is happening to most firms, but because idiosyncratic factors are important, even in the worse recessions, many firms will be thriving. But it is much harder for a firm to succeed in a recession when the overall business climate is poor.

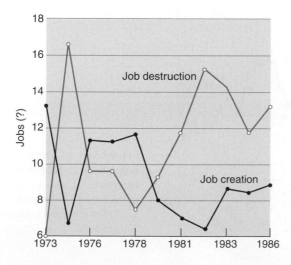

FIGURE 1.5 **Job creation and job destruction in U.S. manufacturing.** In any one year many new jobs are created and many existing jobs are lost. *Source*: Davis and Haltiwanger, *Macroeconomics Annual,* Cambridge, Mass: MIT Press (NBER, 1990).

This does not mean macroeconomics is unimportant to business. Even if aggregate uncertainty only generates 10% of a company's short-term risk, 10% is still a lot of uncertainty and can dramatically affect corporate well being. For instance, in the early 1980s, and again in the early 1990s, the Netherlands experienced a recession where high interest rates combined with extensive corporate debts led (with a lag of a few years) to many corporate bankruptcies. As Figure 1.6 illustrates, these insolvencies can largely be accounted for by aggregate factors.

Aggregate uncertainty is also important because it generates a type of risk that, by definition, all firms and consumers share. Most people today are unlikely to spend their entire career within one firm, or even in one industry; the only source of uncertainty that is fully portable between jobs in different industries is aggregate uncertainty. Understanding macroeconomic uncertainty will therefore prove useful to all future employers and in all future occupations. We think that the knowledge obtained in this course will be relevant throughout your life.

Aggregate uncertainty is more important the more diversified a firm's activities are. A large firm diversified across several markets finds aggregate uncertainty relatively more important because the firm is less dependent on any one product or market. Take, for instance, News International, a highly diversified organization both in terms of its international spread and the media with which it is involved. While profits might be harmed by, say, a mechanical shutdown in one of its plants, the health of the whole company would not be seriously affected. But in the early 1990s, rising interest rates in the world economy combined with a big outstanding debt to generate a substantial negative impact on News International's cash flow. The bigger the firm, the more important macroeconomic risks are relative to idiosyncratic factors. For *all* firms, the macroeconomy contributes to business volatility, but for large firms like News International, it is a *major* factor.

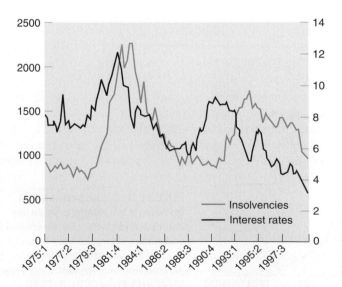

FIGURE 1.6 **Interest rates and bankrupties in the Netherlands.** Interest rates have a major impact on the number of bankruptcies. *Source:* Statistics Netherlands.

CHOOSING PRODUCTION LOCATION

Understanding macroeconomic forces is also useful in another way to large international firms. Over the last few decades, many countries have rejected central planning in favor of more market-based economies. Lack of domestic funds to finance investment has often meant that the firms in these formerly socialist economies required investment from international companies. This created both new business opportunities for Western firms and dilemmas—should a Western firm locate a new factory in, say, Poland or the Czech Republic? As the economy becomes increasingly integrated, and barriers to trade and overseas investment fall, such decisions will become more frequent. These decisions involve assessing what relative productivity will be between the two countries over the ensuing decades (precisely the topic of economic growth that we address in the first part of this book). These issues are the central focus of macroeconomics.

LONG-RUN FACTORS

The most important reason for studying macroeconomics is its long-run significance. In the previous section, we suggested that only around 10% of corporate uncertainty in any one year is due to aggregate or macroeconomic uncertainty. However, the further ahead one looks, the more important aggregate uncertainty becomes. As we stressed earlier, macroeconomics reflects the decisions and actions of all agents in the economy. For instance, if one firm or sector makes a significant technological innovation, then eventually this will spread to the rest of the economy. Thus macroeconomics is about dynamics that eventually change the nature of a firm's markets, its competitors, and the demands the firm places on its own managers and workforce. Consider, for instance, the case of two U.S. car manufacturers—General Motors (GM) and Ford. Thirty years ago they were among the very largest U.S. companies. During this 30-year period, the managements of GM and Ford have had to cope with many changes in how the economy operates. For instance, one of the major technical innovations of the last decade has been the IT revolution. This has led to substantial changes in how cars are manufactured and marketed and also increased the importance of the skilled workforce. The world economy has also become more internationalized, and competition between car producers in different countries has become intense. Coping with this technical change, ensuring a sufficient number of suitably trained workers, and battling against foreign competitors have been an important part of how GM and Ford have tried to remain profitable. The longer-term factors that GM and Ford have had to cope with (international competition, technological progress, training the workforce) are all macroeconomic compared to more short-term issues, such as whether to drop price, what the appropriate level of output is, and whether the firm should focus on niche sectors of the market.

The important forces that will influence whether the successful corporate organizations of today will be thriving in 10, 15, or even 20 years are probably already beginning to manifest themselves in the economy. We should never underestimate the ability of the economy to develop new products, new techniques, and new industries.

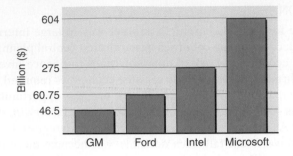

FIGURE 1.7   **Stock market valuation January 2000.** At the dawn of the twenty-first century the industrial giants of the past had been overtaken. *Source:* © 2001 Bloomberg LP. All rights reserved. Reprinted with permission. Visit www.bloomberg.com

Understanding how these factors develop over time and how they spread through the economy is a matter for macroeconomics. These dynamic processes have immense implications. As Figure 1.7 illustrates, even though GM and Ford have enormous annual sales and employ small armies, at the start of the twenty-first century the largest firms (in terms of market capitalization on the New York Stock Exchange) were IT-related. It was hard to foresee even in 1990, let alone 30 years ago, that in January 2000 a software company would be worth more than Ford and GM put together.

Economy-wide trends mean that corporate success today cannot guarantee success in the future, no matter how well a firm operates; new technology, new products, and new opportunities all threaten an established firm. Understanding these long-run forces and responding appropriately to them are crucial for the health of any company you might work for and for your family; it is the subject of much of this textbook.

SUMMARY

Economics is the study of the allocation of scarce resources. Macroeconomics studies how the economy as a whole allocates resources, for instance, how the overall level of saving in an economy is determined; how the total level of investment is generated; how the level of unemployment evolves; the pattern of overall imports and exports; what determines the level of training. Macroeconomics is therefore essentially about the backdrop of economic activity against which firms, governments, and consumers make their decisions. However, this backdrop of economic activity represents nothing other than the overall effect of the thousands of decisions made by millions of different consumers and managers.

Depending on the size of the firm, macroeconomics is either a significant or a major factor in determining an individual firm's performance. Because macroeconomic factors have a huge impact on financial markets and on the demand for goods and services produced by companies, they are an important determinant of corporate performance. Businesspeople are increasingly expected to contribute to the policy debate, and because the long-run trends in the business world are driven by macroeconomic factors, a crucial part of a business education must be the study of macroeconomics.

CONCEPTUAL QUESTIONS

1. Three important macroeconomic variables are:
    Per capita production: the overall level of production in an economy divided by the population.
    The overall rate of unemployment: the percentage of people who want to work but are not working.
    The ratio of the total imports of a country plus its exports to its total production: a measure of the degree of openness of the economy.

    For most developed economies two of these variables have risen fairly steadily over the past 60 years: production and openness. The third variable, the unemployment rate, fluctuates a good deal but has shown no general tendency to rise in developed countries. In the light of these trends, how would you assess the following claims:

    a. "The more imports come into our country, the fewer jobs there will be for our people."
    b. "If you produce more output with fewer people, then unemployment will rise."
    c. "In the future robots will do most things; there will just not be enough work to go around."

2. Suppose a government is considering cutting the rate of tax on corporate profits in half, say from 30% to 15%. An unsophisticated, but not necessarily stupid, forecast for the impact on tax revenue is that it fall by about 50%. It is likely that such a tax cut would affect incentives companies have to invest and to employ workers. This, in turn, would have trickle-down effects upon the incomes of households and the profits of companies making investment goods. Think about how you might try to take account of all these factors in creating a more sophisticated estimate of the impact on overall government tax revenues.

3. Suppose I am in my early thirties and own a modest house. I am about to start a family and contemplate moving to a bigger house. I check out the value of my current house at the local real estate agent. To my horror their valuation is only about 60% of my guess. My guess was based upon my recollection of house values when I purchased the house about 5 years earlier; since then I have not kept in touch with house prices at all. Then I ask about valuations of houses in general and find that the expert valuations are pretty consistently around 60% of my own guess. What I had considered to be a nasty idiosyncratic shock to the value of *my* house appears to be a systematic shock to all house prices. How does this affect my position now and what does it tell you about how to measure the risk of investing in housing?

4. Suppose you live in an economy where most companies borrow money from banks to finance investment and most households have some savings in the form of bank deposits. In this simple economy the banks direct the savings of households toward corporations who use the funds to finance investment expenditure. One day the central bank increases interest rates sharply. Representatives of many leading companies appear on the evening news explaining to the people how this is a very bad thing because it will inevitably slow the economy down. Are these corporate spokespeople missing something?

5. Consider the big economic stories in the newspapers over the past week or so. What proportion of these stories would you classify as being about microeconomic issues and what proportion are macroeconomic? How hard is it to make this classification?

ANALYTICAL QUESTIONS

1. Two countries start out with the same level of per capita output. In the first country population grows by 1% a year steadily and total output grows by 2.25% a year. In the second country population falls by 0.5% per year and output rises by 1.0% a year. What is the difference in per capita output between the two economies after 10 years?

2. Suppose the chances of a person seeking a job in any year reflects both idiosyncratic and aggregate factors. Let the probability that person I is unemployed be denoted p_I:

   $$p_I = 0.05 + b \, U$$

   where b is a coefficient reflecting how sensitive to aggregate unemployment the chances of a person becoming unemployed are. U is the aggregate rate of unemployment. Suppose b is 0.25 and every person has the same probability of being unemployed. What is the aggregate unemployment rate?

3. A country decides to cut its consumption by the equivalent of 25% of total output for a year in order to make a massive investment in new information technology. As a result its rate of growth rises permanently from 1.5% per annum to 1.6%. How long is it before the level of total output is higher by 25% of current output? Does it take that long before the gain from higher output matches the lost consumption?

4. The more regionally diversified across a country the sales of a company are the more important aggregate, as opposed to idiosyncratic, risk becomes. Suppose that the percentage of a company's total risk that is aggregate risk (denoted Agg risk) is described by the following equation:

   $$\text{Agg risk} = 10 + b*(\text{regions})$$

   where the value of "regions" is the number of different regions in the economy in which the company sells its output. Suppose the total number of regions in the country is 20. Would it make sense for the value of b to be 4.5? What would be the highest value for b that you would find plausible?

5. How long does it take an economy to double in size if the annual rate of growth of output is 3%? Suppose the growth rate falls to 2%. Now how long does it take for output to double? Finally, suppose that the economy suffers a decline in its annual growth rate from 3% to 2% that lasts for 25 years. Obviously the growth rate for the next 25 years will need to exceed 3% if the level of output by the end is to equal the level that would have been achieved with constant 3% growth throughout. By how much will growth in the second 25-year period need to exceed 3%?

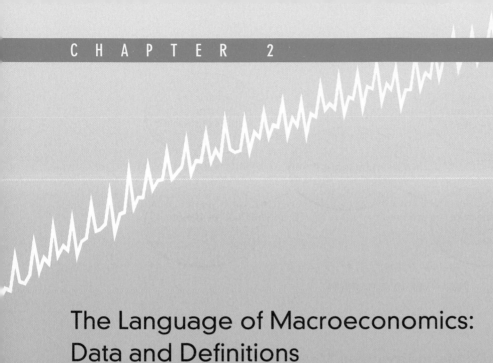

The Language of Macroeconomics: Data and Definitions

Overview

Economics has a strong empirical bias that is reflected in a near obsession, at least in the media, with data and statistics. But knowing how to interpret data depends on understanding what the statistics are trying to measure, and this requires a conceptual framework. In this chapter we explain the concepts behind key macroeconomic variables and how measures of them are constructed.

Getting to grips with the concepts underlying macroeconomic variables sounds like a very mundane task—more a chore than a voyage of discovery. In fact, to understand what economic data are trying to measure requires that we do a lot of conceptualizing and theorizing. This is not a chore; but neither is it trivially easy. Defining the variables that interest economists and providing a framework that relates these definitions to each other represent a substantial intellectual contribution.[1]

In this introductory chapter we will not go into elaborate detail about the hundreds of different measures of economic performance that the media quotes daily (e.g., retail sales, industrial productivity, consumer confidence, bank lending, etc.). Instead we introduce a central but minimal set of concepts that you need to understand the chapters that immediately follow this one.

[1]Simon Kuznets (Harvard, USA) and Richard Stone (Cambridge, UK) each received a Nobel Prize in recognition of precisely this sort of work.

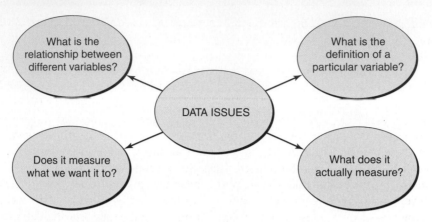

FIGURE 2.1   **Output changes for various reasons.**

2.1   What Do Macroeconomists Measure?

At the foundation of macroeconomics is a concern with human welfare. Economics seeks to help allocate resources most efficiently among competing uses in order to better satisfy the needs and desires of people. But this is rather a vague notion: human welfare is notoriously hard to calculate. This is a particular difficulty in macroeconomics where the relevant measure of welfare is what society as a whole enjoys. Even if we could accurately measure individual welfare, it would be enormously difficult to construct an aggregate measure—how can you compare levels of happiness across individuals and construct a consistent interpersonal measure?

WELFARE AS OUTPUT?

Rather than try and directly measure welfare, macroeconomists take a short cut—they focus on the amount of goods and services—the "output"—produced within an economy. The justification for this is simple—if an economy produces more output, then it can meet more of the demands of society. The more resources there are, the more needs that can be satisfied and society should be better off.[2]

This short cut is only an approximation and is subject to many problems. For instance, what really matters for welfare is not the quantity of goods *produced* in an economy but how much is *consumed*. Between 1928 and 1937, for example, industrial production in the USSR increased by 11.3% per year and gross domestic product (or *GDP*, which is a measure of total output of all goods and services) increased by 4.8% per year.[3] However, most of this increased output was used either for investment or to

---

[2]Of course, the extra output may go only to a few people, and this may add much less to overall welfare than a situation where everyone shares equally.

[3]Bergson and Kuznets (eds.), *Economic Trends in the Soviet Union* (Cambridge, MA: Harvard University Press, 1963).

meet the government's needs. Soviet consumers barely benefited from higher production. In fact, during this period of rising output, the USSR suffered one of the worst famines in history.

This example shows how limited some measures of economic performance are. Many things determine human welfare other than simply the level of output, or even consumption, in an economy. A country may be rich in economic terms, but its citizens may not have democratic rights, a just legal system, or a rich culture that encourages self-expression. The welfare of that country may be lower than that of a poor country whose people enjoy all these things.[4] By focusing on output, macroeconomists do not intend to deny the value of these social and cultural characteristics. Some economists argue that historically only healthy growing economies can support democracy and a creative cultural environment. They argue that high output economies are therefore also high welfare societies. Most economists would subscribe to a weaker position. They argue that standards of living tend to increase when output in an economy grows and usually decline if output falls.[5]

ECONOMICS AND MATERIALISM

Of course, even the statement that the welfare that the people of a country enjoy tends to rise as the level of output increases can be criticized for being too simplistic. Consider the ascetic who believes that true happiness involves rejecting the material world and embracing the spiritual. This person might be made deeply unhappy by seeing an economy produce ever more goods and services. But one need not be an ascetic to regard some increases in output as undesirable—many people bemoan the spread of McDonalds and computer games. Built into the macroeconomist's focus on output is a simple form of materialism. We will return to these issues later in this chapter. But now we need to analyze what we mean by "total output" and how we measure it.

2.2 How Do Macroeconomists Measure Output?

Imagine that a country produces only one good—onions. To measure output in this economy you only have to count the number of bags of onions that are harvested. (Assuming that the size of the bags does not change over time!) But what if the country also starts growing garlic? The first, and obvious, response is to count both the number of bags of onions and of garlic. But this raises difficult issues. What if one year there is a

[4]The comparison of the Soviet Union and ancient Greece is a good one. For all its extraordinary academic achievements and cultural sophistication, the ancient Greek economy was not particularly successful.

[5]Sachs and Lipton ("Creating a Market Economy in Eastern Europe: The Case of Poland," April 1990, Brookings Papers on Economic Activity, 1990:1) describe an example where this simple rule may have been misleading. In the transition to a market economy, output in Poland collapsed. Sachs and Lipton argue that this did not necessarily reduce welfare. They argue that under communist rule consumers spent large amounts of time waiting in line for scarce goods. Using the wage rate to value this time they argue that the move to a market economy substantially increased welfare (because people had more discretionary leisure time) even though output may have fallen.

harvest of four bags of onions and two of garlic, and the next year there are two bags of onions and four of garlic? Has output increased, decreased, or remained the same? While this example might seem trivial, the question it raises is not; before the Second World War there was no clear answer. As a consequence, rather than have a single measure of overall output in the economy, we had a collection of disparate production numbers concerning such fascinating data as pig iron production and railway freight tonnage (and probably onion and garlic production, too!).

The main problem is knowing how to add onions and garlic together or, which is the same thing, what weight to apply to onions relative to garlic. In the real economy, the problem is even more complicated—how to add together Big Macs, computers, cars, haircuts, university courses, and so forth. In essence, the economist's answer to this question is a simple one: *multiply each good by its price and then add them all to-gether*. For instance, if onions sell at $1 and garlic at $2 then in Year 0 we have:

Output Year 0

2 garlic @ $2 (= $4) +   4 onions @ $1 (= $4) = Total Output of $8

If prices are unchanged in Year 1 we have:

Output Year 1

4 garlic @ $2 (= $8) +   2 onions @ $1 (= $2) = Total Output of $10

Therefore, we could say that output has increased by $2, or 25%, between Year 0 and Year 1. In practice the arithmetic is more complicated, but this example illustrates the essentials of how economists measure economy-wide output. When we measure output we include both goods and services. Output in an economy includes not only physical goods that you can touch (and for garlic, smell), but also the services that lawyers, ac-countants, dentists, etc., provide. This method of measuring output assumes that it makes sense to multiply each good by its price. If prices were simply arbitrary numbers, this assumption would have little justification. However, at the heart of economics is the notion that prices reflect the value society places on different goods, so that by multi-plying each unit of output by its price, we can measure how society values total output.

But measuring output is not this simple. Multiplying the quantity sold of each com-modity by its price measures revenue generated, but this is not the same as the value of output created. Consider the case of a table that a retailer sells for $400. If the retailer sells 10 tables, then this amounts to $4000 of output. However, before the retailer can sell the table, other steps in the chain must occur. First, the retailer must purchase the tables from a manufacturer for, say, $200 per table. Second, the manufacturer has to purchase the wood from a lumberyard at a cost, say, of $100 for the wood per table. If we were to count every stage of the production process, then output might seem to be $7000. That is:

$1000 (output from lumberyard = $100 × 10) + $2000 (manufacturing output = $200 × 10) + $4000 (output from retailing = $400 × 10) = $7000

But this would be incorrect—the $4000 gives the value to society of the tables; that is how much consumers are prepared to pay for them. The $7000 figure is misleading because it *double* (actually triple) *counts*. For instance, it includes the value of the wood three times—in the wood the lumberyard sells, in the table the manufacturer sells to the retailer, and then again when the retailer sells the table to the consumer. To overcome this multiple counting, we need to *either* ignore all the intermediate steps and the intermediate industries (the lumberyard and the manufacturer) and just focus on final sales *or* calculate the *value added* of each industry (including the intermediate industries) and then calculate output as the sum of each industry's value added.

Value added is the difference between the value of the output sold and the cost of purchased inputs used to produce the output (such as raw materials or semifinished products). Thus, in our example, the value added of the lumberyard industry is $1000. Value added in the manufacturing industry is also $1000 (10 tables sold at $2000 *minus* the input cost of wood of $1000). Finally, the value added of the retail outlet is $2000 (10 tables sold at $400 but purchased at $200). Combining all these, we arrive at a measure of output or valued added of $4000—exactly equal to the final sale value of all the tables. Focusing on value added makes it clear that the contribution of each sector depends on the *additional* value it creates. In our example the retailer adds more value than any other sector (presumably through point of sale information, delivery, warranties, etc.). However, the key point is that consumers and producers, not economists, decide the relative importance of each sector by the prices they set and are prepared to pay. If prices reflect social value, then this will produce a direct link between measures of output and welfare.

While this example shows the methodology used to measure output, it leaves unanswered many questions about detail. For instance, should we measure the output of the Italian economy by the output produced by all Italians (both individuals and firms) or the output produced by everyone living in Italy? Which of these alternatives is more appropriate depends on the issue being studied, so governments produce two measures of output in an economy:

> **D E F I N I T I O N**
>
> - **Gross domestic product (GDP)** is the output of goods and services produced within a country (including nationals and resident foreigners).
> - **Gross national product (GNP)** is the output of goods and services produced by the nationals of a country (excluding foreign residents but including nationals resident abroad).

In both cases output is measured as the sum of the values added created by all those who produce goods and services. Thus, Italian GDP would include the output produced within Italy by Italians and anyone else, such as Germans or Albanians, who are working in Italy. However, if Albanians send some of the income they earn in Italy back to Albania, then these remittances would *not* be included in Italian GNP (only in Italian GDP) but would be included in Albanian GNP (but not in Albanian GDP). We need to draw a similar distinction for corporate profits. Consider the case of a German bank based in Rome. The valued added that the bank creates will be paid out in wages to its workforce and profits to its owners. The part of the profits that the bank remits to the head office of the bank in Germany will be included in German but not Italian GNP. However, these profits will be included in measurement of Italian, not German, GDP.

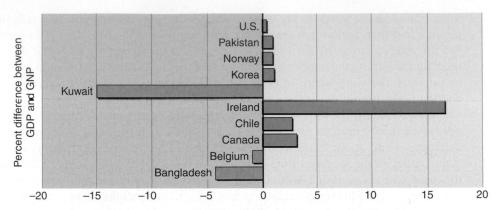

FIGURE 2.2   **Percentage difference between Gross Domestic Product and Gross National Product, 1999.** Net income from abroad is large relative to domestic income for many smaller countries. *Source*: International Monetary Fund, *International Financial Statistics 2000*.

For some economies the distinction between GDP and GNP is trivial, but for others (see Figure 2.2) the difference can be huge. In Ireland, GDP has been substantially in excess of GNP because so many overseas firms moved there in the 1980s and 1990s. These firms pay wages and make profits that boost both Irish GDP and GNP. But profits repatriated out of Ireland are excluded from Irish GNP. This means that Irish GNP is about 16% less than Irish GDP. In contrast, Kuwait has invested much more in overseas assets than international firms have invested in Kuwait. This means that value added by Kuwaiti labor and capital exceeds the total value added created in Kuwait, so that Kuwaiti GNP substantially exceeds GDP.

GDP (or GNP) is the most common measure of output in an economy, and whenever you read in a newspaper that overall output has risen or fallen, the report will refer to one of these magnitudes. We devote much of this book to analyzing why GDP differs across countries and why within a country it changes from year to year or decade to decade.

REAL VERSUS NOMINAL GDP

Crucial to measuring GDP is the multiplication of quantities produced for each good by its market price (excluding any consumer or producer taxes). However, the introduction of prices adds a potential distortion—what happens if prices rise over time? For instance, assume that in Year 2 the quantity of goods provided in our onion/garlic economy does not change but that all prices double—so that a bag of onions now costs $2 and a bag of garlic $4. Using the same methodology as before, we arrive at the following measure of output:

Output Year 2

4 garlic @ $4 (= $16)   +   2 onions @ $2 (= $4)   = Total Output of $20

This reveals an immediate problem—even though the amount of onions and garlic harvested has remained the same, our calculation suggests that output has doubled. This leads macroeconomists to distinguish between *real* and *nominal* GDP, or alternatively between GDP in *constant* and *current* prices.

The calculations of output in the onion/garlic economy we performed thus far have been for *nominal GDP*. We constructed them by multiplying the output of each good by the *current* price of that good in each year. Economists calculate *real GDP* by using *constant prices* (from one particular year). Real GDP increases because the quantity of goods being produced has increased, not because prices have changed. To calculate real GDP, we need to choose the prices in a particular year (called the base year), and then use them to calculate real GDP in every year. For instance, let us choose prices in Year 0 (onions cost $1 and garlic $2) as our base year. Then we would calculate real GDP (in Year 0 $) as shown in Table 2.1.

Because we have used constant prices (onions $1, garlic $2), our calculations of output no longer show any increase in Year 2 output compared to Year 1. Nominal GDP changes every year because of output changes and because the weights (prices) attached to each output have altered. By using real GDP, we abstract from the latter and focus purely on changes in output across different industries. Because economists are ultimately interested in welfare, they want to measure the *production* of output and thus prefer to focus on real GDP.

The calculation of real GDP depends on which base year we choose. (To see this, recalculate real GDP but use the year 2 prices of $4 for garlic and $2 for onions.) If real GDP measures differ depending on the prices chosen, then which year should be the base year? This question has no correct answer, but it is probably best to use a recent year. We use prices to weight together the output of different industries to calculate GDP because prices reflect social value. By using contemporary prices, we therefore get measures of GDP (both current and historical) that reflect contemporary values. This is what statisticians actually do. They choose a base year, calculate GDP, and then periodically (normally every five years) change the base year and recalculate real GDP. This is why you often see statistical tables that report GDP in 1990 or 1995 prices—the year referenced refers to the base year from which prices have been chosen.

Because changes in nominal GDP reflect both increases in output in each industry and changes in prices, while changes in real GDP only reflect output, we can use the gap between the two to measure prices. In our example the nominal, or current price, level of output in year 2 is 20. The real value of output (using Year 0 prices) is 10. So a measure of how prices, on average, have moved between Year 0 and Year 2 is by how

TABLE 2.1 The Onion-Garlic Economy (in Year 0 $)

	Onions	Garlic	Output
Year 0	4	2	8
Year 1	2	4	10
Year 2	2	4	10

much current price GDP differs from constant price GDP. We call the resultant index of overall prices the GDP deflator:[6]

$$\text{Current price GDP/constant price GDP}$$

The percentage change in this price index from year to year is a measure of overall inflation. In our example, the price index rises from 1 to 2 in Year 2—inflation is 100%.

THE INCOME MEASURE OF GDP

We have so far focused on the *output measure of GDP*. But to create the value added produced, we have to use various factors of production: labor, buildings, machines, and so forth. Each of these factors of production gets rewarded by a slice of the value added, which is paid in the form of wages, rents, interest payments, and profits. So another way to calculate the total value of what is produced in an economy is to add together the incomes that production generates—the *income measure of GDP*.

Table 2.2 shows the income measure of U.S. GDP in 1998 and how much was paid out to the suppliers of various *factors of production*—labor, corporate capital stock (machines, buildings, and so on, that companies own), capital rented to the corporate sector, and productive assets owned outside the corporate sector.[7] In the United States in 1998, wages and salaries made up about 70% of total income, and income from capital (both machines and buildings) made up the remaining 30%. These shares are typical for industrial economies.

TABLE 2.2   **U.S. National Income for 2000**
Figures are billions of U.S. dollars
(percentages of total in parentheses)

Compensation of employees:	5638	(70%)
Corporate profits	946	(12%)
Rental Income	140	(2%)
Proprietor's Income[a]	710	(9%)
Net Interest	567	(7%)
Total National Income	8002	

[a]Income from non-corporate business activity, e.g., profits of family-run businesses. *Source:* www.bea.doc.gov

[6]We examine other measures of prices and inflation in Chapter 12.

[7]Information used to construct the various measures of GDP comes from many sources including income-tax returns, surveys of retail sales, companies' income statements, and trade statistics collected by customs and excise authorities.

THE EXPENDITURE MEASURE OF OUTPUT

There is one further means of calculating GDP: the expenditure method. The idea behind the expenditure method is that consumers, governments, and firms purchase *all* the value added produced in an economy. Therefore, we can measure GDP by adding up all the separate expenditure categories. Because supply equals demand, this expenditure measure of GDP should in theory also equal the output measure of GDP (and also the income measure). So we can measure total output either by adding up the expenditure on domestic output, or by adding the incomes generated from domestic production, or by adding the extra output produced by everyone engaged in production (summing the values added). With the expenditure method we are looking at one set of transactions in this triple-entry bookkeeping system; we are focusing on the uses to which output is put.

The goods and services produced within an economy have four basic uses:

- consumption by individuals (C)
- consumption and investment by government (G)
- investment by the private sector (I).
- exports (X)

So it is useful to think of four different categories of expenditure, or demand, in the economy as:

Aggregate Demand = Consumption + Investment + Government Expenditure + Exports

or

$$AD = C + I + G + X$$

Two sources satisfy this aggregate spending in the economy: domestically produced output (Y, i.e., GDP or GNP) and inflows of goods from abroad, imports (M). Because expenditure on goods must equal sales of goods (demand must equal supply), we therefore have

Output + Imports = Consumption + Investment + Government Expenditure + Exports

Or as symbols:

$$Y + M = C + I + G + X$$

With a little bit of rearranging, this equation leads to the key equation in the national accounts of a country:

Output = Consumption + Investment + Government Expenditure + Net Exports

or

$$Y = C + I + G + (X - M)$$

Therefore, the expenditure method of measuring GDP involves adding up these four components of spending. In this framework it is a matter of accounting that supply

TABLE 2.3   Canadian GDP 1999 (C$bn) and Expenditure Components

GDP	949.4	
Consumption	553.6	58.3%
Government Expenditure	200	21.6%
Investment	167.7	17.7%
Exports	411.6	43.4%
Imports	383.7	40.4%

Source: http://www.statcan.ca/english/Pgdb/
Economy/Economic/econ04.htm

equals demand. Changes in inventories represent a firm's unsold output and, in a way, measures the gap between supply and demand. However, the national accounts treat inventories both as a firm buying its own output and as an investment by the firm. Because by definition investment includes inventories it is trivial that supply equals demand.

Table 2.3 breaks Canadian GDP in 1999 into its four expenditure categories. The largest expenditure component is consumption, which accounts for 58% of total GDP. Investment and government expenditure are both roughly 20%. Exports and imports are each more than 40% of GDP—but what matters for GDP is net exports, and the difference between exports and imports is small.

This detailed breakdown of GDP is specific to Canada in 1999. Figure 2.3 shows a similar breakdown for a number of developed countries as an average between 1970 and 1999 (net exports are the missing component, which makes everything add to 100%). In all cases consumption accounts for most of the output produced in an economy—ranging from 55% in Germany to 66% in the United States. There is a wider range of variation in investment and government expenditure, and as we shall see in Chapter 5, differences in investment rates are crucial to understanding differences in the standard of living across countries.

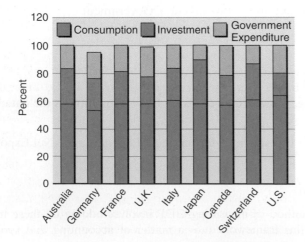

FIGURE 2.3   **Expenditure components as percentage of GDP, 1970–1999.** Investment has been slightly larger than government spending in most developed countries in recent decades, but consumption is far larger than either. *Source*: International Monetary Fund, *International Financial Statistics 2000*.

Investment is the amount of resources used in increasing the capital stock. It is important to note here that what economists mean by investment is spending on new machines, buildings, roads, and so on. They do *not* mean buying existing financial assets—purchasing some corporate equity, for example. What we are measuring is spending on additions to the capital stock of the country, not financial transactions that record the exchange in paper claims like bonds or stocks. There are, however, very important links between physical and financial investment which we examine in detail in Part VI of this book

But investment, as measured in practice, does not equal the change in the capital stock. Over time machines depreciate—for instance, in a car manufacturing plant, the continual use of machines leads to breakdowns that require repairs. Investment includes the resources used in these repairs even though they do not *increase* the capital stock between different time periods. Instead these repairs prevent the capital stock from declining. This leads economists to distinguish between gross and net investment. *Gross investment* (sometimes called gross domestic fixed capital formation, or g.d.f.c.f.), is simply the amount of resources spent over a period on the capital stock and does not allow for depreciation or obsolescence. By contrast, *net investment* is gross investment less depreciation and so is a measure of how much the capital stock has increased between time periods. For machines that depreciate, or become obsolescent, quickly (for example, computers) the distinction between gross and net investment is an important one. Ideally we would use net investment rather than gross investment when measuring output and arrive at a measure of *net domestic product* rather than *gross domestic product*. However, statistical authorities have little faith in their ability to measure depreciation accurately on a timely basis, so instead we focus on gross measures of output and investment. This is yet another reason why GDP and welfare may not correlate well—some of GDP represents not output that can be consumed but resources that are required to make repairs.

2.3   How Large Are Modern Economies?

Figures 2.4 and 2.5 give some idea about the overall size of modern economies and which economies are the largest. Figure 2.4 shows a snapshot of the global economy taken in 1999. It reveals that the economies of the United States and the European Union (EU) were roughly equal in terms of output. Although the EU as a whole is the same size as the United States, none of its constituent economies is anything near as large (see Figure 2.5). The largest EU economy, Germany, had a total GDP of $2115bn, barely a quarter of U.S. GDP of $8230bn. The Japanese economy is a little under half the size of the U.S. and EU economies. The economies of the rest of the world added together generate about one-quarter of world output. Given that the population of China alone is greater than those of the United States, the EU, and Japan combined, world output is clearly unevenly distributed

In making international comparisons, we are confronted by the reliability of data—can we use national estimates of GDP to say one economy is larger than another? An immediate problem is the need to convert all measures of GDP into a common currency. For instance, the Japanese economy is measured in yen and the United States in dollars. To compare their relative size, we need to convert these measures into common

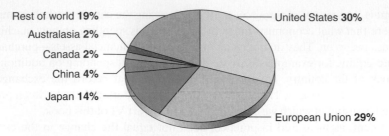

FIGURE 2.4   **Output of major economic areas in 1999 ($bn).** Europe and the USA produce about 60% of World GDP. *Source*: International Monetary Fund, *International Financial Statistics 2000*.

units, say, by multiplying the Japanese GDP statistic by the current dollar–yen exchange rate. This is the method used in Figures 2.4 through 2.6.

There are, however, other ways of making international comparisons, and one popular alternative is to use purchasing power parity (PPP) exchange rates, not market exchange rates, when converting GDP into a common currency.[8] Current market exchange rates do not accurately reflect differences in prices between countries. A Japanese tourist in India who converts yen into rupees at the market exchange rate will find everything cheap. The PPP exchange rate makes commodities in Japan cost, on average, the same as in India. When a currency is temporarily strong against the dollar, its economy will seem large when converted into dollars. For instance, in 1999 the pound sterling was strong against the euro, and as a result in Figure 2.5 the UK economy is the same size as the French economy. The strength of sterling also made the UK seem more expensive than France. However, PPP estimates of the sterling–franc exchange rate suggested that the market exchange rate was overvalued, and so using PPP exchange rates to calculate UK GDP in dollar terms would have reduced its size relative to France. PPP exchange rates tend to reduce the discrepancy in size between the wealthy economies shown in Figure 2.4 and the poorer nations.

Because countries have different sized populations, simply using output to measure economic performance can be misleading. For instance, the Greek economy in 1999 was worth $125bn compared to only $19bn for Luxembourg. However, because the

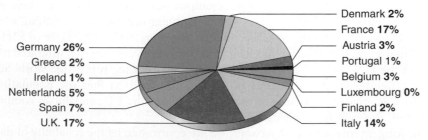

FIGURE 2.5   **EU GDP by country, 1999.** Germany produces about one-quarter of European Union output. *Source*: *WEO Databases 2000*, www.imf.org

[8]In Chapter 18 we offer a comprehensive analysis of purchasing power parity.

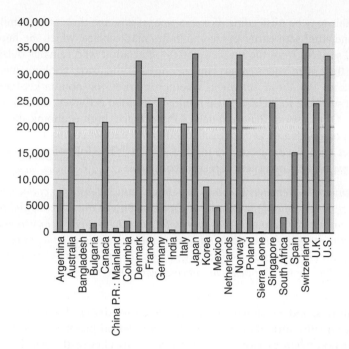

FIGURE 2.6 **GDP per capita, 1999 ($)**. *Source*: WEO Database September 2000, www.imf.org

population in Greece is nearly 30 times that in Luxembourg, Luxembourg has a per capita GDP over four times larger than Greece. Whether to use GDP or GDP *per capita* depends on the issue at hand. To compare standards of living across countries or over time, one should use *per capita* measures. To measure the scale of economic activity in a country, GDP is more appropriate.

Figure 2.6 shows estimates of GDP per capita (calculated using market exchange rates) for 25 economies. This measure reveals enormous differences in the standard of living—from about $35,000 in the United States to about $450 in India and $800 in China.[9]

2.4 Total Output and Total Happiness

Output, or income, is a far from perfect measure of welfare, satisfaction, or happiness. Some even doubt whether the correlation between welfare and output is positive. Some people believe that economic growth is bad because it invariably uses scarce natural resources that are nonrenewable. Macroeconomists, for good reasons, are reluctant to accept that economic growth is bad—economic growth over the last two centuries has led to an enormous increase in the standard of living across many countries. However, the exhaustion of nonrenewable resources is a cause for grave concern.

Even if we adjust output for the depletion of nonrenewable natural resources, focusing on production still concentrates on measuring goods and services that are exchanged in

[9]Using PPP exchange rates would reduce these discrepancies.

the marketplace, and this may be misleading. For instance, at any one time many families in an economy have one adult who earns an income in the marketplace, which the family uses to buy goods and services from the market, and another adult who remains outside the market but nevertheless provides goods and services—child care, cooking meals, household administration. All these activities, whether market- or nonmarket-based, produce output, and if we were to include these nonmarket-based activities, GDP would be substantially larger. Obviously we ignore much of importance, both economically and socially, if we focus just on goods and services exchanged in markets where money changes hands. Many exchanges take place outside the market system.[10] The following quotation sums up well this critique of the narrowness of macroeconomics:

> *Successive governments—over several countries—have found it easier to collect statistics in the marketplaces rather than round the dinner-tables of the nations, and our idea that we are dominated by commerce is an artefact of government's convenience: it is easier to describe market transactions, and to tax them to raise revenue, than it is to measure Sunday lunch, or children's birthday parties. The idea that the field of exchange is circumscribed by what appears in national economic statistics . . . is a severe limitation.[11]*

There is much truth in this, and we should be careful when we discuss "output" to remember that it ignores a substantial part of social life, and social production. But, we should also remember that macroeconomists do not arbitrarily choose the part of economic life they measure. Governments find it far easier to influence the value of inflation than they do the cultural importance of Sunday lunch, and the reported profits of corporations depend crucially on the result of market, rather than nonmarket, activity. Just because macroeconomics does not completely measure economic activity does not mean that the measure it does use is unenlightening.

OUTPUT AS WELFARE?

We have said that macroeconomists are ultimately interested in output as a measure of welfare. But does GDP correlate with welfare or happiness? Tables 2.4 and 2.5 show measures based on survey questions asking U.S. and European citizens over nearly 20 years about their level of happiness. During this period output has increased substantially in all of these countries, and in most of them the proportion of citizens who are "very happy" or "very satisfied" has also risen (although not for the citizens of Belgium, Ireland, and the UK). These tables therefore support the view that increases in aggregate output lead to higher levels of welfare in general, although the link is clearly not perfect.

---

[10]For a good example of the arbitrariness of what activity counts as market-based, consider the case in which you take your parents out to a restaurant for a meal. GDP includes the entire value added of this transaction. If by contrast, you buy the ingredients and cook the meal yourself, then GDP includes only the value added of the ingredients. However, the economic activity is still the same—someone is still cooking the meal. GDP includes a chef getting paid for cooking but not you cooking at home. Of course, if you are a lousy cook then perhaps your value added is zero or negative.

[11]Davis, *Exchange* (Oxford: Open University Press, 1992).

TABLE 2.4 Happiness in the USA, 1972–1990

	1972	1980	1990
Very happy %	30.3	33.9	33.4
Pretty happy %	53.2	52.7	57.6
Not too happy %	16.5	13.3	9.0
Number in sample	1606	1462	1361

Source: Blanchflower, Oswald, and Warr, "Well-Being over Time in Britain and the USA," London School of Economics, mimeo 1999.

For economists measures of aggregate output are still the dominant indicators of the standard of living, but alternative measures have been suggested. Prominent among these is the United Nations Human Development Index (HDI), which combines information on output, life expectancy, and education (some variants also measure income inequality). This index rests on the notion that the amount of goods a country can potentially consume is not the sole measure of the standard of living. Instead, what matters is whether individuals have the resources (or capabilities) to participate in society and fulfill their potential.[12] In the HDI, increases in output lead to an increase in the index only below a certain level—once an economy passes a certain threshold of development, increases in output do little or nothing to increase HDI. This is because the HDI seeks to assess the average degree of poverty in the countries it surveys. Using this

TABLE 2.5 Life Satisfaction in European Countries
Proportion of samples who report themselves as "very satisfied."

Country	Average 1973–81	Average 1982–90	Well-being increased?
Belgium	39.5	24.7	No
Denmark	51.7	62.8	Yes
France	12.4	13.7	Yes
W. Germany	18.8	23.4	Yes
Ireland	38.8	31.1	No
Italy	9.0	13.2	Yes
Luxembourg	34.6	39.1	Yes
Netherlands	41.3	41.8	Yes
UK	31.7	30.9	No

Source: Oswald "Happiness and Economic Performance," *Economic Journal* (1997) 107, 1815–1831.

[12]See Sen, *The Standard of Living* (Cambridge: Cambridge University Press, 1987).

alternative to GDP as a measure of the standard of living leads to different conclusions about changes in prosperity across countries over the last 130 years. For instance, output per head in India in 1992 was around 40% of Belgian per capita GDP in 1870. In other words, contemporary India apparently has a lower average standard of living than nineteenth-century Belgium had as measured by output per head. However, according to the HDI index, India today has roughly the same level of welfare as Belgium in 1870. The major factor in explaining this equality is life expectancy in the two countries. Life expectancy was around 40 years in Belgium in 1870 and is over 50 in contemporary India. In other words, the higher life expectancy in India today offsets the lower GDP per head compared with Belgium in 1870.

2.5   How Does Output Change Over Time?

One of the main issues in macroeconomics is how the level of output changes over time. Consider the behavior of Austrian (quarterly) GDP since 1964, as shown in Figure 2.7.[13]

We can break down the movements in output into four separate components.

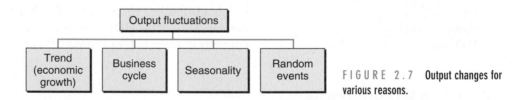

FIGURE 2.7   **Output changes for various reasons.**

LONG-RUN TREND GROWTH

The most noticeable feature of Austrian GDP (as it is for most developed nations) is that it rises gradually over time (Figure 2.8). While there are short-term "wiggles" in GDP, the sustained growth over decades is clear—the level at the end of the sample period is much higher than its initial level. We call this sustained growth over long periods of time the "trend component" of GDP. What determines the long-run, underlying

---

[13]It is common to chart variables that change substantially over time in logarithmic form, as in Figure 2.7. This makes charts easier to read by standardizing the behavior of a variable over time. Changes in the natural logarithm are in most cases roughly equal to the percentage growth of a variable, e.g., if the logarithm changes by 0.02, it approximately equals to 2% growth. The change in the logarithm is simply the gradient of the line in Figure 2.7. A constant slope therefore means a steady growth rate, while a steeper slope means an increase in the growth rate.

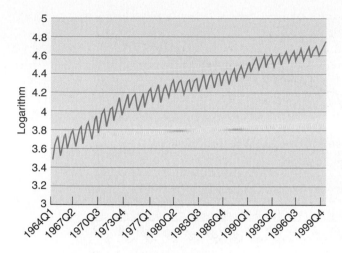

FIGURE 2.8 **Austrian GDP 1964–1999.**
Output tends to trend upwards over time, display medium-term cyclical fluctuations and be highly seasonal with regular patterns of peaks and troughs within each year. *Source*: International Monetary Fund, *International Financial Statistics*, 2000.

trend in different economies is enormously important for the evolution of standards of living and is the focus of Part II of this book. Figure 2.9 estimates this trend for Austria. As the diagram shows, while the actual level of GDP often deviates from its trend value, to understand the long-run performance of the Austrian economy, we have to work out what drives this trend growth in output. This is what we do when we study the economics of growth.

Table 2.6 shows that the trend rate of growth varies both over time and across countries.

TABLE 2.6 **Estimated Trend Rates of Annual Growth in Output per Capita**

	1860–1914	1920–39	1951–73	1974–89
Belgium	0.90	1.01	3.90	2.09
Denmark	1.77	1.58	3.46	1.59
France	0.96	0.78	4.92	1.42
Germany	1.47	2.91	5.11	1.26
Italy	1.47	0.21	5.31	2.05
Sweden	1.52	3.03	3.42	1.62
UK	1.04	1.56	2.24	1.83
USA	1.70	0.86	1.54	1.89

Source: Crafts and Toniolo, *Economic Growth in Europe Since 1945* (Cambridge: Cambridge University Press, 1996).

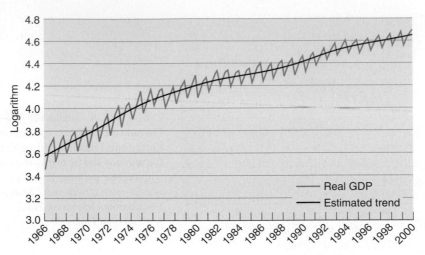

FIGURE 2.9   **Trend in Austrian GDP.** Output fluctuates around a rising trend in most developed economies. *Source*: International Monetary Fund, *International Financial Statistics 2000* and author's own calculations.

BUSINESS CYCLES

The trend component of GDP captures the overall tendency of output to increase over decades. However, from year to year output does not necessarily increase. Sometimes output in economies declines from one year to another, and if this is substantial or persistent, we call it a *recession*. At other times, output increases from year to year, and this is an *expansion*. Recessions and expansions together make up the business cycle—an important determinant of the medium-term behavior of an economy. Business cycles

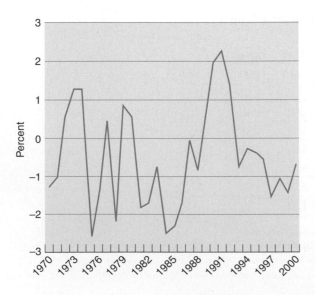

FIGURE 2.10   **Austrian business cycle.** Business cycles are medium-term fluctuations around trend—note the duration and volatility of cycles varies across episodes. *Source*: International Monetary Fund, *International Financial Statistics 2000*.

are a major reason why actual output rarely follows a smooth trend. When we try to explain business cycles, we are trying to account for quarterly or annual changes in output *within* the decade. By contrast, analysis of trend rates of growth tries to account for changes *across* decades. Figure 2.10 shows an estimate of the business cycle in Austria.

SEASONALITY

Although economic growth and business cycles are the subject of much economic research, output also changes for other reasons. Because of the weather, the timing of holidays, and individual choice, economic activity is seasonal—with output in many countries being highest in the final quarter of the year and lowest in the first. These seasonal fluctuations are separate from the trend and cyclical component we mentioned earlier and affect the allocation of activity only *within* a year. Seasonality will influence how much output is produced in the first half of 2002 compared to the second half but not whether 2002 is a higher output year than 2001.

Nevertheless, seasonal fluctuations are large even in nonagricultural economies. Figure 2.11 shows seasonal fluctuations in Austria as a percentage of output (so 0.04 means a 4% increase in output due to seasonal factors). Further investigation of the diagram shows that the peaks and troughs in the seasonal component of GDP have changed over time. While Christmas and summer always occur at the same time of the year, the economy's response to these seasons alters over time.

Because seasonal effects only allocate expenditure within a year, rather than affect the level of expenditure over the entire year, they are often considered uninteresting— at least from an economic standpoint. This is certainly misleading for the many businesses that produce products that are in demand at particular seasons. For instance, between 1960 and 1994, UK consumption at Christmas has risen from £1.6bn to £4bn

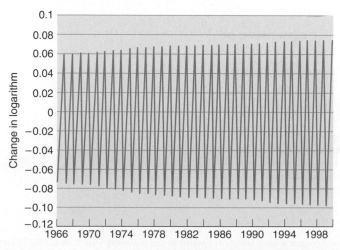

FIGURE 2.11 **Seasonal fluctuations in Austrian GDP.** The figure show the logarithmic change in output by quarters—roughly the percentage movement. The seasonal component of output fluctuations is often large and changes over time. *Source*: Authors calculations using IMF data.

(in constant prices)—this is significantly faster than the rise in GDP over the same years. Naturally this increase led to a bonanza for some firms (card manufacturers, Christmas decoration manufacturers, etc.), but most firms benefited to some extent because much of this expenditure was on general gifts rather than specific Christmas products.

RANDOM EVENTS

Finally, completely random factors cause output to vary from quarter to quarter. These factors do not follow a regular pattern—like seasonal or cyclical fluctuations—and do not grow over time—like trend effects. This random component is really the residual part of the change in GDP; that part of the movement in output that we cannot describe as a trend or seasonal factor and is unrelated to the regular pattern of the business cycle. These influences tend not to be the subject of much study. They are normally due to easily recognizable and one-time events (e.g., an economy-wide transport strike, France winning the soccer World Cup, unusually severe weather). They are therefore of greater interest to the historian than the economist.[14]

2.6   What Produces Output?

We have not yet given much thought to how an economy actually produces goods and services. We have simply focused on measurement. We shall consider how an economy creates goods in great detail in the next few chapters, but for now we assume that an economy produces output by combining the physical capital available (i.e., machinery, factories, computers) with employed labor.

TABLE 2.7   Service Life (in Years) for Machines and Non-Residential Buildings, 1948–89

	USA	UK	Germany	France	Japan
Equipment	12	13	15	11	6
Structures	40	66	57	34	42

Source: O'Mahoney, "Measures of Fixed Capital Stocks in the Post-War Period: A Five Country Study," in van Ark and Crafts, *Quantative Aspects of Post-War European Economic Growth* (Cambridge University Press, 1996), 165–214.

---

[14]Some one-time events trigger a long-lasting response in the economy—such as dramatic increases in oil prices. This is not what we mean here by temporary events. Our focus here is on one-time shocks that only influence this period.

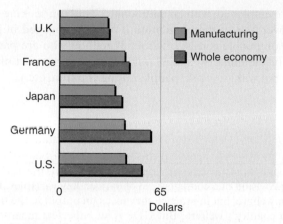

FIGURE 2.12 **Gross tangible physical capital stocks per worker hour, 1989 (1985$).** The amount of capital per worker hour varies considerably across developed countries. *Source*: O'Mahoney, 1996.

The capital stock of a country is the collection of durable physical assets that help generate output of goods and services. The capital stock is normally divided into three components: residential buildings, nonresidential buildings, and equipment (e.g., machines).

As Table 2.7 shows, physical capital, especially buildings, lasts for years. As a result, the capital stock evolves over time, as new investment augments the capital stock already in place. As with most macroeconomic variables, the size of a nation's capital stock varies widely from country to country (see Figure 2.12).

The other factor that helps produce output is labor input—machines still cannot work entirely on their own. One surprising fact about industrial economies is that only a relatively small proportion of the population is actually in employment, and this does not necessarily reflect the level of unemployment. Consider the breakdown of the U.S. population shown in Figure 2.13.[15] Out of a total population of just over 270 million

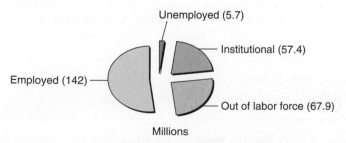

FIGURE 2.13 **U.S. population by labor market status, 2000.** Around one-half of the U.S. population is in work (excluding the military). *Source*: Bureau of Labor Statistics.

[15]Chapter 8 will present us with the opportunity for a more detailed look at data definitions relevant to the labor market.

people, only about 142 million are employed, with an additional 5.7 million seeking employment. Therefore, only just over half of the population is actually engaged in producing GDP. The other 125 million people consist of about 57 million who are part of an institution (in school, prison, or the military) and 68 million who are not part of the labor force (kids, those who may not want to work, people raising children, etc.).

CHAPTER SUMMARY

Central to macroeconomics is the provision of a consistent set of data on key variables. Ultimately economists are interested in welfare, but in practice they focus on output in the belief that increases in output increase a country's welfare. But GDP is an imperfect measure of welfare; it ignores many important factors, such as education, distributional matters, and social and political freedom.

Macroeconomists measure output by adding up the value of all the goods and services an economy produces. Depending on whether we focus on all the citizens of a country, or only on the people producing within its borders, we generate either GNP or GDP. To avoid double counting, economists focus on value added in production. They distinguish between real and nominal GDP. Nominal GDP captures how both changes in prices and shifts in production affect value. By contrast, movements in real GDP reflect changes due to different levels of output and is the better measure of the health of an economy. The most common simple measure of the standard of living in an economy is real GDP *per capita*.

The level of output in an economy fluctuates due to four factors: long-term trend growth, business cycle movements, seasonality, and purely random factors. The trend component of growth represents sustained increases in output and focuses on long-term phenomena that reveal themselves across decades. Business cycle fluctuations determine the medium-term behavior of an economy, and seasonality influences the distribution of economic activity within the year.

An economy creates output by combining capital (equipment and buildings) with employed labor. The value of capital in modern economies is typically about 2.5 to 3.5 times the size of annual output. Employment represents less than 50% of the population in many industrialized economies. The output an economy produces is used for four purposes: consumption, investment, government expenditure, and exports. Consumption is by far the largest component.

CONCEPTUAL QUESTIONS

1. The Beatles claimed that "I don't care too much for money, money can't buy me love." (Shortly after first making this claim they joined the ranks of the richest people in the world.) Does their claim undermine the use of GDP to measure welfare?

2. Do you think it is easier to evaluate the relative welfare of different generations of people in one country (by comparing per capital GDP over time), or to compare the relative standards of living in different countries at a point in time (by converting current per capita GDPs into a common currency)?

3. Try to explain to someone who had never thought about measuring the value of economic activity why the output, income, and expenditure ways of measuring national production should give the same answer. It helps to think of a simple economy producing only two or three different things.

4. Would you expect that a country where the share of wages and salaries in GDP was falling, and the share of profits and interest was rising, to be one where consumption as a percent of national income was also shifting? Why? Would you expect the distribution of income to become more unequal? Suppose the trends were due to demographic shifts, more specifically to a rapidly aging population. Would this change your answers?

5. How would you treat the activities of criminals in GDP accounting? What about the activities of the police force?

ANALYTICAL QUESTIONS

1. Consider an economy with three productive sectors: mining and farming; manufacturing; and retailing. Manufacturers produce goods each year with a sale value of 500. They sell 400 to retailers and 100 direct to the private sector and to government for consumption. Retailers buy goods for 400 from manufacturers and buy 50 from the agricultural sector. Retailers sell goods for consumption for 500. Manufacturers buy goods worth 200 off mining and agricultural firms. Farmers also sell 100 direct to the private sector for consumption. Mining companies sell nothing directly to government or households for consumption.

   What is value added in each sector and what is total output for the economy?

2. The price of the four sorts of goods produced in an economy in 2000 are:

Good	A	B	C	D
Price	8	9	4	2
Quantity	1000	400	600	1000

   The prices of the goods in 2001 are:

Good	A	B	C	D
Price	9	6	8	3

   What is the overall rate of inflation between 2000 and 2001? Would it help to know the levels of output of goods in 2001? How might that information be used to construct an alternative measure of inflation?

3. A country has overseas assets worth 12% of GDP. Overseas assets earn a return of 7%, which is distributed back to the home country. Other countries own assets in the domestic economy worth 8% of GDP and these assets earn a return of 11%. What is the difference between GDP and GNP?

4. The national accounts for a country reveal the following:

Total consumption	$520 billion
Investment	$120 billion
Government spending	$85 billion
Total exports	$229 billion
Total imports	$198 billion

What is GDP? Suppose consumption increases by 10% but output only rises by 5%. Investment and government spending both increase by 3%. What happens to the gap between exports and imports?

5. Suppose the ratio between the capital stock of a country and annual output is 3.5. Capital lasts, on average, for 12 years. By what proportion is total output, gross of depreciation of capital, in excess of output net of depreciation?

6. Suppose that the trend rate of output growth for a country is 2%. In any year output deviates from the trend path for two reasons: a cyclical factor that can persist from one year to the next; a random factor that has no persistence from one year to the next. Specifically consider the following model:

$$Y_t = Ytrend_t + Ycyclical_t + Yrandom_t$$

Y_t is output at time t.
$Ytrend_t$ is the trend component at time t; this grows at 2% a year.
$Ycyclical_t$ is the cyclical component at t. This equals 0.9 times its value in the previous period, i.e.,

$$Ycyclical_t = 0.9\,(Ycyclical_{t-1})$$

$Yrandom_t$ is the random component and there is no link between its value today and the value tomorrow. On average over time the random component is zero.

If $Ytrend_t = 1000$; $Ycyclical_t = -200$; and $Yrandom_t = 50$, then what is the expected growth of output between this period and the next? Assume that your best guess for the random component tomorrow is that it is zero. Suppose $Yrandom_t$ were -50 today. How does this change your answer?

Analytical Overview: Introducing Fundamental Tools

Overview

In Chapter 2 we introduced a core set of macroeconomic variables and explained how they are measured. We now introduce a core set of theoretical tools with which to analyze the behavior of these variables. We will use these tools often in this book. Our aim in this chapter is to outline important ideas that we can apply in many contexts and which offer a unifying framework to the book. Each chapter in this book is intended to be self contained. However, in this chapter we provide an overview of the key relationships between chapters that act as a route map as you read the text. As with most maps, you will understand it better as you proceed through the book, and will want to refer back to it along the route.

3.1 Supply, Demand, and Equilibrium

We noted earlier that because statisticians treat inventories as a firm buying its own output, then the expenditure measure of GDP should equal the output measure. In other words, demand equals supply. However, there is an important distinction between relations that holds true as a matter of accounting identities and *equilibrium* relations that holds as a result of individual behavior. In a **market equilibrium**, the amount of output producers *wish to supply at the current set of prices* coincides with the amount that households, governments, and firms demand *at the same prices*. In macroeconomics, output means GDP (or GNP), and prices refer to the overall level of prices of goods and services. In microeconomics, we expect the supply of output of a particular good to increase with its price. The reasoning is straightforward. A rise in this price (*holding other prices and wages constant*) makes it profitable to produce more, so if we draw a graph with price measured on the vertical axis and quantity on the horizontal axis, the supply curve slopes upward—a higher price generates more supply. By contrast, the demand curves we focus on in microeconomics generally slope downward—a rise in the price of a particular good makes it less attractive to consumers, so they demand less. There are reasons to believe that *aggregate* supply and demand curves have the same shapes as their microeconomic counterparts, although as we shall now see, the explanations for this are different.

Consider the relationship between **aggregate demand**—the sum of consumption, investment, government spending, and net exports—and the overall price level. We might expect a negative relation between them because central banks (e.g., the Federal Reserve Board in the United States or the European Central Bank—the institutions that set interest rates) are likely to react to higher prices in the economy by raising interest rates.[1] We shall consider why they react this way in more detail in Chapter 17. We shall also see (in Part IV) that increasing interest rates reduces spending—particularly on consumption and investment—and thus lowers demand. Therefore, higher prices lead to lower demand and a downward-sloping demand curve, as in Figure 3.1. A second reason for expecting a downward-sloping aggregate demand curve is that higher prices make the output of domestic firms more expensive compared to overseas competition.

There is a third reason to expect overall demand to be lower the higher are prices—the real value of notes and coin, what you can purchase with your money, is lower when prices are higher. The nominal, or face, value of this type of money is fixed, so as the price of goods rises the amount of goods a given amount of money buys falls. That part of household and corporate wealth in the form of noninterest bearing money is relatively

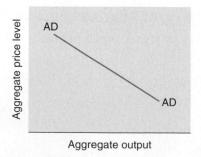

FIGURE 3.1 **Aggregate demand curve.** The higher are prices the lower the demand for output (AD) is likely to be.

---

[1]We need to be careful here. If the central bank has a target for the price level it wants, the proposition is straightforward. But if the central bank has a target for inflation—that is, the rate of change of prices—things are less clear. Of course, a sudden rise in the price level does generate inflation, and if the rise is unanticipated, the inflation rate will be higher than the central bank had expected. Central banks are likely to respond to unanticipated inflation by raising interest rates. So with an unanticipated upwards shift in prices, we are likely to see higher interest rates when there is either a central bank target for actual inflation or for the level of prices. (We will consider this in detail in Chapter 17.)

small in developed countries, so the impact may not be very large, but it is still a negative effect on demand.

So there are at least three reasons why a higher level of overall prices in the economy, other things equal, tends to make the level of demand for domestic output lower. It is important that we focus here on the demand for real output—in Figure 3.1 we measure *real* values, and not money (or nominal) values, on the horizontal axis.

What about **aggregate supply**? Aggregate supply is the total quantity of goods and services firms are willing to produce. *In the short run*, wages and import prices are not likely to fully reflect a sudden change in domestic prices. If that is so, and assuming firms are producing below full capacity, firms may be willing to produce more output if the price level increases because this raises profit margins. As Figure 3.2 shows, this will generate an upward-sloping supply curve.

The upward-sloping supply curve shown in Figure 3.2 comes because wages are fixed in the short run and firms are willing to supply more output as prices increase because profit margins rise. However, wages do not remain fixed forever, and in response to higher prices, employees will soon seek higher wages. Eventually wages will increase by at least as much as prices, in which case profit margins will no longer be higher, and firms will not wish to produce higher levels of output. So in the longer run, we should not expect supply to be higher at higher prices. In fact, we should expect supply to be independent of the price level—**the long-run supply curve** will be vertical. Figure 3.3 illustrates this.

Look at it this way. Suppose one could permanently increase output with a higher price level—then wouldn't countries with very high inflation find that output was rising very fast? Countries that had enjoyed the greatest growth in living standards would tend to be those with the most inflationary pasts. But this is strikingly at odds with the facts.

We can make the point illustrated in Figure 3.3 in another way. To produce a higher level of output over a sustained period, either the amount of labor supplied or the amount of capital (machines, etc.) employed needs to be greater. (We hold constant

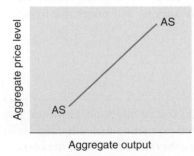

FIGURE 3.2 **Short-run aggregate supply curve.** The higher are prices of output the greater is the incentive of firms to supply output, at least in the short run before all input prices react. So the aggregate supply curve is upward sloping.

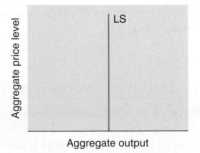

FIGURE 3.3 **Long-run aggregate supply curve.** If wages and other costs eventually move up in line with prices of output, firms will find it no more profitable to produce at high overall levels of prices than at low levels. Then the long-run supply curve will be vertical.

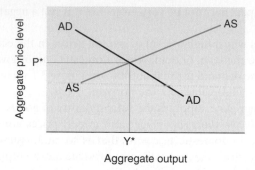

FIGURE 3.4 **Equilibrium with aggregate supply and aggregate demand.** The price level that matches aggregate demand (AD) to aggregate supply (AS) is the equilibrium level of prices (P*). At this price output is Y*.

the rate of technical progress for this comparison.) Both firms and workers care about **real wages**—money wages measured relative to the prices of goods bought and sold. To induce people to work more, the real wage will probably need to move. But why should *real* wages change just because the overall level of prices in the economy is higher (or lower)? Because there is no obvious long-run connection between real wages and the overall level of prices, there is also no reason to expect a link between prices and labor input. We can make the same point about a link between real investment (or the capital stock) and the general level of prices—there is no reason to expect them to be related. If in the long run neither the level of capital nor of labor employed is plausibly linked to the general level of prices, then neither is the supply of output. Hence we see the vertical long-run aggregate supply curve of Figure 3.3.

Figure 3.4 shows how the interaction of particular supply and demand curves determine prices and output in the short run in the economy. At this *equilibrium*, where prices are P* and output Y*, the amount of output firms are willing to produce (given the price) is exactly equal to what agents wish to buy at that price.

What happens when prices are too high for equilibrium—that is, when prices are above P*? At such a high price, firms wish to produce more output than consumers demand. This leads to excess supply, which causes prices to fall as goods remain unsold. If instead prices are below P*, then demand exceeds supply, and prices rise toward their equilibrium value.

3.2   A Conceptual Overview of This Book

We can now use these basic tools to outline the rest of this book. However, remember that this is only an *outline* of a far more detailed exposition that will unfold over the next 20 or so chapters. Its purpose is to give you a coherent overview of the book.

LONG-RUN ECONOMIC GROWTH (CHAPTERS 4–9)

In Chapter 4 we document how much output has increased over time in a range of countries. We also introduce the concept of a production function that links together the factors of production (essentially capital and labor), the state of technological knowledge, and the level of output produced. The production function shows how increases in either the capi-

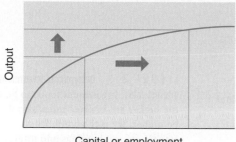

FIGURE 3.5 **The production function.** The production function shows the relation between inputs (capital or labor) and output.

tal stock or hours worked lead to an increase in output—as shown in Figure 3.5. In drawing the production function as a concave function—one whose slope flattens as we move to the right—we are assuming that increases in inputs—labor employed or capital—tend to generate less extra output the higher employment (or capital) is. This assumption of **diminishing marginal returns** is a common one, though the empirical evidence in its favor is mixed, and the implications of dropping it are important. We shall consider them in Chapter 7.

It takes years to change the capital stock of a country substantially. The equilibrium unemployment rate also changes slowly. As a result, the full capacity (or sustainable) level of output moves slowly—if the capital stock and employment cannot change much in the short run, then neither can output produced. However, over decades the full-capacity (long-run) supply curve can shift substantially (as shown in Figure 3.6) and this accounts for improvements in the standard of living over time.

Chapter 4 establishes that increases in the capital stock have been an important source of growth for all economies, so Chapter 5 focuses on capital accumulation. We start by considering how much investment an economy will make each period (e.g., each year) in its capital stock. A useful way to examine this is to consider the financial markets of an economy. Each economy has a financial sector that provides savings for firms to invest. The higher the interest rate in the economy, the more savings the financial sector is likely to provide.[2] The amount of investment firms wish to make depends

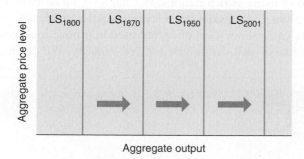

FIGURE 3.6 **Increasing capacity through long-run growth.** Over time the capital and labor that a country uses in production rises. Long-run supply curves move to the right.

___

[2]We talk here about "the" interest rate as if people could only invest in one asset. In reality people can invest in tens of thousands of different assets—we consider the most important types in Part VI. For the moment we should just think of "the" interest rate as a sort of average of the returns on the many different sorts of assets in the economy.

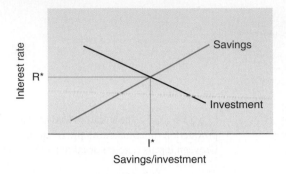

FIGURE 3.7 **Determining investment and interest rates.** Investment tends to be lower the higher are interest rates; savings may be higher. R* is the equilibrium interest rate where total savings and total investment are equal.

on how profitable they think extra spending will be and how high interest rates are. The higher interest rates are, the less firms wish to borrow and the lower their investment will be. Figure 3.7 shows equilibrium in the financial sector. Here the point where the savings and investment schedule intersect determines the interest rate. This equilibrium—where the interest rate is R* and the level of investment is I*—pins down investment and also determines the long-run capital stock of the economy. In Chapter 5 we model how investment leads to changes in the capital stock and, using the production function, show how this helps explain the long-run shifts in the full capacity output level shown in Figure 3.6.

Chapter 6 focuses on an alternative mechanism for driving economic growth: technological progress. Technological progress is the process whereby discoveries and inventions improve how we do things—which to an economist means producing more output from a given set of inputs of labor, capital, and materials. Technological progress leads to an upward shift in the production function and drives economic growth—as Figure 3.8 shows.

Chapter 5 focuses on the accumulation of *physical* capital, that is, machines and buildings. Chapter 7 extends this to include *human* capital, the skills and knowledge that society accumulates. Human capital can dramatically change the implications of the model for long-run growth that we outline in Chapters 5 and 6. In particular it raises the possibility that growth might continue indefinitely and that poor countries may not converge to the same standard of living as rich nations. In Chapter 7 we describe how this changes our theoretical analysis and consider the relevant empirical evidence.

As well as determining the equilibrium level of capital used in production we also need to analyze the amount of labor that can be used at full capacity. We do this in

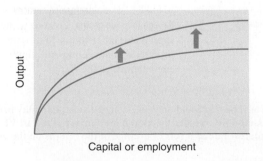

FIGURE 3.8 **Technological progress leads to higher output.** Technological progress moves the production function up—it generates more output for given inputs.

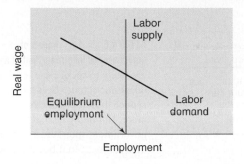

FIGURE 3.9 **Determining long-run employment.**
The equilibrium, or natural, rate of employment
is the level where workers and firms are offering
and hiring as much work as they want and where
supply equals demand.

Chapter 8, where we outline the determinants of the **natural rate of unemployment**—an equilibrium concept that links together the supply and demand for labor. Figure 3.9 shows the essence of this analysis. Here the natural rate, or equilibrium level, of employment is the rate that equates supply and demand and determines how much labor will be used at full capacity. For simplicity Figure 3.9 shows a case where the supply of labor is invariant to the wage—a case, as we shall see, that is consistent with long-run trends in labor markets. This equilibrium employment rate, shown in Figure 3.9, influences the level of output an economy can produce via the production function.

Chapter 8 considers in detail what influences the equilibrium wage and the equilibrium level of employment in an economy and how these change in response to long run productivity developments and differences in institutional structure. We consider a world where as wages increase, firms demand fewer hours worked, but supply remains unchanged—no matter how high the wage rate may go, people will only work a certain number of hours.

Chapter 9, the final chapter of Part II, concerns trade between countries. Here the emphasis is less upon how much output a country can produce than on what *type* of output it produces and exports.

GOVERNMENT POLICY IN THE LONG RUN (CHAPTERS 10–12)

A constant theme throughout this book is how the government influences the economy. In Part III we focus explicitly on the behavior of the government and the long-run framework within which fiscal policy and the money supply influence the economy.

Chapters 10 and 11 consider the role of the government in rectifying market failures and the relationships between taxes, government expenditure, fiscal deficits, and the stock of government debt. The government strongly affects the supply side of the economy. Through government investment in infrastructure—in roads, telecommunications, railways, etc.—it increases the capital stock, and via the production function, enables output to increase. But governments also have to raise revenue to finance this expenditure, and that means imposing taxes, which can result in less investment and a lower capital stock and thus in less output.[3] However, through spending on education and research and development (R&D), the government can also boost the amount of

---

[3]We will consider the mechanisms involved, and the evidence for their operation, in detail in Chapters 10 and 11.

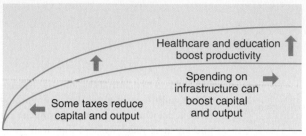

FIGURE 3.10 **Impact of government on long-run output.** Taxes are likely to reduce the level of economic activity because they reduce the supply of capital and labor. But many elements of government spending are forms of investment that boost output.

output that a particular level of capital or hours worked can produce. Figure 3.10 illustrates the different impacts of fiscal policy on the long-run productive potential of the economy.

In Chapters 10–12 (as in Chapters 4–9), we focus on the supply side of the economy—that is, we analyze the evolution of capital and labor, which drive trends in the amount of output supplied to the market. We do so without considering explicitly the aggregate demand curve. Our underlying assumption is that in the long term supply creates its own demand. As we saw when discussing how to measure GDP, all the output produced in an economy must be paid out in income. We also saw that all the output produced is also sold. Therefore we assume that in the long run demand will always expand (or sometimes contract) along with supply. Of course, by focusing only on the supply side of the economy, we cannot discuss prices. When we are most concerned with trends in the standard of living, focusing just on real GDP and ignoring prices makes sense. But the overall price level, and how it changes, is still important, and Chapter 12 analyzes how prices are determined.

In Chapter 12 we close our analysis of the long-run side of the economy by examining the determinants of the price level. We introduce a demand curve into our analysis and use it to pin down the price level in the economy and provide us with a long-run theory of inflation. We outline (and assess) the **quantity theory of money** which forms the basis of monetarism—the theory that changes in the money supply determine the overall level of prices. In this model the full-capacity (or long-run) supply curve determines output, while the amount of money in the economy influences the demand curve.

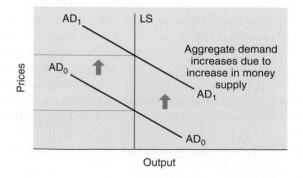

FIGURE 3.11 **Money supply influences long-run price level.** The equilibrium price level moves as aggregate demand shifts up or down a supply curve. Movements in monetary conditions—the amount of money and its cost (interest rates)—generate shifts in the demand curve.

As the money supply increases, so does demand and therefore so do prices, as Figure 3.11 illustrates. With this final analysis, we have a complete—though highly stylized—long-run model of output and prices in the economy.

BUSINESS CYCLES (CHAPTERS 13–17)

The second half of the book turns attention away from the long run, where developments occur across decades, and focuses on shorter-term (annual or quarterly) fluctuations in output. To focus on shorter-run issues, we make two amendments to our earlier long-run analysis. We introduce a more significant role for the demand curve, and instead of the vertical long-run supply curve, we focus on the short-run, upward-sloping supply curve of Figure 3.2.

Chapters 13 and 14 focus on consumption and investment and analyze how they vary over the business cycle. We examine their sensitivity to interest rates and income (among many other variables) and how they affect aggregate demand over the business cycle. We show that cuts in interest rates, expectations of higher profits and income, or reductions in taxes all tend to boost consumption and investment and shift the aggregate demand curve out. By contrast, higher interest rates, the threat of recession, or higher taxes can all cause the aggregate demand curve to shift in. Chapters 13 and 14 help explain why aggregate demand shifts may cause output fluctuations over the business cycle.

To account for business cycle fluctuations, we need to move away from the long-run, vertical supply curve of Figure 3.3 and instead use the upward-sloping, short-run supply curve. Figure 3.13 illustrates how shifts in demand that happen over a time frame where the supply curve slopes up generate movements in output. This shows how the short-run supply curve (AS) interacts with the shifting demand curves of Figure 3.12 and can explain business cycle fluctuations in output and prices.

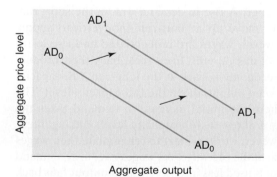

FIGURE 3.12 **Shifting demand curve as source of business cycle fluctuations.** Aggregate demand is the sum of spending on consumption and investment plus government expenditure and net exports. Movements in any of these cause shifts in the aggregate demand curve.

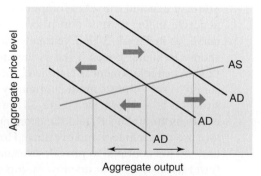

FIGURE 3.13 **Aggregate demand (AD) shifts and the business cycle.** Increases or decreases in aggregate demand generate output shifts in the short run when the aggregate supply curve is nonvertical.

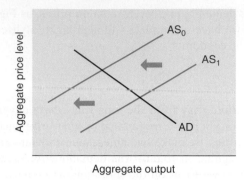

FIGURE 3.14   **Shifting supply curve and business cycle fluctuations.** An adverse shift in conditions for producers—for example a rise in input prices—moves the supply curve inwards (from AS_0 to AS_1).

Chapter 15 offers a detailed theoretical and empirical explanation of the differences between the short-run and long-run supply curves. As we noted above, one explanation for the short-run supply curve and its positive slope is that previous wage settlements fix the level of wages in the short run. As prices increase this means that real wages fall, profit margins rise, and firms are willing to supply more output. Firms can, for short periods, produce above full capacity (by utilizing overtime and working machines above their optimal intensity).

Figure 3.14 shows the case where movements in the supply curves, not shifts in the demand curves, cause business cycle fluctuations in output. One change that shifts the supply curve is an increase in oil prices. For a given level of goods prices, this leads to an increase in costs and a reduction in the profit margin that persuades firms to provide less output—the supply curve shifts inwards. A fall in the price of oil generates an opposite effect and leads to the supply curve shifting out.

LINKING THE SHORT RUN AND THE LONG RUN

Shifts in demand can cause output to change. A rise in demand will, in the short run, generate higher output and prices if we move up a short-run (nonvertical) supply curve, as in Figure 3.13. Eventually, however, wages are renegotiated and rise in response to higher prices. Then as the profit margin falls, firms scale back their production. When adjustment is complete, the economy is back at the long-run, full-capacity supply curve—firms cannot continually keep output above the full-capacity level. The situation is as shown in Figure 3.15 where the initial increase in demand takes the economy from A to B, and the economy is above its full-capacity level, making intensive use of machinery and overtime. However, workers start to renegotiate their wages and will not continue to provide overtime at the old wage. As wages rise, firms demand fewer hours from their employees, capital is used less intensively, and output falls back to its long-run equilibrium level, C. The full-capacity level of output represents the trend level of output. Figure 3.15 shows that business cycle fluctuations are deviations around the trend line. As we discussed above, Part II of the book focuses on how this trend level of output changes over time; in Part IV we discuss the fluctuations around this trend.

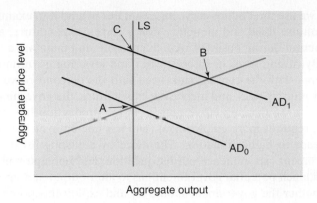

FIGURE 3.15 **Business cycles as deviations from trend output.** A shift in demand (from AD_0 to AD_1) generates higher output in the short run—a move from A to B. But as prices of inputs adjust, output moves back (B to C).

Two other key variables for business cycle analysis are inflation and unemployment, which are linked together via the **Phillips curve**—shown in Figure 3.16. The Phillips curve is named after Bill Phillips, who noted a relation between the level of unemployment and the rate of inflation. His curve traces out a negative relation between inflation and unemployment—a relation based more on empirical regularities from history than theory. One explanation for the negative relationship which has existed in many economies between inflation and unemployment is similar to that which lies behind the upward-sloping, short-run supply curve. If labor negotiations fix the wage level, then, in the short-run, as inflation rises, the real wage (what wages cost relative to the price of commodities produced) falls and labor becomes cheaper. This encourages firms to hire more workers and leads to a fall in unemployment (a rise in employment). By contrast, if inflation is unexpectedly low, then real wages are higher than anticipated, the demand for labor is lower, and unemployment rises. However, this negative relationship between inflation and unemployment is only a short-run phenomenon. Eventually wages are renegotiated, and employment (and unemployment) returns to its equilibrium level (look back at Figure 3.9). Therefore, in the long run, the Phillips curve is vertical—there is no relationship between inflation and unemployment, and unemployment settles at its equilibrium level.

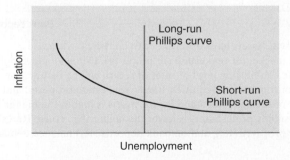

FIGURE 3.16 **Phillips curve.**

In Chapters 16 and 17, we use the Phillips curve and what lies behind it to examine whether the government can use fiscal and monetary policy (taxes, expenditure, and interest rates) to stabilize output during business cycle fluctuations and maintain a low and steady inflation rate. By raising taxes or interest rates and lowering government expenditure, the government—with the central bank—can shift the demand curve inwards. By lowering taxes or interest rates and increasing expenditure, the government can increase demand and shift the demand curve out. From the production function, we know that higher output requires more employment (and less unemployment) and, using the Phillips curve, leads to higher inflation. Therefore by adjusting fiscal and monetary policy, the government can influence output, inflation, and unemployment. In Part IV we consider how much potential government has to alter output and unemployment and, crucially, whether the government should try and exploit this potential if it exists.

ASSET MARKETS AND ASSET PRICES (CHAPTERS 14–24)

A key feature of the economy is how asset markets and asset prices behave. Asset markets both reflect and influence developments in the economy. In Parts V and VI, we show how macroeconomic factors help determine the level of asset prices and how changes in them affect the macroeconomy.

If a global capital market exists, then we can use Figure 3.7 again, but this time to determine a world interest rate, R*, at which all countries can borrow or earn returns on their savings. If there is an integrated world capital market, then savings flow between countries, and investors in one country can allocate their savings across a menu of assets that cover the globe. Global savings and investment balance each other at a world interest rate. At this interest rate, the amount of savings in the

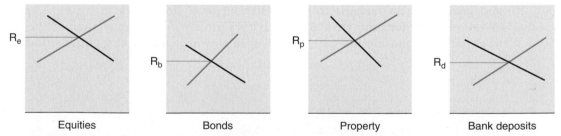

FIGURE 3.17   **Rates of return in asset markets.** Assets have different characteristics—risks are different in the equity market than in the market for real estate (or property). Demand and supply curves are distinct in each market, and the equilibrium level of rates of return will be distinct for different assets. Here we show markets for four assets—equities, bonds, real estate property, and bank deposits. In each market the supply of saving (or demand for the asset) is higher the higher the return, while the demand for saving (the supply of the asset) is lower the higher the return. Rates of return on equities (R_e), or bonds (R_b), or property (R_p), and on bank deposits (R_d) balance demand and supply in each market.

world economy is enough to finance the desired level of global investment *at that particular interest rate*. While savings and investment are the same at a global level, this does not have to be the case for each country when the world financial market allows free movement of capital across borders—a country can finance a high level of investment by borrowing from overseas. In Chapter 20 we examine global capital markets and assess whether a single world interest rate exists and the extent to which countries can finance high levels of investment through overseas borrowing. We also consider the validity of recent demands to control these global capital flows and the role of the major international institutions (particularly the International Monetary Fund [IMF] and the World Bank).

In the global markets for financial assets—for equities, bonds, and bank deposits—savers meet those who wish to raise funds to finance investment. The prices set in these markets, which are rates of return on various types of financial assets, move to balance the supply of new finance (saving) against demand for funds (which reflects investment demands). In Figure 3.7 we should really think of R* as an average of rates of return on different types of assets—equities, bonds, property, and bank deposits. As Figure 3.17 shows, the rates of return on these different assets will not all be equal and will reflect the demand/supply balance in the particular market. Chapters 21 through 24 examine in detail the interaction between these asset markets and the economy. We focus there on four of the most important asset markets: the market for equities (Chapter 21), for bonds (Chapter 22), for real estate (Chapter 23), and for bank deposits (Chapter 24).

3.3 Bringing It All Together: The Link between the Domestic Economy and the Wider World

The capital account of the balance of payments measures the extent to which a country borrows overseas in a period. It measures the net inflow (or outflow) of savings from (or into) a country. It tells you whether a country is a net lender or net borrower in the world financial markets. If domestic savings exceed domestic investment, then the country is lending funds overseas and has a *capital account deficit*—it is buying more overseas assets than it is selling of its own. When investment exceeds savings, the country has a *capital account surplus*. We can use the national accounts framework of Chapter 2 to establish an important relationship between the capital account and net exports. From our expenditure approach to measuring GDP, we have

GDP = Consumption + Investment + Government Expenditure + Net Exports (exports, X, less imports, M)

or $Y = C + I + G + X - M$

which we can write as

$Y - C = I + G + X - M$

We also know that the expenditure measure of GDP equals the income measure, so we can also think of Y as reflecting income. It must therefore be the case that

Income = Consumption + Savings + Taxation

or   Y = C + S + T

where S is savings and T tax payments. Rearranging this gives

Y − C = S + T

If we combine this with our earlier expression, we have

Y − C = S + T = I + G + X − M

or   (S − I) + (T − G) = X − M

S − I is net savings of the private sector, while T − G is the net savings of the government sector. Therefore, total savings in the economy (private plus government sector) must equal net exports. If an economy is borrowing from overseas and running a capital account surplus (I > S), then it must also be generating a negative level of net exports— or what we call a *current account deficit* (X < M).

Net exports are brought into balance with net savings through changes in the real exchange rate (which measures the relative price of goods in different countries). The link comes because when exporters sell goods, or importers buy overseas goods, it stimulates a demand for currencies that is the counterpart to the demand for overseas goods. If a German manufacturing company buys raw materials from a Canadian mining company and pays in Canadian dollars, the transaction is likely to involve a sale of euros and a purchase of Canadian dollars. Flows of financial capital also shift the supply and demand for currencies. If a Canadian pension fund sells domestic shares (equities) to another Canadian pension fund and buys shares in a German company from a French pension fund, then there is likely to be a sale of Canadian dollars against euros. This will affect—though probably not much—the euro/Canadian dollar exchange rate.

A high real exchange rate means that a country's output is expensive, so its exports will be low, and it will import goods from abroad. Therefore, a high real exchange rate leads to low net exports. Figure 3.18 shows how the real exchange rate adjusts, so that net exports equal net savings.[4] If net exports exceed net savings, the demand for the currency exceeds supply, generating an increase in the real exchange rate, which makes exports more expensive and imports cheaper. Therefore, net exports fall until eventually they equal net savings. Similarly, if net exports are less than net savings, the real exchange rate falls. Chapter 18 examines the behavior of the real exchange rate and its determinants.

The real exchange rate refers to how expensive a country's output is, but also important is the nominal exchange rate—the rate at which one currency can be exchanged for another. This is the focus of Chapter 19 where we focus in particular on the relationship between interest rates and the nominal exchange rate.

---

[4]In Figure 3.18 we have assumed that net savings in an economy do not depend on the real exchange rate. Alternative assumptions can easily be made.

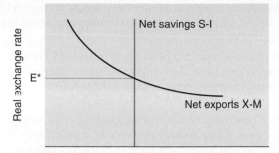

FIGURE 3.18   **Real exchange rate determination.** Aggregate net savings must equal aggregate net exports—movements in the exchange rate help maintain this equality. Here we assume that as the real exchange rate rises exports become less attractive to foreigners and imports become more attractive to domestic residents. As a result net exports (exports minus imports) fall the higher is the real exchange rate. Here we assume net savings is relatively insensitive to the exchange rate.

SUMMARY

Throughout the book we will use the simple, but powerful, ideas we have introduced here. The key notions we have defined—the concept of an equilibrium; the difference between the short run and the long run; the production function—will prove valuable in analyzing many issues. A unifying theme behind the analysis of all markets is that prices and quantities adjust to balance supply and demand. In this chapter we have used this fundamental idea to think about the determination of aggregate output and prices in the short run and in the longer run. We have also looked at equilibrium in the labor market and in the markets where the demand for savings from companies and governments is balanced against the supply of savings from households. The distinction between the short run—where some prices may be slow to adjust—and the long run—where all prices have adjusted to new conditions—is an important one. We have illustrated how in the markets for output and labor the short-run response of activity (the volume produced and the number of hours worked) to shifts in demand is likely to be different from the long-run response.

CONCEPTUAL QUESTIONS

1. Do you think that for most companies the price of their output is changed more frequently than the wage rates they pay their workers? Are there industries in which wages are more flexible than prices? If sectors of the economy in which wage rates are relatively more flexible become more numerous, what might you expect to happen to the slope of the aggregate supply curve?

2. Give some reasons why the overall real level of demand in the economy might be affected by the average level of prices. Is it plausible that the level of nominal demand might fall as the general level of prices rises?

3. As the general price level for produced goods in an economy rises, would you expect firms to have an incentive to produce more? Make clear exactly what you assume about the cost of producing goods when you answer.

4. The Phillips curve shows the relation between the rate of unemployment and the rate of inflation. What do you expect this curve to look like? How might you assess whether the long run relation between inflation levels and unemployment rates and the short-run relation are different?

5. If there is a global capital market, then how much investment companies in a particular country undertake and how much saving is done in that country need not be equal. If there is not a global market for capital, domestic saving and investment need to be closely matched. What are the advantages of having a global capital market? Are there any disadvantages?

6. Is it obvious that when interest rates are higher people save more? Think of some reasons why someone might save less when interest rates are higher.

ANALYTICAL QUESTIONS

1. Assume that consumption of households in an economy depends on how much they expect their wage income to be in the future. Suppose there is a new discovery that is likely to increase labor productivity, and wages, *in the future*. Using aggregate demand and supply schedules show the impact this might have on prices and output (a) immediately and (b) once the discovery actually starts to increase productivity.

2. The supply of output from firms is lower the higher are real wages. Write this supply relation in a simple form:

$$S_t = a - b(W/P)_t$$

where S_t is supply at time t, a and b are positive coefficients, and W_t/P_t is wages (W) relative to prices (P) at time t—i.e., real wages.

Assume that wages this period are set at a level that reflects the prices in the previous period. Let:

$$W_t = P_{t-1}$$

Trace through the impact of a sudden jump in prices at time t on supply. What is the effect of higher inflation (i.e., a consistently more rapid rate of growth of prices)?

3. In Figure 3.7 we assumed that the supply of saving increased with interest rates and that the level of investment declined the higher was the interest rate. Suppose that savings initially increase as interest rates rise from low levels, but that beyond some point savings start to fall as interest rates rise further. Draw a diagram which illustrates how there might be more than one equilibrium interest rate. Is there any way of knowing which of these interest rates will be the equilibrium? Could there be more than two equilibrium interest rates?

4. Suppose a small country is cut off from the global capital market so that domestic saving must match domestic investment. The domestic equilibrium interest rate is above the interest rate in the rest of the world capital market. Now suppose that the country is able to borrow and lend abroad and becomes integrated into the world capital market. What will

happen to domestic saving and to the level of investment? What do you expect to happen to the gap between exports and imports?

5. If workers know that prices in the economy are about to rise, they are likely to push for higher wages in labor negotiations. For this reason we would expect real wages to be *unexpectedly* low only when prices were *unexpectedly* high. The distinction between price rises that are expected and those that are unexpected therefore becomes important. How does this distinction change the way you interpret the Phillips curve? Does it affect the nature of the aggregate supply curve?

The Increasing Wealth of Nations

Overview

In this chapter we document the substantial increase in output that many countries have achieved over the last 100 years or more. This increase has profoundly affected welfare, supporting a larger population, generating longer life expectancy, and creating more income per head. Long-run growth is the most important topic in macroeconomics and one of the most important in the social sciences. Relatively small increases in long-run growth rates can lead, over time, to enormous benefits.

4.1 Increasing Output Over Time

To understand the mechanism that has produced increased output, we focus on the production function—a technological relationship between inputs to the production process and output produced. We concentrate on three inputs: capital, labor, and total factor productivity (TFP). (Total factor productivity is the term economists use to explain the influence of a range of factors that affect the efficiency with which capital and labor combine to produce output.) Some combination of increases in these three factor inputs are the cause of increases in output. To calculate which factors have been most important, we need to know how an increase in each factor leads to higher output. This extra output is the **marginal product**, and different assumptions about whether the marginal product is increasing or decreasing with the scale of production play a crucial role in understanding the growth process. Using empirical observations about the marginal product, we shall see in this chapter that capital accumulation has historically been the key to growth. TFP has also been important for growth in mature industrial economies, while increases in labor input have been more important for growth in emerging markets.

THE FACTS OF GROWTH

Since the Industrial Revolution began in Western Europe in the late eighteenth century, most of the world's economies have witnessed an unprecedented increase in output. Figure 4.1, parts *a* and *b*, show how GDP has increased for several nations.

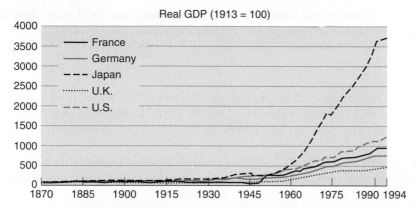

FIGURE 4.1a **Real GDP 1870–1994 for France, Germany, Japan, the UK, and the United States.** Output growth in the twentieth century has been dramatic. *Source*: Maddison, *Monitoring the World Economy 1820–1992* (Paris: OECD, 1995). Copyright OECD.

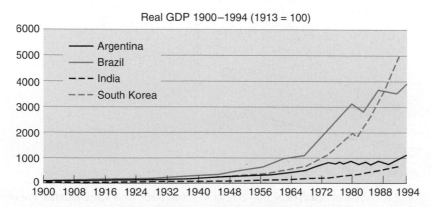

FIGURE 4.1b **Real GDP 1870–1994 for Argentina, Brazil, India, and South Korea.** Production has risen substantially in newly industrialized countries. *Source*: Maddison, *Monitoring the World Economy 1820–1992* (Paris: OECD, 1995). Copyright OECD.

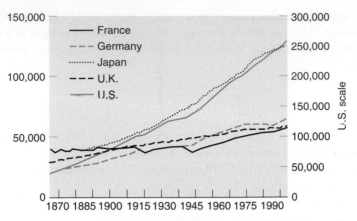

FIGURE 4.2a   **Population trends ('000s) 1870–1994 for France, Germany, Japan, the UK, and the United States.** World population has increased sharply over the twentieth century. *Source*: Maddison, *Monitoring the World Economy 1820–1992* (Paris: OECD, 1995). Copyright OECD.

While all nations have seen an increase, the magnitude varies from a sevenfold increase since 1913 for India to a 48-fold rise in South Korea. This part of the book seeks to explain why these increases have occurred and the cross-country pattern in growth.

As we remarked in Chapter 2, the best measure of the standard of living in a country is not the amount of output its economy produces but output *per capita*. Because of

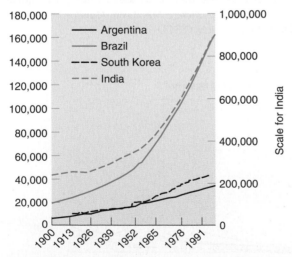

FIGURE 4.2b   **Population trends ('000s) 1900–1992 for Argentina, Brazil, South Korea, and India.** Population growth has been faster in developing countries. *Source*: Maddison, *Monitoring the World Economy 1820–1992* (Paris: OECD, 1995). Copyright OECD.

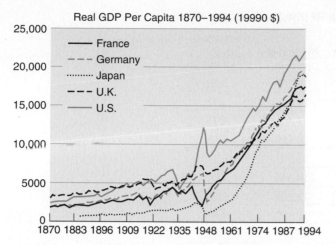

FIGURE 4.3a **Real GDP per capita 1870–1994 (1990s) for France, Germany, Japan, the UK, and the United States.** Per capita output increased rapidly in the period since the Second World War. *Source*: Maddison, *Monitoring the World Economy 1820–1992* (Paris: OECD, 1995). Copyright OECD.

significant population growth (see Figure 4.2*a* and *b*), output *per capita* shows a less substantial increase over time than output alone (see Figure 4.3*a* and *b*). However, all the countries cited in the figures still display very substantial increases in the standard of living across time periods (see Table 4.1 for evidence on other economies). As a result of this economic growth, most of the world enjoys a standard of living that would have been undreamt of 100 years ago.

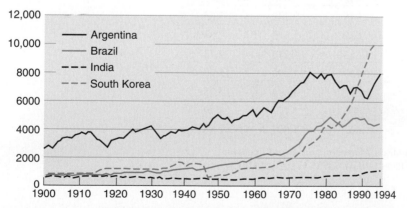

FIGURE 4.3b **Real GDP per capita 1900–1994 for Argentina, Brazil, India, and South Korea**
Source: Maddison, *Monitoring the World Economy, 1820–1992* (Paris: OECD, 1995).
Copyright OECD.

TABLE 4.1   Growth in Real GDP (1990s) per Capita 1900–1992

Country	1900 Real GDP per capita	1992 Real GDP per capita	Growth Multiple (1992 GDP/ 1900 GDP)
Australia	4,299	16,237	3.78
Austria	2,901	17,160	5.92
Belgium	3,652	17,165	4.7
Canada	2,758	18,159	6.58
Denmark	2,902	18,293	6.3
Finland	1,620	14,646	9.04
Italy	1,746	16,229	9.29
Netherlands	3,533	17,152	4.85
New Zealand	4,320	15,085	3.49
Norway	1,762	18,372	10.43
Sweden	2,561	16,710	6.52
Switzerland	3,531	20,830	5.9
Czechoslovakia	1,729	6,845	3.96
Hungary	1,682	5,638	3.35
USSR	1,218	4,671	3.83
Chile	1,949	7,238	3.71
Colombia	973	5,025	5.16
Mexico	1,157	5,112	4.42
Peru	817	2,854	3.49
Venezuela	821	9,163	11.16
Bangladesh	581	720	1.24
China	652	3,098	4.75
Indonesia	745	2,749	3.69
Pakistan	687	1,642	2.39
Philippines	1,033	2,213	2.14
Taiwan	759	11,590	15.27
Thailand	812	4,694	5.78
Egypt	509	1,972	3.79
Ghana	462	1,007	2.18

Source: Maddison, *Monitoring the World Economy 1820–1992* (Paris: OECD, 1995). Copyright OECD.

4.2 The Benefits of Economic Growth

Economic growth has deeply affected human welfare. In this section we outline the extent of this contribution by detailing the increase in population it has supported, improvements in life expectancy, and increases in the quality of life.

GROWING POPULATION

A huge increase in the population of the world has been both produced by and supported economic growth. Thomas Malthus (1766–1834), an English clergyman, wrote his *Essay on the Principle of Population* in 1798 in which he prophesied that limited natural resources constrained population size.[1] With the stock of natural resources fixed, he reasoned that the only way of producing more output was to use more labor. However, with a finite amount of natural resources, there was a limit to the size of the population and thus also a limit to the amount of output that population could produce. But what Malthus did not fully appreciate was that if we add more capital and increasing technical knowledge to a fixed amount of natural resources, then output can increase even with a constant level of labor input. Over the last 200 years, this interaction of capital accumulation and increasing technological knowledge has meant that Malthusian fears of a limit on the population of the world have not been realized (see Figure 4.4). Since Malthus wrote, world population has risen more than fivefold.

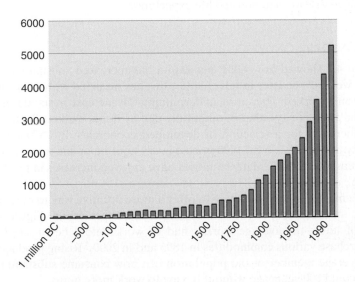

FIGURE 4.4 **World population (in millions) from 1 million BC.** World Population has grown exponentially. *Source*: Kremer, *Quarterly Journal of Economics* (1993) vol. 108, pp. 681–716. © 1993 by the President and Fellows of Harvard College and the Massachusetts Institute of Technology.

[1]The following gives a good taste of Malthus's work:

The power of population is so superior to the power in the earth to produce subsistence for man, that premature death must in some shape or other visit the human race. The vices of mankind are active and able ministers of depopulation. They are the precursors in the great army of destruction; and often finish the dreadful work themselves. But should they fail in this war of extermination, sickly seasons, epidemics, pestilence, and plague advance in terrific array, and sweep off their thousands and ten thousands.

TABLE 4.2   Survival Rates in England 1662 and United States 1993

Age	0	6	16	26	36	46	56	66	76
England 1662	100	64	40	25	16	10	6	3	1
USA 1993	100	99	99	98	97	95	92	84	70

Source: Peter Bernstein, *Against the Gods* (New York: John Wiley, 1996). © 1996 John Wiley. Reprinted by permission of John Wiley and Sons, Inc.

LIFE EXPECTANCY

Table 4.2 shows the proportion of a group of newborn babies in England in 1662, and in the United States in 1993, who could be expected to survive to different ages.

In 1662 a newborn baby in England had a 64% chance of surviving to age 6 compared to a 99% chance in modern America. The table makes for sobering reading—in 1662 English babies had only a one in four chance of surviving to age 26. Life expectancy depends on many things, not least medical knowledge and diet. Higher income leads to better nutrition and finances the production of medicines and medical research. While increased life expectancy was not solely due to economic growth, increased output and wealth undoubtedly were important in promoting it. As one economic historian pointed out, the relatively banal innovations of the widespread availability of affordable clothes, made from washable cotton, and cheap soap improved hygiene, reduced disease, and boosted life expectancy.[2]

IMPROVEMENTS IN THE STANDARD OF LIVING

Figure 4.3 and Table 4.1 showed how GDP per capita has increased substantially in most economies. As we shall see later in this chapter, this has occurred without a similar increase in total hours worked. Therefore, underpinning this increase in standards of living is a rise in labor productivity—that is, output divided by hours worked. Table 4.3 shows productivity increases for a selection of developed economies. In 1870 a U.S. worker produced output worth $2.26 (in 1990 prices) every hour he or she worked, but by 1992 this had increased to $29.10. Many countries have enjoyed increases in productivity of a similar size.

We can use these increases in productivity to offer a more intuitive way to measure improvements in the standard of living than resorting to GDP per capita. Figure 4.5 shows the number of hours the average worker had to work before he or she had earned enough to purchase various commodities in 1895 and in 2000.[3] Rising productivity means that the average member of the population can now consume substantially more then he or she could 100 years ago without having to work more hours.

[2]Landes, *The Wealth and Poverty of Nations* (New York: Norton Publishers, 1998).

[3]The 1895 numbers are calculated using the mail-order catalog of Montgomery Ward and are for the United States. See de Long, 2000. *Cornucopia: The Pace of Economic Growth in the Twentieth Century*, NBER Working Paper 7602.

TABLE 4.3   Labor Productivity (GDP per Hour Worked) 1870–1992 (1990$)

	1870	1913	1929	1938	1950	1973	1992
Austria	1.39	2.93	3.31	3.36	4.07	15.27	24.21
Belgium	2.12	3.60	4.81	5.27	6.06	16.53	28.55
Denmark	1.51	3.40	5.11	5.31	5.85	15.94	21.81
Finland	0.84	1.81	2.57	3.07	4.00	13.42	20.45
France	1.36	2.85	4.15	5.35	5.65	17.77	29.62
Germany	1.58	3.50	4.37	4.84	4.37	16.64	27.55
Italy	1.03	2.09	2.89	3.79	4.28	15.58	24.59
Netherlands	2.33	4.01	6.32	6.26	6.50	19.02	28.80
Norway	1.09	2.19	3.42	4.30	5.41	14.05	25.61
Sweden	1.22	2.58	3.29	4.27	7.08	18.02	23.11
Switzerland	1.75	3.25	5.38	5.90	8.75	18.28	25.37
UK	2.61	4.40	5.54	5.98	7.86	15.92	23.98
Japan	0.46	1.03	1.78	2.19	2.03	11.15	20.02
Australia	3.32	5.28	6.47	7.16	8.68	16.87	22.56
Canada	1.61	4.21	5.21	5.26	9.78	19.09	25.32
USA	2.26	5.12	7.52	8.64	12.66	23.45	29.10

Source: Maddison, *Monitoring the World Economy: 1820–1992* (Paris: OECD, 1995). Copyright OECD.

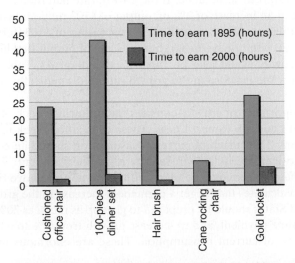

FIGURE 4.5   **Productivity improvements in the United States, 1895–2000.** Workers now enjoy dramatically higher material rewards than 100 years ago. *Source*: de Long, *Cornucopia: The Pace of Economic Growth in the Twentieth Century*, NBER Working Paper 7602 (2000).

4.3   The Importance of Economic Growth

All of the above suggests that the benefits of growth are enormous; considerable economic research has focused on analyzing long-run economic growth. This research is of immense significance because even small changes in growth rates can have substantial long-run implications. For instance, since 1870 the U.S. economy has grown at an annual rate of 1.75% (in *per capita* terms), and the United States is now one of the richest industrialized countries in the world. If instead the U.S. economy had grown at only 1% per annum over this period (as some countries did), then U.S. *per capita* output would now be at roughly the same level as in contemporary Mexico and Hungary and would be *lower* than in Greece or Portugal. Conversely, if the United States had grown at an annual rate of 2.75% over this period (basically the rate at which Taiwan and Japan did), then current *per capita* output in the United States would be more than three times what it currently is. As a leading macroeconomist has written :

> *Is there some action a government of India could take that would lead the Indian economy to grow like Indonesia's or Egypt's? If so, what exactly? If not, what is it about the "nature of India" that makes it so? The consequences for human welfare involved in questions like these are simply staggering: once one starts to think about them, it is hard to think about anything else.[4]*

Small changes in the growth rate can dramatically affect economic performance for a simple reason—the mathematics of compounding. Assume, for example, that the annual growth rate of an economy increases from 2% to 3% and that initially output in the economy was valued at 100 million U.S. dollars. At the end of the first year of higher growth, output would be higher by just $1 million. However, in year 2 the effect of the higher growth rate would start to accumulate. If the growth rate had remained at 2%, then year 2 would have seen an increase of 2% on output of $102 million. Instead under the higher growth rate, there would be growth of 3% on output of $103 million. Not only would the percentage growth rate be higher, but the level of output that benefits from the higher output growth would also be rapidly expanding. As Table 4.4 shows, it would not take long for the increase in the growth rate to dramatically affect the output level.

To emphasize again the importance of growth, consider the following "back of the envelope" calculation of Nobel Laureate Robert Lucas. These calculations seek to answer the following two questions: How much of current consumption should an economy be prepared to give up to increase its growth rate by a specified amount? How much current consumption should an economy be prepared to give up to remove business cycle fluctuations?[5] Lucas calculates that to get a permanent increase in the growth rate from 2% to 3% the United States should be prepared to give up as much as 20% of current consumption in a one-time payment, and to increase growth from 3% to 6%, it should give up as much as 42% of current consumption. These are enormous num-

---

[4]Lucas, "On the Mechanics of Economic Development," *Journal of Monetary Economics* (1988 vol. 22, pp. 3–42).

[5]This is only a thought experiment—Lucas is not saying that spending this money will produce these results.

TABLE 4.4 The Force of Growth Compounding

	2% Growth	3% Growth
Year 0	100	100
Year 1	102	103
Year 2	104	106.1
Year 3	106.1	109.3
Year 4	108.2	112.6
Year 5	110.4	115.9
Year 10	121.9	134.4
Year 25	164.1	209.4
Year 50	269.2	438.4
Year 100	724.5	1921.9

bers—42% of U.S. consumption is nearly 2 *trillion* dollars. By contrast, to remove all business cycle fluctuations, the United States should give up only 0.1% of its current consumption. Undoubtedly, these calculations neglect many important factors, and many have criticized them (see Chapter 14 for a fuller analysis), but they make a basic point: **economic growth is big business compared to business cycle fluctuations and indeed to most other economic issues**.

For the intuition behind this result, remember from Chapter 2 that business cycles are fluctuations around the trend level of economic activity. In other words, the business cycle reallocates output over time periods but does not directly influence the average long-term growth rate.[6] We can see this in Figure 4.6, which shows GDP for an imaginary economy growing at an underlying trend rate of 2.5% per year. The business cycle is defined as fluctuations around a trend, in other words, the movement from A to B and then to C and D. These business cycles contribute substantially to the volatility in

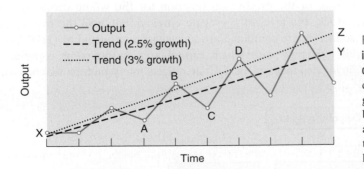

FIGURE 4.6 The relative importance of growth and business cycles. Trend growth is what determines where output goes over the longer term; business cycle fluctuations are relatively insignificant the longer is the time horizon.

[6]This is a simplification; even temporary shocks can have lasting effects. Furthermore, many economists argue that what are called business cycle fluctuations are not temporary deviations from a smooth trend path to which the economy returns but rather reflect shocks that permanently influence sustainable output. We return to these important issues in Chapter 17.

GDP but do not influence trend growth. Therefore we can link the value people place on avoiding business cycles to how much they dislike short-run uncertainty. By contrast, how much they should pay to increase the growth rate depends on how they value higher output. If the economy could somehow shift the long-term growth rate from 2.5% to 3%, then instead of ending up at a point like Y, it would be at Z where output is much higher.

So how important business cycles are depends on how much volatility they produce and how much society dislikes uncertainty. Given the relatively small size of U.S. business cycles (consumption growth nearly always varies between −2% and 5%), Lucas concluded that the main benefits flowed from higher growth—issues of growth are much bigger and more important than the volatility of short-term fluctuations.

Of course, none of this means that business cycles are unimportant, only that the cost of business cycle uncertainty is relatively small compared to the benefits of higher long-run growth. The benefits of boosting the long-term growth rate are substantial.

4.4   How Does Your Output Grow?

To analyze the mechanisms that have led to this increase in output, we return to the "production function" that we introduced in Chapter 3. The best way to understand the production function is to think of a single firm. To produce output, a firm combines its physical capital (buildings and machinery) with labor input (the number and efforts of its workforce) to produce output. Exactly how much output the firm produces when it uses these factors depends on many things: the firm's technological knowledge, whether it promotes efficiency in production, and so forth. All of these factors influence the efficiency with which the firm produces output from a given stock of capital and labor. As a result, we can think of three factors as providing output. Economists call how these factors interact the *production function* (see Figure 4.7).

Although we have introduced the production function for only a single firm, we can, by analogy, also think of the production function for the whole economy. The economy-wide capital stock, the level of aggregate employment, and the overall efficiency with which these factors are combined produce aggregate output or GDP. Economists call the overall efficiency with which capital and employment combine to produce output *total factor productivity*, or TFP. It reflects many factors: technological

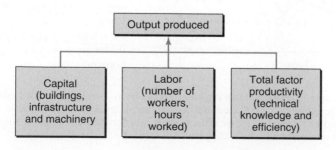

FIGURE 4.7 **The production function.**

progress, social and political institutions, cultural norms, etc., that influence the amount of output an economy can produce from given capital and labor.

Using the concept of a production function, we can investigate why output has increased over time and why the level of output produced differs across countries. Only three candidates can explain these things: different levels of capital, different levels of employment, or that some countries are more efficient or have increased their efficiency at different rates over time.

THE ROLE OF CAPITAL ACCUMULATION

Figures 4.8*a* and *b* show the substantial increases in machinery and structures that a sample of OECD countries have experienced over the last 100 years.[7]

The capital stock has increased dramatically for many reasons, and in succeeding chapters we will focus on the economic explanations for this increase. But noneconomic factors also help explain this historically unprecedented increase in capital accumulation. One important factor is the establishment of individual property rights against those of the monarchy or church. Another is the dramatic increase in life expectancy

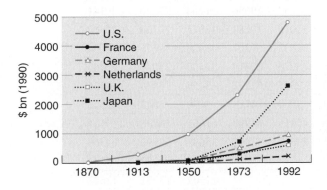

FIGURE 4.8a **Stock of machinery and equipment, 1870–1992 (1990$).** *Source*: Maddison, *Monitoring the World Economy: 1820–1992* (OECD, 1995). Copyright OECD.

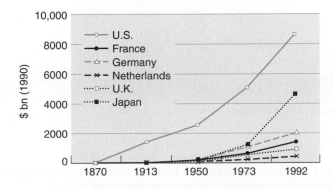

FIGURE 4.8b **Stock of nonresidential structures, 1870–1992 (1990$).** The capital stock in developed economies rose substantially over the twentieth century. *Source*: Maddison, *Monitoring the World Economy: 1820–1992* (Paris: OECD, 1995). Copyright OECD.

[7]The OECD is the Organization for Economic Cooperation and Development. It is a forum for developed countries to discuss economic policy issues.

that occurred from the eighteenth century onwards. Longevity encourages personal sector saving and helps to fund a greater capital stock. A third reason is the increase in our knowledge of risk and probability, a crucial factor behind the establishment of capital markets, which help finance capital accumulation.[8]

INCREASED LABOR INPUT

While countries' capital stocks have increased substantially over time, the statistics on labor input are more ambiguous. Table 4.5 lists employment (in thousands) for a range of countries. In every case employment has risen substantially.[9] However, what matters

TABLE 4.5   Total Employment 1870–1992 (000s)

	1870	1913	1929	1938	1950	1973	1992
Austria	2077	3122	3282	3113	3215	3160	3546
Belgium	2141	3376	3636	3316	3341	3748	3802
France	17800	19373	20170	18769	19663	21434	22557
Germany	9511	16039	17647	19656	21164	27160	29141
Italy	13770	17644	19016	19287	18875	22708	25652
Norway	706	984	1132	1267	1428	1676	2004
UK	12285	18566	18936	20818	22400	25076	25465
Australia	630	1943	2355	2592	3459	5838	7736
Canada	1266	3014	3960	4183	5030	8843	12316
USA	14720	38821	47915	44917	61651	86838	119164
Japan	18684	25751	29332	32290	35683	52590	64360
Greece		2018			2600	3232	3634
Spain		7613			11662	13031	12642
Argentina					6821	9402	11603
Chile					2256	2896	4588
Mexico					8563	15044	26412
Venezuela					1571	3331	6055
South Korea					6377	11140	18376
Taiwan					62872	5327	8632

Source: Maddison, *Monitoring the World Economy: 1820–1992* (Paris: OECD, 1995). Copyright OECD.

[8]The highly accessible book *Against the Gods* by Peter Bernstein (New York: John Wiley, 1997) gives an excellent account of these developments and their economic importance.

[9]A rising population means that increased employment does not necessarily equate with less unemployment.

TABLE 4.6   Annual Hours Worked per Person Employed 1870–1992

	1870	1913	1929	1938	1950	1973	1992
Austria	2935	2580	2281	2312	1976	1778	1576
Belgium	2964	2605	2272	2267	2283	1872	1581
France	2945	2588	2297	1848	1926	1771	1542
Germany	2941	2584	2284	2316	2316	1804	1563
Italy	2886	2536	2228	1927	1997	1612	1490
Norway	2945	2588	2283	2128	2101	1721	1465
UK	2984	2624	2286	2267	1958	1688	1491
Australia	2945	2588	2139	2110	1838	1708	1631
Canada	2964	2605	2399	2240	1967	1788	1656
USA	2964	2605	2342	2062	1867	1717	1589
Japan	2945	2588	2364	2391	2166	2042	1876
Greece					2200	2000	1720
Spain					2200	2150	1911
Argentina					2034	1996	1826
Chile					2212	1955	2005
Mexico					2154	2061	2062
Venezuela					2179	1965	1868
South Korea					2200	2683	2800
Taiwan					2200	2570	2500

Source: Maddison, *Monitoring the World Economy: 1820–1992* (Paris: OECD, 1995). Copyright OECD.

for the production function and for aggregate output is not the number of individuals working but the total number of hours that a country's labor force works. If we are concentrating on output per head, rather than the aggregate level of output, what really matters is hours per person and capital per person. Table 4.6 estimates the annual hours worked per person employed and shows that for most economies (South Korea and Taiwan excepted) employees were working fewer hours in 1992 compared with the past. One way in which people have benefited from higher standards of living is to have more leisure time. Therefore total hours are the product of one factor which is rising over time (employment) and another which is declining (average hours worked). As a result, in many economies, especially in the more mature OECD economies, total hours worked declined during the second half of the twentieth century. The situation is different in Japan, Canada, and Australia and in the emerging market nations listed in Table 4.7. In these countries rising populations and employment have produced an overall increase in total hours worked. These numbers suggest that the importance of labor input in accounting for the growth in the overall level of output varies across countries but that for most OECD economies it is fairly small.

TABLE 4.7   Total Hours Worked (millions) 1870–1992

	1870	1913	1929	1938	1950	1973	1992
Austria	6096	8055	7486	7197	6353	5618	5588
Belgium	6346	8794	8261	7517	7628	7016	6011
France	52421	50137	46330	34685	37871	37960	34783
Germany	27972	41445	40306	45523	49016	48997	45547
Italy	39740	44745	42368	37166	37693	36605	38221
Norway	2079	2547	2584	2696	3000	2884	2936
UK	36658	48717	43288	47194	43859	42328	37968
Australia	1855	5028	5037	5469	6358	9971	12617
Canada	3752	7851	9500	9370	9894	15811	20395
USA	43630	101129	112217	92619	115102	149101	189352
Japan	55024	66644	69341	77205	77289	107389	120739
Greece					5720	6464	6250
Spain					25656	28017	24159
Argentina					13874	18766	21187
Chile					4990	5662	9199
Mexico					18445	31006	54462
Venezuela					3423	6545	11311
South Korea					14029	29889	51453
Taiwan					6318	13690	21580

Source: Maddison, *Monitoring the World Economy: 1820–1992* (Paris: OECD, 1995). Copyright OECD.

4.5   The Link between Input and Output Growth

The production function is a key building block for our analysis of economic growth. Particularly important is how increases in each of the factors of production affect increases in output. The **marginal product of capital** or the **marginal product of labor** captures this information. The marginal product of capital is the increase in output that adding one further piece of machinery generates—keeping unchanged the level of hours worked and total factor productivity. The marginal product of labor is the increase in output that results from adding one further unit of labor, but where the capital stock and TFP remain unchanged. It is crucial to the definition of the marginal product that only one factor input is being changed—the idea is to isolate the role each input plays on its own.

Consider the case of a printing firm that has 20 employees and has to decide how many machines to purchase. Table 4.8 lists the output and marginal product of capital that the firm can produce using different numbers of machines when the firm has 20

TABLE 4.8   **Output and the Marginal Product of Capital**

Number of Machines	1	2	3	4	5
Output produced	10	19	26	31	34
Marginal product of capital	10	9	7	5	3

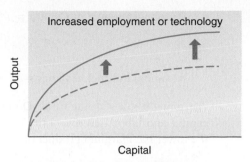

FIGURE 4.9   **Production function and technology/employment shifts.** Technological improvements raise the production function.

employees and each machine embodies the same technology. Figure 4.9 shows the relationship between output and capital for the printing firm.

Table 4.8 shows that the marginal product of capital declines as the firm buys more machines. Each machine leads to higher output, but the increase gets smaller the more machines the firm buys. As a consequence, the production function in Figure 4.9 starts to flatten out as the capital stock increases. This is a case of *decreasing marginal product of capital*. Other technologies may lead to constant or increasing marginal product. As the following chapters show, assumptions about the behavior of the marginal product of capital are a key determinant of cross-country patterns of growth.

Remember in Figure 4.9 we are not altering the number of workers or the technology, only the number of machines used. If the firm decides to hire more workers, then for any given level of the capital stock, it will be able to produce more output—the production function will shift up, as Figure 4.9 shows. The production function also shifts up if the firm decides to invest in better quality, or more technologically advanced, machines.

TECHNICAL DIGRESSION

Economists often assume that a *Cobb-Douglas* function characterizes the production function. With a Cobb-Douglas function

$$\text{Output} = \text{TFP} \times \text{Capital Stock}^a \times \text{Hours Worked}^{1-a}$$

It can be shown that for this production function[10]

---

[10]It requires only straightforward differentiation of the production function because the marginal product of capital equals $\partial y/\partial K$. Write the Cobb-Douglas production function $y = \text{TFP } K^a H^{1-a}$ where y is output, K is capital, and H is hours worked. $\partial y/\partial K = a \text{ TFP } (H/K)^{1-a}$ and $\partial y/\partial H = (1 - a) \text{ TFP } (K/H)^a$. If capital earns its marginal product then the total payments to those who supply capital is $K \partial y/\partial K = ay$, and if the hourly wage is the marginal product of labor the total wage bill is $H\partial y/\partial H = (1 - a)y$. Thus a is the share of profit (the returns to capital) in total value added (y) while $1 - a$ is labor's share.

Marginal Product of Capital = $a \times$ TFP $\times$ (Hours Worked/Capital Stock)$^{1-a}$

and

Marginal Product of Labor = $(1 - a) \times$ TFP $\times$ (Capital Stock/Hours Worked)^{a}

Assuming $0 < a < 1$, the Cobb-Douglas production function has a marginal product of capital and labor that are both decreasing—the more machines (workers) a firm has, the lower the marginal product of capital (labor).

4.6   What Caused the Output Growth?

We can use the production function and data on inputs and output to estimate the role of each factor of production in producing long-run increases in GDP—an exercise known as growth accounting. From the production function we have

Change in Output = Change in TFP

+Marginal Product of Capital $\times$ Change in Capital

+ Marginal Product of Labor $\times$ Change in Labor

For the Cobb-Douglas production function, this equation takes a particularly easy form as the marginal product of capital is $\{a \times Y/K\}$ (where Y is output and K the capital stock) and the marginal product of labor is $\{(1 - a) \times Y/L\}$ (see footnote 10). Denoting the change in output by ΔY (and in capital by ΔK and labor ΔL) we have for the Cobb-Douglas production function that

ΔY = Change in TFP + $\{a \times Y/K\} \times \Delta K + \{(1 - a) \times Y/L\} \times \Delta L$

which can be written as

$\Delta Y /Y$ = Change in TFP/Y + $\{a \times \Delta K/K\} + \{(1 - a) \times \Delta L/L\}$

or in other words:

% Change in Output = % Change in TFP

+ $a \times$ % Change in Capital Stock

+ $(1 - a) \times$ % Change in Hours Worked

Therefore we can calculate the amount of output growth that results from capital accumulation $\{a \times$ % change in capital stock$\}$ and similarly for the contribution of hours worked $\{(1 - a) \times$ % change in hours worked$\}$. We attribute whatever output growth is left unexplained by changes in capital and hours worked to TFP, the unobserved factor input. All that we need to undertake growth accounting (aside from data on output, capital, and employment) is to find out the appropriate value of a. We can do this if we assume that capital and labor get paid their own marginal product—that is, workers' wages reflect the value of the extra output they produce and the return earned by the owners of capital reflects the extra output that capital generates. In this case capital income is MPK × K and labor income is MPL × L. Assuming a Cobb-Douglas production function capital income is $\{a \times Y/K\} \times K = aY$ and labor income is $\{(1 - a) \times Y/L\} \times L = (1 - a) Y$. Therefore we can measure a by calculating the share of GDP paid out to capital. In most OECD economies, around 30% of GDP is paid out to owners of capital, and the remaining 70% is paid out as income to labor, so that a is approximately 0.3.

Note two things about this overview of growth accounting:

1. The TFP term is a residual—it is the output growth that the measured factor inputs do not explain. As a consequence, any errors in measuring output, capital, or labor will affect our estimates of the importance of TFP.
2. We have shown a production function that has only two factors of production. The TFP term will capture all other influences. Of course, we can refine the approach and add additional factors of production, for example, education. As we include more measured inputs in the production function, TFP should account for smaller amounts of growth.

Figure 4.10 shows how growth accounting works where for ease of analysis we assume no change in hours worked. Between Year 1 and Year 2 the capital stock of the country has increased (from K_1 to K_2) and the technology available has improved, so the production function also shifts up as well. As a result of these changes, output in the economy has increased from Y_1 to Y_2. Growth accounting seeks to work out how much of this extra output has arisen from capital accumulation and how much from technological progress. Y_1 to Y_K gives the contribution from capital accumulation alone—that is, the output increase that comes from keeping the technology fixed but increasing just the capital stock, that is, staying on the old production function. Y_K to Y_2 gives the growth that results from technological progress—this shows the extra output that technological progress produces *keeping fixed the capital stock*. Note that growth accounting distinguishes between

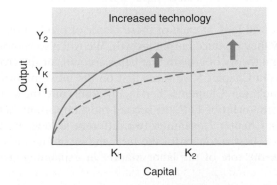

FIGURE 4.10 **Growth accounting.**
Technological improvements and capital deepening drive growth.

investment in additional machines (moving along a given production function) and changes in technology (upward shifts in the production function), whereas in reality new technology comes embodied in the machines purchased this year. However, in growth accounting we are performing a *logical* analysis—how much output growth would have occurred *if* new technology were not available this year? How much growth would there be if technology had not changed, but the firm had purchased more of the old machines? For this logical exercise, it does not matter if capital and technology increases are always implemented simultaneously. We can in principle disentangle the two influences.

4.7   Accounting for Growth

Figure 4.11 shows the results of a growth accounting exercise for Japan, the UK, the United States and Germany for the period 1913–1992. Figure 4.11a shows the results for 1913–1950. During this period in Japan, capital accumulation could account for 1.2% annual growth in output, increased labor input for 0.3% growth per year, and TFP 0.7%. Therefore annual growth in GDP was 2.2% per year over this period (1.2 + 0.3 + 0.7). Close examination of Figure 4.11 shows that

(a) 1950–1973 (the so-called "Golden Age") was a period of rapid output growth.
(b) For the UK and Germany, increases in labor input do not contribute output growth.
(c) In 6 out of the 12 cases, capital accumulation was the most important factor in explaining growth. TFP was the most important component on five occasions. Only once—in the United States between 1973 and 1992—was labor input the most important.

Figure 4.12 shows the results of a similar growth accounting exercise for economies that started their growth process later. As in Figure 4.11 the most important component of growth was capital accumulation. However, unlike the more mature industrialized countries in Figure 4.11, for these emerging nations, TFP played a surprisingly small role in accounting for growth. Instead increases in labor input were the second-most important component.

Over the next few chapters, we will look at each of these factor of productions in turn and examine more closely how they produce output growth. We will also combine all the factors of production to offer a theory of growth that helps account for the cross-country differences outlined above. In Chapter 5 we focus first on the most important component of growth: capital accumulation. Chapter 6 then incorporates into the analysis technological progress—a key component of TFP, the second-most important factor of production for advanced nations. Chapter 7 examines two different models of economic growth and assesses which one best accounts for the facts shown in Figures 4.11 and 4.12. Chapter 8 then examines the role of the labor market in explaining cross-country differences in output.

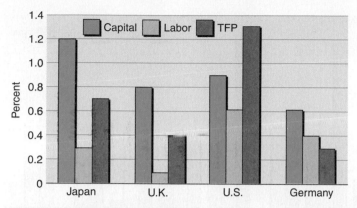

FIGURE 4.11a   Growth accounting for Japan, Germany, the UK, and the United States, 1913–1950.

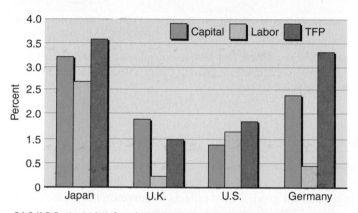

FIGURE 4.11b   Growth accounting for Japan, Germany, the UK, and the United States, 1950–1973.

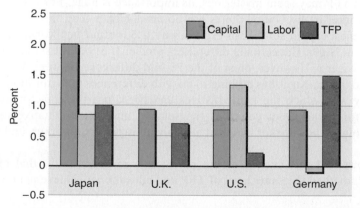

FIGURE 4.11c   Growth accounting for Japan, Germany, the UK, and the United States, 1973–1992. TFP and capital growth have accounted for the largest parts of growth in developed economies. *Source*: Crafts, Globalization and Growth in the Twentieth Century, IMF Working Paper 00/44.

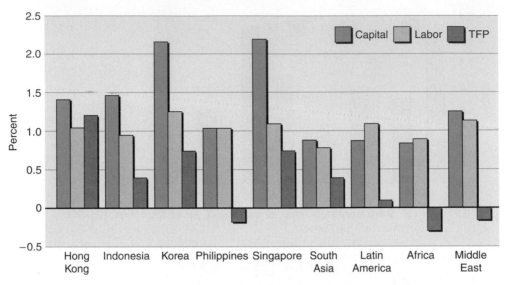

FIGURE 4.12   **Growth accounting in emerging markets, 1960–1994.** In emerging economies labor force growth has been more important than in developed economies. *Source*: Crafts, Globalization and Growth in the Twentieth Century, IMF Working Paper 00/44.

4.8   What Is Total Factor Productivity?

We have defined TFP as a measure of the efficiency with which factor inputs are combined to produce output. Anything that increases (or decreases) the amount of output that can be produced for given inputs reflects an increase (decrease) in TFP. As this definition makes clear, TFP reflects a range of different influences—from technological progress to social conventions that dictate which careers are respectable. While the exact nature of TFP may seem mysterious, its importance is huge. For instance, in 1988 output per worker in the United States was 35 times higher than that of Niger.[11] Differences in physical capital stocks can explain why U.S. output per worker should be 1.5 higher than in Niger. Educational differences predict U.S. output should be 4.7 times higher than Niger's. However, most of the 35-fold difference between U.S. output per worker and that in Niger has nothing to do with differences in factor inputs but with the efficiency with which the United States and Niger use these factor inputs. Table 4.9 shows for a variety of countries the relative magnitude (relative to the United States) of output per worker, physical and human capital per worker, and total productivity.[12]

Table 4.9 shows that the level of output per worker in India is 9% that of the United States. If India had the same level of TFP and educational achievement as the

---

[11]Hall and Jones, "Why Do Some Countries Produce So Much More Output per Worker Than Others?" *The Quarterly Journal of Economics* (February 1999), vol. 114, no. 1, pp. 83–116.

[12]As we remarked earlier, TFP is the output that factor inputs cannot explain. Table 4.9 measures education (or *human capital*) as an input in addition to capital and labor.

TABLE 4.9   Explaining Differences in Output per Head.
(All figures are relative to the United States.)

	Capital	Education	TFP	Output per Worker
Canada	1.00	0.90	1.03	0.93
Italy	1.06	0.65	1.21	0.83
France	1.09	0.67	1.13	0.82
UK	0.89	0.81	1.01	0.73
Spain	1.02	0.61	1.11	0.68
Japan	1.12	0.80	0.66	0.59
Mexico	0.87	0.54	0.93	0.43
Korea	0.86	0.76	0.58	0.38
Iran	0.98	0.47	0.64	0.30
Chile	0.99	0.66	0.40	0.26
Peru	0.94	0.62	0.41	0.24
Egypt	0.45	0.58	0.72	0.19
Pakistan	0.58	0.39	0.57	0.13
India	0.71	0.45	0.27	0.09
Sudan	0.84	0.34	0.23	0.07
Lesotho	0.68	0.48	0.19	0.06
Kenya	0.75	0.46	0.17	0.06
Rwanda	0.44	0.34	0.29	0.04
Uganda	0.36	0.39	0.22	0.03

Source: Hall and Jones, "Why Do Some Countries
Produce So Much More Output Per Worker Than
Others?" *The Quarterly Journal of Economics* (1999)
Vol. 114, No. 1, pp. 83–116. © by the President and
Fellows of Harvard College and the Massachusetts
Institute of Technology.

United States, then its output per worker would be 71% that of the United States. If the only difference between the countries was in educational achievement, then Indian output would be 45% of the U.S. level. However, the most important factor explaining differences in output per worker in the United States and India is total factor productivity. Even if India had the same capital stock and educational achievements as the United States, its output would only be 27% of the U.S. level. Therefore low output in India is not just due to low factor inputs but due to the relative inefficiency with which India uses these factor inputs. As Figure 4.13 shows, this finding is not restricted to India—differences in total factor productivity can account for much of the differences in output per worker across countries.

Why do some countries use factor inputs more efficiently than others? One factor is technology, which differs across nations and which we study in detail in Chapter 6. Also important is the social infrastructure of a nation, reflecting economic, social, and cultural institutions and mores. A good social infrastructure links social and private

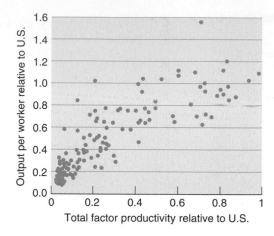

FIGURE 4.13   **Output and TFP across countries.** *Source*: Hall and Jones, *Why Do Some Countries Produce So Much More Output Per Worker Than Others? The Quarterly Journal of Economics* (1999) Vol. 114, No. 1, pp. 83–116. © by the President and Fellows of Harvard College and the Massachusetts Institute of Technology.

returns. This means that individuals benefit from pursuing activities that also benefit society. Just as the internal organization of the firm is an important determinant of corporate performance, so the structure of society affects the growth of the economy. We shall focus in the following chapters mainly on the economic determinants of long-run growth. However, in the remainder of this chapter, we will briefly investigate some of the sociocultural factors that also influence growth.

Economic historians believe that modern economic growth originated in the social changes of the Renaissance period with its increasing emphasis on rationality, individuality, and the introduction of a legal system that defined individual property rights. The result was a social system that encouraged individuals to take up commercial activity to earn profit but that also encouraged higher output and greater productivity. Another aspect of social infrastructure that is much discussed is democracy. Robert Barro examined the interaction between democracy and economic growth and suggests that for low-output economies democracy may actually be a hindrance.[13] At low output levels, the incentive to enact redistributive policies may be so great that it could blunt individual incentives and prevent a sustained increase in output. He also argues that because of vested interests democracy may block necessary structural reforms. This may have hindered the move to a market economy in many Central and Eastern Europe economies after the collapse of communism in 1989–1990.

What economists call the "allocation of talent" also has a major impact on growth. As a leading social historian has commented, *"It is often assumed that an economy of private enterprise has an automatic bias towards innovation, but this is not so. It has a bias only towards profit."*[14] The ultimate sources of economic growth lie in innovation and in creating output. However, individuals can earn money either by innovating and boosting output or by taking fees/profits from those who do innovate and boost output. The former activity we shall call "entrepreneurship" and the latter "rent seeking." For the good of society as a whole, as few people as possible should engage in rent-seeking

[13]Robert Barro, "Democracy and Growth," in *Getting It Right* (MIT Press, 1995).

[14]Hobsbawm, *Industry and Empire from 1750 to the Present Day* (Penguin: Harmondsworth, 1969).

activity. The higher the proportion of the population involved in rent-seeking activities, the slower an economy's growth will be. Rent seeking lowers growth in three ways:

- The rent-seeking sector absorbs labor that would otherwise go into entrepreneural activities.
- By earning income from the value added that entrepreneurs create, rent seekers act as a tax and decrease the amount of output entrepreneurs produce.
- If the rewards to rent seeking are high, the most talented people become rent seekers, and the quality of entrepreneurs suffers.

The costs of rent seeking can be enormous. For instance, in 1980 rent seeking cost the Indian economy the equivalent of an estimated 30–45% of GDP[15] and lowered Indian TFP growth by 2% per year between 1950 and 1980.[16] Mancur Olson argued that rent seeking also helped explain relatively slow growth in Europe due to the influence of vested interest groups in economic and social policy.[17]

Issues regarding the allocation of talent may also help explain why the industrial revolution happened in Western Europe in the eighteenth century rather than 400 years earlier in China. As Figure 4.14 shows, in 1400 China had a higher level of *per capita* output than Western Europe and had introduced many innovations.[18] Yet by 1820, Chinese output had not changed, while that of Europe had soared.

One explanation for this poor relative performance is the allocation of talent in China and the weak social incentives to take part in entrepreneurial activity. As one author notes:

What was chiefly lacking in China for the further development of capitalism was not mechanical skill or scientific aptitude, nor a sufficient accumulation of wealth, but scope for individual enterprise. There was no individual freedom and no security for private enterprise, no legal foundation for rights other than those of the state, no alternative investment other than landed property, no guarantee against being

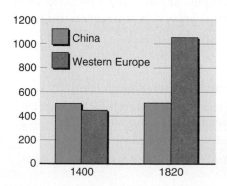

FIGURE 4.14 **Output per capita in Western Europe and China ($1985).** China failed to match the growth of Western Europe over the past 500 years. *Source*: Maddison, *Dynamic Forces in Capitalist Development* (Oxford: Oxford University Press, 1991).

[15]Mohammed and Whalley, "Rent Seeking in India: Its Costs and Policy Significance," *Kyklos* (1984) vol. 37.

[16]Hamilton, Mohammed, and Whalley, "Applied General Equilibrium Analysis and Perspectives on Growth Performance," *Journal of Policy Modelling* (1988) vol. 11.

[17]Olson, *The Rise and Decline of Nations* (Yale University Press, 1982).

[18]Many of which were amazingly lost to future Chinese generations, see Mokyr, *The Lever of Riches* (Oxford University Press, 1990).

penalised by arbitrary exactions from officials or against intervention by the state. But perhaps the supreme inhibiting factor was the overwhelming prestige of the state bureaucracy, which maimed from the start any attempt of the bourgeoisie to be different, to become aware of themselves as a class and fight for an autonomous position in society. Free enterprise, ready and proud to take risks, is therefore quite exceptional and abnormal in Chinese economic history,[19]

While medieval China may be a good example of rent seeking, there are many other historical and current examples.[20] Given its importance, what factors determine the proportion of the population that go into rent-seeking or entrepreneurial activities? The precise determinants are hard to pin down, but we can identify some of them (see Table 4.10).[21]

If a large bureaucracy exists, and property rights are poorly defined, then individuals will be attracted to the rent-seeking sector. Without clearly defined property rights, if someone becomes an entrepreneur, they run the risk of the government simply confiscating their goods and capital (which has happened often in history). Better to be one of the confiscators than risk being exploited in this way. Good property rights are crucial for avoiding rent seeking. Rent seeking is also minimized if large markets exists, which in turn may hinge on whether or not capital markets can make big loans to entreprenuers. Large markets tend to encourage the existence of large firms and this gives entrepreneurs significant social power in their conflict against rent seekers. As a result, governments that promote rent-seeking activity normally try to keep firms and markets small. Not only does this restrain firm power, but the means by which the government restricts market size (by selling of licenses, etc.) gains it additional revenue.

The above analysis assumes that it is fairly easy to identify a rent seeker and an entrepreneur, but this is not necessarily so. For instance, is a lawyer engaged in an expensive lawsuit a rent seeker or an entrepreneur? We shall, for fear of an expensive lawsuit, leave you to decide for yourself. Another question is whether rent seeking is a problem for modern industrialized economies or not? Murphy, Shleifer, and Vishny (to widespread amusement in the economics profession) identify lawyers as rent seekers and suggest that

TABLE 4.10   Factors Behind Wealth Creation

Factors Encouraging Entrepreneurship	Factors Encouraging Rent Seeking
Large markets	Large resources to "official" rent-seeking sectors (army, government, church, etc.)
Good communications	Poor property rights
Easy entry and expansion for firms	Authority invested in rent-seeking sector
Good capital markets	
Clear property rights	

[19]Balazs, *Chinese Civilization and Bureaucracy* (New Haven: Yale University Press, 1964).

[20]Baumol, "Entrepreneurship: Productive, Unproductive and Destructive," *Journal of Political Economy* (1990) vol. 98, pp. 893–921. This article has numerous fascinating historical examples, including China, ancient Rome, and medieval Europe.

[21]This table is an abbreviated version of Murphy, Shleifer, and Vishny, "The Allocation of Talent: Implications for Growth," *Quarterly Journal of Economics* (1991) vol. 106, pp. 503–530.

the number of students enrolled in engineering courses is the best measure of how much talent a society allocates into value-added endeavors. They then studied the growth performance between 1960 and 1985 of 91 countries. In particular they examined what influence student enrollments in engineering and law have on economic growth. The results suggest that every 10% increase in engineering enrollments boosts growth by 0.5% and that every 10% increase in legal enrollments *lowers* growth by 0.3%.[22] It would probably be unfair to change educational policy on the basis of these results (and one wonders what the analysis would be if either engineers or lawyers were replaced by MBA enrollments or economists with Ph.D.s), but it does show that what matters for growth is not just education but the use that a society makes of that education. It also shows that social incentives to take part in rent-seeking activity can be of enormous importance.[23]

Corruption is another example of how the political, social, and legal characteristics of an economy influence growth. Is corruption good or bad for growth? Corruption may inhibit growth because it is a form of rent seeking that acts as a tax on economic activity. But corruption may also help boost growth if it "oils the wheels of trade." To examine this question empirically, we need a measure of corruption. Every year a firm called Business International (now part of the Economists Intelligence Unit) publishes a report based on a questionnaire sent to its national correspondents about bureaucracy, corruption, and so forth. Answers are on a scale of 1 to 10, with 1 showing extreme corruption and 10 a virtuous administration. In Table 4.11 we report the average answer to three questions covering the degree of corruption in a country, the extent of red tape, and the efficiency and integrity of its legal system.

T A B L E   4 . 1 1   Average Score of Corruption Indices

1.5–4.5	**Egypt, Ghana, Haiti, Indonesia, Iran, Liberia, Nigeria, Pakistan, Thailand, Zaire**
4.15–5.5	**Algeria, Bangladesh, Brazil, Colombia, India, Jamaica, Kenya, Mexico, Philippines, Saudi Arabia, Turkey, Venezuela**
5.5–6.5	**Angola, Dominican Republic, Ecuador, Greece, Iraq, Italy, Korea, Morocco, Nicaragua, Panama, Portugal, Spain, Trinidad/Tobago**
6.5–7.5	**Argentina, Ivory Coast, Kuwait, Malaysia, Peru, South Africa, Sri Lanka, Taiwan, Uruguay**
7.5–9	**Austria, Chile, France, Germany, Ireland, Israel, Jordan, Zimbabwe**
9–10	**Australia, Belgium, Canada, Denmark, Finland, Japan, Hong Kong, Netherlands, New Zealand, Norway, Singapore, Sweden, Switzerland, United Kingdom, United States**

Source: Mauro, "Corruption and Growth" *The Quarterly Journal of Economics* (1995) Vol. 110, No. 3, pp. 681–712. © 1995 by the President and Fellows of Harvard College and the Massachusetts Institute of Technology.

[22]For those of you with an aversion to law, the results are not as good as they seem—only the positive effect from engineers is statistically significant. If you rib lawyer friends you had better hope they haven't read the article or don't understand the meaning of a *t*-statistic!

[23]We should avoid gratuitous lawyer bashing. As an aggrieved MBA student (with a legal background) remarked, we have only just been stressing the importance of intellectual property rights and contract law and without lawyers such property rights and contracts would be unenforced. This would clearly be disastrous for the economy.

While these measures of corruption are imperfect (they reflect the subjective views of foreign correspondents), they do enable us to assess the relationship between growth and corruption. It is striking that those countries considered to be most (least) corrupt are typically the poorest (richest).

In the rest of this book, we shall focus on the economic determinants of growth, but as the above shows, we must be aware of the wider social determinants.

SUMMARY

Since the mid-ninetheenth century world output has increased by an unprecedented extent. While initially focused in a small group of countries, this growth has spread to most of the world's economies. This increase in output has vastly increased output per head and has also supported a huge increase in the global population. Underlying this increase in the standard of living are substantial increases in labor productivity.

The welfare implications of economic growth are enormous. If governments could achieve even small increases in growth rates, the benefits would probably outweigh those of stabilizing the economy against business cycle fluctuations. Small changes in growth rates have big effects because of the force of compounding.

Combining physical capital with labor input produces output in the economy. To explain increases in output over time or differences in the level of output among countries, one therefore looks to differences in capital stock, differences in labor input, or differences in the efficiency with which economies combine capital and labor to produce output.

The most important variable explaining this increased output across countries over the last 100 years has been capital accumulation. The next most important factor varies. For the mature industrialized nations, TFP has been important. For emerging markets, it has been increases in labor input. TFP reflects many phenomena, including technological progress and various social influences. While TFP is not the most important factor explaining historical growth patterns, it is crucial in accounting for the substantial cross-country variation in the standard of living. One important social influence on TFP is "the allocation of talent." Individuals can take part in either entrepreneurial or rent-seeking activities. Because society as a whole benefits most from entrepreneurial activities, an important determinant of growth is what influences the occupational choices of individuals. As a result, the use that societies make of education may be more important for growth than education itself.

CONCEPTUAL QUESTIONS

1. Would you rather earn an average income today or be a wealthy nobleman in fifteenth century Europe? How broad is the measure of welfare you use to evaluate this question?

2. "In the future we will need to worry less about the quantity of output produced and more about the quality of life." Discuss.

3. Which careers in your society have the highest prestige? Is there a strong link between private and social return in these careers?

4. The United States is one of the richest nations in the world and benefits from high levels of TFP. What features of U.S. society do you think can explain this?

5. The Republic of Arden has experienced a 5% increase in output this year, a 2% rise in its capital stock, and a 3% increase in hours worked. Assuming a Cobb-Douglas production function where capital income accounts for 30% of GDP, calculate how much output growth is explained by capital accumulation, labor, and TFP.

ANALYTICAL QUESTIONS

1. Over the past 150 years life expectancy has risen a great deal. Now people can anticipate living 10 to 20 years beyond their retirement. This is likely to affect savings behavior and the rate of investment. Suppose people begin work at age 20 and stop work at 60. They earn a real wage of $40,000 every year. Assume that the after-tax real rate of return on saving is zero. Finally, assume that at age 20 people have no assets and aim to have a constant level of consumption throughout their life. (a) How much will people save each year while they work if they know they live to 70? (b) How much wealth will they have accumulated by retirement at age 60? (c) What happens to saving and wealth at retirement if life expectancy is 75?

2. GDP in an economy is growing at 3% a year in real terms. Population is constant. The government decides to allow a significant increase in immigration so that the population (and the workforce) start to grow by 1% a year. Output is produced in the economy according to a Cobb-Douglas production function. The share of labor income in GDP is 70%. How much higher will GDP be as a result of the new immigration policy after 20 years? How much higher will per capita GDP be?

3. In an economy the number of hours each person is willing to work depends on the real hourly wage. Assume that a 1% rise in wages increases labor supply by 0.25% (and a 2% rise in wages increases hours worked by 0.5%, and so on). The population is rising at an annual rate of 1%. Suppose real wages are increasing at 1.5% a year. How much greater is the total number of hours worked in 2050 relative to 2010? Now assume that once wages reach their 2050 level further increases in wages *reduce* the number of hours people want to work. From 2050 every 1% rise in wages reduces labor supply by 0.1%. Assuming no change in population growth or in wage growth, what is the total number of hours worked in 2100 relative to the 2050 level?

4. Output in an economy is produced when labor hours (H) are combined with capital (K) in a way which reflects TFP to produce output (y). The relation is: $y = \text{TFP} . K^{0.27} H^{1-0.27}$ What is the share of labor income in output? What happens to the share of profits (i.e., capital's share in output) when there is a change in TFP? (Comment on your answer.)

5. Use the production function of Question 4 to calculate
   a) What happens to the marginal product of labor if H rises 10% with no change in other inputs?
   b) What happens to the marginal product of capital if K increases by 15% with no change in other inputs?
   c) What happens to the marginal product of labor and to output per person employed if labor and capital both rise by 7%?

6. "Declining marginal product of labor means that the best way to increase real wages is to work less. So we can all be better off if we just took more leisure." Show what is wrong with this "logic." Use the Cobb-Douglas production function to illustrate.

Capital Accumulation and Economic Growth

Overview

In this chapter we examine the relationship between increases in the capital stock and economic growth. We first discuss whether an economy can always grow if it increases only its capital stock. Under certain plausible assumptions, we show this is not possible, and that poorer countries should therefore grow faster than wealthy ones, whose economies will depend more on technological progress than capital accumulation. We then discuss why countries with high investment rates also have high standards of living. We show that to have a high standard of living a country must, over the long run, have a high level of savings and investment. We then examine why some countries have such low savings rates and whether governments can alter this. Finally we consider the rapid growth of the Southeast Asian economies and the extent to which they have relied on capital accumulation.

5.1   What Is the Capital Stock?

THE LINK BETWEEN CAPITAL AND OUTPUT

As we outlined at the end of Chapter 4, increases in the capital stock are a major factor in explaining growth in industrialized countries over the last 100 years and in accounting for differences in the standard of living among countries. Figure 5.1a plots

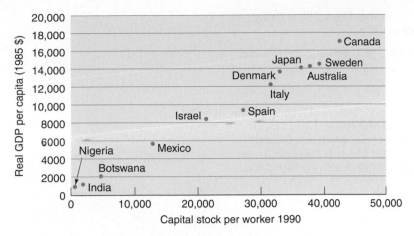

FIGURE 5.1a **GDP per capita versus capital stock per worker in 1990.** *Source*: Summers and Heston dataset, Penn World Tables 5.5, http://pwt.econ.upenn.edu

per capita real gross domestic product (GDP) and the per capita capital stock for a group of industrialized and developing countries. Figure 5.1*b* focuses on the growth in GDP and the growth in the capital stock between 1965 and 1990 for the same group of countries. Countries that have had large increases in their capital stock have also seen large increases in their GDP. For instance, Botswana during this period has seen a near 20-fold increase in its capital stock, and largely as a consequence, its GDP per capita has more than quadrupled. This represents both the largest increase in capital and the largest increase in GDP per capita of all of these countries. Similarly Japan had both the second highest proportional increase in its capital stock and the second highest percentage increase in GDP. Evidently capital accumulation matters greatly for both a country's standard of living and its rate of growth.

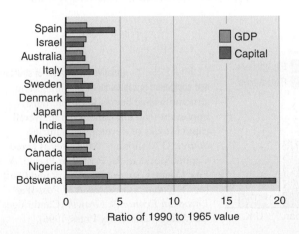

FIGURE 5.1b **Capital growth and GDP growth 1965–1990.** Countries that have accumulated substantial stocks of productive capital have reached higher standards of living. *Source*: Summers and Heston, Penn World Table 5.5, http://pwt.econ.upenn.edu

TABLE 5.1   **Average Length of Life of Physical Capital (in years)**

	USA	UK	Germany	France	Japan
Equipment	15	23	14	15	10
Structures	40	66	57	34	42

Source: O'Mahoney, "Measures Of Fixed Capital Stocks in the Post-War Period: A Five Country Study," in van Ark and Crafts (eds.), *Quantitative Aspects of Post-War European Economic Growth* (Cambridge: Cambridge University Press, 1996).

WHAT IS CAPITAL?

Before considering how capital accumulation boosts output, we have to be more precise about what we mean by capital. Broadly speaking, there are two categories of capital: machines and buildings (sometimes called equipment and structures, respectively). Production requires both types of capital—car firms could not operate without a site that protected machines and workers from the elements, and even service sector firms need machinery (telephones, computers, etc.) to produce their output.

Capital is long lasting—it provides a flow of services over several time periods, often lasting decades. A firm invests in more capital to produce more output in the future, not just today. By contrast, when a firm hires a worker or uses raw materials in the production process, the services provided are instantaneous. Table 5.1 indicates how long lasting equipment and buildings are for five industrialized nations. For instance, in the United States a new machine can be expected to boost production for 15 years, while a building provides 40 years of productive services. This durability is an essential element of capital.

Our interest is in the ability of the capital stock to boost output. Therefore we *exclude* from our measures of the capital stock factors that do not boost GDP. We also exclude most of the capital stock of the household sector, which consists of a vast array of consumer durables found in households, such as refrigerators, microwaves, and televi-

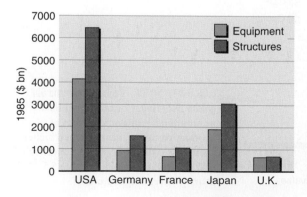

FIGURE 5.2   **Relative importance of structures and equipment in capital stock.** Buildings and structures have been somewhat more important than equipment in the overall capital stocks of developed countries. *Source*: O'Mahoney, "Measures of Fixed Capital Stocks in the Post-War Period: A Five Country Study" in van Ark and Crafts (eds.), *Quantitative Aspects of Post-War European Economic Growth* (Cambridge: Cambridge University Press, 1996).

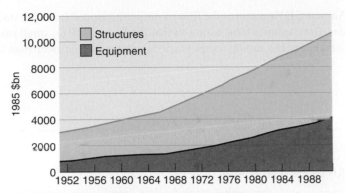

FIGURE 5.3 **U.S. capital stock 1948–1992.** In the period since the Second World War, U.S. stocks of equipment and of buildings and other structures have grown broadly in line. *Source*: O'Mahoney. "Measures of Fixed Capital Stocks in the Post-War Period: A Five Country Study," in van Ark and Crafts (eds.), *Quantative Aspects of Post-War European Economic Growth* (Cambridge: Cambridge University Press, 1996).

sions. These commodities should last (hopefully!) for years and provide a flow of services, but these services are not recorded in GDP.[1]

We should therefore think of our measure of the capital stock as the machines and buildings used in the production of GDP. This raises the issue of which form of capital—machines or buildings—is more important. Figure 5.2 shows that for industrialized nations buildings account for around 60% of the capital stock. Figure 5.3 illustrates (for the United States) that the trend in both forms of capital is the same. Economic growth comes about through increases in *both* equipment and structures.

HOW LARGE IS THE CAPITAL STOCK?

The other important fact to note about the capital stock is its size relative to the economy. Table 5.2 shows the ratio of the capital stock to GDP for a range of industrial countries. The capital stock is generally between two and three times the size of GDP (it would be much larger if we included the residential housing stock). We would expect this given the

TABLE 5.2 **Capital Stock Divided by GDP, 1992**

	USA	France	Germany	Netherlands	UK	Japan
Machinery and Equipment	0.86	0.74	0.70	0.78	0.65	1.07
Nonresidential Structures	1.57	1.52	1.63	1.53	1.17	1.95
Total	2.43	2.26	2.33	2.31	1.82	3.02

Source: Table 2.1 Maddison, *Monitoring the World Economy: 1820–1992* (Paris: OECD, 1995). Copyright OECD.

[1]GDP does include the rental services of residential property. However, our focus is on the production process, so unless we state otherwise, our capital stock measures will also exclude the residential housing stock.

durability of capital. Annual GDP measures the flow of output produced from the stock of capital over a given year. But capital is long lasting so that the flow (GDP) is small relative to the stock (capital), and hence the capital–output ratio is substantially greater than 1.

5.2   Capital Accumulation and Output Growth

HOW MUCH EXTRA OUTPUT DOES A NEW MACHINE PRODUCE?

We now discuss how increases in the capital stock lead to increases in output, our first step in constructing a model of economic growth. First we consider a purely technological question about the production function, namely, *what happens to output when a country increases its capital stock*? The answer will strongly affect how we view the process of economic growth.

As we discussed in Chapter 4, this technological question is about the marginal product of capital—how does output increase when a country increases its capital stock? Remember that the marginal product of capital is about what happens to output when *only* the capital stock changes: in other words, when a country invests in capital but leaves unchanged the amount of labor employed and the technology in use. Note that we are not taking any account of whether there will be demand for the additional output created—our sole concern is the technological relationship between increased capital input and increased output.

The key question is how the marginal product of capital varies. In particular, how does the extra output that *another* unit of capital produces compare with the output that the last unit of capital installed produced? Consider the case of a firm that publishes textbooks and has four printing presses. The introduction of the fourth printing press enabled the firm to increase its production by 500 books per week. Will a fifth machine increase production by more than 500 books, by less than 500 books, or just 500 more books? If the fifth machine leads to an increase in production of more than 500 books (the increase the fourth machine generated), then we have *increasing marginal product of capital*. If the increased production is less than 500 books, then we have *decreasing marginal product*, and if the increase equals 500, then we have a *constant marginal product of capital*.

Answering this question is about technology, not economics. It is a question about what the world is actually like, and we can answer by observing what happens in particular firms or industries. Marginal product may be increasing in some industries and decreasing in others. Over some range of capital, an industry may face an increasing marginal product, but beyond a certain stage of development, the marginal product may begin to fall.

DECREASING MARGINAL PRODUCT, OR IT DOESN'T GET ANY EASIER

In this chapter we shall assume that the marginal product of capital is decreasing for the aggregate economy and discuss what this implies for economic growth. In Chapter 7 we consider alternative assumptions and the empirical evidence for them.

Why might the marginal product of capital be decreasing? Consider again the publishing company and assume that it has 10 employees, each working a fixed shift. With four machines, there are two and a half employees per machine. But as we increase the number of machines but hold fixed the technology and hours worked, we are going to encounter problems. There will be fewer and fewer operator hours to monitor the machines, so each machine will probably be less productive. Even if each new machine produces extra output, the boost in output will probably not be as high as from the previous machine. Note the importance of assuming that labor input and technology remain unchanged.

Obviously not all technologies will be characterized by decreasing marginal product. Consider the case of a telephone. When a country has only one telephone, the marginal product of that initial investment is zero—there is no one to telephone! Investment in a second telephone has a positive boost to output; there is now one channel of communication. Investment in a third telephone substantially increases communications— there are now three communication links, and so the investment increases the marginal product of capital. Adding more and more telephones increases even further the number of potential communication links.[2] Telephones are an example of a technology that benefits from network effects, as is the case with information technology generally (see Chapter 6). Network effects operate when the benefits of being part of a network increase with the number of people using the network. Therefore not all technologies have to have decreasing marginal product.

Figure 5.4 shows the case of diminishing marginal product of capital. At point A the country has little capital, so new investment leads to a big boost in output. At point B the capital stock is so large that each new machine generates little extra output. Note that we have assumed that new machines always increase output—albeit by small amounts—when the capital stock is high.

Figure 5.4a shows how the capital stock is related to *increases* in output (the marginal product of capital), but we can also use this relationship to draw a production

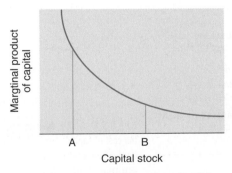

FIGURE 5.4a **Marginal product of capital.**

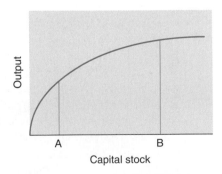

FIGURE 5.4b **The production function.**
A concave production function implies a declining marginal product of capital.

[2]If the number of telephone lines is n, then addition of a new line creates n new potential connections.

function summarizing how the stock of capital is linked to the *level* of output. This is shown in Figure 5.4*b*. At low levels of capital, the marginal product is high, so that small increases in the capital stock lead to a big jump in output, and the production function is steeply sloped. Thus point A in Figure 5.4*b* corresponds to the same level of capital in Figure 5.4*a*. However, at high levels of capital (such as point B), each new machine generates only a small increase in output, so that the production function starts to flatten out—output changes little in this range even for large changes in the capital stock. Figure 5.4*b* will feature prominently in the rest of this chapter as we discuss how far a country can grow through capital accumulation.

 5.3   Capital Stock and Interest Rates

CHOOSING THE CAPITAL STOCK

The marginal product of capital is crucial for determining how much capital a firm or a country should accumulate.[3] The extra revenue a new machine contributes is the price at which output is sold (p) multiplied by the marginal product of capital (MPK). If this amount is greater than the cost of a new machine (which we shall denote r) then it is profitable for a firm to install the machinery. So if MPK $> r/p$ it is profitable to add to the capital stock. Therefore in Figure 5.5 at A, the marginal product of capital is higher than the cost of an additional machine (given by the horizontal line r^0/p), so the firm increases its capital stock until it reaches B, where the last machine contributes just as much to revenues as it does to cost. By contrast, at C each new machine loses money, so the capital stock should be reduced.

This discussion raises the issue of what determines the cost of capital. For the moment we shall consider just one element: the interest rate.[4] We can think of the cost of

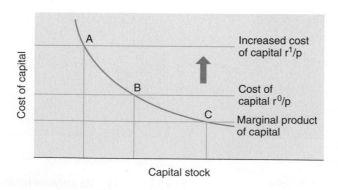

FIGURE 5.5 **Investment and the cost of capital.** Increases in the cost of capital reduce the optimal capital stock.

---

[3]Note once again that what we mean by investment here are increases in the capital stock rather than the more common usage in newspapers where investment refers to the purchase of financial assets.

[4]Chapter 14 considers in far more detail the investment decision and shows that the cost of capital must also include allowance for depreciation, changes in the price of capital goods, and taxes.

the machine as the interest rate (r) that would need to be paid on a loan used to buy it. If we assume that it costs 1 to buy a unit of capital (so we measure everything in terms of the price of a machine) then the interest cost is just r. An alternative way of seeing the point is to note that rather than purchase a new machine, a firm could invest the funds in a bank account and earn interest. Therefore to be profitable, the investment project must produce at least the rate of interest. If the marginal product of capital is above the interest rate, then firms will continue to invest in more machines until, because of decreasing marginal product, there is no additional advantage from doing so—the marginal product equals the interest rate. As the interest rate changes, so does the desired level of capital—if the interest rate increases, then the cost of capital shifts to r^1/p (as in Figure 5.5) and the firm desires less capital, while if the interest rate falls, investment demands will be high. Therefore the relationship between investment and the interest rate is negative, as shown in Figure 5.5.

DETERMINING INTEREST RATES

However, while a firm may wish to increase its capital stock, given the level of interest rates, it has to finance this increase. The firm has to either use its own savings or borrow those of other economic agents. Let us assume that as interest rates increase, so does the level of savings. In other words, as banks or financial markets offer higher rates of return on savings, individuals and firms respond by spending less and saving more. Therefore the relationship between savings and the interest rate is positive. Figure 5.6 shows this relationships among savings, investment, and the interest rate.

Consider the case where the interest rate is R_A. At this level interest rates are so low that savers are not prepared to save much, and savings are at S_A. However, low interest rates make capital investment attractive as the marginal product of capital is higher than the interest rate. As a result, firms are keen to borrow and desire investment I_A. There are not enough savings to finance this desired level of investment, which frustrates some firms' investment plans. Because of the gap between the marginal product of capital and the interest rate, firms are prepared to pay a higher interest rate to raise funds for investment. This puts upward pressure on interest rates, which in turn

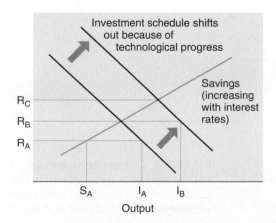

FIGURE 5.6 **Investment, savings, and interest rates.** Technical progress increases investment and may also drive rates of return (interest rates) up.

leads to increases in savings, which can be used to finance the desired investment. This additional savings will in turn help alleviate the imbalance between savings and investment. This process will continue—with interest rates increasing—until savings equal investment at the interest rate R_B. At this point the cost of capital just matches the value of the extra output produced; with decreasing MPK any further investment will generate a lower value of further output than the extra cost involved.

5.4   Why Poor Countries Catch Up with the Rich

We return now to our discussion of the marginal product of capital. From the technological assumption of a decreasing marginal product of capital, we can derive strong implications about economic growth. Consider two economies that have similar levels of unemployment and access to similar technologies. This means that we can think of both economies as sharing the same marginal product curve of Figure 5.4a or equivalently the same production function as in Figure 5.4b. However, one economy has a much higher capital stock. Figure 5.7 shows these two economies as being at K_A and K_B. Diminishing marginal product implies that the economy at K_A will find it easier to grow through investment than the economy at K_B. Assume both countries increase their capital stock by the same amount. The low capital stock country increases capital from K_A to K_B while the wealthier economy moves from K_B to K_C. The result is that output in the low capital country rises from Y_A to Y_B and in the richer economy from Y_B to Y_C. Therefore, the *same* investment will bring forth a *bigger* increase in output in the poorer economy than the richer one. In other words, because of decreasing marginal product, growth from capital accumulation becomes more and more difficult the higher the capital stock of a country becomes. This "catch-up" result implies a process of convergence among countries and regions—for the same investment poorer countries will grow faster than wealthier ones, so wealth inequalities across countries should decrease over time.

Figure 5.8, which displays the dispersion (as measured by the standard deviation) of income per head across U.S. states, shows some evidence for this. Since 1900 the in-

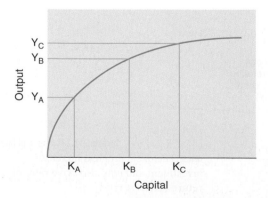

FIGURE 5.7 **Poor countries grow faster than wealthier countries.** A given increase in the capital stock generates more extra output for a country with relatively low capital.

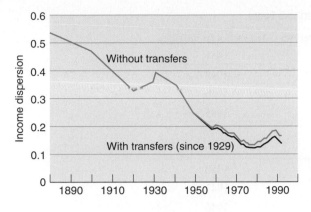

FIGURE 5.8 **Income dispersion across U.S. states.** Income inequality between states in the United States has declined greatly since the end of the nineteenth century. *Source*: Baro and Sala-I-Martin, *Economic Growth* (New York: McGraw Hill, 1995). (Transfers are government transfers of income.)

equalities of income across states have been dramatically reduced as poorer states, such as Maine and Arkansas, have grown faster than wealthier ones, such as Massachusetts and New York. This is consistent with the assumption of decreasing marginal product and its implication of catch-up.

Comparing income across U.S. states is a good test of the theoretical predictions of catch-up because our analysis depends on countries or regions sharing the same production function (i.e., similar unemployment rates and access to similar technology). This is likely to be the case across U.S. states. But finding other examples of countries that satisfy these conditions is not easy—low capital countries like India or Botswana also tend to have access to lower levels of technology than countries such as Japan or Australia. However, the circumstances of war and subsequent economic recovery offer some further support for assuming decreasing marginal product. Figure 5.9 shows that between 1945 and 1946, just after World War II, West German capital stock and output

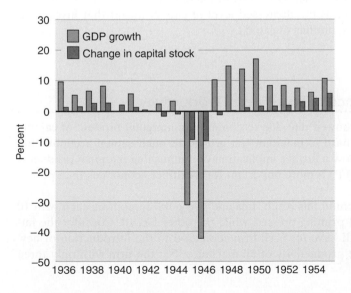

FIGURE 5.9 **West German GDP and capital growth 1936–1955.** West German GDP grew rapidly in the 1950s as the capital stock was rebuilt after the war. *Source*: Capital stock data from Maddison, "Macroeconomics Accounts for European Countries," in van Ark and Crafts (eds.), *Quantitative Aspects of Post-War European Economic Growth* (Cambridge: Cambridge University Press: 1996).

TABLE 5.3   **Post-War Reconstruction in Europe**

	Pre-War Year GDP Same as 1945	Year Reached Pre-War High
Austria	1886	1951
Belgium	1924	1948
Denmark	1936	1946
Finland	1938	1945
France	1891	1949
Germany	1908	1951
Italy	1909	1950
Netherlands	1912	1947
Norway	1937	1946

Source: Crafts and Toniolo, "Postwar Growth: An Overview," in Crafts and Toniolo (eds.), *Economic Growth in Europe Since 1945* (Cambridge: Cambridge University Press, 1996).

both fell. However, between 1947 and 1952, the German economy grew far more rapidly than over the previous decade. It achieved this rapid growth with only small increases in the capital stock—the ratio of output growth to capital growth during this period was extremely high. In other words, small levels of investment produced high levels of output growth compared to the years before 1945—exactly what decreasing marginal product would predict. The large drop in the capital stock between 1944 and 1947 meant that investment in 1947 would benefit from a much higher marginal product of capital compared to 1943. Table 5.3 shows a similarly sharp bounce back in output after WWII for other European nations. As a consequence of the war, European output declined. By the end of the war, GDP and the capital stock had fallen to the level they had been several decades earlier. However, within only a few years these countries had regained the lost output as the depressed level of capital meant that investment benefited from high marginal product of capital.

5.5   Growing Importance of Total Factor Productivity

The previous section showed that due to diminishing marginal product of capital, wealthier countries find it hard to maintain fast growth through capital accumulation *alone*. In this section we show a further implication of diminishing marginal product—total factor productivity (TFP) is more important for wealthier economies than poorer ones.

To see the intuition behind this result, imagine two publishing firms each with 10 employees. One firm has 3 printing presses, while the other has 10. Consider the impact one more machine will have for each firm compared to the introduction of new software that improves the productivity of all machines. For the firm with only three

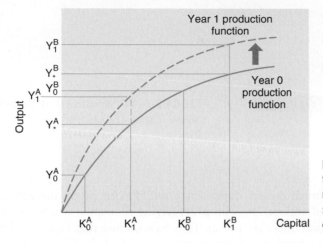

FIGURE 5.10 The impact of technological progress and economic maturity. Technological progress is more valuable the greater is the capital stock.

machines, the technological progress (the new software) will have only a limited effect—with only three machines, the software will not improve productivity a lot. However, this firm gains significantly from the introduction of a new machine because its capital stock is so low that its marginal product of capital is high. By contrast, the other firm already has as many machines as employees, so it will benefit very little from an additional printing press. However, with 10 machines to operate, the technological progress will have a more substantial impact. Therefore we can expect capital accumulation to be more important for growth relative to TFP for poorer nations, whereas for capital rich countries we expect the opposite. This is exactly what we saw in Figure 4.12 in Chapter 4 for the more mature industrialized nations and emerging markets.

To show this argument graphically, consider the production function in Figure 5.10. In Year 0 the production function is the solid line, but because of technological progress, the production function shifts up—for a given level of capital, the improved technology increases output. Now consider two economies—A and B—both of which increase their capital stock by the same amount. For country A the capital stock has risen from K_0^A to K_1^A. Without technological progress, the increase in output would have been Y_0^A to Y_*^A However, because of technological developments more output can be produced for any given level of capital, so that with a capital stock K_1^A country A can produce Y_1^A in Year 1.

In Figure 5.10 we see that output has increased by a total of $Y_1^A - Y_0^A$, of which $(Y_*^A - Y_0^A)$ is due to the addition of extra capital and $(Y_1^A - Y_*^A)$ to technological progress. We can use the same argument for country B and show that capital accumulation (without technological progress) leads to an increase in output of $(Y_*^B - Y_0^B)$, whereas at this new higher level of capital (K_1^B), the improved technology increases output $(Y_1^B - Y_*^B)$. As the diagram shows, the proportion of growth that TFP explains is higher in country B than country A—technological progress has a bigger impact for capital rich countries. This implies that wealthier economies, such as those belonging to

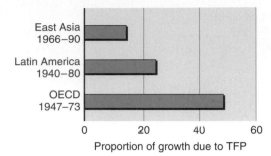

FIGURE 5.11 **Importance of TFP in growth.**
Source: Crafts, "Productivity Growth Reconsidered" *Economic Policy* (1992) vol. 15, pp. 388–426.

the OECD, will have a much greater dependence on TFP for producing economic growth than less developed nations. By contrast, emerging economies will be more reliant on capital accumulation than they will on TFP, a conjecture that Figure 5.11 supports. For the periods considered in the figures, we suggest that the OECD countries were high capital stock countries, the Asian economies low capital stock countries, and Latin American economies in the middle. Clearly TFP has been much more important for growth among the more developed nations.

5.6   The End of Growth through Capital Accumulation

THE STEADY STATE—A POINT OF REST

We have just shown that with a declining marginal product of capital the relative importance of capital accumulation declines as the capital stock increases. In this section we go further and show how countries *always* reach a point where they cannot grow any more from capital accumulation alone. Crucial to this section is the notion of a "steady state":

> **DEFINITION**
>
> A **steady state** is a point where capital accumulation alone will not increase output any further.

As this definition makes clear the steady state is the point at which the economy ceases to grow because of capital accumulations alone.[5] The steady state is a point of rest for the capital stock—efforts to raise or lower the capital stock are futile, and it will always return to this equilibrium level. Why is this so?

---

[5]Although, as we shall see in Chapter 6, technological progress will provide incentives for further capital accumulation. This section shows that without technological progress the capital stock does not change.

INVESTMENT AND DEPRECIATION

Two factors cause the capital stock to change over time. The first is that firms invest in new machinery and structures, so that the capital stock is increasing. But another factor, "depreciation," reduces the capital stock. Whenever they are used, machines are subject to wear and tear and breakdown. This means that over time machines become less effective in production unless they are repaired or maintained. Economists call this process of deterioration *depreciation*—the reduction over time in the productive capabilities of capital. Note that economists use the term "depreciation" in a different sense than accountants do. In accounting, "depreciation" refers to the writing down of the book value of an asset, which may bear little relation to the physical ability of a machine to produce output.

Because of depreciation, we need to distinguish between different measures of investment. In Chapter 2 we discussed investment as a part of the national accounts of a country. This is often called *gross fixed capital formation*, where gross means that no allowance is made for the loss of capital through depreciation. Gross investment is the amount of new capital being added to an economy and includes both the repair and replacement of the existing capital stock as well as new additions to it. Net investment is equal to gross investment less depreciation and represents the increase in the net capital stock—in other words, it deducts repairs and replacements from the new capital stock being added to an economy. Net investment is therefore equivalent to the increase in the capital stock from one year to another. Figure 5.12 shows, for a sample of developed economies, gross investment and depreciation as a percentage of GDP and suggests that net investment is typically about 5–10% of GDP.

Allowing for gross investment and depreciation, the capital stock evolves over time as

$$K(t) = K(t - 1) + I(t) - D(t)$$

where $K(t)$ is the capital stock at time t, $I(t)$ is gross investment, and $D(t)$ is depreciation: $I(t) - D(t)$ is net investment. The steady state is the point where the capital stock does not change, so that $K(t) = K(t - 1)$, which can only occur when $I(t) = D(t)$ or where gross investment equals depreciation. The country purchases just enough machinery each period to make good depreciation.

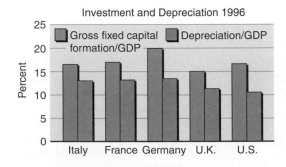

FIGURE 5.12 **Investment and depreciation in selected OECD countries.** Gross investment is substantially higher than net investment for developed countries because their stocks of capital are high. *Source*: OECD Main Economic Indicators. Copyright OECD.

CONVERGENCE

So far our analysis has been based on only a technological assumption about the marginal product of capital. But to complete our model of growth, we need to make some economic assumptions. The first concerns gross investment, which for simplicity we assume equals a fixed proportion of output: for example, $I(t) = bY(t)$, where $Y(t)$ is current GDP. How much of GDP is invested varies across countries, but let us assume that 20% of output is invested, that is, $b = 0.2$. In Figure 5.13 we show the production function of the economy and the investment function this implics. Because investment equals 20% of output, the investment line is just a scaled-down version of the production function. The other assumption we make concerns depreciation. We assume this occurs at a rate of 5% per year—in other words, each period around 5% of the capital stock is retired or needs to be repaired. Therefore $D(t) = \delta K(t)$, where $\delta = 0.05$. Note that while investment is a proportion of output and thus is related to the production function, depreciation is linked to the capital stock. Figure 5.13 shows depreciation as a straight line—if you double the capital stock, you double depreciation.

Consider point A in Figure 5.13. At this level of capital stock, I_A (20% of the output produced) gives the amount of investment that can be financed. At this level of capital, depreciation is only D_A, so that gross investment exceeds depreciation, net investment is positive, and the capital stock is increasing. As the capital stock increases, the gap between investment and depreciation narrows. Decreasing marginal product implies that each new machine leads to a smaller boost in output than the previous one. Because investment is a constant proportion of output, this means each new machine produces ever smaller amounts of new investment. However, depreciation is at a constant rate—each new machine adds 5% of its own value to the depreciation bill. Therefore the gap between investment and depreciation narrows. At point B the depreciation and investment lines intersect. This defines the steady state capital stock where gross investment equals depreciation. At this point the last machine adds just enough extra output to provide enough investment to offset the extra depreciation it brings. At this point the capital stock is neither rising nor falling but stays constant.

Imagine instead that the economy starts with a capital stock of C. At this point depreciation is above investment, net investment is negative, and the capital stock is

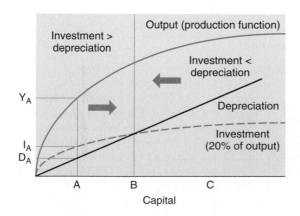

FIGURE 5.13   **The steady state.** If the stock of capital is below B, net investment is positive and the capital stock is growing. If the capital stock is above B, depreciation exceeds gross investment and the capital stock declines.

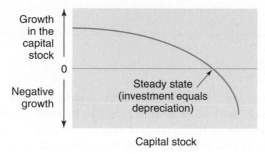

Growth in the capital stock

0

Negative growth

Steady state (investment equals depreciation)

Capital stock

FIGURE 5.14 **Capital growth declines with capital stock.** With a constant rate of investment and of depreciation, the growth of the capital stock declines with the capital stock.

declining. The country has so much capital that the marginal product of capital is low. As a consequence, each machine cannot produce enough output to provide the investment to cover its own depreciation, and so the capital stock moves back to the steady state at B.

Therefore when the capital stock is below its steady state level, it is increasing, and if it is above the steady state level, then capital declines. In other words, *growth in the capital stock* is declining with the size of the capital stock, as Figure 5.14 shows.

Growth in the capital stock slows down purely because of the decreasing marginal product of capital. The change in the capital stock is simply net investment, which under our assumptions equals $bY(t) - \delta K(t)$. Every unit change in the capital stock increases output by MPK, investment by $b \times$ MPK, and depreciation by δ. Therefore net investment changes by $b \times$ MPK $- \delta$. Under the assumption of decreasing marginal product, this expression gets smaller as the capital stock increases. Therefore diminishing marginal product implies that countries play economic catch-up—countries that start richer than others will grow more slowly because of decreasing marginal product.

You can see evidence supporting this catch-up phenomenon in Figure 5.15 which shows real GDP per capita between 1870 and 1999 for four major European countries. In 1870 the UK was substantially wealthier than other European nations. Its GDP per capita was 71% higher than in France, 76% higher than in Germany, and 122% higher than in Italy. However, by 1999 these large gaps in the standard of living had been substantially reduced: the gap between the richest and poorest countries was only 13%, relatively small by historical comparison.

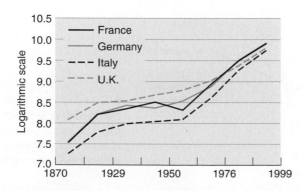

FIGURE 5.15 **Convergence in GDP per capita in Europe.** Levels of output in the major four European industrial countries have converged since the end of the nineteenth century. *Source*: Maddison, *Monitoring the World Economy, 1820–1992* (Paris: OECD, 1995). Copyright OECD. Updated to 1999 from 1994 by author using IMF data.

5.7   Why Bother Saving?

INVESTMENT AND THE STANDARD OF LIVING

Because the steady state is the point at which there is no growth in output through capital accumulation, growth at the steady state must be due either to increases in labor input or to improvements in TFP. Assuming that countries cannot continually reduce their unemployment rate, and that all countries eventually have access to the same technology, this implies that at the steady state countries will all grow at the same rate. In particular whether one country is investing more than another does not matter—*at the steady state, capital accumulation does not influence the growth rate.* Why then should countries encourage high levels of investment if such investment makes no difference to the long-run growth rate?

The answer to this question is simple. While the amount of investment makes no difference to the *growth* of the economy, it strongly influences the *level* of the capital stock in the steady state. In other words, while the growth of output in the steady state does not depend on investment, the level of output does. **The more investment a country does, the higher its steady state standard of living.**

To see this, imagine two countries, one of which invests 20% of its output and the other which invests 30%, as in Figure 5.16. Otherwise both countries are identical—they have access to the same production function, have the same population and the same depreciation rate. For both countries their steady state occurs at the point at which investment equals depreciation—K_L for the low investment rate country and K_H for the high investment country. Therefore the level of output in the low investment country is Y_L, substantially below Y_H. Countries with low investment rates will therefore have a lower standard of living (measured by GDP per capita) than countries with high investment rates. Low investment rates can only fund a low level of maintenance, so the steady state occurs at a low capital stock and, via the production function, at a low output level.

However, at the steady state, both countries will be growing at the same rate—the rate at which technological improvements lead to improvements in the production function.

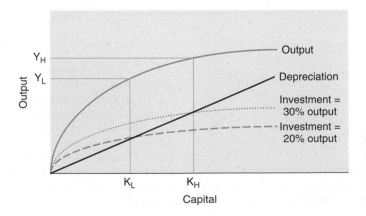

FIGURE 5.16 **Steady state depends on investment rate.** The higher is the rate of investment the greater is the steady state capital stock.

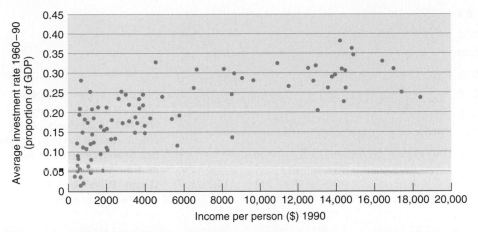

FIGURE 5.17   **Output and investment in the world economy.** Higher investment countries tend to have higher incomes—each point represents the income level in 1990 of a country mapped against its average investment rate from the previous 30 years. *Source:* Summers and Heston, Penn World Table 5.5, http://www.pwt.econ.upenn.edu

Therefore, while long-term growth rates are independent of the investment rate, the *level* of GDP per capita is definitely related to the amount of investment. High investment countries are wealthier than low investment countries, as Figure 5.17 shows.

We can also show the dependence of the standard of living on the investment rate algebraically. At the steady state, gross investment equals depreciation or $bY(t) = \delta K(t)$. Simple rearrangement leads to $K(t)/Y(t) = b/\delta$, so that the higher the investment rate (b) and the lower the depreciation rate (δ), the more capital intensive the economy and, via the production function, the higher the level of output will be. Figure 5.17 shows evidence supporting this result.

THE LONG RUN IS A LONG TIME COMING

Decreasing marginal product of capital and the concept of a steady state suggest that in the long run a country's growth rate is independent of its investment. But the experience of Asia (see Figure 5.18) over the last 20 years is hard to square with this—countries with the highest investment rates have had the fastest GDP growth.

To reconcile Figure 5.18 with the implications of decreasing marginal product of capital, we must stress that only in the steady state is growth independent of the investment rate. Consider the high and low investment countries of Figure 5.16. At K_L the low investment country has no more scope for growth through capital accumulation—it is already at its steady state. However, also at K_L, the high investment country still has gross investment in excess of depreciation, so its capital stock will continue to rise until it reaches its steady state at K_H. Therefore while the low investment rate country shows zero growth, the high investment rate country shows continual growth *while it is moving toward its steady state*. If the transition from K_L to K_H takes a long time (more than 25 years), then our model can still explain why investment and growth are strongly correlated, as in Figure 5.17.

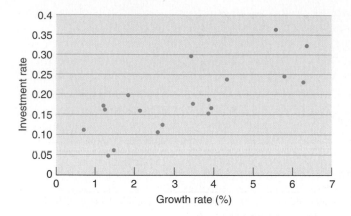

FIGURE 5.18 **Growth and investment in 19 Asian countries, 1960–1995.** In developing Asian countries there has been a positive link between investment and growth. *Source*: Summers and Heston, Penn World Table 5.5, http://www.pwt.econ.upenn.edu

Examining our model and using plausible numbers for investment rates and other key economic parameters shows that the movement from K_L to K_H does indeed take a long time. For instance, after 10 years only 40% of the distance between K_L and K_H has been traveled; after 20 years just under two-thirds of the gap has been reduced. Therefore decreasing marginal product of capital can explain sustained correlations between investment rates and economic growth over long periods, as economies move to their steady state.

5.8   How Much Should a Country Invest?

The previous section showed that countries with high levels of investment will also have high levels of GDP per capita (other things being equal). Does this mean that countries should seek to maximize their investment rate?

THE GOLDEN RULE AND OPTIMAL LEVEL OF INVESTMENT

The answer to this question is no. Output per head is an imperfect measure of the standard of living. We are really interested in consumption. The trouble with investment is that for a given level of output, the more a country invests the less it can consume. For instance, an economy with an investment rate of 100% would have an enormous level of GDP per capita, but it would only produce investment goods. However, at the opposite extreme, an economy with an investment rate of zero would have high consumption today but low consumption in the future because depreciation would cause its capital stock to continually decline leading to lower levels of future output. The situation is like that in the fishing industry. Overfishing reduces the stock of fish and diminishes the ability of the fish to breed, making future catches and thus also future consumption low. However, catching no fish at all would lead to a rapid increase in fish stocks but none to eat. Ideally we want to catch enough fish every day to sustain a constant stock of fish but that also enables us to consume a lot of fish.

Economists have a similar concept in mind when they consider the ideal rate of investment. This ideal rate is called the "Golden Rule" rate of investment—the investment rate that produces the steady state with the highest level of consumption. We have shown that countries with different levels of investment will have different steady states and thus different levels of consumption. The Golden Rule compares all of these different steady states (i.e., examines different investment rates) and chooses the investment rate that delivers the highest consumption in the steady state.

If for simplicity we ignore the government sector and assume no trade, then consumption must equal output less investment ($C = Y - I$). In the steady state, investment also equals depreciation ($I = \delta K$), so steady state consumption, C^{ss}, must equal output less depreciation ($C^{ss} = Y - \delta K$). According to the Golden Rule, the capital stock should be increased so long as steady state consumption also rises. Using our expression for steady state consumption, we can see that increases in capital boost consumption as they lead to higher output. Each extra unit of capital boosts output by the marginal product, so that steady state consumption—other things being equal—is increased by MPK. But other things are not equal because the addition of an extra unit of capital also increases depreciation by δ, which tends to lower steady state consumption. Therefore the overall effect on steady state consumption from an increase in capital is

change in steady state consumption from increase in capital = marginal product of capital − depreciation = MPK − δ

For low levels of capital, the MPK exceeds δ and steady state consumption increases with the capital stock and higher investment. But as the capital stock increases, the marginal product of capital declines until eventually MPK = δ. At this point steady state consumption cannot be raised through higher investment. Further increases in the capital stock would decrease MPK to less than δ—steady state consumption would be declining. Therefore the Golden Rule says that to maximize steady state consumption, the marginal product of capital should equal the depreciation rate.

What level of investment does the Golden Rule suggest is optimal? To answer this question, we need to make an assumption about the production function. We shall assume, as previously, that output is related to inputs via a Cobb-Douglas production function. In Chapter 4 we stated that this leads to :

MPK = aY/K

so that the Golden Rule implies that steady state consumption is maximized when

MPK = aY/K = δ

However, we also know that in the steady state investment equals depreciation, or using our earlier assumptions

I = bY = δK = depreciation

or

bY/K = δ

Comparing the Golden Rule condition and this steady state definition, we can see they can only both be true when $a = b$. That is, the term that influences the productivity of

TABLE 5.4   **Investment as Percentage of GDP, 1965–1990**

Country	Investment Rate	Country	Investment Rate	Country	Investment Rate
Algeria	23.2	Chile	14.7	Germany	30.9
Cameroon	7.9	Venezuela	19.2	Italy	31.4
Egypt	5.2	India	17.2	Netherlands	27.9
South Africa	21.8	Israel	29.9	Norway	34.9
Canada	25.4	Japan	36.6	Spain	28.2
Mexico	18.3	Singapore	32.6	Sweden	26.4
USA	24	Austria	28.3	UK	20.7
Argentina	14.8	Denmark	29.2	Australia	31.3
Brazil	21.7	France	29.7	New Zealand	26.8

Source: Summers and Heston, Penn World Table 5.5, http://www.pwt.econ.upenn.edu

capital in the production function (*a*) equals the investment rate (*b*). When we discussed the Cobb-Douglas production function in Chapter 4, we showed how *a* was equal to the share of capital income in GDP, which empirically was around 30–35%. Therefore the Golden Rule suggests that the optimal investment rate is approximately 30–35% of GDP.

Table 5.4 shows average investment rates for a wide range of countries. Singapore and Japan stand out as having high investment rates, and Germany fares reasonably well, but the United States and the UK score poorly according to this test.[6] The United States and the United Kingdom are underinvesting relative to the Golden Rule, and if this continues will eventually have a much lower future level of consumption than if they invested more (all other things being equal).

HOW TO BOOST SAVINGS

Because investment rates in many countries are lower than the prescription of the Golden Rule, governments often to try to boost savings and investment. Thus many countries create special tax-favored savings accounts: for example, in the United States, IRAs and 401ks; in the UK, ISAs. The idea is to provide tax incentives for savings, which can then be used to finance a higher investment rate. However, this approach only boosts savings if individuals are responsive to changes in rates of return. Assume investors are taxed at the rate of 25% on their investment income and the interest rate is currently 4%, or 3% after tax. If savings become tax exempt, the net interest rate increases from 3% to 4% for taxpayers. However, many empirical studies show that individuals only increase their savings by a small amount in response to such a tax benefit. As a result, these schemes probably only have a modest impact on national savings.

---

[6]Of course, the financial sector must use savings efficiently and allocate it to high productivity investment projects. We return to this issue in Chapter 20 when we discuss the Asian crisis of 1998.

Another approach is to make high levels of savings compulsory—a policy pursued successfully in Singapore where the government has operated a compulsory pension scheme. Both employers and employees have to pay a percentage of the worker's salary into a pension scheme. The pension scheme is in the name of the worker and cannot be used to fund anyone else's pension. The government uses these pension funds to invest in the economy. While many countries operate similar systems, contributions in Singapore have been extremely high. At certain times in the 1980s contributions reached nearly 50% of a worker's gross salary. This has helped support the high levels of investment in Singapore that we examine later in this chapter.

Why don't all countries levy a similar high contribution rate into a compulsory pension scheme? The answer is in part political. The Golden Rule gives the level of investment that would maximize the level of consumption *in the steady state*. But it takes decades for a country to reach a new steady state. For instance, if the United States were to increase its investment rate by 10%, it would take more than 40 years to move only two-thirds of the way to this higher steady state. Therefore several generations of voters would not benefit from the eventual higher consumption but would suffer from lower consumption during the transition to the new steady state because of the higher investment rate. The generations that suffer would be the current working generation, and those that would benefit are as yet unborn. This creates a problem at election times.

The problem is that different groups experience the costs and benefits of higher investment. But even if we assume that all individuals receive the future benefits of higher consumption, we might still not abide by the simple Golden Rule. Because of discounting, individuals prefer current consumption to future consumption. Therefore if consumers discount the benefits they will get from future consumption at a sufficiently high rate, the eventual outcome of higher consumption may not compensate them for the displeasure they incur during the transitional period of higher investment and lower consumption.

ARE ECONOMIES EFFICIENT?

The Golden Rule suggests that an economy can have too much capital—the investment rate can be so high that maintaining the capital stock becomes a drain on consumption. A simple test determines whether economies are efficient, that is, whether they do not have too much capital.[7] If an economy is capital efficient, the operating profits of the corporate sector should be large enough to cover investment. If they are, then the corporate sector has been a provider of funds for consumption. But if investment exceeds profits, then the capital stock has been financed at the expense of consumption. Table 5.5 shows, for a sample of OECD countries, the value of profits less investment relative to GDP. In every case the number is positive, suggesting that these countries' stock of capital is not too high. However, the South Korean numbers are particularly interesting. By the end of the sample period, the South Korean capital stock was close to becoming a drain on the corporate sector—a point we shall return to when we consider the Asian crisis in Chapter 20.

---

[7]This test is explained in detail in "Assessing Dynamic Efficiency" by Abel, Mankiw, Summers, and Zeckhauser, *Review of Economic Studies* (1989), vol. 56, pp. 1–20.

TABLE 5.5 **Contribution of Capital Sector to Consumption** (Cash flow less investment [less depreciation less residential investment] expressed as a percentage of GDP.)

Year	USA	UK	South Korea	Germany	France
1984	8.8	5.3	14.6		5.3
1985	7.6	6	15.2		5.6
1986	7.1	5.4	16		8.1
1987	8.3	5.8	13.8		7.9
1988	8.6	5.5	12.9		7.8
1989	9	3.9	9.3		8.1
1990	8.3	2.5	3.6		7.5
1991	8.3	2.9	2.9	4.1	6.6
1992	8.3	6	2.8	3.2	6.8
1993	8.8	9	3.2	4.1	6.6
1994	10	10.7	4	6.9	9.2
1995	9.7	10.2	2.5	8.3	9.4
1996	9.9	10.3	0.6	9.6	9

Source: OECD *National Accounts Volume II 1998*. Copyright OECD.

5.9 The Asian Miracle—A Case Study in Capital Accumulation?

RAPID SOUTH ASIAN GROWTH

This chapter has focused only on the contribution capital accumulation makes to economic growth. It is useful to see how far this framework helps explain the dramatic economic growth in Southeast Asia since 1960. Figure 5.19 shows the average GDP growth rate between 1966 and 1990 for a selection of countries. The performance of the Asian Tigers over this period—Japan, Hong Kong, Singapore, Taiwan, and South Korea—was exceptional, with average growth rates in excess of 6% per annum.

Such rapid increases in GDP have transformed the standard of living in these economies. Table 5.6 lists real GDP per capita for a variety of OECD and Asian economies. In 1950 the wealthiest Asian country was Singapore, which was ranked seventeenth among our sample—slightly richer than the poorest European nation, Greece. Between 1950 and 1976, the European nations approximately doubled their level of GDP per capita, but the Asian economies performed substantially better. The most impressive growth occurred during 1973–1996 when the level of GDP per capita rose almost fourfold in Singapore; in less than one generation its standard of living

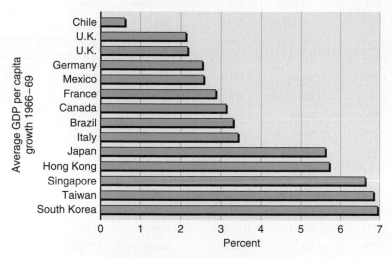

FIGURE 5.19 **Growth in GDP per capita, 1966–1990.** The growth record of the Asian Tigers in the 25 years from the mid 1960s was exceptional. *Source*: Summers and Heston, Penn World Table 5.5, http://www.pwt.econ.upenn.edu

quadrupled. Most of the Asian economies experienced similar large increases in the standard of living. By contrast, OECD nations saw relatively little growth—although Ireland and Norway both doubled their standard of living, most other European countries had only a 20–40% improvement. This "Asian miracle" and what the OECD nations could learn from it were much discussed by academics and in the media.

As Table 5.7 shows, the performance of these Asian countries really was exceptional. In 1960 South Korea and Taiwan had a similar standard of living as Senegal, Ghana, and Mozambique. Between 1960 and 1990, these African countries had static or declining standards of living, whereas the Asian standards of living increased 6- or 7-fold. What made these Asian Tigers grow so fast, or alternatively, why didn't growth like this occur in Africa?

INCREASE THE INPUTS AND INCREASE THE OUTPUT

The production function implies that to increase output it is necessary to increase either factor inputs, labor and capital, or the efficiency with which the production process combines capital and labor, growth in TFP. Because the OECD countries are probably at or near their steady state, they are unlikely to grow much through capital accumulation and depend instead on improvements in TFP. By contrast, countries with low capital stocks can grow rapidly and catch up with economically more mature nations by increasing the capital stock and labor used in the production process.[8]

---

[8]The work of Alwyn Young suggests that most economic growth in East Asia is the result of a dramatic increase in the factors of production. Paul Krugman further elaborated this point in a seminal article, "The Myth of the Asian Miracle" in *Foreign Affairs* (1994).

TABLE 5.6 Real GDP per Person in 1950, 1973, and 1996 (Constant Prices, 1990 $)

Country	1950	Country	1973	Country	1996
USA	9573	Switzerland	17593	USA	23719
Switzerland	8939	USA	16607	Norway	22256
UK	6847	Sweden	13494	Hong Kong	21201
Sweden	6738	Denmark	13416	Singapore	20983
Denmark	6683	West Germany	13152	Switzerland	20252
Netherlands	5850	France	12940	Denmark	19803
Norway	5403	Netherlands	12763	West Germany	19622
Belgium	5346	UK	11992	Japan	19582
France	5221	Belgium	11905	Netherlands	18504
West Germany	4281	Austria	11308	France	18207
Finland	4131	Japan	11017	Austria	17951
Austria	3731	Finland	10768	Belgium	17756
Italy	3425	Italy	10409	Sweden	17566
Ireland	3325	Norway	10229	UK	17326
Spain	2397	Spain	8739	Italy	16814
Portugal	2132	Greece	7779	Finland	15864
Singapore	2038	Portugal	7568	Ireland	15820
Hong Kong	1962	Ireland	7023	Taiwan	14222
Greece	1951	Hong Kong	6768	Spain	13132
Japan	1873	Singapore	5412	Korea	12874
Malaysia	1696	Taiwan	3669	Portugal	12015
Philippines	1293	Malaysia	3167	Greece	10950
Taiwan	922	Korea	2840	Malaysia	7764
Korea	876	Philippines	1956	Thailand	6112
Indonesia	874	Thailand	1750	China	4551
Thailand	848	Indonesia	1538	Indonesia	3464
China	614	China	1186	Philippines	2369

Source: Crafts, "East Asian Growth Before and After the Crisis," IMF Working Paper 98/137, 1996.

TABLE 5.7 Asia and Africa in 1960

Country	GDP per Capita 1960	GDP per Capita 1990
South Korea	883	6206
Taiwan	1359	6207
Ghana	873	815
Senegal	1017	1082
Mozambique	1128	756

Source: Summers and Heston, Penn World Table 5.5, http://www.pwt.econ.upenn.edu

TABLE 5.8   Asian Investment Rates, 1981–1996

China	Hong Kong	Indonesia	Korea	Malaysia	Philippines	Singapore	Taiwan	Thailand
35.5	28.4	32.0	33.5	35.8	22.3	39.1	22.8	35.4

Source: Crafts, "East Asian Growth Before and After the Crisis," IMF Working Paper 98/137, 1996.

The data supports this idea. For instance, Table 5.8 shows the higher average investment rate in East Asian economies from 1981 to 1996 compared to the OECD numbers in Table 5.4. Therefore we would expect more rapid growth in these Southeast Asian economies for two reasons. First, they began with lower levels of capital, so as a result of diminishing marginal product of capital, they should catch up with wealthier nations. Second, high investment rates mean the steady state level of capital is high. Therefore, as in Figure 5.16, the East Asian economies have further to grow before they reach their steady state.

Increases in capital are not the only explanation for this rapid Southeast Asian growth—other factors of production also increased. For instance, while OECD countries were experiencing a declining birth rate and sometimes falling populations, the proportion of the Southeast Asian population aged between 15 and 64 years—the crucial working age population—was increasing rapidly. Average hours worked also rose—see Table 5.9.

In a controversial study, Alwyn Young claimed that a growth accounting exercise for these fast-growing Southeast Asian economies suggests that growth was almost

TABLE 5.9   **Employment Growth** (Percentage change in hours worked per person between 1973 and 1996)

Country	Average Growth	Country	Average Growth
Austria	−2.15	Switzerland	−10.99
Belgium	−17.36	UK	−11.26
Denmark	−5.34	West Germany	−19.09
Finland	−18.67	Hong Kong	11.80
France	−23.37	Indonesia	19.76
Greece	−11.46	Japan	−8.35
Ireland	−18.47	Korea	37.71
Italy	−17.92	Philippines	−12.5
Netherlands	−14.45	Singapore	36.81
Norway	−5.76	Taiwan	6.23
Portugal	11.06	Thailand	13.14
Spain	−31.66	USA	19.05
Sweden	−7.47		

Source: Crafts, "East Asian Growth Before and After the Crisis," IMF Working Paper 98/137, 1996.

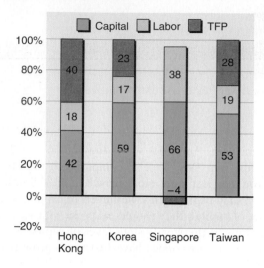

FIGURE 5.20 **Growth accounting for Asian Tigers, 1966–1990.** Increases in inputs of labor and capital accounted for most of the growth of the Asian Tigers over the period when they increased output most rapidly. *Source*: Young, "Tyranny of Numbers: Confronting the Statistical Realities of the East Asian Growth Experience," *Quarterly Journal of Economics* (1985) vol. 110, pp. 641–680.

entirely due to capital accumulation and increased labor input (see Figure 5.20). For each country the most important factor behind economic growth has been capital accumulation. TFP only contributed a substantial amount to economic growth in Hong Kong. In Singapore, Young calculates that TFP growth has actually been negative. In other words, Singapore should have witnessed an even larger increase in GDP given the extraordinary increase in capital and labor that occurred there. Young suggests this negative TFP growth is a result of Singapore's ambitious development plans. The government intervened in many facets of the economy—from the provision of compulsory savings via the pension scheme to choosing which industries to develop. As a result, the industrial structure has frequently changed, with the economy moving from textiles to electrical goods to financial services and currently to the IT and communications industry. Young argues that this frequent reorientation of the economy has been a source of inefficiency. Rather than learn how to optimally exploit the technology of the existing industrial structure, Singapore has grown through massive investment in new industries. As a result, it has had minimal TFP growth.

WHERE'S THE MIRACLE?

Not surprisingly, Young's findings have generated much debate. Subsequent studies argued that Young's calculations were incorrect and that TFP growth had actually been far more substantial for Singaporean growth.[9] Whether TFP growth in Singapore has been significant remains contentious. If true, Young's result puts the Asian growth "miracle" in a different perspective. For mature industrialized economies at their

---

[9]Collins and Bosworth, "Economic Growth in East Asia: Accumulation versus Assimilation," Brookings Papers in Economic Activity (1996) vol. 2, pp. 135–191; and Sarel, "Growth and Productivity in ASEAN Countries," IMF Working Paper 97/97, 1997.

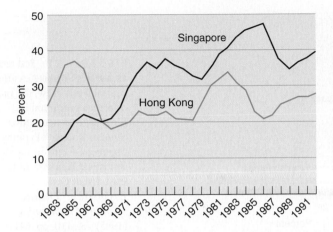

FIGURE 5.21 **Investment rates for Hong Kong and Singapore.** Starting at the beginning of the 1960s, for 30 years Hong Kong and Singapore invested an unusually high proportion of GDP.
Source: IMF *Financial Statistics*.

steady state, the important source of growth now is TFP—these nations have already achieved their growth through capital accumulation. If anything is mysterious about economic growth, it surely relates to this TFP category. Increasing output by increasing factor inputs via capital accumulation or increases in employment is not a miraculous process. However, growth through TFP means that economies can produce more output even without using extra factor inputs. Young's calculations suggest that as far as TFP growth is concerned the world may not have much to learn from the Asian Tigers.

While East Asian growth has come mainly from increases in factor inputs, the sheer scale of these increases is impressive. Figure 5.21 shows that investment rates in Hong Kong and Singapore are higher than in most other nations. Therefore other economies could benefit from studying how the Asian economies achieved such high savings rates. The increase in labor input has also been impressive although there may be less to learn from this aspect of Asian growth. The Asian economies have benefited from large increases in the working age population combined with a shift in the working population away from low productivity agriculture to higher productivity industrial activities. This has been combined with either a constant or increasing level of hours worked per worker, in stark contrast to the declines seen in many OECD economies (see Table 5.9). Such increases in employment are either no longer physically possible in OECD nations or politically infeasible.

DOES IT MATTER?   Does it matter if increases in factor inputs drove Southeast Asian economic growth? At one level, the answer is no—the huge increases in the standard of living these economies attained cannot be denied. That Singapore now has one of the highest standards of living in the world is not a statistical mirage. On the other hand, it does matter, for two reasons. The first is to emphasize that this growth has not been miraculous but has required sacrifices. Singapore has such high levels of capital today because it had high investment rates in previous decades. Lower consumption in previous decades paid for current prosperity. The current generation of Singaporeans are benefiting from these sacrifices, but their high standard of living has come at a cost.

The second reason for concern is the implications that decreasing marginal product of capital have for future economic growth in the region. If technology is characterized by

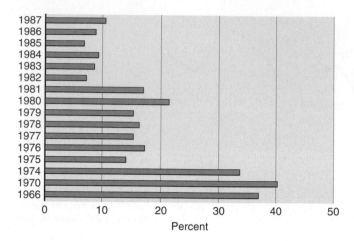

FIGURE 5.22   **Real return on capital in Singapore.** As the capital stock grew, the rate of return on capital in Singapore trended down. *Source*: Young, "Tyranny of Numbers: Confronting the Statistical Realities of the East Asian Growth Experience," *Quarterly Journal of Economics*, (1985) vol. 110, pp. 641–680.

decreasing marginal product of capital, then the Asian Tigers will eventually reach their steady state, if they are not already there. Figure 5.22 shows Young's calculations of the marginal product of capital and suggests that by the end of the 1980s decreasing marginal product had already set in. Because of their high investment rates, this steady state will be at high levels of output per head. However, once at this steady state the economy will cease to grow very fast through capital accumulation, and instead these countries will have to pay attention to the factors that drive TFP. Just because Singapore, according to Young's calculations, has no history of strong TFP growth does not mean that it cannot produce strong TFP growth in the future. However, our analysis suggests that at some point the development strategy of Singapore and the Asian Tigers will have to turn away from just boosting factor inputs and focus on TFP improvements. For instance, between 1966 and 1990 Singapore saw employment rise from 27% to 51% of the population, and investment as a proportion of GDP rose from 11% to 40%; in 1966 half the population had no formal education, but by 1990 more than two-thirds had completed secondary education. As a result of this huge improvement in factor inputs, the country witnessed remarkable growth. But a similar increase in factor inputs over the next 30 years is impossible.

5.10   China—A Big Tiger

The previous section suggested that Southeast Asia grew rapidly because of a substantial increase in factor inputs based around high investment rates and a fast-growing population. The result has been a huge increase in the standard of living of these countries. However, while these economies have grown substantially, they remain small-to-medium-sized economies due to the size of their population. For instance, South Korea has a population of around 50 million, while Hong Kong and Singapore have only about 6.5 million and 3.8 million, respectively. Therefore the rapid growth in these countries has not substantially affected the world's economy. However, the same cannot be said of China with its enormous population of 1.3 billion. China seems to be

TABLE 5.10 **Chinese Employment Growth**

Years	Percentage Growth
1980–85	17.7
1986–90	28.1
1990–95	6.3
1996–97	2.4

Source: International Financial Statistics, IMF.

embarking on the same growth pattern as East Asia 30 years ago, with a huge increase in population and employment (see Table 5.10), high levels of investment (see Figure 5.23*a*), and a substantial shift of resources from agriculture into industry. The result has been rapid rates of growth (see Figure 5.23*b*) suggesting that China may be able to repeat a similarly rapid economic transformation as the other East Asian economies.

But China faces difficulties. In particular the need to shift an enormous part of the economy from state-controlled means of production and distribution to more

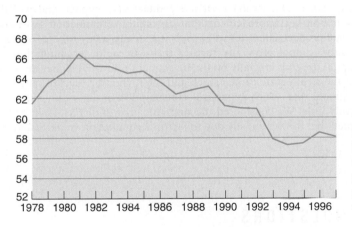

FIGURE 5.23a **Chinese investment as proportion of GDP.** China invests a very high proportion of GDP, and its growth rate in the 1990s was very rapid. *Source*: IMF.

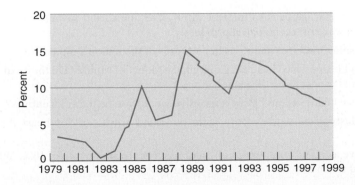

FIGURE 5.23b **Chinese real GDP growth 1979–1998.** *Source*: IMF.

market-oriented systems. Moreover, tensions over the weakness of China's financial system, in particular its banks, and the conflict between economic reform and the political status quo are growing. Pollution is also a major problem. All this means that Chinese economic growth is not guaranteed and that future economic growth may be volatile. However, China is pursuing a development path similar to that of the East Asian Tigers of 30 years ago—large capital accumulation and increases in employment. Our analysis suggests that China can produce decades of fast growth based solely on high capital accumulation rather than reliance on technological progress. China will not need to focus on improving TFP to improve its standard of living for many years.

SUMMARY

This chapter has examined the link between the capital stock and the standard of living and economic growth. Central to our discussion was the concept of the marginal product of capital—the additional output that investment in a new machine brings. We discussed the consequences of assuming decreasing marginal product of capital whereby each new machine leads to a smaller increase in output than the last machine. We showed how this assumption implies that capital poor countries will grow faster than capital rich ones, so that countries or regions will show convergence. Decreasing marginal product also implies that wealthier countries will depend more on TFP improvements than on capital accumulation. Eventually, under decreasing marginal product, countries will arrive at a steady state—where for a given investment rate, a country cannot grow any further through capital accumulation. The steady state level of capital depends crucially on the investment rate—the higher the investment rate is, the larger the steady state capital stock and the higher the level of output are. Compared to the investment rate, which maximizes consumption in the steady state, most countries invest relatively little. We considered the dramatic growth of East Asia between 1960 and 1995 and argued that this was mostly due to factor accumulation, in particular, high investment rates.

CONCEPTUAL QUESTIONS

1. Using Figure 5.6 show what happens to interest rates, investment, and savings when the economy experiences a wave of technological progress.

2. Should we include washing machines and irons in measures of the nation's capital stock?

3. What technologies might experience increasing marginal product of capital? Do they experience increasing marginal product over all ranges?

4. What influences your savings decisions? How responsive would you be to tax incentives?

5. What can mature industrialized nations learn from the rapid growth of Southeast Asian nations?

6. A nation wishes to have a capital output ratio of 2 and has a depreciation rate of 10%. What investment rate should it aim for?

ANALYTICAL QUESTIONS

1. Gross investment in an economy (I) is a fixed proportion, λ, of output (Y). Depreciation (D) is a fixed proportion, α, of the capital stock (K). Output is produced with the Cobb-Douglas production function: $Y = A . L^{0.7} K^{0.3}$. What is the long-run impact of a rise in λ from 0.15 to 0.20 if α is 0.05? What happens to the rate of return on capital?

2. The steady state level of consumption in an economy (Css) is equal to steady state output (Y^{ss}) minus steady state depreciation. The latter is the depreciation rate (α) times the steady state capital stock (K^{ss}). We assume here that there is no technological progress. Thus

   $$C^{ss} = Y^{ss} \quad \alpha \, K^{ss}$$

   What is the impact on steady state consumption of a small increase in the steady state capital stock? What level of the capital stock maximizes the steady state rate of consumption?

3. The simple Golden Rule says that the optimal level of capital is one where the marginal product of capital equals the depreciation rate. If people attach less weight to the enjoyment they get from consumption in the future than consumption today, then does it make sense to abide by the Golden Rule? Is there a better rule? If such an economy ever found itself with the Golden Rule level of capital should it preserve the capital stock by setting gross investment equal to depreciation?

4. Consider an economy where output (Y) is produced by labor (L) and capital (K) according to

   $$Y = A . L^{0.7} K^{0.3}$$

   Investment is always 25% of output and the depreciation rate is 6%. If $A = 10$ and $L = 100$, what is the steady state level of K?

5. Suppose that the economy described in Question 4 enters the twenty-first century with a capital stock of 15,000. Assume that the labor force in year 2000 is 100 and remains constant and there is no technical progress. Calculate output and investment in 2000 and derive the capital stock in 2001. Use the relation

   $$K_{t=1} = K_t + I_t - \alpha K_t \quad \text{where } \alpha \text{ is the depreciation rate } (= 0.06).$$

   Then calculate output, investment, and the capital stock for each year up to 2005. Plot the evolution of the capital stock on a graph and show the steady state that you calculated in Question 4 on the same figure.

CHAPTER 6

Technological Progress

Overview

Technological progress enables output to rise even if the capital stock or hours worked do not increase; and has been a major force behind economic growth over time. Technical progress boosts output directly through the production function and also by increasing the steady state capital stock. Foreign direct investment (FDI) is increasingly important for transferring advanced technology from developed nations to the emerging world and for fostering convergence. In this chapter we examine each of these issues and consider how research and development (R&D) spending generates technological progress. We also investigate how government policy for R&D affects market failure.

Technological progress is often blamed for higher unemployment. We consider the theoretical and empirical arguments and conclude that while technological progress does not cause higher aggregate unemployment, it can have important distributional effects. We consider the sharp slowdown in productivity growth that the world economy experienced in the early 1970s. We then focus on the substantial increase in investment in the 1980s and the advent of the "computer revolution."

6.1 | What Is Technological Progress?

The production function tells us that we can boost output in three ways: by increasing the capital stock, by increasing employment, or by boosting total factor productivity (TFP). The problem with the first of these is that to increase the capital stock, investment

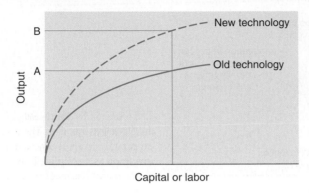

FIGURE 6.1 **Technological progress and output.** An improvement in technolgical knowledge increases output for a given capital stock

has to increase, so that consumption, at least in the short run, has to be reduced. A similar disadvantage relates to the second channel—to boost output, hours worked have to increase and leisure time decrease. But if we can increase TFP, we can boost output without having to lower consumption even temporarily and without having to work harder.

A key component of TFP is technological progress—through technological progress, we can produce more output from the same level of employment and capital. We illustrate the benefits of technological progress in Figure 6.1. The solid line shows the original production function; after technological progress, the production function shifts up. For a given level of factor input (whether capital or labor) the economy can now produce more output (B instead of A) without spending less or saving more. Truly, technological progress is wonderful.

Technological progress can and has taken many different forms.[1] One useful distinction is between *invention* and *innovation*. Invention is the discovery of new ideas, while innovation is about implementing them. Although we give inventions a higher social status, historically innovations account for most of economic growth. When new technologies are invented, it is often impossible or too costly to implement them (for instance, Leonardo da Vinci allegedly designed the world's first submarine and helicopter long before people could construct such machines). Further, the first implementations of a new invention are often not efficient or productive. For instance, during the Industrial Revolution in the UK in the eighteenth century, technological progress led to substantial increases in productivity in the textile industry. However, even here innovation and improvement had more impact than invention. In 1738, Lewis Paul invented and patented the use of rollers to replace fingers in spinning wool, but the technique was too unreliable to be widely adapted. The technology did not begin to be successful until 1768 when Sir Richard Arkwright introduced a machine that used two rollers in spinning. Even then production did not soar until after 1779 when these techniques were incorporated into the mule—41 years after the original invention.

In reviewing the history of technological change Mokyr distinguishes between "macroinventions" and "microinventions." Macroinventions are radical changes in the nature of technology—such as the use of animals to provide power, and the shift first to

[1]See Mokyr *The Lever of Riches* (Oxford: Oxford University Press, 1990) for a fascinating tale of technological development and its causes and influences over the last 2000 years.

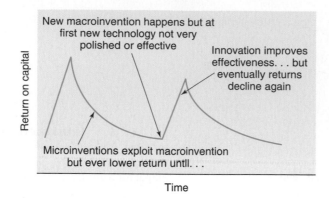

FIGURE 6.2 **Macro- and microinventions over time.** The return on capital increases *after* a major invention as its implications are realized and it is incorporated in new investment.

wind power, then to steam, and then to electricity. In each case a new and better way of organizing production was discovered, and the discovery set in motion a widespread process of adoption that boosted investment and output. By contrast, microinventions improve existing processes within the existing technological paradigm. For instance, the introduction of wind power and the use of windmills were a macroinvention, but productivity could still improve through microinventions—selecting the optimal number of blades on the windmill, angling these blades, making the windmill moveable to maximize wind power, and so forth.

This distinction between macro- and microinventions suggests that economic development follows the process shown in Figure 6.2. Over time the marginal product of capital varies considerably. When a macroinvention occurs, the productivity of capital rises and continues to increase as a sequence of microinventions boosts its effectiveness. However, eventually the marginal product of capital starts to decline as future microinventions, while profitable, boost output less and less. This process of declining returns to capital continues until a new macroinvention renews the process. At the end of this chapter, we shall return to this distinction between macro- and microinventions and consider which category best describes recent developments in information technology.

6.2 Technological Progress and the Steady State

In Chapter 5 we showed that if the marginal product of capital declines with the level of the capital stock, eventually the economy must reach a steady state in which investment equals depreciation and the capital stock is constant. At this point output ceases to grow through capital accumulation.

We now show that technological progress can produce continual growth in the economy through two channels. First, technological progress enables more output to be produced from a given stock of capital and labor—as we saw in Figure 6.1. Second, technological progress enables a country to support a larger steady state capital stock and thus a higher level of output. In terms of the growth accounting of Chapter 5, we

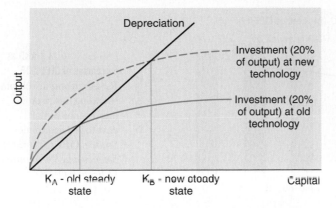

FIGURE 6.3a **Technological progress causes higher steady state capital.** An improvement in technological knowledge pushes up the production function and increases the steady state capital stock.

will find that both TFP and capital accumulation have contributed to growth, although capital accumulation would be lower without technological progress. Thus, technological progress means that a steady state is not fixed but changes over time.

In Figure 6.3a we consider the same model used in Chapter 5 in which investment equals 20% of output leading to a steady state capital stock K_A. Technological progress causes the production function to shift up, so that more output can be produced for a given level of capital, which in turn means more investment. But at K_A this higher level of investment exceeds the amount needed to cover depreciation, so that net investment is positive. Therefore the capital stock increases until it reaches a new steady state where investment equals depreciation—K_B in Figure 6.3a

In Figure 6.3b, the shift in the steady state leads to an increase in output of $Y_B - Y_A$. $Y_B - Y_C$ gives the direct increase in output from technical progress. However the additional capital accumulation resulting from technical progress leads to an increase in capital and a further rise in output of $Y_C - Y_A$.

This analysis suggests that the incentives for firms to engage in R&D increase as firms approach their steady state. Without technological progress there is no growth in the steady state. With technological progress both TFP and capital accumulation contribute to growth. We would therefore expect mature economies to focus more on

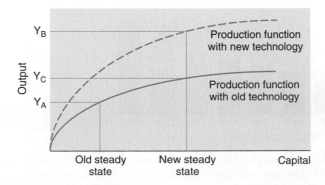

FIGURE 6.3b **Technological progress and growth accounting.** Technical progress increases output directly and has a further effect though its impact upon the equilibrium capital stock.

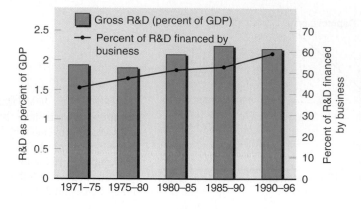

FIGURE 6.4   **R&D as percentage of OECD GDP.** Research and development spending has risen in importance in the developed economies. *Source*: OECD, *Main Science and Technology Indicators* (1998). Copyright OECD.

R&D than emerging markets, which will focus more on capital accumulation. Figures 6.4 and 6.5 support this hypothesis by showing increasing levels of R&D among OECD economies and a substantive increase in South Korea as a rapid process of capital accumulation led to falling marginal product of capital.

6.3   Foreign Direct Investment and Technological Progress

Consider Figure 6.3*b* again and assume that Y_A is the level of GDP in an emerging economy and Y_B GDP in an OECD (i.e., developed) country. For convergence to occur, the emerging market needs *both* to increase its capital stock *and* gain access to the new technology. Capital market flows can accelerate this process—if the advanced nations invest funds in the emerging market, the funds can be used to finance capital accumulation.

Whether these capital flows occur depends on the relative return to investing in the advanced and emerging markets. Figure 6.6 shows the marginal product of capital curve under different assumptions about technology (or, more generally, TFP). If the emerging market has access to the same technology as the advanced nation, the return to

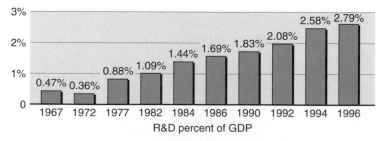

FIGURE 6.5   **South Korean R&D as percentage of GDP.** As the Korean economy developed and its capital stock rose, R&D spending became important. *Source*: OECD, *Main Science and Technology Indicators* (1998). Copyright OECD.

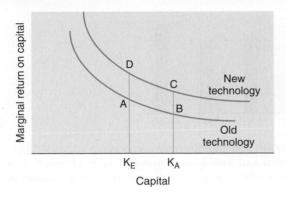

FIGURE 6.6 **Return on capital in emerging and advanced nations.** The marginal return on capital may be greater in a capital-intensive economy if its TFP is high enough.

investment is greater in the emerging market (A rather than B) because the capital stock is lower. As a result, emerging markets receive capital inflows, and will converge on advanced nations. However, things may be different if emerging markets do not use the most modern technology. Depending on the relative productivity of the new technology, the return to investing in the advanced nation may even *exceed* the return in the emerging economy (C compared to A in Figure 6.6). We can use Figure 6.6 to show the importance of foreign direct investment (FDI)—that is, foreign firms building plant and machinery in the recipient country, as when Ford or GM constructs a factory in Thailand or Phillips builds an assembly plant in Malaysia. As Table 6.1 shows, FDI has grown substantially during the 1990s, although not all regions have benefited equally from it.

In 1975 FDI accounted for only 0.3% of world GDP, but by 1985 it had reached 0.5%, and in 1999 over 1.5%. One reason for increasing FDI is the growing importance of multinational enterprises (MNEs)—see Figure 6.7. As we show in Chapter 9, falling impediments to trade and declining transportation and communication costs have substantially increased world trade. Much of this trade is internal trade between different parts of the same parent MNE, as global companies have taken advantage of lower trading costs by slicing production up across different countries. As components are then shipped across countries to complete assembly, world trade rises.

FDI performs two roles: it increases the recipient country's capital stock, and often improves its technology. From Figure 6.6 we can see that if an MNE brings new technology to the emerging market, the return will be D, compared to C in the advanced nation. The MNE therefore performs the investment and helps fuel

TABLE 6.1 **Net Foreign Direct Investment (US$ bn)**

	1992	1994	1996	1998	1999
Total	35.4	84.0	113.2	143.3	149.8
To Africa	0.6	2.3	4.8	5.2	9.5
To Asia	15.7	47.1	53.1	58.3	49.9
To Middle East	0.2	5.4	1.4	2.0	2.6
To Western Hemisphere	13.9	23.1	39.5	56.1	63.6

Source: IMF, *International Capital Markets 2000.*

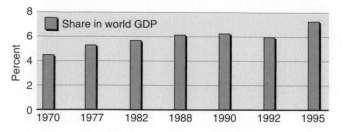

FIGURE 6.7   **Growing importance of multinationals.** Multinational corporations are growing in importance. *Source*: Lipsey, Blomstrom, and Ramsletter, "Internationalized Production in World Output. In *Geography and Ownership as Basis for Economic Accounting, Studies in Income and Wealth,* Vol. 59, edited by Baldwin, Lipsey and Richardson. The National Bureau of Economic Research, Inc. (1995).

convergence by boosting both capital and technology in the emerging market. Studies of firms support the TFP-enhancing role of FDI. For instance, a study of Venezuelan firms between 1976 and 1989 found that across all sectors firms that received FDI tended to have 70% higher productivity, 60% higher wages, and more than eight times higher exports than domestic firms.

If FDI is linked to trade and if it helps foster convergence through capital accumulation and technological transfer, we should expect to find stronger evidence for convergence among open economies. We see this in Figures 6.8a and 6.8b in which we compare the growth in per capita output in a country between 1960 and 1985 and the initial level of output in 1960. If catch-up occurs (and this is a theme we shall consider in detail in Chapter 7), we would expect to find a negative correlation between output growth and

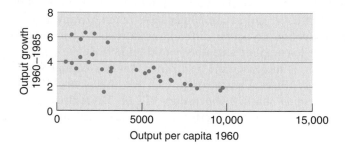

FIGURE 6.8a   **Economic catch-up among open economies.** There is evidence of catch-up in economies that are open to world trade, but less so for relatively closed economies.

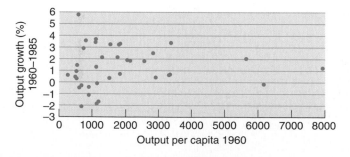

FIGURE 6.8b   **No convergence among closed economies.** *Source*: Sachs and Warner, "Economic Reform and the Process of Global Integration,"*Brookings Papers on Economic Activity* (1995) vol. 1, pp. 1–95.

the starting level of output—richer countries in 1960 will have grown relatively slowly if catch-up occurred. Figure 6.8 compares two groups of countries—one group has relatively low trade restrictions, while the other has high trade tariffs and other barriers.[2] The data suggest that open economies display convergence, while closed economies do not.[3]

6.4 R&D and Knowledge

The output of R&D is knowledge (even learning that something does not work is valuable output). Knowledge is an unusual economic commodity—it is both "nonrivalrous" and "nonexcludable." Nonrivalrous means that more than one person can own the knowledge—your learning about technological progress in this chapter in no way lessens the knowledge of anyone else about it. Nonexcludability means that it is hard to prevent people gaining access to the knowledge you have. For instance, if a computing firm discovers how to make a flatter and better quality computer screen, its competitors can examine the new product and also discover the new technology. That knowledge is both nonrivalrous and nonexcludable creates substantial problems for a market economy. R&D is an uncertain activity—the money spent may not yield a successful outcome. Because the output of R&D activity is both uncertain and, largely, nonexcludable, firms would prefer to let other firms discover successful new technologies and then copy them. But this means that no firm will want to spend money on R&D because as soon as they are successful the technology will be stolen, and the firm that spends money will be unable to make any profit. As a result, a market economy with competitive firms will not produce enough R&D.

To overcome this problem, all governments use patents—a form of legislation that gives a firm sole right to use the technology it has developed for a fixed number of years. In other words, to encourage firms to pursue R&D, governments give them a temporary monopoly. The monopoly gives firms an incentive to develop new ideas without fear that they and their associated profits will be stolen. However, monopolists earn their profits by keeping prices high, and to do that they restrict output. This is why the monopoly position is only temporary—after a fixed number of years, all firms can utilize the new technology, and then its price will decline and its use will become much more diffuse, which benefits the economy.

As one firm or industry develops a new technology, not only can it be used elsewhere, it will also generate other innovations that will benefit the economy. Economists call these "spillover effects"—R&D in one sector improves productivity in other sectors. One author[4] measured knowledge in each industry in the U.S. economy between 1953 and 1980 by cumulating the amount of scientific articles published in academic

---

[2]We take this measure of openness from Sachs and Warner, "Economic Reform and the Process of Global Integration," *Brookings Papers on Economic Activity* (1995), Vol. 1, pp. 1–95, who also establish the result econometrically.

[3]There are also other explanations for this link, and some studies question the finding (see Rodriguez and Rodrik, "Trade Policy and Economic Growth: A Skeptics Guide to Cross National Evidence," NBER Working Paper 7081 (1999).

[4]Adams, "Fundamental Stocks of Knowledge and Productivity Growth," *Journal of Political Economy* (1990) vol. 98, no. 3, pp. 673–702.

journals relevant to the industry and multiplying this by the number of scientists (to give an indicator of the number of people with access to technological knowledge multiplied by the amount of knowledge).

He found that between 1953 and 1990 increases in this stock of industry-relevant knowledge accounted for around 0.35% growth in output per year. However, he also found that spillover effects from increased knowledge elsewhere in the economy generated an additional 0.25% growth per year. Moreover, these spillovers can also occur across countries, although their extent depends on how open an economy is to trade—the more closed the economy is, the less benefit it receives from R&D in other countries. These spillover effects can be substantial—it has been estimated that a 1% increase in U.S. R&D leads to a 0.23% increase in U.S. TFP and, on average, a 0.04% boost to TFP in other OECD countries.[5]

6.5 Technological Progress and Unemployment

Ever since the Industrial Revolution gathered momentum, there has been concern that technological progress causes unemployment. The most famous example is the Luddites who in nineteeth-century England smashed the machinery that they felt would make them unemployed. Suspicion of technological progress is a recurrent theme. One commentator on the impact of information technology (IT) states:

> *While the entrepreneurial, managerial, professional and technical elites will be necessary to run the formal economy of the future, fewer and fewer workers will be required to assist in the production of goods and services.[6]*

We now consider the links between technological progress and unemployment in both theory and practice.

THE LUMP OF OUTPUT ARGUMENT

The basic argument for why technological progress creates unemployment runs like this:

- Firms need to produce a certain amount of output to meet demand.
- Technological progress boosts productivity and means that less labor is required to produce a given output.
- Unemployment therefore has to increase in response to technological progress.

The logic of this argument is impeccable; to deny its conclusions, we have to deny its starting point—that firms have to produce a given level of output. We show in the following pages that this assumption is unlikely to be true. In response to technological progress, output is not likely to remain fixed.

Before proceeding with our analysis, we should consider the historical evidence that technological progress creates unemployment. Figure 6.9 shows aggregate

---

[5]Coe and Helpman, "International R&D Spillovers," *European Economic Review* (1995) vol. 35, pp. 859–887.

[6]Rifkin, *The End of Work* (Harmondsworth: Penguin, 2000).

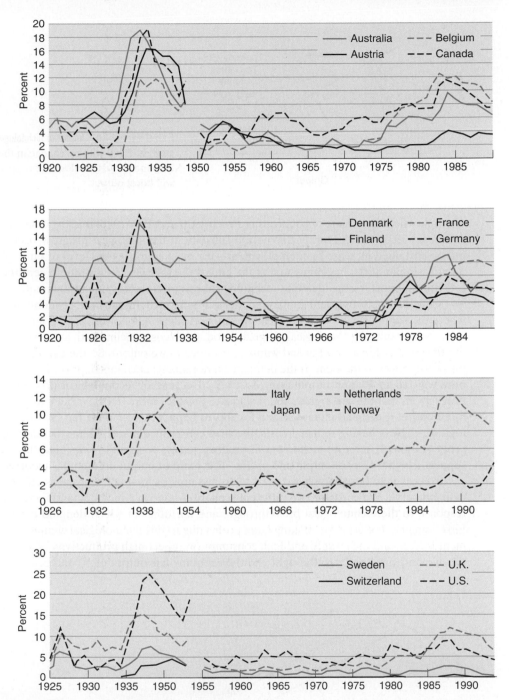

FIGURE 6.9 **Unemployment in the twentieth century.** There is no long-run trend in unemployment in countries that have seen dramatic technological progess. *Source*: Maddison, *Dynamic Forces in Capitalistic Development: A Long-Run Comparative View* (Oxford: Oxford University Press) 1991.

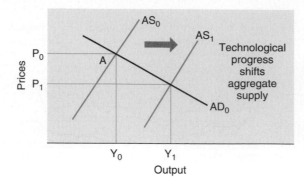

FIGURE 6.10 **Impact of technological progress.** Even with no change in the demand curve techological progress will boost output.

unemployment in a range of countries between 1920 and 1989 (with missing data for the war years 1939–1945). During this period substantial technological progress occurred, but no sustained increase in unemployment—for most countries the level of unemployment is similar at the beginning and at the end of the sample. The twentieth century offers little support for the idea that technological progress creates unemployment.

Consider the supply and demand model in Figure 6.10. Initially the economy is at A where the supply curve AS_0 intersects the demand curve AD_0, prices are P_0, and output is Y_0. As a result of technological progress, production costs decline and, at a given price, the firm makes higher profits and wants to produce more output. So the aggregate supply curve moves to the right. If the demand curve remains unchanged, prices in the economy will fall to P_1, and output will rise to Y_1. Because of technological progress, the firm's profit margins are higher, and it wants to produce more. However, it can only sell more output if demand increases, and for this to happen, prices must fall. With technological progress having reduced costs, the firm can reduce prices without squeezing its profit margins. Therefore technological progress lowers costs and prices and thus helps support a higher level of output and profits—the lump of output argument is incorrect.

To complete our analysis, we need to discuss how technological progress affects the demand curve. We consider two different scenarios—one in which demand increases in response to the technological breakthrough, and the other in which demand collapses. First, imagine that firms are making large profits due to this technological change; investment is high; and high wages and high consumption reflect high productivity. As a result the demand curve shifts to the right and the economy has output of Y_2 and prices at P_2,

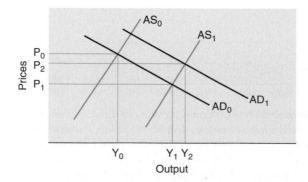

FIGURE 6.11 **Technological progress with positive demand effects.** If demand increases, the rise in output following technological progress will be greater.

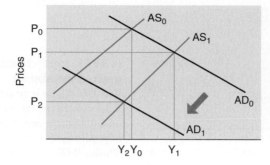

FIGURE 6.12 **Technological progress with negative demand effects.** If demand falls from AD_0 to AD_1 after a rise in technological progress, output could fall; but this is unlikely because demand is more likely to increase.

as shown in Figure 6.11. This boosts output $(Y_2 - Y_1)$ over and above the effect which comes from the shift in the supply curve $(Y_1 - Y_0)$. Again in response to technical progress, an increase in output benefits the economy—in contradiction to the lump of output argument. Note that while the effect on output is unambiguous, prices may rise or fall depending on the relative strength of the supply and demand shift.

Now consider the case in which demand falls after technological progress (this is a logical possibility, not an empirical prediction). Imagine that firms that benefit from technological progress do not invest or pay higher wages; and their shareholders do not spend the extra profits they receive, nor do they deposit the money with financial institutions who lend it to others. In this case demand might fall, and the situation would look like that in Figure 6.12—the economy moves to the point Y_2, P_2.

In this case the shifts in the demand and supply curve have offsetting effects—the technological progress puts upward pressure on output, but the collapse in demand causes downward pressure. The net effect depends on which curve shifts the most—in Figure 6.12 the demand collapse is so pronounced that output falls. To deliver the constant output assumption at the heart of the lump of output argument, Figure 6.12 shows a large contractionary demand shock must coincide with the technology improvement.

To see more clearly how technological progress affects unemployment, consider the definition of labor productivity:

labor productivity = output/employment

so that

% change in labor productivity = % change in output − % change in employment

or with a little rearrangement

% change in employment = % change in output − % change in productivity

The lump of output argument assumes that the change in output is zero, so that the growth in employment is equal to the negative of productivity gains that technical progress induces. By contrast, our theoretical analysis has shown that potentially output can rise or fall in response to technological progress—it is therefore an empirical issue what happens to output. Our historical graphs of unemployment in Figure 6.9 clearly showed no trend increase in unemployment. Figure 6.13, where we plot unemployment and average productivity growth for OECD economies, further supports this view. According to the lump of output argument, those countries with the highest productivity

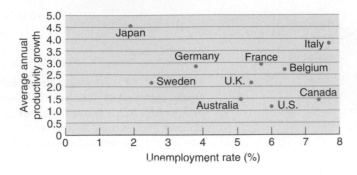

FIGURE 6.13 **Productivity growth and unemployment, 1960–1997.** There is no clear link between the rate of unemployment and the rate of productivity growth. *Source:* IMF.

growth should have the highest level of unemployment, but this is clearly not the case—there is no obvious relationship between unemployment and productivity growth. So technological progress has not caused output and demand to remain constant.

We could argue that this is just historical evidence—future technological progress might generate unemployment. What, for instance, about recent developments in IT? Even here, the evidence to date suggests that productivity improvements associated with IT are not increasing unemployment. As Figure 6.14 shows, unemployment rates in countries with the largest increase in IT investment have actually *fallen*.

6.6   Technological Progress and Structural Unemployment

The evidence is that technological progress does not create *aggregate* unemployment. But new technology does cost *some* people their jobs; the Luddites were not stupid. We have only shown that total unemployment does not increase. In the long run, output increases match productivity increases, so the number of people gaining jobs from the new technology is roughly equal to the number who lose their jobs. For instance, the employees who used to work in the typewriting industry can get jobs in firms

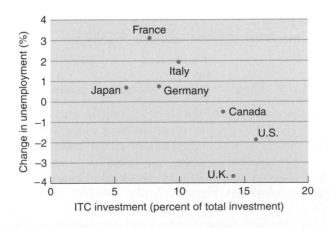

FIGURE 6.14 **IT investment and changes in unemployment, 1985–1996.** At the end of the twentieth century unemployment fell most in countries that did most ITC investment. *Source*: OECD, *Economic Outlook* (June 2000), Table V.3. Copyright OECD.

producing computer keyboards. Technological progress puts the economy through a process of "creative destruction"—some firms and industries decline, while others expand. The pace of this process depends on how efficient the economy is. If banks tend not to lend to new businesses; if housing market restrictions mean that people tend not to move from high unemployment areas to low unemployment ones; if people lack the relevant skills or live where industries are not expanding, this reallocation process can take a long time. In the short run, unemployment may increase before new jobs are created and filled. This process is shown in the film *The Full Monty* in which a group of steelworkers are unemployed and lack the skills to find alternative employment in the area and are unwilling to move away. It takes a while before they can retrain and find alternative employment—albeit as a male strip act!

Therefore, while technological progress does not create additional aggregate unemployment, it does affect the composition of unemployment (across regions and skill categories). Governments, therefore, must ensure that labor markets can deal effectively with this creative destruction by providing training, assistance with job applications, and a safety net for those who cannot find new jobs. While in the *aggregate* the economy benefits from technological progress, it causes distributional problems.

6.7 The Impact of IT on the Economy

In the second half of the 1990s the United States was experiencing its longest business cycle expansion on record; GDP growth averaged over 4%. Such rapid and sustained growth would normally cause inflation to rise, but this did not happen. This caused speculation that a New Economy was emerging—one that benefited from strong productivity growth and rising competition, which led to high output growth and low inflation. Figure 6.11, where rightward shifts in the supply and demand curve lead to big increases in output and no change in prices, shows this situation. Particularly noteworthy was the substantial increase in TFP that occurred in the United States. After 25 years of disappointing productivity performance, the United States experienced TFP growth not seen for a quarter of a century—see Figure 6.15.

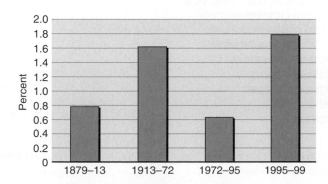

FIGURE 6.15 **Annual output growth due to TFP.** In the second half of the 1990s TFP growth seemed to surge in the United States. *Source*: Gordon, "Does the 'New Economy' Measure up to the Great Inventions of the past," Northwestern University mimeo (2000).

TABLE 6.2   **Annual Percentage Growth in ITC-Related Capital**

	1974–90	1991–95	1996–99
Hardware	31.3	17.5	35.9
Software	13.2	13.1	13.0
Communications Equipment	7.7	3.6	7.2

Source: Oliner and Sichel, "The Resurgence of Growth in the Late 1990s: Is IT the Story?" Federal Reserve Board mimeo (2000).

Along with these productivity gains, substantial investment was taking place in ITC (information technology and communications equipment). As Table 6.2 shows, the stock of ITC-related capital has increased dramatically since the mid 1970s but accelerated after 1995 with the development of the World Wide Web. Many commentators date the beginnings of the New Economy to these rapid developments in ITC.

In this section we review two questions: How important was ITC to the fast growth the United States experienced at the end of the 1990s? Is the New Economy as significant as the second industrial revolution at the end of the nineteenth century when electrical power and the combustion engine were developed? In other words, is ITC a macro- or a microinvention? To answer these questions, we shall focus mainly on the U.S. economy because, to date as Figure 6.16 illustrates, the United States has adopted IT more than any other country.

The importance of ITC in the economy is controversial—estimates of the role of computer hardware in generating annual U.S. output growth vary between −0.27% and 0.82%. While ITC capital stocks have undoubtedly surged, the issue is whether this in-

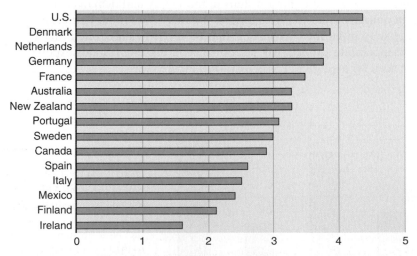

FIGURE 6.16   **GDP share (%) of ITC industries, mid 1990s.** *Source*: OECD, *Economic Outlook* (June 2000). Copyright OECD.

crease has caused output to rise. As Nobel Laureate Bob Solow puts it, "You can see the computer age everywhere but in the productivity statistics." This has become known as the Solow paradox. Computers are all around us, which suggests that they are useful. But if they are so useful, why hasn't their introduction caused productivity to surge?

High levels of investment in computing may not substantially boost output because computers have high levels of depreciation: around 30% per year. Therefore these dramatic increases in gross investment generate much smaller increases in *net* investment. Another factor that helps explain the Solow paradox is that although investment in ITC rose rapidly, it still represented only a small part of the overall capital stock. Between 1985 and 1996, U.S. investment in ITC was around 15% of total U.S. investment, or 3% of GDP. But with the U.S. capital—output ratio of around 2.5, this equates to only a little more than 1% of the total capital stock, even before allowing for depreciation. As a result, proponents of the New Economy argue that it takes several decades for the full impact of substantial technological change to manifest itself.

For instance, Paul David [7]suggests that it took 40 years before electricity substantially affected output. When electricity was first introduced, many factories were located near a water source to make the most cost efficient use of steam power. Electricity introduced some immediate benefits, for instance, a reliable source of lighting and energy for 24 hours a day, but its full impact was not felt for decades. To use electricity most efficiently new machines had to be developed, the factory floor reconfigured, and production relocated. For example, electricity made elevators reliable, which in turn enabled skyscrapers to be built. Obviously this new type of building could not be developed immediately. It may also take decades to realize the full benefits of IT. According to this argument it is too early for the IT revolution to generate a large increase in output, but it will eventually materialize.

Yet after more than a decade of high and accelerating ITC investment, the computing-related capital stock is now substantial. We can no longer, as we could in the mid 1990s, resolve the Solow paradox by claiming that the stock of computers is too small to affect output.[8] Instead, evidence indicates (especially after the substantial national accounts revisions made in 2000) that Solow's paradox may no longer exist—by the late 1990s, the computer revolution *was* affecting the U.S. productivity statistics.

Figure 6.17 illustrates the results of a growth accounting exercise to isolate the contribution of the various components of the ITC capital stock. It shows that the contribution of ITC has risen steadily over the last 25 years, until by 1999 it was boosting GDP growth by 1.2% per year. If true, and there are divergent claims, these numbers suggest that the New Economy was largely responsible for the unusually strong growth performance of the United States in the 1990s.

These growth accounting results suggest that proponents of the New Economy might be correct—ITC may be ushering in a third industrial revolution. However, closer examination of the data suggests a more complex story. As we explained earlier

---

[7]"The Dynamo and the Computer: An Historical Perspective on the Modern Productivity Paradox" *American Economic Review* (Papers and Proceedings) (1990) vol. 80, no. 2, pp. 355–361.

[8]Oliner and Sichel, "Computers and Output Growth Revisited: How Big Is the Puzzle?" Brookings Papers on Economic Activity (1994) vol. 2, pp. 273–317.

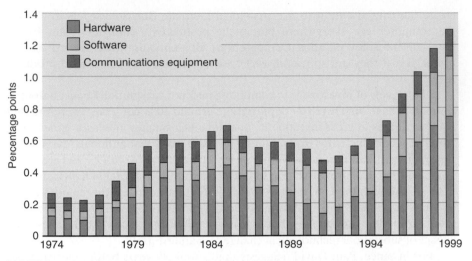

FIGURE 6.17   **Contribution of ITC capital to U.S. non-farm business output.** *Source*: Oliner and Sichel "The Resurgence of Growth in the Late 1990s: Is IT the Story?" Federal Reserve Board mimeo (2000).

in this chapter, technological progress increases output *both* through increases in TFP and indirectly by encouraging wider capital accumulation. We have documented the capital accumulation effect, but the evidence regarding TFP is less convincing.

Figure 6.15 showed evidence of impressive improvements in TFP during the 1990s, but all industries have not gained equally. The durable manufacturing goods sector, which accounts for only 12% of output, achieved much of these gains. Within this sector computer-producing firms, and especially the semiconductor industry, had the most substantive gains. Table 6.3 suggests that around 60% of TFP gains have occurred in the computer sector. In other words, more efficient ways of *producing* rather than *using* computers account for much of the efficiency gains that have boosted U.S. economic growth.

TABLE 6.3   **Sectoral Contributions to TFP Growth in the U.S.**

	1974–90	1991–95	1996–99
Growth Rate Non-Farm TFP	0.33	0.48	1.16
Contribution from Computer Sector	0.12	0.16	0.26
Contribution from Semiconductor Sector	0.08	0.12	0.39
Other Non-Farm Business	0.13	0.20	0.50

Source: Oliner and Sichel, "The Resurgence of Growth in the Late 1990s: Is IT the Story?" Federal Reserve Board mimeo (2000).

TABLE 6.4   Labor Productivity in Manufacturing 1999 (1995 = 100)

	Office, accounting and computing equipment	Radio, television and communications equipment	Manufacturing
U.S.	460	172	125
Japan		112	104
Germany	186	129	117
France		128	115
UK	160		103
Canada	97	141	105
Austria	116	134	130
Denmark	99	151	109
Finland	127	193	119
Korea	454	322	150
Mexico	117	144	119
Portugal		195	122

Source: OECD, *Economic Outlook*, June 2000, p. 183.
Copyright OECD.

Table 6.4 shows how labor productivity has increased dramatically in ITC industries compared to the rest of manufacturing (and also compared to most other nations). As a result of this soaring productivity in producing computers, their prices have fallen dramatically—in 1961 the price index for computer hardware and peripherals was 61640, but by 1999 it had declined to 36—an annual fall in prices of 19.4%. In the second half of the 1990s, productivity improved further, and price declined even faster—the ratio of performance to price increased by a factor of 5 for computers and even more for some components (16 for processors, 75 for RAM, and 176 for hard disk capacity).

Figure 6.18 shows that the inputs into production whose prices have declined the most have seen their use grow fastest. The sharp price declines in ITC equipment (caused by productivity improvements in the computer manufacturing sector) encouraged firms to substitute this newer technology for existing technology, e.g., firms send e-mails rather than faxes; they use PCs rather than typewriters; surf the web rather than scour libraries; fill hard disks rather than filing cabinets. But all this represents substitution between techniques rather than a substantial shift in the productive capacity of the economy.

This analysis reveals that ITC had affected U.S. growth at the end of the twentieth century. Dramatic productivity improvements in the computer manufacturing sector generated significant TFP growth in the United States. The ITC capital stock surged because of the price declines in computing equipment that these productivity improvements caused, which in turn contributed substantially to growth through capital accumulation. However, TFP in the non-ITC U.S. economy increased only a little. The productivity improvements of the New Economy have so far been largely restricted to the durable manufacturing sector.

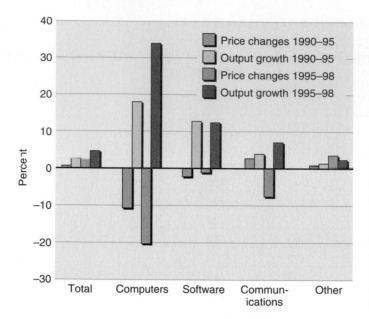

FIGURE 6.18
Substitution between capital inputs. As the price of computers fell their use increased sharply. *Source*: Jorgenson and Stiroh, "Raising the Speed Limit: U.S. Economic Growth in the Information Age," Harvard University mimeo (2000).

Figure 6.19 shows how a few industries account for the increases in productivity. Further, those industries in which productivity had improved the most have not adopted IT the most enthusiastically. Figure 6.20 lists IT intensity across U.S. industries and shows that productivity has grown the least in the most IT intensive industries.

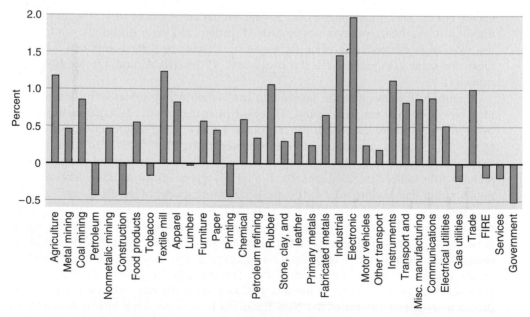

FIGURE 6.19　**Productivity growth in U.S. industries, 1958–1996.** *Source*: Jorgenson and Stiroh, "Raising the Speed Limit: U.S. Economic Growth in the Information Age," Harvard University mimeo (2000).

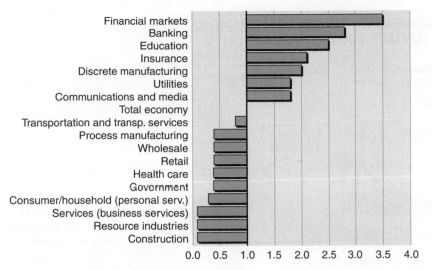

FIGURE 6.20   **IT intensity in U.S. industries.** *Source*: OECD, *A New Economy* (2000). Copyright OECD.

Whether ITC can improve TFP across the economy is controversial. Advocates of the New Economy point to the rapid growth in e-commerce. Sceptics counter that the impact of ITC cannot be compared with that of previous macroinventions such as electricity, the combustion engine, and even internal plumbing! Even the telegraph caused communication costs to fall more dramatically than the Internet did.[9] Moreover, much ITC-based activity involves duplicating existing activities rather than generating extra value added—firms now have to duplicate mail-order catalogs and orders on the Web. Further, much of this commercial activity on the Web is not creating value added but redistributing sales among existing firms—it is competition for market share rather than new markets. Sceptics of the New Economy also point out that ITC is about information, which is an intermediate good and not value added. ITC involves moving information around in the form of binary code. In its own right, this information is not useful—it is only valuable because people require it to produce or consume something. Being able to find out more easily when a concert is scheduled via the Web is useful, but what really matters is attending the concert, not finding out when it is going to start. (Of course, the time you save by finding out about the concert on the Web is valuable.) Finally, computing developments may not automatically improve productivity—employees may also use the Web to pursue their private hobbies rather than boost firm productivity. Figure 6.21 may not be as compelling as some of our previous empirical evidence, but it may nonetheless convince some readers!

We asked ourselves two questions in this section. The first was how important ITC was in explaining the late 1990s U.S. boom—our results suggest that it was important. The second was whether developments in ITC amounted to a third industrial revolution. As we write (in 2000), the data suggest that TFP improvements have been too focused

---

[9]With the telegraph the time taken to send a one-page note from New York to Chicago fell by a factor of 3000—from 10 days to 5 minutes. See Gordon, "Does the 'New Economy' Measure Up to the Great Inventions of the Past," Northwestern University mimeo (2000).

FIGURE 6.21   **Economists Wonder . . .** *Source*: Boston Globe. Reprinted by permission.

on specific sectors of the U.S. economy to support this argument. But, New Economy advocates can point to the slow diffusion of the second industrial revolution and the increase in TFP in the late 1990s to argue that something more dramatic is occurring.

SUMMARY

Technological progress enables us to produce more output for any given level of factor inputs and thus to shift the production function upward. With no technological progress, the capital stock reaches its steady state level, and the economy ceases to grow. Technological progress provides two additional channels for growth: it produces more output from a given level of factor inputs, and it boosts the desired level of capital. The higher level of output that technological progress produces means that for a given investment rate a higher amount of depreciation can be met, so that the steady state capital stock increases, which also increases output.

Foreign direct investment is increasing in importance and encourages convergence among countries. FDI leads both to an increase in the capital stock and a transfer of technology to the recipient country and so contributes to growth in developing nations.

R&D is one way to create technological progress. The output of R&D is knowledge, which is nonexcludable. This means that firms may not be able to capture the profits from an innovation and so will undertake too little R&D. To overcome this problem, governments offer patents, which give firms a temporary monopoly to use their inventions, which encourages R&D.

The relationship between technological progress and unemployment is controversial. Theoretically unemployment can increase if output remains static or grows only weakly after technological progress. However, little evidence supports the notion that technological progress leads to higher aggregate unemployment. While technological progress has only small effects on aggregate unemployment, it does contribute to substantial distributional changes, which create areas where unemployment rises.

The data suggest that the durable manufacturing sector, and in particular the computer-related industries, generated most of the TFP gains in the U.S. economy in the late 1990s. The substantial gains in these industries have led to dramatic declines in ITC equipment prices, which have encouraged large increases in the ITC capital stock and substitution away from older forms of technology. This ITC capital accumulation has increased output and was a factor in the late 1990s U.S. economic boom. However, the lack of widespread TFP improvements throughout the U.S. economy means that the data do not (yet) support the notion of a third industrial revolution.

CONCEPTUAL QUESTIONS

1. In this chapter we have assumed that the level of technology can be adjusted independently of the capital stock. However, in practice investing in new technology means investing in new machines. Use Figure 6.3 to analyze the implications of this.

2. Two economies have the same investment and depreciation rates, but one has access to an inferior technology. Assuming their initial capital stock is the same, how does their output growth and their steady state output and capital stock differ?

3. How would a technological development that boosted output but produced a higher depreciation rate affect output and capital?

4. Is it better to develop your own technological champions or to rely on foreign direct investment?

5. What advantages do industry-wide funded research institutes produce? What problems are they likely to have?

6. If technological progress is so important for long-term increases in the standard of living, why does it make people so anxious?

7. The commercial real estate industry is concerned that IT developments and the rise of tele-working will cause the demand for office space to decline and rents to fall. Is this justified?

8. Which professional categories do you think will see the biggest changes in employment over the next 25 years?

9. How have IT developments affected your productivity?

10. Have developments in biotechnology a better claim than IT to be a macroinvention?

ANALYTICAL QUESTIONS

1. Consider an economy in which output in period t is produced by the Cobb-Douglas production function:

$$Y_t = A_t K_t^b L_t^{1-b}$$

Y_t is output at time t; K_t is capital at time t; L_t is labor employed at time t; A_t is TFP at time t.

Saving, which equals gross investment, is 25% of output. The depreciation rate of capital is 5% a period. Initially TFP is constant at 1 and labor input is constant at 100 and b is 0.3.

   (a) Calculate the initial steady state level of output.
   (b) What happens in the short run if TFP suddenly rises from 1 to 1.2?

(c) What is the new long-run level of steady state output assuming TFP stays at 1.2?

(d) What is the growth in the capital stock between the old steady state and the new one?

2. Suppose there are many companies in a particular sector of the economy. By investing $1 million in R&D one of these companies has a 50% chance of discovering a better way to produce output. If the research is successful, profit will rise by $0.5 million a year so long as other companies do not copy the innovation. If all other companies copy the innovation, profits will be no higher as the gains are competed away and passed on to consumers in lower prices. Assume future expected profits are valued the same as money available today.

   (a) What should the company do if it has a patent on any successful innovation for 3 years?

   (b) What if the patent is for 8 years?

   (c) What is the optimal patent length from the point of view of society as a whole?

3. A company can site a new plant in the domestic economy or in a foreign economy. Wherever it builds the site capital employed will rise by 20. In the domestic economy the relation between output produced and capital employed is

$$Q_d = 10. K_d^{0.5}$$

where Q_d is domestically produced output; K_d is the capital stock in the domestic economy. In the foreign economy output from the capital installed there is

$$Q_f = 3. K_f^{0.5}$$

where Q_f is output produced in the foreign country; K_f is the capital stock in the foreign economy. Initially $K_d = 900$ and $K_f = 50$.

   (a) Where should the company site its new plant?

   (b) At what level of the foreign capital stock is the firm indifferent about where it locates new production, assuming K_d stays at 900?

4. Technical progress in an industry generates a sudden 30% rise in labor productivity. The demand for the output of this industry moves in line with overall GDP but it is very insensitive to price. The companies in the industry collude after the technical progress and decide not to cut prices. The industry is relatively small in the overall economy.

   (a) What happens to employment in the industry?

   (b) Now assume the 30% rise in productivity occurs throughout the economy. What happens to employment now?

5. One hundred years ago a substantial proportion of the labor force in developed economies was domestic servants. Now the proportion of workers who make a living cleaning, cooking, and making fires in other people's homes is substantially smaller. Analyze this trend explaining how technical progress (e.g., the development of central heating, washing machines, microwaves, and convenience foods) has shifted the demand and supply curves for domestic servants.

6. In developed economies the average proportion of people's waking lives spent working has declined substantially over the course of the last 150 years. Would this have happened if there had been no technical progress? Does the decline in working life as a proportion of conscious life mean that per capita GDP growth over the long term underestimates the growth in the standard of living? How might one adjust for this?

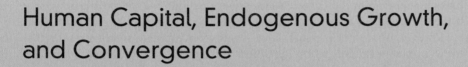

Human Capital, Endogenous Growth, and Convergence

Overview

In this chapter we consider the role of another factor that can boost output: "human capital." We also consider an alternative class of growth theories, known as endogenous growth models, which drop the assumption of diminishing marginal product of capital (MPK). We consider two types of endogenous growth models: one based on human capital and the other on knowledge spillovers between individuals or firms. These models assume that MPK, rather than diminishing, is constant, and as a result, a steady state capital stock does not exist; thus our previous conclusions regarding convergence do not hold. If these spillover effects are pronounced, poverty traps may condemn poor regions not only to grow more slowly than wealthier regions but to remain poor in absolute terms.

    We examine historical growth patterns and find that across a wide sample of countries no pattern of convergence exists; on average poor countries do not grow faster than wealthy ones. However, when we consider similar countries, we find strong evidence in favor of convergence. We reconcile this evidence by introducing the idea of conditional convergence—among countries that share a similar steady state, poorer countries will grow faster than wealthier ones; but comparing across countries with different steady states, we should find no clear patterns of convergence. We then consider what determines a country's steady state and how policy measures might affect it. We conclude by reviewing the poor economic growth performance of Africa.

7.1   Human Capital

By human capital we mean the skills and knowledge that accumulate over time in individuals, the labor force, and society. Both physical and human capital are important inputs into the production process. Like physical capital (buildings and machinery), human capital is durable. Skills that you learn at college or during work remain with you. Human capital also suffers from depreciation—how much of this chapter will you remember tomorrow? Next month? In five years time?

Many skills make up human capital—ranging from learning accumulated at school, to skills learned in the workplace, and to shared social knowledge and conventions. Levels of human capital differ widely across countries (see Table 7.1), which helps to explain many growth anomalies. For instance, real GDP per capita differs greatly between the United States and India, as does the capital stock. If the output differences were due *only* to differences in physical capital, it would imply that the MPK in India was 58 times higher than in the United States due to the low level of the Indian capital stock.[1] If the MPK really was so high in India, then U.S. firms would be investing heavily there. However, we do not see such large levels of investment, which suggests that the return to capital in India is not much different from that in the United States. We can account for this if we allow for differences in human capital. Table 7.1 shows there is much more schooling in the U.S. population than in India. The marginal product of

TABLE 7.1   **Average Schooling Years**

	Primary	Secondary	Higher	Total
Australia	6.52	3.04	0.67	10.23
Botswana	3.40	0.26	0.03	3.69
Brazil	2.39	0.88	0.21	3.48
Canada	5.33	3.87	0.97	10.17
Demark	8.01	1.76	0.56	10.33
Germany	7.43	0.87	0.24	8.54
Ghana	2.26	0.93	0.03	3.22
India	2.11	0.81	0.13	3.05
Japan	5.29	2.65	0.52	8.46
Mexico	3.38	0.82	0.22	4.42
USA	5.85	4.90	1.04	11.79
Venezuela	3.69	1.35	0.34	5.38

Source: Barro and Lee, "International Comparisons of Educational Attainment," *Journal of Monetary Economics,* 1993. Reprinted with permission from Elsevier Science.

[1]R. E. Lucas, "Why Doesn't Capital Flow from Rich to Poor Countries?" *American Economic Review* (1990) vol. 80, pp. 92–96.

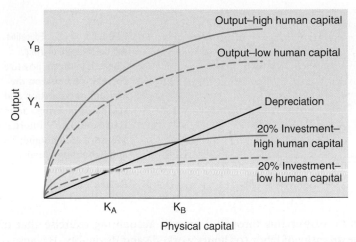

FIGURE 7.1 **Impact of human capital on steady state.** Higher human capital increases output and encourages greater investment in physical capital. Steady state phyical capital moves from K_A to K_B with more human capital.

physical capital increases with the amount of human capital there is in a country—the more educated the workforce, the higher the marginal product of physical capital. Although India has a lower capital stock than the United States (which boosts the MPK in India), it also has a lower level of average human capital. As a consequence, the MPK may not differ much between India and the United States.

A country with a higher level of human capital can produce more output from a given level of physical capital—as shown in Figure 7.1. Therefore for the same investment rate, the country can support a higher level of depreciation and thus a higher steady state capital stock (K_B rather than K_A). Thus higher levels of human capital should be reflected in higher standards of living (Y_B as opposed to Y_A). Note that allowing for human capital alters the catch-up results outlined in Chapter 5. There we showed that diminishing marginal product of physical capital implied that capital poor countries grow faster than capital rich countries. However, the dependence of the marginal product of physical capital on the level of human capital means that we have to modify this result. Countries with low stocks of physical machinery will only grow faster than capital rich countries if they have similar levels of human capital.

SCHOOLING AND THE CLASSROOM

Figure 7.2 shows average years of schooling per person in 1960 for many countries and their GDP per capita in 1985—those countries with higher schooling levels in 1960 had higher levels of output in 1985.

Figure 7.3 shows that education has also increased in most countries over time. How much of historical economic growth do increases in human capital account for?

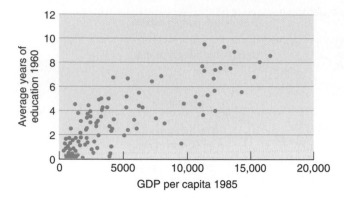

FIGURE 7.2 **Education and the standard of living.** There is a strong positive correlation between the amount of education and standards of living. *Source:* Barro and Lee, "International Measure of Schooling Years and Schooling Quality," (1996) *American Economic Review.*

Table 7.2 attempts to answer this through a growth accounting exercise that distinguishes between the quantity of labor (or hours worked) and its quality. Because of education, the average hour worked in the economy now contains more skill and knowledge than 200 years ago. We therefore need to distinguish between producing more output because of an increase in hours worked and producing more output from the same number of hours worked but increased human capital.[2]

The fourth row in Table 7.2 shows the contribution of increased human capital. For these five countries, increasing human capital accounts for somewhere between 0.2% and 0.5% growth per year. Compared to the role of physical capital and total factor productivity, this is small, but as we pointed out in Chapter 4, small differences in growth rates over long periods add up to substantial differences in welfare. If Germany or the UK could improve its educational and training systems to deliver the same growth benefits as the United States and Japan, then their standards of living could improve substantially over time.

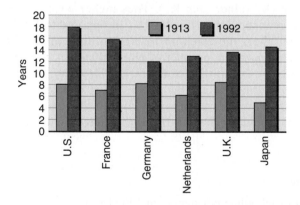

FIGURE 7.3 **Years of education per person aged 15–64.** As countries have become richer people have stayed at school or college longer. *Source:* Maddison, *Monitoring the World Economy* 1820–1992 (OECD, 1995). Copyright OECD.

[2]This is not a trivial exercise. One strategy is to use firm-level studies to estimate the extra income paid to different skill levels of labor. We then assume that high wages reflect differences in productivity. We can then use aggregate data on how the compositions of skill levels in society have changed to calculate how much extra gross domestic product (GDP) growth this would have produced. This is the method used to construct the estimates in Table 7.2.

TABLE 7.2   Contribution of Education to Annual Output
Growth: 1950–90

	France	Germany	Japan	UK	USA
Annual Growth (%)	5.04	5.92	9.27	3.03	3.65
Capital	2.40	3.19	4.33	2.40	1.62
Labor—Hours	−0.09	0.01	0.89	−0.09	0.58
Labor—Skills	0.39	0.19	0.52	0.20	0.48
Total Factor Productivity	2.34	2.53	3.53	0.52	0.97

Source: Crafts "Productivity Growth Reconsidered," *Economic
Politics* (Blackwell Publishers 1991) vol. 15, pp. 387–426.

LEARNING BY DOING

Focusing only on school education as human capital is too restrictive. Learning by doing is also an important source of knowledge. By repeating the same task many times, people become more skillful and productive at the activity—this learning by doing can operate across a range of actions from children learning how to tie their shoelaces to learning how to play a concert-level piano performance or understanding the principles of economic growth. Plenty of evidence supports the notion of learning by doing. One classic example is that of the production of U.S. Liberty ships. Between December 1941 and December 1944, 2458 of these ships were built, all to the same design. Figure 7.4 shows how the number of person hours needed to produce one ship changed as the shipyards had more experience in producing them. This experience in making Liberty ships shows strong evidence of a learning curve—every doubling of cumulative output (e.g.. from 100 ships made to 200 ships, and then to a cumulative 400 ships) reduces costs 12–24%.

The example of Liberty ships focuses on learning by doing within the shipyard—the shipyard learns from its own experience. However, learning by doing also often generates spillover effects—firms learn from the experience of other firms. A study of the U.S. and Japanese semiconductor industry also finds evidence of a learning curve—every cumulative doubling of a firm's output leads to an approximate 20% decline in costs.[3]

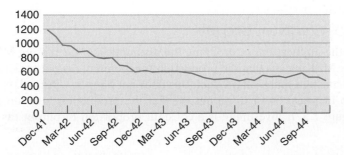

FIGURE 7.4 **Person hours required per Liberty ship.** Building the same model of ship over and over—an example of learning by doing *Source:* Lucas, "Making a Miracle" *Econometrica* (1993) vol. 61(2) pp. 251–271. By permission of *The Economic Society*.

[3]Irwin and Klenow, "Learning by Doing Spillovers in the Semiconductor Industry" *Journal of Political Economy* (1994) vol. 102(6), pp. 1200–1227.

However, the study also detected a learning by doing effect from increases in industry-wide output, albeit at only around a third of the size of the firm specific learning by doing. This industry-wide learning by doing operates across national boundaries—a U.S. firm benefits equally from an increase in industry output regardless of whether it occurs in the United States or Japan. Therefore as industry output expands, all firms learn how to improve productive efficiency.

7.2   Endogenous Growth

We now turn to an alternative model of economic growth called endogenous growth theory. Endogenous means something that is explained within the context of a model or theory. For instance, the weather forecast may explain an impending rainstorm by the presence of a low pressure zone moving over a country. In this case the forecast makes the rainstorm an endogenous variable and explains it via the low pressure zone. However, if then the forecast does not explain the presence of the low pressure zone itself, then it is an exogenous variable within the context of the forecast. Science moves forward by first making phenomena exogenous, working through the implications of those exogenous forces, and then trying to create fuller theories to explain factors that are initially just taken to be exogenous. So what are endogenous growth theories?

Consider again the model we outlined in Chapter 5 based on the assumption of decreasing marginal product of capital. This model explained the steady state and the transition towards it. In the steady state, the model says growth occurs only through TFP. But the model does not explain technological progress. In other words, Chapter 5 offers an *exogenous* theory of economic growth.

By contrast, *endogenous* growth theories try to explain what causes long-run economic growth. There are, of course, many ways of explaining economic growth, and endogenous growth theory refers to a wide range of models. In general, endogenous growth theories try to explain continual economic growth in two ways.[4] One is to rule out the notion of a steady state—without a steady state, the economy can continue to grow without limit. The other route (which can be combined with ruling out a steady state) is to explain what produces technological progress and how it changes over time.

THE WONDERFUL WORLD OF CONTINUAL GROWTH

We now demonstrate the implications of dropping the assumption of decreasing MPK. Assuming a decreasing MPK means that the production function flattens out (as shown in Figure 7.1). With a constant marginal product, this does not happen—instead, every new machine gives an identical boost to output, so that the production function is a straight line, as in Figure 7.5. If investment is a constant proportion of output (as we

---

[4]Both these strands of endogenous growth theory are associated with Paul Romer, in particular his seminal papers "Increasing Returns and Long Run Growth" *Journal of Political Economy* (1986) vol. 94, pp. 1002–10037 and "Endogenous Technological Change" *Journal of Political Economy* (1990) vol. 98, pp. 71–102.

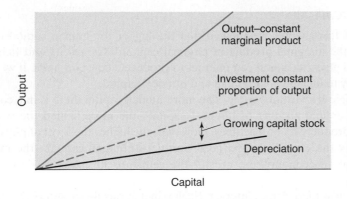

FIGURE 7.5 **Constant marginal product and endogenous growth.** With a constant marginal product of capital there is no steady state level of the capital stock.

previously assumed), the investment schedule is also a straight line. The steady state is the point where the capital stock is not changing—where investment equals depreciation. However, Figure 7.5 shows that no such point exists—investment can always be greater than depreciation, so the capital stock can increase continually, even without technological progress.

The absence of a steady state rules out the convergence result we stressed in Chapter 5—poor countries need no longer grow faster than wealthier nations. Endogenous growth theory also suggests that if government policy can boost investment, it not only increases the capital stock but *permanently* affects the growth rate. To see how growth depends on the investment rate, consider the following. The change in the capital stock equals investment less depreciation. If investment equals a proportion (b) of output and depreciation is a proportion (δ) of the capital stock then

$$\text{change in capital stock} = \text{investment} - \text{depreciation} = bY - \delta K$$

A constant MPK implies that doubling the number of machines doubles output. Therefore output is simply a multiple of the capital stock or $Y = AK$, where A reflects total factor productivity. Therefore

$$\text{change in capital stock} = bY - \delta K = bAK - \delta K$$

The percentage growth in the capital stock is equal to the change in the capital stock divided by capital (K), so we have

$$\% \text{ growth in capital stock} = \text{change in capital stock/capital stock} = bY/K - \delta K/K$$
$$= bA - \delta$$

so that the increase in the capital stock depends positively on the investment rate, b. Therefore, if the government can change the investment rate, it leads not just to a one-time increase in the *levels* of capital and output (as in Chapter 5) but a *permanent* increase in the *growth rates* capital and output.

WHY CONSTANT MARGINAL PRODUCT?

The previous subsection has shown that dropping the assumption of declining MPK leads to different growth implications. But is there a constant MPK?

A BROADER CONCEPT OF CAPITAL

In the first section of this chapter we showed that the higher the human capital of a country, the greater the marginal product of physical capital. We now extend that to show how human and physical capital can interact to produce a constant MPK if we interpret capital broadly to include *both* human and physical capital.

The key to the logic is a virtuous circle. The more human capital there is in a country, the higher the marginal product of physical capital—the more skilled the workforce, the higher the productivity of machines. However, the higher the level of physical capital in an economy the greater the marginal product of human capital—the more machines there are in an economy, the greater the return to investing in skills and education.

Figure 7.6 shows how these forces interact. Each panel in this figure shows the marginal product of human or physical capital, and each marginal product curve is drawn for a fixed level of the other form of capital. *Therefore, holding fixed the other form of capital, both display decreasing marginal product.* Let us assume that an increase in technological knowledge boosts the marginal product of human capital—skilled labor is now more productive. This shifts the marginal product of human capital curve out from A to B in Figure 7.6. Assuming no change in the cost of education, this encourages the economy to increase its stock of human capital to H_1. This increase in human capital boosts the productivity of physical capital—the marginal product curve shifts out to $MPK(H_1)$ in the right-hand panel. Given the cost of capital, this means the economy increases its capital stock to K_1. However, this new higher level of physical capital means that the marginal product of human capital improves, and the marginal product curve for human capital shifts out to C. As a result, more human capital is accumulated to reach the level H_2. This increase in human capital in turn shifts the marginal product of physical capital out [to $MPK(H_2)$], and the virtuous circle continues. Therefore,

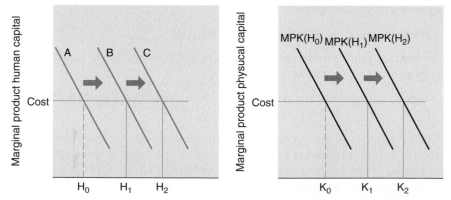

FIGURE 7.6   **Interaction human and physical capital.** Increases in human capital generate more investment in physical capital . . . and vice versa. As the productivity of human capital schedule rises from A to B, the stock of human capital increases from H_0 to H_1, and this raises the productivity of physical schedule from $MPK(H_0)$ to $MPK(H_1)$ The resulting increase in physical capital further boosts the productivity of human capital.

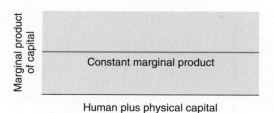

FIGURE 7.7   **Constant marginal product of capital.**

although each category of capital on its own has decreasing marginal product, if we think of capital as including both human and physical capital, then we have constant marginal product of capital, as in Figure 7.7.

What evidence is there that this interaction leads to a constant MPK? Human knowledge is vast and increasing, but we still have much to discover about the implications of what we already know. For instance, with over 130 periodic elements, there are billions of potential combinations, only some of which scientists have logged and many of which they have yet to investigate. To illustrate how this matters, consider the case of a group of French chemists who logged one of these compounds; it took another 10 years before IBM discovered its properties as a superconductor. On a more mundane note, consider the production of a motor bike that consists of 75 separate steps. There are thousands of ways of rearranging the process, so the current one is probably not the optimal one; some rearrangements of the production process will lead to a higher marginal product of capital that will in turn spawn more investment, more R&D, and more learning by doing. This process of exploiting the stock of human knowledge produces the virtuous circle that can lead to a constant MPK. Even if this interaction is not powerful enough to lead to a constant marginal product, it will make marginal product decline far more slowly and so push back the relevance of the steady state.

We can show more clearly how this interaction between physical and human capital works if we return to our analysis of the Cobb-Douglas production function and allow for human capital. In this case the production function becomes

output = A × (human capital)$^{\phi}$ × (physical capital)^{a} × (hours worked)$^{1-a}$

The marginal product of human capital is ϕ × output/(human capital), and for physical capital it is a × output/(physical capital). Both marginal products are declining, keeping fixed the other factors of production. However, if human capital is increasing with physical capital, e.g., human capital = Θ × physical capital, then we can substitute out human capital from the production function and arrive at

output = AΘ^{ϕ} × (physical capital)$^{\phi+a}$ × (hours worked)$^{1-a}$

If $\Phi + a = 1$, then this becomes

output = A* × physical capital × (hours worked)$^{1-a}$

where $A* = \mathbf{A\Theta^{\phi}}$

This is the same AK production function (e.g., Y = AK) that we outlined when we discussed the straight line production function in Figure 7.5. The closer $\Phi + a$ is to 1, the more the production function becomes a straight line.

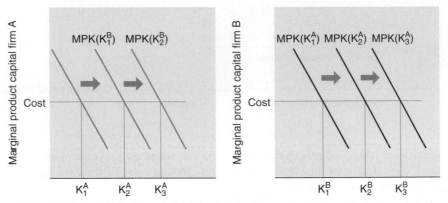

FIGURE 7.8   **Spillover effects and constant marginal product of capital.** The marginal product of each firm is an increasing function of the capital employed of the other firm. As firm A's capital employed rises from K_1^A to K_2^A the marginal product of capital to firm B rises.

EXTERNALITIES AND SPILLOVERS

Earlier in this chapter, we discussed spillovers—firms learning from the production experience of other firms. These spillovers can reinforce the tendency for the MPK to be constant.

Suppose each firm suffers from decreasing MPK when it increases its *own* capital stock. Suppose also that an increase in the aggregate capital stock increases the MPK for each firm due to an industry-wide learning by doing effect (as we documented earlier for the semiconductor industry). The overall result is that while there is declining marginal product in the capital of each firm, there may be constant MPK in the aggregate capital stock.

To see how this process works, assume that the economy consists of only two firms. As shown in Figure 7.8, firm A discovers a new way of arranging production, so that the marginal product of capital curve shifts to the right. As a result, the firm increases its capital stock from K_1^A to K_2^A. But this increase in firm A's capital stock generates spillover benefits to other sectors of the economy. This shifts out the marginal product of capital curve for firm B, which encourages an increase in its capital stock from K_1^B to K_2^B. But the spillovers work in both directions, and this increase in the capital stock of firm B leads to spillover benefits for firm A, which leads to a rightward shift in firm A's marginal product curve. This in turn leads to an increase in firm A's capital stock from K_2^A to K_3^A, and so the process continues. As a result, while there is declining MPK at the firm level, there may be constant MPK in the aggregate.

ENDOGENOUS GROWTH AND GOVERNMENT POLICY

The previous section illustrates some of the features that have made endogenous growth models popular, not just among economists but also among policymakers. The reason is that spillovers are a form of market imperfection—left to its own devices, the market will not arrive at the best outcome, and this suggests a potentially useful role for government intervention. When each firm assesses whether to undertake investment, it compares the benefits and costs of the project. But each firm considers only the benefits

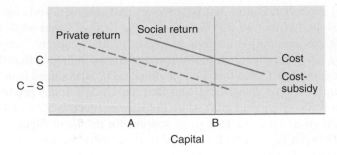

FIGURE 7.9 **Spillovers and subsidies.** A subsidy to bring down the cost of capital can induce firms to undertake the right level of investment (level B) even though they take account only of private returns.

for itself—it does not factor in the additional benefits for other firms that arise from the spillover effects. Because other firms learn from the investment project of the firm, the social return from the investment is greater than the private return that the firm captures. As a result the firm does not do enough investment, as Figure 7.9 shows. Firm A chooses the capital stock in which the private return equals the cost rather than capital stock B in which the social return equals cost. The government can, however, rectify the situation by offering a subsidy, so that the cost to the firm falls to C−S. Thus, while the firm still chooses investment by equating private return to cost, it now chooses the socially optimal investment level B. Therefore endogenous growth theory can provide a rationale for the government to boost long-run economic growth.

7.3 Poverty Traps

We need to investigate a third possibility about the MPK—the case of an increasing marginal product. If marginal product is increasing, this yields even richer growth implications. In particular, we can explain the existence of poverty traps that keep poor regions or countries poor. Figure 7.10 shows two regions in an economy—one with a low capital stock (A) and another with a high capital stock (B). For region A the MPK is less than the cost of investment, so it does not invest. However, because we are now assuming that the MPK is increasing in the capital stock, the capital rich region (B) will make the investment because for it the MPK exceeds the cost of investment. Depreciation and no investment will lead to region A seeing its capital declining and it becoming poorer, while continued investment and increasing marginal product leads to high output and accelerating growth in region B.

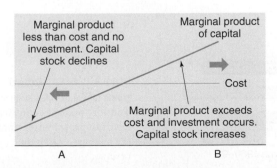

FIGURE 7.10 **Increasing marginal product and poverty traps.** If the marginal product of capital increases as capital employed rises, then poverty traps are possible.

Increasing marginal product therefore not only means that countries and regions don't show signs of catch-up, but that we find *divergence*—the rich get richer while the poor get poorer. Under this assumption one would expect to find economic activity heavily concentrated in a few successful areas that showed continual high growth rather than spread equally across regions. Given that 54% of global GDP is produced from an area that accounts for only 10% of global land, and that the United States produces 50% of its GDP from only 2% of its land mass while the least productive 50% of U.S. land accounts for only 2% of its GDP, there is some support for this view. Figure 7.11 shows the average growth in per capita output between 1960 and 1994, for several countries arranged in five groups. The bottom quintile is the poorest 20% of countries in 1960, the top quintile is the richest 20% of the countries, and the other quintiles reflect intermediate ranks. Overall, the gap between rich and poor countries has widened between 1960 and 1994, with the poorest countries having the lowest growth.

The assumption of increasing marginal product also helps to explain why in global capital markets portfolio investment flows mostly to wealthy nations. Between 1970 and 1994, the poorest 20% of countries received only 1% of total gross global capital flows, or the equivalent of 6 cents per person in those countries. By contrast, the richest 20% of the countries received 88% of total capital flows, which amounted to $189 per person. If the marginal product of capital is increasing, then the return to investment will be highest in the richest nations, and investors will rationally avoid portfolio investment in poor undeveloped nations.

What justification can we give for the assumption of increasing MPK? The most plausible arguments again focus on the key role of human capital. Observing many industries, professions, and even neighborhoods, we can see that individuals tend to associate with individuals of similar levels of human capital. For instance, the quality of economists within an academic department (or students within a university) tends to be similar, although quality will vary widely across different universities and business schools. This may have to do with interdependencies in the production function—it is important to avoid "weak links in the chain." For instance, the space shuttle *Challenger* exploded because one of its many thousands of components malfunctioned. That small imperfection destroyed a complex scientific project. Companies can fail because of bad marketing even if the rest of the firm functions well. With such strong interdependencies (spillovers), we would expect to find highly skilled individuals working with each other, while less skilled individuals also group together. As Michael Kremer notes—Charlie Parker worked with Dizzy Gillespie and Donny Osmond worked with his sister Marie.[5]

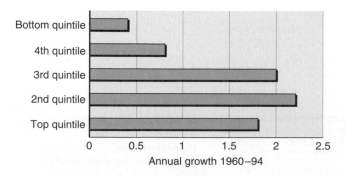

FIGURE 7.11 **Economic growth ranked by initial income.** The very poorest countries have not grown faster than the average—quite the reverse.

Interdependencies also help explain puzzling features of wages. Empirical labor studies have found that secretaries working in investment banks or law firms get paid much more than secretaries working in lower-paid industries. Many explanations have been suggested for this, including an appeal to fairness, but one explanation is that industries with high human capital pay more to attract the best secretaries. With strong interdependencies it is important to avoid weak links because they can hurt the productivity of many other individuals.

These interdependencies are typical of the increasing returns to scale or increasing marginal product that typifies poverty traps. In a poverty trap, the individual's incentive to avoid poverty is poor. If you are surrounded by high-quality human capital, then you have a large incentive to increase your human capital. However, if you are surrounded by low-quality human capital, your incentives are poor—with many weak links in the chain, your gains from increased education are going to be much smaller. This is why individuals and nations can get stuck in a poverty trap.

7.4 Convergence or Divergence?

In previous sections we have shown how different assumptions regarding the MPK have fundamentally different implications for growth. In outlining each of these alternative assumptions on the MPK, we have shown evidence that is consistent with each theory, but which theory best explains the facts?

The key distinction between the Solow or neoclassical growth model based around decreasing marginal product that we outlined in Chapter 5 and the endogenous growth theories of this chapter is convergence. With decreasing marginal product, we expect to find convergence—poorer countries should grow faster than rich ones. According to endogenous growth theories based around constant or increasing marginal product, there should be no simple correlation between initial income and subsequent growth. Therefore, to discriminate between these competing theories, we should simply examine historical evidence to see if there is a negative correlation between initial income and subsequent growth. If there is a negative correlation we have convergence, and the neoclassical model based on decreasing marginal product is the more appropriate.

Figure 7.12 shows the level of GDP per capita in 1960 and the average growth rate between 1960 and 1985 for a sample of 132 countries. Considering all countries together, there is no evidence of convergence; there is no negative correlation between initial income and subsequent growth. While some poor countries grow very fast, there is a range of growth experiences—some grow quickly, while in others standards of living fall further.

Figure 7.12 considers a broad range of different economies including developed (OECD) countries, African countries, emerging markets in Southeast Asia, and some formerly communist economies. If we consider more similar groupings of economies, then different results appear. Figure 7.13 shows the same data, but focuses on just the OECD economies—there is now substantial evidence of convergence. The fastest growing OECD nations were those that were poorest in 1960, i.e., Spain, Portugal, and

[5]The ideas here draw on an interesting article by Michael Kremer, "The O-Ring Theory of Economic Development" *Quarterly Journal of Economics* (1993), August, pp. 551–576.

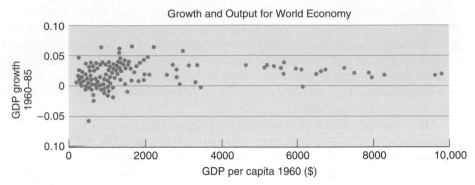

FIGURE 7.12   **Convergence—Exhibit 1, all countries.** There is no tendency for convergence across all countries. *Source:* Summers and Heston Penn World Tables, http://pwt.econ.upenn.edu.

Mexico have grown faster than Germany, France, and the UK. Figures 7.14–7.17 show similarly strong evidence in favor of convergence when we examine U.S. states, regions in Western Europe, provinces in Canada, and prefectures in Japan.

These figures show that when we consider regions or economies that display similar characteristics we find strong evidence of convergence, so that within similar groups relatively poor countries grow faster than the relatively rich. Think of groups of countries as like different species. Elephants are one species—if you find a small elephant, it is probably on its way to becoming the size of an average elephant and will grow fast. But now look at squirrels—all squirrels are small relative to elephants but never catch them up; small squirrels only catch up with average squirrels, not average elephants.

Proponents of the neoclassical model refer to the "iron law of convergence"— when they look at similar groupings of regions, they find that on average about 2% of the discrepancy between rich and poor regions is removed each year. This convergence occurs slowly—it takes 35 years to reduce the discrepancy by half. However, the evidence suggests that while it may be slow, some form of convergence is occurring whereby poorer regions (such as the south of Italy or Maine and Arkansas in the United States) do grow faster than wealthier regions (such as the north of Italy or New York State and Massachusetts).

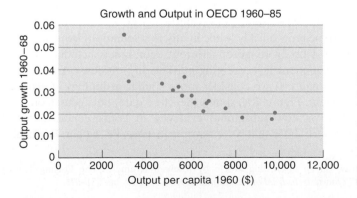

FIGURE 7.13
Convergence—OECD economies.
Within OECD countries convergence seems to exist.
Source: Barro and Sala-i-Martin, *Economic Growth* (Cambridge, Mass: MIT Press, 1995).

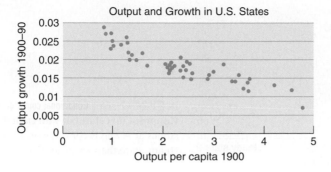

FIGURE 7.14 **Convergence—the United States.** Output converges within the United States.

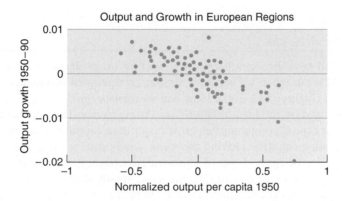

FIGURE 7.15
Convergence—Europe. Output seems to converge within Europe also.

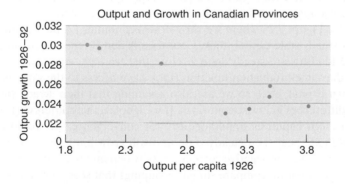

FIGURE 7.16
Convergence—Canadian provinces. Convergence also seems to exist within Canada.

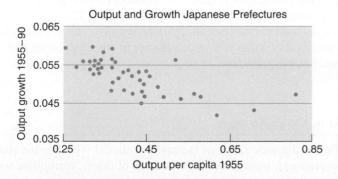

FIGURE 7.17 **Convergence—Japanese prefectures.** The less affluent Japanese regions have tended to catch up with the more affluent areas.

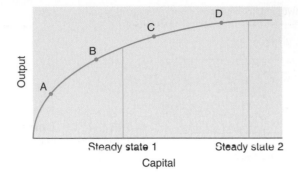

FIGURE 7.18 **Conditional convergence.**
Countries that start out with capital
stocks at A and B converge on a lower
steady state than countries that start
out with capital at C or D.

7.5 Reconciling the Evidence

When we consider all countries simultaneously, we find no evidence in favor of convergence (Figure 7.12), but when we consider similar groupings of economies, we find strong evidence for it (Figures 7.13–7.17). How can we explain this?

The explanation is based on the idea of *conditional convergence*. The neoclassical model does *not* imply that capital poor countries grow faster than capital rich countries. Instead it implies that among countries sharing the *same* steady state we will find convergence. For instance, in Chapter 5 we demonstrated convergence when both economies had the same investment rate and thus the same steady state. Earlier in this chapter, we remarked that capital poor countries will grow faster than capital rich countries only if the former share the same level of human capital as the latter. Therefore, convergence only occurs among countries that have a common steady state.

To see this, consider Figure 7.18 where we show four economies (A, B, C, and D) that differ only in their steady state capital stock. Countries A and B tend toward steady state 1, while C and D tend toward steady state 2. Note that we have assumed that all four economies share the same production function (they have access to the same technology, the same human capital, etc.), so we are also assuming that their steady states differ only because of differences in investment rates. If we ignored their different steady states and examined all four countries simultaneously for convergence, we would find none. Countries B and D are near their steady state and will grow more slowly than A and C. Overall, we will find no clear negative correlation between initial income and subsequent growth. However, when we compare similar groupings that share a steady state (A and B; C and D), then we will find convergence. Conditional convergence helps explain the mixed evidence in support of convergence in Figures 7.12–7.17.

But what determines a country's steady state? Understanding this is crucial both for explaining why the standard of living is so much higher in some countries and also for predicting which countries will grow fastest.

7.6 Determinants of the Steady State

We have already discussed a wide range of factors that should influence the steady state of the economy—investment, human capital, allocation of talent, corruption, social

TABLE 7.3   **Determinants of Steady State**

Variable	Effect on Steady State Output
Human Capital (secondary and tertiary years of education males over 25)	+
Life Expectancy	+
Fertility Rate	−
Goverment Consumption as Share of GDP	−
Rule of Law Index	+
Terms of Trade	+

Adapted from: Barro, *The Determinants of Economic Growth* (Cambridge, Mass: MIT Press, 1997).

infrastructure, to name a few. But what do the data show? Statistically which of these factors accounts for differences in the standard of living? Given the importance of the topic, many empirical studies have investigated it. Table 7.3 shows the results from one of the more prominent scholars in this area. His results suggest that the steady state output level depends positively on education, life expectancy, the terms of trade, and the rule of law.[6] The steady state depends negatively on fertility and the share of GDP that government consumption accounts for. Fertility has a negative impact for two reasons: the greater the population, the lower the level of capital per person and the more children there are, the fewer individuals there are who are working, and the more resources child rearing takes up. The government consumption measure excludes education and defense expenditure and excludes public sector investment. Table 7.3 suggests that the government can do both good and bad—expenditure that raises education or life expectancy boosts the standard of living, while other current expenditure exerts a negative influence on it.

The investment rate is omitted from this list for econometric reasons. However, Barro's work suggests that many of the variables in Table 7.3 influence investment. In other words, some of the variables in Table 7.3 may boost the standard of living indirectly by producing a high steady state investment rate.

Table 7.3 shows the results from one study. Other studies, although broadly in agreement with Table 7.3, suggest that additional variables are important. One is the extent to which an economy is open to trade (in Chapter 5 we showed how open economies showed evidence of convergence while close economies do not). The more open an economy, the more productive its steady state is likely to be. One robust result emerges from all of the studies. The investment rate and the level of human capital always play a substantial role.

GOOD AND BAD STEADY STATES

Table 7.4 shows some of the key variables that influence the steady state for a variety of economies. Given our steady state analysis and the concept of conditional convergence, the table makes for sobering reading. Conditional convergence says that countries that

---

[6]The terms of trade refer to the ratio of export prices to import prices. The higher the terms of trade, the fewer exports a country needs to sell to finance its imports.

TABLE 7.4　Determinants of Steady State for Selected Countries

Country	Civil Liberties	Fertility	Government Consumption	Education	Investment	Life Expectancy
Egypt	4.8	5	28.3	3.14	6.0	59.6
South Africa	5.2	4.6	20.5	4.96	16.4	59.4
Nigeria	6.2	6.6	20.6	—	8.75	50.1
Sierra Leone	5.2	6.5	29.7	1.72	1.64	40.3
USA	1	1.84	11.8	11.79	24.1	74.9
Korea	3.2	2.3	8.1	7.9	33.1	68.7
Italy	1	1.42	11.1	6.3	26.4	76.3
France	1	1.82	13.5	6.5	27.5	76.6
Japan	1	1.73	7.7	8.5	36.7	77.3
Australia	1	1.95	10.9	10.2	29.7	75.8
Brazil	2.2	3.6	11.2	3.49	17.9	64.3
Sweden	1	1.74	20.2	9.5	24.3	76.4
Mexico	3.8	3.8	8.96	4.42	15.0	68.1
India	2	4.48	18.5	3.05	17.7	56.7

The lower the civil liberties index the greater the degree of civil liberties; 1 is the lowest score. Fertility is the number of births per 1000 people. Government consumption is the amount of GDP that government consumption accounts for, excluding education and defense. Education is average years of post-primary education. Investment is proportion of GDP spent on investment, and life expectancy is measured in years.

Source: Barro and Lee, "Sources of Economic Growth," *Carnegie Rochester Conference Series on Public Policy,* 1994. Reprinted with permission from Elsevier Science.

are furthest away from their steady state grow fastest. This is hardly reassuring for Sierra Leone, for example, which has the worst measures for four out of the six criteria shown and second worst for the remaining two categories. This suggests that Sierra Leone has a poor steady state and will not grow much. By contrast, India would appear to have better fundamentals and should benefit from higher growth. These numbers show that being poor does not guarantee growth. But if these poor nations could shift their steady states (and Table 7.3 suggests that government policy can help do this) then their growth prospects would improve.

ARE THERE POVERTY TRAPS?

The theory of conditional convergence maintains the assumption of decreasing MPK and therefore rules out poverty traps. Figure 7.19*a* shows the distribution of real GDP per capita across 132 countries and how it changed between 1960 and 1990. The number of countries with GDP per capita of less than $3000 hardly changed although the more wealthy nations became richer. Figure 7.19*b* shows some evidence that two groups of economies are beginning to emerge: the poor and the rich. The existence of these two groups suggests that convergence clubs may exist—with a group of poor economies

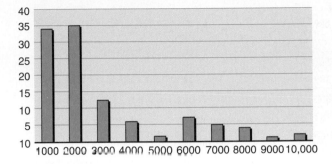

FIGURE 7.19a **Distribution of GDP (US1985$) per capita in 1960.** *Source:* Summers and Heston Penn World Tables at http://pwt.econ.upenn.edu.

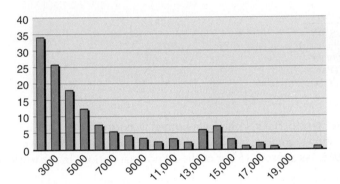

FIGURE 7.19b **Distribution of GDP per capita (US1985$) in 1990.** On the vertical axis we measure the proportion of countries with incomes in the ranges shown on the horizontal axis. The distribution of income across countries has not became more equal between 1960 and 1990.

with bad fundamentals converging on a low income steady state and a group of rich economies with stronger steady states. Why don't poor countries improve their steady state? This is where our insights from poverty traps may be relevant. In poverty traps the poor have weak incentives to improve their lot. Therefore even if poor economies try to increase expenditure on education, health, and family planning to boost the steady state, they may not benefit as much from doing so as advanced economies would. If a region has poor education, low life expectancy, large family size, and poor social infrastructure, then the returns from gaining more education, living longer, or having fewer children may be minimal. In other words, countries may get trapped in a poor steady state.

7.7 Why Is Africa So Poor?

Table 7.5 shows estimates of real GDP per capita for various regions for 1820 and 1992. For the entire period, Africa has been both the poorest and slowest growing region. Taken literally these estimates suggest that in 1992 Africa had a level of output per head just below that of Western Europe in 1820. In this section we consider why Africa is so poor, and why its growth has been so disappointing.

Economic growth in Africa (particularly sub-Saharan Africa) has been continually disappointing. For instance, in 1967 the chief economist at the World Bank listed seven African nations that he felt could reach or surpass a sustained 7% annual growth rate of GDP. Instead, real GDP did not grow in Africa between 1965 and 1990, and the seven

TABLE 7.5   Performance of
Major Regions 1820–1992 (1990 $ GDP
per capita)

	1820	1992
Western Europe	1292	17387
Western Offshoots	1205	20850
Southern Europe	804	8287
Eastern Europe	772	4665
Latin American	679	4820
Asia and Oceania	550	3252
Africa	450	1284
World Total	651	5145

Source: Maddison, *Monitoring the World Economy 1820–1992* (Paris: OECD, 1995). Copyright OECD.

nations about which the World Bank's chief economist was optimistic had negative growth. As Figure 7.20 shows, some sub-Saharan African economies now have lower levels of GDP than in 1965. As a result, 15 out of the 20 poorest nations in the world are in Africa.

Africa has had some success stories over the last few decades. One obvious success is Botswana, which Figure 7.20 shows increased its GDP more than fourfold

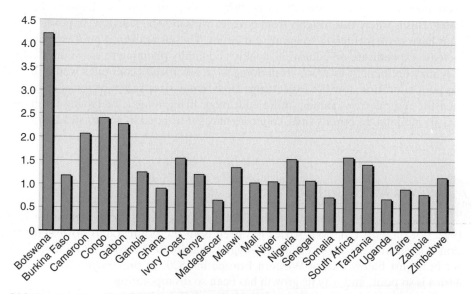

FIGURE 7.20   **Ratio of 1990 and 1965 real GDP for sub-Saharan Africa.** In many sub-Saharan countries growth has been negative over the second part of the twentieth century; overall the record has been abysmal. *Source:* Summers and Heston Penn World Tables at http://pwt.econ.upenn.edu.

between 1965 and 1990 and continues to show robust growth, financed in part by diamond deposits. Even more dramatic is Equatorial Guinea (not shown in Figure 7.20), which has grown on average by 39.5% a year since 1991, largely due to energy discoveries. Mauritius (4% a year) and Uganda (3% a year) have shown less spectacular, but still strong growth rates in the 1990s. But most African countries have not had economic growth.

Our steady state analysis helps to explain why Africa has seen such poor growth. Africa scores poorly on many of the key determinants of the steady state—low investment, low educational achievement, and low scores on measures of social infrastructure. Moreover, Africa's strong protectionist policies have limited its ability to show convergence. But why has Africa had such low investment and consistently inappropriate government policies?

One explanation for Africa's poor growth performance that has been the subject of much research is its ethno-linguistic diversity.[7] Many African countries are composed of several large cultural groups, each with its own language and practices. In part this is the legacy of European colonialism, which at the end of the nineteenth century created national boundaries that served European needs rather than boundaries that created ethnic homogeneity. Ethno-linguistically diverse nations tend to have poor government policy. Such polarized societies may be more prone to competitive rent seeking—each group tries to extract resources from other ethnic groups—and to find it more difficult to reach agreement over public goods (for instance, the location of roads and transport routes). This in turn leads to bad social infrastructure because it produces a gap between the return to individuals and that to society. As one Nigerian academic commented, "the struggle for power [after independence] was so absorbing that everything else, including development, was marginalized."[8] Easterly and Levine found that high levels of ethno-linguistic diversity are associated with the existence of substantial black markets, lower financial development, low provision of infrastructure, and low education. Table 7.6 shows the 15 most and least fractionalized economies, according to one measure of ethno-linguistic diversity. The strong presence of African economies among the most fractionalized suggests that ethno-linguistic diversity may explain some of Africa's poor economic performance.

For instance, Kenya's population consists of around 40 different ethnic groups. Five groups account for 69% of the population, and each of them predominates in a particular region of the country. The result is a polarized political situation. In Kenya's 1992 presidential elections, the Luo tribe candidate achieved 75% of the vote in the Luo region; the two Kikuyu tribe candidates polled 96% of the vote in the Kikuyu region, and the Kalenjin tribe candidate received 71% in the Kalenjin region. As a result, changes in power also change the allocation of government expenditure and the relative strength of different groups in society. According to Easterly and Levine, these variations in ethno-linguistic diversity matter—for instance, if Nigeria had the world average level of ethno-linguistic diversity Easterly and Levine predict it could have doubled its growth rate.

[7]See, for instance, Easterly and Levine, "Africa's Growth Tragedy" *Quarterly Journal of Economics* (1997) vol. 112, pp. 1203–1250.

[8]Ake, *Democracy and Development in Africa* (Washington, DC: The Brookings Institution, 1996).

TABLE 7.6   **Ethno-linguistic Diversity**

Most Fractionalized		Least Fractionalized	
Tanzania	93	Haiti	1
Uganda	90	Japan	1
Zaire	90	Portugal	1
Cameroon	89	Hong Kong	2
India	89	Yemen	2
South Africa	88	Germany	3
Nigeria	87	Burundi	4
Ivory Coast	86	Dominican Republic	4
CAR	83	Egypt	4
Kenya	83	Ireland	4
Liberia	83	Italy	4
Zambia	82	Norway	4
Angola	78	Iceland	5
Mali	78	Jamaica	5
Sierra Leone	77	Jordan	5

Table shows the probability of two individuals drawn at random being members of different ethno-linguistic groups in a country.

Source: Taylor and Jodice, World Handbook of Political Indicators, 3rd ed (New Haven: Yale University Press, 1983).

Ethno-linguistic diversity may also lead to civil war. Civil wars tend to damage an economy more than a conflict between different nations do. Civil wars are fought entirely on a country's own territory and so destroy much of its capital. They tend to leave a legacy of distrust that reduces social infrastructure and hinders economic growth even after the conflicts are over. Further, while wars between countries often strengthen the state, which may be beneficial for the economy, civil wars weaken a government. One study finds, however, that if a society is ethnically either homogenous or very diverse then the risk of a civil war is not high. Only societies with a few large and competing ethnic groups have a high risk of civil war.[9] Moreover, while ethnic diversity contributes to the risk of civil war, the most important factor is poverty. Because Africa is relatively poor, it therefore faces a higher probability of civil war, which in turn leads to poor economic incentives and weak growth.

[9]Collier and Hoeffler, "On Economic Causes of Civil War," *Oxford Economic Papers* (1998) vol. 50 pp. 563–573.

Jeffrey Sachs and his coauthors offer an alternative explanation of Africa's poor growth.[10] They suggest that the key to understanding Africa's weak growth is the combined effect of climate, disease, geography, and poor policies. Throughout the world tropical regions are poorer than nontropical areas. The only successful countries with a mostly tropical climate are Hong Kong and Singapore. In both Australia and Brazil, the tropical regions are substantially poorer than the nontropical regions. The most successful economic areas in Africa are in the north and the south which are the only nontropical areas of the continent. The five North African nations have a GDP per capita (1995) of $4371, nontropical South Africa's 1995 GDP per capita was $7348, while tropical sub-Saharan Africa's was only $1732. In terms of climate, soil, disease, and ecology, tropical regions suffer many handicaps. Agriculture is less productive in tropical areas, and agricultural (and nonagricultural) innovations tend to be designed for the temperate regions, making their adoption problematic in the tropics. Since 93% of sub-Saharan Africa is tropical, this is a major restraint on its standard of living.

Linked to the tropical climate are the acute problems Africa faces from malaria. Every year an estimated 2 million Africans die from malaria (over 20% of total African deaths). Although modern medicine has dramatically reduced the threat of malaria in southern Europe, the Caribbean, and parts of North and South Africa, eradicating malaria from tropical regions still remains a huge task. Historically, malarial countries have grown more slowly than others. Between 1965 and 1990 real output per capita in African countries with severe incidence of malaria grew only 0.4% per year, while other countries in Africa grew by 2.3%.

Africa also faces serious problems from the spread of AIDS. Between 1985 and 1995, more than 4 million Africans died from AIDS-related conditions; by 2005 another 10 million may be dead. Of the 30 million people with the HIV virus, 22 million are in sub-Saharan Africa. This represents 60% of the men, 80% of the women, and 90% of the children in the world who have the virus. With per capita medical expenditure in Africa of around $10–15 per year, even the cost of screening for AIDS is prohibitive, let alone the $16,000 annual cost of drug treatment. Because the incidence of AIDS is highest in the age group that is most economically active, this represents a heavy burden in lost output as well as lost lives.

There is another feature of geography that Sachs and his coauthor suggest restricts Africa's growth: Africa is poorly placed to benefit from trade. As Table 7.7 shows, Africa has the highest proportion of its population living in landlocked regions. As a result, trading costs for African economies are much higher. One way to measure transportation costs is to examine the gap between the cost of exports inclusive of freight and insurance costs, and the cost of exports measured as freight on board. In other words, the cost of a commodity before it is exported and the cost when it arrives. The gap between these prices is 3.6% in the United States, 4.9% in Western Europe, 9.8% in East Asia, 10.6% in Latin America, and an extraordinary 19.5% in sub-Saharan Africa. While part of these costs are undoubtedly due to poor transport infrastructure,

---

[10]See *inter alia* Sachs and Warner, "Sources of Slow Growth in African Economies," *Journal of African Economies* (1997) vol. 6, pp. 335–376; Bloom and Sachs, "Geography, Demography and Economic Growth in Africa," Brookings Papers on Economic Activity.

TABLE 7.7 **Geographical Characteristics of Selected Regions**

	GDP per Capita	Population	Land Area (mill km²)	Land in Tropics (%)	Population w/100km Coast (%)	Population w/100km Coast/River (%)	Landlocked Population (%)	Distance to Core Market (km)	Coastal Density (per/km²)
Sub-Saharan Africa	1865	580	24	91	19	21	28	6237	40
Western Europe	19,230	383	3	0	53	89	4	922	109
East Asia	10,655	1819	14	30	43	60	0	3396	381
South Asia	1471	1219	4	40	23	41	2	5744	387
Transition Economies	3902	400	24	0	9	55	21	2439	32
Latin America	5163	472	20	73	42	45	3	4651	52

Source: Bloom and Sachs, "Geography, Demography and Economic Growth in Africa," Brookings Papers on Economic Activity, Sept. 1998.

TABLE 7.8 **Explaining Growth Differences by Geography**

	Sub-Saharan	South Asia	Latin America
Total Growth	−4.2	−2.8	−3.6
Congergence	1.4	1	−1.1
Total Geography	−3	−0.8	−0.2
Coastal Density	−0.7	0	−0.5
Interior Density	0	−0.3	0.1
Topics	−0.1	0.1	−0.1
Malaria	−1	−0.1	0.3
Life Expectancy	−1.2	−0.5	0
Total Policy	−2.1	−2.1	−1.8
Openess	−1.2	−1.2	−1
Public Institutions	−0.7	−0.9	−0.7
Secondary Education	−0.5	−0.8	−0.6
Unexplained	−0.5	−0.8	−0.6

This table gives a breakdown of overall growth (relative to South East Asia) into elements due to various factors. For example, for sub-Saharan Africa, Bloom and Sachs estimate that geography would have the effect equivalent to losing 3% of productivity growth. Convergence forces (starting with a relatively low capital stock) are worth +1.4%. The overall impact of government policy was to knock about 2.1% off productivity growth.

Source: Bloom and Sachs, "Geography, Demography and Economic Growth in Africa," Brookings Papers on Economic Activity, Sept. 1998.

they also reflect geographical location. Sachs' studies suggest that landlocked countries will experience slower growth and a lower steady state purely because of geography.

But how much of Africa's weak growth is due to geography and how much to bad policy? In Table 7.8 we show the conclusions of Sachs' work.

From 1960 to 1990 growth in sub-Saharan Africa was on average −4.2% below that in South East Asia. Convergence factors (a low initial capital stock in Africa) are estimated to have boosted growth in Africa by 1.4%. However, adverse geographic considerations reduced growth. Much of this growth shortfall was due to malaria and poor life expectancy. Additional effects came from Africa's largely landlocked nature. Bad public policy reduced African output growth by 2.1%. The most unfortunate policy was to restrict international trade, but the poor quality of public institutions and education also weakened growth.

Another important issue in considering African development is foreign aid. OECD governments and international institutions have provided a variety of foreign aid to Africa. Unfortunately, little evidence suggests that this has fostered economic growth. One recent study draws the following conclusions based on 56 developing countries over the period 1970–1993:[11]

(a) Donors tend to give more aid (per capita) to poor countries, small countries, and countries in which the donor has a special interest (for instance, French Africa, British Commonwealth, etc.).

(b) Aid has not systematically boosted either investment or growth, although it may have boosted government consumption. This suggests that aid is fungible—in other words, even if donors specify that aid can only be used for one purpose, governments can use aid money to avoid spending their own money for that purpose and spend their money on something else. As the then deputy director of the World Bank's Economic Development team said in 1947, *"When the World Bank thinks it is financing an electrical power station it is in reality financing a brothel."*

(c) There is evidence that aid given to countries with good economic policies, particularly fiscal, monetary, and trade policies, does boost economic growth, but that aid given to countries with poor policies has no impact.

(d) Aid cannot be used to induce a country to adopt better economic and social policies.

These results do not imply that aid to developing countries should be scrapped, but that it should be targeted to those countries best placed to benefit from it.

We conclude this gloomy section with a more cautious note. Reasonable growth began to occur in many African economies during the late 1990s (see Table 7.9). For the first time in decades there is some optimism about sustained growth in Africa. The key to this optimism has been economic reform in many countries, leading to a more open economy and better social infrastructures. If these policies are sustained, then the analysis in this chapter suggests that this optimism may be warranted. While climate and geography will continue to constrain African economic growth, good policies can do much to remove poverty in Africa.

[11]Burnside and Dollar, "Aid, Policies and Growth," *American Economic Review* (2000) vol. 90 (4) pp. 847–868

TABLE 7.9 Recent African Real GDP Growth

Country	1991	1992	1993	1994	1995	1996	1997	1998	1999
Africa	1.02	−0.71	0.35	2.32	3.15	5.56	2.89	3.14	2.34
Angola	0.32	−5.84	−23.98	1.34	11.55	11.57	5.74	6.39	1.28
Benin	4.72	4.01	3.52	4.37	4.6	5.55	5.72	4.51	4.95
Botswana	7.42	3	2.04	3.41	4.66	6.88	7.76	6	5.02
Burkina Faso	9.95	2.48	−0.78	1.2	3.97	5.98	4.75	6.17	3.73
Burundi	5	0.7	−5.89	−3.68	−7.27	−8.36	0.38	4.48	4.72
Cameroon	−3.76	−3.05	−3.16	−2.49	3.3	5	5.1	5.05	4.4
Cape Verde	−34.06	−18.39	87.87	12.67	2.23	2.62	6.62	8.02	8
Central African Republic	−0.55	−6.42	0.34	4.89	6	−3.22	5.73	4.85	3.06
Chad	10.4	2.39	−2.07	5.67	1.11	3.66	4.08	8.09	−1.14
Equatorial Guinea	−1.14	10.7	6.3	5.11	14.26	29.14	71.19	21.96	15.1
Ethiopia	−4.78	−5.22	13.36	3.49	6.13	10.9	5.89	−1.04	5.69
Gabon	6.12	−3.26	2.39	3.44	6.97	5.06	5.29	2.12	−5.76
Gambia, The	2.16	4.42	6.13	3.83	−3.4	5.32	0.76	9.89	4.17
Ghana	5.35	3.87	5.02	3.78	4.5	3.52	4.2	4.55	5.5
Guinea	2.61	3	4.7	4	4.41	4.6	4.84	4.48	3.75
Guinea-Bissau	5.1	1.05	2.05	3.15	4.41	4.6	5.36	−28.07	8.66
Guyana	6	7.82	8.18	8.53	5.03	7.93	6.2	−1.5	1.8
Kenya	1.44	−0.8	0.35	2.63	4.43	4.14	2.1	2.08	1.83
Lesotho	4.07	4.57	3.69	3.71	5.93	9.44	4.58	−3.8	0.5
Malawi	8.73	−7.33	9.69	−10.24	15.45	8.98	4.84	3.07	6.8
Mali	−0.93	8.36	−2.36	2.24	6.4	2.08	6.79	3.35	5.25
Mauritania	2.61	1.7	5.48	4.61	4.5	4.7	4.8	3.5	4.1
Mauritius	6.36	4.78	6.67	4.32	3.51	5.14	5.49	5.59	5.38
Morocco	6.9	−4.03	−1.01	10.36	−6.58	12.12	−2.04	6.32	0.16
Mozambique	4.9	−8.1	8.7	7.5	4.3	7.1	11.32	11.97	9.74
Namibia	8.19	7.13	−1.71	6.35	3.71	2.14	2.64	2.38	2.42
Niger	2.49	−6.52	1.45	4	2.61	3.42	3.3	8.3	2.28
Nigeria	6.01	2.64	2.2	−0.62	2.59	6.4	3.06	1.91	1.11
Rwanda	−4.3	6.6	−8.29	−49.52	32.76	15.84	12.83	9.51	5
Senegal	−0.4	2.21	−2.22	2.87	5.16	5.14	5.05	5.66	5.07
Sierra Leone	−7.99	−9.65	0.05	3.5	−10.03	5	−17.6	−0.8	−8.1
South Africa	−1.02	−2.14	1.23	3.23	3.12	4.15	2.52	0.63	1.23
Sudan	7.02	3.01	3.77	1.78	8.9	4	6.7	5	6
Swaziland	2.5	1.3	3.3	3.5	3	3.6	3.7	2	2
Tanzania	2.07	0.58	1.21	1.57	3.57	4.54	3.52	3.35	5.33
Togo	−0.7	−3.98	−15.09	14.89	7.85	9.64	4.22	−2.25	2.1
Tunisia	3.9	7.81	2.19	3.3	2.35	7.03	5.41	5	6.54
Uganda	0.99	3.08	8.38	5.4	10.62	7.78	4.54	5.4	7.83
Zimbabwe	5.53	−9.03	1.33	6.86	−0.56	8.66	3.75	2.47	0.49

Source: *World Economic Outlook* (May 2000). Courtesy of IMF.

SUMMARY

We have examined the importance of human capital in producing output and improving the marginal product of capital. We focused on two sources of human capital: learning by doing (including knowledge generated by spillover effects) and formal education. Increases in human capital have played a significant role in driving economic growth.

Assuming that the MPK is constant rather than decreasing leads to dramatically different predictions from our growth model. With constant marginal product, a steady state level of output does not exist, and we should not expect to find convergence across countries. We offered two justifications for constant marginal product. One relied on positive feedback between human and physical capital, while the other assumed knowledge spillovers from industry output to firm costs. If instead we assume that the MPK is increasing, then poverty traps exist. In a poverty trap, individuals have poor incentives to invest in either human or physical capital. As a result, wealthy nations get wealthier while the poorer nations stay poor.

When we examined growth since 1950 among a wide range of countries, we found no evidence of convergence; poor countries do not grow faster than rich countries. This suggests that the assumption of the diminishing MPK is inappropriate. However, when we considered more similar groupings of countries, like the OECD nations, we found strong evidence of convergence. We introduced the notion of conditional convergence; the idea that countries grow fastest when they are furthest away from their steady state, but that different countries will have different steady states. As a result, only similar nations will show any evidence of convergence. We then examined what determines the steady state of a nation and found that investment, education, and an open economy are important.

Finally, we reviewed the disappointing growth performance of Africa. For over two centuries, Africa has been both the poorest and slowest growing region in the world economy. In part this can be attributed to Africa's poor steady state due to low levels of investment, education, the closed nature of African economies, and poor social infrastructure. However, ethnic diversity, the landlocked nature of much of Africa, and its tropical climate and diseases are also important.

CONCEPTUAL QUESTIONS

1. Education is potentially good for output growth. But what type of education do you think is most socially valuable?

2. Endogenous growth theories require that individual educational choices respond to economic incentives. Is this plausible?

3. Do models that assume decreasing MPK offer a theory of economic growth?

4. What do you think are the key features that lead to high levels of social infrastructure? How does your society score on these features?

5. If individuals live in an area characterized by a poverty trap, will they not just move to a prosperous region? Should policymakers therefore worry about poverty traps?

6. Do empirical studies of the determinants of the steady state tell us anything more than that the richest economies are OECD economies? Are OECD economies a successful blueprint for emerging nations?

7. Repeat the analysis of Figure 7.18 when the high investment rate economy also has access to more productive technology. What does this imply about the scale of inequality we should expect to find across countries?

8. Can conditional convergence explain *any* pattern of cross-country differences in standards of living?

9. Can human knowledge and ingenuity support a constant MPK?

10. Does it matter if development aid just boosts government consumption in poor African economies?

ANALYTICAL QUESTIONS

1. Assume that there are no diminishing returns to capital and that output is simply a constant proportion (*a*) of the capital stock. Investment is also a constant fraction (*b*) of output and depreciation is a proportion (δ) of the capital stock. The change in the capital stock is total investment minus depreciation. Show how the proportionate rate of change of the capital stock depends upon the relative magnitudes of *a*, *b*, and δ. What happens to the growth of capital if *b* doubles from 0.1 to 0.2.

2. Suppose that two economies share a common steady state so that there is convergence between them. The poorer country closes 2% of the income gap between them each year. What proportion of the initial gap in income between the two countries is closed after 20 years? After 40 years how much of the initial gap remains?

3. Output (Q) is produced by three factors in an economy: physical capital (K), human capital (H), and hours worked (L). The production function is:

$$Q = A\, H^a K^b L^c$$

where A is total factor productivity.

Suppose that human and physical capital grow in line so that H = λK where λ is some positive number. (Imagine that this happens because every time money is spent on acquiring new machines it enhances the skills of the workers that get to use them). Explain the relation between the MPK and the coefficients *a* and *b*. If *a* + *b* = 1, what shape is the MPK schedule?

4. In an economy there are two firms (A and B) whose output (Q_a and Q_b) is interdependent. Because of positive spillovers, the higher the output of firm A the more firm B produces for given capital (K) and labor (L). The production function of the two firms is:

$$Q_a = [K_a^\alpha L_a^{1-\alpha}] \cdot Q_b^\theta$$
$$Q_b = [K_b^\alpha L_b^{1-\alpha}] \cdot Q_a^\theta$$

where Θ is 0.1 and α is 0.3.

Initially labor and capital and output of the two firms are identical and both equal to 10. What are the levels of output of the firms? If firm A now increases K to 11, what happens to the output of each firm if we assume firm B does not change its capital or labor? Would firm B be likely to increase its capital stock?

5. Suppose you live in a country where the chances of being caught and convicted for committing fraud are lower the more people commit fraud. If you commit fraud and get away with it, the benefit is worth $200,000. If you get caught and are convicted, the cost to you has a

money value of $500,000. The chances of being caught and convicted are 0.5 if fraud is very rare. If fraud is widespread in the country the chances of capture and conviction are 0.2. Assume you decide whether to commit fraud just by calculating the average money value of the gamble.

    (a) If very few people are committing fraud in the country, what should you do?

    (b) If fraud is widespread, what should you do?

    (c) If most people reason like you, is fraud likely to be rare or widespread?

6. Countries A and B resemble each other and have the same steady state level of output of 100. Countries C and D are also similar and also share a steady state but at a much higher output level of 300. Each year every country closes 5% of the gap between its previous level of income and its steady state level. Initially the levels of income of the four countries are: A = 80; B = 95; C = 60; D = 420.

Use a spreadsheet to calculate how income evolves for each country over the next 20 years. Would you say incomes are becoming more equal?

CHAPTER 8

Unemployment and the Labor Market

Overview

In previous chapters we focused on how the capital stock, technological progress, and social factors affect output. Also important is the number of people employed in productive activity—the subject of this chapter. We begin by reviewing the key data definitions of the labor force and examine how these variables differ across countries and demographic groups. We then complete our analysis of long-run growth by examining the impact of capital accumulation and technological progress on the labor market and show how higher productivity generates higher wages but may not change the unemployment rate. This leads to the notion of a country's natural rate of unemployment—a long-run equilibrium concept that determines what fraction of the workforce is economically active. We propose a model to determine this natural rate that implies that it depends on the structure of product and labor markets and we review the empirical evidence for it. We also examine how the natural rate is related to flows into and out of unemployment and how legislation to protect employment affects the labor market. We analyze labor market policy and discuss whether more market-oriented reforms are necessary to reduce unemployment. Finally, we show how growing income inequality among OECD countries over the last two decades is linked to a sharp decline in demand for unskilled workers and suggest that the fall in demand is mainly due to technological change.

8.1 Labor Market Data

The labor force is that part of the total population willing and able to work; most will have jobs, but some will not. People in prison, in the military, or of compulsory school age are not active in the labor market and so we exclude them from the labor

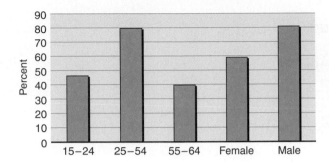

FIGURE 8.1 **OECD Europe participation rates.** Labor force participation rates are higher for men than for women and much higher for those aged between 25 and 64 than those younger or older. *Source:* OECD, *Employment Outlook* (June 1999). Copyright OECD.

force. They are part of the institutional population. The **participation rate** is defined as the labor force divided by the size of the civilian noninstitutional population. Individuals who are out of the labor force fall into one of a number of categories. They include those who go to school beyond the compulsory school age, retired people whether or not they are of retirement age, and people who are not willing to work in the marketplace because, for instance, they are raising a family. This suggests that participation rates will be low for the age group 15–24 years because of higher education, for those aged 55–64 because many of them will take early retirement, and for females because more women stay at home to raise children than men. Figure 8.1, which shows average participation rates for OECD Europe in 1998, confirms this.

TABLE 8.1   Cross-Country Variation in Labor Market Statistics, 1998

Country	Participation 15–24	Early Retirement	Female Participation	% Employment Part Time	% Part-time Jobs Held by Females	Average Weekly Hours Worked	Participation Rate
Australia	67.6	53.4	63.9	25.9	68.6	35.8	73.0
Czech Republic	49.0	61.4	64.0	3.3	70.0	39.8	72.2
Finland	49.7	58.0	69.7	9.7	63.1	33.9	73.2
France	28.0	63.9	60.8	14.8	79.3	31.4	67.4
Germany	49.6	55.5	60.9	16.6	84.1	30.4	70.1
Japan	48.3	32.9	59.8	23.6	67.5	36.3	72.6
Mexico	54.0	45.6	41.5	15.0	63.5	36.1	63.2
New Zealand	65.2	41.6	67.1	22.8	74.3	35.1	75.2
Norway	63.8	31.8	75.9	21.0	79.1	26.9	80.8
Spain	46.4	61.2	48.7	7.7	75.9	35.0	63.1
Sweden	50.0	32.5	75.5	13.5	97.3	29.8	78.1
Switzerland	67.2	27.2	74.2	24.2	83.4	30.4	82.3
UK	69.5	49.0	67.8	23.0	80.4	33.4	75.9
USA	59.0	42.3	70.7	13.4	68.0	37.8	77.4

Early retirement index is 100 − participation rate of 55–64 years.
Source: OECD, *Employment Outlook* (June1999). Copyright OECD.

TABLE 8.2   Unemployment Rates (%) by Age and Gender for OECD Europe, 1998

Age	15–24	25–54	55–64
All	17.8	8.0	7.2
Female	19.2	9.7	7.2
Male	16.7	6.9	7.1

Source: Employment Outlook (1999). Copyright OECD.

As Tables 8.1 and 8.2 show, participation rates of different demographic groups vary across countries. This reflects differences in costs and provision of higher education, the generosity of pension schemes (including both the level of pensions and the number of years people have to work to qualify for a pension), the level of wages, the availability of part-time work, and social attitudes toward female employment.

The final distinction is between those in the labor force who are employed and those unemployed. The unemployment rate is the percentage of the workforce who are unemployed. One complication in measuring unemployment is who counts as being unemployed. The best measure is one based on survey data that counts respondents as being unemployed if they do not have a job but are actively seeking work. However, many countries calculate unemployment numbers on the basis of whether individuals are entitled to receive unemployment benefits. Because not everyone without a job receives unemployment benefits, and because not everyone receiving benefits is looking for a job, this is not a reliable indicator of unemployment. When examining cross-country evidence on unemployment, consistent definitions based on survey data are important.

Figure 8.3 shows unemployment rates also vary across countries. Explaining these cross-country differences is a main aim of this chapter.

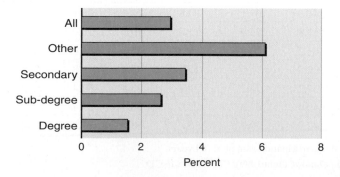

FIGURE 8.2   U.S. unemployment (%) by education, 2000. In the United States the more highly educated are less likely to be unemployed. Those with a university degree are less than half as likely to be out of work than those who left full-time education after secondary school. Source: U.S. Bureau of Labor Statistics, April 2000.

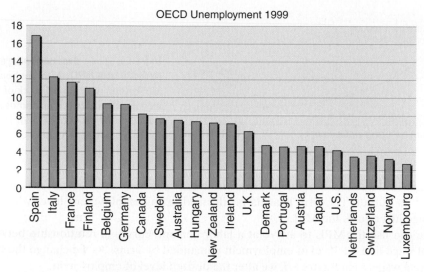

FIGURE 8.3 **OECD unemployment rates, 1999.** Unemployment rates vary significantly across developed countries. In 1999 they ranged from around 3% in Norway, Switzerland, and Luxembourg to over 16% in Spain. *Source:* OECD, *Employment Outlook* (2000). Copyright OECD.

8.2 A Long-Run Model of the Labor Market

Chapters 4 through 7 focused on long-run developments in the economy and on how capital accumulation and technological progress affect output. We now complete this analysis by considering how these factors affect the labor market.

LABOR DEMAND AND THE PRODUCTION FUNCTION

Thus far we have focused on the supply side of the economy, on the ability to produce output, and we have analyzed the production function extensively. For the labor market, the key concept is the marginal product of labor—the amount of extra output that hiring more labor can produce *keeping fixed the stock of capital and the level of technology*. It is analogous to the marginal product of capital that we discussed in Chapters 4 and 6. The *marginal product of labor* (MPL) is assumed to be decreasing with the level of employment: "too many cooks spoil the broth." Figure 8.4 shows this situation.

When the firm considers how many workers to employ, the MPL plays a key role. Each additional worker produces extra output equal to the MPL. If the firm can sell a unit of output for a price P, then hiring one more worker yields additional revenue of P × MPL. However, every additional worker increases a firm's costs—the firm has to pay wages, employment taxes, recruitment and training costs, and so forth. We summarize these costs in a wage term, W. If P × MPL exceeds W, then hiring an extra worker leads to an increase in profits, while if P × MPL is less than W, profits fall. Alternatively, we can say if MPL > W/P, the firm should hire workers, and if MPL < W/P, the firm should reduce its workforce. The term W/P is the

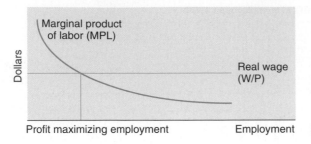

FIGURE 8.4 **Diminishing marginal product of labor (MPL).** As more hours are worked with a fixed stock of machines and a given technology, the marginal product of labor is likely (eventually) to fall.

real wage and reflects how much the firm has to pay its workforce relative to the price of its output. The firm is at its profit maximizing employment level when the real wage just equals the MPL.

We can use the MPL to arrive at a labor demand curve—a relationship between the real wage and the level of employment demanded by firms. As we change the level of the real wage, as in Figure 8.5, we alter the desired level of employment.

Therefore the MPL traces out a negative relationship between real wages and labor demand—in other words, *the MPL curve is the labor demand curve*. We now use this result to show what happens to labor demand when there is capital accumulation and technological progress.

An increase in either the stock of capital or the level of technology means that each worker becomes more productive—for a given level of employment, the marginal product of labor increases, and the MPL curve shifts out—as in Figure 8.6. This means that for a given real wage the demand for labor increases (remember the labor demand curve is the same as the MPL curve) as firms wish to hire these more productive workers.

LABOR SUPPLY

However, in order to analyze the impact of capital accumulation or technological progress on the labor market, we must also consider labor supply. When the real wage increases, it affects the supply of labor in two ways. First, it becomes more expensive *not* to work. The cost of enjoying another hour of leisure is the wage you would have earned if instead you worked. An increase in real wages makes leisure more expensive and in itself leads to an increase in the supply of labor. This is called the *substitution*

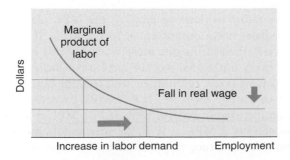

FIGURE 8.5 **Declining real wage leads to higher labor demand.** A fall in real wages will raise the profit maximizing level of labor demand for a firm.

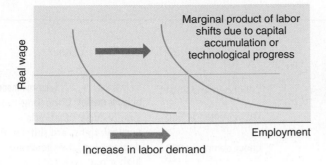

FIGURE 8.6 **Effect of capital accumulation technological progress on labor demand.** More capital, or better know-how, increases the marginal product of labor and raises the demand for labor at a given real wage.

effect—as the price of a good increases (in this case leisure), people substitute something for it (in this case work).

However, there is a second, offsetting effect when the real wage increases. People become wealthier and want to consume more of most goods, including leisure. This *income effect* leads people to consume more leisure and supply less labor as real wages rise. What happens to the supply of labor when wages increase depends on whether the income effect or substitution effect dominates. In Figure 8.7*a* we show the case in which the substitution effect dominates and labor supply is increasing with the real wage; in Figure 8.7*b*, the income effect dominates, and finally in Figure 8.7*c*, we show what happens if the income and substitution effect exactly offset each other.

Which of these labor supply curves is most appropriate? Chapter 3 outlined the long-run facts of the labor market that we are trying to explain:

(a) No long-run increase in hours worked
(b) Substantial increases in labor productivity
(c) Substantial increases in real wages

The only labor supply curve that helps account for these stylized facts about long-run performance is shown in Figure 8.7*c*, where the income and substitution effects cancel out.

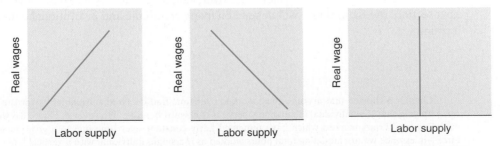

FIGURE 8.7 a **Substitution effect dominates.** b **Income effect dominates.** c **Income and substitution effect cancel out.** How labor supply responds to a wage depends on the relative size of the income and substitution effects.

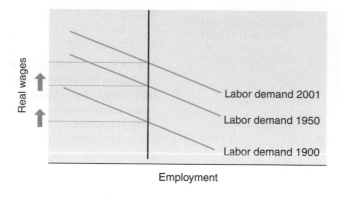

FIGURE 8.8   **Long-run model of labor market.** If the long-run supply curve of labor is vertical, rightward shifts in the demand for labor generate higher real wages at a constant level of employment.

To see how this analysis accounts for long-run developments, consider Figure 8.8. As capital accumulation and technological progress grew between 1900 and 1950, the MPL increased, causing an outward shift of the labor demand curve. But the labor supply curve is vertical—no additional hours are supplied. As a result firms compete among themselves for workers and bid wages up. Firms are prepared to pay these higher wages because productivity has increased. But because of the vertical supply curve, the higher wages do not lead to extra hours worked. Competition between firms continues until the real wage has been bid up to offset the productivity improvements, and firms no longer wish to hire more worker-hours. At this point, labor demand is once more equal to labor supply. The long-run impact of capital accumulation and technological progress is therefore an increase in average wages and no change in employment. Our analysis suggests that in the long run productivity improvements, whether from capital accumulation or technological progress, feed through one for one into real wages.

Figure 8.8 suggests that over time real wages reflect productivity improvements but that employment remains approximately constant.[1] Over the business cycle, employment/unemployment will show short-term fluctuations around this level, but eventually it will return to this *equilibrium* level.[2] Economists refer to this equilibrium as **"the natural rate of unemployment."** The natural rate is a long-run concept that characterizes the average unemployment rate over, say, a decade. As we shall show in the next section, the natural rate will depend on many economic and institutional details in a country.

---

[1]Chapter 3 showed that *average* hours worked over time had declined substantially over the long run, implying that the individual labor supply curve is backward bending. However in Figure 8.8 we are modeling total hours worked which have remained fairly constant over time due to a growing work-force—in essence we are modeling total hours worked as *if* a single individual with a vertical labor supply curve supplied them; we are ignoring compositional effects.

[2]We use employment and unemployment interchangeably here—for a fixed labor force this is appropriate.

8.3 The Natural Rate of Unemployment

Table 8.3 shows OECD estimates of the natural rate of unemployment in 1998 for several countries. The table shows substantial variation across countries—from 3.6% in Japan to an extraordinary 18.6% in Spain. The natural rate of unemployment is not some divinely determined economic constant but reflects the structure of the economy. In this section we outline a model of the natural rate of unemployment in terms of the structure of the product and labor market in the economy.

INTUITION BEHIND THE MODEL—COMPETING MONOPOLY POWERS

In outlining our model of unemployment, we move away from the assumption that the labor and product markets are competitive. Instead, we examine a model where unemployment is the mechanism that reconciles the monopoly demands of firms and workers. The more monopoly power either firms or workers have, the higher the natural rate of unemployment will be.

What the existence of monopoly power for firms implies is easy to grasp—firms can set price above cost. This means they try and set prices at a certain level above wages (an important component of costs) and thus put downward pressure on the real wage (the wage relative to prices). Monopoly power in the labor force reflects workers' ability to influence their own wage rather than have to accept the established market rate. The most obvious form of such monopoly power is labor unions, and this is how we will think of monopoly power in the model. However, you do not need to belong to a labor union to be able to influence your wage. Many workers have some form of monopoly power. For instance, if I leave my post today, my employer will incur a variety of costs. First, my job will be vacant until the firm hires a replacement, and during this period the firm's profits will decrease. Second, the process of advertising, interviewing, and recruiting a new employee is estimated to typically cost about a year's salary. Finally, once installed in the job, the new employee will require training and a period of assimilation which will further reduce the firm's profits. For all these reasons the firm has an incentive to keep me in my post, which gives me some ability to influence my wage relative to the current market average. The more monopoly power that I possess, the greater the wage I can obtain.

TABLE 8.3   **OECD Estimates of Natural Rate of Unemployment, 1998**

Country	Natural Rate	Country	Natural Rate
USA	5.4	Austria	5.6
Japan	3.6	Spain	18.6
Germany	9.2	Greece	9.7
France	10.5	Netherlands	5.0
Italy	10.1	New Zealand	5.8

Source: OECD Fiscal Dataset. Copyright OECD.

We assume that workers seek as high a real wage as possible, but the higher unemployment is, the more cautious they are in their wage demands. When unemployment is high, labor unions face more competition for their jobs from the unemployed and it will take longer for a union member to find a new job if wage demands lead them to lose their current position. This leads unions to moderate their wage demands. A conflict between firms that are seeking to achieve a low real wage (prices high relative to wages) and unions that negotiate for a high real wage causes unemployment. Market equilibrium requires that the demands of firms and workers be in agreement. This can only occur when unemployment is at a level that leads unions to seek real wages consistent with the profit margins firms seek.

8.4   A Diagrammatic Analysis

Figure 8.9 shows the model diagrammatically. The horizontal line is the firm's price-setting curve—it shows the real wage consistent with the firm's desired profit margin. For simplicity we assume that the only costs a firm faces are its wage costs, and that the firm wants a profit margin of x%. The price (P) of the firm's output therefore equals $W(1 + x/100)$, where W is the wage rate (or unit labor cost). This pricing rule sets $P/W = 1 + x/100$ or alternatively $W/P = 1/(1 + x/100)$. For simplicity we also assume in Figure 8.9 that the profit margin (x) that the firm desires is always the same regardless of the rate of unemployment—the price setting curve therefore is a flat line.

The other part of Figure 8.9 is the downward sloping line (the wage setting curve) that shows the real wage labor unions seek for a given unemployment rate. The higher the level of unemployment, the more restrained unions' wage demands are. In equilibrium the real wage that firms are prepared to accept must equal the real wage that the unions demand. The intersection of the price and wage setting curves gives this point, and it determines the natural rate of unemployment. *Only at this level of unemployment are the wage demands of workers consistent with the profit margins firms seek.*

Consider the case where unemployment is at the low rate of U_L. With unemployment so low, the real wage demands of workers are too high for firms, and unemploy-

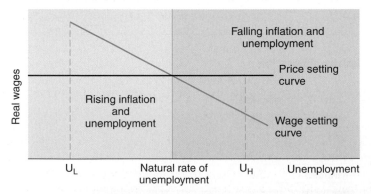

FIGURE 8.9   **Determinants of the natural rate of unemployment.** When unemployment is above the natural rate, the wage that firms are prepared to pay exceeds the wage that labor is able to negotiate; the opposite is true when unemployment is below the natural rate.

ment will start to rise above U_L and toward the natural rate as firms reduce unemployment. Firms will also try to restore their profit margin by raising prices, which will lead to higher inflation. Rising unemployment leads unions to moderate their wage demands until the increase in unemployment produces enough wage restraint that the demands of firms and workers are consistent, and inflation and unemployment stabilizes—the latter at its natural rate.

If instead the unemployment rate is above the natural rate, for instance at U_H, the process works in reverse. At this level of unemployment union wage demands are modest, and firms can achieve a high profit margin. In response they start to hire more workers, so that unemployment falls toward the natural rate. As unemployment falls, the wage demands of unions rises, but until unemployment reaches its natural rate these wage demands still produce a high profit margin and encourage firms to expand production and employment. At the natural rate, the economy is in equilibrium and unemployment and inflation are stable.

8.5 Determinants of the Natural Rate

We have characterized the behavior of firms by the price setting rule

$$W/P = 1/(1 + x/100)$$

where x is the firm's desired markup. We can also characterize the behavior of unions by

$$W/P = A - bu$$

where u denotes the unemployment rate, so that union wage demands are lower when unemployment is high. The constant A reflects the factors that influence the wages labor unions demand, and the coefficient b determines the sensitivity of wage demands to unemployment.

In equilibrium the wage demands of workers must be consistent with the price setting decisions of firms, so that

$$1/(1 + x/100) = A - bu$$

We can rearrange this to arrive at an expression for the natural rate of unemployment:

$$u^* = (1/b)(A - 1/(1 + x/100))$$

Therefore, we can think of three separate influences on the natural rate:

(a) Product market power (x). The greater is monopoly power in the product market the higher is unemployment.
(b) The sensitivity of labor union wage demands to unemployment (b). Unemployment is the means of reconciling the competing demands of firms and workers. The less responsive wage demands are the higher unemployment must be.
(c) The monopoly power of labor unions (A). The greater the strength of unions, the higher their wage demands will be. This leads to higher unemployment.

We now proceed to examine the institutional factors that affect each of these three influences.

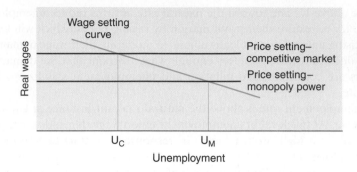

FIGURE 8.10 **Monpoly product markets lead to higher unemployment.** If employers gain market power they will increase the price of goods driving real wages down. Unemployment has to rise to make this consistent with union demands.

PRODUCT MARKET COMPETITION AND THE NATURAL RATE

As we change the monopoly power of firms and the size of their profit margin, we shift the position of the price setting curve and change the natural rate of unemployment. Figure 8.10 compares two economies that share the same labor market structure (i.e., the same wage setting curve) but have different degrees of product market competition. In the country with more powerful monopolies, firms set prices that are high relative to wages. This implies a low real wage, a price setting curve closer to the origin, and a high natural rate of unemployment (U_m). The intuition is straightforward—monopolists charge a higher price and thus produce less output and set a lower level of employment. In order for unions to accept these low real wages unemployment has to be high. Therefore less competitive product markets lead to higher unemployment.

THE INFLUENCE OF LABOR MARKET STRUCTURE

Figure 8.11 shows two economies that differ only in their labor market structure. The economy in which workers have more monopoly power has a wage setting curve further out from the origin and has a higher natural rate of unemployment.[3] The labor force may be able to exercise more monopoly power for five reasons: (1) strong labor union

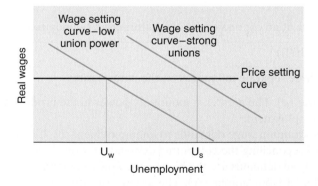

FIGURE 8.11 **Stronger unions lead to higher unemployment.** If labor power increases it may cause higher unemployment with little gain in terms of higher real wages. Here, because the price setting curve is flat, more labor union power simply increases unemployment from U_w to U_s.

---

[3]We focus here on shifts in the wage setting curve (that is changes in A), but the implications are similar for changes in the slope of the curve (changes in b).

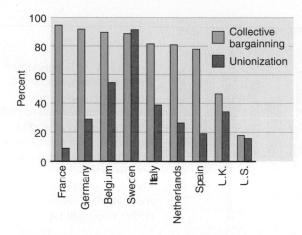

FIGURE 8.12 **Union membership and coverage among OECD economies, 1994.** The significance of labor unions differs substantially across countries. *Source:* OECD, *Jobs Study: Evidence and Explanations* (1994). Copyright OECD.

membership and union rights, (2) generous unemployment benefits, (3) large numbers of long-term unemployed, (4) unemployment is higher in certain regions or among those with fewer skills, and (5) high levels of taxes on labor. We now consider each of these factors and how they vary across countries.

UNION MEMBERSHIP

The more members a union has, or the more people its negotiations cover, the more monopoly power they can exploit. Figure 8.12 shows measures of labor union strength across OECD economies. When considering union influence, we need to distinguish between membership and coverage. Coverage (or collective bargaining) refers to the proportion of the workforce whose pay is determined by union negotiations—within a firm or industry wage negotiations by unions are often extended to nonunion members. Empirical studies suggest that coverage influences unemployment more than union membership does.

UNEMPLOYMENT BENEFITS

If unemployment benefits are high and last for a long time, they increase the monopoly power of those employed in two ways. First, generous benefits cushion the effects of being unemployed and lessen the motivation to look for new work. This reduces competition for jobs. Second, generous unemployment benefits also reduce the cost of becoming unemployed and these make the employed more aggressive in their wage demands.

Figure 8.13 shows the **replacement rate** for a variety of OECD economies where the replacement ratio is unemployment benefits expressed as a percentage of previous earnings. Most countries have reasonably generous replacement rates for the first year, but after this benefits fall substantially. This decline in replacement ratios is intended to give people protection against the initial shock of unemployment while minimizing their negative impact (the rightward shift in the wage setting curve due to the reduced threat of unemployment). The positive effects of unemployment benefits stem from two sources: first, as an insurance policy to workers, and second, because governments are effectively

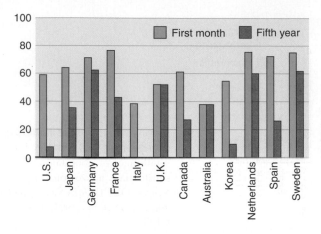

FIGURE 8.13 **Unemployment benefit replacement ratios, 1997.** In most countries the level of benefits to the unemployed falls after a period out of work; in some cases, most notably in the United States, the decline in benefits to those who stay out of work is very large. *Source: Assessing Performance and Policy* (1999). Copyright OECD.

subsidizing job searches. Benefits encourage the unemployed worker to spend more time searching for a job that is more suitable to him or her rather than having to accept a first job offer. The better the match between job and worker, the higher the productivity in a country, so subsidizing job searches has social benefits.

PROPORTION OF LONG-TERM UNEMPLOYED

The monopoly power of those in employment is lessened if the unemployed compete effectively with the employed for jobs. However, the greater the proportion of long-term unemployed, the less intense this competition is. The longer people are unemployed the more work-relevant skills they lose, and the lower their chance of becoming employed becomes. As they become less likely to find a job, they stop searching so intensely, which further reduces their chances of finding employment. As a result, the greater the proportion of long-term unemployed, the more monopoly power that the employed possess. This leads to a rightward shift in the wage setting curve and upward pressure on unemployment.

Figure 8.14 shows, for a variety of economies, the proportion of unemployed who have been unemployed for six months or more and for a year or more. Those countries

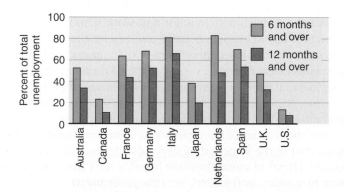

FIGURE 8.14 **Proportion of long-term unemployed among OECD economies, 1998.** In Europe the proportion of those unemployed who have been without work for many months is higher than in North America and Japan. *Source: Employment Outlook* (June 1999). Copyright OECD.

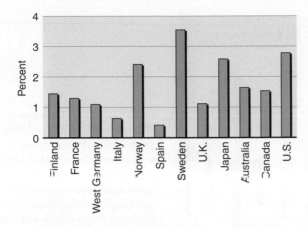

FIGURE 8.15   **Percent of population who change regions per year, 1980–1987.** Labor mobility is higher in the United States than in most other developed economies. *Source. Employment Outlook* (1999). Copyright OECD.

in the figure with high levels of unemployment (e.g., France, Germany, and Italy) also have high levels of long-term unemployed. Note the low levels of long-term unemployed in the United States. As we shall see, the American labor market is particularly effective at finding jobs for the unemployed quickly.

REGIONAL AND SKILL-BASED MISMATCH

If one area of the economy is booming but is in a different part of the country from an area that is doing badly, then the employed will face weaker competition from the unemployed if there is little mobility across regions (see Figure 8.15). Similarly, if the unemployed are mostly unskilled, but the employed have high levels of skill, then unemployment will not effectively restrain the wage demands of the employed. Therefore, for a given level of unemployment, the greater the regional or skill mismatch, the higher the natural rate of unemployment.

LABOR TAXES

Because of taxes it is important to distinguish between the *consumer* and the *producer* real wage—a distinction we have ignored so far. The real wage is the nominal wage divided by the price, but the wage and price concerned differ for the producer and the consumer. For consumers the wage is what they receive after the deduction of taxes relative to prices, which include all retail taxes such as general sales tax (GST) or value-added tax (VAT). The producer wage is the gross wage that firms pay out plus any additional employer taxes or social security contributions. Three tax rates influence the gap between the producer and consumer real wage: payroll taxes (taxes that either the employer or employee pay and that are normally related to social security contributions); income taxes; and consumer price taxes. Because the last two affect both the employed and the unemployed, economists think that payroll taxes influence the natural rate the most. These tax wedges shift the wage setting curve further to the right and thus increase the natural rate. The wage curve shifts out because the higher taxes are, the greater the wage unions seek to provide a given real standard of living for their members. As Figure 8.16 shows, these tax wedges are very large in many developed countries.

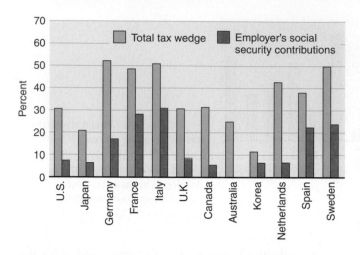

FIGURE 8.16 **Tax wedges in OECD countries.** Tax wedges drive a gap between the real wages workers take home and the real cost of labor to employers. In many developed economies these tax wedges are very large. *Source: Assessing Performance and Policy* (1999). Copyright OECD.

8.6   What Lowers Unemployment?

The previous section focused on factors that increase the natural rate of unemployment. Here we discuss influences that *lower* unemployment. We focus on two such beneficial factors: active labor market spending and coordinated wage bargaining. In each case the effect is to shift leftward the wage setting curve in Figure 8.9 and to lower the national rate of unemployment.

ACTIVE LABOR MARKET SPENDING

Active labor market spending refers to a range of policies that governments use to boost employment and reduce unemployment (see Figure 8.17). One is to assist the unemployed's job search—improving information flows about job availabilities, helping individuals with application forms and interview techniques, and offering retraining. Other active labor market policies subsidize the creation of jobs for the unemployed, e.g., offer loans to individuals who want to start their own businesses, subsidize firms that hire those who have been unemployed for a long time, and so on.

COORDINATED WAGE BARGAINING

In a previous section, we argued that the stronger the monopoly power of unions, the higher the natural rate of unemployment. Yet some countries with the most extensive union coverage (in particular Scandinavia) also have low unemployment rates. To explain this, we need to recognize that whether or not unions are bad for unemployment depends *both* on the degree of monopoly power the workforce possesses *and* how it exercises this power. In particular, if wage bargaining occurs at a highly centralized level between unions and firms, then the adverse unemployment effects may be small.

Consider the case of numerous strong unions which each negotiate separately with their employers and try to achieve as high a wage as possible compared with other unions. Of course, not all unions can do this—they cannot all outperform each other. Their unco-

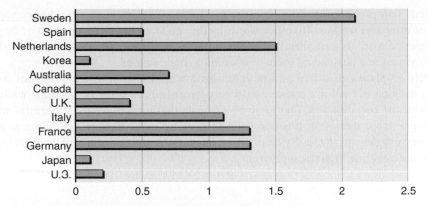

FIGURE 8.17 **Active labor market spending (% GDP).** In Continental Europe governments have devoted substantial resources to trying to make labor markets work better. *Source: Assessing Performance and Policy* (1999), p. 136. Copyright OECD.

ordinated attempts at boosting wages only generate higher unemployment to restrain their wage demands. If instead the unions coordinate their bargaining, they will realize that additional wage demands will only boost unemployment (especially if employer organizations are also coordinating their negotiations). As a result, their wage demands will be more modest, so that unemployment can be lower and still reconcile the competing demands of firms and the workforce. The intuition behind this result is straightforward. Monopoly power interferes with the work of the invisible hand—this is why unemployment

TABLE 8.4 **Centralization of Wage Bargaining across OECD**

Country	Ranking	Country	Ranking
Canada	1	New Zealand	9
USA	2	Belgium	10
Switzerland	3	Netherlands	11
Japan	4	West Germany	12
Italy	5	Finland	13
UK	6	Denmark	14
France	7	Sweden	15
Portugal	7	Norway	16
Spain	7	Austria	17
Australia	8		

The higher the index, the greater the degree of centralization in wage bargaining.

Source: Calmfors and Driffill (Blackwell Publishers, 1988) "Centralisation of Wage Bargainning and Macroeconomic Performance" *Economic Policy* vol. 6 pp. 15–61.

is created. This problem can only be overcome in two ways, by removing the monopoly power of firms and workers (in other words by deregulating the labor market) or by getting firms and workers to realize that exploiting their monopoly power will only produce unemployment and persuading them to coordinate their actions.

Table 8.4 shows estimates of how centralized wage bargaining is in different countries—a ranking of 1 is for a country with very decentralized wage bargaining, while 17 denotes strong coordination. Our analysis suggests that unions are most harmful when they have a strong monopoly position (as measured by, say, coverage) and wage negotiations are very decentralized. By contrast, strong unions and coordinated wage bargaining may not generate high unemployment.

8.7   A Flow Approach to the Natural Rate of Unemployment

To enhance our understanding of the labor market, we now focus on flows into and out of unemployment. This is simply a different perspective—it does not contradict the analysis in the previous section. It will enable us to review the effectiveness of employment protection legislation (EPL), which aims to reduce unemployment by restricting the ability of firms to fire people.

Every period some of those who are employed lose their jobs. This may be for voluntary reasons—they did not like their current job and quit—or involuntary ones—their firm is downsizing, and they are fired. This inflow increases unemployment. However, in every period other people cease to be unemployed either because they withdraw from the labor force or find work. The natural rate of unemployment is an equilibrium at which there is no tendency for unemployment to change. But for unemployment not to be changing, the inflow into unemployment must equal the outflow. We can use this fact to derive an expression for the natural rate of unemployment.

The inflow *into* unemployment equals the number of people employed (L) multiplied by the probability that a person loses his or her job (p). The outflow *from* unemployment equals the number of people who are unemployed (U) multiplied by the probability of an unemployed person finding a job (s). Figure 8.18 (where for simplicity we focus on flows only between employment and unemployment and ignore flows out of the labor force) shows this situation.

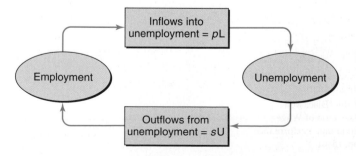

FIGURE 8.18   **Job market flows.** L is the level of employment; U is the level of unemployment; s is the chances of getting a job each period; p is the chance of losing a job.

The natural rate of unemployment occurs when inflows and outflows equal each other, that is

unemployment inflows = $pL = sU$ = unemployment outflows

We know, by definition, that employment plus unemployment equals the labor force (LF), so that $LF = L + U$ or $L = LF - U$. We can therefore write our equilibrium condition as

$$p(LF - U) = sU$$

As the unemployment rate (u) equals the unemployed divided by the labor force (U/LF), we can write this expression as

$$p(LF/LF - U/LF) = sU/LF$$

or

$$p(1 - u) = su$$

where u is the unemployment rate (U/LF). Rearranging this gives us an expression for the natural rate of unemployment

$$u^* = p/(p + s)$$

In other words, the natural rate of unemployment depends positively on p, the probability that an employed person becomes unemployed, and negatively on s, the probability an unemployed person finds a job.

THE IMPACT OF EMPLOYMENT PROTECTION LEGISLATION (EPL)

EPL is a label for a variety of measures that governments take to protect those in employment from dismissal, e.g., formal dismissal practices, severance pay, formal notice periods of dismissal, the number of warnings firms have to give a worker before he or she can be fired, and whether government has to approve a corporate downsizing, and so forth.

Table 8.5 shows considerable variation in the scale of EPL severity among OECD economies. For instance, according to the OECD, U.S. employers face no meaningful administrative processes before they can dismiss workers and legally have to offer no notice or severance pay, even after 20 years of service.[4] By contrast, in Belgium firms have to give nine months notice to workers with more than 20 years of tenure. Most countries require no severance pay within the first year of employment, but Portugal and Turkey require 20 months of severance pay after 20 years of work. Such large institutional differences in EPL significantly affect the operation of labor markets. Figure 8.19 shows the OECD's overall assessment of the severity of employment legislation. The higher the index, the more expensive and difficult it is for a firm in that country to reduce its workforce. Southern European countries tend to have the highest level of EPL, while the English-speaking countries have the lowest levels.

[4]Table 8.5 shows the legal minimum requirement. Individual contracts or collective bargaining may lead to firms offering more generous conditions.

TABLE 8.5   Indicators of Strictness of Employment Protection in OCED, Late 1990s

Country	Procedure	Notice Period (months) for Length of Employment			Severance Pay (months) for Length of Employment		
		9 months	4 years	20 years	9 months	4 years	20 years
Austria	2.0	1.0	1.2	2.5	0.0	2.0	9.0
Belgium	0.5	2.0	2.8	9.0	0.0	0.0	0.0
France	1.8	1.0	2.0	2.0	0.0	0.4	2.7
Germany	2.5	1.0	1.0	7.0	0.0	0.0	0.0
Ireland	1.5	0.3	0.5	2.0	0.0	0.2	2.2
Netherlands	3.0	1.0	1.0	3.0	0.0	0.0	0.0
Switzerland	0.5	1.0	2.0	3.0	0.0	0.0	2.0
UK	1.0	0.2	0.9	2.8	0.0	0.5	2.4
Greece	2.0	0.5	1.5	8.0	0.3	1.0	5.8
Italy	1.5	0.3	1.1	2.2	0.7	3.5	18.0
Portugal	2.0	2.0	2.0	2.0	3.0	4.0	20.0
Spain	2.0	1.0	1.0	1.0	0.5	2.6	12.0
Turkey	2.0	1.0	2.0	2.0	0.0	4.0	20.0
Canada	0.0	0.5	0.5	0.5	0.0	0.2	1.3
Mexico	1.0	0.0	0.0	0.0	3.0	3.0	3.0
USA	0.0	0.0	0.0	0.0	0.0	0.0	0.0
Australia	0.5	0.2	0.7	1.2	0.0	1.0	1.0
Japan	1.5	1.0	1.0	1.0	0.0	1.5	4.0
Korea	1.8	1.0	1.0	1.0	0.0	2.0	6.0
New Zealand	0.8	0.5	0.5	0.5	0.0	1.5	5.0

Procedure column shows OECD ranking of administrative restrictions on dismissal process where 0 is free from restrictions and 3 where restrictions are most severe.

Source: OECD, *Employment Outlook* (June 1999) p. 55. Copyright OECD.

EPL seeks to make it costly for firms to fire people and so leads to a lower value of p (probability of becoming unemployed) and a reduction in the natural rate. It may also increase a sense of job security among the employed, which in itself is valuable. However, EPL also adversely affects s—the probability of the unemployed finding a job. When hiring employees, firms have to remember that at some future date they may wish to terminate the employment. Therefore the more costly it is to fire people, the more expensive it is to hire them. When bargaining over wages, firms could try and exploit this to negotiate a lower wage, but EPL increases the bargainning power of the employed, so this is not an option. Therefore we can expect EPL to have offsetting effects on unemployment—it lowers job destruction rates but reduces job creation. Its overall impact on unemployment therefore is an empirical question.

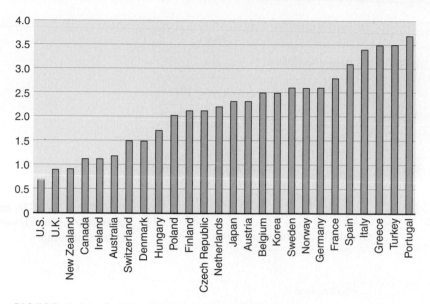

FIGURE 8.19   **Overall employment protection legislation strictness.** In the United States it is relatively easy to dismiss workers; in Greece, Portugal, and Turkey it is very hard. *Source:* OECD, *Employment Outlook* (June 1999), p. 66. Copyright OECD.

Figures 8.20*a* through 8.20*f* (and associated econometric work) show that for OECD economies:

(a) Countries with strong EPL have low employment rates—increased hiring costs reduces the demand for labor.

(b) EPL is not correlated with unemployment. This suggests that the reduction in employment is matched by a similar fall in the participation rate and in the size of the labor force because EPL makes part-time jobs less attractive for employers and the absence of such jobs reduces female participation in the labor force.

(c) Countries with strong EPL have lower levels of outflows *and* inflows into unemployment (both p and s decline). This explains why unemployment does not vary with EPL—the declines in inflows and outflows offset each other.

(d) Countries with strong EPL have greater job security and longer job tenure, but unemployment also lasts longer. EPL therefore benefits those workers who are employed at the cost of those without jobs.

So EPL has both good and bad effects. However, its benefits tend to accrue to those already in work, while the disadvantages hurt the unemployed. Why would a country adopt legislation that benefits the employed at the expense of the unemployed, who tend to be poorer? Political economy helps answer this question. In most economies around 90% of the labor force is employed. Further, in countries with strong labor unions, the demands of the employed can be easily coordinated and voiced, whereas the unemployed have no such organization. As a result, governments come under political pressure to adopt EPL.

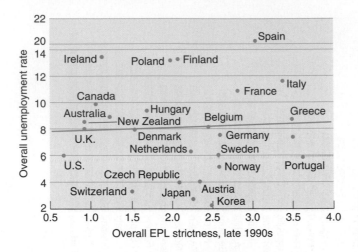

FIGURE 8.20a **EPL and unemployment.** There is very little relationship.

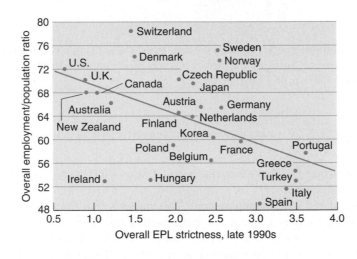

FIGURE 8.20b **EPL and employment rates.** Strong EPL typically means lower employment rate.

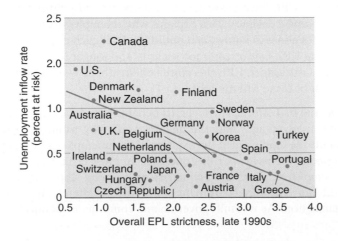

FIGURE 8.20c **EPL and unemployment inflows.** Stronger EPL reduces job losses.

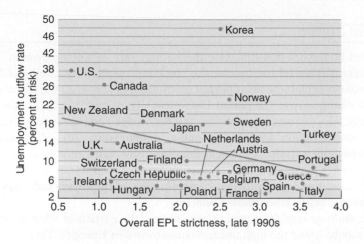

FIGURE 0.20d **EPL and unemployment outflows.** Strong EPL lowers outflow from employment.

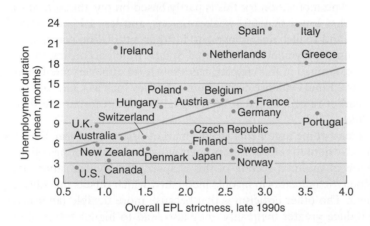

FIGURE 8.20e **EPL and unemployment duration.** Stronger EPL increases length of employment.

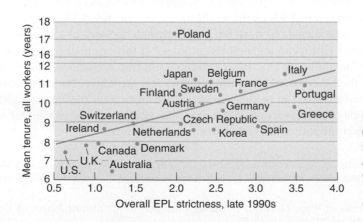

FIGURE 8.20f **EPL and duration of employment.** EPL improves job tenure. *Source:* All diagrams, OCED, *Employment Outlook* (June 1999). Copyright OECD.

8.8   Labor Market Reform

We have looked at factors that influence the natural rate of unemployment. To summarize our results it is useful to consider the empirical results of Nickell and Layard, which are based on explaining unemployment differences across 20 OECD countries and how these changed over the period 1983–1994.[5] They find that the following variables significantly *boost* unemployment : (a) the **tax wedge** (employer social security contributions, consumption taxes), (b) **union membership**, (c) **labor union coverage**, (d) **the replacement ratio**, (e) **benefit duration** (how many months can claim benefits), (f) **home owner occupation rate** (reflecting low regional mobility). The following variables produce *lower* unemployment: **coordination of employers and employees in wage negotiations; active labor market policies**.

What do these findings imply for government policy? In particular what do they suggest is the best way to lower the high unemployment rates in Europe? There is currently growing support for Continental Europe to enact labor market reform, which would remove government restrictions, reduce the power of unions, and increase the role of market forces. The motivation for this is partly based on our theoretical framework, which suggests that lower benefits, weaker unions, and less EPL will stimulate labor market turnover and reduce unemployment. Further motivation comes from the currently low rate of unemployment in the United States, which according to most of the statistics we have examined in this chapter, has a low level of government intervention in the labor market. Final evidence comes from countries such as Chile and the UK that enacted labor market reform aimed at boosting labor market forces and then saw unemployment decline.

But there are at least three arguments against market-oriented reform. One maintains that while market-oriented reform lowers unemployment, it also brings other concerns. As we shall see in the final section of this chapter, deregulated labor markets have experienced dramatic increases in income inequality, which offsets the advantages of low unemployment. The other criticism is that because more flexible labor markets lower wages and produce greater inequality, they also lead to higher levels of crime. Crime is expensive for society (just think how much richer you would be if there was no need to pay insurance premiums against theft or taxes to finance the police force and prisons). One author notes that in 1993, when U.S. employment was at 6.6%, the U.S. prison population amounted to 1.9% of the workforce, and a further 4.3% were on parole, giving a total of those outside of work but physically able to work of 12.8%, which was close to Continental European unemployment rates.[6] If this criminal population is linked to the greater flexibility of U.S. labor markets (and this is by no means an accepted proposition), then labor market reform becomes less attractive. It can cost over $30,000 a year to keep a person in prison—considerably more than paying for Continental European levels of social security. Of course, the key issue here is whether inequality produces the crime rather than other features of a society.

[5]"Labor Market Institutions and Economic Performance," in *Handbook of Labor Economics* Vol. 30 (Elsevier: North Holland, 1999). These results are reasonably consensual, although obviously results differ across researchers.

[6]Freeman, "The Limits of Wage Flexibility to Curing Unemployment," *Oxford Review of Economic Policy* (Spring 1995) vol. 11, no. 1, pp. 63–72.

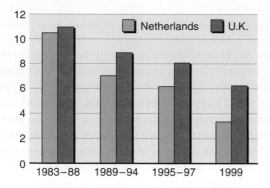

FIGURE 8.21 **Unemployment in Netherlands and the UK.** *Source: Employment Outlook* (2000). Copyright OECD.

The third argument is that market-oriented reform may not be the only way to reduce unemployment. It is useful here to examine why unemployment declined in the 1990s in the UK and the Netherlands (see Figure 8.21).

Table 8.6 shows estimates about why unemployment fell in each country. The differences are clear. The UK has focused on a market-oriented approach by weakening union strength and lowering replacement rates and tax wedges. By contrast, the Netherlands reduced unemployment though increased active labor market spending and coordination measures.

The results suggest that governments may have other options besides just market-oriented reform packages—particularly if they start from a position of strong but uncoordinated unions and low levels of active labor market expenditure. Of course, some countries may have little choice. For instance, in the UK the labor unions were so strong and numerous that coordinating their actions may have been impossible, and so only weakening their rights, powers, and immunities would have worked. But the experience of the Netherlands suggests that this is not the only way to proceed.

TABLE 8.6 **Explaining Netherlands and UK Unemployment Declines**

	Netherlands	UK
Union Density	−0.83	−1.47
Union Coverage	0.58	−1.25
Active Labor Market Spending	−1.09	0.16
Union+Employer Coordination	−2.53	0
Benefit Replacement Rate	−0.41	−0.48
Tax Wedge	−0.24	−0.72
Total	−4.52%	−3.76%

The decline in unemployment rates in the UK and in the Netherlands in the 1990s was substantial, but the factors explaining the fall in joblessness are very different.

Source: Nickell and Van Ours, "The Netherlands and the UK: A European Unemployment Miracle" *Economic Policy* (Blackwell Publishers, 2000) vol. 30, pp. 135–180.

8.9   Limits to Labor Market Reform

Unemployment is a situation of excess supply—those willing to work (the labor force) exceed the demand for labor (employment). In economics, falling prices remove excess supply. Consider the dockside market for fish when ships come in with their hauls. If the price is set too high, then the fishermen will end up with unsold fish, which is useless to them. Therefore the price of fish will fall until demand mops up excess supply. Why then, if there is unemployment, do wages not fall to balance demand and supply? The question we examine in this section is why does the labor market operate differently from the market for fish? We have already outlined two models (the wage-price setting model and the inflow/outflow approach) that provide a detailed framework with which to think about the natural rate of unemployment. Here we pursue a more philosophical approach to how the labor market operates. Key to our analysis is the concept of an *efficiency wage*. Although there are many different efficiency wage models, in essence they all explain why it may not be profit-maximizing for firms to lower wages when unemployment exists. This explains why even countries with competitive labor markets still experience unemployment.

Imagine that unemployment did not exist—anyone who wanted a job could find one immediately. What would you do in these circumstances if your boss refused to let you take a day off to attend the wedding of a close friend? Or if you were asked to do a difficult and unpleasant task? The most obvious thing to do would be to resign and immediately take another job. You would lose nothing from this experience—you would immediately swap one job paying the current market wage for another that pays the same. By contrast, your employer would have to incur the costs of advertising your position and then training your successor. To avoid paying these costs the firm could instead pay you a higher wage, above the market rate. In these circumstances you would be better off keeping your job and doing what your boss wants. But not all firms can set above-average wages, so this policy results in wages that are set too high, and leads to unemployment. Therefore even when unemployment exists, firms may find it profit maximizing not to lower wages. Another reason not to lower wages when unemployment rises is "adverse selection." If applicants for a job are prepared to work for a lower wage, it may signal that they are of lower quality and productivity than the existing workforce, especially if the applicants are unemployed—after all, if they had above average productivity they would probably not have been dismissed in the first place. Thus wages may not fall even when faced with downward pressure from the unemployed.

8.10   Widening Inequality

In the 1980s and 1990s, income inequality increased in several countries. Given that inequality had narrowed for most of the twentieth century these trends generated much comment and analysis. Table 8.7 measures inequality across countries and over time. The closer to zero the measure, the more equal income distribution is;

TABLE 8.7 Inequality Trends in OECD, Economies Mid-70s to Mid-90s

Country	Mid-70s	Mid-80s	Mid-90s
Australia	29.1	31.2	30.6
Belgium		25.9	27.2
Canada	28.3	28.9	28.4
Denmark		22.9	21.7
Finland		21.2	23.1
France		29.6	29.1
Germany		26.5	28.2
Italy		30.6	34.5
Japan		25.2	26.5
Netherlands	22.6	23.4	25.3
Norway		23.4	25.6
Sweden	23.2	21.6	23.0
USA	31.3	34.0	34.3

Source: Burniaux, Dang, Fore, "Index of Income Distribution and Poverty in Selected OECD Countries," OECD Working Paper 189 (March 1998). Copyright OECD.

there is clear evidence for an increase in inequality in most countries over the whole sample.

This rising inequality manifested itself most obviously in a growing gap between the wages of skilled and unskilled workers. Figure 8.22 plots the log of the ratio of wages of college-educated employees to those with only high-school educations in the United States; it shows a significant increase since 1980. This substantial rise in the

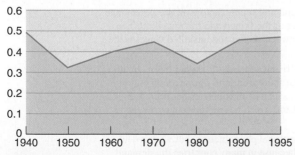

FIGURE 8.22 **U.S. college–high school wage premium.** In the United States those with college education have always earned a premium over those who left full-time education after high school. But the premium increased significantly over the 1980s and 1990s. *Source:* Autor, Katz, and Krueger "Computing Inequality: Have Computers Changed the Labor Market?" *The Quarterly Journal of Economics* (November 1998) Vol. 113, No. 4, pp. 1169–1213 © by the President and Fellows of Harvard and the Massachusetts Institute of Technology.

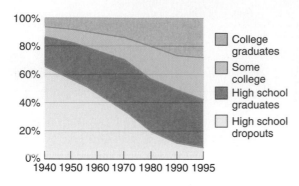

FIGURE 8.23   **Educational composition of U.S. workforce.** The U.S. workforce is becoming better educated—at least in the sense that it tends to have spent longer in full-time education. *Source:* Autor, Katz, and Krueger, "Computing Inequality: Have computers Changed the Labor Market?" *The Quarterly Journal of Economics* (November 1998) Vol. 113, No. 4, pp. 1169–1213 © by the President and Fellows of Harvard and the Massachusetts Institute of Technology.

TABLE 8.8   **Explaining Widening Skill Differentials in 1980s**

Country	Percent Impact on Wage Differential from Demand	Percent Impact on Wage Differential from Supply
France	55.9	−54.4
Germany	17.5	−24.1
Italy	119.9	−111.7
Netherlands	26.7	−33.6
Norway	87.5	−86.2
UK	112.6	−98.4
Australia	42.9	−44.3
Canada	92.9	−89.6
USA	41.4	−28.9

The table shows the impact of demand and supply factors on the percentage change in the gap between the wages of the skilled and the unskilled. The overall change in the differential between skilled and unskilled wages is the sum of the two columns.

The first column shows the effect of rising demand for skilled labor. In all countries this has served to boost the skills premium. The second column shows the effect of changing supply, which in all countries has seen more skilled workers and fewer unskilled and which has served to narrow the differential.

Higher demand for skilled labor is a global phenomenon, but we have not seen higher inequality everywhere because in many countries the demand effect has been cancelled out by the supply effect. This has not been the case in the United States.

Source: Nickell and Layard, "Labor Market Institutions and Economic Performance" in *Handbook of Labor Economics* Vol. 30, 1999. Reprinted with permission from Elsevier Science.

wages of skilled workers is all the more dramatic because the supply of skilled workers increased during this time (see Figure 8.23).

Table 8.8 shows that this increase in the supply of skilled labor is a global phenomenon that has occurred while the demand for skilled workers has also increased. In countries in which the increase in demand has outstripped the increase in supply, the result has been widening inequality between skilled and unskilled workers.

What underlies this surge in demand for skilled workers and the associated decline in the demand for the unskilled? The two most popular hypotheses are the increase in global trade and the spread of new technologies associated with computers and information technology. As we shall see in Chapter 9, trade implies that the demand for factors of production that countries have in abundance should increase. Therefore increasing trade predicts rising demand for skilled workers in the OECD. Although this issue is hotly contested, the current consensus from economists is that trade can only explain around 20% of the increased inequality; trade between OECD and emerging markets is not large enough to have substantially affected inequality. Moreover, increases in inequality have occurred across all industries by roughly the same amount; they have *not* been more acute in industries more exposed to trade.

A more popular explanation for this increase in demand for skilled workers is general technological change associated with computers and information technology. The evidence suggests that computers, capital equipment, and skilled labor are seen as complements in production—computers are used more intensively in industries with skilled labor and high levels of capital intensity. Table 8.9 shows that the near doubling in the diffusion of computers across the U.S. workforce between 1984 and 1993 is heavily concentrated among the more highly educated.

The fact that the skilled have adopted technology more than the unskilled, and that the spread of technology across industries reflects the spread of inequality, makes it plausible that technological change accounts for much of the rising inequality in the 1980s and 1990s.

TABLE 8.9   Percentage Diffusion of Computers Among U.S. Workforce

	1984	1989	1993
All Workers	25.1	37.4	46.6
High-School Dropout	5.2	7.7	10.4
High School	19.2	28.4	34.6
Some College	30.6	45.0	53.1
College Graduates	42.1	58.6	70.2

Source: Autor, Katz, and Krueger, "Computing Inequality: Have Computers Changed the Labor Market," *The Quarterly Journal of Economics* (November 1998) Vol. 113, No. 4, pp. 1169–1213 © by the President and Fellows of Harvard and the Massachusetts Institute of Technology.

SUMMARY

We have completed our long-run analysis of the economy by providing a model of the labor market whereby capital accumulation and technological progress increase the demand for labor to produce rising real wages and a higher standard of living. We have explained the concept of a natural rate of unemployment—a long-run equilibrium to which the economy tends to return. We outlined a model of the natural rate based on the interaction between producers and the labor force where both possess a degree of monopoly power. Unemployment reconciles the conflicting profit demands of firms with the real wage aspirations of workers. Stronger labor unions, high levels of unemployment benefits, a large proportion of long-term unemployed, substantial regional variations in unemployment, high labor taxes, and greater monopoly power among firms lead to higher unemployment.

We also outlined a model of the natural unemployment rate based on inflows and out-flows into unemployment. We showed that EPL varies across countries. The greater the degree of EPL, the lower are inflows into unemployment. But this is offset by the fact that employment protection also reduces outflows from unemployment. As a result the data suggest that employment protection does not influence the aggregate unemployment rate, but instead increases job tenure and the duration of unemployment.

We considered at a more philosophical level how unemployment can persist—why doesn't an excess supply of labor lead to falling real wages and thereby reduce unemployment? We introduced the concept of efficiency wages, which imply that for a variety of reasons (reductions in turnover, pilfering, absenteeism, and improvements in incentives) firms may find it profitable to pay high wages and will be reluctant to lower wages even when unemployment exists. Social and motivational reasons make the market for labor different from the market for many other commodities.

Inequality has widened in many OECD labor markets over the last two decades. We show that this is the result of a sharp decline in the demand for unskilled workers and a large increase in the demand for skilled workers. The most plausible explanation for this trend is technological developments connected to information technology.

CONCEPTUAL QUESTIONS

1. A country has a working age population of 70 million, a total population of 100 million, unemployment of 5 million, and employment of 45 million. (a) What is its labor force? (b) What is its participation rate? (c) What is the participation rate as a proportion of the working-age population? (d) What is its unemployment rate?

2. In Greece the participation rate (as percentage of working age population) in 1998 for men aged 15–24 was 44.3%; aged 24–54, 94.2%; and aged 55–64, 57%. For the United States these numbers were 68.4%, 91.8%, and 68.1%. In Greece the corresponding figures for women were 37.3%, 59.4%, 24.4%, and for women in the United States, 63.3%, 76.5%, and 51.2%. What do you think explains these cross-country differences?

3. If the population was prepared to work substantially longer hours for higher wages, what would be the long-run impact of capital accumulation and technological progress on the labor market?

4. What influences the wage demands you make of your employer?

5. How do the following affect the natural rate of unemployment : (a) an increase in tariffs on imported goods, (b) making unemployment benefits taxable, (c) more expenditure on re-training programs for the unemployed, (d) increases in indirect taxes on product prices, and (e) increases in income tax on labor income?

6. If generous welfare payments support the long-term unemployed, is employment protection legislation a good thing?

7. What type of firms and industries pay above average wages? Can efficiency wages explain this?

8. Are the differences between labor markets and fish markets exaggerated?

9. What type of worker have computers displaced and why have they increased the demand for skilled labor? Will skilled labor and computers always be complements in production?

10. Is there a link between the flexibility of U.S. labor markets and its large prison population?

11. The UK and the United States have highly deregulated labor markets and have also seen much larger increases in inequality due to declining demand for unskilled workers than Continental Europe. What might explain this difference?

ANALYTICAL QUESTIONS

1. A family has a target for the income that it needs to earn of $1500 a week. Both adults in the family work at flexible jobs where they have a choice over how many hours to work. They decide that the relative number of hours they should work should be equal to the ratio of their hourly wage rates. The female earns $20 an hour and the male $15. How many hours do they work? What happens when the female gets a 20% wage rise to $24 an hour? What happens if both adults get a 20% pay rise?

2. Consider the Cobb-Douglas production function:

$$Y_t = A_t K_t^b L_t^{1-b}$$

where Y_t is output at time t; K_t is capital, L_t is labor hours worked, and A_t is total factor productivity at time t, b is 0.3. Analyze how the marginal productivity of labor changes when:

    a.   A increases by 10%
    b.   K increases by 10%
    c.   L increases by 10%
    d. b falls from 0.4 to 0.3

3. In an economy firms set prices at a markup of 20% over costs. Costs are all in the form of wages, so that $P = (1.2) W$. Labor unions enter into bargains with firms on wages. The higher is unemployment the less powerful are unions and the lower is the real wage they can achieve in negotiations. The real wage that gets negotiated is:

    $W/P = 1 - 2u$

where u is the fraction of the workforce unemployed. What is the equilibrium fraction of the labor force unemployed?

4. Consider the economy described in Question 3. The government now decides to charge income tax on wages at a rate of 15%. Companies have to pay tax on their profits of 20%; profits per unit produced are simply price minus cost, and the cost is the wage. Assume that

firms continue to want to get a net of tax profit margin of 20% of costs. Labor unions bargain so that real wages *after income tax* are still given by the expression: $1 - 2u$. What happens to the equilibrium unemployment rate?

5. Suppose the probability of a worker losing his or her job in a year is 2%. The probability of someone unemployed finding a job within a year is 40%. What is the equilibrium unemployment rate? What happens if government measures to free up the labor market double the chances the unemployed have of finding a job and also double the chances of those with jobs becoming unemployed?

6. Suppose that in an economy those with high skills get paid twice the wages of those with low skills. With this pattern of relative wages there are as many low-skilled as high-skilled workers. Technological advances mean that relative wages now change so that the skilled get paid three times the unskilled. This changes the incentives to gain skills and the proportion of those with skills increases to 75%. Consider different measures of inequality in this economy and use them to show how vague the question "has inequality increased?" is.

CHAPTER 9

International Trade

Overview

The modern history of world trade is one of fast growth until 1914, fueled by declining transport costs, and then a dramatic slowdown between the two World Wars when governments erected barriers to trade. The founding in 1946 of GATT (General Agreement on Trades and Tariffs) lowered trade restrictions and increased trade. World trade is now increasing faster than world gross domestic product (GDP), so that the global economy is becoming more interconnected. We consider the advantages of free trade and outline the theory of comparative advantage, which says that all countries can benefit from free trade, even those that are less efficient at production than other nations. Comparative advantage shows how countries gain from free trade but does not tell us what types of commodities they produce. The Heckscher-Ohlin model tells us that countries export commodities that require the intensive use in production of factors that a country possesses in abundance. We examine the evidence for this and consider other factors that help explain the observed pattern of trade. How much a country gains from trade depends on the terms of trade—the price of exports relative to imports—and we examine how this has varied for a range of countries.

We then consider why protectionism enjoys political support. We outline the Stolper-Samuelson Theorem, which states that some groups in society lose because of free trade while others gain, and we consider to what extent increasing levels of trade can explain widening income inequality in many OECD economies. We also consider the arguments in favor of subsidizing key industries to boost a nation's competitiveness and argue that such a debate confuses trade with economic growth. Finally, we consider "New Trade Theory" which maintains that for some industries protectionism or export subsidies can benefit an economy. We conclude by examining the nature of trade restrictions and the role of the World Trade Organization (WTO) in attempting to continue to reduce trade restrictions.

9.1   Patterns of World Trade

World trade has been increasing for centuries as explorers have discovered trade routes and the technology of transport has improved. The great voyages of Christopher Columbus to the Americas in 1492 and Vasco da Gama to India in 1498 are dramatic examples of this long-running process of globalization. However, while these heroic journeys opened up new trading opportunities, the trade tended to be in high value added items that played a relatively small role in the economy. Large-scale trade only began in the nineteenth century; it started in basic commodities like wheat, iron, and textiles.[1] Figure 9.1 shows evidence for this in a narrowing of price differentials in Amsterdam and Southeast Asia for three traded goods: cloves, black pepper, and coffee. If trade is substantial, then prices for the same commodities should be similar in each location. Large price differentials can only persist if traders cannot buy commodities in the cheap location (which pushes up prices) and sell them in the more expensive location (which depresses prices). Trade forces prices to converge.

Figure 9.1 shows a dramatic narrowing of price differentials in the early nineteenth century. Figure 9.2 shows one reason for this—trade was boosted by falling transport prices. Figure 9.3 shows the growth of exports for five major OECD economies. Between 1913 and 1992 French exports increased by a factor of around 18, U.S. exports by around 16, and Japan's (still a closed economy in 1913) by an extraordinary 160.

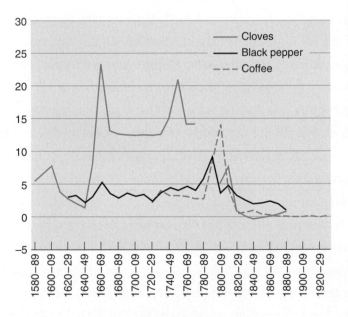

FIGURE 9.1 **Price differentials between Amsterdam and Southeast Asia (%).** As trade in many commodities increased sharply in the nineteenth century, international price differences fell. *Source*: Taken from material contained in *Southeast Asian Exports since the 14th Century: Cloves, Pepper, Coffee and Sugar* compiled by David Bulbeck, Anthony Reid, Lay Cheng Tan, and Yiqi Wu. Reproduced here with the kind permission of the publisher, Institute of Southeast Asian Studies, Singapore, *www.iseas.edu.sg/pub.html*

[1] See O'Rourke and Williamson, "The Heckscher-Ohlin Model between 1400 and 2000," NBER Working Paper 7411 (November 1999).

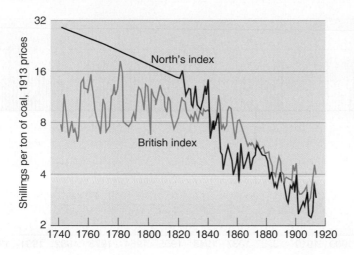

FIGURE 9.2 **Real freight rate indexes, 1741–1913.** Transport costs declined dramatically in the nineteenth century. *Source*: Harley, C. Knick "Ocean Freight Rates and Productivity, The Primacy of Mechanical Invention Reaffirmed 1740–1913," *Journal of Economic History* (1988) vol. 48, pp. 851–876. Reprinted with the permission of Cambridge University Press.

But world trade has not grown at a steady pace—it has risen and fallen during different decades. Figure 9.4 shows the annual growth in world trade over the last 100 years (excluding the periods of the two World Wars 1914–1918 and 1939–1945). Before 1914 world trade grew at an average of around 5% per year, although it fluctuated quite widely depending on the business cycle. After the end of World War I, in 1918, trade re-

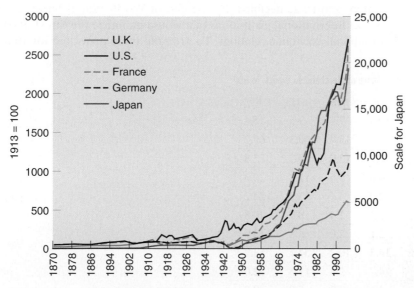

FIGURE 9.3 **Exports for G5, 1870–1997.** Over the last century world trade has increased faster than GDP, and trade between the developed countries has risen dramatically. *Source*: Maddison, "Monitoring the World Economy: 1820–1992" (Paris: OECD, 1995). Copyright OECD. Updated using WTO Annual Report (2000).

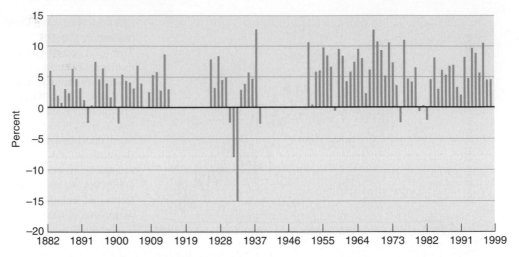

FIGURE 9.4   **Annual Growth in World trade, 1882–1997.** Since the end of the Second World War the volume of world trade has risen at an annual average rate of over 5%. *Source*: Maddison, "Monitoring the World Economy: 1820–1992" (1995). Copyright OECD. Updated using WTO Annual Report (2000).

sumed but collapsed dramatically during the early 1930s. The United States and the rest of the world were in the midst of the Great Depression, and to prevent imports from capturing domestic demand the United States enacted protectionist measures. Other countries retaliated, and trade declined. By the end of World War II, most countries wanted to construct international institutions that would minimize the threat of conflict and foster international economic relations. To promote these goals, the International

TABLE 9.1   **Share of Merchandise Exports in GDP**

	1913	1950	1973	1997
Australia	10.9	7.7	9.5	15.4
Belgium	17.5	13.4	40.3	69.2
Canada	12.9	13.0	19.9	35.8
France	6.0	5.6	11.2	20.8
Germany	12.2	4.4	17.2	24.2
Italy	3.3	2.4	8.7	20.8
Japan	2.1	2.0	6.8	10.0
Netherlands	14.5	10.2	34.1	53.2
UK	14.7	9.8	11.5	22.0
USA	4.1	3.3	5.8	8.8

Source: Maddison, *Dynamic Forces in Capitalistic Development: A Long-Run Comparative View* updated using WTO Annual Report 1998. By permission of Oxford University Press.

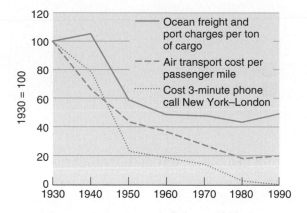

FIGURE 9.5 **Transport and communication costs.** Costs of moving goods and information continued to fall through the twentieth century. *Source: The Economist* (July 20, 1991). © The Economist Newspaper Limited, London (1991).

Monetary Fund (IMF) and the World Bank were founded and the General Agreement on Trades and Tariffs (GATT) was enacted. The latter achieved through a series of negotiations, reductions in trade tariffs and other barriers to trade. As a result, growth in world trade has been rapid over the last 50 years—punctuated only by periods of world recession. World trade has grown more rapidly than GDP, so that the share of output that most countries export has risen substantially. The openness of all economies (the ratio of exports to GDP) is now higher than ever, as Table 9.1 shows.

Decreasing transport costs and declining trade restrictions have fueled this increase in trade. Figure 9.5 shows how transport and communication costs have decreased. Since 1930 sea freight charges have declined by 50%, air transport costs by 80%, and international telephone charges by 99%. This means that goods and services can be traded over greater distances because transport and communication costs have become less important.

Transport costs decreased most dramatically in the first half of the twentieth century, but this decline slowed in the second half even though trade continued to grow because trade restrictions between countries declined. Figure 9.6 shows how trade tariffs have fallen by more than 80% since 1930.

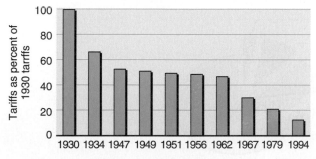

FIGURE 9.6 **Tariffs as percentage of 1930 levels.** The average tariffs on traded goods and services have steadily declined since the Depression. *Source*: Phillipe Lavergne "The Political Economy of U.S. Tariffs" (PhD thesis, University of Toronto, 1981) reproduction Robert E. Baldwin, "U.S. Trade Policy since World War II" in R.E. Baldwin and A.O. Kruegar (eds), *The Structure and Evolution of Recent U.S. Trade Policy*," (Chicago: University of Chicago Press, 1986).

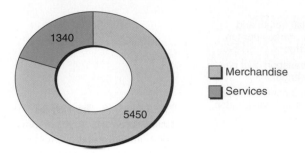

FIGURE 9.7   **Composition of world trade, 1999 ($bn).** *Source*: WTO Annual Report (2000).

What types of commodities are traded? Figure 9.7 shows that merchandise goods—a category that includes manufacturing, mining, and agricultural products—account for 80% of world trade, and services account for the remaining 20%.

Figure 9.8 shows that merchandise trade is overwhelmingly in manufactured goods, which overall make up 60% of *total* world trade. Manufacturing is thus the most exposed economic sector to international trade.

Table 9.2 shows which countries are most involved in international trade. Note that the European Union (EU), the United States, and Japan together account for about 45% of merchandise exports.[2] However, as we saw in Chapter 2, the EU accounts for around 30% of world GDP, the United States for about 30%, and Japan for roughly 13%. Therefore, relative to the size of their economies, these regions are underrepresented in world trade. This is in fact a general rule—large economies tend to be more closed, that is exports are a smaller proportion of their GDP than they are in smaller economies. The most obvious example of this is Hong Kong, which accounts for 4.5% of world trade even though its population is only 3.5 million—around 1% of the population of the EU and 0.66% of the United States. But the large regions account for a much greater proportion of services trade.

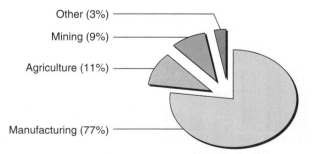

FIGURE 9.8   **Composition of merchandise trade, 1999.** *Source*: WTO Annual Report (2000).

[2]Table 9.2 does not include intra-EU trade.

TABLE 9.2   Top 20 Exporters of Merchandise
Goods and Services, 1999

Share of	Merchandise Trade	Share of	Services
EU	18.9	USA	18.8
USA	16.4	UK	7.6
Japan	9.9	France	5.9
Canada	5.6	Germany	5.7
China	4.6	Italy	4.8
Hong Kong, China	4.1	Japan	4.5
Korea	3.4	Spain	4.0
Singapore	3.0	Netherlands	4.0
Mexico	3.2	Belgium-Luxembourg	2.8
Taiwan	2.9	Hong Kong, China	2.6
Singapore	2.7	Canada	2.4
Malaysia	2.0	Austria	2.4
Switzerland	1.9	China	2.0
Thailand	1.4	Switzerland	2.0
Australia	1.3	Korea	1.9
Saudi Arabia	1.2	Sweden	1.3
Indonesia	1.1	Australia	1.3
Brazil	1.1	Taiwan	1.3
Norway	1.1	Denmark	1.2
India	0.9	Turkey	1.2

Source: WTO, Annual Report (2000).

9.2   Comparative Advantage—How Countries Benefit from Trade

Most economists consider free trade a good thing. This belief is based on one of the oldest, most important, and least well-understood theories in economics: *the theory of comparative advantage*. This says that *all* countries can benefit from trade, even if they are less productive in *every* industry than are other nations. What matters is *not* whether a country is the most productive in the world at producing a commodity. Instead, countries gain from trade by exporting commodities in which their productivity disadvantage is least pronounced; by specializing in what they are least bad at.

The theory of comparative advantage is essentially an invisible hand/free market argument. It says that free trade best promotes the welfare of countries. Comparative advantage says that nations should specialize in their productive activities and should focus on those activities in which their advantage is greatest or their disadvantage least. It implies that all countries benefit from trade *even if they have low productivity*. This is exactly what happens in everyday economic life. Consider the case of a highly qualified lawyer who can earn $1000 an hour. This lawyer has high productivity in whatever she does. For example, she can type twice as fast as her secretary, can make a better meal in less time than the chef in her firm's cafeteria, and drive across New York more directly and quickly than a taxi driver. She is also, of course, more productive as a lawyer than her secretary, the chef, or the taxi driver. In other words, the lawyer has an absolute advantage in all these activities. However, the optimal strategy for her is not to do everything herself. Every hour she spends typing up case notes, making meals, or driving herself around town costs her $1000. Far better to use this time on legal work and then purchase the other services at a cheaper rate. Therefore, the lawyer will focus on the activity that is most productive for her. A similar argument applies to the other characters. The chef would earn little as a lawyer, is a hopeless typist, and cannot drive. His comparative advantage is to cook. Therefore, his best strategy is to specialize as a chef and then purchase whatever legal or transport services he needs. In everyday life we all specialize in activities that we are *relatively* good at—this is the theory of comparative advantage.

To demonstrate in detail the theory of comparative advantage, we consider two economies, Eurasia and Oceania, that each produce two commodities: onions and garlic.[3] Comparative advantage relies on many assumptions, but the two key ones for our purposes are that trade between countries is competitive—countries cannot exploit a monopoly position—and that within a country factors of production (i.e., capital and labor) are mobile, and the economy has a constant natural rate of unemployment (see Chapter 8).

We assume that Eurasia's population is 10 people and that Oceania's is 40. The key to our analysis is productivity levels in each country. We assume that in Eurasia it takes 2 people to produce a bag of onions and 5 to produce a bag of garlic. By contrast, in Oceania it takes 8 people to produce a bag of onions and 10 for a bag of garlic. Table 9.3 shows the state of production technology.

These assumptions imply that Eurasia is more efficient than Oceania in producing both commodities. Oceania therefore has an absolute advantage in neither industry.

TABLE 9.3 **Production Technology for Eurasia and Oceania**

	Eurasia	Oceania
Onions	2	8
Garlic	5	10

Table shows the number of individuals in each country required to produce one bag of commodity listed in the first column.

[3]We discuss a world of two economies and two commodities, but the analysis also holds for many more commodities and countries.

However, because of comparative advantage, both countries can gain from free trade. The key concept is *opportunity cost*.

In economics every activity has an opportunity cost. Opportunity cost is what you could have done had you not pursued your current activity—it is the opportunity you forgo when you make a choice. For instance, the opportunity cost of us writing this textbook is the research papers we could have written instead or the consulting income we might have earned. For you, the opportunity cost of reading this book is meeting a friend, going to a film, or reading a novel. For Eurasia, the opportunity cost of producing more garlic is producing fewer onions. The resources used to produce onions are transferred from the onion industry to garlic production. This happens because if unemployment remains constant, Eurasia can only increase garlic production by moving labor from onions into the garlic fields. Because every bag of garlic requires 5 people to produce it while a bag of onions needs 2 people, the opportunity cost of producing one bag of garlic for Eurasia is 2.5 (=5/2) bags of onions. However, in Oceania it takes 8 people to produce a bag of onions and 10 to produce a bag of garlic. For Oceania the opportunity cost of producing one bag of garlic is therefore 1.25 (=10/8). In other words, it is cheaper in an opportunity cost sense for Oceania to produce garlic than it is for Eurasia. *Oceania is said to have a* **comparative advantage** *in producing garlic.*

We now show diagrammatically how both countries benefit from free trade. We assume that on world markets two bags of onions can be exchanged for one bag of garlic. We shall show that *if* this is the world price, then free trade benefits both Eurasia and Oceania. Note that this is not the only price at which trade benefits both countries. We will discuss how this particular price gets established later.

The solid triangular area in Figure 9.9 shows Eurasia's production possibility set— all the combinations of onions and garlic that Eurasia can produce given its workforce and technology. Eurasia has a workforce of 10 people and requires 2 people to produce one bag of onions. Therefore if everyone specializes in onion production, the country can produce at most five bags of onions and zero bags of garlic. This gives us the top point in the production possibility set. If instead, Eurasia devotes all its resources to garlic production (which requires five people per bag), it can produce two bags of garlic and zero bags of onions. This gives us the other extreme point on the production possibility frontier. However, there are also many intermediate positions where Eurasia does not specialize but allocates some labor to onion production and some to garlic. Eurasia can

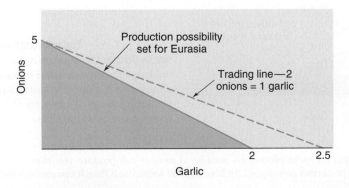

FIGURE 9.9 **Production and trade sets for Eurasia.** Trade allows Eurasia to move on to a higher production frontier, generating the scope for higher consumption.

reach any point on the line drawn between these two extreme points of specialization and the slope of the line reflects the opportunity cost—how much of one commodity is forgone by producing more of the other. All points on this line represent where Eurasia is producing the maximum amount of onions and garlic it can produce given the allocation of labor between the two industries. However, Eurasia can also produce output inefficiently so that the shaded triangular area gives the full set of production possibilities.

The production possibility set shows the consumption possibilities for Eurasia if it does not trade—in this case Eurasia can only consume what it produces. However, if Eurasia starts to trade, it can sell two bags of onions for one bag of garlic (given world prices). Figure 9.9 shows the trading line this implies for Eurasia. If Eurasia concentrates on onion production, it has five bags of onions that it can swap on international markets for 2.5 bags of garlic.[4] Therefore, allowing for trade, Eurasia can consume five bags of onions and zero bags of garlic, or it can consume zero bags of onions and 2.5 bags of garlic. It can also consume any combination between these two extreme points if it decides to sell some, but not all, of its onion production. Figure 9.9 also shows that the trading line lies everywhere above the production possibility set. Therefore Eurasia can do better for itself through international trade than if it concentrates entirely on producing for its own consumption. Figure 9.9 shows that the optimal strategy for Eurasia is to specialize entirely in onion production and then sell onions to acquire the amount of garlic it wants to consume. This is still optimal even if Eurasia does not wish to consume *any* onions at all. Individuals or countries should specialize in producing the commodity they are most efficient at producing and then, through trade, purchase the commodities they wish to consume. After all, even though we are producing an economics textbook, we have no desire to purchase one! This separation of production and consumption enables the economy to operate efficiently.

But Table 9.3 shows us that Eurasia is more efficient at producing both onions and garlic. Therefore it is hardly surprising that the country benefits from free trade. Can we show that Oceania, which is relatively inefficient, also benefits?

Figure 9.10 shows the production and trading possibilities for Oceania. Oceania has 40 people, and it takes 8 to produce a bag of onions and 10 to produce a bag of gar-

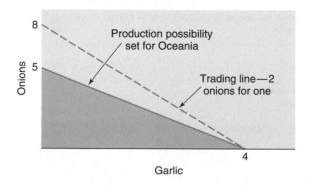

FIGURE 9.10   **Production and trade sets for Oceania.** Oceania too can enjoy the scope to consume more of both goods once it trades and specializes in producing the good where its comparative advantage lies.

---

[4]Eurasia will not focus on garlic production because at most it can produce two bags of garlic, which given international prices can be swapped for four bags on onions, less than it can produce itself.

lic. Therefore at most Oceania can produce five bags of onions and no garlic or four bags of garlic and no onions. Again, the shaded area shows the production possibility set. The same international prices apply to Oceania, so it can swap two bags of onions for one of garlic. Therefore, if Oceania focuses on garlic production and produces four bags, it can trade and obtain up to eight bags of onions—compared to only five if it is self-sufficient. Thus if international prices enable two bags of onions to be swapped for one bag of garlic, then *both* Eurasia and Oceania benefit from trade even though Oceania has no absolute advantage in either industry. That is the theory of comparative advantage.

Trade is beneficial when international prices are different from the opportunity costs in each country (when the trading line differs from the slope of the production set). But how do we know that international prices will reach a level that makes trade beneficial to both countries? We have shown that a price exists that makes trade beneficial for both countries. However, not all possible prices make trade beneficial. For instance, if international prices are 2.5 bags of onions for one bag of garlic, Eurasia is no better off with trade—it can do just as well being self-sufficient. But if Eurasia does not trade, Oceania loses the benefits of free trade. Rather than do that, Oceania can suggest alternative prices (for instance, two bags of onions for one garlic) until both countries benefit. Therefore, unless prices are restricted, they will eventually move to a range that promotes trade. What might prevent prices from moving to this mutually beneficial range? One cause is tariffs—Oceania may impose an import tariff on onions, so that the market price cannot be two bags of onions for one bag of garlic. But without such restrictions, the price will shift until it induces beneficial trade.

This is the comparative advantage result—all countries can benefit from trade. However, there are some things comparative advantage does *not* imply:

(a) Comparative advantage says all countries gain from trade, but not that all countries become wealthy. As we saw in Chapters 4 though 7, the standard of living in a country depends on its *absolute* productivity. In our example, Eurasia is more productive than Oceania and so has a better standard of living (compare the level of onions per capita in each country). However, both Eurasia and Oceania will have *higher* standards of living than if they did not trade with each other. In other words, trade makes all countries better off but not equally well off.

(b) While both Eurasia and Oceania benefit from trade, they do not benefit equally. The greater the price of garlic in world trade, the greater the gains for Oceania and the less the gains for Eurasia. The key concept here is the *terms of trade*—the ratio of the price of a country's exports to its imports. The higher the terms of trade, the more the country benefits from trade.

(c) Comparative advantage only says that a country gains from trade in the aggregate. It does not say that *every* citizen benefits. For example, garlic producers in Eurasia will not benefit from trade with Oceania. We will examine the distributional implications of free trade in detail later.

Figure 9.11, taken from an early seminal study, shows empirical support for comparative advantage. The figure shows for a variety of industries the relative

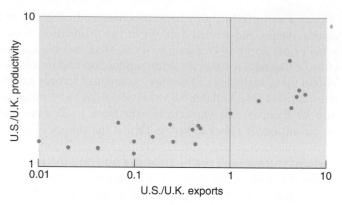

FIGURE 9.11   **Comparative advantage in the United States and UK, 1937.** Just before the Second World War the United States and UK appeared to specialize in production and export of goods where they had comparative advantages— although the United States had an absolute advantage in production of nearly all goods   *Source*: G.D.A. MacDougall, "British and American Exports," *The Economic Journal* (1955) vol. 61, pp. 703–707.

productivity of the United States (compared to the UK) and the relative amount of exports from the United States in each industry. The scale shows that for every industry, productivity in the United States was greater than in the UK. In other words, the United States had an absolute productivity advantage in all industries. Yet the UK still managed to export more than several of these U.S. industries (where the ratio of U.S. to UK exports is less than 1). Figure 9.11 shows that the UK out-exported the U.S. in those industries in which the U.S. productivity advantage was least pronounced. In other words, the United States focused its export performance on those industries in which its productivity advantage was greatest compared to the UK (pig iron and motor cars). This left the UK to specialize in those industries in which its productivity deficit was *smallest* (beer and woolens)—exactly what comparative advantage implies.

9.3   The Terms of Trade

The terms of trade is the ratio of the price of a country's exports to the price of its imports. The higher the terms of trade, the more benefits a nation captures from trade. Figure 9.12 shows variations in the terms of trade between 1950 and 1998 for the United States, Japan, Germany, and the UK.

Over 40 years they show a decline in the terms of trade for the United States, an increase for Germany and the UK, and essentially no change for Japan. The index for the United States terms of trade stood at 132 in 1950 but had fallen to 119 by 1998—a decline of around 10%. Over this period U.S. imports were on average 6.1% of GDP (beginning at around 3% and ending at 11%). Therefore, a 10% increase in the price of imports relative to exports means that the U.S. gains from trade *fell* by around 0.6% of GDP (10% of 6.1%). This does not mean the United States did not gain from trade— comparative advantage tells us otherwise. But adverse shifts in the terms of trade meant that the United States gained *less* than it otherwise would have done.

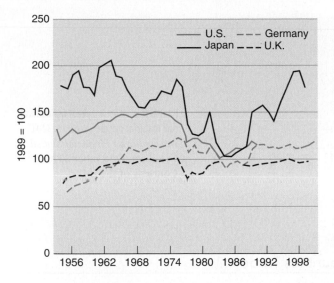

FIGURE 9.12 **Terms of trade for the United States, Japan, Germany, and the UK.** *Source*: IMF, *International Financial Statistics,* CD-Rom, December 2000. Courtesy of the IMF.

Japan's experience shows that the terms of trade can be volatile. Overall between 1950 and 1998, the Japanese terms of trade hardly changed. But between 1950 and 1980 they fell dramatically—from 179 to 100, a fall of around 45%. This is mainly due to the substantial increase in oil prices achieved by OPEC (Organization of Petroleum Exporting Countries) in 1973 and 1979.

Figure 9.13 shows the terms of trade for a different set of countries. It shows a substantial decline for Australia, a lesser decline for Tanzania, and a sharp improvement for Iran, which reflects the increase in oil prices mentioned above. The deterioration for Australia and Tanzania reflects that over this time period non-oil commodity prices fell sharply (Figure 9.14 shows an index for the real value of agricultural raw materials from 1957 to 1998.) For countries that are heavily dependent on such commodities, this decline has reduced the net benefits from trade.

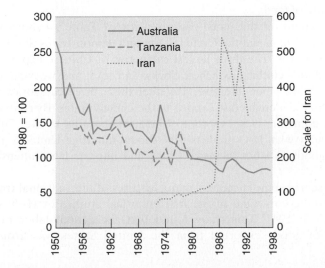

FIGURE 9.13 **Terms of trade for Australia, Iran, and Tanzania.** *Source*: IMF, *International Financial Statistics,* CD-Rom, December 2000. Courtesy of the IMF.

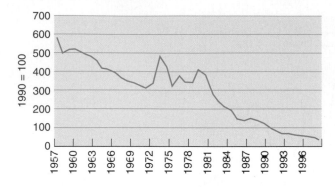

FIGURE 9.14 **Real agricultural raw material prices.** *Source*: IMF, *International Financial Statistics*, CD-Rom, December 2000. Courtesy of the IMF.

9.4 What Goods Will Countries Trade In?

Comparative advantage says all countries benefit from trade and have a comparative advantage in some industries. But what can we say about the type of industry a country has a comparative advantage in?

The Heckscher-Ohlin (H-O) model (named after two Swedish economists) answers this question. Based on certain key assumptions, the H-O model predicts that:

> **KEY POINT**
>
> A country possesses a comparative advantage in a good whose production requires the intensive use of a factor input that the nation possesses in abundance.

In other words, China with its 1.2 billion population should have a comparative advantage in labor-intensive commodities; Saudi Arabia has a comparative advantage in exporting oil-based products; and Canada has a comparative advantage in commodities that require the extensive use of land.

How well does H-O account for the actual pattern of trade? Table 9.4 shows the composition of trade between China and the United States and demonstrates that H-O can explain some trading patterns. The three largest categories of Chinese exports to the United States are children's clothing; watches, clocks, and toys; and weaving and wool products—all of which are labor intensive. Together these three categories account for nearly 60% of Chinese merchandise exports to the United States. By contrast, aircraft parts and engines dominate U.S. exports to China—amounting to over 70%. This pattern of trade is exactly what H-O predicts—the capital-intensive United States exports capital intensive goods to labor-intensive China and imports labor-intensive commodities.

However, while H-O scores some successes, many features of international trade conflict with its simple predictions. One of the first empirical studies of H-O was based on U.S. trade data in 1947. This study found that the capital–labor ratio (or capital per worker) of goods exported from the United States was around

TABLE 9.4   Chinese–U.S. Merchandise Trade

	Chinese Exports to United States (%)	U.S. Exports to China (%)
Periodicals, office, and computing machinery	4.8	7.7
Aircraft parts	2.6	48.8
Engines and turbines	3.9	21.3
Concrete, plumbing, and heating	11.5	4.3
Watches, clocks, and toys	18.9	6.3
Wood buildings and steel	8.2	1.3
Shipbuilding and repairs	4.1	2.8
Cigarettes, motor vehicles	5.2	1.8
Weaving and wool	17.2	0.4
Children's outerware	23.5	5.2

Source: Sachs and Shatz, "Trade and Jobs in U.S. Manufacturing," *Brookings Papers on Economic Activity Macroeconomics* (1994) vol. 1.

$14,000, while for imports it was $18,200. In other words, the United States imported goods that were more capital intensive than the goods it exported, even though the United States had one of the highest capital stocks in the world. This is inconsistent with H-O.

Figure 9.15 shows the composition of U.S. merchandise imports in 2000. While U.S.–Chinese trade is consistent with H-O, Figure 9.15 shows that the United States imports goods whose production is very capital intensive. How can we explain this? In the next few pages, we will try to explain these anomalies for the H-O model by considering a range of factors: differences in tastes across countries; the existence of trade restrictions; whether the U.S. comparative advantage really lies in physical capital intensive goods; differences in technology across countries; and the presence of imperfect competition and increasing returns to scale.

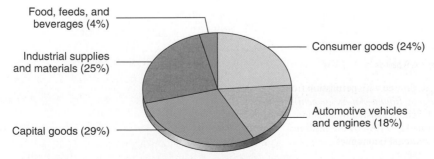

FIGURE 9.15   **Composition of U.S. Merchandise Imports, 2000.** *Source*: U.S. Bureau of Economic Analysis (www.bea.doc.gov).

DIFFERENCES IN TASTES

The H-O model assumes that all countries have the same preferences, so that trade patterns reflect only supply considerations. However, variations in demand also explain trade patterns. For instance, the U.S. state of Virginia exports every month 30 tons of poultry feet to Southeast Asia.[5] The H-O model cannot account for this trade because the United States does not have a comparative advantage compared to Asia in poultry production. This trade literally results from different tastes—Asian cuisine, but not American, uses chicken feet. Therefore, the United States may import capital-intensive goods because the U.S. demand for such goods may be so overwhelming that it also has to import them even though it has a comparative advantage in producing those commodities itself.

However, differences in tastes are unlikely to explain the pattern of trade shown in Figure 9.15. First, U.S. capital-intensive imports are too big to be explained by taste differences. Second, if the United States has a bias for any particular commodity, it is for luxury goods that require substantial amounts of skilled labor as input. Differences in tastes are not, therefore, enough to completely rectify the H-O model.

TRADE RESTRICTIONS

The H-O model assumes the existence of free trade. Even though trade restrictions have been reduced over time, they still distort trade patterns. Table 9.5 shows estimates of the average level of tariffs across countries in 1994. Tariffs are taxes on imports. Such tariffs can distort patterns of trade.

IS THE UNITED STATES CAPITAL INTENSIVE?

We have assumed that only two factors of production exist—capital and labor—but this is simplistic. In reality output is produced using many different inputs—raw materials,

TABLE 9.5 **Average Tariffs**

Region	Average Tariff (%)
Developed countries	3.9
Canada	4.8
European Union	3.6
Japan	1.7
USA	3
Developing countries	12.3
Economies in transition	6

Source: Reprinted with permission from *The Uruguay Round–An Assessment*. Jeffrey J. Schott, assisted by Johanna W. Buurmann. © 1994 by the Institute for International Economics.

[5]This and many other fascinating trade facts are discussed in detail in Yarbrough and Yarbrough, *International Economics* (Fort Worth: Dryden Press, 1997).

skilled and unskilled labor, land, machinery, and so forth. More detailed modeling of these factor inputs, in particular human capital, may explain why U.S. imports are so capital intensive.

While the U.S. has lots of physical capital, its labor force also has high levels of years of schooling. This suggests that its comparative advantage lies in the export of goods that require the intensive use of human capital. The data support this theory. One study finds that U.S. exporting industries use a higher proportion of workers with 13 or more years of schooling, whereas import-competing industries use a higher proportion of workers with 8 or fewer years of schooling.[6]

Table 9.6 breaks down the types of goods that some countries exported or imported in the mid 1960s. If a country exports a good that involves the intensive use of a factor, it is marked as an X. If it imports such a commodity, it is shown by a M. The table reveals some plausible results—the United States exports goods that require the intensive use in production of human and physical capital; Canada exports land-intensive commodities; Germany and Japan have a comparative advantage in goods that require skilled labor; Mexico imports capital-intensive goods; and the Philippines exports commodities that require unskilled labor. Thus a more detailed breakdown of factors of production shows more support for the H-O model. However, the H-O model is still not entirely vindicated. The authors of this study examined whether the export–import patterns in Table 9.6 were consistent with independent

TABLE 9.6   Factor Intensity of Trade for Selected Countries, 1967

	USA	Canada	Germany	Japan	Mexico	Philippines
Capital stock	X	X	M	M	M	M
Labor force	M	M	M	X	X	M
Professional technical workers	X	M	X	X	X	M
Manageral workers	M	M	X	X	X	M
Clerical workers	M	M	X	X	X	M
Sales workers	M	M	M	M	X	X
Service workers	M	M	M	M	X	X
Agricultural workers	X	X	M	M	X	X
Production workers	M	M	X	X	M	M
Arable land	X	X	M	M	X	X
Forest land	M	X	M	M	X	M
Pasture land	M	X	M	M	X	M

M means the country imports the good which uses the factor in the relevant row relatively intensively. X means that the country exports the good.

Source: Bowen, Leamer, Svelkauskas, "Multicountry, Multifactor Tests of the Factor Abundance Theory," *American Economic Review* (1987) vol. 77, pp. 791–809.

[6]Baldwin, "Determinants of the Commodity Structure of U.S. Trade" *American Economic Review* (1971), vol. 61, pp. 126–46.

measures of factor abundance in each country. While there were some successes, there were also many failures—important features of the trade data are inconsistent with the H-O model.

DIFFERENCES IN TECHNOLOGY

As well as assuming that countries are identical in their tastes, the H-O model also assumes that they all have access to the same technology. Therefore the only explanation for trade is supply side differences in factor abundance. However, at any given time, countries will be using different technologies. This is another reason why trade may not agree with the predictions of H-O.

INTRA-INDUSTRY TRADE AND IMPERFECT COMPETITION

Here we outline a more recent theory of trade that combines imperfect competition with increasing returns to scale. This theory seeks to explain why the OECD countries export goods that are similar to those that they import. In other words, why much of international trade is *intra-industry*.

Consider the following measure of intra-industry trade:

1 − absolute value (exports − imports)/(exports + imports)

which is calculated for each industry in a country. The term absolute value (exports − imports) is the value of net exports, ignoring whether they are positive or negative. Imagine a country that specializes in car production and exports many cars but imports none. In this case our measure of intra-industry trade (given that imports of cars are zero) would be 1 − exports/exports = 1 − 1 = 0. If instead the country has no car industry, so that car exports are zero, but imports are large, the measure would be 1 − imports/imports = 1 − 1 = 0. Therefore, if trade in an industry is in only one direction (exports or imports), this measure is 0. When a country both imports and exports cars, so that net exports are zero, the measure is 1 − 0/(exports + imports) = 1. Therefore, the higher the measure, the greater the extent to which trade is intra-industry, e.g., Italy selling Fiats to France, and France selling Peugeots to Italy.

Figure 9.16 shows measures of intra-industry trade for 11 countries and reveals considerable intra-industry trade among the most developed nations. The H-O model cannot explain this—what type of factor endowment can explain why Italy produces Fiats while the French produce Peugeots? We therefore need a different model.

To develop this model, we make two assumptions. The first is that consumers like variety. On entering a car showroom, they wish to select from a range of colors, models, and makes rather than be faced with no choice. Because consumers value variety, the maker of each different type of car has some monopoly power—consumers do not treat Fiats and Peugeots as identical. The second assumption is that car production is characterized by increasing returns to scale—the more cars that are produced, the lower the unit cost. Therefore, if restricted to a small output, the costs—and therefore the price—of the car will be high.

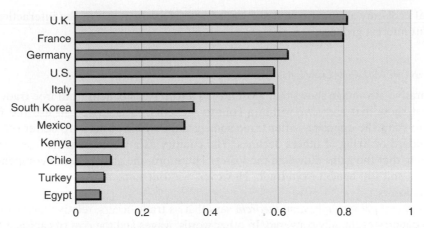

FIGURE 9.16 **Extent of intra-industry trade.** A very high proportion of trade for developed countries represents exports of types of goods or services that the country also imports. *Source*: Grimiracle, *International Trade: New Patterns of Trade, Production, and Investment*. Reprinted with permission of Routledge.

Now consider what happens when the economy is closed to trade. Consumers want a wide range of models to choose from, but this means that production runs have to be inefficiently small and car prices will be high. Although consumers value product variety, there is a limit to what they are prepared to pay for it. As a result, the country will produce a limited range of products to benefit from the increasing returns to scale, e.g., Italian consumers would buy Fiats; the French, Citroens; and the Germans, Volkswagens. Now consider what free trade between countries does. Because car producers can now sell to export markets, they can achieve large production runs with no increase in the level of demand in their domestic economy. Therefore they can keep costs and prices low. Meanwhile, consumers can now choose among different car models at reasonable prices because producers are still benefiting from increasing returns. Therefore German consumers can now choose to buy Volkswagens, Fiats, or Citroens. Trade in this case is still beneficial—production is efficient, and consumers benefit from greater product variety—but the pattern of trade looks different from what H-O predicted. Trade will contain an important intra-industry component as Germany imports Fiats and Citroens while exporting Volkswagens.

9.5 So What's Wrong with Free Trade?

The theory of comparative advantage is unambiguous—free trade is good for a country. Why then do the United States, Japan, the EU, and emerging markets clash so often over trade and why are trade restrictions so common? To answer these questions we focus on four issues: the effect of trade on the distribution of income, concern over a nation's competitiveness, alternative theories of trade (so called "New Trade Theory") that argue that countries can benefit from trade restrictions, and political economy arguments that see trade barriers as the result of the interaction of different interest groups.

TRADE AND INCREASING INCOME INEQUALITY

Comparative advantage shows that a country *as a whole* can benefit from free trade—it does not show that *everyone* within a country benefits. In fact, we can use the H-O model to show the opposite—after trade some groups within society are better off, but the standard of living of others declines. The country as a whole benefits from trade, suggesting that the gains outweigh the losses. Therefore, the gainers *could* compensate the losers and still benefit from trade. However, without some redistribution trade will generate losers.

The *factor price equalization theorem* says that as trade occurs, relative factor prices in each country eventually converge. In other words, wages and the cost of capital adjust until they are in the same ratio across countries. Consider a country that has an abundance of capital (say the United States) and another country whose comparative advantage lies with labor-intensive commodities (e.g., Mexico). H-O says the United States will export capital-intensive commodities to Mexico and import labor-intensive goods. As a result, the demand for capital will increase in the United States, and the demand for labor will rise in Mexico. By contrast, the demand for labor will decline in the United States and the demand for capital will fall in Mexico, which will put downward pressure on both U.S. wages and the Mexican rental price of capital. Before trade, labor is scarce in the United States and capital scarce in Mexico. As a result their factor prices were high, and the United States thus had a comparative advantage in capital-intensive goods and Mexico in labor-intensive goods. *As a result of trade wages should fall in the United States and rise in Mexico, and the rental price of capital should increase in the United States and fall in Mexico.* In fact, we can go further and say that factor prices should be equalized across countries—Mexican and U.S. wages should become the same.

Figure 9.17 shows hourly manufacturing wages for a selection of countries. There is huge variability. Given the factor price equalization theorem, it is understandable that free trade troubles many people. If U.S. wages fall to Mexican levels, then free trade will lead to serious social problems in the United States. However, the situation is not as grim as Figure 9.17 suggests. Factor price equalization implies that *identical factors of production should be paid the same even if they are in different countries*. But unskilled labor in the United States is not the same as unskilled labor in Mexico. In a U.S. factory, unskilled workers have access to much higher levels of capital and probably to higher levels of technology. Therefore, U.S. unskilled workers will have a higher level of productivity than Mexican workers and U.S. firms can pay a higher wage. If the productivity of U.S. workers is twice that of Mexican workers, then their wage can be twice as high. Therefore factor price equalization refers to productivity-adjusted wages rather than to the hourly wage rate. This means that U.S. unskilled wages do not have to fall to equal Mexican wages—only that unit labor costs (the wage costs of producing a unit more of output) should be the same in each country. In Figure 9.18 we plot wages and productivity relative to the United States for a wide variety of countries. The data support the theory: countries with high productivity can pay high wages without violating factor price equalization.

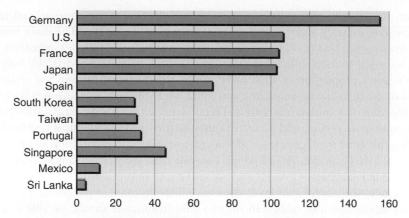

FIGURE 9.17 **Hourly manufacturing wages.** Wage rates differ spectacularly across countries that trade with each other. *Source*: U.S. Bureau of Labor Statistic (http//www.bls.gov/flshome.htm).

However, even though U.S. and Mexican unskilled wages do not have to be equal, the factor price equalization result still implies that unskilled wages fall in the United States as a result of trade with Mexico. The benefits of free trade in the form of lower import prices partly offset this fall. However, we have one more important trade result to outline—the *Stolper-Samuelson* Theorem. This says that trade increases the real income of owners of the abundant factor of production and decreases the real income of owners of the scarce factor. In our U.S.–Mexico example, this means that the real income of U.S. skilled labor increases, while that of unskilled workers declines.

Over the last 30 years imports into the United States have increased from around 5% to 11% of GDP. Inequality in the United States has also increased, as we discussed in Chapter 8. For instance, between 1973 and 1992, the real income of the richest 20% of the U.S. population increased by 19%, while that of the poorest 20% fell by nearly 12%. Given the increase in trade and the Stolper-Samuelson result, the obvious question is whether increased trade explains the recent rise in inequality?

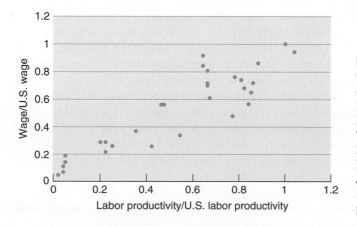

FIGURE 9.18 **Relative wages and productivity.** Wage differences across countries largely reflect differences in labor productivity. *Source*: Trefler, "International Factor Price Differences: Leontief was Right!" *Journal of Political Economy* (1993) vol. 101, pp. 961–987.

In fact, most labor economists estimate that higher levels of international trade were responsible for only about 5–20% of this increase in inequality.[7] The main reasons for this consensus are first that increased inequality is common within all industries, not just those exposed to international competition; second, because imports still only account for a small proportion of U.S. GDP, trade alone cannot explain the observed magnitude of the increase in inequality; and third, while Stolper-Samuelson is based on H-O and the idea of common international relative prices for goods, tariffs, transportation costs, monopoly power, and a host of other factors prevent identical commodities from costing the same in all countries. Moreover, a significant amount of trade is inconsistent with the H-O model. All of which suggests that the Stolper-Samuelson effect may be muted in its impact.

To conclude, we can see that trade does have distributional implications. However, comparative advantage tells us that those who gain from trade should be able to compensate the losers and still experience net benefits—the country as a whole benefits. In other words, free trade should be encouraged but governments need to consider policies that minimize its distributional implications.

9.6   Competitiveness

In the early 1990s, policymakers became increasingly concerned with "competitiveness." New industries were providing high levels of value added, high levels of productivity, and exciting innovative potential. Policymakers believed that advanced nations were in a competitive race to achieve supremacy in these key industries. A successful country would benefit from these new technologies and high productivity levels, leaving other nations behind. A country's competitiveness was taken to mean its ability to outperform its rivals in key industries. With such high stakes, governments felt under pressure to subsidize domestic firms in key areas and erect trade barriers against foreign competition.

Paul Krugman attacked this notion of competitiveness, and the following section is a summary of his critique. In essence Krugman's critique of "competitiveness" tries to spell out what comparative advantage actually implies. It also attacks the common fallacy of drawing analogies between appropriate strategies for corporations and good policies for government—what is good advice to CEOs may not be sensible for heads of state. Krugman's main criticism is that comparative advantage says that *all* countries can benefit from trade, whereas the competitiveness argument implies that trade is a zero-sum game—if one side wins, then the other side loses. In a football match, two teams are competing, and only one can win—each team focuses on its own competitiveness. This is the main idea behind competition. But comparative advantage offers a different perspective—countries that trade with each other both benefit. There is no loser.

Competitiveness makes sense in a business setting. Consider the constant battle for market share between Coca Cola and Pepsi. Coke can only gain market share at the ex-

---

[7]See Chapter 8 for a fuller discussion of the importance of technological progress in this context.

pense of Pepsi, so the notion of competition here is clear. As a result, the CEO of Coca Cola will try to outperform Pepsi and vice versa. In the limit, if Coke captures the entire market, then Pepsi will go bankrupt. Competition between these two firms does appear to be "do-or-die." But does this kind of competitive rivalry carry over to two different countries—say the United States and Japan? The answer is no, not very well.

COUNTRIES DO NOT GO BANKRUPT

If Coca Cola gains 100% market share, then Pepsi goes bankrupt, and this would be disastrous for Pepsi's management, workforce, and shareholders. What happens to the United States if the Japanese dominate the semiconductor industry? The United States does not go bankrupt—companies and governments go bankrupt, but not countries. If the United States loses out to Japan in the semiconductor industry, it retains a stock of physical capital, human capital, and labor and can still produce output. Further, comparative advantage tells us that a country always has a relative advantage in some industry. If the semiconductor industry in the United States starts to decline, then other industries will be expanding—biotechnology, software, or the film industry. Instead of bankruptcy, a country undergoes an industrial restructuring. For instance, those industries in the UK with comparative advantage have continually evolved—from textiles, to coal, steel, and more recently, to financial services, fashion, and music. All these changes have distributional implications, but overall the UK still benefits from trade. Naturally the textile industry will campaign vigorously against cheap foreign imports because that industry may face ruin. But the country itself does not face ruin—a declining textile industry frees resources for another industry to expand.

IS TRADE BETWEEN COUNTRIES ADVERSERIAL?

Imagine that Pepsi introduces a new wonder drink that tastes fantastic and sells for half the price of other soft drinks. This would be unmitigated bad news for Pepsi's rivals. The marketing manager for Coca Cola will not enthuse to its board that employment and wages in Pepsi factories are booming, increasing the potential market for Coca Cola. Neither will the manager stress the benefits to Coke's own workforce of the availability of a cheaper and better tasting product. Pepsi and Coca Cola are adversaries.

But what if Japan announces a new smaller and cheaper computer chip that increases processing speed 20-fold? Is this bad for the United States? It is almost certainly bad news for computer chip manufacturers in the United States, but not for the rest of the U.S. economy. Two things have happened. First, U.S. firms can now get access to cheaper and better products that will improve productivity in a range of industries and therefore increase the U.S. standard of living. Second, the Japanese economy will be performing strongly on the strength of the additional profits, investment, and employment that this innovation generates. This in turn will increase the demand for U.S. goods in Japan. Of course, trade restrictions could prevent the importation of the new technology or prevent U.S. firms from exporting to Japan. Then these benefits will not materialize. But if there is free trade, the innovation will benefit the United States. This example shows clearly the difference in perspective between being the CEO of a company and the president of a country.

Competitiveness confuses two distinct notions: economic growth and comparative advantage, or absolute and relative productivities. Advocates of competitiveness want their country to focus on high productivity industries—which is unquestionably correct. As we saw in Chapters 4 though 7, the higher a country's productivity, the greater its standard of living. Capital accumulation, education, and technological progress are means of increasing productivity. Therefore, government policies that encourage the development of capital- and skill-intensive industries are to be welcomed. However, all of this is about the *absolute* level of productivity. By contrast, comparative advantage tells us that trade is about *relative* productivity. As a result a country always has a comparative advantage in some industries and so will always benefit from trade. However, we also stressed that trade does not make all countries equally wealthy. Countries with high levels of productivity will always have a higher standard of living than countries with low levels of productivity. It is, of course, better for a country to have high productivity, but whether it does or not, free trade policies improve welfare. In other words, a country should invest in education, encourage investment, and try to stimulate technological progress, but these policies should not interfere with free trade between countries.

The danger with a single-minded obsession with competitiveness is that it leads one to think of success as doing better than other countries. But Chapters 4 though 7 suggested that a country should try and maximize productivity growth rather than outperform rivals. Consider the imaginary case in which the French and German economy are both experiencing long-run productivity growth of 2% per year, but the Germans suddenly achieve an increase of 4%. In some sense the French have lost their competitiveness, but what does this mean? France will experience some disutility from this faster German growth rate (individual happiness does depend in part on comparisons with your neighbors, and a much larger German economy would probably affect the role of France in international politics). But in essence nothing has happened to the French standard of living—it is still growing at 2% per year. Further, if the German productivity boost arises from a new technology, then that technology is likely at some point to be transferred to France, which will then experience a similar rise in productivity.

Failure to recognize this distinction between absolute and relative productivities can lead to trade restrictions. Comparative advantage shows that all countries gain from trade, which therefore implies that all countries lose from trade barriers. This reasoning underpins Krugman's statement that competitiveness is a dangerous obsession.

9.7   New Trade Theory

Comparative advantage shows that basing trade policy on the concept of competitiveness makes little sense. Yet popular support for trade restrictions remains strong, and governments continue to subsidize exports and restrict imports. So should we abandon comparative advantage rather than criticize competitiveness?

In recent years researchers have developed models that imply that simply looking for current comparative advantage is not the key to national success. The models in this "new trade theory" vary, but most assume increasing returns to scale and imperfect competition. We have so far taken a passive view of comparative advantage—according to H-O, the resource endowments of a country determine competitive advantage. However, with new trade theory, a country may be able to determine its own comparative advantage. For instance, Switzerland has a comparative advantage in the production of precision engineered luxury watches—an advantage that partly reflects historical accident. At some point in the past, Switzerland had many craftsmen who could produce high-quality watches, so the industry was established in Switzerland. A range of industries then developed nearby to supply components, and an expanding workforce acquired the skills to make watches. Thus Switzerland established a reputation for producing fine watches. The status of the Swiss watch industry reflects a comparative advantage accumulated over many years, an advantage that reputation and know-how have strengthened. This suggests that countries do not need to accept as inevitable their current comparative advantage. Perhaps government policy (e.g., import protection, export subsidy) can develop an industry that will eventually develop into the country's comparative advantage.

Many different types of models make up new trade theory, and in what follows, we outline just one. However, this model illustrates the implications of strategic trade theory compared to (static) comparative advantage.

Consider the aircraft industry, which is characterized by extreme increasing returns to scale—average unit production costs decrease sharply as output increases. Consider the interaction between two firms: the U.S. firm Boeing and the European conglomerate Airbus. This example combines many features: aircraft production involves huge development costs, which explains why the industry has strong increasing returns to scale. The industry is a large and important one—Boeing is the United State's largest exporter. The industry is high tech/high value added and of strategic importance to the United States and Europe. Europe and the United States have continually clashed over whether government support of Boeing and Airbus violates free trade principles.

To develop our model, we utilize tables such as Table 9.7 which is a payoff matrix showing the profits Boeing and Airbus earn in response to different actions by each firm. To keep the analysis simple, we focus on the case in which each firm simply decides whether to enter the market or not. The first number in each cell gives the profits Boeing earns, and the second those Airbus earns.

We treat Boeing and Airbus symmetrically—each gets the same profits if they find themselves in the same circumstances. Table 9.7 shows that if both Boeing and Airbus produce planes, then they each lose $100 million. The reason is that if they share the market, then neither benefits from increasing returns to scale, so costs are high; competition also keeps prices low, and both lose money. However, if Boeing enters but Airbus

TABLE 9.7 Airbus–Boeing Payoff Matrix—No Government Intervention

		Airbus	
		Enter	Don't Enter
Boeing	Enter	−$100mn, −$100mn	$500mn, 0
	Don't Enter	0, $500mn	0, 0

First figure in each cell represents the payoff to Boeing; the second figure is the payoff to Airbus.

does not, then Airbus makes zero profits, and Boeing earns $500 million. Boeing captures the whole market and benefits from increasing returns to scale and a monopoly position. If only Airbus enters the market, it makes $500 million, and Boeing earns zero. Obviously if neither enters the market, they each make zero profit.

The best strategy for each firm depends on what it thinks the other firm will do. If Boeing knows that Airbus is going to enter the market, its best strategy is to withdraw—in this case, it makes zero profit rather than loses $100 million. If, however, it knows that Airbus has no intention of entering the market, then Boeing's best strategy is to enter. The same considerations hold for Airbus. If Boeing is already in the market and is committed to maintaining a presence, Table 9.7 says that Airbus should choose not to enter. Therefore Europe would not have an airplane manufacturing industry and would have to buy planes from an American monopoly provider.

We now show how this model provides different policy implications from those that comparative advantage would indicate. Imagine that Europe decides it needs an airplane manufacturing industry and offers a subsidy to Airbus of $200 million if it produces planes. Table 9.8 gives the payoffs to Boeing and Airbus.

Airbus profits remain unchanged if it does not enter—the subsidy is only paid if Airbus produces. However, if Airbus enters, profits increase by $200 million, the amount of the subsidy. Thus if Boeing enters the market, the subsidy converts the operating loss of $100 million for Airbus into a total profit of $100 million, while if Boeing withdraws from the market, Airbus profits are $700 million (operating profit of $500 million plus the $200 million subsidy). The European subsidy changes the industry; regardless of what Boeing does, Airbus' optimal strategy is to produce planes. Therefore Boeing has to select a strategy by comparing outcomes along the top row of Table 9.8. Given that the subsidy means that Airbus is definitely going to enter the market, Boeing either loses $100 million by producing, or earns zero profits by withdrawing. The best strategy for Boeing is therefore to cease production and leave the market to Airbus. The European subsidy has worked spectacularly. In return for a subsidy of $200 million, Europe gains monopoly profits of $500 million and Europe gains a comparative advantage in an industry perceived as being of strategic economic importance. Moreover, Europe no longer has to buy planes from a foreign monopolist.

This example (based on imperfect competition and increasing returns) makes a focus on competitiveness seem more sensible than a search for comparative advantage. In this model, trade is a zero-sum game—what Airbus captures, Boeing loses. Further, trade protection measures (subsidizing Airbus) increase welfare for Europe contrary to what the static theory of comparative advantage implies. If this model captures important aspects of reality, then free trade policy may not be best, and government interventions in key industries can bring benefits.

TABLE 9.8   Airbus–Boeing Payoff Matrix—European Subsidy $200mn

		Airbus	
		Enter	Don't Enter
Boeing	Enter	−$100mn, $100mn	$500mn, 0
	Don't Enter	0, $700mn	0, 0

TABLE 9.9 Airbus–Boeing Payoff Matrix—United States and European Union Pay $200mn Subsidy

		Airbus	
		Enter	Don't Enter
Boeing	Enter	$100mn, $100mn	$700mn, 0
	Don't Enter	0, $700 mn	0, 0

However, we should not end our account of the model here. By paying a subsidy to Airbus, Europe has captured the market, but the U.S. government is unlikely to remain inactive while its largest exporter ceases production. Table 9.9 shows the payoffs if the United States also pays a $200 million subsidy to Boeing.

The best course of action for Boeing now is to produce no matter what Airbus does. The EU subsidy also means that Airbus' optimal strategy is to produce no matter what Boeing does. Therefore both firms enter the market and the relevant cell is the top left corner of Table 9.9—both firms make profits of $100 million. However, this profit includes the subsidy—each firm has an operating loss of $100 million. Production and cost levels are too high. The U.S. retaliatory action makes the EU intervention no longer advisable. Europe is now paying a subsidy of $200 million so that Airbus can make an operating loss of $100 million. Thus any comparative advantage gains are achieved at a loss to society. In fact only air travelers in other countries gain from the subsidies paid by the United States and Europe. Competition between Airbus and Boeing leads to cheaper airplanes, which in turn leads to cheaper travel. European and American taxpayers overpay for this benefit, but citizens of other countries benefit without having to finance the subsidy.

So does new trade theory support strategic trade policy? We have shown that *under some circumstances* trade can be a zero-sum game and that suitable policy can lead a country to gain a comparative advantage in a key industry. However, the model also suggests many caveats. First, strategic trade policy works only under specific conditions—substantial increasing returns and imperfect competition. Such industries account for only a small part of the economy, and therefore the potential gains from strategic trade policy, even if successfully implemented, are small. Second, the benefits of strategic trade policy depend on how other countries react. Retaliatory responses or trade wars produce losses that outweigh any gains from import restrictions or subsidies. Therefore, new trade theory offers not general prescriptions for trade policy, but insights for specific circumstances.

9.8 Political Economy

Probably the main reason why governments implement trade restrictions stems from political lobbying. The Stolper-Samuelson Theorem says that with free trade some groups in society lose, and others gain. The groups that lose may lobby the government for protection from foreign competition. Whether they succeed depends on how strategically important they are to the government; how forcefully they make their argument; and how strong the arguments of the groups who stand to gain are. Often the group who stands to lose from free trade is a readily identifiable industry that is concentrated in a particular region. Further, although the region may be small relative to the economy, each individual in it stands to lose substantial amounts, e.g., their jobs. By contrast, those who gain may be a large but diverse group each of whose members only benefit slightly from free trade. Consider U.S. tomato producers concerned about cheaper Mexican imports. Millions of U.S. consumers will benefit from cheaper imported tomatoes—but by only a few cents per purchase. By contrast, thousands of workers on U.S. tomato farms will become unemployed and lose their income. Comparative advantage tells us that the combined gains of consumers are greater than the tomato industry's losses. But the many consumers and their small individual gains mean that they will not combine to lobby the government in support of cheap Mexican tomatoes. The tomato industry will lobby vociferously against it. The government will therefore face pressure from an anti-trade lobby but no corresponding support for free trade policies. If the tomato-growing industry is concentrated in a particular region, then the political representatives for that area will be sensitive to the lobbying, as will the government if it is worried about an election. This political economy argument helps explain why governments adopt economic policies that are not economically efficient.

Empirical analysis of industries that are most likely to receive protection from trade pressures in OECD countries shows that they tend to have high levels of employment, high employment/output ratios, a high proportion of unskilled workers, and monopoly power. The adverse distributional implications of free trade, which lead governments to try and protect high-employment, unskilled industries, explain the first three findings. Coordination effects explain the final factor—it is much easier for an industry concentrated around a few firms to finance and coordinate a lobbying effort than for an industry that has many small firms.

9.9   Trade Restrictions in Practice

We now examine what trade restrictions look like in practice and describe the institutions set up to reduce trade barriers. Trade restrictions take many forms. The most obvious is a tariff that levies a charge on imports of certain goods. The charge can be either a fixed rate or a percentage, e.g., $3 a ton or 5% of the value of the goods imported. There are a huge number of tariffs—for instance, the United States has over 8500 different tariffs with rates ranging from 0% to more than 450%. Tariffs must be specified in considerable detail, which means that a lot of time is spent adjudicating whether particular goods are classified as, for instance, sportswear or other apparel or whether toys are counted as dolls or action figures (dolls currently have a 12% tariff; action figures zero).

Another common trade restriction is a quota that allows goods to be imported (normally free of tariffs) until a certain limit (expressed in terms of value or units) has been reached. For instance, Italy used to limit the number of Japanese cars that could be imported from outside the EU to 2200 a year. The EU also imposes a quota on the importation of dolls of nonhuman figures from outside the EU, although it places no such constraint on dolls of human figures.[8] A VER (Voluntary Export Restriction) is a quota under which the exporting country agrees to limit the exports it sells to a country. The Japanese car industry has unilaterally agreed to a VER to U.S. markets for several years. Countries accept a VER to avoid having the importing country set more restrictive anti-trade policies.

Other forms of trade restrictions include Domestic Content Requirements under which a country only accepts imports if a certain proportion of the import has been produced domestically. Countries often reduce tariffs on goods that have a large percentage of domestically produced components. Government procurement policies also frequently favor domestically produced goods. More recently, the imposition of administrative and technical standards have caused considerable tension between countries. For instance, in 1999 France refused to import beef from England on safety grounds that the British government claimed were spurious.

In 1947 the General Agreement on Trades and Tariffs (GATT) was established. This institution sought to provide a forum to reduce multilateral trade restrictions through rounds of trade negotiations. Each round was given a timetable and an agenda, and at the end of the round, countries would agree to accept the results of negotiations. Although GATT had some institutional limitations, it substantially reduced tariffs—as Table 9.10 shows.

To show how GATT worked, we will consider the Uruguay round that began in Montevideo, Uruguay, in 1987 and was scheduled to be completed by 1990. The agenda

TABLE 9.10   Impact of GATT Negotiations on Tariffs

	Average Cut in All Duties (%)	Remaining Duties (% 1930 level)	Number of Participants
Pre-GATT (1934–47)	33.2	66.8	23
First round 1947	21.1	52.7	23
Second round 1949	1.9	51.7	13
Third round 1950–51	3	50.1	38
Fourth round 1955–56	3.5	48.9	26
Dillon round 1961–62	2.4	47.7	26
Kennedy round 1964–67	36	30.5	62
Tokyo round 1974–79	29.6	21.2	99
Uruguay round 1987–94	38	13.1	125

Source: Yarbrough and Yarbrough, *The World Economy* (1997).

[8]Yarborough and Yarborough (*International Economics*, Fort Worth: Dryden Press 1997) discuss some of the absurdities that restrictions produce. Particularly amusing is the case of a firm that could not import Star Trek figures of Mr. Spock even though Captain Kirk could be imported. A legal case decided that even though Mr. Spock had a human mother, his pointed ears meant he had to be classified as a nonhuman figure!

for this round was to extend previous tariff reductions from manufacturing to services and agriculture; to improve the coverage of copyright regulations and intellectual property rights; and to reduce nontariff barriers, which had proliferated when many governments had responded to previous GATT-induced tariff reductions by introducing other forms of restrictions such as quotas.

Negotiations were protracted and the timetable had to be extended to the end of 1993, so the agreement was only signed in 1994. The complexity of trade negotiations, their social importance, and the economic gains from trade liberalization are evident if you examine the details of the Uruguay round. To give only one example among many, consider the importation of rice to Japan. Before the Uruguay round, Japan prohibited the importation of rice unless Japan itself had a poor harvest. As a result, Japanese rice prices were eight times higher than world prices. Considering the importance of rice in the Japanese diet, these trade restrictions imposed a heavy cost on Japanese consumers. As was the case with the EU and its Common Agricultural Policy and with the United States over parts of its agricultural industry, negotiations were difficult. Eventually Japan agreed to allow immediate imports of rice worth 4% of its annual consumption. This import would rise to 8% by the year 2000, when Japan would introduce equivalent tariffs. Equivalent tariffs essentially would make rice imports so expensive that they would only account for 8% of Japanese rice consumption.

At the time of writing, efforts are being made to establish a new round of trade talks with an agenda to reduce tariffs further, to extend trade liberalization to services, to improve intellectual copyrights, and to introduce international standards for environmental issues and employment rights and conditions. However, the first attempt (in Seattle in 1999) to agree on an agenda and a timetable failed, so the round awaits further negotiations.

The Uruguay round also set up the successor to GATT: the World Trade Organization (WTO). The institutional structure of GATT contained two flaws: countries could decide whether or not to agree to any particular round without making any commitment to previous negotiations; and GATT had limited powers to enforce any of its decisions in trade disputes. The WTO attempts to resolve both of these issues. Countries have to apply to belong to the WTO. Membership means that a country must accept the outcome of all previous trade negotiations. It also implies that a country will accept as binding the decisions of the WTO's arbitration courts and committees. Like all international institutions, this raises difficult issues of sovereignty, and the WTO will face many tests of its legitimacy.

The WTO is a global institution that is trying to establish free trade, but many regional trade organizations also exist. These include the European Union (EU), North American Free Trade Association (NAFTA, made up of the United States, Canada, and Mexico), MERCOSUR (Argentina, Brazil, Chile, Paraguay, and Uruguay) and the Asian Pacific Cooperation Forum (APEC), which has 18 members. Progress toward free trade tends to be more rapid within these organizations than in the WTO, but there are tensions between them and the WTO. The WTO is concerned that these organizations often encourage free trade among their members at the expense of restricting free trade with countries that do not belong to the organizations.

SUMMARY

World trade has been increasing at a faster rate than world GDP, so the openness of economies to trade is now at a historical high. Trade is mainly in manufacting goods, although services are becoming more important. Economists' support for free trade is based on the concept of comparative advantage, which says that all countries can benefit from trade if they specialize in goods in which their productive advantage is greatest or their productive inefficiencies are least. The Heckscher-Ohlin model says that countries have a comparative advantage in goods whose production involves the intensive use of a factor that the country possesses in abundance. This prediction accounts for some of the observed patterns of trade, but tariffs and differences in tastes and technology lead to anomalies. The H-O model also fails to account for the substantial amount of intra-industry trade, which requires a model that combines increasing returns with consumers' desire for variety. Even though economic theory clearly shows the advantages of free trade, trade restrictions remain popular. The distributional implications of free trade help explain this support. New trade theories, combining increasing returns and imperfect competition, suggest that under certain circumstances restrictive trade policies can be beneficial. But restrictive trade practices are largely the rational response of governments to lobbying pressures, and they usually come at the cost of economic inefficiency. After World War II GATT and its successor, the WTO, have helped to liberalize trade.

CONCEPTUAL QUESTIONS

1. Review your transactions in the marketplace over the last week. What is your comparative advantage?

2. What is the comparative advantage of your country? Can the Heckscher-Ohlin model explain it?

3. In some OECD countries, agriculture is heavily protected, and governments provide public support at least in part to preserve traditional life styles. What is wrong with using trade restrictions to achieve this aim?

4. The automobile manufacturer VBW is threatening to remove production from your country because productivity in its plants is too low. However, if the government pays a large enough subsidy, the firm will stay. Examine the merits and demerits of such a policy for the firm, government, and consumers.

5. Imagine a reunion in 10 years time with your classmates. Under one scenario you find that although your income rose 50%, everyone else's income rose 100%. Under another scenario, your income fell by 25%, but everyone else's fell by 50%. Which of these scenarios do you prefer? What does this imply about competitiveness?

6. An emerging market wishes to develop a presence in a key high-technology industry. It realizes that it could not possibly compete at the moment with existing firms but believes that if it were sheltered from competition via import restrictions for several years it could compete. (This is the *infant industry* argument for trade restrictions.) What are the likely problems with such an approach?

7. We saw in Chapter 6 that countries that were open to trade showed evidence of convergence. Why do you think that is?

8. Trade between regions of a country is usually much greater than trade between different countries. How far will internationalization make trade between different countries similar to trade between different regions in the same country?

9. In 1999 attempts to achieve an agenda for WTO talks failed. Was it fair for the developed world to seek labor standards on emerging markets?

10. Does popular resentment against free trade simply reflect economic illiteracy or more deep-seated political issues?

ANALYTICAL QUESTIONS

1. In country A it is possible to produce a car with the same resources that would produce 1000 toy cars. In country B to produce a car uses resources that could produce 3000 toy cars. Show with a diagram how both countries can be better off if the international terms of trade between cars and toy cars is 1 car to 2000 toy cars. Suppose the country that is relatively good at making toy cars is poor and feels it cannot waste resources on consuming toy cars. Does this affect your analysis?

2. Consider again the two countries in Question 1. Country A has a per capita GDP 10 times country B. The government of country B decides that concentrating on producing toy cars is harmful because it sees few countries in the rich, developed world that use more resources on building toys than on manufacturing automobiles. It places a 50% tariff on imported automobiles (so that if the world price of an automobile is $10,000 the domestic price will be $15,000). There is no change in world prices as a result of this. What is the impact of the tariff on the structure of domestic production? Is anyone better off? Is anyone worse off?

3. One measure of the "competitiveness" of a country is the price of domestic produced export goods converted into a common currency (say by using the current exchange rate of the country against the dollar) compared with the price of similar goods produced in other countries, also expressed in dollars. In contrast, the terms of trade of a country are the relative prices of the goods it exports to price of goods it imports. What might you expect to be the correlation between movements in competitiveness and movements in the terms of trade? Which of the two is a better guide to the welfare of a country?

4. A small industrialized country initially has no trading links with a large, but closed, centrally planned economy that shares a border. Wages per hour for skilled and unskilled workers are $25 and $12, respectively, in the industrialized economy. The centrally planned economy suddenly undergoes a peaceful revolution and the border with its industrial neighbor is completely opened to trade. In the former centrally planned economy skilled workers get paid $5 an hour and unskilled workers get paid $2 an hour. Productivity in the former centrally planned economy is one-fifth that of the industrial country in all sectors and for all workers. What would factor price equalization imply happens to wages in the industrial country?

5. Suppose that the technology used in street cleaning is similar across countries that have very different standards of living. Assume that in a developed country street cleaner wages are $15,000 a year; in a developing country they are $150 a year. How can this position persist if we assume productivity is roughly equal in street cleaning? What are you assuming about the migration of workers in your answer?

6. A rare and exotic dish is popular in only one country in the world. The key ingredient is the decomposing leaves from a type of tree that is common in only one other country and the leaf has little commercial use there. Could it make sense for the country where the dish is popular to impose a tariff on imports of the leaf? Could it make sense for the government of the country where the tree grows to levy a large tax on export revenues from the leaf?

CHAPTER 10

The Role of Government

Overview

In this chapter we consider the role of government and we ask why government spending varies across countries. We analyze the rationale behind government intervention and the public provision of services and consider empirical evidence on government activities in different countries. We then discuss the implications of the size of government on taxation and how it distorts resource allocation. Contemporary governments redistribute resources—largely through transfer payments and by linking tax payments to household income. We focus on this role, especially the provision of insurance by the public sector. We examine whether current government provision of insurance is sustainable in light of predicted demographic change. Finally we discuss the empirical evidence for the link between the size of the public sector and long-run economic growth.

10.1 Government Spending

By the end of the twentieth century, governments in industrialized, market economies were playing a greater role in the economy than ever before. Figure 10.1 shows the level of general government spending relative to gross domestic product (GDP) in 1998 across the major developed countries. This wide measure of the influence of government on the economy includes spending on goods and services and so-called transfer payments, e.g., benefits to the unemployed, the retired, and the poor. The range of public sector spending programs is wide.

Figure 10.1 shows that the size of the public sector varies considerably across OECD countries. For instance, in Sweden during the 1990s government spending accounted for around 60% of GDP, while in the United States it was around 30%. Some things that governments do are both essential and could not be done by the private sector—it is hard to see how anyone but the government could be responsible for the legal system, the police force, and national defense. Some things that governments do in many countries are essential, but the private sector could do them. For example, in many countries, public sector health and education services comprise much of total spending, but the private sector could provide these services. And some government activities need not be done, and until relatively recently, were not. For example, in most developed countries, governments provide various kinds of social security (unemployment and sickness benefits, old age pensions). This kind of social welfare provision, or social insurance, is a relatively recent phenomenon, but one that accounts for much of the rise in the role of government in market economies.

Not surprisingly, variability in the tax taken out of total incomes mirrors variations in the scale of government spending. Figure 10.2 shows the ratio between tax receipts by central governments and total GDP in 1998. If there were no corresponding differences in tax revenues, government debt would increase indefinitely in countries with a large public sector.

While government spending varies among countries, the public sector expanded in most countries during the twentieth century. Table 10.1 shows the share of government spending in GDP for 14 industrialized nations since the second half of the nineteenth century. In 1870 government spending as a percent of GDP averaged about 8% across these economies. Just after the end of the First World War, expenditure had, on average, almost doubled to over 15% of GDP. By 1960 the average proportion of total spending that government accounted for had risen to almost 30% of GDP. Since then, expenditure has steadily increased in most countries, so that on average the public sector now accounts for over 40% of GDP in developed countries.

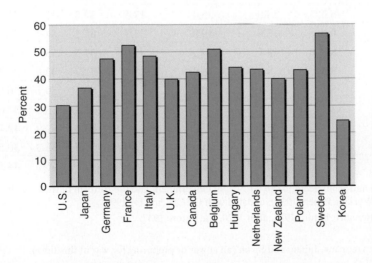

FIGURE 10.1 **General government spending (% GDP, 1998).** The size of government varies across countries, but in all developed economies the state plays a major role in economic life. *Source*: OECD Economic Outlook, 2000. Copyright OECD.

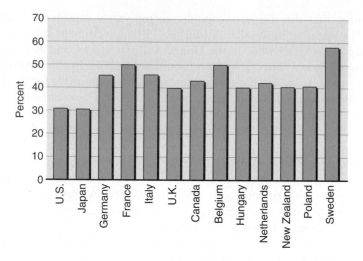

FIGURE 10.2 **General government current receipts (%GDP 1998).** Tax receipts as a proportion of GDP, and therefore average tax rates, broadly reflect the scale of government spending. *Source*: OECD, Economic Outlook. Copyright OECD.

TABLE 10.1   **The Increasing Share of Government Expenditure, 1870–1998 (in percent of GDP)**

	Later 19th century (about 1870)[a]	Pre-World War I (about 1913)[a]	Post-World War I (about 1920)[a]	Pre-World War II (about 1937)[a]	Post-World War II (1940)	1980	1990	1998
Austria	—	—	14.7	15.2	35.7	48.1	48.6	49.7
Belgium	—	—	—	21.8	30.3	58.6	54.8	50.8
Canada	—	—	13.3	18.6	28.6	38.8	46.0	42.6
France	12.6	17.0	27.6	29.0	34.6	46.1	49.8	52.4
Germany	10.0	14.8	25.0	42.4	32.4	47.9	45.1	47.3
Italy	11.9	11.1	22.5	24.5	30.1	41.9	53.2	48.6
Japan	8.8	8.3	14.8	25.4	17.5	32.0	31.7	36.9
Netherlands	9.1	9.0	13.5	19.0	33.7	55.2	54.0	43.5
Norway	3.7	8.3	13.7	—	29.9	37.5	53.8	46.4
Spain	—	8.3	9.3	18.4	18.8	32.2	42.0	39.4
Sweden	5.7	6.3	8.1	10.4	31.0	60.1	59.1	56.6
Switzerland	—	12.7	4.6	6.1	17.3	32.8	33.5	37.6[b]
United Kingdom	9.4	12.7	26.2	30.0	32.2	43.0	39.9	40.1
USA	3.9	1.8	7.0	8.6	27.0	31.8	33.3	30.5
Average	8.3	9.1	15.4	18.3[c]	28.5	43.3	46.1	44.5

Source: Data are from Tanzi and Schuknecht, "The Growth of Government and the Reform of the State in Industrial Countries," IMF Working Paper (1995); updated with OECD data for 1998.

[a]Or nearest available year after 1870, before 1913, after 1920, and before 1937.

[b]1992

[c]Average; computed without Germany, Japan, and Spain (all at war or preparing for war at this time).

Much of the rise in government spending reflects growing government consumption; that is, government spending on wages (of civil servants, soldiers, police, and so on) and on materials and supplies that public sector workers use (e.g., office supplies, arms, fuel, and electricity). This part of government spending absorbs or *directly* uses economic resources, but it excludes investment (e.g., road building). The evolution of government consumption from the nineteenth century to the Second World War roughly mirrors the rise in overall spending. But since 1939 spending has outpaced direct government consumption. Now, on average, less than one half of government spending in developed countries is consumption. The majority of government spending in developed countries now involves transfers; that is, various cash benefits, pensions, unemployment benefits, disability payments, and so on. Unlike government consumption or investment, transfer payments involve the government spending money but without receiving any economic goods or services in exchange. Since the eve of the Second World War, this kind of transfer has been responsible for most of the growth of the government sector in developed countries. Across the seven developed countries for which reliable data are available, transfer payments relative to GDP averaged just under 4% in 1937. That figure had grown to over 15% by the end of the 1990s. Figure 10.3 shows the level of social benefits relative to GDP in 1998.

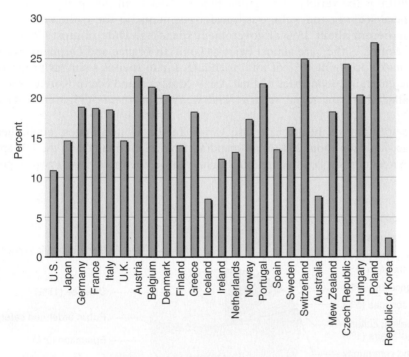

FIGURE 10.3   **Social benefits as % GDP, 1998.** There is a huge variability in spending on social benefits—in the United States they represent about 10% of GDP, while in many European countries they are about twice as large relative to national income. *Source*: OECD, Economic Outlook. Copyright OECD.

TABLE 10.2   Government Spending in Major Economics, 1998 (% of GDP)

	Goods and Services	Social Security	Debt Interest	Total
Italy	18.1	17.1	8.0	48.6
France	23.6	17.9	3.6	52.4
Canada	22.6	12.6	8.4	42.6
Germany	19.0	18.6	3.6	47.3
UK	18.3	13.9	3.4	40.1
USA	14.4	11	4.2	30.5
Japan	10.1	14.5	3.8	36.9

Source: OECD Economic Outlook 2000. Copyright OECD.

While there has been a common trend over the past century for the role of government to expand, the extent of this role still varies among countries. Table 10.2 gives a broad breakdown of spending across the big seven economies for 1998, while Figure 10.4 shows a more detailed picture of how a more diverse sample of countries allocates spending. The first point to note about the figures that show the allocation of expenditure is the variety of programs funded. Nearly all the spending under the heading social security and welfare is transfer payments. In the United States, such transfers represent about 25% of government spending, while in most Continental European countries they are almost twice as large. In France and Germany, welfare payments make up about 40% of total spending. Japan spends a similar proportion. Two of the emerging economies of East Asia—Malaysia and South Korea—spend a much smaller share on social security and welfare payments (Figures 10.4*g* and 10.4*h*).

Public spending on health care also varies. In the United States, public health spending accounts for about 20% of all spending. France, Germany, and the UK spend a smaller percentage on health care; but because those countries have a bigger public

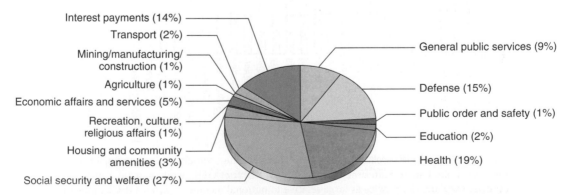

FIGURE 10.4a   **U.S. government expenditure, 1998.** Courtesy of IMF.

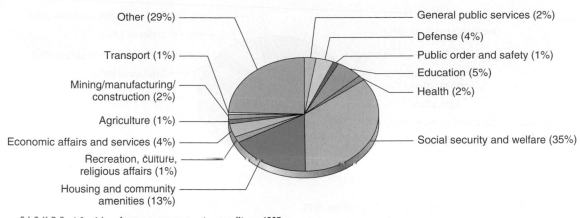

Other (29%)

General public services (2%)

Transport (1%)

Defense (4%)

Public order and safety (1%)

Mining/manufacturing/
construction (2%)

Education (5%)

Agriculture (1%)

Health (2%)

Economic affairs and services (4%)

Social security and welfare (35%)

Recreation, culture,
religious affairs (1%)

Housing and community
amenities (13%)

FIGURE 10.4b   Japanese government expenditure, 1993.

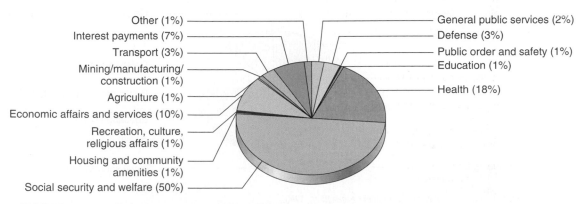

Other (1%)

General public services (2%)

Interest payments (7%)

Defense (3%)

Transport (3%)

Public order and safety (1%)

Mining/manufacturing/
construction (1%)

Education (1%)

Agriculture (1%)

Health (18%)

Economic affairs and services (10%)

Recreation, culture,
religious affairs (1%)

Housing and community
amenities (1%)

Social security and welfare (50%)

FIGURE 10.4c   German government expenditure, 1996.

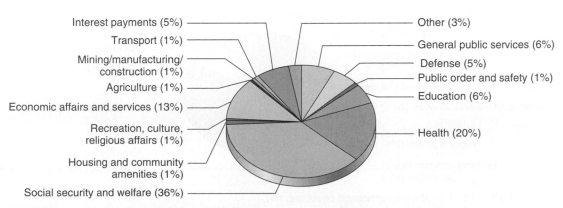

Interest payments (5%)

Other (3%)

Transport (1%)

General public services (6%)

Mining/manufacturing/
construction (1%)

Defense (5%)

Public order and safety (1%)

Agriculture (1%)

Education (6%)

Economic affairs and services (13%)

Recreation, culture,
religious affairs (1%)

Health (20%)

Housing and community
amenities (1%)

Social security and welfare (36%)

FIGURE 10.4d   French government expenditure, 1993.

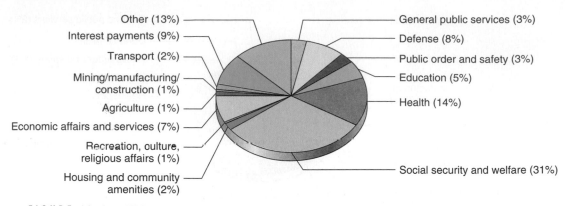

FIGURE 10.4e   **UK Government Expenditure, 1995.**

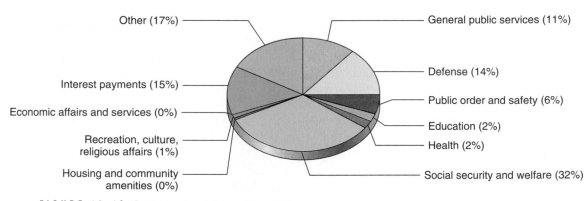

FIGURE 10.4f   **Russian government expenditure, 1995.**

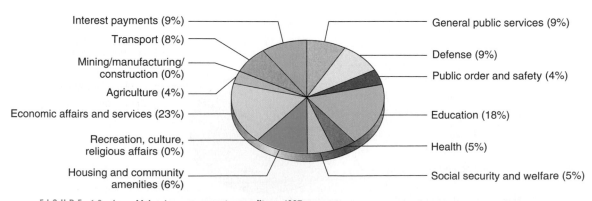

FIGURE 10.4g   **Malaysian government expenditure, 1997.**

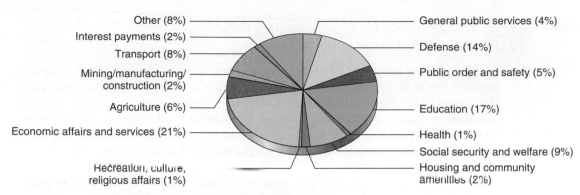

Other (8%)
Interest payments (2%)
Transport (8%)
Mining/manufacturing/ construction (2%)
Agriculture (6%)
Economic affairs and services (21%)
Recreation, culture, religious affairs (1%)

General public services (4%)
Defense (14%)
Public order and safety (5%)
Education (17%)
Health (1%)
Social security and welfare (9%)
Housing and community amenities (2%)

FIGURE 10.4h   **South Korean government expenditure, 1997.** Data for Figures 10.4a–h from IMF Government Finance Statistics Yearbook, 1998.

sector, overall government spending on health care as a proportion of GDP is comparable. However, in Japan, Malaysia, and South Korea, government spending on health care is a much smaller proportion of total national income.

Defense spending also differs significantly across countries. Both the United States and Russia allocate about 15% of all their spending to defense, and South Korea spends only slightly less. In Japan and Germany spending is much lower—largely as a legacy of the Second World War.

We have not distinguished in the figures between investment expenditure and current consumption. Although most governments do give some breakdown into capital and current expenditure, this does not correspond to the economic distinction between investment and consumption. This classification issue is acute for the public sector because governments call much of what they spend on goods and services "current expenditure" (which is often interpreted as consumption) when it is more like investment. Education expenditure helps enhance, or at least preserve, the national stock of human capital. The largest element of this expenditure is wages, but governments generally count them as current expenditure. We could make the same point about health expenditure. Firms count their expenditure to cover the depreciation of physical investment as investment; government health spending is, by analogy, a form of investment to cover depreciation of the national stock of human capital.[1]

These figures show that governments in all developed economies play a major role in the economy and that the range of government programs is wide. Why is this? In the next few sections, we discuss the rationale behind government spending on goods and services and in particular why transfer payments have grown.

---

[1]Of course, these issues also affect the classification of private sector spending into consumption and investment, but to a lesser extent.

10.2 The Rationale for Government's Role and the Failure of the Invisible Hand

The political economist Adam Smith had a truly profound insight. The free operation of forces in decentralized markets would lead not to chaos but to order—resources would tend to be allocated to produce goods that society valued most. He likened the operation of these forces to the workings of an invisible hand. Smith argued that market mechanisms coordinate the actions of companies and households—all serving their own self-interest— to produce things that people want *and* in the right quantities. It was as if some giant benevolent hand were guiding and coordinating the millions of economic decisions made each day. But market outcomes would only be efficient under certain circumstances: when agents understand the nature of the goods that are being offered for sale, when those agents behave rationally, when goods are produced under competitive conditions (i.e., no monopolies), and when all commodities that have value are offered for sale (i.e., when markets are "complete"), then the free operation of markets efficiently allocates resources. Efficiency here has a special, and unusual, meaning. The allocation of resources is efficient if a reallocation of resources (perhaps as a result of government intervention) is unable to make anyone better off without making someone worse off. We call such a situation *Pareto efficient* (named after the Italian economist Vilfredo Pareto (1848–1923)).

The idea that market forces encourage the efficient use of resources is immensely powerful. There is also a simple intuition behind it: free markets tend to be efficient in this sense because if they were not, then profitable opportunities would not be exploited. But to operate this invisible hand requires demanding conditions. And even if those conditions exist, the resulting allocation of resources could be hugely unequal and unsustainable in a society in which citizens vote and governments respond to majority opinion.

Smith himself was aware that the conditions needed for *laissez-faire* (or totally unregulated) capitalism to work well might not hold and that because of this government intervention *could* generate more desirable outcomes. Free markets might not produce certain goods that are desirable because it would be difficult to make people pay for them—some of these are so-called **public goods**; others are goods for which there are **missing markets**. People might not fully take account of the consequences of producing and consuming certain goods; irrationality can make free market outcomes suboptimal and justify a **paternalistic** role for government. Finally, free market outcomes may generate an **undesirable distribution of income**. We will now consider the significance of these phenomena—we might call them market imperfections—and what they imply about the role of government.

PUBLIC GOODS

Even at the height of laissez-faire capitalism in the mid nineteenth century, people recognized that the state had to take responsibility for providing some things. These so-called "night watchmen" duties of the state were largely concerned with ensuring law and order: the legal system (crucial to the functioning of any market economy based on exchange and property rights), policing, and national defense. A secure system of national defense and a well-functioning legal system are goods in much the same way that having a telephone is a good. But these goods are *nonexcludable*—it is hard to exclude any citizen from enjoying their benefits. If I live in a country in which crime is low, the legal system fair, and the borders secure, then I benefit even if I make no contribution to paying for the police force, the army, and the law courts. *My* consumption of these benefits, which are safe streets and peace of mind about the threat of invasion or arbitrary imprisonment, does not affect the cost of providing these services. We call goods that have this characteristic *public goods*.

The problem with public goods is that you cannot easily sell access to them: how can you get *individuals* to pay voluntarily for an army? People who live in the country benefit from the army whether they pay or not. So rational and nonaltruistic people would not pay for the service and instead hope to get a free ride from the contributions of others. But if everyone does this, the market will not provide an army.

When the cost of providing commodities or services to another person is close to zero at the margin and the benefits of providing them cannot easily be blocked, it is hard for commercial enterprises to produce them. It is the difficulty of preventing people from enjoying the benefits of these goods that makes providing them in a market problematic.

Moreover, markets for most standard (nonpublic) goods would not operate well unless some of these public goods were provided. Consider the importance of a police and legal system that is administered fairly and without corruption. This system is essential to the efficient running of an economy (see Chapter 4). We can see this most vividly by looking at cases in which respect for the law has broken down; such situations make the rewards of trying to expropriate the goods of others high and the benefits of actually producing goods (which are likely to be stolen) low. It is worth considering the costs of such situations and how they can trap standards of living at low levels. To do so, we introduce the notion of a Nash equilibrium.

PUBLIC GOODS AND NASTY NASH EQUILIBRIA

Most people who have read Joseph Heller's *Catch-22* remember the catch: if you were crazy, you could be declared unfit to fly dangerous bombing raids; but claiming insanity to avoid flying is the act of a sane man. In one of the scenes in the novel, a character is discovered committing a selfish act that could endanger others and is asked, "What if everyone did that?" After some thought, he answers, "Then I'd be a fool not to." Economists will instantly recognize a Nash equilibrium here (after the mathematical economist and Nobel prizewinner John Nash). A Nash equilibrium is a situation in which, given everyone else's behavior, each person is acting in a way that is individually rational. The example from *Catch-22* suggests that such equilibria may not be pleasant places within which to get trapped.

In a nasty equilibrium, cheating, breaking conventions, or stepping outside the law are individually advantageous, though collectively costly. Laws and social conventions can prevent societies from being trapped in bad equilibria in which standards of living are low. It is useful that a convention forbids standing on your seat at a football game to get a better view—though doing so would be rational if people around you did it, even though it would be collectively self-defeating.

The football example is trivial; but the strength of social institutions (laws, conventions, how rules are enforced and changed) in preventing inefficient equilibria may help explain the massive differences in wealth and income across countries. As we saw in Chapters 4 and 7, the differences in output across countries are far more pronounced than the differences in capital stocks employed. Total factor productivity, in which social institutions and culture play key roles, is hugely important in explaining income differences.

So one of the primary roles of government is to try, in part through the legal and police systems, to reduce corruption, theft, and disrespect for the law. The World Bank tries to reduce corruption, particularly in developing countries, because it sees how corruption can damage economic growth and standards of living.

PATERNALISM AND THE DISTRIBUTION OF INCOME: THE RATIONALE FOR THE WELFARE STATE

Many public goods (e.g., law and order, absence of corruption) are essential—the operation of markets cannot supply them. But Figure 10.4 shows that only a small part of government spending today represents the provision of public goods. In the developed countries, the emerging economies, and in the formerly centrally planned economy of Russia, spending on defense, public order, safety, and general public services does not exceed 25% of all spending and is often lower. But until the middle of the nineteenth century governments' almost exclusive role in the economy was to provide public goods. Starting in Bismarck's Germany, in the 1880s, governments in many countries began to provide social insurance, which almost always involved redistributing income among agents. In 1870 across the industrialized market economies, average spending on transfers was less than 1% of GDP. By the 1990s it was almost 20% of GDP.

Governments have come to play a bigger role here for many reasons. The first is a paternalistic one, reflecting the belief that left to themselves many people will not act in their own longer-term economic interests. For example, people may not perceive how education can benefit their future incomes, and if left to themselves, they would "underconsume" education. So governments subsidize education in most countries and force people to consume it by requiring that they stay in school until a certain age. People might also consume too much today and save too little for their old age—a decision that they might later bitterly regret. To protect people, governments in many countries force them to contribute to pension systems. And people might also fail to see the full benefits of health care, both for themselves and others, so governments subsidize health services.

These paternalistic arguments for the public sector's providing some goods, and for the compulsory consumption of others, are partly behind the growth of the welfare state in many countries. The spending patterns in Figure 10.4 show that all governments spend heavily on health and education, for example. Concern about the distribution of income is another reason for government involvement in the economy. The distribution of income that might arise from free market outcomes may be undesirable for many reasons. One may be that a majority of the population simply finds it ethically unacceptable that many of their fellow citizens should live in poverty. Another reason may be that risk-averse individuals, fearing the consequences of bad luck, bad genes, or bad schools, may want the state to offer them insurance against misfortune in their later lives. This can be a powerful but not altruistic force.

A third factor may also be important. You may not care that other people live in poverty or fear the risks of becoming poor yourself, but you may not like how other people's poverty affects you. Crime, delinquency, and disease are likely to be worse if a large economic underclass has poor economic prospects, bad schooling, and inadequate health care. The worse these problems are, the lower the quality of life for people in general—not just for those in poverty.

Note the distinction between the state offering insurance against uncertain and bad outcomes and the state redistributing resources to the less well off when outcomes are not uncertain, but people are predictably and persistently poor. This is the important distinction between providing insurance and engineering redistribution.

Even if you accept the case for insurance (against illness, unemployment, and so on) and for redistribution, you can still question whether governments should insure people against life's risks and redistribute incomes, rather than have society rely on private charity. Market failures—when the invisible hand result does not hold—provide one set of arguments for the state's role. These arguments are particularly relevant in the case of risk.

MISSING MARKETS, MARKET FAILURE, AND THE VALUE OF INSURANCE

> *The important thing for government is not to do things which individuals are doing already, and to do them a little better or a little worse: but to do things which at present are not done at all.*
>
> —J. M. Keynes "The End of Laissez-Faire" (1937)

Individuals are generally risk averse and value insurance against illness, unemployment, low income, and so forth. Most government transfer payments represent flows of income toward those who have poor health, low wages, or no job. We have seen that these transfer payments have grown in most market economies. But why can't the market provide these forms of insurance? To some extent, of course, it can. People buy medical insurance in many countries. But the market has problems providing various forms of insurance. Consider insurance against low incomes. In this market, problems of *moral hazard* are severe. If I have taken out insurance against my annual salary falling below $100,000, then I may not work quite as hard. If I have to work hard to keep my salary above $100,000 *and I have full insurance against my income falling below that level*, then why not work less hard? Of course, if everyone did that, then insurance companies would not offer that sort of insurance. This is the problem of moral hazard in insurance markets.

Moral hazard probably affects commercial insurance for a range of risks and is why most auto insurance policies make you pay for the first $100 or so of damage. As a result, demand may exist for many forms of insurance that the market mechanism cannot supply. Consider, for example, risks that hit a whole generation of people in a country—such as a war or the temporary collapse in the price of a crucial raw material. If people could enter into risk-sharing agreements with later generations, then everyone (including the unborn!) might be better off. But it is hard to see how in a free market a commercial company could ever credibly offer an insurance contract in which people not yet born agreed to pay out to the current generation if it were hit by an adverse shock. Governments, however, can enforce these kinds of contracts. Pay as you go pension (PAYGO) schemes, for example, have some features of this type of contract. In a PAYGO pension system, contributions from current workers finance the pensions paid to the current generation of the retired. This is a form of intergenerational transfer. If the current generation of workers are working when productivity is growing, and wages are high, then the retired will share those benefits if their pensions are linked to revenues that come from current labor incomes.

Governments can also insure workers because governments need not balance the books on PAYGO pension systems. If wages temporarily fall, governments might decide to honor their promise to earlier generations by still paying pensions but not increasing the rate of contribution that current workers pay. Thus the contributions that current workers make would not be fully financing pensions. The pension system would generate a deficit that could be paid off over time as wages for future generations rose toward some longer-run equilibrium. Therefore governments can redistribute resources between generations in ways that private insurance companies cannot. What the private insurance company cannot do, and what governments can, is force future generations to transfer resources to people alive today. Governments do it by taxing the unborn: for example, when people are born into a society whose government has accumulated a large debt. But no private company can force people not yet alive to pay when they are born and start to work for benefits paid out to people who are alive today.

Of course, governments can only do this up to a point. Unless governments can stop people from leaving a country, then individuals born into economies where the burden of debt from past generations, and consequently levels of taxation, are extremely high may just up and leave. (We will return to these important issues in due course.) The costs of raising the revenues, via taxation, to pay for the insurance government welfare programs offer must be set against the benefits of providing the insurance. Such costs can be high and we will consider them in section 10.5 of this chapter. But because many types of uncertainty are harmful, the benefits of providing insurance that commercial firms cannot provide can also be large.

There are many sources of uncertainty in people's lives. One useful way to categorize them is into those that most people would rather do without (and might pay to avoid) and those that make life more interesting or richer. Sport has uncertain outcomes; without that uncertainty most games would be mere displays of physical virtuosity. And some uncertainty about your love life, or about how good that restaurant or film will be is also attractive.

Most people want less uncertainty against fire or theft. To avoid the consequences of these events, people buy insurance, and markets allow companies to sell these types of risk. Insurance companies can work out what the odds of having to pay out are; with enough customers they can be confident that they will have the resources to deal with claims and still make a profit.

But as noted above, people cannot insure themselves against some of the most important and unpleasant risks they face, and this has important implications for the role of the state. Consider uncertainty over future income from employment. It is hard to insure against a prolonged downturn in your future earnings. You can buy (at high cost) insurance against an illness that prevents you from working for a time; and you can buy insurance to pay your mortgage if you become unemployed. But periodic unemployment or illness are only a part of labor income uncertainty. More important—especially for young people—are the risks that you go into the wrong career; join a firm that is about to go bankrupt; or fail the exams that would have set you off on the fast track.

The kind of insurance contract you might find tempting at the start of adult life would promise to give you the income that someone with your characteristics could, on average, expect over his or her working life; if your actual earnings (as a result of misfortunes) turned out to be much below the average, you would receive payouts from the policy, if you do spectacularly well, you pay the insurance company the excess. Now this contract is excellent in some ways—it removes income uncertainty—but hopeless in others. Why should you put in lots of effort at work, when the insurance company will take the extra income? Why should you to go to work at all, when the insurance contract compensates you if earnings are below average? Only if the insurance company can compel you to work as hard as you would without the policy could this kind of contract work. But since slavery is outlawed, the insurance company cannot enforce this contract.

This absence of a decent market for insurance against income risks is a form of market failure or incompleteness. And it has profound consequences. Income from labor makes up between 60% and 80% of the total value of production in most developed countries; this implies that the value of human capital (the earnings power people embody) is probably three to four times as large as the value of other physical assets (machines, factories, cars, houses, etc.). Financial markets let people insure physical assets (houses and cars), but these assets are less important than human wealth, which is largely uninsurable.

It is therefore crucial to understand exactly what private markets can and cannot do; private firms may be able to do many things more efficiently than the public sector—but it is a bad mistake to believe that this is a universal truth.

10.3 The Impact of Government Provision on Behavior

When governments make transfer payments—whether for insurance or redistribution—they affect behavior. For example, unemployment and sickness benefits may induce risk-averse people to save less. Unfunded state pension systems where contributions are compulsory also tend to reduce private sector saving. People are less likely to save a lot for their retirement if they expect to receive a state pension. And by definition a PAYGO system does not accumulate a stock of public wealth, so there is no stock of public assets to compensate for lower private sector savings. Consequently, national savings may be lower the more generous are unfunded state pensions. Government social welfare programs are also likely to affect labor supply. As we saw in Chapter 8 the generosity of unemployment benefits affects labor supply decisions and the natural rate of unemployment.

Therefore it is easy to think that government welfare provision adversely affects incentives and economic activity. On this view, there is inevitably a tradeoff between the benefits of a "better" (which often means more equal) distribution of resources and the costs of having fewer overall resources because of the adverse impact of dulled economic incentives. But that view is too simplistic. It implies that government welfare programs (including state subsidized health and education spending) generate a more equal distribution of resources. This is far from self-evident. Many transfers are likely to be transfers of resources over an individual's own life cycle: people may pay most taxes and may also have to contribute to PAYGO pensions when they are working and then receive more health care and state pensions toward the end of their lives. Such life-cycle transfers do not necessarily make the distribution of income more equal (though they may, nonetheless, be beneficial). Furthermore, some government programs may benefit the relatively well-off—subsidies to higher education, for example.

Nonetheless, government taxing and spending, overall, typically generate net redistribution to the less well-off. There is an inverse correlation within the developed countries between the size of the government sector and the inequality of incomes and wealth. Yet the view that there is an inescapable tradeoff between equality and efficiency in production ignores the ability of many government welfare programs to enhance efficiency. This is a point worth considering in more detail.

GOVERNMENT PROGRAMS AND RISK TAKING

The United States is often thought of as a country in which people are prepared to take economic risks; without risk-takers capitalism is unlikely to work well, so—the story goes—the most successful economy in the world is naturally one in which the entrepreneurial spirit burns especially bright. But just how bright is that? Recent research throws fascinating light on how much economic risk people in the United States find acceptable. It also sheds light on the value of forms of social insurance and fiscal redistribution that cushion people against such risks. In other words, it tells us a lot about the appropriate size of government and the kind of government programs that are likely to be popular.

First the results. In 1995 economists surveyed the attitudes to risk of over 11,000 U.S. adults.[2] The key question they asked was:

> *Suppose that you are the only income earner in the family, and you have a good job guaranteed to give you your current income every year for life. You are given the opportunity to take a new and equally good job, with a 50–50 chance that it will double your income and a 50–50 chance that it will cut your income by a third. Would you take the new job?*

Note that on average a move to this new job would increase your income for the rest of your working life by 33%. You might think that this looks like a pretty good gamble. If you did, you would be in the minority in the United States. Over 75% of the sample said they would *reject* this opportunity. Even when the downside risk was reduced to at

---

[2]Barsky, Kimball, Juster, and Shapiro, "Preference Parameters and Behavioral Heterogeneity: An Experimental Approach in the Health and Retirement Survey," *Quarterly Journal of Economics* (May 1997) vol. 112, pp. 537–579.

TABLE 10.3   Proportion of U.S. Individuals in Each Group Rejecting the Move to a Risky, But Probably Much More Productive, Job (50-50 chance of doubling income and 50-50 chance of cutting income by one-third)

All	Males	Females	Protestant	Catholic	Jewish	Other
76.2%	75.2%	76.9%	76.2%	73.1%	69.5%	75.9%

Source: Robert B. Barsky, F. Thomas Juster, Miles S. Kimball, and Matthew D. Shapiro, "Preference Parameters and Behavioral Heterogeneity: An Experimental Approach to the Health and Retire Survey," *Quarterly Journal of Economics* (May 1997), 112: 537–579. © 1997 by the President and Fellows of Harvard College and the Massachusetts Institute of Technology.

most a 20% fall in income, but the chance to double income remained the same, about two-thirds of the sample rejected the offer. As Table 10.3 shows, there was more of a difference among people of different religions to this question than there was between men and women.

Now if people are this risk averse, the value of the social insurance that welfare systems and the redistribution of income through taxation will be potentially large. Commentators on welfare and taxation often ignore this point. The more common view is that the welfare system and redistributive taxation generate economic costs, in terms of diminished incentives, but that there is still a strong moral case for helping the worst off. There is then a tradeoff between economic efficiency and helping the disadvantaged.

Clearly there are lots of things right in this view—high taxation and benefits that make working unattractive to many entail efficiency costs, and society should help the least well off. So in certain cases, the tradeoff view is reasonable. But by implying an inevitable tradeoff between economic efficiency and helping the disadvantaged, it ignores powerful mechanisms that work the other way; *some* aspects of welfare and taxation may encourage productivity and increase national output.

Consider what the results of the above research suggest about people's attitudes to more education or training for a specific job. Spending time and money on more education or specialized training probably generates a high expected (or average) return for most people, but it is risky; there may be no job at the end of the training, or the exams may be too hard. Given high risk aversion, the option of a lower paid, but safe, job may seem preferable. From a social view this could be undesirable; if the returns to more training are as high as in the survey question and if the risks for individuals even out in aggregate, then the case for encouraging people to risk investing in themselves becomes strong. Two obvious ways to encourage such risk taking are to subsidize education and to use income support and unemployment benefits to reduce the risk that people may not be able to find a job after their training.

The free market counter to all this is simple: while risk aversion means that insurance is valuable, it does not imply that the state should provide that insurance. In principle this is a good reply, but in practice in those areas in which the effects of risk are likely to be greatest commercial companies may not provide insurance. As we noted before, private insurance markets cannot be expected to work well when insurers cannot know what a person's risks are or how hard people are trying to avoid them. Remember the training examples; would you expect insurance companies to insure against failing exams or against future unemployment? Probably not, because the people who might buy such insurance would not be a random sample of students but predominantly those who either know they may have problems or are not prepared to work to avoid them. Universal government-provided insurance—financed through taxation—cuts through this problem, although it cannot avoid the ensuing moral hazard. In other words, governments may be able to make up for the absence of some markets.

10.4   Taxation and Efficiency

We cannot answer questions about the appropriate size of government simply by focusing on the merits of different spending programs or the relative efficiency with which the private and public sectors provide services. How public spending is financed is also relevant. If government chooses to finance its spending mainly out of taxation, then we must take the economic costs of raising revenue into account when considering the optimal size of government.

We need to be precise about what we mean by the economic costs of raising revenue. We do *not* mean simply how much revenue the government actually raises. There is no efficiency loss, *per se*, from raising the $500 million needed to build a new road by taxing people as opposed to charging fees for using the road. The costs of using one strategy or the other have to do with how particular revenue-raising schemes distort behavior. The invisible hand result is that when markets are complete and competitive the allocation of resources is efficient—prices signal to firms and workers the value that is placed upon the goods and services that the markets provide. Taxes drive a wedge—or create a gap—between what sellers receive for supplying goods and services and the prices buyers pay. This can mean that highly valued activities will be underprovided if suppliers only receive a fraction of the value created. If labor income is taxed at 50%, workers only receive one-half of the price that buyers of labor pay; this is likely to affect labor supply. The higher taxes are—either direct taxes on labor incomes and profits or indirect taxes on the sale of goods—the more they will affect demand and supply decisions.

So the real cost of raising revenue through taxation is to distort patterns of spending and labor supply, savings behavior, or other aspects of economic activity. Virtually any form of tax alters economic behavior. Taxes on labor income are likely to influence people's choice of jobs, the number of hours they work, how hard they try to earn a bonus, or how much costly training and education they undertake. Taxes on corporate profits are likely to affect the investment that companies undertake. Social security contributions levied either on workers or firms will affect the cost of labor and the benefits of work and thus will tend to affect levels of employment, as in Chapter 8. Taxes on wealth and property influence people's incentives to save and accumulate that saving. Taxes on consumption (indirect taxes) affect both the distribution of spending across commodities (because governments may tax commodities in different ways) and the supply of labor, because indirect taxes reduce the real spending power of wages.

TAXATION AND EFFICIENCY

We can measure the costs of the distortions arising from taxes by thinking about how taxes affect the demand and supply for the taxed good. For taxes on earned income, the relevant good is labor. In Figure 10.5, the demand curve shows how many hours of work are demanded at different wages. Labor should be demanded up to the point at which the value of the extra output produced—which is the marginal productivity of labor (MPL)—equals the wage (see Chapter 8 for a full analysis). We can assume that the more hours worked—with a given amount of machines, computers, land, and so on—the lower, eventually, marginal productivity will be. So in Figure 10.5 we show a downward-sloping demand for labor. Because productivity declines with hours, the wage must fall if employers are going to buy more hours of labor. The supply of labor schedule reflects the value people place upon the time they give up when they work one more hour. We can assume that beyond some point people value the leisure they have to give up to work more at increasingly high rates. The money value of the leisure given up will equal the wage a worker has to be paid to induce him or her to do the extra work. So we expect to see an upward sloping supply of labor schedule.

Figure 10.5 shows the demand and supply schedules. On the graph we also illustrate the effect of taxing labor income. The vertical distance t is the tax on wages. This drives a wedge between the wage the employer has to pay and the net wage the worker receives. If we have the kind of demand and supply schedules that economists consider normal (downward sloping demand and upward sloping supply), the number of hours worked will fall at the same gross wage if the tax rate rises. The supply curve will move up by the amount of the tax, since workers' supply is based on net of tax wages and in the figure we measure gross of tax wages (which is what matters to firms) on the vertical axis.

In Figure 10.5 the gray triangle measures the cost of the distortion. It reflects the fall in the number of hours worked *and* the gap between the demand curve (the productivity schedule) and the supply curve (the value of leisure schedule) over that range of hours. This is a good measure of the distortions because it measures the lost benefit of work where the benefit is the difference between what workers actually produced (marginal productivity) and the value of what they gave up (i.e., leisure). The height of the supply schedule at the relevant number of hours gives the value of the leisure because

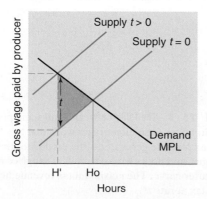

FIGURE 10.5 **Labor Supply, Labor Demand, and Taxes.** Taxation (on wages) is distorting because it alters economic decisions relative to the invisible hand outcome. Hours worked fall from Ho to H′ when tax at rate t is levied.

When a person reduces hours worked:
• MPL measures the loss of output
• the height of a person's supply curve measures the value of the extra leisure gained from working less.
Thus the value of the distortion generated by a tax t is the gray triangle.

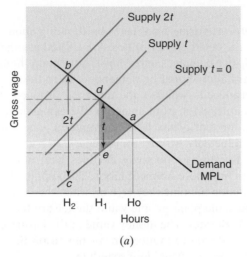

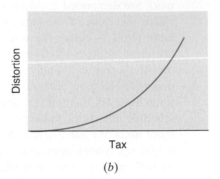

(*a*)   (*b*)

FIGURE 10.6   **Measuring the Cost of Labor Taxes.** When taxes rise from *t* to 2*t* the cost of distortions more than doubles. The area *abc* is 4 times the area *ade*. Thus the cost of taxes is proportional to the square of *t*. If tax *t* is doubled, the distortion will quadruple.

this is the compensation (or wage) that the worker needs to induce him give up an hour of leisure.

This diagram implies that the cost of the tax rises with the tax rate. In fact it will tend to rise more than proportionally because we are multiplying a reduction in hours worked (which depends on the tax rate) by a *widening* gap between productivity and the value of leisure—the distance between the demand and supply curves. In fact, as Figure 10.6 shows, the cost of the tax rises with the square of the tax rate.

Revenue raised increases as the tax is increased from zero but will ultimately fall as taxes deter ever more workers from supplying hours. It follows that the curve describing the relation between tax revenue and the tax rate is hump shaped as in Figure 10.7. This relation is called the Laffer curve.

So a key insight into the economics of taxation is that the distortions to economic behavior that a tax creates are likely to be greater the higher the tax is (Figure 10.8). In

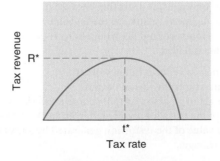

FIGURE 10.7   **The Laffer Curve.** Beyond some point, the rise in tax rates so discourages work that the overall tax revenue generated—the product of the tax rate, wages, and hours worked—falls. That gives rise to the Laffer curve. The maximum tax revenue here is R* with tax at rate *t**.

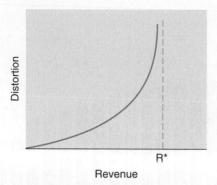

FIGURE 10.8 **Taxation theory.**
Two important conclusions may be drawn from this figure.
- There is a limit to how much revenue the government can raise.
- The marginal cost of taxation, in terms of distortions, increases with revenue.
  –The cost approaches infinity close to R^*, *the maximum revenue.*

simple models of taxation, the welfare cost of taxes rises with the square of the tax rate rather than the level of the tax itself. This implies that the damage that a rise in the tax inflicts is greater the higher the level of that tax to start with. A simple example may help to illustrate this. A rise in the tax rate of 10 cents on the dollar of labor income may have relatively little impact on incentives to work if it takes the overall tax rate from 5% to 15%. Workers still get to keep 85% of the wages employers pay them. But suppose the tax rate was already at the high rate of 80% on marginal (or extra) income. If wages employers pay do not change, then the extra 10 cents on the dollar tax cuts the after-tax earnings of a worker in half—from 20% of the gross wage to just 10% of the wage. This example may seem far-fetched; but in fact marginal tax rates on labor income in several European countries have, at times, been in excess of 70%. However, the implications of Figures 10.6 and 10.7 have been learned. Figure 10.9 shows that by 1997 the marginal income tax rate on the average worker was around 60% in Belgium, Hungary, Finland, and Italy. In Japan, it was 20%, and in South Korea, lower still.

Figure 10.10 shows how the largest OECD governments raised revenue in 1998. Taxes levied directly on individuals (on income, property, or goods and services consumed) have consistently been far more important than taxes raised from corporations. In those countries in which state pensions are generous and account for a big slice of government spending—Germany, France, and Italy—social security contributions are an important source of revenue.

But what remains unclear, even after decades of intensive research, is the scale of the damage done to economies by government intervention. The average level of taxation governments levy varies widely across the developed countries. If higher taxes had dramatic negative impacts on incentives, we would expect that the income levels, the growth of productivity, and perhaps also levels of investment to be lower in countries with high levels of spending than in countries in which the government plays a smaller role. But if government expenditure helps boost education and health, then countries with higher taxes may have high growth.

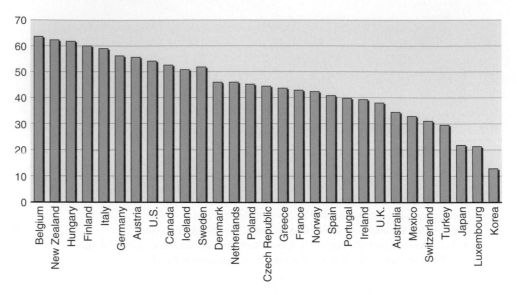

FIGURE 10.9   **Marginal tax rates on earnings of an average production worker,[1] 1997.** The marginal tax rate on income varies hugely across countries. *Source*: OECD, *The Tax/Benefit Position of Employees—1997* (Paris, 1998). Copyright 1998 OECD.

[1]Covering employees' and employers' social security contributions and personal income tax, with respect to a change in gross labor costs, of a one-earner family with two children whose wage level represents 100% of an average production worker.

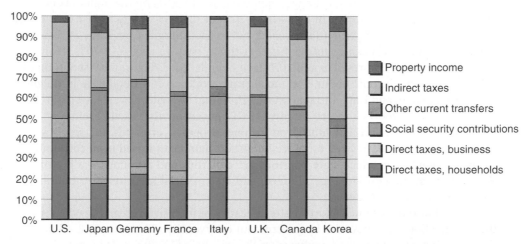

FIGURE 10.10   **Relative importance of different taxes, 1998.** *Source*: OECD, Economic Outlook. Copyright 1998 OECD.

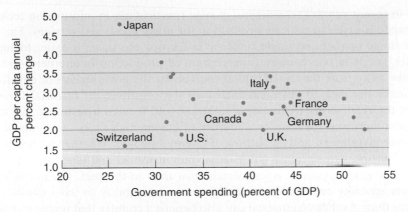

FIGURE 10.11 Government spending and growth—is there a relationship? (OECD countries, 1960–1994). There is no obvious, strong link between growth and the share of output accounted for by government. *Source*: OECD Historical Statistics, 1999. Copyright OECD.

Figure 10.11 shows the relationship between government spending (as a percentage of GDP) and the growth of GDP per capita between 1960 and 1994. The relation between these variables is not strong. Nor have more sophisticated statistical techniques established a clear link between the size of the public sector and the rate of economic growth.[3] The absence of a clear link should not surprise us. What affects efficiency is how effectively the public sector provides goods and services and makes transfers. *Bad* government, not necessarily *big* government, damages a country. Furthermore, the distortions taxes generate depend on the structure of *marginal* tax rates, not on the average tax take out of GDP. A government can raise little revenue and yet impose damaging taxes. An example would be a situation in which marginal tax rates on income were 90% or more and the revenue generated was small but incentives were badly damaged. So we could find that the economic damage taxes inflict is not much related to the overall level of revenue they generate, because the structure of the tax system probably matters more than the overall level of revenue that needs to be generated.

10.5 The Future Role of the Public Sector: Demographic Pressures and Factor Mobility

Whatever the scale of the distortions arising from taxes, they will be greater the more sensitive is the supply of resources (labor, effort, or capital) to remuneration or cost. The sensitivity in supply of scarce factors to changes in tax has probably

---

[3]See Slemrod, "What Do Cross-Country Studies Teach about Government Involvement, Prosperity and Economic Growth?" *Brookings Papers on Economic Activity* (1995) vol. 2, pp. 373–431. See also *The Economic Journal* (1996) vol. 106, no. 439.

increased in recent years. Technological change (particularly in information technology) has made it easier to relocate production for many goods and services. The creation of a single market and single currency in Europe has made it easier to supply demand for goods in one country from centers of production in another. And the steady move away from the use of capital controls by the governments of developed countries over the past 30 years has increased the sensitivity of financial flows to changes in the relative tax treatment of domestic and foreign investment. All these changes have increased the costs to a country of having high taxes—in terms of lost output, lower investment, and an outflow of talented people. Whether a country, especially in Europe, can sustain a much larger public sector, and much higher taxes, than other countries around it is less certain now than in the past. Greater international factor mobility could undermine a government's ability to have significantly higher taxes than in other countries; it can also benefit a country that is able to undercut its neighbor's tax rates.

Whether or not they will ultimately generate net benefits, many countries, particularly Continental European ones, are feeling pressure to reduce the burden of taxes. Taxes on labor (income tax, but also social security and pension contributions that workers and employers pay) are the greatest source of concern. In Europe, unemployment in the 1990s rose to high levels and stayed there. Demographic shifts may put further upward pressure on labor costs as contribution rates needed to finance PAYGO pension systems rise. Practical issues on the optimal size of government and the roles of the public and private sectors will arise most clearly in the area of state pension provision over the next few decades.

THE REFORM OF PENSION SYSTEMS: FUNDED AND UNFUNDED PENSIONS AND THE ROLE OF THE STATE

We have seen that government can play a useful role in providing social insurance when markets cannot. However, governments also spend huge amounts on pensions when private sector alternatives to state provision exist. The United States and the UK, for example, have enormous stocks of private pension assets accumulated from workers' contributions over decades. So the failure of private markets is not a key factor in this area. It is also an area in which demographic change will strain public finances over the next 50 years. And with greater factor mobility and more flexibility in the location of production, governments are more sensitive to how the burden of taxation in their countries compares to their neighbors. This means that reform of state pension systems is almost inevitable—with enormous implications for the pace of capital accumulation and the welfare of different generations.

The key macroeconomic issue is not so much whether the state will pay pensions, but whether pensions will be funded. With funded systems workers make pension contributions that are invested in assets; with unfunded schemes contributions from one generation of workers are immediately channeled to pensions, and there is no accumulated fund of assets. Most state pension systems are unfunded; private systems are almost always funded. In principle the distinction between unfunded and funded pension systems is simple: in unfunded schemes contributions from current workers and firms finance pensions for retired workers; in funded schemes a stock of assets accumulated from contributions finances pensions. In practice the state tends to run unfunded schemes because private agents would find it hard to enforce the intergenerational contract implicit in them; unfunded, state schemes also often redistribute income to the less well off because the level of contributions workers pay (either directly or on their behalf) bears a closer relation to their lifetime income than does the pension they subsequently receive. For example, in the UK all those with a full entitlement to a basic state pension receive the same pension; and a full entitlement does not depend on the value of contributions paid over a person's working life but rather on the number of years a person spends in the workforce (either employed or unemployed).

In many countries—Canada, Denmark, Ireland, New Zealand, the Netherlands—state pensions are essentially the same for all retired people and there is no link between the value of earnings and contributions from the period when a worker makes payments into the system and the value of the pension the worker subsequently is paid. In practice the private sector runs most funded schemes (either occupational pensions or private pensions in which only the individual makes contributions); and while redistribution is often implicit in these schemes, it is not generally from the better off to the less well off. In many occupational pension systems redistribution has more normally been from those who move between jobs relatively frequently to those who stay put; personal pensions are invariably defined contribution schemes in which pensions depend on the value of the fund at retirement, and there is no redistribution among pensioners.

PAYGO (Pay-As-You-Go) schemes fund most state pension schemes in developed countries. Table 10.4 presents information on state pension systems in some of the major economies; it shows total spending, contribution rates, retirement, and the degree of indexation of benefits. There is substantial variability across countries; Continental European state pension schemes tend to be more generous than the U.S. and UK systems, both in terms of replacement rates (the ratio of typical pensions to current average labor income) and in the rate at which entitlements to pensions accrue. As a result, aggregate pension payments and typical contribution rates are also much higher. Few schemes have significant assets—the U.S. scheme is an exception, though even here forecasts suggest that if current policies continue the fund will be exhausted by about 2030.[4]

A combination of rising life expectancy and declining fertility rates will, unless there are dramatic shocks (wars, new fatal diseases) or a steep rise in inflows of relatively young immigrants, cause the proportion of the population aged over 65 to rise over the next 40 years in nearly all developed countries. With an unfunded scheme, if the proportion of the population of working age falls relative to the number over the current typical retirement age, at least one of the following must happen: contribution rates will rise; the average level of pensions relative to wages will fall; the age of eligibility for receipt of pensions will rise; or the system will move into deficit (assuming it started in balance).

[4]Feldstein, "Transition to a Fully Funded Pension System: Five Economic Issues," NBER Discussion Paper, 6149.1997 (1997).

TABLE 10.4 Public Pension Schemes

Country	Financing	Retirement Ages[a] (Men/Woman)	Contribution Period for Full Pension	Replace-ment Rate[b]	Assessed Earnings	Pensions[c] Spending (% GDP)	Social Security Contribution Rate[d]
United States	PF	65/65	35	38.5	Career	5.1	12.6
Japan	PF	60/55	40	19.6	Career	6.2	17.0
Germany	PAYG	65/65	40	52.0	Career	12.2	30.4
France[e]	PAYG	60/60	38	60.1	Best of 12 years	12.6	38.5
Italy	PAYG	62/57	40	53.9	Last 5 years	15.6	30.9
United Kingdom	PAYG	65/60	44	17.5	Career	5.0	11.6
Canada[f]	PAYG	65/65	40	29.2	Career	5.7	n/a
Sweden[g]	PF	65/65	30	39.0	Best of 15 years	13.0	23.2

Sources: Kopits, "Are Europe's Social Security Finances Compatible with EMU?" IMF Fiscal Affairs Department Working Paper (February 1997); Roseveare, Leibfritz, Fore, and Wurzel, "Ageing Populations, Pension Systems and Government Budgets; Simulations for 20 OECD Countries," Economics Department Working Paper no 168 (Paris: OECD, 1996); Chand and Jaeger "Aging Populations and Public Pension Schemes," IMF Occasional Paper no 147 (Washington: IMF, 1996).

PAYG = Pay-As-You Go; PF = Partially Funded.

[a]Statutory retirement ages as of 1995.

[b]The ratio between the pension and average earnings from employment (in 1995).

[c]In 1994.

[d]In percent of gross compensation of employees, including contributions; 1994.

[e]The basic scheme is indexed to prices, while the earnings-related schemes are indexed to gross wages.

[f]For earnings-related scheme only.

The implications of aging populations for the structure and financing of unfunded state pension schemes have been the main factor behind the recent upsurge in analysis of, proposals for, and (in some cases) implementation of switches from unfunded to funded schemes. Figure 10.12 shows United Nations projections of the demographic structure of some of the major economies to 2150. The total population of Europe and North America is projected to change little over the period, but the age structure may change a great deal. The proportion of the population over 60 in Germany and Japan

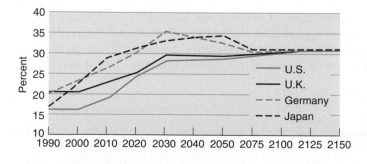

FIGURE 10.12 **Aging populations—over 60s as % of total population.** The proportion of those over 60 is set to rise strongly in the developed world. *Source*: United Nations Population Projections.

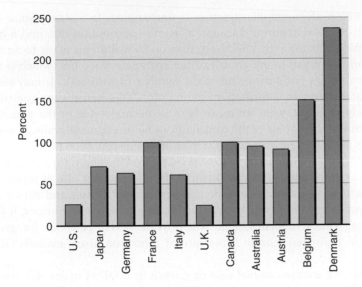

FIGURE 10.13 Present value of public pension deficits (% GDP). These values are based on a 5% discount rate and assume 1.5% productivity growth. *Source*: Roseveare, Leibfritz, Fore, and Wurzel, "Ageing Populations, Pension Systems and Government Budgets: Simulations for 20 OECD Countries," Economics Department Working Paper no. 168, (OECD, 1996). Copyright OECD.

over the next 30 years is likely almost to double. Figure 10.13 shows OECD estimates of the scale of deficits that these demographic shifts could cause to unfunded pension schemes in various countries.[5] The figure shows the OECD estimate of the present value of the future gaps between contributions to state schemes and likely pension payments.[6] Figure 10.13 reveals huge potential deficits in many countries—in present value terms, equal to about annual GDP in Canada, Australia, and France; in Sweden, Belgium, and Denmark, the figures are even higher.

In the United States, proposals for phasing out unfunded pensions have focused on replacing them with personal funds in which contributions go directly into an individual's own account. These accounts are considered a person's property, and bigger contributions to an account will (for a given path of future rates of return) mean proportionately higher future pensions. This implies a close link between the value of contributions and the value of pensions subsequently received; it will also make pensions sensitive to realized rates of return on assets. This raises serious issues about the risk and redistributive characteristics of such funded schemes.

LONG-RUN IMPLICATIONS OF ALTERNATIVE PENSION ARRANGEMENTS

While the scale of the potential burden that aging brings to the financing of unfunded state pensions has generated an interest in switching to funded schemes, advocates make the economic case for a switch most forcefully by focusing on the long-run steady

[5]See Roseveare, Leibfritz, Fore, and Wurzel, "Ageing Populations, Pension Systems and Government Budgets: Simulations for 20 OECD Countries," Economics Department Working Paper 168, (Paris: OECD, 1996).

[6]Unless governments have already announced a phased-in change in male or female retirement ages when such plans are taken into account.

state when, by definition, demographic structure is unchanging. In a steady state—in which population structure is assumed constant, as is the contribution rate into a balanced PAYGO pension scheme—the effective return on contributions made to an unfunded pension scheme is equal to the growth of the aggregate wage bill (which is the sum of growth in real wages per person and of the number of workers).[7] It may seem strange to talk about a return on contributions to an unfunded scheme when contributions are immediately paid out; what we mean here is the real value of the pensions paid to a person relative to the value of the contributions he or she made while at work. If the share of wages in GDP is roughly constant over time, this return on payments to a PAYGO scheme will, on average, be close to real GDP growth. The return on contributions to a (defined contribution) funded scheme is the average, net rate of return on the assets in the portfolio (averaged over time and across asset classes and net of administrative costs and of any tax payable). Abstracting from risk considerations, it follows that in the long run a funded scheme will provide better pensions for given contributions than an unfunded scheme if the rate of return on assets exceeds GDP growth.

Table 10.5 shows the average annual rate of growth in GDP in major developed economies over the 30 or so years from the early 1960s to the mid 1990s. The table also shows the real rate of return that would have been earned over roughly the same period on a portfolio invested equally in domestic government bonds and in domestic equities. In most cases, the average annual real return on the portfolio exceeded the rate of growth of GDP; but in most cases, the difference is also small, and in several cases (Japan, Italy), GDP growth exceeded the return on assets. The picture would, however, be different if we had considered a portfolio only of domestic equities (or stocks). For much of the 1970s inflation in many countries was much higher than had been anticipated, and ex-post real returns on fixed income assets were unusually low; equities proved a much better hedge against inflation. A pure equity portfolio would have generated returns in excess of GDP growth in every country; but it would also have had different risk characteristics from the bond/equity portfolios. A comparison between funded and unfunded pension schemes depends crucially on the portfolio of assets that is acquired with contributions.

Demographic change is likely to have a major impact on GDP growth and on the rate of growth of the aggregate real wage bill; and population shifts and other changes in the macroeconomic environment mean that expected real rates of return on assets over the next 40 years may not be equal to average real returns over the past few decades. So the numbers in Table 10.5 should be interpreted with care. Alternative guides to the relative magnitude of future long-run returns on assets and growth in aggregate wages are yields on long-dated indexed linked bonds and estimates of long-run productivity growth and shifts in population structure. The longest-dated, inflation-proof UK government bonds are probably the best guide to a safe real return on debt; yields over the 1990s have averaged about $3\frac{1}{2}$%. Over the postwar period, GDP in

[7]Samuelson, "An Exact Consumption Loan Model of Interest with or without the Social Contrivance of Money," *Journal of Political Economy*, (1958) vol. 66, pp. 467–482.

TABLE 10.5   Real Rates of Return: Equity and Debt

	Average Annual Real Return (%)[a]			Average Annual GDP Growth (%)
	1962–96	1970–82	1983–96	1961–96
USA	4.31	−0.29	9.2	2.99
Japan	4.67	2.01	7.41	5.80
UK	4.39	−0.14	9.27	2.32
Germany	4.06	0.51	8.60	3.05
France	3.60	−1.05	11.07	3.40
Italy	1.89	−6.32	13.20	3.52
Netherlands	3.92	−0.41	9.72	3.14
Belgium	3.31	−0.63	8.96	3.12
Ireland	4.76	−2.37	11.28	4.27
Denmark	6.42	6.39	8.53	2.83
Spain	3.13	−6.59	11.55	4.21
Portugal[b]	3.82	—	3.82	4.31
Austria	5.43	0.06	11.51	3.31
Norway	4.95	−0.09	15.24	3.74
Sweden	5.34	0.5	11.48	2.46
Mean	4.23	−0.66	10.06	3.48

[a]Real rate of return = $0.5R + 0.5$ (% change $S + d$)

  R = Real long-term interest rate; nominal long-term bond yield minus consumer price inflation

  S = Real share price index

  d = Equity dividend yield

[b]Data refers to 1983–94.

Source: Author's calculations.

most countries has increased by an average of between $2\frac{1}{2}$% and $3\frac{1}{2}$% a year. But over that same period, the population of working age in most OECD economies has increased substantially, whereas over the next 50 years it will not; so a figure of between $2\frac{1}{2}$% and $3\frac{1}{2}$% almost certainly overestimates the average future growth in aggregate real wages. And a yield of $3\frac{1}{2}$% is likely to underestimate the average return on a portfolio with assets such as equities, property, and nominal bonds that are risky and could be expected, over the long term, to outperform sovereign debt with a guaranteed real return.

So it seems likely that the rate of return will exceed GDP growth. But that in itself does not show that switching to a funded scheme will increase welfare; it merely shows that *once a switch had been made*, and capital accumulated, the new long-run average level of consumption could be higher for everyone. A comparison of rates of returns says nothing about the costs of switching from an unfunded to a funded scheme.

Furthermore, the Samuelson analysis is based on a comparison of returns in two steady states in which population structures are unchanging. At the same time, a comparison of rates of return may understate the long-run benefits of a switch from unfunded to a funded scheme because it ignores how labor supply decisions may affect any associated switches in the linkage of pensions to contributions. The lack of a tight link between contributions to most state pension schemes and pensions received means that the contributions act largely as a tax on labor—with associated distortions—rather than as forced savings. The scale of the induced distortions depends on the sensitivity of labor supply to after-tax wages and on the level of other labor taxes to which pension contributions are added. Contributions to a personal fund—the value of which determines future pensions—are, in contrast, a form of saving; if the contributions were to be mandatory part of the saving might be involuntary (and might simply reduce other saving), but the distortion to labor supply would still be lower than with contributions to an unfunded scheme with no linkage between payments and pensions.

All this means that to analyze the overall, macroeconomic effects of having unfunded pension systems, and the long-run implications of a switch to funding, we need work out how a PAYGO system influences private sector labor supply and saving decisions and how the aggregate effects of individual behavior (on the capital stock, rates of return, and tax revenue) feed back on individual behavior.

A useful—perhaps the only—way to gauge the overall impact of alternative pension arrangements on labor supply, private sector saving, interest rates, the capital stock, and GDP is with a model of the economy that explicitly analyzes the interaction of people of different ages over time. Since the pathbreaking work of Auerbach and Kotlikoff in the 1980s several studies using calibrated, overlapping generations models of the economy have analyzed shifts in taxes, alterations in pension arrangements, and movements in population structure.

Miles shows the results of running simulations on such a model of the European economy in which the aim is to estimate the impact of phasing out a PAYGO pension system.[8] The results suggest that the saving rate and the capital stock would be significantly higher if PAYGO pensions were phased out, and that *once a transition had been made*, output and consumption could be higher.

But how can a transition be engineered? The transition costs to specific generations of switching from unfunded to funded pensions can be large. Those costs are not difficult to understand. If an unfunded system is phased out—so that ultimately what were contributions from workers to be paid out immediately to pensioners are instead accumulated on their behalf in a fund—resources still need to be found to pay pensions for those in or near retirement. Just as one set of generations benefits when an unfunded scheme is first established, one set of generations *may* have to "pay twice" when such a scheme is run down. Whether there have to be losers, who they are, and how great their losses might be are the critical issues that governments in all developed countries are now addressing. Whether deficit financing is a means of making a transition is an issue of major political and macroeconomic significance.

---

[8]Miles, "Modelling the Impact of Demographic Change Upon the Economy," *The Economic Journal* (1999) vol. 109, no. 452, pp. 1–36.

SUMMARY ON PENSION PROVISION

In the long run people might be better off if pensions were funded. But in the transition to such a scheme, funds need to be accumulated, and that requires higher national saving. While deficit financing can, under certain circumstances, help spread the burden of the transition across generations, the scale of extra debt that many developed countries might need is problematic. Ultimately, a transition toward greater funding of pensions will probably make some people worse off. The problems that the Italian, French, and Austrian governments have had in the late 1990s in scaling back the generosity of state pension schemes testify to the difficulty of making the transition. In short, getting widespread support for the transition to a funded scheme may be hard to manage. The task is harder the more generous are existing state pensions, the more rapid is the aging of the population, and the more constrained the government is in using deficit financing. Given all this, the United States and the UK are in a relatively good position (vis-à-vis Europe) to make a transition. Things are much tougher in Continental Europe and in Japan.

10.6   Political Factors behind the Role of Government

Once one looks at the reasons why governments now play such a big role in the economy, the attractions of simple slogans begin to fade. "Less government is better government" is a simple message, and in a simple world, it might be true. But we do not live in that world. Central planning of all economic activity has not proved effective, at least in peace time.[9] But market failures in some areas can be so severe and persistent that governments moving to the opposite extreme and reverting to a night watchman role is unlikely to be desirable.

In fact, rolling back the state to a night watchman role is not even remotely likely because many government programs benefit particular groups while their costs are spread widely. When governments cut spending in any area, the cost tends to fall heavily on a readily identifiable group that stands to lose a lot. Such a group often has the ability and incentive to fight back. But the benefits of lower government spending—in terms of reduced taxation and lower distortions—are generally spread thin; indeed, it is sometimes hard to identify who the beneficiaries are. So governments usually get more trouble from losers than thanks from winners if they reduce spending. This is one important political factor behind the strong rise in the role of the state over the past century. Many OECD countries have vastly increased both the role of government and the size of government debt outstanding. In Italy and Belgium, for example, government spending since the Second World War rose strongly as a percent of GDP while tax revenue failed to keep up, so that the stock of government debt increased sharply. In these countries government could not reduce spending or raise taxes enough to prevent sustained

---

[9]In war time it can achieve awesome results. As Paul Krugman has noted, Russia was able to fight the German army to a standstill in the Second World War because of its staggering ability to apply labor and capital to produce armaments.

periods of large fiscal deficits. Much evidence links these forces and the nature of the political system.

The more pressure a government is under to hold together a coalition of parties, the less it can afford to lose friends. Controlling public spending and raising taxes rarely make friends—at least in the short term—and often loses them. Governments that are in danger of losing power in the near term find it harder to take tough decisions with beneficial long-run effects. Countries that use proportional representation—which often generates short-lived, coalition governments—tend to have higher spending and government debt than majoritarian or presidential systems, which are less likely to hold government hostage to the defection of some political group.

SUMMARY

Governments are important because their spending represents a high proportion of overall total expenditure—on average around 40% in the developed economies. But the range of activities undertaken by governments varies greatly across countries. If markets worked perfectly, and if the free-market distribution of incomes were considered acceptable, there would be no role for government. But if there are market imperfections, this invisible hand result no longer holds, and government can make the economy work more effectively. But financing government spending through taxes creates distortions—labor supply is affected by income taxes and investment by companies and households is influenced by corporate taxes and taxes on saving.

The optimal scale of government is one that perfectly trades off the benefits from government rectifying forms of market failure against the costs of raising the funds to finance spending. But governments are run by people who face political constraints and have to answer to pressure groups. Vested interest groups can be powerful and have clear incentives to exert pressure—sometimes pressure for governments not to spend money, but more often pressure for more spending. Benevolent dictators might be willing and able to resist these pressures. But any system of government that allowed a benevolent dictator to come to power could get other sorts of dictators, too.

CONCEPTUAL QUESTIONS

1. Suppose that companies have enormous flexibility in where they can locate production. Suppose also that governments want firms to locate in their countries. Governments might then compete to attract firms by offering greater incentives—for example, low corporate tax rates and generous subsidies. In this environment consider the potential costs and benefits of a multicountry system of minimum corporate tax rates. Do the forces at work here justify *complete* harmonization of tax systems?

2. Resource allocation will be less distorted if taxes are levied on goods and services (including types of labor) that are in inelastic supply—that is, where changes in the price sellers receive

does not change supply much. But would this generate a fair system of taxes? What conflicts might arise between the design of a tax system that generates small distortions and one that is equitable?

3. Should governments force people to be in school?

4. For much of the 1980s and 1990s, different UK governments tried to reduce the share of government spending in the economy below 40%, with little success. Was this a worthwhile goal, and if so, why?

5. Some of the things that governments spend money on are luxury goods (goods for which the proportion of people's income that is spent on them is likely to rise as income grows). Health care and education may be such goods. If most goods that government provide are of this type, the pressure for the share of government spending in total GDP to rise over time will grow. Should such pressures be resisted?

6. Market failures often arise because of information problems; for example, some insurance contracts are hard to price because the insurance company does not know enough about the risks of potential buyers of insurance. Given the advances in information technology, would you expect market failures to be becoming less serious? What does that imply for the role of government in providing forms of insurance?

ANALYTICAL QUESTIONS

1. Suppose the average person in a city places a value of $10 on having an extra 1000 policeman for a year out on the streets. Some people have a higher value and some a lower value. The population is 7 million. The city government decides to ask people how much they value an extra 1000 police to see if it is worth spending the $50 million a year needed. The first version of the questionnaire asks people to assess the value to them of the extra police and explains that people will pay the amount they answer on the condition that the total of answers is at least $75 million. The second version of the questionnaire asks people to reveal how much they value the extra police but says that everyone will pay the same amount if the police are hired, provided the sum of the personal valuations exceeds $75 million.

   (a) What would be the results of the different surveys?
   (b) Which is better?
   (c) Do either surveys give people the incentive to tell the truth?
   (d) Can you devise a survey that does make people reveal the truth?

2. Suppose that income is distributed within a country so that one-third of the population earns exactly one-third the average wage, one-third earn exactly two-thirds of the average-wage, and the richest one-third earn exactly twice the average wage. Initially there are no taxes and no benefits. The government then introduces a system of redistributive taxes and benefits. Those earning more than the average wage are taxed at 25% on total earnings and those earning less than the average wage each receive the same flat rate benefit. Total taxes received and benefits paid are equal. Assuming no change in pretax wages, what is the new distribution of income? Now assume that one-half of those with above average incomes leave the country in response to the tax. What does the distribution of income look like then?

3. Suppose that the costs of the distortions from levying income tax at a flat rate of t on all incomes in an economy is $billion $\times$ $(20t)^2$. The government decides to follow a policy of balancing the budget every year. Incomes on which tax can be levied are $700 billion a year. Over a three-year period government spending is $100 billion, $150 billion, $50 billion. The government could borrow money at 5%. Would the government do better to borrow to finance the unusually high spending in year 2 rather than see taxes rise, then fall? Assuming the debt issued to finance any deficits is all sold to domestic residents, does it matter what the interest rate is in evaluating the tax-smoothing option?

4. The pain that I suffer from studying hard for my exams can be given a monetary value. The harder I work, the more I suffer now, but the greater are future wages because my productivity is higher the more I know. But if I study too much, my brain overheats and I learn less. Suppose the pain function is

monetary value of pain = $20 $\times$ H
where H is the annual hours I work when studying now.

The money value of all the gains in later life from studying more now is given by

$(1 - t) (60 \times H - 0.01 H^2)$

where t is the tax rate which is equal to 30%.

(a) What is the optimal number of hours to work this year in preparing for my exams?
(b) What happens if the tax rate rises to 40%?
(c) What if the tax is abolished and replaced with a poll tax (everyone pays the same regardless of qualifications, productivity, or income)?

5. Suppose you had information on the impact of spending on public education on the productivity of the labor force. You also have information on how education spending reduces crime (with a time lag). Finally, you have estimates of how raising extra taxes creates distortions to labor supply. Explain precisely how you would use this sort of information to help determine optimal spending on public education. What extra information would be valuable?

Fiscal Policy

Overview

In this chapter we consider the implications of governments running fiscal deficits; that is, not covering their current expenditure out of tax revenue. First we look at the facts, focusing particularly on the United States. We discuss how deficits and the stock of debt have evolved over the last century. We then consider the implications of governments running unbalanced budgets for saving, investment, and international capital flows.

Key to the impact of government fiscal policy is the response of the private sector to governments not matching expenditure against tax revenues. We consider in detail how the private sector might respond to government deficits and surpluses. The response of the private sector to changes in fiscal policy depends crucially on what governments' running current surpluses or deficits implies about the future balance between government taxing and spending; it also depends on how farsighted the private sector is.

We also discuss the long-run implications of current deficits and show how the relative magnitudes of rates of return and growth of GDP are critical to the sustainability of the fiscal position. Finally, we analyze the advantages of unbalanced budgets, particularly during war and when other temporary shocks hit the economy.

11.1 Government Spending and Taxing over the Long Term: The U.S. Case

In Chapter 10 we saw that the role of government in most developed countries had expanded over the twentieth century. Government expenditure is now much higher relative to gross domestic product (GDP) than it was at the end of the nineteenth century in nearly all market economies. Taxation also takes a much greater share of national output. But taxes and spending do not 'typically match each other from year to year. Governments, like households and companies, can run deficits and incur debt. In fact, governments have far greater ability to spend more than they raise in tax revenue than individual households have to borrow to finance their current consumption. Governments can raise revenue in the future through the tax system, and unlike households and companies, they do not have to sell commodities at market prices to raise revenue.

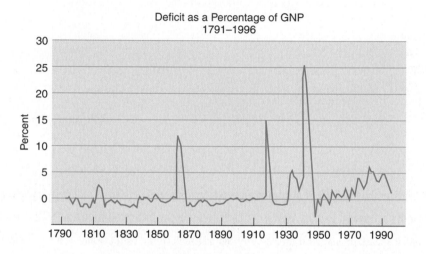

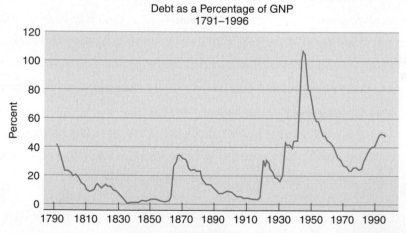

FIGURE 11.1   **U.S. Debt as a percentage of GNP, 1791–1996.** The stock of U.S. government debt has fluctuated greatly over time, while the deficit has shown even greater variability from year to year. *Source*: Elmendorf and Mankiw, "Government Debt." In J. Taylor and M. Woodford (eds.), *The Handbook of Macroeconomics*, vol. 1. p. 1618. (North Holland, Amsterdam: Elsevier Science, 2000). Reprinted by permission from Elsevier Science.

This means that governments can usually borrow more, and at lower cost, than companies or individuals can.

Figure 11.1 shows the difference between annual U.S. government spending and the revenue the government raised over the last 200 years (the total deficit). The size of the deficit is shown relative to gross national product (GNP). The three major peaks in deficits reflect wars; the Civil War of the 1860s, the First World War, and the Second World War. But except for during these wars, the U.S. government typically ran (close to) balanced budgets; indeed, after the Civil War and the First World War, the government ran surpluses for several years and reduced the stock of debt. But for much of the period since the early 1970s the U.S. government has run a deficit; the first sustained period in peacetime when the government did not balance expenditure against revenue. For most of the period from the mid 1970s to the end of the 1990s, the U.S. government ran deficits close to 4% of GNP. Only at the end of the 1990s did the U.S. government move back into surplus.

When a government is running a deficit, it is borrowing to finance the gap between expenditure and taxation. As a result, the stock of outstanding debt increases. Figure 11.1 shows how the stock of U.S. government debt relative to GNP has evolved. Again, major wars generated a sharp rise in the stock of debt relative to GNP. But the stock of debt fell in postwar periods. However, since the 1970s, the stock of debt has increased steadily relative to GNP, at least until the end of the 1990s. The experience of the United States since World War II is not unusual. Many governments in developed countries have run deficits on a scale previously only seen in wartime. Figure 11.2 shows the combined fiscal deficits of the seven largest economies (the G7 countries) from 1981 to 1999. Through several business cycles, the G7 countries, in aggregate, have consistently run deficits; over the 1980s and 1990s deficits have averaged close to 3% of GDP. As a result, the stock of debt relative to GDP has risen to high levels, by historical standards, in most developed countries.

But focusing purely on the stock of debt ignores the financial assets of the public sector, and so can mislead us about public sector indebtedness. Table 11.1 shows instead the stock of net debt (in 1999) as a percentage of GDP for OECD countries.

In measuring the stock of net debt, we are subtracting from the stock of gross debt any financial assets the public sector holds. The figures reveal substantial variability across countries in the stock of net debt. In Belgium and Italy, for example, net debt in

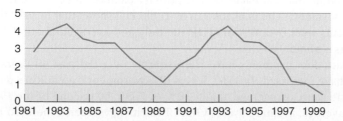

FIGURE 11.2 **Budget deficits—G7 countries (% GDP).** Budget deficits across the world's largest seven economies (the G7) have fluctuated with the economic cycle: in the downturns in the early 1980s and 1990s deficits rose sharply; in the upturns in the second half of the 1980s and 1990s, deficits fell. *Source*: OECD "Economic Outlook." Copyright OECD.

TABLE 11.1   Net Government Debt (percent of GDP), 1999

United States	49.7	Belgium	107.6
Japan[a]	37.7	Denmark	31.6
Germany[b]	47.0	Finland	−28.3
France	43.0	Iceland	25.8
Italy	104.4	South Korea	−21.7
United Kingdom	38.7	Netherlands	51.0
Canada	55.3	Norway	−47.8
Australia	13.8	Spain	47.6
Austria	51.7	Sweden	13.0
		OECD Average	46.4

[a]Includes the debt of the Japan Railway Settlement Corporationa and the National Forest Service.

[b]Includes the debt of the German Railways Fund from 1994 onwards and the Inherited Debt Fund from 1995 onwards. *Source:* OECD Economic Outlook. Copyright OECD.

1999 was in excess of annual GDP. But in South Korea and Norway, net debt was substantially negative; the public sector had significant net financial assets. The figures show that the U.S. net debt position in 1999 was not unusual; the ratio of net debt to GDP of just under 50% is close to the average across all countries. But the U.S. was running a budget surplus in 1999, and was projected to run much larger surpluses for several years. Table 11.2 shows the size of government deficits in 1999, again relative to GDP. The first column shows the overall balance between revenue raised and total spending. What is unusual here is that most governments in 1999 were running deficits at a time when no country was fighting a major war. The average deficit was about 0.8% of annual GDP. But most governments were covering their expenditure if we exclude interest on outstanding government debt. The second column in Table 11.2 shows the primary balance—the difference between revenue and spending excluding debt interest. Among developed countries, only Japan was running a primary deficit in 1999. The difference between overall financial balances and primary balances reflects the importance of debt interest payments. The final column of Table 11.2 shows that in 1999 these annual interest payments were over 6% of GDP for Italy and averaged about 3% for developed countries as a whole.

In OECD countries debt payments have risen sharply over the past 40 years because stocks of debt have increased. In 1960, levels of government expenditure across the industrialized world were, on average, under 30% of GDP; by the end of the 1990s, expenditure was, on average, around 50% of GDP. Deficits have been generated consistently over the intervening period because the tax take out of GDP has not risen fast enough to offset increasing spending. The stock of net debt relative to GDP has risen in each of the G7 countries over the past 20 years, often sharply (Figure 11.3). This

TABLE 11.2   Government Deficits

	General Government Financial Balances 1999	General Government Primary Balances 1999	General Government Debt Interest Payments 1999
United States	1.0	3.8	2.8
Japan	−7.0	−5.7	1.3
Germany	−1.1	2.0	3.1
France	−1.8	1.2	3.0
Italy	−1.9	4.5	6.4
United Kingdom	1.1	3.3	2.2
Canada	2.8	7.4	4.7
All OECD	−0.8	2.1	2.9

Source: OECD Economic Outlook (2000). Copyright OECD.

Column 1 = column 2 − column 3.

process can become unstable as interest payments on the accumulated stock of debt rise. Because of increases in the stock of debt, interest payments since 1960 have roughly tripled as a proportion of GDP. Whether governments can continue to run deficits while preventing the stock of debt from rising continuously as a percentage of GDP is important, and we analyze it in detail below. In fact, in most industrial countries, the cost of government debt, as measured by the interest rate that the government has to pay to sell bonds, has not increased over the past 30 years. Financial markets, by implication, do not consider the rise in the stocks of government debt in developed countries an indication that governments are likely to default or go bankrupt. If they

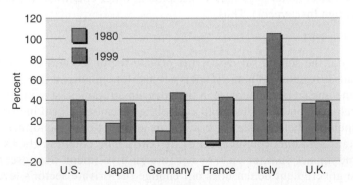

FIGURE 11.3   **Ratio of net government liabilities to GDP, 1980 and 1999.** For much of the 1980s and 1990s most governments ran fiscal deficits and the ratio of net debt to GDP rose. *Source*: OECD Economic Outlook. Copyright OECD.

did, one would expect interest rates on government debt to be rising over time to compensate for increasing default risks.

But even if running deficits has not significantly increased fears of default for most industrialized countries, those deficits nonetheless can affect the economy. In the next three sections of this chapter, we consider in detail how those effects may come about.

11.2 Government Saving, National Saving, and the Balance of Payments

Let's go back to one of the basic national accounts identity:

$$Y = C + S + T$$

Where Y is national income, C is private consumption, S is private saving, and T is net tax payments. The identity reflects an obvious economic fact: income is consumed, saved, or handed over to the government as tax.

National income *also* equals the sum of consumption expenditure (C), investment (I), government expenditure (G), and net exports (NX). Thus:

$$Y = C + I + G + NX$$

If we put together these two relations, we have a well-known equation that states that private savings (S) plus government savings (T − G) must equal the sum of investment (I) and net exports (NX):

$$S + (T - G) = I + NX$$

Net exports generate an international flow of money from the payment for goods and services, and these must be matched by flows of money across the capital account if the demand and supply of the currency is to be balanced. In other words, net exports (NX) must equal net investments by domestic residents in other countries. We denote this by NFI (Net Foreign Investment). Thus,

$$S + (T - G) = I + NFI$$

This equation says that the sum of savings by the private sector (S) and government savings (T − S) equals investment at home (I) plus net investment abroad (NFI).

Now consider the impact of an increase in the government deficit, starting from a position of, say, a balanced budget. This could arise either because of a cut in taxation with government spending held constant, or a rise in government expenditure with taxation held constant (or some combination of the two). The equation shows that there has to be some impact on S, or on I, or net foreign investment. Suppose, first, that the shift in the government deficit does not change the private sector's level of savings. Then either domestic investment must fall or net foreign investment overseas must be reduced. In an open economy, in which the incentive to invest domestically reflects productivity of capital relative to the world real required rate of return, a change in the government deficit need not affect domestic investment. In this case, and once again assuming that private sector saving is unchanged, any increase in the government deficit simply shows up as a reduction in net foreign investment. So, for example, a rise in the government deficit would show up as an increase in the balance of payments deficit (or a fall in the surplus), which is the counterpart to the fall in net foreign investment (NFI = NX).

In a closed economy, of course, net exports and net foreign investment are zero, in which case, if increasing government deficits do not affect private savings, they must, as a matter of identity, reduce domestic investment. This might happen through induced effects on real interest rates. Imagine that changes in government deficits do not affect private sector saving. If the government then increases the size of the deficit (or moves from surplus into deficit), it will have to sell more government debt. To induce the private sector to hold a higher proportion of its financial assets in government debt—as opposed to equity, property, or other assets—the rate of return on that debt will have to increase. This will generate a rise in yields on bonds that is likely to adversely affect stock market values and increase the rates of return that corporations need to earn on new projects. The level of investment will typically fall as a result, thereby ensuring that the national accounts identities hold (as, of course, they must).

This is a standard "crowding out" argument; more government spending squeezes out private sector investment. Of course, it is only a good guide to what might happen if we assume that changes in the size of the deficit do not themselves affect private savings, and that might be a poor assumption. First, shifts in the deficit themselves may have expansionary effects on the level of income in the economy. This is a standard Keynesian argument. Whether extra government demand really will boost output depends on whether there is slack in the economy to start with. If there is, and if domestic firms react to higher demand by expanding output and employment, then domestic incomes may rise and, assuming not all the extra income is spent, private sector savings may rise along with them. So we could imagine a situation in which private sector savings increase in line with the government deficit because the level of output and incomes themselves have increased. Then there need be no crowding out. Indeed, if firms become more optimistic about future demand, they might increase investment; we would have crowding in rather than crowding out.

Whether we would expect these Keynesian effects to be significant in the longer run is a moot point. Over the longer term, it is plausible that supply side factors (people's willingness to work, the productivity of capital, and so on) determine levels of output in economies. In this case, governments cannot expect to have long-run, positive effects on levels of output by increasing demand through larger fiscal deficits (of course, we are ignoring any productivity-enhancing effects of extra government expenditure).

Clearly the impact of government deficits or surpluses on the wider economy depends on how the private sector responds. And that response depends on how *current* fiscal policy affects taxes and spending in the *future* and on how households respond to what they anticipate different taxes or spending levels will be. We consider these impacts in the next section.

11.3 Government Budget Constraints and Ricardian Equivalence

Let's assume that governments do not go bankrupt. In this case the stock of debt cannot increase indefinitely, relative to GDP, for if it did, the burden of repaying the interest on the debt would rise over time relative to the ability of the economy to generate taxes. Then the government could not even raise enough taxes to pay the interest on the stock of existing debt. In this case, even if government revenue could cover the noninterest payments element of government spending, the stock of debt would continue to rise ever faster, and the government would default on interest payments within a finite period. None of this implies that governments cannot consistently run deficits; they can and do. We will see below that provided the economy is growing and the rate of interest is not above some critical level, then governments may be able to run primary deficits consistently. (Remember, the primary deficit is the gap between government expenditure, *excluding* debt interest payments, and tax revenue.)

For the moment let's leave aside the effects of growth in the economy over time and discuss a case in which there is no long-term rise in GDP. In this case, if a government is not to ultimately default on its debt obligations, then at some point in the future, a primary surplus must offset a higher deficit today. Suppose that were not the case, and that we started from a position of no debt and a balanced budget. From that initial position, assume that the government cuts taxes for some period, so that it runs a temporary deficit. It would then emerge from this period of unbalanced budgets with a positive stock of debt. Suppose also that the government did not subsequently run a primary budget surplus, so that its tax revenue was only enough to pay its noninterest expenses. In this case the government would not be raising enough revenue to pay the interest on its positive stock of debt, and thus the stock of *nominal* debt would have to rise year after year. As long as the real interest rate was positive, the *real* stock of debt would also continue to rise. In an environment in which real national income was not rising over time, this would imply that the ratio of debt to GDP was exploding. The total tax take would, eventually, not even cover the interest on existing debt and would then fall ever further behind it. This would not be sustainable.

So in an economy without growth but with a positive real interest rate, to avoid insolvency, government must balance any deficit today with a primary surplus in the future. It is possible to show that, assuming governments do not go insolvent, then the value of government debt today equals the net present value of future primary surpluses. In other words, past deficits must be offset by future surpluses. This implication of the government intertemporal budget constraint can profoundly affect the impact of running current deficits (or surpluses) on private sector savings. The great English economist David Ricardo (1772–1823) first noted this almost 200 years ago. Until recently, economists neglected Ricardo's analysis of the implications of the intertemporal budget constraint on governments. But Robert Barro's 1974 paper, "Are Government Bonds Net Wealth?" revived interest in Ricardo's arguments.[1]

---

[1]Barro, "Are Government Bonds Net Wealth?" *Journal of Political Economy* (1974), vol. 82, pp. 1095–1117.

Ricardo's analysis of the options facing a government in financing a war neatly illustrates his argument. Elmendorf and Mankiw recount how in an article written in 1820 Ricardo analyzed the issue.[2] Ricardo considered an example of a war that might cost the British government £20 million. Suppose the interest rate were 5%; then the government could finance the war by issuing £20 million of perpetual government bonds that required interest payments of £1 million a year forever. Or it could simply increase taxes now by £20 million. A third option would be to increase taxes by more than £1 million, but by less than £20 million, for a limited number of years: if taxes were £1.2 million higher for 45 years, the war costs would be paid off—interest and capital on the initial debt of £20 million would be eliminated after 45 years. Ricardo then observed:

> *In points of economy, there is no real difference in either of the modes; for £20 million in one payment, £1 million per annum forever, or £1,200,000 for 45 years are precisely the same value. . . . It would be difficult to convince a man possessed of £20,000, or any other sum, that a perpetual payment of £50 per annum was equally burdensome with a single tax of £1,000. He would have some vague notion that the £50 per annum would be paid by posterity, and would not be paid by him. But if he leaves his fortune to his son and leaves it charged with this perpetual tax, where is the difference whether he leaves him £20,000 with the tax or £19,000 without it?*

Ricardo was saying that if a government were to run a deficit of £20 million and increase government debt by that amount, the present value of the extra taxes that it would have to levy in the future to ensure that the debt was ultimately repaid would be precisely £20 million. If the private sector understands this, it should consider its own wealth to be the same whether the government raises taxes by the full amount today or runs a deficit and issues bonds of that value. Either way, the private sector pays the equivalent of £20 million. The key implication is this. *If* the level of spending and saving by the private sector depends on its overall wealth (taking into account future incomes and future taxes that have to be paid), then there shouldn't be any difference between levels of consumption and national saving if the government levies £20 million in tax today or issues debt of £20 million but has to levy future taxes of the same present value.

Barro showed what the implications of all this were with an economic model that took account of the responses of rational, forward-looking individuals. Because there is no difference between government levying taxes today and in the future, consumption cannot be any different in the two cases. If that is so, then a decision to increase the deficit by cutting current taxes results in higher savings by the private sector *by an amount that exactly matches the deficit.* One way to think about this is to note that if the private sector's plans for future consumption are to be unchanged, then the increase in its current wealth must exactly match the extra obligations to pay taxes in the future that the current deficit creates. This requires that all the tax cut is saved. If we go back to our national income equations, we will note that if S (private sector saving) moves to

[2]Elmendorf and Mankiw, "Government Debt." In Taylor and Woodford (eds.), *The Handbook of Macroeconomics* (North Holland: Amsterdam 2000).

exactly offset any change in $(T - G)$, then changes in the size of the government deficit will not affect $I + NFI$. In this case government deficits would not crowd out investment, either domestically or overseas: government debt policy would be neutral.

For this result to hold, individuals must look to the distant future. But, as Ricardo noted, people do not live forever. Yet so long as they consider the effects of higher future taxes on their own children, their grandchildren, and their great grandchildren . . . then they still may take higher future taxes into account today. What needs to happen, as Barro showed clearly, is that individuals plan to make bequests to their children, and that their children should also plan to make bequests to their children, and so on. If that is the case, any increase in the fiscal deficit today implies a higher burden of taxation for some generation in the future. If all people alive today were planning on making a bequest to their children (because they were concerned about the levels of consumption that their children could enjoy), then they can exactly offset the impact of higher future taxes by bequeathing more wealth. The increase in the size of the current generation's bequest that would be needed to ensure that higher future taxes made it, *and all subsequent generations*, no worse off is precisely equal to the size of the deficit today.

In fact, Ricardo did not think that people would respond to higher deficits by saving more themselves. In part, this may be because they do not calculate correctly what current deficits imply. But their failure to save more need not reflect myopia or irrationality. Many people might like to borrow off future generations but can't; after all it is difficult for people to hand over personal debt to the next generation. But governments can. By running deficits today and cutting current taxes, government helps ease a binding constraint on the private sector, which responds by consuming much of the tax cut. In this case national savings will fall, which will affect either domestic investment or net overseas investment, depending on whether we are in a closed or open economy. Either way, there is crowding out.

Since Barro resurrected the Ricardian idea, a huge amount of research has investigated whether so called Ricardian equivalence holds; that is, whether financing government spending out of revenue raised from taxes today is equivalent to financing it from taxes in the future. If Ricardian equivalence does hold, then deficits don't have much effect on the real economy. If it does not hold, some form of crowding out may occur with implications for long-run growth (which we will consider in more detail later). One line of research is to investigate whether changes in deficits have affected real interest rates. If Ricardian equivalence does not hold, then shifts in government spending are unlikely to have an offsetting impact on private savings, in which case one would expect real interest rates to be affected as savings become more scarce. In practice, empirical research to identify an impact of government deficits on real interest rates has proved difficult. Movements in real interest rates are hard to explain, and the fact that measures of government deficits don't appear to have much impact reflects the difficulty more than it indicates Ricardian equivalence.

So the jury remains out on whether shifts in private sector savings offset government deficits. But if they do offset them, it is probably less than complete, because many households cannot borrow as much as they would like. And those households that do not have children, or decide that they do not wish to leave a bequest to them, clearly would not satisfy the Ricardian conditions. Because many households are in this position, we would not expect, in theory, Ricardian equivalence to hold.

Nonetheless, the Ricardian argument does highlight the importance of the impact of fiscal deficits or surpluses on different generations.

11.4 Intergenerational Redistribution and Fiscal Policy

Government spending and taxing patterns often reallocate resources between people of different ages. They can also reallocate resources between people alive today and those not yet born. Laurence Kotlikoff has studied countries to show the net impact of spending and taxing on people of different ages. Figure 11.4 shows estimates of the net effects of spending and taxing on people of different generations in the United States and Japan in 1995. The figure allocates elements of government spending (e.g., on health, education, pensions) to different cohorts. The authors also work out how tax rates need to evolve to ensure that government debt remains sustainable. With these tax rates, and given assumptions about who benefits from different types of spending, they work out the balance between payments of tax and receipts of benefits over the entire lives of people born at different times. Figure 11.4 shows this balance. It reveals that in both Japan and the United States those aged 60 or more in 1995 tended to be net gainers; that is, the present value of the benefits they receive from government spending programs exceeds the value of taxes they will pay over their lives. In contrast, those who were aged less than 50 in 1995 were likely to pay substantial net taxes over their lives. In this context, by net taxes we mean the difference between tax payments and receipts of benefits due to government expenditure (direct receipts in the form of pensions or unemployment benefits but also indirect receipts in the form of medical

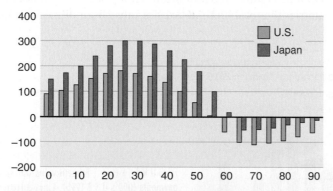

FIGURE 11.4 **Generational accounts (000s U.S.$, 1995)[1].** The young pay taxes and the old receive net benefits—therefore unchanged policies and demographic shifts mean large projected deficits. *Source*: Kotlikoff and Leibfritz, "An International Comparison of Generational Accounts," NBER Working Paper W6447 (March 1998).

[1]Present value of net tax payments (until death) by different generations indexed by age in 1995.

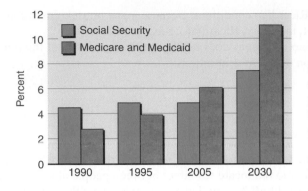

FIGURE 11.5 **U.S. social security spending, 1990–2030 (% GDP).** The aging population is likely to lead to large increases in pensions and health care. *Source*: Kotlikoff and Leibfritz, "An International Comparison of Generational Accounts," Working Paper 6447 (March 1998).

expenditure and government expenditure on education, for example). If governments consistently ran balanced budgets and there were no intergenerational redistribution through pay-as-you-go (PAYGO) pension systems, then you would expect that net taxes paid over each individual's life would be roughly the same for people of different ages. But in the United States and Japan, a combination of relatively generous un-funded pensions in the past and rising old-aged dependency rates into the future means that people now in their 20s and 30s are likely to have to pay far more in net taxes than those who were relatively young when unfunded pension systems were young them-selves. The result will be substantial net intergenerational transfers from today's young (and those yet to be born) to today's old.

Figure 11.5 reveals the main factor behind intergenerational transfers in the United States. The projected dramatic increase in the size of federal government expenditure on social security, medicare, and medicaid reflects the aging of the U.S. population. Be-cause it is likely that future workers will largely pay for this expenditure, it will redis-tribute resources from today's young to today's old.

Figure 11.6 illustrates that this kind of redistribution is not just a U.S. phenomenon. It shows that for many countries the total lifetime taxes of those born in 2015 are likely

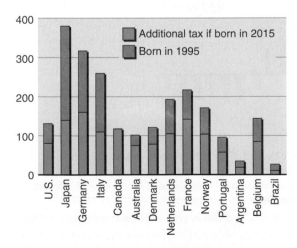

FIGURE 11.6 **Present value tax payments (000's U.S.$ 1995).** Large future tax increases await younger generations. *Source*: Kotlikoff and Leibfritz, "An International Comparison of Generational Accounts," Working Paper 6447 (March 1998).

to be substantially higher than the present value of all the taxes paid by those born in 1995. Again, the large future tax increases awaiting younger generations are an implication of demographic change and reflect intergenerational redistribution.

There are economic and moral reasons why redistribution toward today's old is reasonable. Many of the generations born in the first part of this century lived through the First World War, the Great Depression, and the Second World War. In contrast, those people born since 1960 have enjoyed a substantially higher standard of living than their parents and grandparents and (at least at the time of writing!) have not faced the kind of world wars and economic depressions that occurred between 1900 and 1945. So it may be reasonable that people born after 1950 should make substantial transfers to those born earlier in the century.

These calculations of intergenerational accounts assume that the stock of debt, relative to GDP, does not rise dramatically over time. They depend crucially on assumptions about the real interest rate and the growth of GDP. If GDP rises over the next 50 years substantially faster than it did over the past 50 years, then governments will have more scope to run deficits, while keeping the ratio of debt to GDP from rising. Were that to occur, governments would not need to raise taxes on today's young and unborn to anything like the extent that Figure 11.6 implies. So in thinking about the long-term implications of government spending and taxing, the relative magnitudes of the growth of GDP and the real interest rate on government debt are central. We consider these issues in more detail in the next section.

11.5   Long-Run Sustainability

In this section we want to consider when governments could consistently run budget deficits and how great those deficits might be. Let's begin with a simple case. Consider an economy in which the primary deficit is zero. In that situation government revenue is exactly equal to noninterest expenditure. Let the nominal interest rate on government debt equal R and the growth in *nominal* GDP equal g (which is equal to the inflation rate plus long-term real growth). Let the initial stock of government debt equal D and denote GDP by Y. The government's debt position is sustainable when the ratio D/Y is not rising over time. If the government is in primary balance, then because of interest payments on the existing stock of debt, it will not be covering its overall spending; remember, primary balance means that tax revenue just covers spending *excluding* debt interest. In this case, the stock of debt will be rising. But inflation and real growth will mean that GDP is also rising. If R is greater than g, and assuming primary fiscal balance, then the accumulation of interest payments will dominate, and D/Y will tend to infinity. In this case, the fiscal position is unsustainable. If, however, R is less than g, and again we are in perpetual fiscal primary balance, then the growth of output will dominate the rise in debt due to rolling up interest, so the debt to GDP ratio will eventually tend to zero.

We might define sustainability as a position of a constant debt GDP ratio.[3] This implies that if g is *greater* than R, governments can run a primary deficit every period and

---

[3]There are other ways to think about sustainability, but this is probably the most natural one.

still keep the debt-to-GDP ratio constant. Of course, if the deficit is too large, then the debt will become unsustainable; nonetheless, if g exceeds R, governments can run primary deficits, *up to some critical level*, indefinitely.

It is useful to set out the key relations more formally. If we denote the primary deficit by (G − T), that is the difference between government spending excluding interest payments (G) and taxation (T), then the evolution of the stock of debt is given by

$$D_t = D_{t-1} (1 + R) + (G - T)_t \tag{1}$$

The ratio of debt to GDP is

$$D_t/Y_t = D_{t-1} (1 + R)/Y_t + (G - T)_t/Y_t \tag{2}$$

We can write this as

$$D_t/Y_t = (D_{t-1}/Y_{t-1} [(1 + R)/(1 + g)] + (G - T)_t/Y_t \tag{3}$$

where $1 + g = Y_t/Y_{t-1}$ so that g is the rate of growth of the economy.

If we have a constant debt to GDP ratio of d and a constant primary deficit to GDP ratio of p, equation 3 implies:

$$d = d [(1 + R)/(1 + g)] + p \tag{4}$$

Rearranging equation 4 gives a relation between sustainable debt/income ratio and sustainable primary deficit:

$$d = p \{1/(1 - [(1 + R)/(1 + g)])\} \tag{5}$$

Equation 5 reveals how important the relative size of R and g is. If R exceeds g, the term in brackets on the right-hand side of equation 5, which multiplies p, is negative. This implies that a sustainable positive debt to income ratio ($d > 0$) requires a sustained primary surplus ($p < 0$). But if the growth rate exceeds the interest rate (R < g), then it is possible to run sustained primary deficit ($p > 0$) and have a steady debt to GDP ratio.

Using some numbers may help to illustrate the result. Suppose a country wants to have a debt to income ratio of 0.6. If R is 7% (0.07) and G is 3% (0.03), then equation 5 implies that p needs to be −0.023: the country needs to run primary surpluses of 2.3% to generate a steady debt to income ratio of 60%. But suppose R fell to 4% while g rose to 6%. Plugging these numbers into equation 5 reveals that the necessary value of p is now 0.011: the country can run a primary deficit of 1.1% indefinitely.

Table 11.3 illustrates the dynamics of debt by showing two situations. In both cases g exceeds R. Interest rates are 3%, while the growth in real GDP plus inflation adds up to 5%; we assume 2% inflation, which implies real interest rates of plus 1%. In the first case, we start with a stock of public debt of $350 billion, but the primary deficit is $35 billion. The primary deficit to GDP ratio is 5%. But we see from the table that this implies a rising stock of debt and a rising interest burden. The debt–GDP ratio would eventually settle down on this path but at a much higher level than 50%. Only when the debt to GDP ratio is 250% is it sustainable. But if the deficit–GDP ratio were initially 1%, then although the stock of debt would continue to rise (because the government would consistently be running a deficit), the stock of debt to GDP would remain constant at 50%.

TABLE 11.3   Sustainble and Unsustainable Deficits

Assume 5% growth in money GDP—3% real + 2% inflation; interest rates are 3%

Unsustainable	GDP	Public Debt	Deficit	Interest	Debt/GDP	Deficit/GDP	Interest/GDP
Year 1	£700bn	£350bn	£35bn	£10.5bn	50%	5%	1.5%
Year 2	£735bn	395.5bn	£36.8bn	£11.9bn	53.8%	5%	1.6%
Year 3	£771.8bn	£444.1bn	£38.6bn	£13.3bn	57.5%	5%	1.7%
Year 4	£810.4bn	£496.0bn	£40.5bn	£14.9bn	61.2%	5%	1.8%
Sustainable							
Year 1	£700bn	£350bn	£7bn	£10.5bn	50%	1%	1.5%
Year 2	£735bn	£367bn	£7.35bn	£11.0bn	50%	1%	1.5%
Year 3	£771bn	£385.9bn	£7.72bn	£11.6bn	50%	1%	1.5%
Year 4	£810.4bn	£3405.2bn	£8.1bn	£12.2bn	50%	1%	1.5%

Because of output growth the government can always run a primary deficit of 1% and its debt is sustainable (in the sense that D/Y stays at 50%). An economy with a 5% deficit eventually sees D/Y stabilize at 250%.

Clearly whether g exceeds R matters. Most empirical evidence suggests that rates of return on assets in *general* do, over the long term, exceed GDP growth. What is really relevant in the context of sustainable fiscal policy is the real interest rate that governments themselves face in the bond market. This is not easy to judge because most of the debt that governments in industrialized countries have issued is not inflation proof (or index linked), that is, it offers a *nominal* (and not real) interest payment. The key issue is whether the real cost of debt exceeds or falls short of the long-run, real sustainable rate of growth of GDP. The sustainable rate of growth of real GDP probably does not exceed 2.5% for mature, developed economies. But what about the real rate of return on government debt? One measure is to take nominal yields and subtract inflation. But actual inflation over the last 20 to 30 years has probably, on average, exceeded expected inflation in many countries. So the ex-post (or realized) average real rate is a poor guide to the real cost of government borrowing going forward. Perhaps a better indication is to look at inflation proof (index-linked) bond yields. However, few governments have issued index linked bonds. The biggest market is in UK government index-linked bonds. Since that market was created in the early 1980s, index-linked yields on medium-dated (10 year) government bonds have fluctuated, but the average has been close to 3%—above the likely sustainable long-run rate of growth of developed economies.

So it would appear likely that R does exceed g, which implies that sustainability of fiscal policies requires that governments do *not* consistently run primary deficits. *Governments with existing debt will need to run primary surpluses at some point to keep the debt-to-GDP ratio from exploding.*

Of course, governments can still run substantial deficits from time to time. Indeed, not only *can* governments do this, but they probably should. We consider the potential benefits of running temporary deficits in more detail in the next two sections.

11.6   Optimal Budget Deficits

Budget deficits can be a problem or a blessing. There are powerful justifications for governments running deficits. First, governments may be running deficits to finance investment. Government spending to build a lavish presidential palace is clearly different from government spending to improve the transport system. So we should always ask what governments are spending their money on. If net government investments in productive assets more than match a deficit, then such deficits need not be a problem. Certainly they need not be unsustainable, because the level of spending is likely to improve future government revenues and GDP growth itself.

Deficit financing can also be desirable when the economy suffers a temporary shock. Consider a major war, one of the biggest shocks that can hit any economy. Increasing taxation to balance a budget during wartime could significantly raise corporate and income tax rates. In terms of equity, the generation that is paying for the war—in the direct sense of fighting it—should not also have higher taxes reduce its net resources for consumption. So on a pure *equity* argument, there are grounds for running a sustained deficit during wartime. But there is also a tax-smoothing argument—an *efficiency* argument—about distortions.

Taxes distort individual behavior—they force people to do things differently, for example, work less hard, spend less, and so forth. These distortions discourage activities that are taxed heavily, even though using resources in those areas may be economically beneficial. Taxes move resources toward activities that are taxed less heavily, rather than toward those that are of greatest value. Moreover, as we showed in Chapter 10, the level of the distortions typically rises more than disproportionately with the tax rate. This implies that governments should keep taxes at a smooth average level rather than change them every period in order to balance a budget. To illustrate the point, consider the results of two tax policies. One would keep tax rates constant at 20% through booms and recessions. The other would raise tax rates to 30% in recessions (when tax revenue would otherwise tend to fall and unemployment benefit expenditure might be high) to balance the budget and lower tax rates to 10% in boom times to stop a surplus from being generated. Under both policies the average tax rate over the cycle is the same, but because of tax distortions and inefficiencies, the constant 20% rule is better. Figure 11.7 shows why. Here the welfare loss from distortions due to taxation rises more than proportionately with the tax rate. Keeping tax rates constant at 20% would generate average welfare losses of level W_A. In contrast, setting tax rates sometimes at 10% and sometimes at 30% will generate an average welfare loss from taxation of level W_B—exactly halfway between the loss from a 30% tax and that from a 10% tax.

If there are sharply rising costs of tax distortion costs, then to minimize the harm of taxation, governments should *not* try to balance the budget every period, but instead try to keep tax rates steady over the business cycle and thereby ensure an average budget balance rather than try to balance budgets with different tax rates from year to year. If the economic cycle lasts long, tax smoothing can justify prolonged periods of deficit, provided, of course, that the government expects offsetting surpluses in the future.

This tax-smoothing idea has strong implications for how to deal with unexpected expensive events, such as wars (or German unification). Governments should only

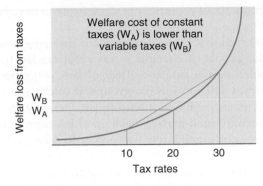

FIGURE 11.7 **Distortionary cost of taxes rises faster than tax rates.** Keeping taxes stable generates fewer distortions than having taxes sometimes well above, and sometimes well below, average.

increase tax rates by a small amount when faced with an expensive, one-time event, but keep them at this higher level for a long time. This will spread the burden across many periods. Governments have followed this policy during wartime. We noted above that government deficits in the United States have risen dramatically during wartime, but that the stock of debt had tended to fall again after the war.

The implications of all this are clear. The level of taxes should reflect the level of expenditure not just for today, but for today and in all future periods. Governments should avoid changing taxes frequently. Taxes should be set to ensure the long-run solvency of the government and not a balanced budget from year to year. Governments should expect to switch from surpluses (in booms) to deficits (in recessions). Indeed, if governments did not loosen fiscal policy in recessions and tighten it in booms, they would be switching off automatic stabilization mechanisms. That would aggravate recessions and stoke up demand in booms. Raising tax rates at times of slow output growth (or falling output) and rising unemployment is likely to be destabilizing; cutting taxes when demand in the economy is rising fast is likely to have the same destabilizing effect. Shifting tax rates over the economic cycle to ensure balanced budgets at all times would override automatic fiscal stabilizers and generate volatility in tax rates over the cycle. Such a policy is undesirable for microeconomic reasons (to do with tax smoothing) and for macroeconomic reasons (to do with stabilization).

11.7   Political Factors behind Fiscal Policy

We noted above that since the early 1970s the average size of budget deficits across nearly all developed economies has increased; as a result, the stock of debt relative to GDP has also increased in most countries. But the extent to which debt levels have risen, and the levels they have reached, differ significantly across countries. In some countries—Belgium and Italy, for example—stocks of debt have soared past 100% of annual GDP. Thus far we have focused on economic factors behind fiscal policy and the scale of budget imbalance—demographic shifts and the evolution of the business cycle. But these factors do not explain the different path of debt levels among OECD countries; after all, the impact of the economic cycle and of shifts in population structure is broadly similar. The different experiences across countries are more likely to have been the result of political differences.

At the end of Chapter 10 we observed that cuts in government spending tended to affect particular groups, while the impact of changes in tax rates tended to be more widely spread across the population. Because the effect of cuts in particular government spending programs typically falls on specific groups, if interest groups have significant political power governments will find it hard to cut spending. A system of government that gives influence to small parties, each of which represents a particular group of interests, and gives correspondingly less power to a single large party that represents a wider group, has more difficulty cutting government spending. In a political system with many parties, where none has a majority in the legislature, then most governments are coalitions in which the largest party might have to make concessions to smaller parties, which could involve agreeing to preserve (or increase) spending on particular programs. Furthermore, the greater the difficulty of forming governments, and the more often coalitions fall apart, the shorter the life of any government is likely to be. This encourages short-term behavior. So the government is likely to avoid the unpleasantness associated with tax increases and cuts in spending and pass a higher level of debt and a greater long-term fiscal problem on to the next government.

Evidence shows that these political considerations are relevant. Figure 11.8 shows the average size of the deficit to GDP ratios across the OECD countries in the 1980s. Here we distinguish among three types of country: those where some form of representative (or coalition) governments are common—often as a result of election to the legislature by proportional representation; those where the majority party forms a government; and those with a presidential system. The figure shows that deficits were significantly higher in the "representative" systems than in the majoritarian or presidential countries in which power tends to be centralized in the hands of one party or even one person. Figure 11.9 shows that the same ranking is true when we focus on debt levels rather than deficits. The more centralized power is likely to be, the lower debt levels tend to be: presidential systems have debt levels that are about 70% of those in majoritarian systems and only around 40% of those in "representative" systems.

Ultimately the structure of government and the nature of voting systems may be more significant factors behind fiscal policy than concerns about tax smoothing and macroeconomic stabilization. For that reason some commentators have advocated

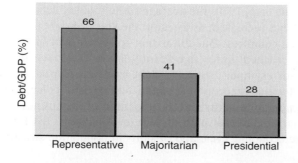

FIGURE 11.8   **Debt and politics, 1989.**
Source: Alesina and Perotti, "The Political Economy of Budget Deficits," IMF Staff Papers (March 1995) vol. 42, pp. 1–31.

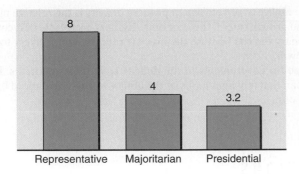

FIGURE 11.9   **Average deficit/GDP (1980–89) in OECD by political system.** *Source*: Alesina and Perotti, "The Political Economy of Budget Deficits," IMF Staff Paper (March 1995) vol. 42, pp. 1–31.

reform of the constitutional framework to limit the ability of governments to run deficits. In the United States the Republican party has advocated a balanced budget amendment that would make it illegal for an administration to plan to run a budget deficit. The rationale for such an amendment is that politicians rarely have the political willpower to run the budget surpluses that are required to offset the impact of past and future deficits. Governments with limited time horizons are likely to see the benefits of cutting taxes and raising spending more clearly than those of bringing deficits down. The balanced budget amendment aims to remove fiscal discretion from politicians—just as the establishment of an independent central bank removes much of politicians' influence over monetary policy.

Balanced budget amendments reflect a belief that politicians' interests may be different from the real needs of current and future citizens. But, for tax smoothing and macroeconomic stabilization reasons, taking away government's options to run budget deficits for what might be significant periods (and certainly for more than one quarter or even one year) is unlikely to benefit citizens. How well politicians' interests can be brought into line with those of citizens is the ultimate test of a political system. The design of optimal constitutional constraints on discretion over fiscal policy is an important aspect of the overall political system. Getting the tradeoff right between the benefits and the dangers of government's having discretion over fiscal policy is profoundly difficult.

SUMMARY

Governments rarely match spending to tax revenue—fiscal deficits or surpluses are the norm. In the period since the Second World War deficits have been much more common than surpluses. The economic impact of deficits depends crucially on how the private sector responds. Ricardian equivalence would imply that the actions of the private sector offset the impact of deficits or surpluses and leave national saving, consumption, and investment unchanged. But the conditions required for Ricardian equivalence to hold are very stringent and it is implausible they hold exactly. So deficits and surpluses probably do have economic effects.

A crucial determinant of the ability to run persistent primary deficits is the relative magnitude of the interest rate and the growth rate of the economy. Evidence suggests that countries cannot persistently run primary deficits because the interest rate on debt is likely to be above the sustainable rate of growth.

Finally, controls on the scope for governments to run deficits have their advocates. But the benefits of tax smoothing mean that any tight limits of the ability to run unbalanced budgets would come at a substantial cost.

CONCEPTUAL QUESTIONS

1. Consider the governments that have ruled in your country over the past 40 years. Is there any link between the strength of those governments and the fiscal stance?

2. Does the fact that substantial amounts of wealth are bequeathed in most economies suggest that Ricardian equivalence holds?

3. Because future generations are likely to enjoy higher real incomes than the current generation, shouldn't we aim to run up the stock of debt so that those most able to pay face the higher taxes?

4. If you were designing a constitutional amendment to limit the ability of the government to run unbalanced budgets, how might you set the limits to the scale and duration of deficits and surpluses? Would you set tighter limits on the size of deficits than on surpluses? If so, why?

ANALYTICAL QUESTIONS

1. In a closed economy the level of private sector saving is $250 billion. Government spending is $190 billion and the government does not undertake any investment. Tax revenue is $178 billion. What is the level of investment? Now assume that taxes rise to match unchanged public spending. Assuming that 20% of the tax raised from the public would have been saved, what is the new level of overall investment?

2. A government is running a balanced budget. An election is approaching and the government decides on a one-time, temporary massive tax cut which will cut tax revenue by $50 billion in one year; after this tax rates and tax revenue returns to normal. The government decides to issue perpetual bonds of $50 billion to cover the cost of the tax cut. The interest rate on these bonds is constant at 6%. The tax to pay the interest in the future will be levied on the private sector. Suppose that one-half of the population plans ahead and wants to leave enough in bequests to the next generation so they are not harmed by future higher taxes. The other half of the population spends all they can now. The government can sell bonds domestically and on a world capital market:

    (a) What is the impact of the tax cut on domestic saving?

    (b) What happens to consumption?

    (c) Who buys the $50 billion of debt?

    (d) What might happen if the government could not borrow abroad?

3. Consider the initial situation shown for the two economies in Table 11.3. Using a spreadsheet calculate the evolution of the stock of debt, debt interest payments, and the overall deficit if interest rates are 4% rather than 3%. How much lower would the initial stock of debt need to be for the second country for the situation to generate a constant ratio of debt to GDP?

4. A government receives revenues from tax on extraction of domestic natural resources worth $25 billion a year. The natural resources are all exported. The government initially expects the real revenue to remain constant indefinitely. A major war suddenly drives the price of the natural resources up hugely so that tax revenue doubles to $50 billion. Higher prices are expected to last for three years. The real interest rate is 5%. By how much could the government *permanently* cut tax revenue from *other* sources to preserve the overall fiscal position?

5. Suppose that the real interest rate in an economy is 6%. Real GDP grows by 2.75% a year. The new chief economic adviser to the government argues that a tax increase of $20 billion will generate huge benefits because the real interest rate is much larger than the growth of GDP, so that tax rates will be lower on future generations forever. What is wrong with this argument?

CHAPTER 12

Money and Prices

Overview

This chapter focuses on the nominal side of the economy—the money and prices we use to measure economic activity. We examine the historical behavior of prices and the surge in inflation that occurred in the later twentieth century. We consider how to measure prices and inflation and compare their different meanings. We discuss why policymakers want to control inflation and what are the costs of inflation.

Intimately linked to prices is money—after all, we quote prices of goods and services in terms of money. We review the historical development of money—from commodity money to paper money—and examine how governments and the banking sector create money and credit.

We then consider the interaction between money and inflation. We first discuss hyperinflations—inflations of more than 50% per month—and show that they really always originate in fiscal policy when governments print money to finance their activities. We review the concepts of seignorage and the inflation tax and compare them across countries. We then discuss a more general link between money and inflation and outline the quantity theory of money, which forms the basis of monetarism—the idea that inflation can be controlled by controlling the money supply.

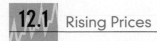

12.1 Rising Prices

THE HISTORICAL RECORD

Although historical evidence regarding the scale of economic activity is often obscure, we have much more evidence about the price of different items. The various receipts, invoices, and advertising leaflets that accumulate in pockets and wastepaper baskets amount to a substantial historical legacy. From these we can construct price indexes over time that reflect the costs of buying a representative collection of consumer goods. For example, we could go to a supermarket on January 1, 2001 and buy a typical household's weekly groceries for $120. When purchased on January 1, 2002, the same groceries cost $125. With this information we can construct a price index that has a value of 120 in 2001 and 125 in 2002. This implies an inflation rate (the annual percentage change in prices) of 4.2% [(125 − 120)/120]. Price indexes often are set at a value of 100 in a particular year—usually the year used to construct the average basket of goods. Therefore, in our example, the index would have been 100 in 2001 and 104.2 in 2002.

Figure 12.1 shows the behavior of UK prices between 1661 and 2000.[1] A detailed examination and a cross-reference with UK history reveals many interesting events,[2] but we want to see the broad characteristics of price behavior. Between 1661 and 1930, prices showed no persistent upward trend. Sometimes prices rose (1730 to 1820), but at other times, they fell (1820 to 1900). Similarly, prices sometimes rose sharply (e.g., during the Napoleonic Wars (1790s to 1815) and the First World War (1914–18)) but then

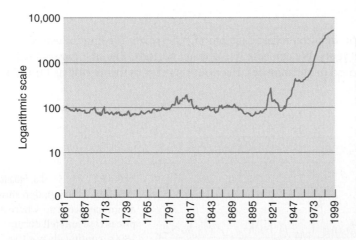

FIGURE 12.1 **UK prices, 1661–2000.** Until the twentieth century prices showed no upward trend, experiencing both increases and decreases. In the twentieth century, prices increased sharply. *Source*: B. R. Mitchell, *British Historical Statistics* (London: Cambridge Univ. Press, 1988). Updated using Office of National Statistics data.

---

[1]We have linked together a number of different price indexes because the average basket of goods has clearly changed over this time!

[2]See Fisher, *The Great Wave: Price Revolutions and the Rhythm of History* (New York: Oxford University Press, 1996), for an ambitious attempt to summarize 1000 years of inflation and its causes across a range of countries.

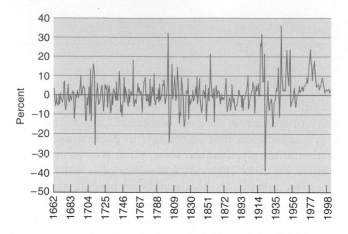

FIGURE 12.2   **UK inflation, 1662–2000.** Since 1950 inflation in the UK has been consistently positive. *Source*: Authors' calculations from Figure 12.1.

fell sharply. However, after 1930 things changed. Whereas previously prices ebbed and flowed, so that increases were followed by declines, after 1930 prices continued to increase—by 27-fold between 1945 and 2000. As Figure 12.2 shows, after 1945 annual inflation was always positive. Before 1945 the UK had experienced extreme inflation, large deflations (falls in prices), and frequent small deflations, which all kept the price level reasonably constant over long periods.

Although not all countries experienced the UK's price stability between 1661 and 1930, most countries did see prices surge during the second half of the twentieth century—Figure 12.3 shows the same pattern for the United States.

THE RECENT EXPERIENCE

Figure 12.4 shows the inflation experience among the seven leading industrialized nations over the last 30 years. We can note five distinct periods. The first covers 1973–1976 when inflation increased in all countries. Economists refer to this period as OPEC I . In

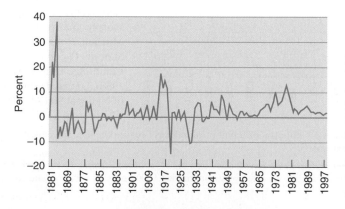

FIGURE 12.3   **U.S. Inflation, 1861–2000.** U.S. inflation shows a familiar pattern—whereas prices rose and fell during 1800s, continually positive inflation in the twentieth century caused big increases in prices. *Source*: *www.nber.org/macrohistory/ m04NNN.db* historical data.

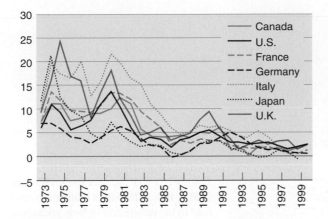

FIGURE 12.4 **G7 inflation, 1973–2000.** Inflation surged after increases in oil prices in 1973 and 1979 and after high global growth in late 1980s, but it was subdued by the end of the century. *Source*: IMF, *International Financial Statistics* (September 2000). Courtesy of IMF.

October 1973 Arab nations, through the Organization of Petroleum Exporting Countries (OPEC), a cartel of oil producers, embargoed oil sales as part of the Yom Kippur War with Israel. As a result, oil prices increased from $3 a barrel to $11.65 (see Figure 12.5 for the history of oil prices over this period). Industrialized nations were heavy importers of oil and had low oil stocks in the early 1970s, so the increase in oil prices led to a rapid increase in inflation.

By 1977 most countries had stabilized their inflation in response to OPEC I, but in 1979 OPEC again raised oil prices (OPEC II), which peaked at over $36 a barrel in 1980. Inflation surged again, although as Figure 12.4 shows, the increase was more restrained. The increase in oil prices and the associated rise in interest rates led to a global recession. This slowdown in the economy and a sharp fall in oil prices produced the third stage in Figure 12.4—low inflation among the industrialized nations in the 1990s. Inflation continued to fall, and in the 1980s, economic growth increased significantly in the industrialized world. The strength of this boom and the strong growth in all countries led to another increase in inflation by the end of the decade, so that governments again raised interest rates, and economic growth slowed. In the 1990s inflation continued to fall until by 2000 it was at its lowest level since the 1970s.

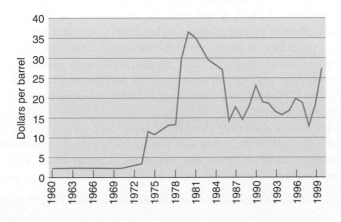

FIGURE 12.5 **Oil prices, 1960–2000.** Previous high inflation periods occurred at the same time as oil prices at historical highs. *Source*: IMF, *International Financial Statistics* (2000, observation is for 12/14/00). Courtesy of IMF.

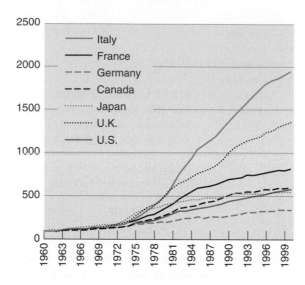

FIGURE 12.6 **G7 price levels, 1960–2000 (1960 = 100).** Differences in inflation rates lead to big differences in how prices have changed over time. *Source:* IMF, *International Financial Statistics* (September 2000). Courtesy of IMF.

We have stressed the co-movements in inflation across countries, but differences are also significant. High inflation means something different to an Italian than to a German. These differences in annual inflation rates lead to big differences in price changes over long periods. Figure 12.6 shows how prices have changed across countries. Prices are set equal to 100 in each country in 1960, so that an index of 500 in 2000 means that prices have risen fivefold. Germany has had the lowest inflation over this time period, so goods that used to cost DM1 now cost around DM3. By comparison, Italy has seen large increases in prices—a commodity that used to cost 1000 lira now typically costs around 19,000 lira.

12.2   Measuring Inflation

Price indexes measure the cost of purchasing a bundle of commodities. However, different agents buy different bundles of commodities, and each bundle defines a different price index. The most important indexes are consumer price indexes (CPIs) (sometimes called retail prices indexes (RPIs)), which measure the cost to the consumer of purchasing a representative basket of commodities. This basket includes both goods and services; commodities purchased in shops, through mail order or the Internet, and commodities produced either domestically or from abroad. Consumer prices also include any consumption taxes (e.g., general sales tax or goods and services tax (GST) or value added tax (VAT)). The CPI is the most important inflation measure because central banks often use it as a policy target.

We can also construct price indexes for producers' *input* and *output* prices. Producer input prices measure the cost of the inputs that producers require for production. Industrialized nations import many of these raw materials, so that fluctuations in exchange rates will affect changes in producer input prices.[3] Producer *output* prices,

---

[3]This is less important for the United States because many commodities are priced in U.S. dollars.

or "factory gate prices," reflect the price at which producers sell their output to distributors or retailers. Factory gate prices exclude consumer taxes and reflect both producer input prices and wage and productivity terms.

Governments and central banks pay attention to producer prices because they can help predict future changes in consumer prices. Consider an increase in oil prices that increases producer input price inflation. Because commodity prices are volatile, the firm may not immediately change its factory gate prices—customers dislike frequent changes of prices. Instead, firms will monitor oil prices, and if they remain high for several months, eventually output prices will increase. However, this may not immediately result in higher consumer price inflation. Instead, retailers may decide to absorb cost rises and accept a period of low profit margins—they may think that the increase in output prices is only temporary or intense retail competition means they are unable to raise their own prices. However, if output prices continue to increase, eventually retail prices will follow. Therefore, consumer price inflation will typically lag behind increases in producer input and output prices.

The gross domestic product (GDP) deflator is another common measure of prices and inflation. In Chapter 2 we discussed the difference between nominal and real GDP. Changes in nominal GDP reflect changes in both output and inflation, whereas changes in real GDP only reflect changes in output. Therefore, we can use the gap between nominal and real GDP to measure inflation. We define the GDP deflator as nominal GDP / real GDP. Because it is based on GDP, this measure of inflation only includes domestically produced output and not import prices. Further, because GDP is based on the concept of value added it does not include the impact of taxes on inflation.

Each of these different inflation measures reflects different commodities, so on a year-to-year basis, they can behave differently from each other. However, the various prices tend to move in a similar manner over long periods, as Figure 12.7 shows.

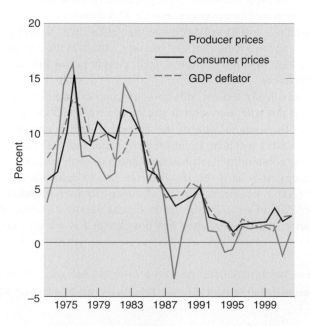

FIGURE 12.7 **Different measures of Danish inflation, 1970–2000.** Although inflation measures differ from one another each year, over time they show similar patterns. *Source*: IMF, *International Financial Statistics* (September 2000). Courtesy of IMF.

All measures of inflation tend to mismeasure actual inflation. Every year the quality of existing products improves, and firms introduce new products. If a toothpaste manufacturer increases its price when introducing a new tube that is easier to squeeze, how should our price index reflect this? The toothpaste costs more, but in part this reflects its improved quality. Therefore, some of the increased cost of purchasing the representative basket of goods reflects improvements in product quality rather than the increased cost of buying *exactly the same* commodity.

Improvements in computers and medical services illustrate this problem dramatically. Virtually no households had computers 40 years ago. Twenty years ago some households did have machines, but their capabilities were massively inferior to even the cheapest desktops available today. No PC today has as little computing power as a state-of-the-art machine had in the early 1970s. Medical services pose even deeper measurement problems. Some operations that are now relatively routine—cataract removals or hip replacements—were not feasible a few decades ago. Many drugs that exist today were not available even five years ago; how do we work out the impact on average prices of Viagra?[4] People might have paid fortunes for Viagra or hip replacements in the past, but the technology and know-how did not exist. In a fascinating article, Matthew Shapiro and David Wilcox show how issues around pricing medical services over time suggest that price indexes in the United States probably overstate inflation by around 1% a year.[5]

12.3   The Costs of Inflation

As a result of the high levels of inflation in the latter part of the twentieth century, the control of inflation now dominates economic policy. Public opinion seems to support the notion that inflation damages an economy. Figure 12.8 shows survey evidence from the United States, Germany, and Brazil over whether individuals would prefer low inflation at the cost of high unemployment or low unemployment at the cost of high inflation. Except for Brazil, a high inflation economy, most people prefer low inflation even if it entails high unemployment.

While public opinion seems firmly against inflation, economists find it more difficult to explain why people feel this way. Economists use money and prices to measure economic activity; they reflect the *nominal* side of the economy. This is analogous to using miles or kilometers to measure distance. Inflation means that something that cost $10 last year now costs $11; the commodity itself has not changed—only its price is different. To continue our analogy, it is as if the distance we use to define a mile has changed, so that one year (2001) we measured the distance between London and Boston as 3250 miles (using "2001 miles"), but in the next year we say it is 3500 miles (using "2002 miles"). Of course, the true distance has not changed at all, all that has

---

[4]See Krugman, "Viagra and the Wealth of Nations," *New York Times Magazine* (Aug. 23, 1998).

[5]Shapiro and Wilcox, "Mismeasurement in the Consumer Price Index: An Evaluation," NBER Working Paper W5590 (May 1997).

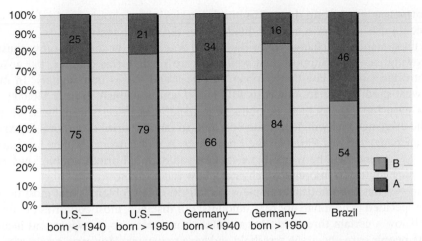

FIGURE 12.8 **Public attitudes to inflation.** Defeating inflation is seen as hugely important for the general population. *Source*: Shiller, *Why Do People Dislike Inflation?* in Romer and Romer, (eds.), *Reducing Inflation: Motivation and Strategy* (Chicago: Univ. of Chicago Press, 1997).

A is the proportion of people who prefer 10 years of 2% inflation and 9% unemployment, and B is the proportion of those who prefer 10 years of 3% unemployment and 10% inflation.

changed is the units we use to measure distance—"2002 miles" are a bit shorter than "2001 miles." The same is true for inflation—after 10% inflation, a dollar buys 10% less.

Economists refer to money as "a veil"—it is merely a system used to price things and should not influence the real economy. It does not matter whether I measure the distance between London and Boston in miles or kilometers—the actual distance that needs to be traveled does not change. Similarly it does not matter if we use 2001 prices or 1960 prices in the economy the real side of the economy remains unaltered. This belief that in the long run money is neutral helps explain the different results shown in Table 12.1; 84% of ordinary citizens agree that preventing high inflation is

TABLE 12.1 **How Important Is Preventing Inflation?**

	1	2	3	4	5
	Fully Agree		Undecided		Fully Disagree
All U.S. Citizens	52	32	4	8	4
Economists	18	28	11	26	18

The table shows response to question, "Do you agree that preventing high inflation is an important national priority, as important as preventing drug abuse or preventing deterioration in quality of our schools?" Whereas the general population believes defeating inflation is hugely important, there is less consensus among economists.

Source: Shiller "Why do people dislike inflation?" In Romer and Romer (eds.), *Reducing Inflation*: Motivation and Strategy (Chicago: University of Chicago Press, 1997).

as important as preventing drug abuse and deteriorating school standards. By contrast, economists are almost equally divided over the same question.

To understand why changes in prices should be neutral for the economy, consider the following example. Suppose that while you are reading this chapter, the government introduces a new law that doubles all prices and wages immediately. In other words, what used to cost $5 now costs $10, and if you previously earned $40,000, you will now earn $80,000. All bank accounts, loans, and asset prices will likewise be doubled. The exchange rate will depreciate by a half, so that the price of imports or exports remain unchanged in real terms for their purchases. A new currency will be introduced, and all old currency will be worth twice its face value. So all prices double,[6] but aside from causing confusion (more of which later), how is it costly to society?

However, this hypothetical example is unrealistic. One problem is that most tax systems are specified in nominal, not real, amounts. For instance, most countries do not tax income below a certain threshold. But as inflation increases, so do wages and income, and more people earn above the threshold and have to pay tax. However, wages are only increasing in line with inflation; real incomes are not changing. But the increase in nominal income means that more people are paying tax and thus are worse off.

The taxation of interest rates causes a similar problem. Tax is usually levied on the nominal interest rate, e.g., if interest rates are 10%, and the tax rate is 50%, the net of tax interest rate is 5% [$10\% \times (1 - 0.5)$]. However, two components make up the nominal interest rate—one term reflects expected inflation, the other reflects the real interest rate. The term reflecting inflation compensates the saver for rising prices. If inflation is 5%, then a good that costs $100 at the beginning of the year costs $105 by the end of the year. Therefore, investors need to earn at least 5% if they are not to lose by investing their money. The reward to saving is the difference between the nominal interest rate and expected inflation. This is called the *real* interest rate. With an interest rate of 10% and an inflation rate of 5%, the real interest rate is 5%. After a year, the saver's $100 becomes $110, and after allowing for inflation (what used to cost $100 now costs $105), the real return is $5 or 5%. However, taxation applies to the whole nominal interest rate—even the part that compensates for inflation. For instance, with 50% tax rates, 5% interest rates, and 0% inflation, the pretax real interest rate is 5%, and net *of tax* it is 2.5% ($0.5 \times 5 - 0 = 2.5$). If inflation and interest rates both increase by 5%, the pre-tax real interest rate remains unchanged, but the net of tax real interest rate falls to 0% ($0.5 \times 10 - 5 = 0$). If interest rates and inflation reach 15% and 10%, respectively, the pretax real rate remains 5%, but the net real rate is now -2.5%, i.e., $0.5 \times 15 - 10$.

Inflation also exerts a cost by reducing the value of cash. Unlike bank deposits, notes and coins do not earn interest, so there is no compensation for inflation. As a result, the value of notes and coins falls as inflation increases (this is called the *inflation tax*, which we will return to later). As inflation increases, firms and individuals will hold less cash at any one time, so they will need to make more trips to the bank to withdraw cash, and spend more time keeping their cash balances at low levels. We call these costs "shoe leather costs." Taken literally, this phrase refers to the wear and tear that repeated trips to the bank to withdraw funds exact on peoples shoes! But it also captures

---

[6]Technically this doubling of prices is not inflation—inflation is a *sustained increase* in prices.

a more general tendency to spend time managing finances (when inflation is 20% per month, unpaid invoices become urgent) rather than engaging in productive activity. Despite their trivial sounding names these costs can be substantial—shoe leather costs can exceed 0.3% of GDP when inflation is 5%.[7]

Another cost of inflation is *menu costs*. Changing prices is costly for firms. One obvious cost is physically changing prices—printing new menus or catalogs, replacing price labels and advertisements in stores and the media. The higher inflation is the more often these prices have to change and the greater the cost to firms. Moreover, marketing departments and managers have to meet regularly to review prices, which is also costly. The lower is inflation, the less often these meetings need to be held.

Another unrealistic feature of our example of a costless increase in prices was that all prices simultaneously increased by exactly the same amount. As a result, there were no relative price changes, e.g., CD players did not become relatively more expensive than concerts, there was only a general increase in prices. In practice, although all prices might eventually increase by the same amount, they will not increase at the same time, which reduces the overall efficiency of the price system. For the market to work well, firms and consumers must respond appropriately to relative price changes. If the demand for a firm's product increases, its price will rise. This will encourage firms to produce more of that commodity and less of others. Prices therefore signal what consumers want. But inflation interferes with this signal. Producers may not know whether a price increase largely reflects increased demand for their product or just reflects a general increase in prices. Furthermore, some prices respond quicker than others, which redistributes income among individuals. For instance, if wages respond slowly to rising commodity prices, inflation will hurt consumers because their real income will fall. Table 12.2 suggests that this may help explain public resentment against inflation.

The volatility of inflation is also a problem because it leads to uncertainty—with very volatile inflation firms and consumers do not know whether inflation will be 1%

TABLE 12.2   Does Income Lag Inflation?

	Up to a Month	Next Negotiation	Several Years	Never	Don't Know
USA	0	7	39	42	11
Germany	0	8	40	40	12
Brazil	2	19	17	28	14

Response to "How long will it be before your income catches up with inflation?" One reason individuals dislike inflation is a belief that their wages rise slower than inflation.

Source: Shiller, "Why do people dislike Inflation?" In Romer and Romer (eds.), *Reducing Inflation: Motivation and Strategy* (Chicago: University of Chicago Press, 1997).

[7]Fisher, "Towards an Understanding of the Costs of Inflation II," *Carnegie Rochester Conference Series on Public Policy* (1981) vol. 15.

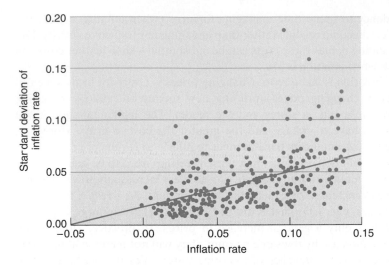

FIGURE 12.9 **Inflation and inflation volatility.** Countries with high inflation also have more volatile inflation. *Source*: Barro, Inflation and Economic Growth, NBER Discussion Paper 5326 (1995).

or 10%. If inflation is predictable, contracts can be written to minimize its costs. But if inflation is different from what was expected when contracts were written, the parties to the contracts will not get the return they were expecting. These are redistribution effects—some parties gain, others lose—but they can still have an overall impact on society. For instance, unexpectedly high inflation is particularly hard on retired people whose savings are invested in banks. Interest rates only compensate for expected inflation, so unpredictable inflation will tend to impoverish the elderly. Further, *ex ante* no one knows whether inflation will be less than or greater than what they expected it to be. Inflation makes writing such contracts riskier, so fewer contracts will be written, and less money will be saved. All of this will hurt the economy. While these costs come from volatility in inflation, they are also indirectly related to the level of inflation. As Figure 12.9 shows, countries with high inflation tend also to have volatile inflation.

Inflation also harms long-run growth. Evidence suggests that an increase in inflation of 10% leads to a decline in growth per year of between 0.2 and 0.3% and a fall in investment/GDP ratio of 0.4–0.6%.[8] However, we can only identify these costs if we focus on countries whose inflation rates exceed 15%. At lower rates inflation does not seem to adversely affect long-run growth.

Inflation may also seem costly for another reason—it complicates economic life. Imagine that every year the distance that we called a mile got smaller by a variable amount. This is analogous to how inflation every year reduces the value of what money can buy. Dealing with these changes would be a computational burden. What year was the atlas printed that tells you how far apart two cities are? In what year was the speed control in your car installed or the speed limit signs on the highway erected? The scope for confusion and mistakes would be considerable. Not only do these annual changes in

[8]Barro, "Inflation and Economic Growth," NBER Working Paper 5326 (1995).

TABLE 12.3   It's Just an Illusion?

	1	2	3	4	5
	Fully Agree		Undecided		Disagree
U.S. Citizens	28	21	11	14	27
Economists	0	8	3	13	77

Responses to "I think that if my pay went up I would feel more satisfied in my job, more sense of fulfillment even if prices went up just as much." Individuals seem to react inappropriately to purely nominal variables.

Source: Shiller, "Why Do People Dislike Inflation?" In Romer and Romer (eds.), *Reducing Inflation: Motivation and Strategy* (Chicago: University of Chicago Press, 1997).

value lead to costly calculations, but people may not respond rationally to price changes. Table 12.3 shows that when people's salary rises by the same amount as inflation, so that their real income remains unchanged, nearly half of respondents would feel better off. Table 12.3 shows evidence of what economists call *nominal illusion*—people mistake nominal changes for changes in a real variable. If prevalent, this behavior will be another source of inflation costs.

12.4   The Nature of Money

In everyday conversation, when people talk about someone having lots of money, they really mean that she is rich—she has wealth. In calculating a person's wealth, we convert the components of that wealth—cars, stocks and shares, houses, gold, pension rights, yachts, works of art—into money values. But just because we can put a dollar value on your car or the current assets in your pension fund does not make them money, in the sense an economist uses the word. A car or a house is not money because money by definition can be used to make a transaction, which implies that it is an acceptable means of payment. Try paying for a pair of Nike sneakers with a few bricks from the side wall of your house!

What counts as money is a matter of convention and convenience. For instance, in North Carolina in 1715, 17 commodities were declared to be legal tender including wheat and maize. Money is whatever people will accept in return for handing over goods. What is acceptable as money to *me today* depends crucially on what I expect its acceptability will be for *others tomorrow*. Acceptability limits what items can serve as money. Historically the need for acceptability led societies to use precious or rare commodities as money, but over time we have switched to money that has value only because government legislation says it has value, what we call *fiat money*.

Money makes an economy much more efficient. Suppose money did not exist and that people had to rely on barter—swapping goods directly rather than accepting money as payment for them. To get through the week in a barter economy, you would need to have some goods that the producers of gasoline, milk, electricity, bread, movies, newspapers, etc., each wanted to swap with you. As economists we make money by giving lectures, writing books, and thinking profound thoughts on, for example, the role of money. But how could we find someone willing to swap 10 gallons of gasoline on a wet night at 11:30 PM for some economics advice? And how does the person who sells gasoline buy this book (assuming we don't frequent the gas station)? She needs to find a bookseller who wants to trade a few cans of gasoline in his bookstore in exchange for this fine text. Tricky—to put it mildly.

Barter relies on a double coincidence of wants—you need to find someone who has the commodity you want and who also wants the good that you are willing to trade. This is costly in three ways:

(a) Transaction costs are high; you have to find out what commodities people are willing to exchange and then you have to decide on a price.
(b) When you go shopping, you have to carry around with you many different commodities in the hope that you can barter some of them.
(c) You can not consume this sample of commodities because you need them to make transactions.

THE ROLE OF MONEY

Money avoids these costs because everyone accepts it in exchange for commodities. The publisher sells this book for money and can then use money to buy gasoline. Note that the publisher values not the money itself but only what it can purchase. Similarly, the owner of the gas station accepts money for gas only because she can then use it to buy what she wants.

Money offers substantial efficiency gains over barter because it fulfils three key roles: it acts as a medium of exchange, a unit of account, and a store of value. We have already discussed the importance of money as a medium of exchange. But also important is its role as a unit of account—the language in which prices are quoted. We could measure the prices of commodities in terms of almost anything, for example, a loaf of bread. But it is bizarre to quote prices in terms of a commodity when transactions do not actually involve the exchange of that commodity. Why would we quote the price of boots, cellophane, computers, and motor bikes in terms of numbers of loaves of bread when nobody would pay for those things at a store with a truck full of loaves? It makes sense to quote prices in terms of what we will hand over when we purchase goods.

The final role for money is as a store of value—money needs to be a durable commodity that can transfer purchasing power from one period to another. Even in the simplest preindustrial societies, there was a gap between the times when people wanted to sell what they produced and the times when they wanted to buy what they consumed. As the local baker, I may want to sell all my loaves by 10 AM each day. Due to the drudgery of my life, I tend to want to spend much of the proceeds of my bread sales on alcohol, which I generally consume after 6 PM. So I need a means of holding the revenue from my bread sales until the bars open at 6 PM. Holding my bread revenues in the form of money lets me do this.

COMMODITY AND PAPER MONEY

Until the nineteenth century, most money in most countries was commodity money; that is, money that itself was a durable and physical commodity as opposed to pieces of paper. To use money as a medium of exchange, the seller has to be persuaded that she is receiving something valuable. If the commodity used as money is scarce or not easily reproduced, then sellers are likely to be persuaded to accept it. Therefore common forms of money have been cowrie shells, gold, silver, and even stones (Native Americans used *wampumpeag* as currency—strings of mainly white beads).[9]

Commodity money is a satisfactory way of establishing a medium of exchange because people will accept in payment a valuable commodity. But it also has disadvantages. First, because money is a valuable commodity, people like to use it for other purposes, e.g., gold can be used for jewelry or in industry or in dentistry. But because money is used as a medium of exchange, it will be in short supply for these other uses. For instance, during World War II, cigarettes were used as money in prisoner of war camps. This puts smokers in an expensive dilemma! Second, commodity money has intrinsic value. This gives individuals (or governments!) an incentive to adulterate coins with less precious metals, and as a result the public loses faith in the value of money.

For these reasons, most countries over time moved from commodity money to paper money. To see how this process occurs, consider the practice on the Pacific islands of Yap where large circular stones (called feis) were for many centuries the only form of money.[10] Feis were so large that holes were drilled through them so that they could be carried around on poles. Because the stones were unwieldy, they were not carried around to pay for goods. Instead claims to the stones circulated as money. Now as long as you have a piece of paper that proves that you own a stone (which may be stored miles away and never moved), you have something valuable. If you can transfer that claim to another person, he should be willing to accept it in exchange for goods and services. So this is one (big!) step removed from pure commodity money. We are talking about a system in which paper claims circulate as money. The confidence in the pieces of paper ultimately rests on the knowledge that somewhere a stock of physical commodities could in principle be delivered when the paper claim is presented. Furthermore, the physical commodities are in limited supply and hard to fake.

This describes a system of paper money in which people accept bits of paper as payment because they can go to the monetary authority and swap them for a precious commodity. However, in normal circumstances people are too busy to keep swapping paper for the precious commodity. Therefore the paper money circulates with increasingly less use made of the underlying precious commodity. At this point the government may be able to switch to a fiat currency by abolishing convertibility into the precious commodity and legislate that people *have* to accept intrinsically worthless pieces of paper as money.

---

[9]See Davies, *A History of Money: From Ancient Times to the Present Day* (Cardiff: University of Wales Press, 1994) for a broad survey of the history of money.

[10]The rather unusual nature of currency in the Islands of Yap is a source of great fascination for numismatologists. A large sample of a fei stands in the courtyard of the Bank of Canada in Ottawa.

As long as everyone accepts this convention, and they have done so historically, the fiat money system works as well as the commodity money system.[11]

The Chinese are widely believed to have been the first to introduce fiat paper money. Marco Polo lived in China between 1275 and 1292 and in Chapter XVIII, "Of the Kind of Paper Money Issued by the Grand Khan and Made to Pass Current throughout His Dominions," of his *Travels*, he writes:

> *In this city of Kanbalu is the mint of the grand khan, who may truly be said to possess the secret of the alchemists, as he has the art of producing paper money. . . . When ready for use, he has it cut into pieces of money of different sizes. . . . The coinage of this paper money is authenticated with as much form and ceremony as if it were actually of pure gold or silver . . . and the act of counterfeiting it is punished as a capital offense. When thus coined in large quantities, this paper currency is circulated in every part of the grand Khan's dominions; nor dares any person, at peril of his life, refuse to accept it in payment. All his subjects receive it without hesitation, because, wherever their business may call them, they can dispose of it again in the purchase of merchandise they may have occasion for; such as pearls, jewels, gold or silver. With it, in short, every article may be procured.*

This captures the essence of paper money—note how the grand Khan enforces its acceptance!

Most countries now use fiat money. If you go to the European Central Bank or the U.S. Federal Reserve Board with a euro or a dollar you will not be given gold or silver. The one modern exception is countries that operate a currency board (see Chapter 20), such as Hong Kong and Argentina, which is committed to swapping the national currency for dollars at a fixed rate. In this case U.S. dollars fulfill the role of a precious commodity.

12.5 The Money Supply

Much of a person's wealth is in some form of money, but most of it is not. While people own notes and coins, they may also hold part of their wealth in various types of bank deposit. They also may hold stocks and shares, either directly or through pension schemes. Many people also own their homes, though often they also have a large liability in the form of a mortgage. People can use some of the forms in which they hold wealth to quickly and easily buy other commodities. I can easily use money in my bank account to buy goods and services. But other financial assets are harder to exchange for goods and services. I cannot easily get my hands on the assets in my pension fund until I retire. And even if I own stocks and shares, I have to sell them and transfer the proceeds into a bank account before I can write a check on that account to buy goods.

---

[11]Mankiw recounts another story from the Island of Yap. During a severe storm, some large feis were sunk irretrievably. It was agreed that the owners of the stones were not to blame and that their paper claims were still valid, *even though no feis backed them up*. This shows perfectly how an economy moves from commodity money, to paper money backed by commodities, to a system where the link between paper claims and the original commodity money becomes tenuous. (*Macroeconomics*, New York: Worth, 1992).

Financial assets therefore have a spectrum of spendability, or *liquidity*. Some financial assets are readily available to use to buy goods and services—notes and coins, for example—and we will certainly want to call them *money*. Others (stocks and shares, life insurance policies, or pension fund assets) are less liquid and should not count as money. Somewhere in between notes and coins and stocks and shares held in pension funds, are assets whose availability to buy commodities is less clear. I cannot use a 90-day deposit with a bank to finance a last-minute weekend at a ski resort unless I can switch the deposit into a checking account. However, the 90-day deposit is clearly closer to being "money" than are the stocks and shares in my pension fund. So when we think about measuring the money supply, we should be aware that in modern economies the answer to the question "What is the money supply?" has no simple answer. It depends on what measure of money you want to use.

We can start with the narrowest definitions of money (notes and coins) and then add in increasingly less liquid assets. Notes and coins are readily acceptable in exchange for goods and services almost anywhere. In fact, most bank notes state on them that people *have to* accept them, by law, in exchange for goods and services. But often people are less willing to accept a check. So checking accounts are *somewhat* less liquid than dollar bills. Other types of bank accounts that do not have checking facilities are even less liquid because we would usually need to transfer the money from them to a checking account, or else cash those deposits in (i.e., turn them into notes and coins), before we could use them to complete a transaction.

Table 12.4 shows increasingly wider definitions of the U.S. money supply and illustrates how the stock of different definitions of money stood at November 2000. The narrowest definition in the Table is M1, which is made up of currency plus demand deposits (that is, money available at short notice) and other deposits against which checks can be written (including traveller's checks). M1 represents funds that can readily be used to make transactions. Adding savings deposits to M1 gives us M2. (M2 includes other liquid forms of savings, including money market mutual funds and short-maturity eurodollar deposits.) If we add in large denominations time deposits, and other longer-maturity financial assets, we reach M3, a wider definition of the money supply.

DEFINITIONS:

M1 = currency + traveler's checks + demand deposits + other checkable deposits
M2 = M1 + retail money market mutual funds + savings and small time deposits + overnight repurchase agreements
M3 = M2 + large time deposits + term repurchase agreements + eurodollars + institutional money market mutual funds

TABLE 12.4   U.S. Money Supply ($bn), November 2000

Currency in Circulation	M1	M2	M3
522.7	1091	4887	6955

Source: www.federalreserve.gov/rnd.htm

The U.S. money supply consists mostly of credit rather than currency.

TABLE 12.5 European Monetary Union Money Supply (Euro Bns), October 2000

Currency	M1	M2	M3
343	1990	2947	4162

Source: www.ecb.int

As in the United States, the European money supply is mainly made up of credit money.

Table 12.5 shows the levels of M1, M2, and M3 in the European Monetary Union in October 2000. The definition of the various money stocks is close to, but not identical with, those used in the United States.

DEFINITIONS:

M1 = currency + overnight deposits

M2 = M1 + deposits with agreed maturity up to 2 years + deposits redeemable at notice up to 3 months

M3 = M2 + repurchase agreements + money market mutual funds + debt securities up to 2 years' maturity

12.6 How Banks Make Money—The Money Multiplier

As Tables 12.4 and 12.5 show the stock of currency (that is, notes and coins) is a small part of the wider definition of the money supply in both the United States and Europe. Notes and coins are only 8% of total M3 in the United States, 7% in the European Monetary Union, and 3.5% in the UK. In this section we will show how from a relatively small amount of currency, the commercial banking sector can create many more large bank deposits through a mechanism called the money multiplier. The money multiplier means that only a relatively small part of the money supply is under the *direct* control of the monetary authorities. In Chapter 17 we shall explain how central banks try to control the money supply and set interest rates. Here, however, we focus on how commercial banks create credit—literally how they make money, or create the gap between M3 and currency.

RESERVES

A critical variable for commercial banks is their reserves, which are either cash held in the banks' vaults or money the banks hold on deposit with the central bank. How much a bank can lend depends on its level of reserves. If a bank extends too much credit, it risks exhausting its reserves. If a high proportion of its customers simultaneously write checks or make payments from their account, the bank will not have the cash to honor its commitments to the other banks that have received these payments. Banks and the monetary authorities thus closely monitor the level of reserves. Most countries set a *reserve requirement*—a floor below which the ratio of reserves to checkable deposits must not fall. For instance, if the reserve ratio is 5%, a bank that has deposits worth $100 billion must have reserves of at least $5 billion. The value of the reserve requirement varies across countries. Some countries set a low ratio, and banks themselves often choose to use a higher one. Historically, many countries used the reserve requirement as a key part of monetary policy and used it to control the money supply. More recently, countries have used the reserve requirement to ensure a stable and prudent financial system.

Although the reserve requirement limits the ratio of reserves and deposits, in effect it also constrains banks' ability to issue loans because every time a bank issues a loan, *it also creates a deposit*. When you get a loan, the bank either sends you a check for you to deposit in another bank or credits your own account with the funds. This is how commercial banks create money—they essentially swap a bank deposit, which counts as money, for a loan note, which doesn't count as money. Therefore, a $10,000 loan creates a $10,000 deposit, and with a 5% reserve requirement, requires an additional $500 of reserves. If the bank already has a reserve-to-deposit ratio of 5% and cannot obtain new reserves, it cannot grant this additional $10,000 loan.

THE MONEY MULTIPLIER

To see how the money multiplier works, consider the case of LoansR'us, which has reserves of $5 million and deposits of $100 million, so that it satisfies the minimum reserve requirement of 5%. The central bank purchases from LoansR'us $1 million worth of government bonds by placing $1 million in LoansR'us bank account at the central bank. LoansR'us reserves are now $6 million against deposits of $100 million—it now exceeds the minimum 5% requirement, so it can lend $1 million to Greedyforfinance.com and credits their account with $1 million. LoansR'us now has reserves of $6 million and deposits of $101 million. It has lent the full $1 million of extra reserves out, but the reserve requirement ratio is still close to 6%. LoansR'us can lend *another* $19 million until its deposits reach $120 million, and the reserve requirement reaches 5%. At this point Loans R'us can lend no more. Therefore, an extra $1 million of cash or reserves enables the commercial banking sector to create $20 million of additional deposits. In this example the money multiplier is 20—$1 million of reserves is turned into $20 million of M3. The magnitude of the money multiplier depends on the reserve requirement. In fact, we have

money multiplier = 1 / reserve requirement

so that a reserve requirement of 10% (0.1) would lead to a money multiplier of 10 (1/0.1).

The principle at work with the money multiplier is similar to our discussion of how the government issues paper currency backed up by its holdings of precious commodities. Because people only take a certain amount of paper currency a day to the central bank and demand to swap it for a precious metal, the central bank can issue more paper money than it has precious metal. For instance, if on average 5% of people want to swap paper for metal, then if the central bank has $5 million of gold, it can issue $100 million of paper money. This is exactly what commercial banks do. If on average only 5% of their customers want to come and withdraw their account in cash, the commercial bank can issue $100 million of loans backed by its own reserves of $5 million.[12]

---

[12]The money multiplier is not a modern invention. Sir William Petty, Professor of Anatomy at Oxford University, wrote in his 1682 work, *Quantulumcunque Concerning Money*, "We must erect a Bank, which well computed, doth almost double the effectiveness of our coined money."

TABLE 12.6   **The Money Multiplier**

	Deposit	Required Reserves	Loan
Ms. A	$ 100.00	$ 5.00	$ 95.00
Mr. B	$ 95.00	$ 4.75	$ 90.25
Mrs. C	$ 90.25	$ 4.51	$ 85.74
Dr. D	$ 85.74	$ 4.29	$ 81.45
⋮	⋮	⋮	⋮
Total	$2000.00	$100.00	$1900.00

Using a reserve requirement, banks can make loans and dramatically increase the money supply.

Table 12.6 shows this process. Ms. A deposits $100 in cash with LoansR'us, which increases its reserves by $100. But LoansR'us has to pay interest on this deposit and thus wants to lend money out to earn interest. However, LoansR'us cannot lend all $100 out because tomorrow Ms. A may wish to withdraw her cash. Based on its experience, LoansR'us calculates that on average its customers withdraw 5% of their deposits a day in cash, and therefore it decides that it can only lend out $95, which it does to Mr. B whose deposit increases by $95. However, on average, Mr. B will only want to withdraw 5% of these funds tomorrow (0.05 × 95 = $4.75), so LoansR'us can lend the remainder ($95 − $4.75 = $90.25) to Mrs. C whose account is credited with this amount. But like the other customers, Mrs. C will only withdraw on average 5% of her deposit (= $4.51), so that LoansR'us can lend another $85.74 to Dr. D. We could carry on this way for many pages (which would be very boring), but eventually we would find that from the original $100 deposit the bank increases the money supply by $2000.

12.7 Seignorage and the Inflation Tax— How Governments Make Money from Money

Issuing paper money is a high profit margin activity—the face value of currency normally far exceeds its production costs. The profit made from printing money is called *seignorage* and equals the amount of new currency that the monetary authority issues. Along with raising taxes and issuing debt, printing money is one of the three ways in which a government can finance its activities.[13] Historically, seignorage was an important source of revenue for monarchs whose one reliable source of revenue was the profits from minting coins.[14] However, in the modern economy, taxation revenues are much more substantial, and with highly developed government debt markets,

---

[13]Strictly speaking a government finances its activities through taxation or by selling bonds either to the private sector or the central bank, with bonds being purchased by issuing new currency.

[14]Loans from the nobility were often politically costly, as was taxation. Plunder from wars and ransoms were other important sources of revenue.

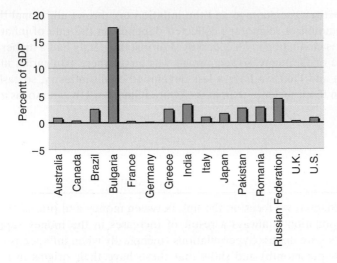

FIGURE 12.10 **Seignorage, 1997–1998 (% GDP).** For most countries seignorage is an unimportant source of revenue, but for some countries it is substantial. *Source*: IMF, *International Financial Statistics*. Calculated as change in monetary base divided by nominal GDP. Courtesy of IMF.

seignorage for most countries is a relatively small source of finance. As Figure 12.10, shows, for most OECD nations, seignorage accounts for less than 1% of GDP, although it is more important for emerging markets in which tax and bond market infrastructure is less developed.

Closely related to seignorage is the *inflation tax*. Seignorage looks like a good way to raise revenue because it means that governments have to collect less revenue through taxes. However, this ignores a crucial link between issuing money and creating inflation—the subject of the rest of this chapter. Notes and coins do not earn interest; bank deposits do. Therefore inflation reduces the value of the cash holdings of individuals—after 10% inflation a $10 bill is worth only $9 in real terms; it is as if the government has taken a dollar from your wallet. However, $10 in a bank account earning 12% interest (2% real interest and 10% for anticipated inflation) does not lose its value. Therefore

inflation tax = inflation × currency[15]

How is seignorage linked to the inflation tax? By definition

Seignorage = change in currency

Expressing everything relative to the size of the stock of currency, we have

inflation tax / currency = inflation rate

seignorage / currency = change in currency / currency

Therefore, if the inflation rate equals the growth in the money supply, then seignorage and the inflation tax are equivalent. In a later section, we outline this claim exactly—in the long run, changes in the money supply are proportional to inflation. Therefore, in the long run, the inflation tax is also proportional to seignorage.

[15]Strictly speaking, this should read noninterest-bearing assets.

This equivalence between seignorage and the inflation tax throws additional light on Figure 12.10. The amount of seignorage collected depends on the rate of inflation and on how much cash is circulating in an economy. For instance, Italy had a higher inflation rate than France or Germany, so seignorage was larger there (Bulgarian inflation was 1082%). India and Pakistan have a less developed credit industry, so cash is much more important in these societies than in the United States or UK, and so, as a result, is seignorage.

12.8 Hyperinflation

In the rest of this chapter, we focus on the link between money and prices, and in particular, on whether inflation is always a result of increases in the money supply. However, before doing so, we discuss hyperinflations (technically when inflation is running at more than 50% per month) and show that these have their origins in fiscal rather than monetary policy.

While many countries have experienced hyperinflations, it has been a particular scourge recently in two regions—Latin America and the formerly socialist economies, as shown in Tables 12.7 and 12.8.

TABLE 12.7   Latin American Inflation (%), 1981–96

	Argentina	Bolivia	Brazil	Nicaragua	Peru
1981	104	32	102	24	75
1982	165	124	101	25	64
1983	344	276	135	31	111
1984	627	1281	192	35	110
1985	672	11750	226	219	163
1986	90	276	147	681	78
1987	131	14	228	911	86
1988	343	16	629	10205	667
1989	3080	15	1430	47770	3399
1990	2314	17	2947	7485	7482
1991	172	21	432	2945	410
1992	25	12	951	23	74
1993	10.6	9	1977	20	49
1994	4.2	8	2075	6.7	24
1995	3.4	10	65	10.9	11
1996	0.16	12	16	11.6	12

Latin American experienced numerous hyperinflationary examples during the 1980s.

Source: IMF, *International Financial Statistics (*various issues*)*. Courtesy of IMF.

TABLE 12.8   Inflation (%) in Formerly Socialist Economies, 1992–98

	Belarus	Bulgaria	Kazakhstan	Romania	Russia	Ukraine
1992	967	91		211		
1993	1190	73		255	875	4735
1994	2221	96	1877	137	307	891
1995	709	62	176	32	197	377
1996	53	123	39	39	48	80
1997	64	1082	17	155	15	16
1998	73			59	28	

Reform in formerly socialist economies is hampered by hyperinflation.

Source: IMF, *International Financial Statistics* (various issues).
Courtesy of IMF.

In all these cases, the cause of high inflation was the same: a large fiscal deficit that without tax increases or the ability to issue bonds led governments to finance their activities through the inflation tax and by printing money. Unless a government reforms its fiscal position, it will have to print money and create inflation. Further, inflation will increase continuously while the authorities pursue this policy.

To see why inflation increases when the government resorts to seignorage, consider again the definition of the inflation tax as inflation multiplied by noninterest-bearing money. We can think of the inflation rate as the tax rate and the stock of noninterest-bearing money as the tax base, that is, the thing that is getting taxed. As tax rates increase, all other things being equal, the tax base shrinks as individuals shift to commodities with lower or zero taxes. Therefore, as inflation increases, people try to get rid of their cash holdings by spending them—in other words, the demand for money falls.[16] When the demand for a good falls, its price also declines, which for money means it buys less as inflation increases the price of other goods. In other words, the real money supply falls. But the government has to raise all its revenue from the inflation tax, so as the real money supply falls, the inflation rate has to rise. But, of course, this only causes the demand for money to fall further and the inflation tax to rise. Lags in the collection of taxes exacerbate the situation. If inflation is running at 5000% per month, then tax revenues collected with a lag of a few months are effectively worthless, which increases the fiscal deficit. This is an example of the Laffer curve we documented in Chapter 10—a higher tax rate does not necessarily bring forth greater tax revenue.

Therefore, hyperinflations create a vicious circle of inadequate tax revenue leading to a reliance on the inflation tax, which in turns leads to a decline in the demand for money and rising inflation. Rising inflation further reduces the real values of tax revenue collected and encourages the demand for money to fall further, leading to ever-rising inflation. The only way to end a hyperinflation is therefore to solve the underlying fiscal problem.

---

[16]China has the strongest claim to have invented paper money and also had one of the first experiences of hyperinflation around 900 AD. China had a novel way to boost the demand for money in the face of hyperinflation: *"a perfumed mixture of silk and paper was even resorted to, to give the money wider appeal, but to no avail; inflation and depreciation followed."* Goodrich, *A Short History of the Chinese People* (London: Macmillan 1957).

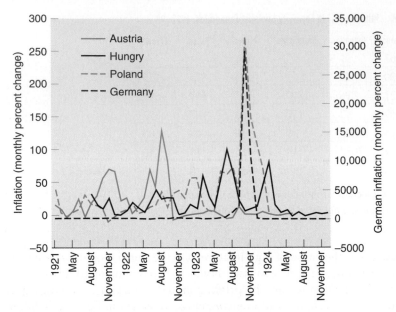

FIGURE 12.11 **Hyperinflations in Central and Eastern Europe, 1921–25.** Austria, Germany, Hungary, and Poland all resorted to printing money to finance expenditure in the 1920s, resulting in hyperinflation. *Source*: Author's calculations from data in T. Sargent, "The End of Four Big Inflations," in *Rational Expectations and Inflation* (New York: Harper and Row, 1986) pp. 41–98. Reprinted by permission of Addison, Wesley, Longman.

The classic examples of hyperinflation are those that occurred in Central and Eastern Europe in the 1920s after the First World War (1914–1918).[17] Figure 12.11 shows the *monthly* inflation rates between 1921 and 1925 for Austria, Germany, Hungary, and Poland. All these countries experienced horrendous hyperinflations. In Germany, inflation peaked at over 29,500% in October 1923.

These hyperinflations show all the signs that we documented above—large fiscal deficits, excessive reliance on monetary financing, and large reductions in the real money stock as people sought to avoid the inflation tax, which required even larger increases in inflation. For instance, in Austria between 1919 and 1920, the government issued currency to finance 63% of expenditure; in Hungary 48% between 1920 and 1921, in Poland in 1923, 62%; and in Germany in 1923–1924, 88%. Between the beginning and end of hyperinflation, the real money stock fell by 67% in Austria, 89% in Hungary, 63% in Poland, and 99.9% in Germany. These hyperinflations ended the same way—with a new currency, fiscal reform, a return to a fiscal surplus that removed the need to print money, and the establishment of an independent central bank with the constitutional ability to ignore the demands of the fiscal authority.[18]

[17]See Sargent, "The End of Four Big Inflations," in *Rational Expectations and Inflation* (New York: Harper and Row, 1986).

[18]Germany's fiscal problems were mainly a result of reparation payments to the Allies after its defeat in the First World War. In 1921–1922 reparations amounted to 77% of all government expenditure. Refusing to pay reparations was a key part of German fiscal reform.

12.9 Monetarism and the Quantity Theory of Money

We have throughout this chapter been discussing the nominal side of the economy and referred often to the link between money and prices. We now focus on this in more detail by considering the claims of monetarism—that money supply growth causes inflation. One of the famous results in economics—the Quantity Theory of Money—underpins this belief.

Nobel Laureate Milton Friedman is one of the most famous exponents of monetarism. In a seminal work, he and his co-author Anna Schwartz studied the relationship among money, output, and inflation.[19] Friedman concluded that *"Inflation is always and everywhere a monetary phenomenon."* Some critics of monetarism argue that this statement is meaningless. Inflation is essentially a change in the price of money—a $10 bill buys less because of inflation. Therefore, to claim that inflation is always and everywhere a monetary phenomenon is as true but as meaningless as saying that, in the words of Frank Hahn, "The price of peanuts is always and everywhere a peanut phenomenon."

To give Friedman's quote its full significance, we must theorize. We start with a relationship that has to hold by definition—the *quantity equation*. Let M denote the stock of money, P the price level in the economy, and T the volume of transactions. In a monetary economy, money has to back transactions, but the money supply can be less than the value of all transactions if the same bank notes are used repeatedly. For instance, if I pay the baker $5, the baker pays the butcher $5, and the butcher pays the gas attendant $5, a single $5 bill can finance $15 worth of trade because it is used three times. Economists call the number of times that money is used for transactions in a period the velocity of circulation (V). By definition

$$M \times V = P \times T$$

Rather than focus on transactions, it will be easier to focus on the overall value added in the economy, in other words, the level of total output (GDP or Y). Value added is a different concept from the number of transactions, but the two are likely to be closely linked. We can therefore rewrite the quantity equation as

$$M \times V = P \times Y$$

which implies that

% change in money supply + % change in velocity $\cong$ % change in prices (inflation) + % change in output

So far we have only developed an identity—a relationship that has to hold true by definition. To convert this into a theory of inflation, we need to make two more assumptions.

---

[19]Friedman and Schwarz, *A Monetary History of the United States 1867–1960* (Princeton, N.J.: Princeton University Press for NBER, 1963).

STABLE DEMAND FOR MONEY

The first is that the velocity of circulation does not change—the percentage change in velocity = 0. For the moment assume that M measures a narrow monetary aggregate, such as M1, and that an individual wishes to keep around two months of her annual expenditure in a checking account or in cash. Her annual expenditure is simply $P \times Y$, so money demand $(M^d) = (2/12) \times P \times Y$. But the quantity equation tells us that $M \times V = P \times Y$, so this assumption about money demand means that $V = 6$, which is, of course, a constant. Therefore, the percentage change in velocity = 0, and the quantity equation becomes

$$\% \text{ change in money} = \% \text{ change in prices} + \% \text{ change in output}$$

The same conclusion holds for any alternative assumption about how many months of expenditure the individual wants to hold in her bank account.[20]

LONG-RUN NEUTRALITY—OUTPUT INDEPENDENT OF MONEY

Assuming that the velocity of money is constant means that increases in the money supply feed through into increases either in prices or in output. Our second assumption is that changes in output are independent of changes in the money supply—in other words, money is neutral. In discussing the costs of inflation we outlined the logic behind this argument. Money is a nominal variable that we use to measure economic value. Just as whether we use miles or kilometers does not influence the distance between Tokyo and New York, neither should it matter if things cost $10 or $20, as long as all prices double. Consider again our analysis in Chapters 4–9 of what determines a country's level of output. We discussed how, via the production function, capital, labor, and total factor productivity influenced output. We never mentioned the role of money or prices. Our analysis holds irrespective of whether things are priced in euros, dollars, Disney dollars, or whether things are priced as they were in 1950 or 2000.

Over the long term, the level of real output (Y) should be independent of shifts in the money supply and in prices. When we described the evolution of real output in the earlier parts of this book, we focused on the accumulation of capital, the supply of labor, the stock of human capital, shifts in technology, and movements in productivity. These were links between *real* variables. We discussed many factors behind long-run growth, but did not mention the average level of prices or the money supply. We never gave a plausible explanation of a significant long-run link between movements in total productive output in the economy and shifts in the price level or movements in the number of notes and coins or increases in the level of nominal bank deposits.

Over the long run, real factors like the efficiency with which machines are used, the numbers of new and useful inventions, the willingness of people to work, and so on determine a real magnitude like total output. We would not expect shifts in the price level or in the stock of money to substantially affect these factors. Instead output grows at a rate (g) that is independent of the money supply but dependent on technology and

---

[20]Our result will also hold, with only minor modifications, even if there are predictable changes in velocity. Only large unpredictable changes in velocity undermine our results.

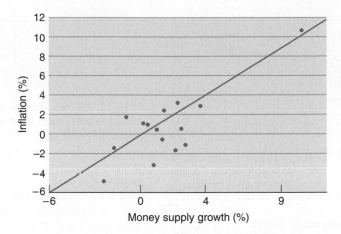

FIGURE 12.12   UK money supply and inflation, 1799–1929. Long-run UK data supports the notion that high money supply growth produces high inflation. *Source*: B. R. Mitchell, *British Historical Statistics* (London: Cambridge Univ. Press, 1988). Updated using Office of National Statistics data.

other factors. This implies that the percentage change in output = g, so we can rewrite our quantity equation as

% change in money supply = % change in prices + g

or

% change in money supply − g = inflation

In other words, inflation should be strictly related to changes in the money supply. If the long-run growth rate does not change over time, every 1% increase in the money supply will increase prices by 1%. Therefore, by assuming that the velocity of money is constant and that money as a nominal variable cannot influence real output, we arrive at a version of monetarism—changes in the money supply directly affect inflation.

Figures 12.12 and 12.13 support this monetarist view. Figure 12.12 shows money supply growth and inflation for each decade between 1799 and 1929 in the UK. Figure

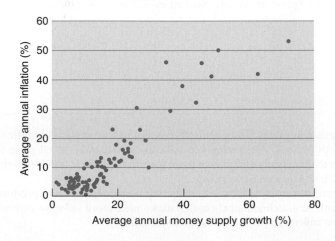

FIGURE 12.13   Cross-country evidence on money supply growth and inflation, 1980–1999. *Source*: IMF, *International Financial Statistics*, (September 2000). Courtesy of IMF.

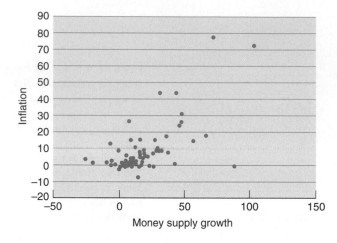

FIGURE 12.14 **Cross-country evidence on money supply growth and inflation, 1999–2000.** There is no evidence in the short run that money supply growth and inflation are connected. *Source*: IMF, *International Financial Statistics* (September 2000). Courtesy of IMF.

12.13 shows inflation and money supply growth between 1980 and 1999 for a cross-section of 90 countries. Both figures support the conclusion of our monetarist argument—inflation is a monetary phenomenon, high money supply growth means high inflation.

However, although Figures 12.12 and 12.13 support our quantity theory, they focus purely on long-run data—cross-country trends over 20 years and averages of decades for the UK. If we focus on the shorter term the evidence is much less impressive. Figure 12.14 shows the same countries as in Figure 12.13 but focuses on money supply growth and inflation between 1999 and 2000. The evidence is less supportive—countries with low inflation have a range of outcomes for money growth. Therefore in the short run, money is a poor indicator of inflation trends.

Figures 12.12–12.14 tell us that the assumptions underlying our quantity theory—stable velocity of money and output being independent of inflation—are only true in the long run. In Chapter 17 we will examine why the quantity theory does not explain short-run inflation trends and show that as a result most governments have now moved away from the idea that they can control inflation by controlling the money supply. However, the lesson from this section is clear: as a long-run theory, the quantity equation does explain inflation. Sustained inflation is always a monetary phenomena.

SUMMARY

Inflation is a sustained increase in prices. The twentieth century has witnessed dramatic inflation compared to previous periods. After surges in inflation in the wake of oil price increases in 1973 and 1979 and after strong global economic growth in the late 1980s, inflation at the turn of the millennium was once more very low.

There are many different measures of inflation, reflecting both consumer and producer prices. Quality improvements and technological change make measuring inflation difficult, and it is widely believed that official statistics overestimate inflation.

The defeat of inflation is currently a main aim of macroeconomic policy, one which receives widespread public support. To understand why, we have to find ways in which nominal variables, such as prices, affect real variables, such as output. One explanation is nominal illusion—individuals become confused and make erroneous decisions when inflation is high. Shoe leather costs, menu costs, inflation volatility, adverse interactions with the tax system, and negative effects on long-run growth all add to the costs of inflation.

Money is an asset used for transactions. Originally money was a form of precious commodity, but over time the link with commodities has disappeared. Paper money now has value and is accepted in exchange as a result of government legislation and social convention. In addition to paper currency issued by the government, the money supply also consists of credit created via the banking system.

The ability to issue paper currency provides governments with a source of revenue, called seignorage. Seignorage is equivalent to the inflation tax. Hyperinflations are caused by governments resorting to seignorage as their main source of financing.

Monetarism derives from the quantity theory of money and states that sustained inflation is caused by increases in the money supply. Assuming that the velocity of money is constant and that output is not influenced by the money supply, increases in the money supply feed through into inflation. The long-run evidence behind monetarism is compelling, but the short-run support is poor.

CONCEPTUAL QUESTIONS

1. Suppose thieves hijack a truckload of old bank notes on the way to the incinerator. The old currency is worth $1 billion. Who, if anyone, loses if the thieves get away with the cash?

2. Some right-wing "thinkers" believe that a return to gold-backed currencies is highly desirable to control inflation permanently. The price of gold in terms of consumer goods, rather than in terms of currency (which you could think of as the real price of gold), has fluctuated since gold ceased to be convertable into U.S. dollars in 1971. Does this undermine the argument of the advocates of the gold-regime?

3. Rich people tend to hold more money than poor people; so is the inflation tax fair?

4. Suppose a new drug can cure cancer. It costs a few cents to make the pill, and one pill can stop a malignant growth with zero side effects. The drug goes on sale for a few cents a pill, and although the manufacturer makes millions, the money value of the production is tiny. Is it right that GDP has not really changed much? What would the price index, both before and after the invention and sale of the drug, look like?

5. Which of these is money: a credit card; lunch vouchers; a portfolio of blue-chip equities; a $100,000 revolving credit facility; a $100 dollar bill in Moscow; one million Russian rubles in New York; one million Russian rubles in Des Moines, Iowa.

6. Suppose people could walk around with electronic charge cards that they could use to buy anything; they never need to carry currency. People would have accounts that were invested in bonds, equities, and other financial assets into which their salaries, dividends, and interest were paid. The portfolio manager would automatically sell assets whenever the card was used. In such a world would money exist? Would it matter?

ANALYTICAL QUESTIONS

1. The UK price index in Figure 12.1 has the value 109 in 1661, 83 in 1691, 81 in 1891, 231 in 1919, 208 in 1946, 1103 in 1975, and 5350 in 2000. Imagine a one pound note which is accidentaly left in the attic of a stately home when it is built in 1661. Calculate the real value of this bank note for each of the years listed above.

2. In the United States of Albion expected inflation is 5% and the real interest rate is 2%.
   (a) What is the nominal interest rate?
   (b) If inflation turns out to be 10% instead, what is the *ex post* real interest rate? Who gains and who loses from this error in forecasting inflation?
   (c) Recalculate your answers for (a) and (b) for net interest rates when the tax rate is 50%.

3. Main Street Bank sets its loans on the basis of a 5% reserve requirement and has $100 million cash in its vaults.
   (a) What is the maximum amount of loans the bank can make?
   (b) If the bank has made $50 million of loans to real estate firms, and is required to keep a 50% reserve requirement against such loans, how does this change your answer?

4. Let the demand for money in the economy be given by 150,000 − [Inflation (%)].[3] Calculate the amount of revenue raised through the inflation tax for inflation rates up to 50% (a spreadsheet would help!). What inflation rate maximizes revenue?

5. The Central Bank of Arcadia has an inflation target of 2%, and forecasts real GDP growth of 2.5% and no change in the velocity of money.
   (a) What money supply growth should it target?
   (b) If the Central Bank revises its velocity forecast to 3% growth, what does this do to its money supply target?
   (c) Assume a forecast of no change in velocity. Interest rates are currently 4%, but inflation is 3% and the money supply is growing at 5.5%. Every 1% increase in interest rates leads to a 1% fall in money supply growth, a 0.5% reduction in output growth, and a 0.25% increase in velocity. What level do interest rates have to be to achieve the 2% inflation target?

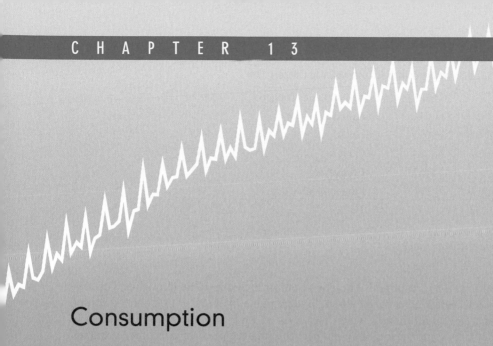

CHAPTER 13

Consumption

Overview

This chapter examines the determinants of consumption. Consumption is the largest component of demand in the economy and plays an important role in business cycle fluctuations. Saving is whatever income is not spent on consumption, so analyzing consumption is also important for understanding capital accumulation and economic growth. We consider the influence of current and future income on consumption and how borrowing restrictions and financial deregulation influence savings. The response of consumers to uncertainty over future incomes, movements in interest rates, and expectations of future shifts in taxes and wages are key determinants of the impact of government policy. We also consider how concern for future generations and the desire to leave bequests can affect savings and wealth accumulation.

13.1 The Importance of Consumption

Economists pay enormous attention to consumers' expenditure because they are interested in welfare which ultimately comes from the utility people get from consuming goods and services. Table 13.1 shows that the average U.S. household in 1998 spent $35,577 on consumption. The two most substantial components were housing—including rent/interest payments, maintenance, and utilities—and transportation—including automobile expenses. Figure 13.1 shows how over time the type of commodities that consumers buy has changed.[1] The largest component of consumption is of services, with

---

[1]Durable consumption consists of named categories for motor vehicles, furniture, and household equipment; nondurables are food, clothing, and shoes, gas and energy; services consist of housing, housing operations, transportation, medical care, and recreation.

TABLE 13.1   U.S. Average Household Consumption by Category, 1998

Food	$4,801	Alcohol and Tobacco	$581
Housing	$11,711	Apparel	$1,671
Transportation	$6,616	Health	$1,902
Entertainment	$1,744	Personal Care	$400
Reading	$162	Education	$580
Miscellaneous	$1,969	Financial Services	$3,380
		Total	$35,577

Source: Consumer Expenditure Survey, Bureau of Labor Statistics,
http://www.bls.gov/csxhome.htm

nondurable goods the next largest. There is a notable increase in the importance of consumer durables, which to a large extent is explained by Figure 13.2—the price of durables has fallen continuously which has boosted their expenditure. Whether it is televisions sets, computers, or mobile phones, the relative price of consumer durables has tended to fall over time.

Another reason for macroeconomists' interest in consumption is that it represents the largest part of overall spending and is a key determinant of gross domestic product (GDP). Table 13.2 shows the proportion of GDP accounted for by consumption in a

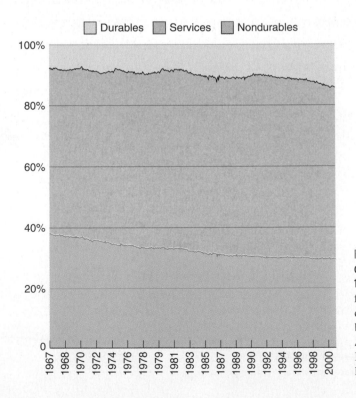

FIGURE 13.1 **U.S. consumption by category, 1967–2000.** Services account for the largest part of consumption; durables are becoming more important. *Source*: Bureau of Economic Analysis, http://www.bea.doc.gov/.

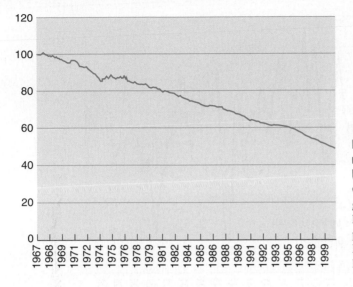

FIGURE 13.2 **Falling relative durable goods prices in the United States, 1967–2000.** Consumption of durable goods is boosted by sharp long-term decline in their prices. *Source*: Bureau of Economic Analysis, http://www.bea.doc.gov/.

sample of countries. The size of consumption varies across countries. For the majority of economies it lies around 50–65% of GDP. Among the OECD (developed) countries displayed in the table consumption varies from 48% in Korea to just over two-thirds in the United States. There is a greater range for the non-OECD economies—from 70% in Argentina to 37% in Botswana.

The importance of understanding the role of consumption in business cycle fluctuations is illustrated in Figures 13.3*a* and *b* where we show that the cyclical fluctuations in

TABLE 13.2 **Consumption as a Proportion of GDP, 1999**

ARGENTINA	69.74
BANGLADESH	77.51
BOTSWANA	37.29
CHILE	65.20
CHINA, P.R.: MAINLAND	48.06
DENMARK	50.46
GREECE	70.25
JAPAN	61.93
NORWAY	48.48
SWEDEN	50.55
THAILAND	56.08
USA	67.41

Source: IMF, *International Financial Statistics,* (September 2000).

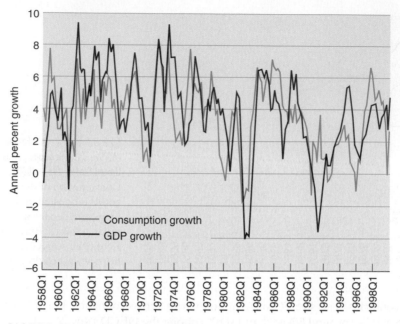

FIGURE 13.3a   **Consumption and GDP growth in Canada, 1958–1999.** *Source*: IMF, *International Financial Statistics* (September 2000). Courtesy of IMF.

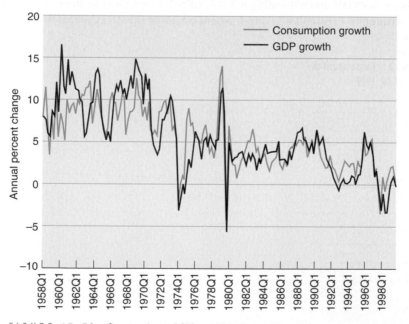

FIGURE 13.3b   **Consumption and GDP growth in Japan, 1958–1999.** Consumption tracks GDP very closely over the business cycle. *Source*: IMF, *International Financial Statistics* (September 2000). Courtesy of IMF.

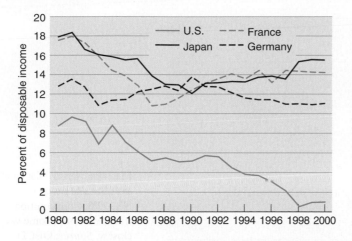

FIGURE 13.4 **Savings rates in the United States, Japan, France, and Germany.** There is substantial variation in savings rate over time and across countries. *Source*: OECD Economic Outlook (2000). Copyright OECD.

Canadian and Japanese GDP are closely mimicked by fluctuations in consumption. These figures also illustrate another fact—*while consumption closely follows GDP fluctuations, it is not so volatile.* For instance, whereas Canadian annual GDP growth between 1958 and 1999 varies between −3.9% and 9.3%, the growth in consumption varies between −1.7% and 8%. Understanding why consumption changes are smoother than output changes will be a major focus in this chapter.

What people do not spend out of their disposable income (that is total income, including wages, interest payments and dividends, and social security payments, less tax payments), they must save. As we saw in Chapter 5, the level of savings in a country is a crucial determinant of its long-run steady state so that in understanding the determinants of consumption we are also modeling saving decisions. Figure 13.4 shows that the savings rates vary significantly both across countries and over time.

13.2 The Basic Keynesian Model

The economist John Maynard Keynes stated that "*The fundamental psychological law, upon which we are entitled to depend with great confidence both a priori from our knowledge of human nature and from the detailed facts of experience, is that men are disposed, as a rule and on the average, to increase their consumption as their income increases, but not by as much as the increase in their income.*"[2] In other words, we should expect to see a very close relationship between current consumption and current income—both for an individual and for an economy. Evidence in support of this can be seen in Figure 13.5 which shows that in the UK consumption rises strongly with disposable income.

---

[2]*The General Theory of Employment, Interest and Money* (New York: MacMillan, 1936) p. 96.

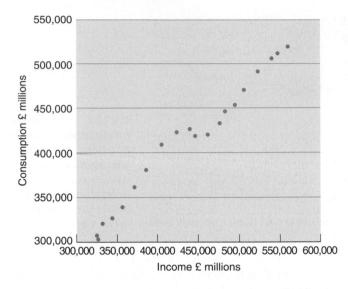

In Keynes' work an important concept is the **marginal propensity to consume**, or m.p.c. The marginal propensity to consume is the extra amount an individual will spend if you give them an extra $1. If the m.p.c. is 80%, or 0.8, then from every extra dollar of income the individual spends 80 cents. A key task of this chapter is to examine the determinants of the m.p.c. The m.p.c. may not be constant—it may vary with income. But for the moment we will assume people spend a constant fraction of every dollar they receive.

However, the m.p.c. only tells us how much *additional* income an individual spends. What about someone who receives no income? This individual will still need to consume goods and services, whether financed by begging, borrowing, or stealing. Therefore, even at zero income an individual will have positive levels of consumption. In Figure 13.6 we show how individual consumption is linked to income according to this simple Keynesian model.

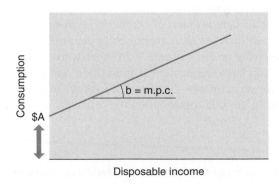

FIGURE 13.6 **The Keynesian consumption function.** The Keynesian consumption function has consumption rising with current income but by less than 1:1. The m.p.c. (b) is less than 1.

At zero income the individual spends \$A; e.g., A could be 100 or 1000. For every extra dollar, they spend b dollars, where b is the m.p.c.; e.g., if they spend 80 cents out of every dollar then $b = 0.8$. Therefore consumption is given by

Consumption = A + b × Disposable Income

or

C = A + b × Y

The m.p.c. is given by b, but we can also define the *average propensity to consume*—how much of an individual's total income he or she spends (the m.p.c. is about how much of your *additional* income you spend). The average propensity to consume (a.p.c.) is just consumption divided by income, or C/Y. Given our expression for consumption this is

C/Y = A/Y + b

As income gets larger, the term A/Y goes toward zero so that eventually the a.p.c. is the same as the m.p.c. Because consumption plus savings equals income (C + S = Y), the a.p.c. equals 1 minus the savings rate (S/Y).

Why have we spent so much time outlining the concept of the m.p.c.? For Keynes, the level of demand in the economy is key to understanding business cycle fluctuations and in turn the m.p.c. is the key concept in influencing demand. To see why, consider again the national accounts identity from Chapter 2:

Output = Consumption + Government Expenditure + Investment

or

Y = C + G + I

where we have for ease of analysis ignored net exports (X-M). We showed in Chapter 2 how the income and output measure of GDP were equivalent, so using this fact and our expression for consumption we can rewrite this as

Y = A + b × Y + G + I

which can be rearranged as

Y − bY = A + G + I

or

Y = [1/(1 − b)] × {A + G + I}

In other words, GDP equals the sum of A plus government expenditure and investment all divided by (1 − b). If the government can increase G by \$100 million, then according to this expression GDP will increase *by more than \$100 million*. If G increases by \$100 million, then Y rises by \$100 million/(1 − b). If $b = 0.8$, then GDP increases by \$500 million, while if the m.p.c. (b) equals 0.9, GDP increases by \$1000 million. The expression [1/(1 − b)] is called the **multiplier** and it represents the total impact on the economy of an initial increase in demand. The larger is the m.p.c., the bigger the multiplier.

Why does this multiplier exist? When the government spends $100 million it purchases goods with this money, which increases the income of the firms that produce these goods and their workers. Because of the m.p.c. this extra income is spent on other goods and services, further increasing income and consumption elsewhere in the economy. But this additional income is also spent so that the initial increase in government expenditure sets in motion a sequence of rising incomes and consumption throughout the economy, which serves to magnify the initial demand boost. The higher is the m.p.c. the greater the impact on consumption at every stage of the process and so the greater the ultimate increase in demand.[3]

Whereas current consumption undoubtedly depends on current income, the model we have outlined is rather simplistic. According to this model an individual looks at his or her monthly salary check and spends a constant proportion of it. But consider whether this insight holds true for the following characters:

1. A senior in college has a current income of $3000 from various part-time jobs, but Merrill Lynch offers her a job when she graduates with a starting salary of $70,000.
2. A bond trader at Goldman Sachs is currently earning $500,000 a year, but rumors of layoffs are rife.
3. The tax authorities refund $25,000 to someone in a steady job who has mistakenly overpaid taxes in recent years.

If we are thinking about how consumption is linked to current income, e.g., what is the marginal propensity to consume, then in each of these three cases we would arrive at different answers. Although the student's current income is low, she will probably wish to spend substantially more than she is currently earning because of her high future income (assuming the bank will loan her the money). The Goldman Sachs trader has a very high current income, but uncertainty about the future will lead him to accumulate savings in order to prevent consumption from crashing if he loses his job. The third case involves a one-time windfall receipt of income which will not be repeated. The consumer therefore has to choose between spending it all today or spreading it out over several years.

13.3   The Permanent Income Model

All of these examples suggest, as does common sense, that when deciding how much to consume households think about their income over the future as well as what they currently earn. These ideas lead us to a broader theory of consumption, called the **permanent income** theory,[4] which provides a much richer model of the determinants of the m.p.c. To understand this theory we outline a simple and stylized model of income over a person's life.

---

[3]We stress this is an uncritical exposition of basic Keynesian economics. The validity of this analysis is much contested. Note that it ignores completely prices and any consideration of the supply side.

[4]Friedman, *A Theory of the Consumption Function* (Princeton, NJ: Princeton Univ. Press for National Bureau of Economic Research), 1957.

THE INTERTEMPORAL BUDGET CONSTRAINT

Any model of consumption must contain two ingredients: the constraints consumers face and also their preferences. We focus first of all on their constraints.

Consider a person whose life consists of two periods (if it cheers you up, let the periods last for many years). Denote labor income in the first period by $Y(1)$ and in the second period as $Y(2)$. For instance, if the individual is a student in the first period, $Y(1) = 0$, but $Y(2)$ will be positive—her salary. If instead the individual is currently working but will retire next period, then $Y(1)$ is positive and $Y(2)$ zero. We shall denote consumption in the first period by $C(1)$ and in the second by $C(2)$. For ease of analysis we also assume the individual has no wealth at the beginning of the first period. This means that at the end of the first period the individual's bank balance is $Y(1) - C(1)$. If the individual has saved money, $Y(1) > C(1)$, the bank balance is positive. If instead he borrowed money to finance high consumption [$Y(1) < C(1)$], then he owes the bank money. Assuming the bank pays out interest r, (or charges an interest rate on loans of r), then at the beginning of the second period the bank account has funds worth

$$(1 + r) \times (Y(1) - C(1))$$

Therefore, the maximum amount of money the individual has to spend in the second period is given by

$$Y(2) + (1 + r)\,[Y(1) - C(1)]$$

Assuming the individual does not wish to leave any inheritance she will spend this entire amount on second period consumption so that

$$C(2) = Y(2) + (1 + r)\,[Y(1) - C(1)]$$

In order to arrive at the intertemporal budget constraint we need to do a little rearranging. First we collect on one side all the consumption terms and on the other all the income terms. This gives

$$(1 + r)C(1) + C(2) = (1 + r)\,Y(1) + Y(2)$$

If we finally divide through by $(1 + r)$ we have the **intertemporal budget constraint**

$$C(1) + C(2)/(1 + r) = Y(1) + Y(2)/(1 + r)$$

When we divide a number by $1 + r$ we *discount* the number. Discounting is a way of valuing future amounts of income or spending in terms of today's money. Imagine that I have $100 and the interest rate is 10%, i.e., $r = 0.1$. Therefore I can turn $100 of cash today into $110 in a year's time. This also means that if I were to calculate today the value of $110 received in a year's time I would put it no higher than $100, i.e., 110/1.1. The intertemporal budget constraint therefore says that current consumption plus discounted future consumption must equal the sum of current income and future discounted income. In other words, the key constraint that the individual faces is a *lifetime* budget constraint. While in any one particular year an individual can save or borrow, over his or her lifetime, total discounted expenditure must equal total discounted income. The intertemporal budget constraint reveals immediately the importance of the future. How much the consumer can spend today $C(1)$ depends on their expectations of future income $Y(2)$ as well as future consumption $C(2)$ and current income $Y(1)$.

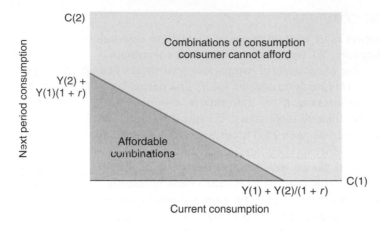

FIGURE 13.7 **The intertemporal budget constraint.** The intertemporal budget constraint shows combinations of first and second period consumption an individual can afford given lifetime income.

In the case of two periods we can show the intertemporal budget constraint diagrammatically. Figure 13.7 shows the different combinations of first and second period consumption the individual can afford on the assumption that today's income is $Y(1)$ and tomorrow's $Y(2)$. Assuming individuals can borrow against future income, they could choose to consume the whole of today's income ($Y(1)$) plus an amount equal to the maximum they could borrow against tomorrow's income—$Y(2)/(1 + r)$. Therefore the *maximum* first period consumption is given by the point on the horizontal axis at which $C(1) = Y(1) + Y(2)/(1 + r)$ and $C(2) = 0$. At the other extreme, if an individual were to save all her current income, i.e., $C(1) = 0$, she would start the final period of her life with accumulated wealth of $Y(1)(1 + r)$, to which she would add final period income $Y(2)$ to enjoy a maximum final period consumption of $Y(2) + Y(1)(1 + r)$. These two extreme points involve setting consumption to zero in one period, but the consumer can of course reallocate consumption between time periods. Every $1 of reduced period 1 consumption translates into an extra $(1 + r)$ in period 2, so the slope of the line linking these two extreme points is simply given by one plus the interest rate. Any point on the straight line joining these two extremes or any point within the shaded triangle represents consumption bundles the consumer can afford given lifetime income.

CONSUMER PREFERENCES

The intertemporal budget constraint shows what the consumer can afford; it does not say what he or she prefers. To find this out we need to know about consumer preferences. Economists draw **indifference curves** to characterize preferences between commodities (and we can think of consumption today and consumption tomorrow as two distinct commodities). Indifference curves show combinations of consumption of the two commodities between which an individual is indifferent. Consider the points A and F in Figure 13.8. Point A involves high first period consumption but very little in the second period. By contrast, F involves a lot of second period consumption but not much in the first period. However, both points are on the same indifference curve which means the consumer is equally happy with either bundle. The additional second period consumption that F implies just compensates for the loss of first period consumption compared to A.

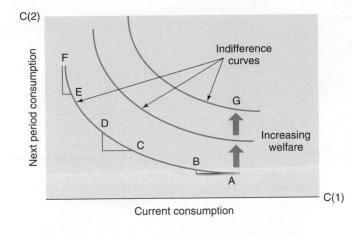

FIGURE 13.8 **Consumer indifference curves.** Indifference curves indicate consumption bundles which yield equal pleasure.

The slope of the indifference curve tells us how willing a consumer is to substitute between first and second period consumption. Consider points A and B. At point A the consumer has very little second period consumption but lots of first period consumption and we have drawn a very flat indifference curve. This means that the consumer is prepared to give up quite a lot of first period consumption in return for only a small amount of extra second period consumption. We are in effect assuming that when a consumer has a lot of one commodity but very little of another, he places a higher value on the scarce commodity. The same logic explains why the indifference curve is so steep between points E and F. In this case the consumer has an abundance of second period consumption and so is prepared to forgo quite a lot of this in return for a small increase in initial consumption. Finally, between points C and D the consumer is willing to trade roughly equal amounts of first and second period consumption—when they have similar amounts of both commodities they are valued roughly equally.

The previous discussion was about different combinations of first and second period consumption which yield the same welfare. However, comparing points A and G we see that they both have the same amount of first period consumption, but G involves more second period consumption. Therefore the consumer prefers bundle G to bundle A and these different combinations are on different indifferent curves. The higher the indifference curve the more the consumer prefers the consumption bundles.

THE CONSUMER'S CHOICE

If we put together the intertemporal budget constraint and the indifference curves we have a complete analysis of the consumer's consumption decisions. Assuming that consumers' want to maximize their welfare they will want to choose the combination of first and second period consumption that puts them on the highest indifference curve that their intertemporal budget constraint makes feasible. This is shown in Figure 13.9 as point A—where the budget constraint just touches the highest achievable indifference curve. We have drawn Figure 13.9 to produce roughly equal amounts of first and second period consumption. This result is achieved by an indifference curve with the curved shape shown. As explained above, these indifference curves imply that consumers

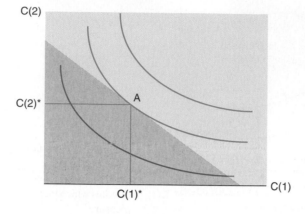

FIGURE 13.9   **Consumer's optimal choice.** Consumers choose the affordable consumption bundle that gives the highest welfare.

dislike volatile consumption—they prefer roughly equal amounts of consumption in each year. This is why they are prepared to give up a lot of second period consumption at F (see Figure 13.8) for only a small gain in terms of first period consumption.

RESPONSE TO INCREASE IN CURRENT INCOME

Figure 13.10 shows how we can use our model to analyze the effect of a temporary one-time increase in current income. It considers the case in which current income is higher by \$100,000 but no change is expected in period 2. If all income is used to finance current consumption, then instead of consuming $Y(1) + Y(2)/(1 + r)$ the consumer can now spend $Y(1) + 100,000 + Y(2)/(1 + r)$. Similarly, if the consumer saves everything, then maximum second period consumption rises from $Y(1)(1 + r) + Y(2)$ to $(Y(1) + 100,000)(1 + r) + Y(2)$. The effect in Figure 13.10 is for the whole intertemporal budget constraint to shift out. The increase in lifetime income means that consumption increases, but the increase in current income leads to a roughly equal increase in *both* first and second period consumption. This is because of our assumption on indifference curves—that the consumer prefers to divide consumption equally between both periods

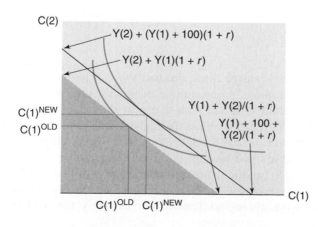

FIGURE 13.10   **Impact on consumption of increase in current income.** Both current and future consumption increase when current income rises in the forward-looking model.

rather than experience substantial swings. This implies that in response to a temporary increase in income the m.p.c. in this two-period model will be approximately 50%—half the income is spent now and half later. Arguing analogously we also note that if there are ten more periods then the m.p.c. would be about 10%.[5]

RESPONSE TO INCREASES IN FUTURE INCOME

Now consider the case in which first period income remains unchanged but tomorrow's income is expected to be $100,000 higher. The maximum amount of first period consumption that can be financed (by borrowing on the basis of all future income) is $Y(1) + (Y(2) + 100,000)/(1 + r)$ and the maximum second period consumption is $Y(1) (1 + r) + Y(2) + 100,000$ (see Figure 13.11).

As in the previous case the consumer's lifetime income has risen and she responds by spreading the increase equally between both periods. The result is that current consumption rises even though current income has not changed. This would suggest that our graduating student will respond to her employment letter from Merrill Lynch by going out and spending even though current income has not changed.

PERMANENT INCOME

Our previous two examples show that current consumption rises by a similar amount in response to an increase in current income and an increase in future income.[6] This is very different from the simple Keynesian model in which current income is all that matters. In the forward-looking model the consumer sets consumption considering lifetime

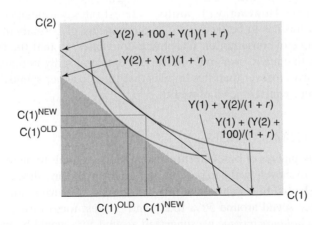

FIGURE 13.11 Impact on consumption of increase in future income. Because of borrowing both current and future consumption increase when an agent expects higher future income.

[5]Because of discounting and interest rates the increased lifetime income is not spread *exactly* equally between periods. The higher the rate at which people mentally discount future satisfaction, the more is spent today because consumers are impatient, and the higher the interest rate, the less is spent today because consumers have more of an incentive to save.

[6]The reason why there will be a difference is due to interest rate effects. If interest rates are high, then the consumer will be tempted to save more of any first period increase in income. Similarly, it is more expensive to borrow against news of higher future income.

rather than current income and, given our assumptions on indifference curves, does so in a manner that tries to avoid large changes in consumption. Consider the extreme case in which the consumer wishes to set first and second period consumption to be the same and for simplicity assume that interest rates are zero. Under these assumptions the intertemporal budget constraint is

$$C(1) + C(2) = Y(1) + Y(2)$$

If the consumer sets consumption to be the same in each period, then $C(1) = C(2) = C$ so we have

$$2C = Y(1) + Y(2) \text{ or } C = (1/2)[Y(1) + Y(2)]$$

that is, consumption is set equal to average lifetime income or what is called **permanent income**. Any change in permanent income is immediately reflected in current consumption. When first (or second) period income increases by $100,000, then permanent income (and consumption) increases by only (1/2)($100,000) = $50,000 and the m.p.c. is 50%.

Therefore, the forward-looking model has as its main relationship the link between consumption and permanent rather than current income, and the m.p.c. is determined by the influence that current income has on permanent income. This permanent income model helps explain one of the key facts of Figure 13.3—in a recession consumption does not fall by as much as GDP nor rise by as much in a boom. In a recession GDP and income are temporarily low and so the fall in current income is greater than the fall in permanent income. As a consequence the m.p.c. is low and consumption falls by less than income. Exactly similar reasoning holds during a boom so that over the whole business cycle consumption fluctuates by less than income.

The assumption of zero interest rates means that permanent income only depends on labor income in our example. However, with positive interest rates consumers earn interest on their wealth and this has to be factored into our concept of permanent income. Once again the principle of consumption smoothing dominates, so that the consumer spends from this wealth equally over time. In the extreme and sadly unrealistic case in which the consumer lives forever then this implies that the consumer spends the interest payments to maintain a constant level of wealth.

TEMPORARY AND PERMANENT INCOME CHANGES

We can combine our previous analysis of how current consumption responds to increases in current and future income to show how the m.p.c. out of permanent income shocks differs from that of temporary shocks. In response to a $100,000 increase in current income we found the consumer would spend around 50% today and the rest tomorrow. In response to a $100,000 increase in *future* income we suggested around 50% would be spent now and the rest tomorrow. A permanent increase in income of $100,000 is simply extra income today *and* next period and so combining these two results we have that the consumer has an m.p.c. out of additional permanent income of around 100% in the current period as well as next period. Therefore, the m.p.c. out of permanent shocks to income is much greater than out of temporary income. In the case of permanent shocks to income, the implications of the forward-looking model and the Keynesian consumption function are very similar—consumers will spend most of any increase in current income.

SAVING FOR A RAINY DAY

The permanent income model has important implications for savings. Consider the case in which savings are negative; that is, consumption is greater than current income. This in turn implies that average lifetime income is greater than current income, e.g., the individual feels that his or her income will rise in the future. By contrast, consider the case in which savings are positive so that current income exceeds consumption and average lifetime income. In these circumstances the individual thinks his or her income will fall in the future. Therefore, according to the permanent income model, savings is for a "rainy day"—people only accumulate assets if they believe their income is going to fall. For instance, if the individual is retiring from work in the next period his income will fall to zero and he should be saving now in order to finance his retirement. Conversely, the student who is waiting to begin employment with Merrill Lynch should be borrowing heavily and then using her high future income to repay her bank loan.

13.4 The Importance of Current Income Revisited

The forward-looking model of consumption is not consistent with the central assumption of the Keynesian consumption function that there is a simple and stable relationship between current consumption and current income. Instead it emphasizes the importance of future income in influencing current consumption decisions. In this section, however, we add two different features to the forward-looking model, each of which reinstates the importance of the link between current income and consumption. The first factor we add is consumer uncertainty about future income; we then examine the implications of constraints on how much individuals can borrow.

THE IMPORTANCE OF UNCERTAINTY

So far we have been assuming that people have knowledge of current and future incomes. In practice, however, future earnings are highly uncertain. This is likely to affect savings and consumption decisions through influencing the m.p.c. One recent study[7] suggests that as much as 46% of personal sector wealth is the result of higher savings aimed at insuring against future income uncertainty.

Let's consider two different people. Mr. Gray has taken a safe job with the tax authorities that pays a steady income forever. He is a reliable and boring type—a James Stewart character from a Frank Capra film. Then there is Ms. Purple who has piled all her savings into setting up a software company that has generated her a first-year income of $80,000, but whether she will even have a company in two or three years is anyone's guess—she is more a Sharon Stone type in a 1980s thriller. Let's assume that Mr. Gray also earns $80,000 doing his repetitive tasks. Mr. Gray is probably not going to worry about volatility in his future income and as a result will be inclined to spend more—in

---

[7]Carroll and Samwick, "How Important Is Precautionary Saving." *Review of Economics and Statistics* (1998) vol. 80, no. 3, pp. 410–419.

other words, he will have a high m.p.c. By contrast, the entrepreneur must remember that her income could fall to zero any day, and since dramatic swings in consumption are unpleasant, she will likely save in order to accumulate assets for precautionary reasons. Note that these savings are for precautionary reasons and are different from the rainy day savings we mentioned above. Savings for a rainy day are because my best guess is that my income will fall. In contrast, **precautionary savings** provide individuals insurance against their income turning out worse than they forecast. The more uncertainty there is about income and the more risk averse consumers are, the greater is precautionary savings.[8]

Introducing precautionary savings makes current income more important than future income. Future income is uncertain—I may fall ill and be unable to earn, my boss may be replaced by my arch rival who forces me out of the firm, and so forth. Given news about a $100,000 increase in both current and likely future income, the m.p.c. will be a lot higher out of the former. There is no need to do any precautionary savings in respect to current income.

BORROWING CONSTRAINTS

There is another way of reinstating the close link between current consumption and current income that characterizes the basic Keynesian model. For the forward-looking model to be relevant, individuals must be able to borrow. Consider again the student with a job offer from Merrill Lynch. The only way she can spend more than her current income is if a bank is persuaded to loan her funds. If banks refuse, then it does not matter what the student's permanent income is—she can only finance consumption equal to current income. This situation is shown in Figure 13.12. If the

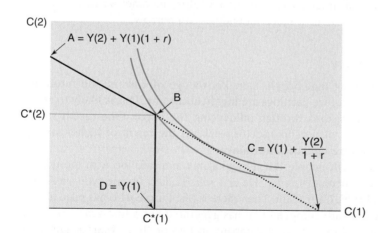

FIGURE 13.12 Borrowing constraints make consumption equal to current income. If consumers are unable to borrow, then current consumption depends on current rather than permanent income.

<hr />

[8]You may have spotted an obvious problem with this argument. James Stewart was the worrying type (which is why he takes the safe job with the tax authorities), while Sharon Stone doesn't give a damn about tomorrow and loves risk. So maybe Stewart saves more than Stone. This is an example of *sample selection bias*. The point we make in the text refers to holding attitudes to risk constant. Thus the person in the safe job would save less than the person running the new company. But running a company attracts risk-lovers and working for the tax authorities attracts the risk-averse. However, our James Stewart character will save more if he is starting up a new firm than if he is employed with the IRS.

consumer could borrow from the bank, her budget constraint is given by the line ABC. However, if the bank does not grant her credit, then first period consumption cannot exceed first period income and the budget constraint becomes ABD. With this budget constraint the consumer chooses first period consumption C*(1) and then C*(2). Therefore, she consumes too little in the first period and then too much in the second period. The inability to borrow reduces her welfare because she is on a lower indifference curve.

We can use Figure 13.12 to examine the impact of credit liberalization on the economy. During the 1980s a number of European economies instituted a process of financial deregulation. The result was a much greater degree of competition between financial institutions and the introduction of overseas banks eager to grab market share. The consequence was a surge in bank lending as banks competed among each other for new customers. In order to attract market share banks became willing to lend on anticipations of future incomes and large loans were offered for house purchases. The budget constraint thus shifted from ABD to ABC and current consumption rose strongly. Further, if consumers expect rising future income, then according to our "rainy day" story, savings will go negative as consumers avail themselves of the opportunity to smooth their consumption over time. Figure 13.13 shows this is exactly what happened in Sweden, Norway, Finland, and the UK.

In the case of borrowing constraints the m.p.c. is very high—individuals have too low first period consumption and too high second period consumption. They would like to reallocate this consumption but cannot because they cannot borrow. Therefore, when they receive more current income they will spend most of it—there is no point in saving money when consumption next period will already be too high. This situation is shown in Figure 13.14 where the increase in current income shifts the budget constraint from ABD to EFG. In this case the increased income leads entirely to higher extra first period consumption and has no effect on second period consumption.

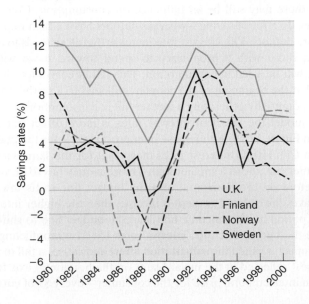

FIGURE 13.13 **Impact of 1980s financial deregulation on UK and Scandinavian savings.** The increased ability of banks to lend in the 1980s led to dramatic falls in the savings rate in the UK and Scandinavian economies. *Source*: OECD Economic Outlook (various issues). Copyright OECD.

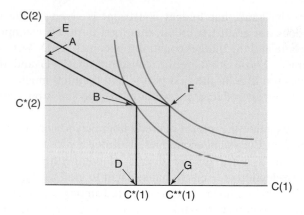

FIGURE 13.14   **Increases in income have high m.p.c. under borrowing constraints.** With borrowing constraints, increases in current income feed through into current consumption only.

Therefore, if borrowing constraints are important, it is current income rather than future income that matters.

13.5   The Influence of Interest Rates

Because of the importance of consumption as a component of GDP the influence of interest rates on consumption is an important aspect of monetary policy. In the basic Keynesian model all that matters for consumption is current income so that interest rates have only an indirect effect. For savers a higher interest rate means greater income because of higher interest payments. However, for debtors the higher interest rates reduce their income available for discretionary consumer spending. The extra income gained by creditors should equal the income loss to debtors so overall aggregate income has not changed. However, there may still be an influence on consumption. Creditors tend to have low m.p.c.—they do a lot of saving—whereas debtors have a high m.p.c.—this helps explain why they are debtors. The interest rate increase therefore leads to a redistribution of income from those with a propensity to spend toward those with a tendency to save. The result will be a fall in consumption. This fall in consumption, via the multiplier effect outlined at the beginning of the chapter, will lead to a further fall in GDP, rising unemployment, potentially generating a further fall in consumption.

In the forward-looking model the effect of interest rates is more direct but also more ambiguous, as shown in Figure 13.15. An increase in interest rates leads the budget constraint to tilt from AB to CD. Higher interest rates mean that for the same second period repayment the consumer can afford a smaller loan—more money has to be spent on interest payments. Therefore on the horizontal axis the budget line shifts inward. However, if the consumer saves his or her first period income, then the higher interest rates lead to greater second period interest income and lead the budget line to shift *up* on the vertical axis. Because the budget line tilts, interest rates have two conflicting effects on consumption. One impact is called the **substitution effect** and causes a fall in first period consumption and is best reflected in the inward shift on the horizontal axis from B to D. The interest rate is an intertemporal price for the consumer—every $1 of current

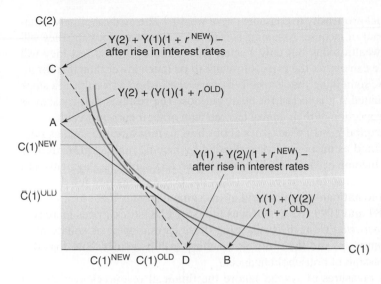

FIGURE 13.15 **Impact of interest rates on consumption.** Increases in interest rates lead to lower consumption as a result of income and substitution effects.

consumption means $(1 + r)$ less future consumption. If the interest rate increases, this makes first period consumption more expensive and so the consumer substitutes away toward second period consumption by saving more. The other influence is the **income effect**. When interest rates increase, savers receive higher interest payments and can afford to spend more—this is the reason why the intercept on the vertical axis shifts up from A to C. This higher income means the consumer can spend more over his or her lifetime, and because of consumption smoothing, this will lead to an increase in first and second period income.

For savers the income effect leads to higher current consumption. However, for debtors, the higher interest rates mean higher debt interest payments and so *lower* lifetime income and lower current consumption. Therefore, for debtors, the income effect of higher interest rates leads to lower current consumption. For borrowers, the effect of higher interest rates is unambiguous—current consumption falls. For savers, however, consumption can either rise or fall depending on the relative strength of income and substitution effects. In Figure 13.15 we have shown the substitution effect dominating so that consumption falls; this outcome is also supported in the aggregate consumption data. However, the impact of interest rates on consumption is relatively small, partly due to offsetting income and substitution effects.

13.6 The Role of Wealth and Capital Gains

We have so far focused only on income and interest rates as influences on consumption, but another important influence is wealth. The household sector does not hold all its money in a bank account but also owns stocks, bonds, and real estate. Changes in the value of these other assets will affect consumer wealth and also consumer spending.

What is the marginal propensity to consume out of wealth? The analysis closely parallels that for the m.p.c. out of income. Assuming consumers are forward looking, they will not consume all their wealth today but only a small proportion of it—the rest they will leave for later years. We can expect the m.p.c. of wealth to be much lower than that for income. Income is a *flow*, something that is received every year, whereas wealth is a *stock* and needs to be maintained if it is to last for many periods. The result is that consumers spend a much higher proportion of their annual income than of their current wealth.

The existence of capital gains raises issues about how to measure the savings rate. The savings rate is defined as unspent income divided by income, and as measured by the national accounts, income *excludes* capital gains but *includes* interest payments and dividends. As we saw in Figure 13.4, in the late 1990s the U.S. savings rate fell dramatically, as measured by the national accounts, but at the same time the U.S. stock market boomed—between 1989 and 1999 the Dow Jones index of U.S. stock prices increased fivefold. Consumers borrowed from the bank using these capital gains as collateral in order to finance consumption, and the result was a sharp fall in savings. But does this give a misleading impression of household finances?

National accounts measures of savings ignore the financial resources available to the consumer through capital gains. Including capital gains dramatically changes the performance of the U.S. savings rate. Figure 13.16 shows the national accounts (NIPA) measure of savings along with an alternative measure that includes realized capital gains (e.g., capital gains that have been banked via selling stock) in its concept of income. This adjusted series suggests that U.S. consumers save a much higher proportion of their income and that this proportion has changed very little. Figure 13.16 also shows the savings rate for U.S. consumers including unrealized gains in the measure of disposable income. Far from showing a dramatic decline in U.S. savings, the chart suggests that *savings* has actually increased so that U.S. consumers were being cautious in the rate at which they are spending these capital gains. Given the sharp falls in stock prices in 2001 such caution was amply justified by subsequent events.

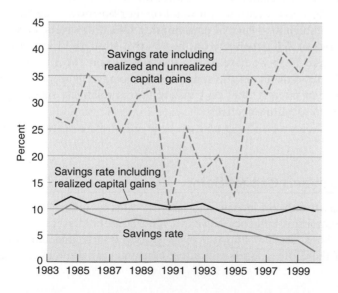

FIGURE 13.16 **U.S. savings rate and importance of capital gains.** The U.S. savings rate would be much higher if capital gains were factored into the concept of disposable income. *Source*: Peach and Steindal, "A Nation of Spendthrifts?" *Current Issues in Economic and Finance* (September 2000), vol. 6, no. 10, pp. 1–30.

POLICY PROBLEMS

Earlier in this chapter we outlined the key role of the m.p.c. in determining the efficacy of government spending in influencing GDP. If the m.p.c. is a stable and large number, then governments have a powerful influence on the economy which they can use to try and stabilize the business cycle. However, the forward-looking permanent income model illustrates some of the problems policymakers face. The dependence of the m.p.c. on consumers' expectations of future income, whether they perceive income increases to be temporary or permanent, the importance of uncertainty, and the variable impact of capital gains, combined with the issue of whether they have access to credit—all make the m.p.c. a difficult number to pin down. This suggests that governments have limited ability to reliably influence consumption by shifting taxes or moving interest rates.

13.7   Demographic Influences in the Life Cycle Model

We have omitted much of the richness of individual lives in the simple two period models that we looked at above. But this richness affects both consumption and savings. The profile of income over individual lives is likely to be uneven, and as a consequence, we can expect people's savings behavior to be different at different points in their **life cycle**. Most people earn low amounts in their teens and often into their twenties as they get a formal education. They then (usually) start work, and their income tends to rise as they become better at what they do and get promoted. At some point senility replaces experience, productivity declines, and earnings fall. The profile of earnings over working life depends on the work people do. Professional football players' productivity declines sharply in their 30s but a professor of English literature might not peak until her late 50s (at which point she can understand *Finnegan's Wake*). The Rolling Stones' earnings seem to rise even as they approach their 60s. But usually income tails off sharply as people move near or into retirement.

Consumption is also likely to vary dramatically over the life cycle. Most people spend their early adult life single, during which period consumption is relatively low. However, as they become older they may have a family, with consumption increasing as a result. Eventually children grow up, leave home, and (hopefully) stop relying on parental income, at which point household consumption falls. During retirement, consumption tends to continue to fall (perhaps the desire for extravagant skiing holidays in Aspen declines as the ability to get out of bed in the morning diminishes).

Support for these demographic shifts in consumption and income is shown in Figure 13.17 and Table 13.3. These show how consumption and income vary across a large sample of 107,000 U.S. households as the age of the reference adult in the household varies. The income profile is exactly what we outlined, except that income remains significant at the end for people older than 75 because measured income in this survey includes interest earnings and pension payments.[9]

---

[9]It is important to note that Figure 13.17 is based on data covering different individuals of different ages and not consumption over a single individual's life. Because of productivity growth, income differs across generations.

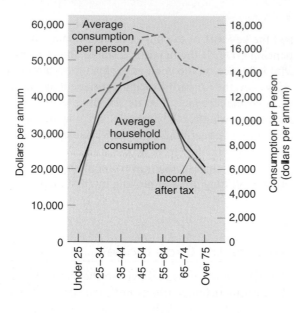

FIGURE 13.17 **Consumption and income over the life cycle—average U.S. consumer, 1998.** Consumption and income vary with age, peaking in middle age and then declining. *Source*: Consumer Expenditure Survey, Bureau of Statistics, http://www.bls.gov/csxhome.htm

This survey data is based on households and the number of individuals in the household changes over time. Table 13.3 shows that household size peaks during the 35–44 age band as children per household peak at 1.4. To avoid any confusion from changes in the size of households, Figure 13.17 also shows average consumption per household member. Household consumption peaks during the 45–54 age band, as does income, but individual consumption peaks during the "golden years" of 55–64 when children have left home. After this point, consumption continues to decline, as does income.

With income and consumption following such different paths, the household has to use savings to offset the differences. Table 13.4 shows the savings that accompany Figure 13.17: Early in adult life consumers borrow and then repay their loans and accumulate funds, which they then run down slightly during retirement.

Although the life cycle model achieves many empirical successes, it does have some problems. In particular, older generations tend not to spend their savings at a very rapid rate, if at all. Two possibilities are frequently stressed to account for the reluctance of older generations to reduce their savings dramatically: uncertainty and bequests. First,

TABLE 13.3   **Average Household Size and Number of Children, 1998**

	Under 25	25–34	35–44	45–54	55–64	65–74	Over 75
Persons	1.8	2.8	3.3	2.7	2.2	1.9	1.5
Under 18	0.4	1.1	1.4	0.6	0.2	0.1	0.0

Source: Consumer Expenditure Survey, Bureau of Labor Statistics, *http: www/www.bls.gov/csxhome.htm*

TABLE 13.4   Savings Rates by Age, United States, 1998

Under 25 Years	25–24 Years	35–44 Years	45–54 Years	55–64 Years	65–74 Years	75 and Over
−21.3	9.7	9.3	14.8	7.8	−8.6	−8.2

Source: Consumer Expenditure Survey, Bureau of Labor Statistics, *http://www.bls.gov/csxhome.htm*

uncertainty is critical. People, thankfully, don't know exactly when they are going to die. So the simple life cycle theory that says that people should decumulate wealth in retirement and have negative savings rates doesn't translate easily to a model in which people are uncertain about how long they will live. You may be afraid that you will live too long and run out of money and thus not exhaust your stock of wealth in retirement. And, of course, many people want to hand over substantial bequests to their heirs. The relative importance of uncertainty over longevity and the desire to leave a bequest are controversial as explanations for the surprisingly high savings rates of retired individuals, with some studies suggesting these motives account for more of U.S. wealth than life cycle savings.

SUMMARY

Consumption accounts for around 60% of GDP and is closely tied to GDP growth over the business cycle. Consumption decisions also determine savings, which is a key determinant of the long-run standard of living. Traditionally, Keynesian economics has given a key role to consumption in influencing how fiscal policy impacts the economy. The key concept is the *marginal propensity to consume*—how much of an extra dollar of income is spent by an individual.

The basic Keynesian model has consumption depending on current income. The permanent income model offers a richer framework and has consumers smoothing their lifetime income by setting consumption equal to permanent income. The m.p.c. then depends on whether changes in income are perceived as temporary or permanent. It also explains savings as dependent on future income expectations—if income is expected to grow, then savings is negative. The forward-looking model can also produce a close relationship between current consumption and income as in the Keynesian model but for different reasons. One is that individuals are unable to borrow; the other, that individuals are unsure of future income expectations and so base their current expenditure decisions on current income. In the forward-looking model the impact of interest rates is ambiguous depending on the relative strength of income and substitution effects. For borrowers, the effect is for current consumption to fall, but for savers, the net effect is indeterminate.

As well as depending on future income expectations, the pattern of consumption is also influenced by demographic considerations—in particular, the number of children in a household. Both profiles of income and consumption vary systematically with age, meaning that savings rates are also age dependent.

CONCEPTUAL QUESTIONS

1. Is there a distinction to be made between consumers' expenditure and consumption for (a) services (b) nondurable goods, (c) durable goods? Is this distinction important for the business cycle?

2. Draw indifference curves for a patient consumer compared to an individual with an instant need for gratification.

3. What would the budget constraint look like if it were only possible to borrow at an interest rate higher than the deposit rate?

4. In practice the m.p.c. out of current income is very high—is this necessarily inconsistent with the forward-looking model?

5. When inflation increased sharply in the 1970s, the savings rate increased. Evaluate the role of interest rates and current and future income in explaining this phenomena.

6. The permanent income model assumes that you treat your current financial wealth and the present value of your discounted future income in the same way. Discuss the plausibility of this result.

7. What variable does the forward-looking model suggest is best for measuring income inequality in society?

8. In the two-period model the consumer aimed to die with zero assets. What would be the planning horizon of parents who wished their children to enjoy the same standard of living they experienced in the family home after they have grown up? What is the planning horizon if every generation feels this way?

9. How would an increase in the popularity of annuities affect levels of inheritances in a country? (Annuities are contracts where in exchange for handing over a lump sum of money today, a person receives a certain [known] amount of money each year until death.)

10. What would be the impact on savings of the government introducing an unemployment insurance scheme?

ANALYTICAL QUESTIONS

1. A consumer expects to earn the following sequence of income over the next five decades

    4   7   10   19   0

    (a) Using the forward-looking consumption smoothing model, calculate consumption, savings, and wealth for the consumer in each decade (assuming interest rates are zero).
    (b) The government introduces a tax system to pay benefits to all those earning less than 8. As a result, the net of tax income the individual earns (including benefits) changes to

    8   8   10   14   0

    Recalculate consumption, savings, and assets for each decade. What impact does the benefit system have on consumption?

2. Consider the same consumer as in Question 1, but now the consumer is unable to borrow—wealth always has to be positive.

    (a) How does your answer to Question 1a change?
    (b) How does your answer to Question 1b change?
    (c) What difference is there in the way fiscal policy influences the economy in these two situations? Why?

3. Ms. A and Mr. B both live for two periods. In the first period both Ms. A and Mr. B expect to earn 50. However, in period 2, Ms. A will earn 30 with probability 50% or 110 with probability 50%. By contrast, Mr. B earns either 40 or 60 with equal probability.

    (a) Assuming no precautionary behavior and a desire to smooth consumption, calculate consumption, savings, and wealth for each individual for each period.

However, in response to income uncertainty these consumers set their consumption equal to a risk-adjusted permanent income rather than just permanent income (PI). Assume that risk-adjusted permanent income (PIRA) is given by the following expression

    $PIRA = PI - R \times (Ymax - Ymin)/PI$

where Ymax is the maximum second period income they will receive, Ymin is the minimum second period income, and R reflects their aversion to risk. The larger is R, the more risk averse are consumers.

    (b) Calculate consumption, savings, and wealth for each consumer and for each period, assuming R = 2.5. Which individual does the most saving? Is this consistent with the "rainy day" interpretation of savings?
    (c) Redo your calculations with R = 20. Explain how your results have changed.
    (d) Which job is someone with R = 20 most likely to take? Explain the implications this has for finding evidence for precautionary saving in cross-sectional data.

4. Consider an individual who is planning his consumption over five periods during which he expects his income to be 4, 10, 16, 12, and 8.

    (a) What is his permanent income?
    (b) What is his marginal propensity to consume out of a temporary increase which boosts first period income to 6?
    (c) What is the m.p.c. if the income increase of 2 is expected to continue into period 2?
    (d) What is the m.p.c. if the income increase of 2 is expected to continue for every period of the consumer's life?

5. Consider a consumer who expects to receive income in the following five periods of 4, 12, 23, 16 and 0. In response to 5% interest rates, the consumer defers savings and aims for her consumption to grow by 1 every period. If interest rates are 10%, then she wishes her consumption to increase by 2 every period.

    (a) Calculate consumption and savings in each period when interest rates are 5%.
    (b) Repeat these calculations for interest rates at 10%. Comment on the relative income and substitution effects.

Investment

Overview

In this chapter we focus on capital spending in economies—investment in machinery, plant, buildings, and infrastructure. Investment is the means by which a country preserves and enhances its productive potential; it is also a major source of demand for output. Investment expenditure, especially when it is taken to include the accumulation of inventories of goods (stockbuilding), is not only a significant element of overall demand, it is also a volatile one. Because investment also tends to be procyclical, it is a force behind business cycle fluctuations. We explore the determinants of investment expenditure and analyze why it is volatile. We also look at the distribution of spending among different types of capital goods and where that spending is done—domestically or overseas. Overseas investment (sometimes called foreign direct investment) has become more important to both developed and developing countries over the past 30 years, and we discuss this trend and its implications.

14.1 Investment and the Capital Stock

We have noted several times the staggering differences in standards of living across countries. Income per head in the United States is over 40 times as great as in many African countries. One factor behind this is differences in capital per worker. What we mean by this is capital in the form of physical assets (steel mills, PCs, laboratories, trucks, buildings, telephone systems). Differences in the overall value of physical

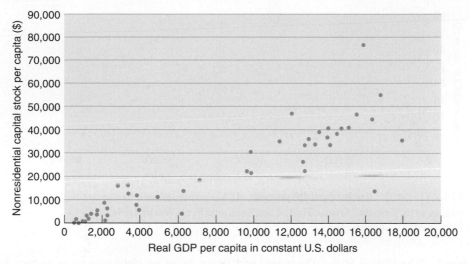

FIGURE 14.1 **Physical capital and real output.** There is a clear relation between capital per worker and the standard of living. *Source*: Heston and Summers Penn World Table 5.5, http://pwt.econ.upenn.edu

capital between countries are themselves dramatic and can account for a substantial part—but by no means most—of the differences in standards of living.[1]

Figure 14.1 plots physical capital per worker (excluding residential capital) against gross domestic product (GDP) per head. The data are from 1992 and cover about 50 countries, including some of the poorest and the richest in the world. The variability in capital per worker is marked; in some African countries, capital per worker is only a few hundred dollars; in Switzerland, capital per worker in the early 1990s was around $80,000. There is a clear, positive, correlation between output per head and capital per head. This suggests that the accumulation of physical capital is a critical determinant of the standard of living. But there is almost certainly also a feedback from income to investment. Figure 14.2 shows that there is a positive link between the average level of income in a country (GDP per capita) and investment as a share of GDP. Rich countries tend to invest a higher proportion of their output than do poor countries. This is particularly noticeable at low levels of income where some countries are so poor that they can hardly set aside any income for capital accumulation.

Investment expenditure is important not just because it determines the evolution of the capital stock, but also because it is a volatile component of the overall level of demand. Movements in investment expenditure tend to be sharper than shifts in other components of expenditure. Figures 14.3–14.5 show a time series of the percentage change in real GDP and private sector investment for the three largest economies in the

[1]We are careful to use the term "account for" rather than "causally explain." The level of capital available to workers is an important factor behind productivity. But unless we understand how capital comes to be accumulated, and the link between accumulation and incomes, we will not have an explanation of why labor productivity differs among countries.

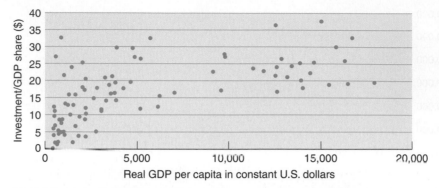

FIGURE 14.2   **Investment and GDP per capita.** Richer countries tend to allocate more of aggregate output to investment. *Source*: Heston and Summers Penn World Table 5.5, http://pwt.econ.upenn.edu

world: the United States, Germany, and Japan. Here we define investment broadly to include spending on new plant and machines, buildings (including residential house-building), and inventory.

The long-run trend in investment expenditure and in GDP is similar in each of the big three economies. But investment is much more volatile than GDP. For the United States, Germany, and Japan, changes in investment are about four times as volatile as changes in GDP. But the changes are highly correlated; investment is procyclical. When output in the economy as a whole is rising rapidly, investment expenditure tends to increase sharply; and when output growth falls, investment expenditure tends to decline markedly. Movements in investment expenditure may be disproportionately important in driving the business cycle. Understanding what drives investment is critical for understanding both movements in the standard of living of countries and also the volatility of activity from year to year.

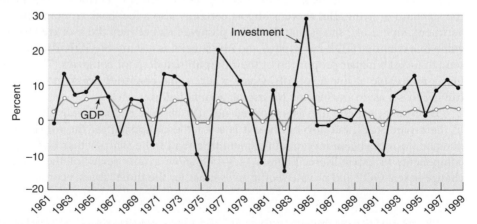

FIGURE 14.3   **Percent change U.S. GDP and total private sector investment.** Investment is procyclical and much more volatile than GDP. *Source*: OECD *Economic Outlook*, various issues. Copyright OECD.

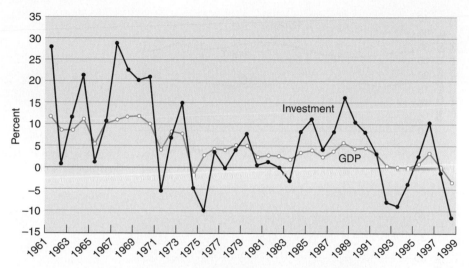

FIGURE 14.4   Japan: percent change real GDP and total private sector investment (including stockbuilding).
Source: OECD *Economic Outlook*, various issues. Copyright OECD.

When we talk about investment, we should be precise about what we mean. In this chapter investment means the accumulation of physical capital. We are not talking about expenditure on the education system or on research and development. What we mean is investment in machines, buildings, and so on—tangible assets used in the production process. Expenditure on these kinds of capital assets is extremely important. Figure 14.6 shows investment as a proportion of GDP in some of the major economies from 1980 to the late 1990s. Two things stand out from these figures. First, investment expenditure is a substantial proportion of overall spending in developed economies—accounting for

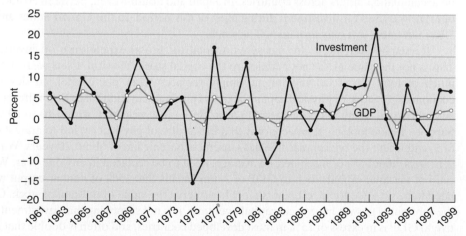

FIGURE 14.5   Germany: percent change real GDP and total private sector investment (including stockbuilding).
Source: OECD *Economic Outlook*, various issues. Copyright OECD.

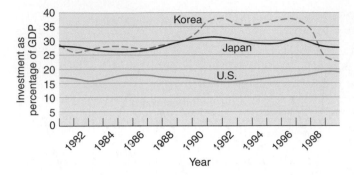

FIGURE 14.6a   **Total fixed investment as % GDP.**

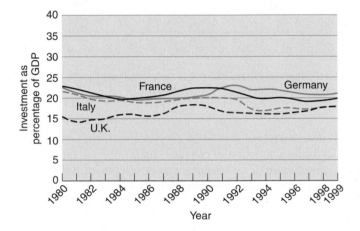

FIGURE 14.6b   **Total fixed investment as % of GDP.** Investment averages bout 25% of GDP across the developed economies—but there is substantial and persistent variation. *Source*: OECD *Economic Outlook*, various issues.

around one quarter of GDP. But that part of overall production that is set aside for capital accumulation differs across countries. In Japan and South Korea, between 30 and 35% of GDP was used for investment during most of this period. In the United States and the UK, investment was only around half as much.

Remember that these are measures of total (or gross) expenditure on investment. This is not the same as the net addition to the capital stock. Physical assets wear out, and much of total (or gross) investment simply replaces worn out capital. In developed economies the stock of physical capital often has a value of around three times the value of annual output. Many machines become obsolete, or just wear out, within 10 to 20 years. Suppose we are looking at an economy that has a ratio of physical capital to annual GDP of 3, and where the typical machine has a useful economic life of about 20 years. With 20-year lives, about 5% of machines, on average, need to be replaced in any one year. With a ratio of the total capital stock to GDP of 3, this means that 15% of annual output would need to be set aside for investment simply to preserve the value of the capital stock. Given the substantial growth in physical capital over time, it is not surprising that investment relative to GDP is in excess of 15% in most developed countries, and often is double that level.

Even in the United States, where investment relative to GDP has been lower than in most other developed countries, the scale of net accumulation of capital has been substantial in the postwar era. Figure 14.7 shows the path that the measured market

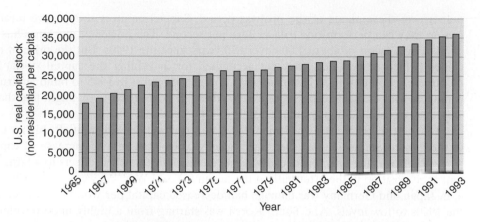

FIGURE 14.7 **U.S. Capital Stock per Capita.** The per capita stock in the United States has risen steadily over time. *Source*: Heston and Summers Penn World Tables 5.5, http://pwt.econ.upenn.edu

value of capital per worker in the United States took over this period. Between 1965 and the early 1990s, the value of the physical capital per worker in the United States roughly doubled from about $17,000 to $35,000 (at 1985 prices). Capital per worker continued to rise through the 1990s. In fact, investment increased particularly fast between 1992 and 1999 as output and corporate profits grew rapidly (see Figure 14.8). By the end of the century, the average U.S. worker had more than three times the capital that was available in 1945 at the end of the Second World War.

Such figures almost certainly underestimate the growth of effective machine power. Consider, for example, how computers have changed over the past 40 years. At the end of the 1940s the largest computers could perform a few thousand floating point operations per second (flops). Such machines were enormous—the largest was so big and used so much electricity that when it was running at full power street lights in neighboring areas were often dimmed. Such machines were housed in large buildings and were valued at hundreds of thousands of dollars. Today, the most basic desktop PC can

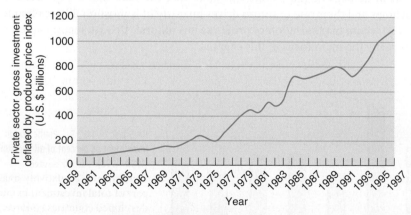

FIGURE 14.8 **Total U.S. investment.** U.S. Investment rose sharply in the 1990s. *Source*: OECD Economic Outlook, various issues. Copyright OECD.

outperform these giants of the postwar period. Supercomputers today have teraflop power; they can perform one *trillion* flops per second. The power of machines has increased by a factor of about 1,000 every 20 years since the 1940s. But the price of machines (which reflects how they get accounted for in valuing the capital stock) has plummeted. If you were to calculate what it might have cost in 1945 to build and run a computer with the same capacity as a $1000 desktop PC of today, you might find that it would have cost several percentage points of GDP.

In countries where the investment to GDP ratio has been substantially higher than in the United States—Japan, Germany, South Korea—the rate of increase of capital per worker over the past few decades has been much faster. This reflects to a large extent their position in the aftermath of the Second World War. As we noted in Chapter 4, in Japan and Germany war damage had decreased capital per worker by the end of the 1940s to low levels. And South Korea was starting from a highly underdeveloped position when industrialization began to accelerate a few decades ago. So much of what we see in recent trends in investment in these countries reflects "catch-up." Pictures of Tokyo, Berlin, Dresden, and Hiroshima from 1945 reveal the almost complete destruction of infrastructure, buildings, and factories. By contrast, the capital stock of the United States was unscathed. Of course, in the war years, U.S. military expenditure increased sharply, which probably squeezed out some domestic investment.

The notion of catch-up, which seems plausible for Germany and Japan, is based on a simple idea: at any point in time, there is a capital stock that is optimal and reflects the relative sizes of the cost of machines against the extra profits that could be earned from their installation. This optimal capital stock level is likely to be different from the actual stock of capital in place in the economy. For a country emerging from a devastating war—where the capital stock has plummeted—the desired, or optimal, capital stock is likely to be substantially more than the actual capital stock. Because installing new capital is costly and time consuming, it may take years to close most of the gap between the actual capital stock and the desired capital stock. So one would expect that levels of investment would remain high for a prolonged period. This simple idea doesn't seem controversial. But we have not yet specified in detail the key element: namely, the determinants of the optimal, or desired, stock of capital. In the next section, we will consider this in detail. For the moment we note that the idea that a gap between the cost of machines and their rate of return drives investment is most readily applied to the private sector, where maximization of profits seems natural. Private sector capital accumulation is really the main focus of this chapter.

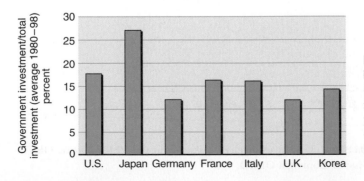

FIGURE 14.9 **Public sector investment as percent of all investment (1980–1998).** Public sector investment is a relatively small part of total investment in most developed countries. *Source*: OECD Economic Outlook, Copyright OECD.

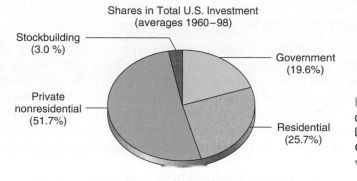

Shares in Total U.S. Investment
(averages 1960–98)

Stockbuilding
(3.0 %)

Government
(19.6%)

Private
nonresidential
(51.7%)

Residential
(25.7%)

FIGURE 14.10a **The composition of investment in the largest economies.** *Source*: OECD, Economic Outlook, various issues.

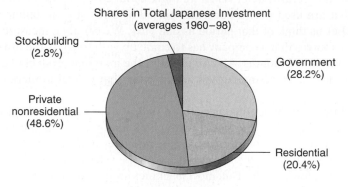

Shares in Total Japanese Investment
(averages 1960–98)

Stockbuilding
(2.8%)

Government
(28.2%)

Private
nonresidential
(48.6%)

Residential
(20.4%)

FIGURE 14.10b

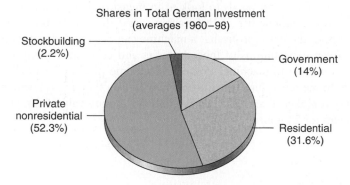

Shares in Total German Investment
(averages 1960–98)

Stockbuilding
(2.2%)

Government
(14%)

Private
nonresidential
(52.3%)

Residential
(31.6%)

FIGURE 14.10c

Figure 14.9 shows that public investment accounts for a relatively small, though not trivial, part of total investment. (We considered public sector expenditure and the appropriate role of the state in Chapter 10.) The major part of investment, or capital, expenditure in the developed economies is private sector spending on business capital (machines, offices, vehicles, and so on).

Figure 14.10 shows that private, nonresidential investment accounts for 50% or more of overall investment in the three largest economies. But residential investment—new homes—is also a major part of overall spending and one that we will consider in more detail in Chapter 24.

14.2 The Optimal Stock of Capital

It makes sense for a company to expand its stock of capital if the cost of the additional investment turns out to be lower than the value of the extra profit the new machines generate. And it also makes no sense to continue investing if the extra revenues from the new machine do not at least cover its cost. So we can think of the optimal capital stock as being that level beyond which extra returns are lower than cost, and below which extra returns exceed cost. Figure 14.11 shows a simple illustration of the determination of the desired capital stock. On the horizontal axis, we measure the total value of machines in place (that is, "the capital stock"), and on the vertical axis, we measure costs and marginal rates of return. It is important to be clear about the units in which we are measuring costs and returns here. When we think about costs, we are measuring the *extra* resources that are used over a particular period as a result of installing one extra unit of capital. Let us think of that period as one year. We can then measure the cost of capital as the resources that a company has to come up with to enjoy the use of a particular lump of capital for 12 months. And we measure the marginal product of capital as the *extra* profit that the company derives from having that capital in place over that period.

Of course, it is arbitrary to think of the period over which we measure extra profits, and the cost, as precisely 12 months. We should really think about how long the capital is in place and the stream of extra profit that it can generate over that period. If we can buy a machine today and sell it again in a few months, then the relevant period to calculate profits against cost is a few months. But, most machines aren't like this. Once a machine is in place, trying to sell it in a couple of months would generate little revenue. So the relevant time horizon that a firm needs to look at in measuring costs and benefits might be the whole useful economic life of the machine, and that might be 10 or 20 years. When we think about the extra profit that a machine can earn and about its cost, then we may need to form expectations of those benefits and costs over many years. But this will vary from machine to machine. You can hire some pieces of capital for a day. If I hire a van to help me move furniture into my new house, then the relevant cost of capital is the one-day rental cost, and the gain is whatever money value I can put on the benefits of using a van for 24 hours.

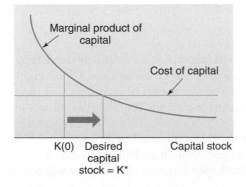

FIGURE 14.11 **What determines investment?** The optimal level of the capital stock is where the cost of capital just equals the marginal productivity of capital.

So in practice it matters a lot what type of capital we are talking about when we think about measuring costs and benefits. Let us, for the moment, return to the somewhat abstract world depicted in Figure 14.11 and focus on how we actually measure the cost of capital. We need to think about the extra resources that using a piece of capital for "a period" consumes. This cost reflects several things. First, there is the opportunity cost of the funds tied up in the machine. Suppose that you bought a piece of capital machinery on January 1 and borrowed the money to finance the purchase. A major element of the cost of capital would then be the interest rate on the borrowed funds. If you sold the machine again at the end of the year, a second element of cost would be the change in its value, which itself reflects both depreciation (or wear and tear) and the change in the market price of that sort of capital.

So two of the major elements in the cost of capital are changes in the value of the machine and the cost of using funds. That second element—the cost of funds—is more subtle than simply the rate of interest. Most corporations, in fact, do not finance their investment expenditure by borrowing from banks. So we need to think about more than just a bank interest rate. Companies finance investment from many sources: they issue shares, retain profit, issue bonds, and sometimes rely on credit from suppliers of capital goods. So funds come from many sources, and the cost of capital should reflect the cost of each type of finance and its relative importance. Table 14.1 shows that in the recent past companies in Germany, Japan, the United States, and the UK have, in aggregate, relied on internal funds for a far higher proportion of their investment than borrowing from banks or issuing new debt or equity.[2] Of course, internal finance is not free!

When a company uses some of its profits to finance investment it is using money that it could otherwise pay out to shareholders as dividends. And once the dividends

TABLE 14.1   The Financing of Investment:
Flow-of-funds Estimated (%) (1970–1994)

	Germany	Japan	UK	USA
Internal finance	78.4	69.9	95.6	94.0
Bank finance	12.0	30.1	15.0	12.8
Bond finance	−1.0	3.4	3.8	15.3
New equity	−0.02	3.4	−5.3	−6.1
Other	10.6	−6.8	−9.1	−16.0

Note: Internal finance comprises retained earnings and depreciation. The other category includes trade credit and capital transfers. The figures represent weighted averages where the weights for each country are the level of real fixed investment in each year in that country.

Source: Corbett and Jenkinson, "How Is Investment Financed?" *The Manchester School* (1996) vol. LXV, pp. 69–94.

[2]Internal funds means profit not paid out to shareholders that is available to finance expenditure.

are distributed to shareholders, they could earn a rate of return that reflects the investment opportunities open to investors. So we should think of the cost of internal finance as reflecting the rates of return that investors might earn on funds if they were available to them. Those funds could be invested in the stock or bond markets or put in banks, so the overall cost to a firm of using internal finance reflects rates of return that could be earned on a whole range of financial assets.

And then, of course, there is risk. The shareholders in a company may perceive investments in that company as more risky than putting money in the government bond market or buying a diversified portfolio of equities. In this case, the cost of capital to the individual firm will reflect not just the rates of return that could be earned on other assets, but also a risk premium to reflect greater uncertainty over returns.

In figuring out the cost of capital, as well as the required rates of return that investors might expect on different assets, there is also the impact of the tax system. Interest on debt is usually tax deductible to corporations, so this helps determine both the relative attractiveness of debt and equity to companies and the overall level of the cost of capital. And tax plays a key role in calculating the marginal product of capital. Companies pay tax on profits that they earn, and these taxes are a deduction from the available profits. In fact, the tax system is much more complicated than this. Depreciation of capital is often tax deductible, and companies may enjoy tax incentives to undertake investment.[3] We shall see below that the impact of taxes on investment differs in important ways across countries.

PUTTING IT ALL TOGETHER . . .

An example may help to draw together some of the key factors that determine the cost of capital and the marginal returns on extra investment, the factors we expect to influence optimal capital accumulation. Suppose a company is trying to figure out how many new PCs to buy for its workforce. It reckons that 1000 computers would increase productivity, such that gross revenues would be $3 million higher over a year. They would need to hire more people (software and hardware support), but netting off these extra labor costs should generate net higher revenues of $2.8 million. More computers would probably generate yet more revenue; fewer would probably give less revenue. We are concerned with extra after-tax profit, so we need to take account of extra taxes that will have to be paid on increased revenues. We assume the corporate tax rate is 25% and show in Table 14.2 the extra post-tax revenues as well as the gross figures. The machines cost $1000 dollars each and will be sold at the end of the year. The resale price of a PC is estimated to be $500 dollars. The company will be able to deduct the depreciation of 50% (or $500 dollars) from

---

[3]Governments in developed countries have often introduced tax breaks to encourage investment expenditure, especially when investment looks low and the economy is in a slump. The effectiveness of tax breaks, which may prove temporary, is questionable given the length of life of much capital equipment. Temporary tax breaks may also affect the *timing* of investment expenditure more than the *amount* of capital accumulation.

TABLE 14.2   Revenues, Costs, and Optimal Investment

Numbers of New PCs	Estimated Net Extra Revenue ($ million over a year)	
	Gross	After Tax
250	937,500	703,125
500	1,650,000	1,237,500
750	2,250,000	1,687,500
1000	2,800,000	2,100,000
1250	3,100,000	2,325,000
1500	3,200,000	2,400,000
1750	3,250,000	2,437,500

its taxable profit, so we must take this into account in calculating the cost of having the machines for one year. So a key element of cost is that each machine is bought for $1000 and sold for $500 dollars, generating a gross cost of $500 but a post-tax cost of $0.75 \times \$500 = \$375$.

The company still needs to find $1000 dollars to pay for each machine bought at the start of the year. Suppose that the investment cost will come from retained profit and that shareholders (who would otherwise get the funds) can earn a nominal rate of return of 12%. The cost of using $1000 of shareholders' funds for a year is therefore the $120 dollars they could have earned on the cash. So the overall cost of each machine over one year is this $120 dollars plus the $375 coming from the depreciation; this generates a flat per-machine cost of $495. We can now draw up a schedule of the extra cost of installing various numbers of machines versus the extra net revenues they generate; this makes it easy in Table 14.3 to see the optimal level of investment.

The best bet would be to buy about 1250 machines. Buying this many PCs generates a net gain, having taken account of all the costs of using the machines for a year, of about $1.71 million; this is more extra profit than when fewer or more new machines are used. A useful way to find the same answer is to draw up a schedule showing the

TABLE 14.3   Revenues, Costs, and Optimal Investment

Number of PCs	Extra After-Tax Revenue	Extra Cost	Net Gain
250	703,125	123,750	579,375
500	1,237,500	247,500	990,000
750	1,687,500	371,250	1,316,250
1000	2,100,000	495,000	1,605,000
1250	2,325,000	618,750	1,706,250
1500	2,400,000	742,500	1,657,500
1750	2,437,500	866,250	1,571,250

TABLE 14.4   Revenues, Costs, and Optimal Investment

Number of PCs	Marginal Revenue	Marginal Cost	Net Marginal Profit
250	703,125	123,750	579,375
500	534,375	123,750	410,625
750	450,000	123,750	326,250
1000	412,500	123,750	288,750
1250	225,000	123,750	101,250
1500	75,000	123,750	−48,750
1750	37,500	123,750	−86,250

extra cost, and extra after-tax revenues, of having a *further* 250 machines starting from different points. You can easily calculate the schedule from the last one by simply taking the difference between successive entries in each column. This generates *marginal* (or incremental) revenue and *marginal* cost for each *marginal* 250 machines.

The first two columns in Table 14.4 correspond to the marginal product and cost of capital schedules in Figure 14.11. So long as marginal product exceeds marginal cost (the latter is constant in this example), expanding the number of PCs generates a net increment to profit, so the total profit figure will increase. Between 1250 and 1500 machines, net revenue from the extra machine dips below the extra cost. So total profit is maximized when the firm buys a few more than 1250 machines, at a point where the cost of a machine (the cost of capital) equals the extra revenue it generates (its marginal productivity, or marginal revenue).

Figure 14.11 depicts a situation that is consistent with our numerical example and where the marginal product of capital itself falls with the value of the capital stock. This is probably plausible for an individual company. The greater is the capital stock, the larger is the level of output, and beyond a certain point, price probably has to fall to sell more of a product, so marginal profitability declines. If the cost of capital is either flat or is increasing, and the marginal product of capital schedule, at least beyond some point, begins to decline, then there will be a unique desired capital stock. In Figure 14.11 initial capital is at level K(0) and desired capital is at level K(*). If there are costs in adjusting the capital stock quickly, then investment will be undertaken to close the gap between K(0) and K(*) over some period; but we will not jump straight to the new level. The amount of time taken to close the gap between current capital and optimal capital itself reflects the size of the gap and the costs of installation of capital.

We can use this framework to analyze the impact of changes in some of the main determinants of the capital stock. Figure 14.12 shows what happens when the cost of capital increases. If firms were initially at their optimal capital stock, so that K(0) coincided with K(*), then anything that causes the cost of capital to increase will take the new optimal level of capital *beneath* the current level (to K(1)). Many things could increase the cost of capital. Investors may suddenly come to see the risks of investing in corporations as having increased, in which case the risk premiums on corporate capital

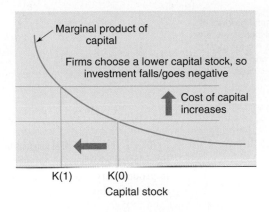

FIGURE 14.12   **What happens when interest rates increase?** A rise in the cost of capital, other things remaining equal, reduces the optimal capital stock.

will rise, meaning that the required rates of return on new investment need to be higher. Or, the monetary authorities may increase interest rates, which may cause bond prices to fall, thereby increasing companies' nominal cost of borrowing. (The lower are bond prices, the greater is the cost for firms in selling bonds to finance investment; we explore the link between bond prices and the required rates of return of investors in Chapter 22). Unless there is an offsetting increase in expectations of inflation, then the *real* cost of borrowing has risen, and the cost of the capital schedule will move up. Clearly some changes in the tax system (for example, reductions in the generosity of deductions of interest charges against taxable profit) could have the same impact.

For whatever reason, if the cost of capital increases, the optimal stock of capital will be lower. However, companies may not be able to reduce their capital stock instantly to a lower level. For example, the resale value of many of their machines may be close to zero and simply selling them may be far less effective than not replacing them and waiting for them to wear out. If resale values of existing machines are low, then getting rid of them is not worthwhile; that they may have cost a lot only a year or so ago, when you expected their revenue-generating ability to be huge, is irrelevant—sunk costs are sunk costs. So long as using the machines generates extra revenue (enough to cover any ongoing expenses), you might as well keep them going until they no longer add to net revenues.

All this implies that the transition from K(0) to K(1) following a rise in the cost of capital may be far from instantaneous and could, in fact, take years. If a firm finds that its optimal capital stock is substantially beneath its current level of capital, then it may decide to undertake zero *gross* investment for some years and allow depreciation to gradually reduce its capital.

Note that all this tends to make investment expenditure volatile. Small movements in the cost of capital could take the equilibrium level K* from being slightly in excess of K(0) to well beneath it. If a company found that K* was in excess of K(0), it would want to undertake positive net investment, which, given depreciation, could imply substantial levels of *gross* investment. But if K* then dipped beneath K(0), the firm might find it optimal to reduce gross investment to *zero*. We can see already why

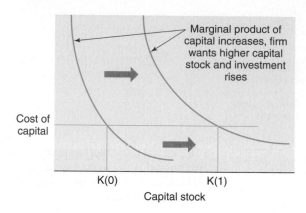

FIGURE 14.13   **What happens with technological breakthrough?** An increase in productivity raises the optimal stock of capital.

[Figure labels: "Marginal product of capital increases, firm wants higher capital stock and investment rises", "Cost of capital", "K(0)", "K(1)", "Capital stock"]

investment expenditure might be more volatile than consumption expenditure. We expect consumption expenditure to move up and down with changes in the current level of income and in response to shifts in expectations of future income. Whereas it would be unusual for an individual to decide to cut consumption to *zero* in response to news about interest rates or future incomes, it is not unusual for firms to move from substantial *net* investment to zero *gross* investment from one year to the next. So in most economies aggregate investment expenditure is typically substantially more volatile than consumption expenditure.

One of the main driving forces behind investment expenditure is technological advances. Many companies spend so much on computer systems because computer hardware and software technology has advanced so dramatically in the last 20 years that one generation of machines is virtually obsolete within a few years. Again, we can use the simple framework we have developed to analyze the impact of technological breakthroughs. If a new invention dramatically increases the productivity of capital, then the marginal product of capital schedule will shift significantly outward. Figure 14.13 illustrates this. After a technological breakthrough, you might expect dramatic investment for substantial periods of time. You might also expect existing machines that have become obsolete to be scrapped. Technological progress can simultaneously increase both gross investment and the scrapping of existing machines. So its overall impact on the value of the net capital stock may not be dramatically positive. But its impact on productivity may, nonetheless, be profound. We see here another reason why investment expenditure is likely to be more volatile than consumption expenditure. Technological breakthroughs often profoundly affect the structure of the capital stock and can be sudden and hard to predict.

14.3   Investment and the Stock Market

We noted above that in the largest developed economies, corporations finance most of their investment expenditure from internal resources; ultimately this is shareholders' capital. The stock market valuation of companies' existing capital reflects the return that shareholders might earn on funds. So we should expect to see a link between levels of investment companies undertake and the stock market. In fact, the link was elegantly and formally set out many years ago by James Tobin, who developed the so-called q theory of investment. Tobin noted that if the value of a company on the stock market was substantially more than the replacement cost of the assets that the firm employs (most of which we will assume are some form of capital equipment), then in principle that company has a major incentive to increase investment. When we think about the replacement value of capital here, we mean the current cost of buying the sorts of machines that the company uses. If the ratio between the value of its shares and the replacement cost of that firm's capital stock is greater than 1, then the stock market is valuing the firm at more than it would cost to replace all its capital by buying new machines. If that were the case, a company would have an incentive to replicate itself by expanding its capital stock, and its stock market valuation would rise by more than the cost of the investment. The company could finance the purchase of the new machines from its existing shareholders who would enjoy immediate gains as the firm's stock market value increased by more than the cost of the new machines. The ratio between the value of a firm's shares (or its stock market valuation) and the replacement cost of its capital stock is Tobin's "q".

DEFINITION

- q = stock market valuation of company / replacement cost of company's net assets
- If q > 1, then the stock market values a firm at more than it would cost to replace all the firm's capital. In this case, the firm should expand the capital stock, and stock market valuation will rise more than cost of investment. The firm will continue to issue equity and invest until q = 1.
- If q < 1, then the firm can sell its capital stock and buy out / pay back its shareholders. It will reduce its capital stock until q = 1.

Let's take a simple example. Suppose the stock market valuation of a small company that produces specialized pistons for high-performance car engines is $200 million. The assets of the company are really of two sorts: the physical plant, machinery, and buildings with which it produces pistons and its less tangible assets, like the experience of its workforce and the value of the techniques that the firm has developed. Suppose that the firm can hire more workers with the same skills as the current workforce and at the same cost and that it can sell more pistons on the same terms as existing output. This means that doubling the productive capacity—buying new machines, getting new buildings, hiring more workers, and so on—should double the value of the firm. Suppose that the existing machines, buildings, and such have a replacement cost of $150 million. Because the existing company is valued at $200 million, and it costs $150 million to double productive capacity, the company could increase its market value by $200 million by spending $150 million; obviously this is a good deal.

In this example, Tobin's q is well in excess of 1 (it is 200/150 = 1.333), so there is a clear incentive to invest. Note that we specified that the firm could expand production by taking on extra workers who were no more costly and no less productive than the existing ones. We also assumed that the firm could sell the extra pistons at no lower a price and that the techniques they had developed (whose worth the market value of the existing firm reflected) could be as productively applied to the operation of the new machines. These assumptions ensured that the value of existing assets was a guide to the increase in value that expanding capacity would bring. (Put more technically, we needed to ensure that the average q on the exiting assets was equal to the marginal q on new investments.)

The q theory has a simple prediction for the relationship between the level of investment and the value of the stock market, and Figure 14.14 depicts it. If the q of a company exceeds 1, that company should find that the cost of buying machines is below the value that the stock market will then place upon those machines. This is an incentive for a firm to expand and start investing, which will be in the interest of its shareholders. By the same token, if Tobin's q is less than 1, then the stock market is valuing the capital of a company at less than its replacement cost. This means that were a company to undertake investment, it would find that the cost of buying the machines was greater than the value the market placed on those machines. Firms would have no incentive to invest under such circumstances. In fact, they should start selling their capital because they would get more for it on the secondhand market than the value shareholders placed on it.

The q theory is closely linked to the idea that firms should invest if the rate of return on new capital exceeds the cost of capital. To see this, assume that a firm can get a return on new investment that is close to the return on its existing capital. Then a good way to measure the marginal rate of return is to take the ratio between the profits earned on the existing capital and the replacement cost of that capital. (For simplicity we assume here that it is an all-equity-financed firm, but this is not essential to the logic of the argument.) This ratio tells you the average rate of return given the actual purchase price of machines, and this is the relevant number when considering buying a new machine. So our measure of the rate of return is

profits / replacement cost of capital

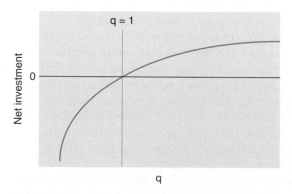

FIGURE 14.14   **The q Theory of Investment.** When *q* is above 1 there is an incentive to undertake net investment because the rate of return on capital is larger than the cost of capital.

What about the cost of capital? If a firm is just generating enough profits to satisfy its shareholders, we would expect that the ratio of profits to stock market value is equal to their required rate of return. So a measure of the cost of capital is

profits / stock market value of firm

The ratio of our measure of the rate of return to the cost of capital is therefore

[profit / replacement cost of capital] / [profit / stock market value of firm]
= stock market value of firm / replacement cost of capital = q

Thus q is the ratio of the rate of return to the cost of capital. If $q > 1$, the rate of return exceeds the cost of capital, and the capital stock should be expanded. If $q < 1$, the rate of return falls short of the cost of capital, and the capital stock should not be expanded. The q theory of investment implies that there should be a positive link between stock market valuations (relative to the purchase cost of plant, machines, buildings, etc.) and the level of investment. But empirical evidence suggests that there is no such clear link. Figure 14.15 plots changes in the level of investment expenditure in the United States charted against the change in real stock prices (that is, nominal stock prices deflated by an index of capital goods prices). While the two move roughly in line, the correlation between them is low. Similar pictures could be drawn for all the major economies.

What are we to make of the relatively weak link between stock prices and levels of investment? The most natural interpretation may be that corporations do not find sudden shifts in stock market valuations informative when it comes to predicting rates of return they can earn on new investment. Given the volatility in stock prices, often apparently unrelated to shifts in fundamental factors that might influence profitability, they may be right. If stock prices have a tendency to become unconnected with fundamental economic forces—supply and demand for goods—then firms would not

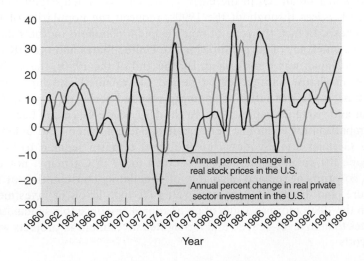

FIGURE 14.15 **U.S. stock prices and investment.** There is at best only a weak link between movements in stock prices and changes in investment. *Source*: Datastream and U.S. Department of Commerce, Bureau of Economic Analysis.

be helping their shareholders by undertaking massive bouts of investment every time the stock market moved up sharply, only to slam on the brakes when stock prices plummet.

Paradoxically, in the light of the failure of q theory to account for much of the variability in investment, many commentators have blamed relatively low levels of investment in the United States and the UK over the past 40 years on the greater role that stock markets might play in allocating resources in those countries. During the 1980s and for much of the 1990s, the "short termism" hypothesis gained ground in those countries. Its advocates claimed that in countries where the stock market was really significant (for example, where the total values of stocks were large relative to GDP) and where takeovers often shifted corporate control, that firms had to pay too much attention to their stock price and that short-term movements in equity prices had undue influence. Furthermore, they argued that companies in the United States and the UK were far less inclined to think about long-term profitability of investment expenditure and had a tendency to underinvest as a result. In contrast, companies in Germany and Japan, where it appeared that stock market values were less important and borrowing through the banking system relatively more important, were more inclined to invest in the long term.

The British finance minister Nigel Lawson asserted in the 1980s that

The big institutional investors nowadays increasingly react to short-term pressure on investment performance . . . (and) . . . are increasingly unwilling to countenance long-term investment.

At about the same time as Lawson made his claim, the actor Michael Douglas, playing the role of Gekko in the film "Wall Street," was asserting that greed was good and was the ultimate driving force behind the efficient allocation of resources.

In the 1980s many agreed with Lawson and felt that Gekko was trying to defend the indefensible (which is what the film's director Oliver Stone believed). However, the depression into which Japan fell in the early 1990s, and sustained expansion in U.S. output and stock prices throughout the 1990s, reduced the popularity of the short termism hypothesis. In fact, the tone of much popular comment on the role of stock markets and the efficiency of corporations in the United States and the UK relative to Germany and Japan was transformed. By the end of the 1990s, the United States had enjoyed an almost unprecedented period of sustained and high GDP growth, and in contrast, Japan was suffering an unprecedented period of stagnant (indeed falling) output and rising unemployment. In the UK, where Germany had long been a point of comparison for economic performance, unemployment had fallen to about one-half the German rate. Suddenly all the short termism seemed to be in Japan, and in Europe the creaking inefficiency seemed to be in Germany, not the UK! In Japan, the government seemed incapable of stimulating consumption or investment expenditure, and the media now interpreted the high levels of investment undertaken there in the 1980s more as a sign of an irrational response to a speculative bubble in asset prices than to level-headed and far-sighted investment in projects with solid long-term payoffs.

TABLE 14.5   Balance Sheet Measures of Gearing (%)

	Germany	Japan	UK	USA
Market value				
median	15	17	11	23
aggregate	6	28	13	31
Book value				
median	18	37	16	33
aggregate	10	49	19	45

Notes. Estimates are for 1991. Gearing is measured broadly as total debt over total assets. The sample of firms comprises those nonfinancial companies covered by the Global Vantage data set that reported consolidated balance sheets in 1991. These figures are the adjusted estimates provided by the authors. Adjusted liabilities are defined as total liabilities, less pension liabilities (in Germany), less cash. Adjusted debt is measured as the book value of debt, less cash and marketable securities. Adjusted assets are total assets, less cash and short-term securities, less pension liabilities (in Germany), less intangibles. Adjusted book value of equity is book equity, plus provisions, plus deferred taxes, less intangibles.

Source: Rajan and Zingales, "What Do We Know About Capital Structure: Some Evidence from International Data" *Journal of Finance* (1995) vol. 50, pp. 1421–1460.

In fact, the whole short-termism debate now seems wrongheaded. The United States, the UK, Japan, and Germany have far more in common in financing and investment than is generally perceived. Table 14.1 showed that in all four countries *new* equity finance[4] was, in aggregate, unimportant and that debt finance was also much less important than internal funding. Table 14.5 shows that gearing—the ratio between a company's debt and its overall assets—does not vary much across countries. The UK and Germany have similar corporate balance sheets, at least in terms of the relative use of debt and equity. The same is true of the United States and Japan.

---

[4]As opposed to retained profit, which we can think of as *old* equity finance, i.e., funds that shareholders allow the company to use to finance company expenditure that could otherwise have been paid to them as dividends.

14.4 Cash Flows and Investment

Relatively heavy reliance on internal resources to finance investment suggests that shifts in current profits may have more influence on levels of investment expenditure than do movements in stock prices, or even shifts in expectations of future profits. Of course, this isn't how we analyzed investment expenditure in the abstract models outlined above. There, what really mattered was the relative magnitude of the cost of capital and the marginal rate of return on new investment. Current cash flow or the amount of internal revenue that the company generated played no role. Investment depended completely on the *potential* returns and costs of new investment rather than on the revenue existing capital generated. So if current profits were, in fact, a key determinant of investment expenditure, it would not only be in marked contrast to the simple model, it would also suggest that resources could become significantly misallocated. If existing cash flow, rather than potential profitability, determines investment, then in periods of buoyant profits, companies might tend to overinvest and they might underinvest when current profits were low. Investment could also destabilize the macroeconomy. Corporate profits and revenues would tend to be high during booms, and if investment also tended to be high, it would exacerbate the economic cycle; similarly corporate revenues would tend to fall in recessions, and investment expenditure might also decline.

So whether the cash flow story of investment is correct matters. This is a controversial area, and the evidence is not straightforward. The problem is that movements in current profits not only generate shifts in available resources (i.e., in cash flow), they also, plausibly, should influence expectations of the *future* profitability of investment expenditure. Even a high correlation between current profits and levels of investment would not prove that available cash flow is the key variable that drives investment. It could simply reflect a strong correlation between expectations of high future profitability on capital and high current profitability. It would be bizarre if such a correlation did not exist.

So an apparent link between current cash flows and investment expenditure does not indicate that something has gone wrong with how corporations make investment decisions. There are, nonetheless, worrying signs. Surveys in the United States[5] and in the UK[6] in the 1990s revealed that companies seemed to apply unusual criteria in deciding whether to undertake investment projects. Specifically, they appeared to require rates of return on investment expenditure that are often dramatically higher than the rates of return that investors typically receive on funds. It looks, at face value, as if firms are requiring hurdle rates of return[7] on potential new investment projects that are much larger than rates of return that you might expect investors to be content with. Could this affect the relatively low levels of investment expenditure in the UK and in the United States? Again, the evidence is far from conclusive. Managers of corporations, who are used to inflated forecasts of profits about projects from those in the company who have the most to gain from expansion, may tend to correct for this excess optimism by applying a higher discount factor. Of course, this isn't the right way to handle excess

---

[5] By Jim Poterba and Lawrence Summers.

[6] By the Bank of England.

[7] That is, minimum required rates of return on new investment projects.

optimism: a better strategy would be to scale back the inflated expectations of profits that come from the planning department. But as a rough and ready response to institutionalized excess optimism, it is at least understandable.

14.5 Lumpy Investment and Business Cycles

We have assumed that if a firm finds a gap between its existing and desired stock of capital it will aim to close it through new investment. But how quickly will the gap be closed? This depends on the costs of installing new machines. Consider this description of retooling in the U.S. auto industry:

When the line was stopped at the end of the model run, the bulk of the production force would be laid off, new machinery would be installed, new dies moved into place, and the assembly line rearranged for the production of the new model.[8]

The auto industry evidently has major costs updating and replacing machines—production is disrupted (indeed it halts!). This is likely to be true in many companies. If the disruption costs of installing capital are high, then it makes sense for companies to concentrate their investment in particular periods; better to do a major overhaul of equipment once every three years and close down production for a while than have production continually disrupted by installing some new capital every month.

Empirical evidence supports the idea that investment is lumpy. In the United States a study of plant-level investment in the 1970s and 1980s showed that companies concentrated their spending on particular plants and in particular periods. U.S. economists Doms and Dunne found that firms tended to do more than 50% of their total investment over a 17-year period in the years on either side of their peak spending year. Figure 14.16 indicates how bunched expenditure can be. It shows the proportion of total investment a sample of U.S. firms undertook per year over 20 years. Across the sample of firms almost 17% of investment over the 20-year period was, typically, undertaken in the year of heaviest investment. Less than 1% of investment was typically undertaken in the year when spending was lowest.

This bunching of investment would not have any obvious macroeconomic significance if different firms bunched spending at different times. Aggregate investment would be smooth even if company-level expenditure was irregular as long as companies did not all tend to bunch their spending at the same time. But in fact, companies will tend to bunch spending together if common factors are driving the optimal level of capital. Shifts in interest rates set by the central bank, or tax rates set by government, will move the cost of capital for all companies in the same direction at the same time and will also move their optimal (or target) capital stocks in the same direction. General productivity shocks will have common effects and will also tend to make investment procyclical because improvements in productivity will boost current output and

[8]Sidney Fine, quoted in Cooper and Haltiwanger "The Macroeconomic Implications of Machine Replacement: Theory and Evidence" *American Economic Review* (1993) vol. 83, pp. 360–382.

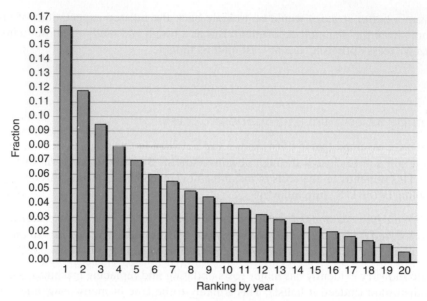

FIGURE 14.16 **Investment bunching in particular years.** Proportion of investment done in different years ranked from heaviest to lightest years by form. *Source*: Cooper, Haltiwanger, and Power, "Machine Replacement and the Business Cycle: Limps and Bumps," *American Economic Review* (September 1999) vol. 89, no. 4, pp. 921–946.

simultaneously increase the desired capital stock which encourages new investment. Firms in general are also likely to become more optimistic about the future when aggregate output is growing fast.

The lumpiness of investment, its concentration in particular periods, and its tendency to be high when output is already rising mean that movements in investment expenditure significantly affect business cycle fluctuations as we saw in Figures 14.3 through 14.5. That role is greater the more volatile are companies' expectations about future demand, and the more sensitive are those expectations to shifts in current spending. Keynes argued that those expectations of future demand conditions were unstable and that waves of optimism and pessimism among firms generated investment booms and slumps that exacerbated business cycle fluctuations. The evidence on the volatility of investment, and its procyclicality, supports the Keynesian view. But alternatively, if shifts in technology, which generate surges in productivity, are the real force behind business cycle fluctuations, then this would also explain why investment is volatile and procyclical.

14.6 Foreign Direct Investment and the Global Capital Market

Increasingly firms in the developed world make their investment decisions by asking not just what the optimal stock of capital is but also where in the world that capital should be installed. Figure 14.17 shows the stock of foreign direct investment (FDI)

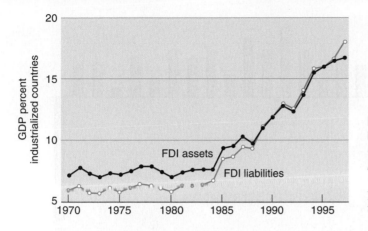

FIGURE 14.17 **Foreign direct investment in the 1980s and 1990s (% GDP).** Average FDI position. *Source*: Lane and Milesi-Ferretti, "The External Wealth of Nations," IMF Working Paper WP/95/115 (August 1999).

relative to GDP for the industrialized countries. In 1970 the stock of productive capital that companies in the developed economies had built up in other countries (in both the developed world and developing countries) was worth about 5% of GDP. By the end of the 1990s, it had risen to about 20%. The stock of *inward* foreign investment (shown in Figure 14.17 as FDI liabilities) has risen broadly in line. This represents a huge increase in the internationalization of investment flows. Figure 14.18 reveals that richer countries (those with higher GDP per capita) tend to hold larger stocks of investment overseas.

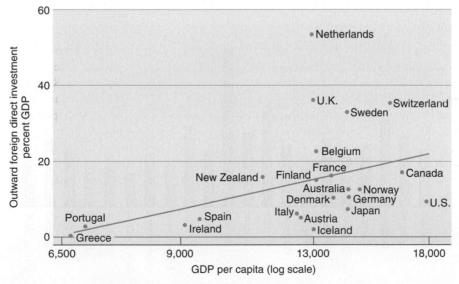

FIGURE 14.18 **Outward FDI and GDP per capita.** Richer countries tend to invest more overseas. *Source*: Lane and Milesi-Feretti, "The External Wealth of Nations," IMF Working Paper WP/95/115 (August 1999).

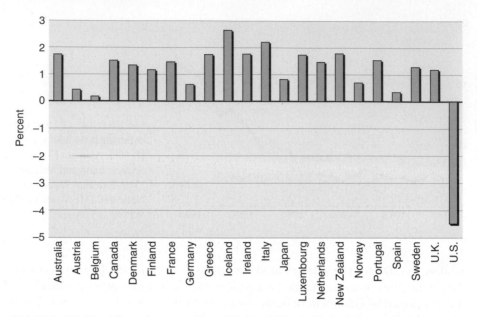

FIGURE 14.19a   **Tax wedges on machinery investment, 1996.** *Source*: OECD calculations (Gordon and Tchilinguirian, "Marginal Effective Tax Rates on Physical, Human and R&D Capital," OECD Discussion Paper 199 (1988). Copyright OECD.

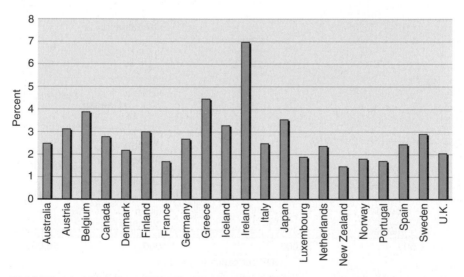

FIGURE 14.19b   **Tax wedges on inventory investment, 1996.** *Source*: OECD calculations (Gordon and Tchilinguirian, "Marginal Effective Tax Rates on Physical, Human and R&D Capital," OECD Discussion Paper 199 (1998). Copyright OECD.

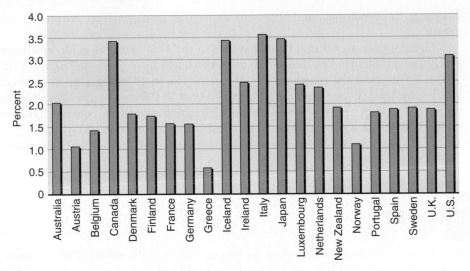

FIGURE 14.19c **Tax wedges on building investment, 1996.** Tax systems differ greatly across countries, creating a wide range of incentives and disincentives to invest. *Source*: OECD calculations (Gordon and Tchilinguirian, "Marginal Effective Tax Rates on Physical, Human and R&D Capital," OECD Discussion Paper 199 (1998).

Over the past 30 years, corporations in the developed economies have channeled an increasing proportion of their capital expenditure overseas; these economies have been sending more investment to other countries *and* have been receiving more inward investment from abroad. When we think of which factors influence a company's investment, we should focus on the cost and productivity of capital not just in the domestic economy but wherever in the world the company could invest. There are obvious reasons why both the marginal productivity of capital and the cost of capital can differ across countries. If technology is common across countries (and a multinational corporation can use the same know-how in Mozambique as in Manhattan), then differences in capital–labor ratios and wages can generate big differences in the marginal returns on new investment. Differences in taxation can also be a big factor, both on the cost side (e.g., differences in the rate at which interest payments can be deducted against the company tax bill) and on the revenue side (e.g., differences in tax rates on profits). Figure 14.19*a, b,* and *c,* show an estimate of different overall tax rates on various sorts of capital investment across developed countries.

These calculations take into account the taxation of corporate income and the value of allowances that companies can claim against tax. They also reflect the tax treatment of income to those who provide funds. Because the tax investors pay generally depends on their income, we have to make some assumption about who the investor is before we can calculate the overall impact of the tax system on the incentives to invest in different types of physical capital. The OECD data in the figures assume that the investor is someone earning average income. The figures show the so-called tax wedge on various types of capital investment relative to a bank deposit. This is the difference between the required pretax return on the relevant capital (machinery, buildings, or inventories) and on a bank deposit, so as to generate the same after-tax return.

Figure 14.19*a* shows that the tax system in the United States made investment in machinery profitable even though the machines might have generated a pretax (gross) return 4.5% below the return on a bank deposit. So in 1996, the United States effectively subsidized investment in machinery. Figures 14.19*b* and 14.19*c* show that investment in buildings and inventories in the United States was, in contrast, taxed more heavily than bank deposits. These figures reveal that tax on various types of capital investment varies across countries, which has influenced cross-border flows of investment.

SUMMARY

Investment expenditure is important for two reasons: it is the means whereby the capital stock grows (or at least is preserved) and it is a significant, volatile, and procyclical element of overall spending. Investment depends upon expectations of the profitability of new capital relative to its cost. The cost depends upon interest rates, the tax system, depreciation, and movements in the price of capital goods.

Increasingly firms are undertaking investments that produce, or are designed to produce, abroad as well as in the domestic economy. Investment has become increasingly footloose and therefore sensitive to cost and rate of return differences across countries.

Investment is a means to an end, and not an end in itself. When we judge the performance of countries, it would be bizarre to rank them in terms of levels of investment expenditure. What really matters is how productive is the investment that has been undertaken. We noted in earlier chapters that productivity in the United States has remained higher than in Japan. Japan has invested about twice as much of its annual income as the United States has. Until the 1990s economic pundits often said that Japan was going to overtake the United States within the next 5 to 20 years (the more the pundit wanted to be listened to in the short term, the lower that number tended to be). One of the factors the pundits pointed to was the high level of investment by Japanese companies. But those pundits forgot that what really matters is the rate of return on investment and not just the level of investment. Rates of return on much of the investment expenditure undertaken in the 1980s in Japan turned out, by the end of the 1990s, to have been low. The pundits retreated into themselves and had to think of a new story to sell those paperbacks at airports.

CONCEPTUAL QUESTIONS

1. Suppose interest rates rise sharply but are expected to fall again in a year or so. How do you think this would affect the level of investment in machines with short and long useful lives?

2. Suppose firms extrapolate from recent growth in demand to future growth. They invest when capital is insufficient to meet projected demand. If current capital exceeds what is required to meet expected demand, investment is cut to zero. How could an economy that worked like this generate investment-led business cycles?

3. Suppose an invention renders much of existing production techniques in a sector of the economy obsolete. What would happen to the stock prices of firms and to investment in the sector? What does this tell you about q theory?

4. Should governments give incentives to overseas firms to invest in the economy? Should incentives be the same for domestic firms? What if other governments offer incentives?

5. How would you assess whether a country is undertaking an optimal amount of investment? Can a country invest too much?

6. Labor leaders often claim that firms underinvest. What might they mean and how could you test the claim?

ANALYTICAL QUESTIONS

1. The capital output ratio in an economy is 2.5. Capital depreciates at 6% a year. Output grows at 3% a year. What is the ratio of gross investment to output that keeps the capital–output ratio constant?

2. A delivery company can buy a new van for $50,000. It can finance the purchase with a bank loan. The annual interest rate is 12%. Interest payments are tax deductible and the corporate tax rate is 30%. The company estimates that it will be able to sell the van a year later for $30,000. Any capital loss is tax deductible. What is the annual user cost of a van?

3. Consider again the delivery company in Question 2. The company estimates how much extra pretax income a given number of new vans will bring in. Here is the schedule:

Extra vans	Extra income (pretax $)
10	300,000
20	570,000
30	840,000
40	1,000,000
50	1,150,000

How many vans should the firm buy?

4. An all-equity company (which has no debt) has a stock market value of $540 million. Its tangible assets comprise land, buildings, and machines. The land is worth $100 million. The buildings are worth $120 million. The replacement value of the machines is $300 million. What is Tobin's Q? Why might Q differ from unity? The intangible assets of the company include the value of its reputation. Does the fact that these assets might have value imply that the company should expand?

5. Suppose that the corporate sector in an economy aims to do enough investing to preserve a ratio of the capital stock to output of 3. If the capital stock is less than 3 times output, firms invest; if the capital stock is above 3 times output, firms do not scrap capital or sell it because the scrap or secondhand values are very low. Instead, companies can cut gross investment so net investment can be negative. Capital wears out and companies need to invest 4% of their existing capital just to preserve the value of capital. Initially companies expect output to grow at 2% a year next year and plan their investment accordingly. What will be the level of investment if total current output is $1000 billion? Firms suddenly change their view on output growth cutting expected growth from 3% to 0. What happens to investment? Finally,

firms become despondent and expect output to fall by 3%. In each case calculate the ratio of investment to output.

6. Suppose companies can deduct interest payments on their debt against their taxable income: they pay tax on profits, *net* of interest payments on debt. The revenue that a company generates from some new investment is taxed, but it can offset depreciation of the capital. Suppose the government introduces a 100% deprecation allowance—so companies can immediately deduct all investment spending from taxable profit. But to offset this very generous measure they set the corporate tax rate at a high level of 60%. Is the resulting tax system advantageous or disadvantageous to investment—take as your benchmark a situation with no taxes at all. Assume companies use debt to finance investment.

Business Cycles

Overview

Business cycles are medium-term fluctuations in the economy; that is, fluctuations that are normally completely contained within a decade. The business cycle involves oscillations between periods of high and low activity or expansions and contractions. In this chapter we outline the main statistical facts that characterize business cycles—how the business cycle affects different industries and different individuals. We consider whether or not business cycle fluctuations are bad for the economy or whether they may have beneficial effects. Understanding the business cycle requires identifying what are the shocks that trigger fluctuations and the various economic mechanisms that propagate these shocks over time. We view a range of different business cycle theories and outline the shocks and propagation mechanisms they assume and review the evidence in support of each. We describe a simple supply and demand model with which to view the effects of these shocks and propagation mechanisms.

15.1 What Is a Business Cycle?

One way of defining the business cycle is that it is the fluctuations in output around its trend. The production function tells us that for a given level of capital, labor, and technology a certain amount of output can be produced. This is what we have referred to as the trend level of output. However, at any point in time, output does not have to equal its trend value. Firms can always produce less output if they do not work at full capacity utilization or if they do not work their labor force at full efficiency during its working shift. Therefore, output can always be below this trend level. But output can also exceed the trend level predicted by the production function. For instance, workers can be persuaded to work overtime for short periods and machines can be utilized at more than full capacity during intense periods of production. Firms cannot maintain these high levels of activity indefinitely—eventually the workforce needs a rest, and if machines are used too intensively they will break down and there will be stoppages. However, for short periods this intensive use of factors of production enables output to be above its trend. One definition of the business cycle is these fluctuations of output around this trend level.

Figure 15.1 shows an estimate (by the OECD) of the trend (or potential) level of output for Italy as well as its gross domestic product (GDP). Figure 15.2 shows the gap between Italian GDP and potential output, which is one measure of the business cycle. When output is above trend, the economy is in the boom phase of the cycle, and when it is significantly below trend, the economy is in recession.

The measure shown in Figure 15.2 is sometimes referred to as the "**output gap**"— the distance between potential output and current GDP. The output gap is a popular concept used to explain how monetary policy operates. When the output gap is large and negative, GDP is far below its potential level and factors of production are not being used intensively. By contrast, when the output gap is positive and large, GDP exceeds potential output by a large margin. This can only be the case if factors of production are being used intensively so that overtime is high and machines are operating a full shift. In these circumstances inflation is likely to be rising. If firms are already at full capacity when they receive additional orders, the orders cannot be met, so the firm will start to increase prices to choke off demand. With overtime costing more than normal working hours, costs will increase which will put upward pressure on prices. Therefore, a large positive output gap is associated with either high or rising inflation, while a large negative gap leads to subdued inflation.

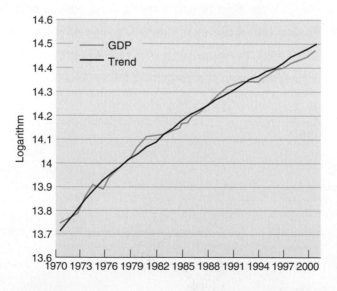

FIGURE 15.1 **Italian GDP and trend GDP**. GDP isn't always equal to its trend level but fluctuates around it—these are business cycle fluctuations. *Source*: OECD Economic Outlook, various issues. Copyright OECD.

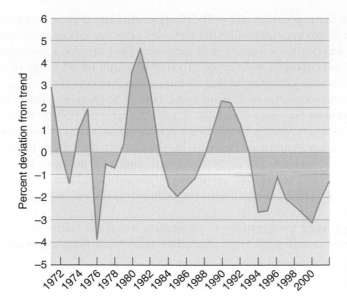

FIGURE 15.2 **Italian output gap, 1970–2000.** The output gap is a measure of the business cycle. *Source*: OECD Economic Outlook, various issues. Copyright OECD.

As Figures 15.1 and 15.2 make clear, business cycles are only temporary—whether in an expansion or a recession, output is eventually expected to return to its trend level. However, the economy can remain either above or below its trend level for several successive years. In other words, expansions last for several years and then are replaced by recessions, which are also persistent. The business cycle is the continual process whereby the economy enjoys an expansion, endures a recession, and then again experiences an expansion. In this chapter we will try to explain why the economy experiences these oscillations and also try to document how persistent each stage of the business cycle is.

15.2 Measuring the Business Cycle

We do not actually observe the business cycle—we only observe GDP. To measure the business cycle we have to make assumptions about trend output. To further complicate matters, economists use a variety of terms when discussing business cycles—booms, recessions, expansions, contractions, depressions, growth recessions, and other expressions. What do these terms mean?

One often cited definition of a **recession**, particularly in the United States, is when an economy has experienced two successive quarters of negative growth. Therefore, if an economy grows by −0.3% and −0.5% in two quarters, it is in recession. Unfortunately this definition is somewhat restrictive. Imagine that over the last three quarters output growth had been −15%, 0.01%, and −35%. This economy is clearly in recession but not according to our two consecutive quarter ruling. Therefore we need a more flexible way of defining recessions. The authoritative National Bureau of Economic

Research in the United States provides one such definition. A business cycle committee, which examines recent trends in output and other variables as well as different sectors of the economy, decides whether the economy is in recession. They declare a recession if economic activity contracts across a wide range of variables and a broad range of sectors—see Table 15.5 later in this chapter for their dating of U.S. business cycles.

In many economies recessions—that is, genuine falls in output—are quite rare. However, **growth recessions** are more common. A growth recession occurs when, although the economy is still expanding, i.e., showing positive growth, the growth is less than the economy's long-run trend rate of growth. In other words, the output gap is increasing during a growth recession. For instance, growth may slow down to 1% even though over the last three years it has been expanding at 5% per year. Such a slowdown is a growth recession, but not a recession itself—the economy is still expanding but not as fast as previously.

Another term used when the economy is performing weakly is "*depression.*" As with much business cycle terminology, depression does not have a precise definition.[1]

TABLE 15.1
Percentage Output Declines during the Great Depression

Argentina	−13.72
Australia	−5.78
Austria	−19.79
Belgium	−7.09
Canada	−24.08
Chile	−30.02
France	−14.66
Germany	−23.50
Mexico	−17.66
New Zealand	−14.64
UK	−5.09
USA	−26.99
Venezuela	−21.20

Source: Maddison, *Monitoring the World Economy 1820–1992* (OECD Paris, 1995).

Depressions are characterized by dramatic and long-lasting falls in output.

[1] Although it is sometimes said that a recession is when you know someone who has become unemployed and a depression is when you become unemployed!

Loosely speaking, it signifies a bad recession—one that is both long lasting and in which output declines substantially. This does not specify how bad or long lasting a recession has to be to be called a depression. Probably the key difference between a recession and a depression is that, as Figure 15.2 shows, recessions tend to be short-lived and output soon returns to its trend value. The economy therefore shows momentum between good and bad periods. However, in a depression the economy seems to have lost all momentum—the downturn lasts so long that the economy seems unable to recover on its own without a dramatic policy intervention.

The most famous example of an economic depression is the one that affected many countries between 1929 and 1932. Table 15.1 shows the percentage decline in output between 1929 and 1932 of the countries that were most affected by the Great Depression. Throughout this three-year period, output in these countries fell sharply. Both the extent of these declines and the duration of the contraction make this period a depression rather than a recession.

15.3 Characterizing Business Cycles

Business cycles are not just a feature of modern OECD economies—even the bible describes seven years of feast followed by seven years of famine. Figure 15.3a shows annual growth in Swedish real GDP between 1862 and 1905 and reveals a pattern of oscillation between periods of high and low growth. Figure 15.3b plots the same series for Germany and Peru. Nineteenth-century Sweden and modern Germany and Peru are obviously very different economies, yet all of them show a pattern of business cycle fluctuations.

The nature of these fluctuations differs across countries—for instance, Peruvian growth varies much more than the postwar United States—but they all show the general pattern of expansions followed by contractions. Why do such different economies experience business cycle fluctuations? Later we will provide a model to explain these

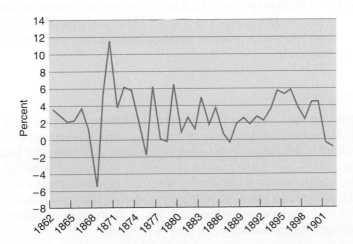

FIGURE 15.3a **Growth in Swedish GDP, 1862–1905.** *Source*: Data used in Basu and Taylor, "Business Cycles in International Historical Perspective," *Journal of Economic Perspectives* (1999), pp. 45–68. Reprinted by permission of the American Economics Association.

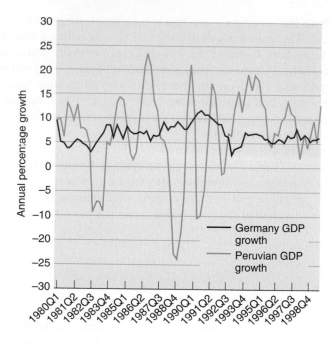

FIGURE 15.3b **Annual GDP growth in Germany and Peru, 1980–1999.** Although their frequency and amplitude change, all countries in all historical periods have experienced business cycle fluctuations. *Source*: IMF, *International Financial Statistics*, (September 2000). Courtesy of IMF.

fluctuations, but for now we shall use a simile. The economy is like a reservoir. With no wind or disturbance the water will be still. However, as soon as something is thrown into the water, it sets in motion a wave-like pattern on the surface. If a pebble is thrown in, the waves will be small and will not extend far. If an automobile is thrown in, the waves will be bigger and more pronounced. In other words, different disturbances evoke different fluctuations in the water, but all disturbances evoke a wave like motion. If the structure of water were different, these disturbances, the pebble or automobile, might simply disappear under the water and create no wave. Economists think in a similar way about the economy. Its structure is such that any disturbance, such as an increase in the price of oil or in interest rates, sets in place a long-lasting reaction in which output fluctuates between high and low periods of activity. Different economies will experience different shocks, and the magnitude and duration of business cycles may vary, but such fluctuations are inevitable.

WHAT DO BUSINESS CYCLES LOOK LIKE?

We have said that a business cycle consists of two stages: an expansion and a contraction. There are many differences between these two stages of the business cycle. The first is that expansions tend to last longer than recessions. Figure 15.4 shows (for industrial output rather than GDP) how many months expansions and contractions last in different countries. The number shown is the average length of expansions and contractions from 1969 to 1992. Expansions last three to four times longer than recessions—recessions last around 12 to 15 months and expansions 3 to 5 years in most countries. Note that these are averages—each business cycle may be different.

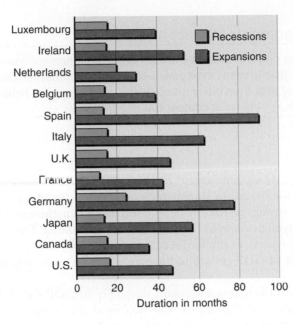

FIGURE 15.4 **Duration of business cycle expansions and contractions.** Expansions typically last longer than contractions. *Source*: Artis, Kontolemis, and Osborn, "Classical Business Cycles for G7 and European Countries," CEPR Discussion Paper 1137 (1995).

However, while recessions are shorter than expansions, they are characterized by more dramatic monthly changes in output. Figure 15.5 shows for the same countries the average monthly percentage decline in output during recessions and the average monthly increase in expansions. In nearly all cases output declines much more dramatically during recessions. Therefore, short periods of sharp declines in output tend to characterize recessions, while expansions are longer lasting. During expansions the economy regains the losses of output that occurred during recessions, but at a more leisurely pace.

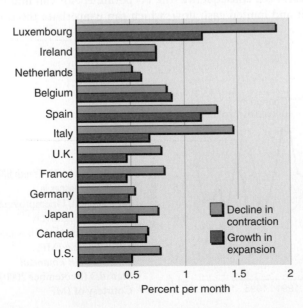

FIGURE 15.5 **Monthly percentage increases and decreases in industrial production in expansions and contractions.** During recessions output changes more rapidly than during expansions. *Source*: Artis, Kontolemis, and Osborn, "Classical Business Cycles for G7 and European Countries," CEPR Discussion Paper 1137 (1995).

15.4   Business Cycles as Aggregate Fluctuations

The key feature of business cycles is that they are an aggregate phenomenon. Co-movement characterizes them; that is, many economic variables from different sectors and regions of the economy, and also from different countries, display similar behavior at roughly the same time. In this section we document this co-movement.

CO-MOVEMENT ACROSS VARIABLES

Over the business cycle, GDP and unemployment move in opposite directions. Figure 15.6 shows this with data for France (a similar picture emerges for other countries). When GDP growth is strong, unemployment falls, but when the economy moves into recession, unemployment starts to rise (and employment falls). The labor market is normally a lagging indicator of the business cycle—it usually takes around six months for a rise in the rate of GDP growth to have an affect on employment or unemployment.

In Chapter 2 we showed how the national accounts decomposed GDP into different demand components. Figure 15.7 shows how the two most important components—consumption and investment—vary over the business cycle in France. As in all OECD economies, consumption growth follows the same cyclical path as GDP but tends to be less volatile—as explained in Chapter 13. However, if consumption is not very volatile, other variables have to be more volatile, and Figure 15.7 shows that investment is extremely volatile relative to GDP. Whereas GDP growth fluctuates between −1% and 5%, investment growth varies between −7% and 9%. Over the business cycle, the personal sector does its best to maintain a smooth level of consumption. However, with GDP declining, this can only be achieved if resources are switched to the personal sector. As a consequence, the corporate sector can find itself with reduced access to credit and limited cash flow, which can exacerbate the downturn in investment spending.

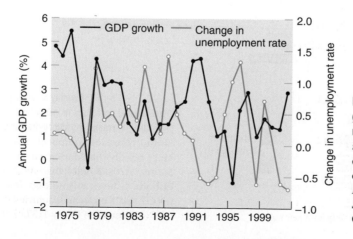

FIGURE 15.6   **French GDP growth and changes in unemployment.** Unemployment and GDP negatively correlated over the business cycle *Source*: IMF, *International Financial Statistics* (September 2000). Courtesy of IMF.

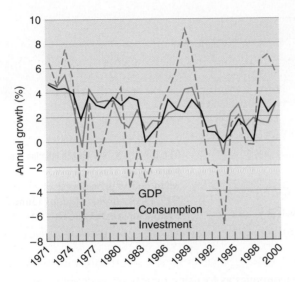

FIGURE 15.7 **Consumption, investment, and output growth In France, 1971–2000.** Consumption and investment are all procyclical—consumption tends to fluctuate less than GDP and investment by considerably more. *Source*: IMF, *International Financial Statistics* (September 2000). Courtesy of IMF.

Although most aggregate economic variables display a strong cyclical pattern, some do not. Particularly important for understanding business cycle behavior are wages. As Figure 15.8 shows, wage growth displays little volatility over the business cycle and a much lower correlation with GDP than other economic variables. Trying to explain why wages show such a weak cyclical pattern when unemployment and employment are so strongly cyclical is a key challenge to business cycle theorists and an issue we will examine in Section 15.7 of this chapter.

Figure 15.9 shows that inflation is also cyclical—when output growth is high, so on average, is French inflation. However, inflation is also a lagging cyclical variable. It takes many months—often as long as one or two years—before higher GDP growth starts to be reflected in higher inflation.

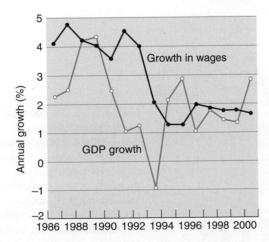

FIGURE 15.8 **French output and wage growth, 1986–2000.** Wages show a modest degree of procyclicality. *Source*: OECD, *Economic Outlook* (June 2000). Copyright OECD.

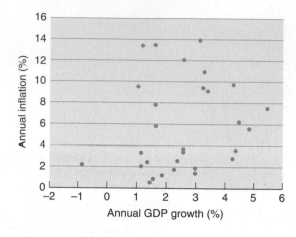

FIGURE 15.9 **French inflation and output growth.** Inflation tends to be higher when output growth is strong. *Source*: OECD, *Economic Outlook* (June 2000). Copyright OECD.

CO-MOVEMENT ACROSS SECTORS

In Chapter 1 we defined macroeconomics as focusing mainly on aggregate uncertainty; that is, events that many agents tended to experience. The business cycle is a prime example of a macroeconomic phenomenon. In a recession many firms and industries will be performing poorly. As we saw in Chapter 1, this doesn't mean that all firms are doing badly—in a recession bankruptcy advisers' workload will soar, and firms can still get lucky by introducing a new product consumers really want. In other words, idiosyncratic uncertainty is important. However, most firms in most industries will be performing below average in a recession.

Figure 15.10 shows this common aggregate experience by examining four main productive sectors of the UK economy: manufacturing, services, construction, and the public

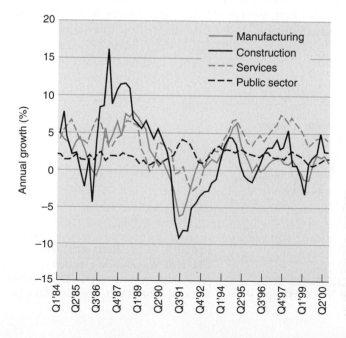

FIGURE 15.10 **UK output growth by industrial sector, 1984–2000.** All sectors rise and fall together over the business cycle, but volatility is most pronounced in manufacturing and construction. *Source*: Economic Trends, UK Office for National Statistics, various issues.

sector. These figures show that when one sector is doing well, so normally are the others—all four sectors' output tends to move together. However, although output moves in a similar direction across industries, the magnitude of the fluctuations differs greatly.

The most exposed sector to the business cycle shown in this figure is construction—output growth in this industry has hit peaks of 17% and declines of −9% in a year. As Chapter 24 shows, the output of the property industry is extremely cyclical. The manufacturing sector is also as volatile—over the same time period, growth was as high as 8% and declines as large as 8%. By contrast, the service and public sectors show muted business cycle fluctuations. Output growth in the public sector has varied between 4% and 0%, although for most of the time it lies in the range of 0 to 2%. The service sector shows more variability, with fluctuations between 7% and −7%, but this is still less volatile than either manufacturing or construction output. Therefore, while most sectors show a business cycle pattern, some are more exposed than others.

CO-MOVEMENTS ACROSS REGIONS

Regions within a country are strongly connected, so we would expect to find positive co-movement between them. Table 15.2 shows the correlation of output across U.S. states between 1971 and 1998. If the correlation is positive, then output growth tends to be high in each state when overall U.S. output growth is high. The closer the correlation is to 1, the stronger the co-movement. If the correlation is negative, then output in the state tends to be

TABLE 15.2   Output Correlations across U.S. States, 1978–1998

State	Corr.	State	Corr.	State	Corr.
Alabama	0.83	Louisiana	0.49	Ohio	0.92
Alaska	0.14	Maine	0.69	Oklahoma	0.24
Arizona	0.79	Maryland	0.81	Oregon	0.71
California	0.79	Massachusetts	0.78	Pennsylvania	0.89
Colarado	0.49	Michigan	0.81	Rhode Island	0.77
Connecticut	0.75	Minnesota	0.90	South Carolina	0.87
Delaware	0.54	Mississippi	0.77	South Dakota	0.54
District of Colombia	0.61	Missouri	0.83	Tennessee	0.77
Florida	0.77	Montana	0.32	Texas	0.53
Georgia	0.84	Nebraska	0.64	Utah	0.59
Hawaii	0.12	Nevada	0.59	Vermont	0.72
Idaho	0.51	New Hampshire	0.73	Virginia	0.86
Illinois	0.93	New Jersey	0.79	Washington	0.59
Indiana	0.87	New Mexico	0.17	West Virginia	0.63
Iowa	0.76	New York	0.83	Wisconsin	0.87
Kansas	0.73	North Carolina	0.92	Wyoming	0.29
Kentucky	0.87	North Dakota	0.31		

The business cycle is a common experience across geographical regions.

Source: Author's calculations from data from Bureau of Economic Analysis, www.bea.doc.gov

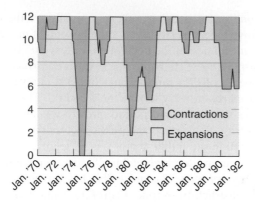

FIGURE 15.11 **Number of countries in recession or expansion.** Business cycle conditions tend to be similar in different economies.

low when the rest of the economy is doing well. If the correlation is zero, then there is no consistent pattern between how output at the state level varies with the national business cycle. Table 15.2 shows the co-movement across regions—26 of the states have a correlation coefficient greater than 0.75, 41 of more than 0.5, and none of them have a negative correlation. Clearly the majority of regions face similar business cycle experiences.

CO-MOVEMENT ACROSS COUNTRIES

It is understandable why sectors within an economy tend to share a common business cycle. If the manufacturing sector is doing well, it will generate demand for new buildings that will encourage the construction industry and will also generate increased demand for the service sector (increased realtor services, mortgage demands and insurance policies, etc.). National economies are also linked together—when the U.S. economy is growing fast, it generates demand for non-U.S. goods and that helps output grow faster in other countries. As a result, we should expect to see signs of a common business cycle across countries.

Figure 15.11 shows how many of the 12 countries in Figures 15.4 and 15.5 have been in expansions or contractions at the same time between 1970 and 1992. It is very rare for only a few economies to be in recession; normally several countries experience a downturn simultaneously. However, these regions do not have to share a common business cycle. For instance, in 2000 the United States had been experiencing a long and sustained economic boom; Continental Europe experienced modest growth and Japan was mired in recession. Therefore, while national economies tend to experience similar business cycle timings, this is not inevitable.

15.5 Have Business Cycles Changed?

While business cycles have been a feature of economies for most of recorded history, their nature is not constant. Table 15.3 shows how volatility (as measured by the standard deviation of output growth) has declined since 1950—according to these numbers, business cycle volatility has fallen by around 30–40% in most industrialized countries.

TABLE 15.3   Standard Deviation
of Output Growth

Country	1885–1939	1950–1999
Argentina	6.49	5.12
Australia	6.10	2.05
Belgium	5.31	1.97
Brazil	8.65	5.38
Canada	6.32	2.23
Finland	5.06	2.67
Italy	4.32	3.84
Netherlands	6.25	2.82
Portugal	8.68	3.07
Sweden	4.71	2.17
Switzerland	3.07	2.84
UK	4.86	4.31
USA	4.95	2.83

Business cycles seem less volatile
after 1950.

Source: Authors' calculations from
Basu and Taylor dataset from data
used in Basu and Taylor, "Business
Cycles in International Historical
Perspective," *Journal of Economic
Perspectives* (1999), pp. 45–68;
updated using IMF, *Internatioinal
Financial Statistics* (September
2000).

Figure 15.12 shows this reduced volatility in U.S. output growth. The abrupt
change in the nature of this volatility has lead to much discussion—particularly because
from 1950 onwards, many governments used fiscal and monetary policy to try to reduce
business cycle volatility. Figure 15.12 and Table 15.3 support the idea that governments
succeeded in reducing this volatility.

Has business cycle volatility really declined? A study by Christina Romer of Berke-
ley suggests otherwise. The reason lies in how we measure the economy. Before 1950
governments did not measure GDP. Instead economists used to monitor the behavior
of a wide range of different industries. Historical series of GDP are therefore constructed after the event—economic historians use the measured output of industries for
which there are data and combine them to estimate GDP. However, the GDP data
measured from 1950 are based on many more industries than economic historians have
data for before 1950. Therefore GDP data before 1950 is an average of a smaller range
of industries, and as a result, we would expect it to be more volatile. Imagine estimating
the average height of the population by measuring only the people living in your household. This is unlikely to be close to the national average, and comparing estimates

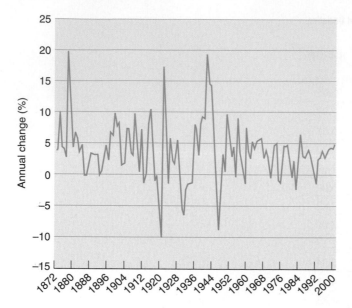

FIGURE 15.12 **U.S. Output growth, 1871–2000.** The figure shows the significant decline in volatility of measured U.S. output. *Source*: From data used in Basu and Taylor, "Business Cycles in International Historical Perspective," *Journal of Economic Perspectives* (1999), pp. 45–68; updated using IMF, *International Financial Statistics* (September 2000).

across different households will vary widely. However, if we take averages of households in each street or even in each town, then these averages will get closer to the national average and will show much less variation across streets or towns. In the same way, measuring GDP by sampling only a few industries will lead to much more volatility in GDP than when we sample many industries.

Romer showed that this measurement difference can account for the reduced volatility in U.S. GDP. To examine whether volatility has declined in the U.S. economy, she considered only the industries for which there are data before and after 1945 (40 in all), and then compared the volatility of industry output both before and after 1945. Table 15.4 shows her results. Using midpoints of the intervals as measures of volatility, we find that 22 industries have a pre-1939 volatility of output the same or less than post-1945. In other words, no strong evidence suggests that U.S. GDP fluctuations are less dramatic after 1945.

However, while we cannot conclude that the volatility of business cycles has fallen, the nature of U.S. business cycles has changed. Table 15.5 shows the dates for U.S. expansions and contractions and shows the duration of each.

TABLE 15.4   **Ratio of pre-1939 to post-1945 Volatility in U.S. Industries**

<0.75	0.75–1.25	1.25–1.75	1.75–2.25	2.25–2.75	2.75–3.25
8	14	13	2	2	1

Evidence suggests that in each individual industry volatility has not increased.

Source: Romer, "The Cyclical Behavior of Industrial Production Series 1889–1984, *Quarterly Journal of Economics* (February 1991), pp. 1–31.

TABLE 15.5 Dating of U.S. Business Cycles

| Trough | Peak | Duration (in months) of | | |
		Contraction	Expansion	Business Cycle
12/1854	6/1857		30	
12/1858	10/1860	18	22	40
6/1861	4/1865	8	46	54
12/1867	6/1869	32	18	50
12/1870	10/1873	18	34	52
3/1879	3/1882	65	36	101
5/1885	3/1887	38	22	60
4/1888	7/1890	13	27	40
5/1891	1/1893	10	20	30
6/1894	12/1895	17	18	35
6/1897	6/1899	18	24	42
12/1900	9/1902	18	21	39
8/1904	5/1907	23	33	56
6/1908	1/1910	13	19	32
1/1912	1/1913	24	12	36
12/1914	8/1918	23	44	67
3/1919	1/1920	7	10	17
7/1921	5/1923	18	22	40
7/1924	10/1926	14	27	41
11/1927	8/1929	13	21	34
3/1933	5/1937	43	50	93
6/1938	2/1945	13	80	93
10/1945	11/1948	8	37	45
10/1949	7/1953	11	45	56
5/1954	8/1957	10	39	49
4/1958	4/1960	8	24	32
2/1961	12/1969	10	106	116
11/1970	11/1973	11	36	47
3/1975	1/1980	16	58	74
7/1980	7/1981	6	12	18
11/1982	7/1990	16	92	108
3/1991		8		

U.S. business cycles vary in their duration—on average, contractions are shorter than recessions.

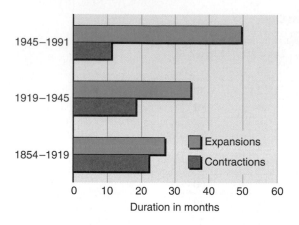

FIGURE 15.13 **Changing nature of U.S. business cycles.** Expansions seem to be getting longer in the United States. *Source*: Authors' calculations from NBER business cycle dates at www.nber.org

Table 15.5 illustrates a point we made earlier—business cycles are not uniform in length. Between 1919 and 1920, one business cycle lasted only 17 months, and between 1980 and 1981, another cycle lasted only 18 months. By contrast in the 1880s, 1960s, 1980s, and 1990s, business cycles occurred that lasted for longer than 100 months. Contractions during the period covered in Table 15.5 have been as short as 6 months and as long as 65 months, while expansions have varied between 10 and 106 months. Table 15.5 also suggests that U.S. business cycles have changed over time—in particular, expansions have been longer since 1945, while contractions have become shorter, as Figure 15.13 shows.

15.6   Are Business Cycles Bad?

In Chapter 4 we outlined an argument of Nobel Laureate Robert Lucas that said that the benefits to boosting the long-run rate of economic growth were enormous and that the gains from eliminating business cycle fluctuations were fairly small. In this section we reexamine this argument. Lucas is correct in saying that the benefits from boosting long-run growth are large *relative* to the gains from removing business cycles. However, are the gains from eliminating business cycles so small?

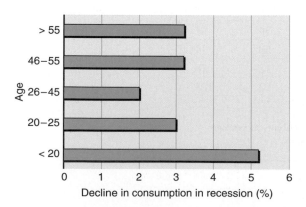

FIGURE 15.14 **Impact of recession on consumption by age.** The impact of recession is felt the most by the young and the least by those of prime working age. *Source*: Clark, Leslie, and Symons, "The Cost of Recessions," *Economic Journal* (1994), vol. 104, pp. 10–37. Reprinted with permission of Blackwell Publishers.

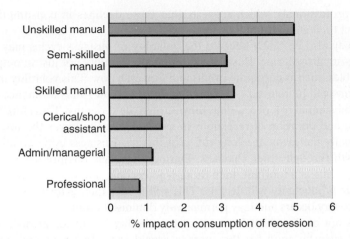

FIGURE 15.15 **Impact of recession on consumption by occupation.** Recessions are particularly costly for those with fewer skills. *Source*: Clark, Leslie, and Symons, "The Cost of Recessions," *Economic Journal* (1994), vol. 104, pp. 10–37. Reprinted with permission of Blackwell Publishers.

In essence, Lucas' argument is that consumption does not vary much over the business cycle, and that according to some measures, investors do not need to be compensated much for bearing risk (although our analysis of equity markets in Chapter 21 suggests that this is not uncontroversial). However, Lucas considers fluctuations in *aggregate* consumption, but Figure 15.10 showed that business cycle volatility affects some sectors more than others. Therefore, for some individuals, consumption volatility may be greater than Lucas' calculations suggest. Figures 15.14 and 15.15 show that this is indeed the case. These are taken from a study of UK households that examines the impact of the 1990–91 recession on consumption of different individuals and households. Recessions hit the young and the unskilled much more than they affect prime working-age professionals. Therefore, focusing on aggregate consumption underestimates the volatility some consumers face.

Table 15.6 shows how the consumption costs of recession are distributed across the population. Most of the population (57.7%) experiences small declines in consumption as a result of recession—between 0 and 2%. In all, nearly three-quarters of the people suffer at most a 4% decline in their consumption. For this group Lucas' calculations would seem to apply—business cycles involve relatively small variations in consumption. However, although recessions affect most people only minimally, a small group suffers disproportionately. For 1% of the population (and if the sample is representative of the UK population that is 600,000 people), consumption declines more than 10%, and for 15% of the population, it falls more than 6%. Figures 15.13 and 15.14 also suggest that those who suffer the most tend to be the poorest in society, e.g., unskilled

TABLE 15.6 **Distribution of Consumption Costs of Recession**

0–2%	2–4%	4–6%	6–8%	8–10%	10–12%	12–14%	>14%
57.7	16.5	13.4	5.4	3.4	0.3	0.3	0.3

The majority of individuals suffer very little from recessions, but a sizeable minority are badly hit. *Source*: Clark, Leslie, and Symons, "The Cost of Recessions," *Economic Journal* (1994), vol. 104, pp. 10–37.

workers rather than professionals, which suggests that these declines in consumption will substantially affect their standard of living.

Business cycles may also be costly because the volatility of business cycles may be connected to the long-run growth rate. Business cycles create volatility not just in output but also in other variables, such as corporate profits and firm cash flow. This volatility may retard investment. Firms will be reluctant to commit cash or borrow funds to finance investment if there is a substantial risk of a serious downturn in the economy. Therefore the greater the magnitude and duration of recessions in an economy, the lower the investment rate and potentially the lower the long-run growth rate. Business cycle volatility may also hinder growth through other channels. During recessions unemployment increases. If learning by doing is important, then those who become unemployed will lose certain skills, and their productivity will decline. This will hinder their efforts to regain employment when recovery occurs and may permanently diminish output.

Nonetheless, it is not obvious that business cycle volatility is bad for growth. Indeed, recessions may even be good for the average growth rate. In an expansionary phase, when the economy is growing strongly, it is costly for firms to stop production and add new machinery or rearrange the production process to boost efficiency. While order books are full it will be expensive to invest and reorganize. However, during a recession machines are idle and workers have spare time and this is a good time for firms to restructure and try to boost productivity. Intense competition during recessions also gives firms the incentives to reorganize. In other words, recessions may act like a pit stop for the economy during which efficiency and productivity improve, so that growth can accelerate when the economy recovers.

Figure 15.16 shows the volatility of output growth between 1961 and 1989 for 85 countries plotted against the average growth rate for each country over this time period. Overall the data suggest a weak, but negative, relationship—in other words, volatile business cycles are probably bad for growth—although clearly other things also affect growth. One study finds that every 1% increase in business cycle volatility leads to a 0.2% reduction in growth.[2] This implies that if Portugal could reduce its business

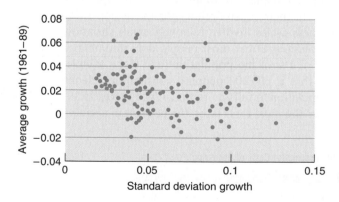

FIGURE 15.16 **Trend growth rates and business cycle volatility.** There is some evidence that volatile business cycles lead to low growth, but the link is very weak. *Source*: Summers and Heston dataset, http://cansim. chass.utoronto.ca:5680/pwt/

[2]Ramey and Ramey, "Cross-country Evidence of the Link between Volatility and Growth," *American Economic Review* (1995) vol. 85, pp. 1138–1151.

cycle volatility to the U.S. level, its trend growth rate would be 0.4% higher, or if the United States could reduce its business cycle volatility to that of Sweden, U.S. trend growth would be higher by 0.15%.

15.7 The Frisch-Slutsky Paradigm

We have already implicitly discussed the main ideas behind the Frisch-Slutsky paradigm when we drew an analogy between business cycles and reservoirs.[3] The Frisch-Slutsky paradigm identifies three components in business cycle fluctuations—as shown in Figure 15.17.

The first component is an impulse or a shock that triggers business cycle fluctuations. In terms of our metaphor, the impulse is the pebble or automobile that is thrown into the reservoir. However, as in our metaphor, the fluctuations that are produced may have a different pattern from the impulse that started them. This is because the impulse acts through a propagation mechanism that converts one-time shocks into persistent business cycle fluctuations—the pebble interacts with the structure of water to produce a wave.

Most economists agree about what business cycles look like. Therefore, debate focuses on the first two components of the Frisch-Slutsky paradigm—which shocks are most important and what economic factor converts these shocks into the business cycles we observe. There is broad agreement over which candidates might cause business cycles—monetary and fiscal policy shocks; shifts in desired consumption and investment; terms of trade shocks (including oil prices); technology shocks; shocks to the financial structure. But economists disagree over which of these shocks is most important in explaining observed output fluctuations. Yet the most substantial debate is over what mechanism propagates business cycles. This is because the nature of the propagation mechanism determines how policymakers should respond. Policymakers can do little to reduce the likelihood of technology or terms of trade shocks. The issue is instead whether policymakers should offset the business cycle fluctuations these shocks cause.

In the rest of this section, we outline two different views of business cycles. One says that business cycles are the efficient response of markets to shocks that have affected the economy—in other words, business cycles are a sign that the market is working correctly. The other viewpoint, which we shall call Keynesian, is that business cycles are a sign that the market is failing to operate.

FIGURE 15.17 Frisch-Slutsky business cycle paradigm: a theoretical characterization of business cycles.

[3]Named after two 1930s economists: Norwegian Ragnar Frisch and the Italian Eugene Slutsky.

REAL BUSINESS CYCLE THEORY

The last 20 years have seen substantial debate in academic journals about business cycles, Real Business Cycle theory has generated much of this debate.[4] Real Business Cycle theory created several controversies, but here we focus on only two. The first is its claim that technology (or more generally total factor productivity, TFP) shocks cause business cycles. Traditionally economists believed that variations in demand caused business cycles and that changes in TFP drove long-run growth but not business cycles. Real Business Cycle theory's rejection of demand shocks and its use of the same model to explain growth *and* business cycles are therefore radical. The other controversy concerns the propagation mechanism. Real Business Cycle theory says that the profit maximizing decisions of consumers and firms convert technology shocks into business cycle fluctuations. When technology improves, firms want to hire more workers and capital. The capital stock cannot be increased instantaneously, but once in place, it leads to high demand for labor and rising wages. This in turn leads to higher personal income and thus higher consumption. The effect of the positive technological development is thus spread over several periods.

This view that the propagation mechanism is the efficient operation of the market is particularly controversial. In essence Real Business Cycle theory says that booms are a time of high productivity and good technology shocks. As a result firms want to produce high levels of output, to employ many workers, and to invest in new machinery. Because productivity is high, firms will pay high wages. So economic expansions happen because it is a good time to be economically active. By contrast, recessions happen because productivity/technology is poor. It is a bad time to produce, and firms will not wish to pay high wages, invest, or hire workers. With wages low, workers will not be eager to work. Recessions are simply bad times to be economically active. Note that in this theory, individuals make the decision not to engage in high levels of economic activity in the recession having seen market prices, and the invisible hand result tells us that the market is efficient. Of course, this doesn't mean that recessions are good—everyone would prefer to be in a boom than a recession. It does, however, mean that because the economy is experiencing low productivity, it is optimal for the economy to be in recession—in other words, governments should not try to kickstart the economy.

To see this, consider agricultural production and employment which vary substantially over the year, reaching a peak at harvest time and a trough during the winter. Governments do not respond to the dramatic decline in output, investment (sowing), or employment during these winter months by aggressively cutting interest rates or trying to boost government expenditure. They recognize that winter is a bad time for farmers and employees to work, so output is low. Real Business Cycle theorists make essentially the same argument regarding business cycle fluctuations. This implies that while recessions may be bad in the sense that we would rather not have them, given the circumstances (bad weather, adverse technology shock), the economy is inevitably in recession, and the government should not try to alter output or employment.

---

[4]Many have contributed to Real Business Cycle theory, but its origins are in the work of Finn Kydland and Ed Prescott, "Time to Build and Aggregate Fluctuations," *Econometrica* (1982). Far more sophisticated Real Business Cycle theories have been developed than that we outline here.

This claim that recessions are optimal market responses to bad economic events is understandably controversial. As our seasonal analogy suggests, it also raises interesting issues. In Chapter 2 we saw that economies experience substantial seasonal fluctuations that are actually more dramatic than those observed over the business cycle. However, governments do not express concern over seasonal downturns, economists rarely use anything other than seasonally adjusted data. This suggests that volatile output is not necessarily bad—the key issues are what produces this volatility and how the economy responds to it. So are Real Business Cycle theorists correct in their claims that recessions are an optimal response by the market to bad technology shocks?

To answer this question we need to look more closely at Real Business Cycle theory model by focusing on a model of the labor market. As we showed in Section 15.3 of this chapter, over the business cycle, wages fluctuate relatively little but employment fluctuates a lot. How does Real Business Cycle theory explain this? Changes in technology trigger real business cycles which, as we saw in Chapter 6, shift the marginal product of labor and thus also the labor demand curve. When the economy experiences a positive technology shock, then the marginal product of labor is high. At a given wage, firms now want to hire more workers, so the labor demand curve shifts to the right. How this increase in labor demand affects wages and employment depends on the slope of the supply curve. Figure 15.18 shows two different possibilities. In Figure 15.18a the labor supply curve is steep—in response to higher wages, firms are not able to employ more people. In this case fluctuations in labor demand lead to large changes in wages but no change in employment. However, this is inconsistent with the business cycle facts we documented earlier.

But if we assume a flat labor supply curve, so that in response to small changes in wages individuals are prepared to dramatically change their hours worked, then this model can explain the high employment variability and low wage movement that we see over the business cycle. Here is the crux of the argument. To explain business cycle fluctuations, the Real Business Cycle model needs to assume that labor supply is very responsive to

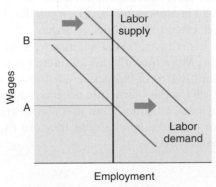

FIGURE 15.18a **Business cycles with inelastic labor supply.**

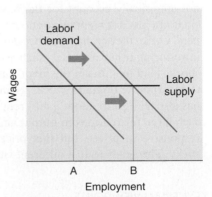

FIGURE 15.18b **Business cycles with elastic labor supply.** To explain the observed business cycle pattern of employment and wages requires an elastic labor supply curve.

changes in wages, as in Figure 15.18*b*. In other words, individuals are highly responsive to market prices. Over the business cycle, we see volatility in output, employment, and investment, but much less volatility in interest rates, inflation, and wages. In other words, quantity variables are more volatile than price variables. To explain this, we have two main camps. One camp, which the Real Business Cycle model belongs to, says that markets work well and that individuals are very responsive to changes in prices. The other camp, which includes the Keynesian models we will soon discuss, says that markets do not work well and that prices are sluggish. As a result, the economy can only respond to adverse shocks through big changes in output or employment.

Are Real Business Cycle models justified in assuming such a flat labor supply curve as in Figure 15.18*b*? This flat labor supply curve assumes that individuals want to work an average number of hours over the business cycle. However, they will work more hours when wages are high and will reduce their hours when wages are below average. If individuals are highly responsive to changes in wages, employment and unemployment will fluctuate a lot. According to Real Business Cycle theory, therefore, recessions are periods of low total factor productivity, which means a low marginal product of labor, so firms are not prepared to pay high wages. People respond to these low wages by choosing not to work many hours, which leads to a fall in employment and a rise in unemployment.

However, studies suggest that people are not very responsive to changes in wages. In fact, studies of the responsiveness of prime working age males reveal that their labor supply hardly varies with changes in wages—Figure 15.18*a* would capture their behavior much better. Other demographic groups show more responsiveness but never enough to justify the flat labor supply curve in Figure 15.18*b*. We see some support for Figure 15.18b when we consider those who change their employment status over the business cycle rather than just vary the hours they work. For instance, some people may not find it worthwhile to seek employment when wages are low because they have to pay for, say, daycare for their children. However, when wages rise above a certain level, these people do find it profitable to work a full shift. As a result, their employment is very responsive to changes in wages. However, even this variation of employment does not empirically account for the business cycle facts—most people's labor supply decisions are just not responsive enough to changes in market prices. As a result, Real Business Cycle theory has had to develop and extend the model of Figure 15.18*b* by introducing other impulses, such as changes in tax rates, that in addition to technology shocks lead to shifts in the labor supply curve. More recently this literature has started to incorporate demand shocks as an important source of business cycle fluctuations. It has also started to adopt a different view of why we see such little price variability and such large fluctuations in output and employment. It assumes not that people are very responsive to prices, but that prices do not change much because they are fixed or sticky. This leads us to a different view of business cycles.

THE KEYNESIAN VIEWPOINT

In 1936 John Maynard Keynes (1883–1946) published *The General Theory of Employment, Interest and Money*. This was a defining moment for macroeconomics. Keynes wrote his masterpiece with the Great Depression of 1929–1932 in mind. His basic message was that in certain circumstances the market mechanism may not work. For various reasons he argued that prices, wages, and interest rates might be unable to change, or to change by enough, to prevent the economy getting caught in a period of low output and high unemployment. If the market works well, then prices and wages should fall until demand and employment increase. Keynes argued that prices may not be able to fall, and even if they did, it may exacerbate matters. Keynes was essentially arguing that microeconomics—the study of the marketplace and how prices and individuals interact—may not be relevant for studying the aggregate economy. In other words, macroeconomics needed different models and tools.

The General Theory was innovative not just in its analysis of the Great Depression but in its suggested remedy. If markets could not on their own restore prosperity, then governments had to. If prices could not be relied on to change to create demand, then government had to pump demand into the economy by raising government expenditure, cutting taxes, or lowering interest rates. The differences between this approach to business cycles and that of Real Business Cycle theory are many. This Keynesian perspective says that recessions are caused not by adverse supply shocks but by too low a level of demand. Further, recessions are occasions not when individuals optimally choose to produce low output but periods when the market does not work properly, leading to suboptimally low output. In other words, recessions are bad, and the government should and can improve things.

The General Theory is a fascinating book. However, Keynes tended to prefer words to diagrams and math. As a result, what he means, or how the effects he details operate, is not always entirely clear. The book has so many ideas that it is not always obvious which idea Keynes put most emphasis on. As a result, a huge literature is dedicated to sorting out what Keynes really meant to say. However, given that Keynes died in 1946, it is hard to reach a definitive view on this issue, so the literature has recently focused less on what he meant to say and more on developing his insights into how market failures may lead to business cycles.

Essentially Keynesian economics is about malfunctioning markets. Of course, a market can fail in many ways and there are many different markets to fail. As a result, Keynesianism has many different strands—some Keynesians think that it is the labor market that does not function well and that wages do not change, so unemployment can become too high. Others argue that product market monopolies keep prices too high and output too low, so that unemployment is too high. Another camp argues that flaws in the credit markets and banking sector produce fluctuations and recessions. Of course, all three markets could operate poorly and the interactions among them could produce large fluctuations and inefficient business cycles.

Keynesian models are therefore many and varied, linked by the common theme of market failure. In many of these models, the market failure is of a particular form— what economists call a "**strategic complementarity**"—a situation in which whether a person acts in a particular way depends on whether someone else is also acting that way. Consider whether you want to go to a party this evening. You are probably more likely to go if you think that your friends will be there. Knowing the cost of attending the party, e.g., cab fares, gifts, etc., is not enough information to decide whether to go. This is an example of a strategic complementarity, in which you are more likely to do an action if others are as well.

Keynesian models invariably involve strategic complementarity. Consider the example of an economy dominated by two large industries—A and B. Each industry is contemplating a major investment program that will substantially increase productivity and output but be extremely costly. The investment will only prove profitable if the economy has enough demand to purchase the extra output. If each industry makes the investment, productivity and wages will be so high the economy will have enough demand to make the investment profitable. If only one industry undertakes the investment, demand will not be high enough, and the expanding industry will make a loss. In this situation each industry will only undertake the investment if it thinks the other industry will, too. As a result, the invisible hand does not work—firms cannot simply look at the market price and make their decisions; they also need to know what other industries will be doing. This raises the possibility of a coordination failure—what if each industry wants to make the investment but thinks the other industry won't? Then neither industry will invest and the economy remains at a low level of output. If each industry could be persuaded that the other will invest, then the economy would be at a high level of output.

This example introduces another common feature of Keynesian models: multiple equilibria. This example has two outcomes—either both industries invest, and the economy booms, or neither does, and the economy remains at low output. This offers a different perspective on business cycles—expansions are periods when everyone is confident, and the economy performs well, but recessions are periods of coordination failure when pessimism takes hold, and the economy is at a low activity level. In this case recessions are clearly bad—it is better to be at the high output level. What should the government do? In our example the solution is simple. The government has to promise that it will always provide enough demand in the economy to purchase the production of firms. Then each industry knows that if it makes the investment it can sell its output and make profit no matter what other industries do. As a result, all industries make the investment and the government never actually needs to buy anything—because all firms expand, there is enough demand from the private sector.

Another form of strategic complementarity is what economists term *thick market effects*. Consider the housing market. The decision whether to put your house up for sale depends on what price you think you can sell it for, on how easily you can find a buyer, and on how quickly you will be able to find another house that you want to buy. When few houses are up for sale, few people are looking to buy houses (apart from first-time buyers) and few houses are on the market to choose from. As a result, this is a bad time to try to sell your house and buy another. This makes it less likely that you will try to sell your house, so the number of houses for sale remains low. This also makes other people less likely to try to sell their house, so the level of activity remains low. However, when the level of activity increases, the opposite happens. The more people there are in the market looking to buy and sell, the more likely you are to put your own house on the market. This swells the number of people on the market, which in turn encourages other people to enter the market. Therefore, the market may oscillate between periods of low and high activity. In this case the thicker the market—the more people participating—the more people who want to be economically active.

A popular strand of Keynesian thought is that prices and wages are sticky—that they do not adjust in response to changes in output or employment. As a result, over the business cycle, we get large fluctuations in output and employment but little fluctuation in prices and wages. One explanation for this price stickiness is that firms are monopolists and set too high a price—as a result, their output is lower and they need fewer employees, so unemployment will be higher.

To see how this fits in with our discussion of strategic complementarities, consider that the demand for a firm's product depends essentially on two factors: the price of the product relative to other commodities and the total amount people want to spend. The latter factor depends on the stock of money in the economy. However, what this money can buy depends on the price level. The higher the price level, the fewer commodities this money can buy. When a firm sets its price, it tends to think only of how its price affects its attractiveness relative to other commodities. This gives it an incentive to lower its price, but it ignores an additional channel. If a firm lowers its price, then it increases the amount that individuals are prepared to spend on all commodities—the amount of money they hold can now buy more. However, this effect is small if only one firm lowers its price, and it boosts demand for all products (this is the strategic complementarity) not just those of the firm itself. Therefore, the firm ignores this additional benefit from cutting prices when it selects its own price and as a result sets prices too high. But the same reasoning leads all firms to set prices too high so that output and employment are too low.

If somehow all firms could be persuaded to lower their prices, then the economy would have more demand and output and employment would be higher. This problem can only be overcome if government tries to boost the demand for all commodities. In this simple model, if firms won't lower prices, then the government should increase the money supply.

These have only been sketches of Keynesian models, and when more fully elaborated, each model reveals both insights and pitfalls. However, the contrast with Real Business Cycle models is obvious—in Keynesian models markets do not function well, individuals may act in an uncoordinated way and arrive at a bad equilibrium, and in these circumstances, the government can and should improve things.

15.8 Aggregate Demand and Aggregate Supply

Broadly speaking, two categories of impulses might trigger business cycle fluctuations: aggregate demand shocks and aggregate supply shocks. In this section we use fluctuations in the aggregate supply and demand curve to construct a simple way of thinking about business cycle fluctuations.

AGGREGATE DEMAND

Aggregate demand measures the claims made on output produced. We saw in Chapter 2 that we can categorize the use made of output produced into four components: consumption, investment, government expenditure, and net exports. As Table 15.7 shows (for Canada), consumption is the largest component of demand, net exports the smallest, and investment the most volatile domestic component.

TABLE 15.7 Canadian National Accounts

	% of GDP	Standard Deviation
Consumption	58%	0.96
Government Expenditure	19%	1.44
Investment	20%	2.44
Exports	43%	3.03
Imports	40%	3.15

Percent of GDP is calculated for 1999 and standard deviation from quarterly data between 1961 and 1999.

Source: IMF, *International Financial Statistics* (September 2000).

To construct our model of business cycles, we need to use the concept of an aggregate demand curve that we first introduced in Chapter 3. Figure 15.19 shows this negative relationship between demand and prices. When prices are high, demand is low—output is too expensive. We are interested in shifts in the demand curve; that is, changes in the amount of demand in the economy even without a change in prices. Figure 15.19 shows the example of an increase in aggregate demand that shifts the demand curve to the right. This means that at the price P, demand in the economy is now Y(1) and not Y(0). Note that this shift has nothing to do with changes in prices—at unchanged prices individuals wish to buy more.

What might cause such a shift? Table 15.7 shows that aggregate demand consists of consumption, government expenditure, investment, and net exports. We are looking for shocks to aggregate demand—unexpected increases in any of these components. For instance, consumers may decide that they would rather save less out of their income than they have previously—perhaps because the population is getting younger on average, or social forces glamorize conspicuous consumption, or the population just feels more optimistic about the future. Any of these events would lead to an increase in aggregate

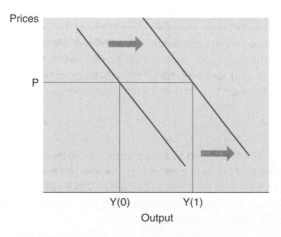

FIGURE 15.19 **Shifts in aggregate demand curve.** The aggregate demand curve shifts right when, at a given price, the level of demand increases.

demand through a shift in consumption. Similarly, an increase in the optimism of firms regarding investment prospects, a change of government to a party that favors increased government expenditure, or a sudden shift in world demand towards the products a country produces will all lead to shifts in aggregate demand and affect business cycle fluctuations.

However, a complete model of business cycles needs to contain both supply and demand features. Chapters 4 through 7 outlined in detail the development of the supply side of the economy. There we listed the determinants of supply as the capital stock, employment, and total factor productivity (TFP). However, our analysis omitted prices—if all prices are doubled (including wages and the rental cost of capital), then this should make no difference to the capital stock, employment, or TFP, and so no difference to output. In other words, Chapters 4 through 7 suggest that the supply curve should be vertical. We introduced this idea first in Chapter 3 and we illustrate it again in Figure 15.20. There is a fixed level of output that can be provided, which the capital stock, employment and TFP determine, regardless of the price level.

However, Figure 15.20 shows that with this model of the supply side we cannot account for the business cycle properties we observe through shocks to aggregate demand. When the demand curve shifts out this means that at a given price the economy has more demand. However, firms cannot provide any more output to meet this extra demand—they can only produce their full capacity output and no more, and capital, labor, and TFP pin this level of output down. The extra demand only pushes up prices—from P(0) to P(1). As prices rise, they choke off demand until demand equals the output that firms can produce. This model implies that when demand varies output does not change, only prices fluctuate—clearly this is no good as a model of business cycle fluctuations. However, if the supply curve is not vertical but upward sloping, then changes in demand evoke both changes in output and changes in prices—as in Figure 15.21. The flatter the supply curve, the more output varies and the less prices change—similar to what we observe over the business cycle.

Figure 15.21 implies that when firms start to receive increased orders they meet this extra demand by some combination of raising prices and increasing output. Therefore Figure 15.21 can account for business cycles, but its plausibility depends on the answers to two questions: Are firms prepared to meet increases in demand by expanding output

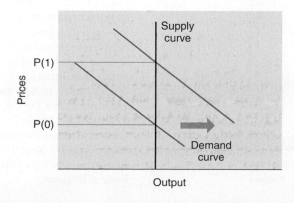

FIGURE 15.20 **Business cycles with vertical supply curve.** With a vertical long-run supply curve an increase in demand only raises prices and leaves output unaffected.

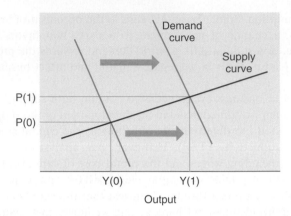

FIGURE 15.21 **Business cycles with short-run supply curve.** With an upward-sloping short-run supply curve, firms respond to increases in demand by raising output.

rather than just raising prices? And why would firms not just raise prices when demand increases?

Figure 15.22 shows the results of a Bank of England survey that asked firms how they respond to increases in demand. The huge percentage of respondents who would increase output even if this means working more overtime, hiring more workers, or increasing capacity is striking. Only 12% of firms gave increasing prices as one of their main responses. Figure 15.22 gives very strong practical justification for the flat supply curve in Figure 15.21.

Firms seem willing to increase output rather than raise prices when demand increases for two reasons. The first is that firms only periodically review prices, so that for significant periods prices are fixed. For instance, mail order firms and restaurants print catalogs and menus in advance and cannot alter prices between printings. This makes prices sticky and costly to change, an example of what economists call "nominal rigidities." Figure 15.23 shows that firms from the same Bank of England survey only occasionally review their prices—the rest of the time prices are fixed, and either output

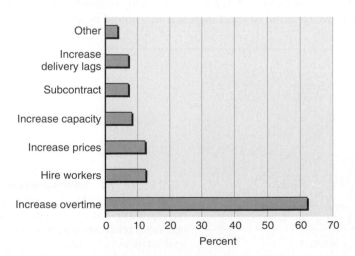

FIGURE 15.22 **How firms respond to increased demand.** Survey evidence suggests most firms respond to higher demand more by raising output than increasing prices. *Source*: Hall, Walsh, and Yates, "How Do UK Companies Set Prices?" Bank of England Working Paper 67 (1997). Reprinted with the permission of the Bank of England.

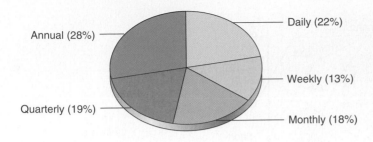

FIGURE 15.23 **Frequency of price reviews.** The majority of firms review their prices once a month or less. *Source*: Hall, Walsh, and Yates, "How Do UK Companies Set Prices?" Bank of England Working Paper 67 (1997). Reprinted with the permission of the Bank of England.

or delivery lags vary when demand changes. While 22% of firms review their prices daily, over a quarter review them once a month, and another 19% only once a quarter. Therefore, firms may not change prices in response to every change in demand—prices are sticky.

Prices are also sticky because firms may be unable, or may choose not to change them. Figure 15.24 shows from the Bank of England survey the number of price changes firms made over a year. Even though 22% of firms review their prices daily, only 6% change their prices more than 12 times a year. In total, 80% of firms change their prices every six months or more—firms do not adjust prices frequently in the short run.

But if we assume that firms are maximizing profits, why don't they increase prices by more when they have the opportunity to increase them? Firms don't raise prices for many reasons. The first is that when firms raise prices they lose customers and thus revenue. If the firm has many competitors, none of which has raised prices, then the firm will be wary to do so itself for fear of losing revenue and profit. The second reason is costs. A standard result in microeconomics is that firms maximize their profits when they set price equal to a markup over their marginal cost, where the markup depends on how much monopoly power the firm has. According to this formula, firms should only change prices when either the markup they demand, or their costs, change. Therefore, the behavior of marginal costs is crucial in determining the slope of the supply curve. If marginal costs do not alter much when the firm increases output, then it should increase output, not change its prices. Therefore it can be profit maximizing for firms not to increase prices even if they have the opportunity—this is what economists call "real rigidities." Similarly even if marginal costs increase with output, firms may not change prices if they are prepared to take a lower markup. Therefore, a combination of nominal rigidities (that is, firms cannot change prices because of fixed contracts),

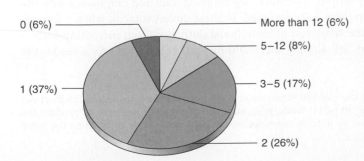

FIGURE 15.24 **Frequency of price changes.** But the majority of firms change prices twice a year or less. *Source*: Hall, Walsh, and Yates, "How Do UK Companies Set Prices?" Bank of England Working Paper 67 (1997). Reprinted with the permission of the Bank of England.

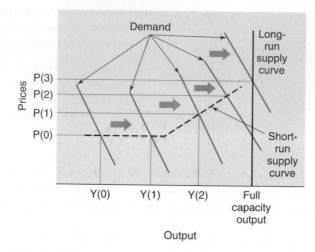

FIGURE 15.25   **Supply and demand model of business cycle.**

existing advertising, or price stickers, and real rigidities (that is, firms not wanting to raise prices even when they make a price review), means that in the short run the supply curve is not vertical and variations in demand lead to changes in output and prices, as in Figure 15.25.

RELATIONSHIP BETWEEN SHORT-RUN AND LONG-RUN SUPPLY CURVES

Where does this leave our supply side model outlined in Chapters 4 through 7? The answer is that the analysis in those chapters focused on long-run developments in the economy, how the level of output varied from decade to decade. However, when we analyze business cycles, we are considering fluctuations that complete themselves within a decade. We can therefore think of the vertical supply curve of Figure 15.20 as being a long-run supply curve and the flat curve of Figure 15.21 as a short-run supply curve.

The long-run supply curve shows the level of output that an economy can produce when machines and labor are working at full capacity for a given level of TFP. As Figure 15.25 shows, demand increases at this full capacity level produce price increases because firms cannot produce any more output—the marginal cost of output soars as firms find it increasingly difficult to produce any more, so prices rise.[5] However, firms are not always at this full capacity output. Machines may be lying idle, and employees may not have enough work to keep them fully occupied. In these circumstances, when a firm receives new orders, it has the spare resources to boost output without increasing costs—the machines and workers are already there and are not being used. As a result, the

[5]Another way of drawing the long-run supply curve is for it to be placed just before the short-run supply curve becomes vertical. In other words, price increases occur when firms try to produce too far above the full capacity level by utilizing machines more than is sustainable or by using too much overtime.

supply curve will be flat, and as Figure 15.25 shows any increases in demand boost output rather than prices. However, as output increases, fewer machines are idle, and all potential employee hours are being used. Under these circumstances firms will have to use overtime, hire more workers, or invest in new machinery to meet rising orders. As a result, marginal costs begin to increase, and the firm responds to extra demand by a combination of raising output and raising prices. The supply curve is no longer flat but increasingly slopes upwards.

Figure 15.25 suggests the following pattern for prices and output over the business cycle. Consider an economy in recession with output Y(0)—the economy has a large negative output gap because GDP is far below its capacity level. However, as demand increases, the economy grows to Y(1) but experiences little inflation—firms meet the increase in orders by boosting output, not prices. At Y(1) the output gap has shrunk, so that when demand continues to increase firms still increase production but also start to pass along price increases to customers. Output rises to Y(2) and prices to P(1), and the economy grows until it reaches full capacity output, and prices are at P(3). At this point the economy is on the long-run supply curve, and firms cannot boost output—any additional increase in demand feeds straight through into inflation. Therefore, in the latter stages of an expansion, output growth slows and inflation increases. Policymakers will try to allow growth during the recovery stage but prevent demand from increasing when the economy is at full capacity. Figure 15.25 shows why central bankers analyze information about the output gap so closely—it indicates potential inflation.

WHEN DOES THE SHORT RUN BECOME THE LONG RUN?

How do we link the short- and long-run supply curves? The long-run supply curve moves over time as the capital stock and the level of technology changes, so that the full capacity level of output increases. However, the capital stock and technology change slowly and only increase substantially over decades. Within a business cycle, which tends to last less than a decade, they change little, so that the full capacity output level is roughly fixed—in other words, over the business cycle, the long-run supply curve does not move. This is consistent with the approach of Section 15.2 in this chapter where we defined the business cycle as medium-term fluctuations around the trend level of output.

DO SUPPLY SHOCKS CAUSE BUSINESS CYCLES?

Figure 15.25 shows fluctuations in demand causing business cycles while the supply curve remains fixed. However, supply shocks can also affect business cycle fluctuations. When we discussed Real Business Cycle theory, we mentioned one source of supply shock: technological innovations. There are, however, many other sources of supply shock. The most obvious example is an increase in the price of commodities such as oil. As Figure 12.5 showed, the price of oil has varied considerably over the last 30 years, with particularly large increases in 1973 and 1979.

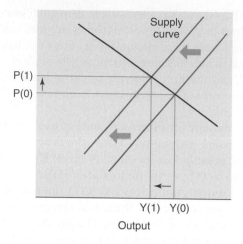

FIGURE 15.26 **Adverse supply shock causes recession.**

Oil is an important input into the production process of many commodities. If the price at which firms sell their product does not change, but their input costs have risen, then the profit margin will decline and the firm will start to scale back production. For the same price, firms will now want to supply less output, and the supply curve shifts in, as in Figure 15.26. As a result of this adverse supply shock, output falls, and the economy goes into recession. However, while a demand shock moves the economy into recession, a negative supply shock also increases prices. In other words, with oil price increases, producers cut back on production but also try and recapture their profit margins by raising prices.

Increased inflation and a slowdown in output growth were exactly what occurred after the two oil price increases in 1973 and 1979—as Figure 15.27 shows for the G7, the seven largest industrialized nations (the United States, Japan, Germany, France, the

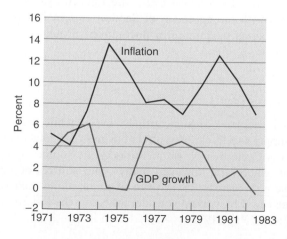

FIGURE 15.27 **G7 inflation and output growth, 1971–1982.** *Source*: IMF, *International Financial Statistics* (September 2000).

UK, Italy, and Canada). Inflation rose immediately in response to the oil price hike, and within a year, output growth had slowed—consistent with the mechanism in Figure 15.26.

There are wider sources of supply shocks than oil price increases—anything that alters the output firms provide at a given price shifts the supply curve. For instance, increases in indirect taxes will act as a negative supply shocks because for the same retail price, firms now receive a lower profit margin. Another source of supply shocks is structural reform—collapsing output and rising inflation, as you might expect following a negative supply shock, characterized the early years of economic reform in Central and Eastern Europe.

15.9   So What Causes Business Cycles?

In outlining the Frisch-Slutsky approach to business cycles, we commented that although there was broad agreement over the list of candidate shocks for explaining the business cycle, there was no consensus over which of these many shocks is most important. The problem is partly that we have to infer from the data which shocks are hitting the economy, and different assumptions lead to different conclusions about the importance of shocks. Table 15.8 shows the results of one study that attempted to discover the ultimate source of business cycles in the three largest European nations. It distinguishes among three distinct causes of business cycle fluctuations: nominal demand shocks (due to variations in the money supply), real demand shocks (shifts in consumption, investment or fiscal policy not related to monetary policy), and supply shocks. The results vary from country to country but essentially show that demand shocks tend to cause most business cycle volatility. Therefore, while economists accept a role for supply side shocks in the business cycle, they see fluctuations in demand as the major source of business cycle volatility.

TABLE 15.8   Causes of G7 Business Cycles, 1973–1995

	Percentage of Nominal Demand Shocks	Output Volatility Real Demand Shocks	Explained by Supply Shocks
USA	37	52	11
Germany	98	2	—
UK	57	43	—
France	3	67	30
Italy	35	—	65
Canada	45	—	55

Demand shocks explain the majority of business cycle fluctuations.

Source: Canova and Nicolo, "On the Sources of Business Cycles in the G7," Universitat Pompeu Fabra mimeo (2000).

SUMMARY

Business cycles are medium-term fluctuations in the economy around its long-run trend rate of growth. Business cycle fluctuations are normally, although not always, finished within a decade. Expansions tend to last longer than recessions, although the economy changes more dramatically each period in a recession. The key feature of the business cycle is co-movement—economic variables tend to move up and down together as do different sectors and regions of the economy. To a lesser extent countries also tend to show similar cyclical movements, although this is not always the case. There is some evidence that business cycle expansions have become longer since 1945.

The benefits from eliminating business cycle fluctuations are not trivial and arise from the beneficial impact on growth through encouraging investment by reducing uncertainty. Because the impact of recessions tends to fall disproportionately on the poorer members of society, reducing business cycle fluctuations also reduces inequality. For Keynesians the business cycle reflects a market failure and recessions are a time of suboptimally low output. The market failure can be caused by numerous factors and often relates to coordination failures in either the product, labor, or asset market. In contrast, Real Business Cycle theory says that recessions are the result of bad technology shocks which make it optimal for firms to produce little and workers not to work many hours. However, to account for the observed high variation in output and employment but low volatility in prices and wages, the Real Business Cycle model has to rely upon an implausibly high sensitivity of individuals' labor supply to changes in market prices.

A simple supply and demand model can be used to account for business cycle fluctuations, although to account for the low variability in prices but high volatility in output we have to utilize a short-run supply curve. The short-run supply curve describes the fact that in response to new orders firms may not just increase price but will also boost production. We argued that there are real and nominal rigidities such that firms decide only infrequently whether to change prices and often decide not to. Empirically the most important sources of business cycle fluctuations are changes in demand with variations in supply playing only a supporting role.

CONCEPTUAL QUESTIONS

1. If the economy goes into recession, how will it affect you? Consider not just your income but the prices of any assets you might own or commodities you purchase. How can you minimize this impact?

2. If rising inflation after an oil price increase leads the Central Bank to dramatically increase interest rates, what is the impulse behind this business cycle and what is the propagation mechanism?

3. How much of your weekly shopping is on commodities with "sticky" prices—prices that firms cannot immediately change? Are these sticky prices relevant or can they be negotiated? How do you think the introduction of barcoding and computer pricing will influence price behavior?

4. Travel on a train between Paris and Madrid and the view from the window changes—fluctuating between green land and a heavy concentration of economic activity. What explains this bunching of activity over space? Could similar factors explain the bunching of activity over time (the business cycle)? If so, how should governments respond to the business cycle?

5. In a recession share prices tend to be low and companies can be bought at low prices and workers hired for low wages. Given that recessions are only temporary, what stops you from buying loads of companies in a recession and then selling them during an expansion?

6. Why are recessions shorter than expansions?

7. What role do you think consumer and firm psychology has in driving the business cycle through fluctuations in demand?

8. Real Business Cycle theory implies that negative total factor productivity shocks cause recessions. What do you think such shocks might be?

9. Are recessions a good time for reorganizing and improving the efficiency of firms?

10. What are the impulses and propagation mechanisms of Real Business Cycle theory and Keynesian models?

ANALYTICAL QUESTIONS

1. Consider the Real Business Cycle model of Figure 15.18a. How does the labor supply curve need to shift for the model to explain business cycle fluctuations? What might cause such a shift?

2. Output in an economy is given by the following numbers

Year	1	2	3	4	5	6	7	8	9	10
Output	1	1.2	2.8	4.3	5.2	6.1	6.7	7.4	8.9	10

   (a) Assume a simple straight line between Year 1 and Year 10 is a good estimate of trend GDP. Calculate the output gap.
   (b) In Year 11 output is measured at 10.5—how does this change your estimate of trend output? What about your estimated output gap in Year 10?
   (c) In Year 11 output is instead measured as 12. What happens now to your estimate of trend output and the output gap? Discuss the problems this suggests in using the output gap to measure the current state of the business cycle.

3. (You will find a spreadsheet useful in answering this question.) Let the output gap in Year 0 and Year 1 be 0. Further let the output gap today equal 0.9 of yesterday's output gap less 0.9 of the output gap two periods ago, e.g., $Y(t) = 0.9*Y(t-1) - 0.9*Y(t-2)$.

   (a) Calculate the output gap for Years 1 to 20.
   (b) An unexpected shock in Year 2 increases the output gap to +1. What happens to the output gap now until Year 20?
   (c) What happens to the amplitude and duration of business cycles when the shock is +2 instead?

(d) What happens to the amplitude and duration of business cycles when the output gap follows the rule $Y(t) = 0.5Y(t-1) - 0.5*(T(t-2)$?
When it is $Y(t) = 0.1Y(t-1) - 0.1Y(t-2)$?
What about $Y(t) = Y(t-1) - Y(t-2)$?

(e) Consider again the case where $Y(t) = 0.1Y(t-1) - 0.1Y(t-2)$. What happens to fluctuations when $Y(2)$, $Y(3)$, and $Y(4)$ are increased by 1 and $Y(5)$, $Y(6)$, and $Y(7)$ are lowered by 1 and the same three-period oscillatory pattern is imposed for the remaining years? What does this tell you about the relative role of propagation and shocks in explaining persistent business cycle fluctuations?

4. Use a supply and demand model to analyze the impact of an oil price shock on the economy. After an increase in oil prices, what is likely to happen to profits, unemployment, income, and consumer confidence? How will this further affect your analysis? How useful is the distinction between supply and demand shocks?

5. An economy is dominated by two industries, both of which are considering whether to initiate a major investment project. If both industries invest, then employment and productivity are high and each industry makes profits of $5 billion. However, if neither industry invests, the economy is weaker and each industry makes $1 billion profit. If only one industry invests, then the industry that doesn't makes $2 billion profit but the additional costs of the investing industry mean that it loses $1 billion.

   (a) If each industry assumes the other one will not invest, what is their optimal course of action?
   (b) What if they assume the other industry will invest?
   (c) What is the role of changing business optimism in this economy?
   (d) How do your answers change when government offers an investment subsidy worth $3 billion to each industry? Is society better off?

Stabilization Policy

Overview

In this chapter we ask a big question: Can governments use fiscal and monetary policy to stabilize the economy? We saw in Chapter 15 that economies do not grow smoothly. Most advanced industrialized countries go through periods when economic growth is above the long-run average, unemployment falls, and inflation is high. In other periods output is far more sluggish, unemployment rises, and inflation falls. In this chapter we consider whether fiscal policy and monetary policy can be used to make the path of output, unemployment, and inflation smoother than it otherwise would be. We analyze whether tradeoffs between inflation and output exist. We consider whether governments and central banks operate macroeconomic policy better when they have maximum flexibility (or discretion) or whether binding rules exist that generate better long-run outcomes although they reduce discretion in the short run.

16.1 Output Fluctuations and the Tools of Macroeconomic Policy

Figure 16.1*a* and *b* shows the output gap—the difference between gross domestic product (GDP) and its trend level—for a sample of countries between 1970 and 2000. In Chapter 15, we introduced the output gap as one measure of the business cycle. Figure 16.1 shows these business cycle fluctuations to be large—in Canada

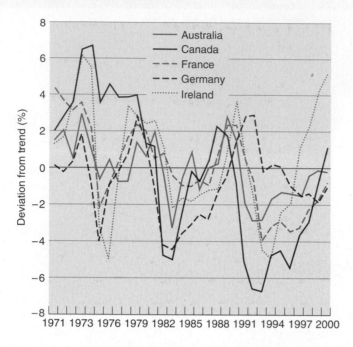

FIGURE 16.1a   **Output gaps in industrialized countries, 1970–2000.** Courtesy of IMF.

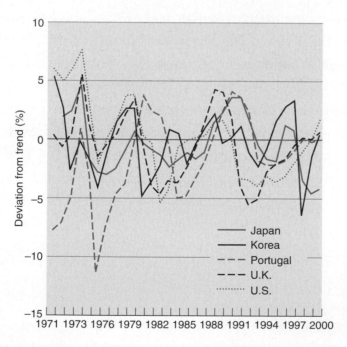

FIGURE 16.1b   **Output gaps in industrialized countries, 1970–2000.** Output shows substantial volatility over the business cycle. *Source*: IMF, *World Economic Outlook* (October 2000). Courtesy of IMF.

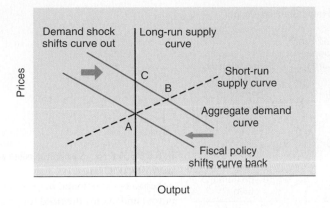

FIGURE 16.2 **Stabilization policy with demand shocks.** By changing monetary and fiscal policy, government may be able to adjust demand to stabilize pries and output in the face of aggregate demand shocks.

+7% to −7%. What can the government do to reduce these fluctuations? Can the government stabilize the economy by using fiscal and monetary policy?

We can use the aggregate demand and supply analysis of Chapter 15 to show what might be feasible. Consider Figure 16.2, which shows the case of an economy which has experienced an aggregate demand shock (e.g., an investment boom caused by "animal spirits," a consumption surge or an increase in government expenditure). In the short run, the economy moves from A to B—prices rise and output increases. However, at B the economy is producing above its trend level—the output gap is positive—so prices are rising. As prices increase, demand and output fall until the economy reaches C. The result is an increase in prices but no long-run increase in output. While moving from A to C output and prices show considerable volatility. If the government could control the demand curve, it could reduce demand, for instance, by raising taxes, reducing government expenditure, or increasing interest rates, and shift the demand curve back again. Prices would remain at A and output would not change. A similar logic holds for negative demand shocks. In this case, by boosting demand (interest rate and tax cuts, increases in expenditure) the government could avoid the recession. By using fiscal and monetary policy to change demand, Figure 16.2 suggests that governments might be able to stabilize output and prices.

Figure 16.3 shows the role of stabilization policy after an adverse supply shock—for instance, an increase in oil prices. The increase in oil prices causes the supply curve to shift leftwards, which produces an increase in prices and a fall in output as the economy moves from A to B. B is below the trend level of output and so is not a long-run equilibrium. For the economy to return to equilibrium either prices have to fall and the economy moves from B to A (which given price stickiness could take a long while), or the government boosts demand and shifts the economy from B to C. If the government does the latter, it will be stabilizing output but destabilizing prices.

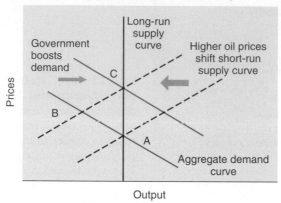

Boosting Demand Helps Stabilize Output

FIGURE 16.3 **Stabilization policy and supply shocks.** Using fiscal and monetary policy to boost demand helps stabilize output and avoids the need for prices to fall.

The idea that governments could manipulate demand and, in doing so, stabilize the business cycle was the essence of Keynesian economics in the 1950s and 1960s. There was considerable optimism that the adoption of such demand management policies would eradicate events such as the Great Depression. The main issues concerned how best to boost demand—whether interest rates, tax cuts, or increases in expenditure were most effective.

Events in the 1970s and 1980s substantially reduced this optimism. Later in this chapter we will outline a powerful argument which says that governments should not try to use fiscal and monetary policy in such a discretionary way. Instead they should follow fixed rules and avoid the temptation to try to stabilize the economy. We shall show that in certain cases we reach the counterintuitive result that by doing so the government achieves a better outcome than if it tried to manipulate the economy. This is a positive argument for not using stabilization policy—there are better ways of doing things.

There are also negative arguments—that stabilization policy will not work if it is tried. The first set of arguments applies to both monetary and fiscal policy and is based on the limited information that policymakers have at their disposal and the lags involved between the economy experiencing a problem and the policy response affecting the economy.

 16.2   General Arguments against Stabilization Policy

UNCERTAINTY

In Figures 16.2 and 16.3 we assumed that the government knew by exactly how much the demand or supply curve had shifted and also what the trend level of output is. However, one of the key problems of stabilization policy is working out what is happening in the economy. Figure 16.4 shows a variation on Figure 16.2. In this case, the

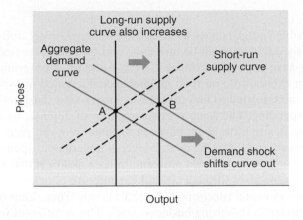

FIGURE 16.4 **Business cycle expansion due to demand and supply boost.** Stabilization policy is complicated by the need to work out whether fluctuations are caused by temporary demand shocks or permanent supply improvements.

long-run supply curve has shifted out, presumably because of some technological development, at the same time as the positive demand shock has happened. The government needs to decide how much of the increase in output has been caused by demand factors and how much by permanent supply changes. If it mistakenly assumes that it is nearly all demand shocks, then fiscal and monetary policy will be tightened too much and the economy will experience a sharp recession. Therefore, the government runs the risk of being the source of volatility if it uses stabilization policy when it is uncertain of the structure of the economy.

POLICY-MAKING LAGS

Monetary and fiscal policy are also subject to long lags. Stabilization policy faces three types of lag: informational lags, decision lags, and implementation lags. Informational lags arise because economic data are published only with a delay and even then are normally revised later. For example, in December we usually only have provisional estimates of GDP in June. Therefore, governments will only have statistical evidence of a boom or a recession several months later. Decision lags arise because even when the government has obtained the data it has to decide how to respond. For monetary policy, when all that has to be decided is the interest rate, this can be done relatively quickly. However, fiscal policy involves many different tax rates, tax thresholds, and thousands of government procurement decisions; fiscal policy cannot be adjusted so rapidly.

Finally, even when a government has identified an economic problem and adjusted its policy accordingly, it will take several periods before it has its full impact on the economy. This is the implementation lag. First, the policy actually has to be changed. In the case of interest rates this can be done swiftly, but for tax and expenditure plans the process is more cumbersome and may even require legislation. Second, once policy has been changed it has to have an effect on the economy. Empirical estimates suggest that it takes around two years before the peak impact of changing fiscal and monetary policy is achieved. Long uncertain lags mean that stabilization policy may actually be destabilizing. By the time a government has boosted demand in response to a recession, the economy may well have recovered, thus the policy is simply adding demand to an already strong recovery.

PROBLEMS WITH FISCAL POLICY

Fiscal policy is not a very flexible tool. Changes in taxes are administratively difficult and take time. Government expenditure cannot be turned on and off like water from a tap. Government departments have to plan in advance. No one could run a government transport department in which expenditure on road maintenance fluctuated massively from year to year as the government tried to fine-tune the economy with sharp movements in the overall level of spending. The same is obviously true of defense, health, and education spending. There is a tension, then, between sensible long-run planning for providing public sector services and using the overall level of government spending to regulate demand in the economy. An additional problem for fiscal policy is that governments wish to achieve many objectives through tax and expenditure policies—long-run growth, redistribution, environmental concerns, and political ends. These aims may conflict with the role of fiscal policy in stabilizing business cycles. This is different from monetary policy in which the sole instrument is interest rates and the government seeks to achieve only limited aims.

The other complication in using fiscal policy is uncertainty over the impact changes in taxes or increases in expenditure will have on demand. There are three channels through which attempts by the government to boost demand may be offset by the behavior of the private sector: Ricardian equivalence, consumer expectations, and crowding out.

RICARDIAN EQUIVALENCE

We outlined the notion of Ricardian equivalence in detail in Chapter 11. This results says that the impact of government expenditure on the economy does not depend on whether higher taxes or government debt is used to finance it. In other words, government deficits have no effect on the economy. Ricardian equivalence is a special result which relies on several strong assumptions. Ricardian equivalence is unlikely to hold exactly. However, it is the case that sometimes increases in fiscal deficit have little effect on demand because of increases in private sector saving. Unless the multiplier effects of fiscal deficits are predictable, using fiscal policy to stabilize the economy can be destabilizing.

CONSUMER EXPECTATIONS

As we saw in Chapter 13, how consumers respond to tax cuts depends on whether they perceive them as transitory or not. If consumers believe tax cuts will be reversed as soon as the economy recovers from recession, consumption will respond only weakly to a tax cut, if at all. Only if the tax cuts are perceived as being permanent will consumption respond strongly. As tax cuts made to stabilize the economy are only temporary, this not only suggests they will have only a small effect on the economy, it also adds an additional element of uncertainty as to how fiscal policy will work.

CROWDING OUT

There is another way in which government attempts to boost demand are offset by the actions of the private sector. There are a variety of different ways in which "crowding out" works, but all have the same essential mechanism: increases in the fiscal deficit lead to higher interest rates and lower private sector demand. If private sector demand is highly sensitive to interest rates, these crowding out effects can be substantial. The classic way in which crowding out operates is through a larger fiscal deficit reducing the amount of funds available to other borrowers, including the corporate sector. This leads to higher interest rates, which leads to lower investment and consumption. The expenditure plans of the private sector have to be reduced in order to provide the financing for the fiscal deficit.

For this channel to work the fiscal deficit must be large relative to the amount of funds available in the loan market. Given the size of global capital markets very few economies are likely to have a large enough fiscal deficit for crowding out to work through this channel. This argument is probably only relevant for the case of an extremely large U.S. fiscal deficit. However, in the 1950s and 1960s, when global capital flows were very small, deficits had to be financed largely through the domestic loan markets and so this channel would have been more important. There are, however, alternative ways for crowding out to work. With monetary policy set mostly by independent central banks, if governments run large fiscal deficits this may persuade central banks to raise interest rates in order to reduce inflationary pressures. These higher interest rates would lower consumption and investment and, through a higher exchange rate, lead to lower exports.

MONETARY POLICY

In many ways monetary policy is a more useful tool for stabilization. Central banks can change interest rates at very short notice. The U.S. Federal Reserve, the European Central Bank, and central banks in Japan, Australia, New Zealand, and in the UK have regular meetings to discuss monetary policy after which, literally within minutes, the decisions on interest rates that have been made are implemented. The lag between a decision and the implementation of monetary policy is virtually zero.

Nonetheless, many of the problems with fiscal policy are common to monetary policy. Private sector expectations about the aims of policy are critical. Time lags between the implementation of policy (a change in interest rates) and its impact upon expenditure decisions are long and variable. On average most of the affects of interest rates on output and inflation may only come through after two or three years.

Finally, although the ability to move official interest rates and other short-term interest rates is substantial, central banks do not control *real* interest rates of any maturity. So when they set monetary policy, central banks have a very indirect impact on the prices that really matter for many private sector spending decisions. One would expect that investment decisions, precisely because they have long-term implications, would be most sensitive to shifts in long-term, real interest rates. But central banks only set short-term, nominal interest rates. This means that unless movements in interest rates set by the central bank can influence expectations of inflation and of future interest rates, they are unlikely to have a substantial impact upon spending.

Therefore, using stabilization policy is problematic and assumes a great deal of knowledge and proficiency among economic policymakers. Fiscal policy is not flexible enough and its impact too uncertain to be extensively used for stabilization purposes. Although monetary policy also has drawbacks, it is more suitable as a short-term demand management tool. We shall now examine whether, using monetary policy, governments should seek to stabilize output.

16.3   The Inflation Output Tradeoff

Historically there has been a correlation in most developed economies between the rate of unemployment and the rate of inflation. Bill Phillips, who spent most of his life as a professional economist at the London School of Economics, first noted this link.[1] Phillips observed an empirical regularity between unemployment and inflation. Specifically, he documented a negative correlation between the level of unemployment and the rate of increase in prices and of wages. The lower was unemployment, the higher inflation tended to be. The data he considered and the curve that explains this data is shown in Figure 16.5.

To understand this correlation, let's suppose that at some point in time people expect that inflation will be 3%. We will assume that the labor market is in equilibrium (at the existing level of real wages all those who want to work can, and firms are employing precisely the number of people that maximizes their profits). In this case, if unemployment remains constant, wages should be increasing at the rate of expected inflation, so that real wages are expected to be steady (for the moment we ignore technological progress, which would allow wages to grow by inflation plus the rate of productivity

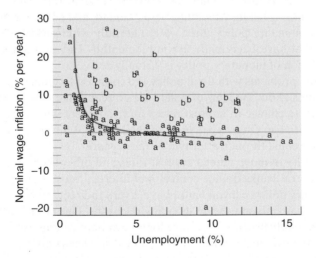

FIGURE 16.5 **Wage inflation and unemployment, UK, 1856–1997.** Phillips used UK historical data and found a negative relationship between (wage) inflation and unemployment. *Source*: Reprinted from Haldane and Quah, *Journal of Monetary Economics* (1999), vol. 44, pp. 259–278. Copyright (1999). Reprinted with permission from Elsevier Science.

[1]Alban William Housego "Bill" Phillips was an inventive man (as well as being a polymath, a crocodile hunter, and a school dropout at the age of 15). He built probably the first working model for macroeconomic experiments. The machine was made up of tanks and pipes with different colored water to represent levels of consumption, exports, and a variety of taps and plugs to help show how demand circulated through the economy. For a fascinating account of Phillips and his life see Leeson, "A.W.M. Phillips MBE (Military Division)," *The Economic Journal* (May 1994).

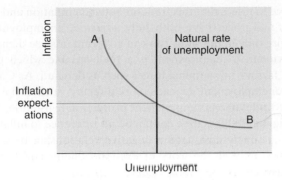

FIGURE 16.6   **The Phillips curve.** The Phillips curve shows a negative relationship between inflation and unemployment. Unemployment equals the natural rate when inflation equals inflation expectations.

growth). Suppose that instead of wages and prices both increasing at 3%, as people had anticipated, demand for the output of firms turned out to be higher than producers had anticipated, and in response companies increased their prices by more than 3%. If wages are fixed in nominal terms in the short run, then real wages will have fallen (nominal wages will have risen at 3% while the prices of goods will have increased by more than 3%, so real wages—the ratio of nominal wages to the price level—will have fallen). Because labor is now cheaper, firms will hire more workers to supply more output, particularly when demand is high. The end result is a negative correlation between inflation and unemployment, as illustrated in Figure 16.6.

Figure 16.6 depicts the Phillips curve for a given level of inflation expectations; it is, the relation between unemployment (horizontal axis) and inflation (vertical axis) holding anticipated inflation constant. We can represent the Phillips curve in a simple formula

inflation = inflation expectations + A
     × (natural rate of unemployment − actual unemployment)

Where A is a positive number. This version of the **Phillips curve** states that actual inflation will equal expected inflation if output and unemployment remain at their equilibrium levels (see Chapter 8 for a full analysis of the natural rate of unemployment). This means that the point at which the Phillips curve crosses the line depicting the natural rate of unemployment gives an inflation rate equal to inflation expectations. If the level of inflation expectations changes, then the Phillips curve will shift to a new position.

Suppose A = 0.5 and the natural rate of unemployment is 6%. Suppose too that everyone thinks that inflation is going to be 5%, and unemployment is 6%. The Phillips curve says that in these circumstances, inflation will turn out to be 5%. But if unemployment were 2%, inflation would need to be 7%: that is, the 5% expected inflation plus an extra $0.5 \times (6 - 2)$.

In explaining why there is a negative relationship between inflation and unemployment we made the assumption that wages could not adjust as rapidly as prices. It was because of this that the real wage changes, which in turn affects labor demand and unemployment. However, as soon as wages do adjust, the real wage returns to a value consistent with unemployment being at its natural rate. Therefore, the negative relationship between inflation and unemployment is only a short-run phenomenon—it is only while wages are sticky relative to prices that this tradeoff between inflation and unemployment exists. When wages and prices have both fully adjusted, unemployment will be at its natural rate. Therefore only in the short run can governments use demand management to affect unemployment. Unemployment is a real variable which ultimately must be explained by real factors, not nominal forces such as demand. As Chapter 8 showed, the natural rate of unemployment depends on real factors such as the tax and benefits system, the power of trade unions, employment protection legislation, and monopoly power in firms. The original Phillips curve contained no reference to inflation expectations or the natural rate, it simply envisaged a negative relationship between inflation and unemployment. It was through the work of Edmund Phelps and Milton Friedman that these additional aspects of the Phillips curve were introduced. As we shall see, the introduction of expectations and the natural rate profoundly changes the government's policy options.

There is one further addition to the Phillips curve that we have to make. We saw in Chapter 15 that supply shocks also contributed to inflation through adverse shifts in the supply curve. Further, these negative supply shocks cause output and employment to fall. We need therefore to amend our Phillips curve to

inflation = inflation expectations + A
    × (natural rate of unemployment − actual unemployment)
    + supply shocks

Supply shocks introduce another reason why the Phillips curve can shift. The negative tradeoff between inflation and unemployment only exists for changes in demand—adverse supply shocks cause inflation and unemployment to rise together. *Therefore the Phillips curve exists as a short-run tradeoff the government faces when it uses demand management; it is not necessarily a strongly observed relationship in the data.* Figure 16.7a, b, c show inflation and unemployment for the United States, Japan, and France between 1983 and 2000. For Japan and to some extent France a negative relationship exists, but certainly not for the United States during this time period. However, this does not mean the Phillips curve does not exist. Any changes in inflation expectations, the natural rate of unemployment, or supply shocks will shift the Phillips curve, but at any moment in time the government still faces the Phillips curve tradeoff in operating demand management policies.

If there is a known, stable, and predictable Phillips curve, governments have a tool to help operate stabilization policy. Using Keynesian demand management, it seems that the government could usefully increase or reduce demand depending upon events in the economy. Therefore, it appears possible to achieve a preferred level of unemployment. The role of the Phillips curve is to tell policymakers the costs of a particular unemployment rate in terms of the inflation it will generate. If governments want to reduce unemployment and are prepared to pay the price of higher inflation, they simply need to increase demand within the economy, which will bid up prices and generate more inflation. To the extent that this inflation is unexpected, unemployment will be lower as we move along the Phillips curve from B to a point like A in Figure 16.6. Alternatively, a government may decide that inflation is too high, and the Phillips curve will tell the policymaker how much unemployment it has to accept to reduce inflation. If governments believe that the inflation and unemployment combination of point A in

Figure 16.6 is suboptimal and inflation too high, then the level of unemployment at B might be a price they would pay to reduce inflation.

So the Phillips curve *appears* to provide a menu of choices for policymakers. It seems to imply that we can have 1% less inflation, but only at the expense of (1/A)% more unemployment. *But, crucially, the addition of the natural rate into the Phillips curve limits this tradeoff to the short run—while wages do not adjust.* However, as we saw in Chapter 15, Keynesian macroeconomics tends to view price and wage adjustment as lengthy processes, if they occur at all. If this is the case, then the tradeoff may exist for a substantial period of time.

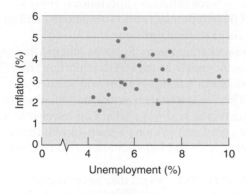

FIGURE 16.7a Inflation and unemployment, United States, 1983–2000. *Source*: International Financial Statistics.

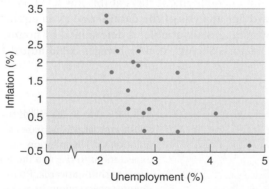

FIGURE 16.7b Inflation and unemployment, Japan, 1983–2000. *Source*: International Financial Statistics.

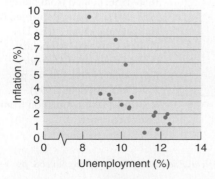

FIGURE 16.7c Inflation and unemployment, France, 1983–2000. The Phillips curve is not always seen clearly in the data as changes in the natural rate, supply shocks, and changing expectations shift the curve around. *Source*: OECD, *Economic Outlook* (June 2000). Copyright OECD.

16.4   The Phillips Curve and Shifting Expectations

During the 1950s and 1960s the Phillips curve was crucial to understanding how governments ran fiscal and monetary policy in an effort to stabilize the economy. However, Milton Friedman warned that the Phillips curve could not be used for this purpose and, if it were, the result would be ever higher inflation rates.[2] Key to Friedman's analysis is the fact that a different Phillips curve exists for each level of inflation expectations. If inflation expectations increase, then the Phillips curve shifts upwards, while a decrease in expectations leads to a downward shift. That such shifts occur is shown in Figure 16.8 which shows UK wage inflation and unemployment. Between 1856 and 1957 (points labeled *a*) inflation was low and so were inflation expectations. However, between 1957 and 1997 (points labeled *b*) UK inflation increased substantially and so did expectations. The result was the Phillips curve shifting upwards.

Figure 16.9 illustrates Friedman's powerful argument. Suppose initially that inflation expectations are 2% and unemployment equals its natural (equilibrium) rate. The government, however, wishes to achieve lower unemployment and so increases demand by raising government spending. This leads to higher prices and inflation moves above 2%, and because of wage sluggishness the real wage falls. This lower real wage leads to a fall in unemployment. The economy moves along a short-run Phillips curve to a point such as B—with lower unemployment and inflation above 2% (we have assumed it at 4%).

At point B one of three things will happen. First, wages may never adjust; the real wage remains permanently lower and unemployment stays at this low level. However, for this to happen we have to discard our analysis of the natural rate as an equilibrium concept and assume that unemployment, a real variable, is determined by nominal demand rather than real supply side factors. Second, nominal wages could adjust to the

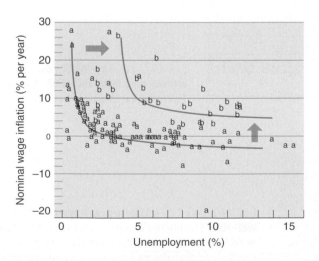

FIGURE 16.8 UK Phillips curve and shifting expectations. Increases in inflation led UK inflation expectations to rise and the Phillips curve to shift outwards. Point *a* denotes observations in period 1856–1956; point *b* from period 1957–1997. *Source*: Reprinted from Haldane and Quah, "The UK Phillips Curve and Monetary Policy." *Journal of Monetary Economics* (1999), vol. 44, pp. 259–278. Copyright (1999). Reprinted with permission from Elsevier Science.

[2]Friedman, "The Role of Monetary Policy," *American Economic Review* (1968), vol. 68, pp. 1–17.

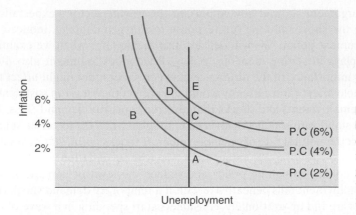

FIGURE 16.9 **The long-run Phillips curve.** Because inflation expectations adjust to higher inflation outcomes the government does not face a usable tradeoff between inflation and unemployment.

higher inflation level; the real wage returns to its equilibrium level and the economy returns to A. However, for this to happen individuals have to display slightly strange behavior. At B inflation is at 4% and the economy can only be at A if individuals expect inflation of 2%. In deciding what level of wages to bargain for, workers have to form an expectation of inflation. In doing so surely they will consider the current level of inflation. The government has already revealed it prefers B to A, so if workers negotiate wages on the basis of 2% inflation expectations, inflation is once again likely to be 4%. The third possibility therefore is that workers revise upwards their inflation expectations to 4% and the Phillips curve shifts upwards to the line we have marked PC 4%. If that happens, then if inflation remains at 4%, unemployment will move back to its natural rate (point C).

If the government wants to keep unemployment beneath its natural rate it must increase demand again but now has to generate inflation *above* 4% in order to lower the real wage. So we could move to point D with unemployment beneath its natural rate, but the inflation rate now has to be higher again, at 6%. But if the economy remains at point D, we would have to assume that workers begin to anticipate 6% inflation and inflation remaining at 6% would then imply that unemployment would move back to its natural rate at point E.

Therefore, if individuals adapt their inflation expectations in response to changes in observed inflation, attempts by governments to exploit the Phillips curve produce only higher inflation and no long-run benefits in terms of unemployment. There is a *vertical* long-run Phillips curve positioned at the natural rate. Friedman's crucial insight is that there is no usable long-run tradeoff between inflation and output. The key assumption is that the natural rate of unemployment is itself independent of nominal variables and is determined by fundamental supply side factors.

Friedman's analysis of the Phillips curve is a forceful argument against using demand management to achieve "full" employment. If full employment is incompatible with the natural rate of unemployment, then attempts at demand management will just result in higher inflation. However, Friedman's argument does not necessarily imply that *stabilization* policy must fail. After all, stabilization policy is designed to stabilize output and unemployment *around* some long-run trend rather than to try to drive the level of output (or unemployment) permanently *above* (or *below*) that long-run trend.

The Friedman argument showed how important the private sector's expectations were in determining the short-and long-run response to shifts in demand, induced by movements in government policy. We will develop this theme later when we examine the role credibility plays in setting monetary policy. Friedman's argument also illustrated the enormous importance of the difference between shocks that might affect the natural rate of unemployment (and certainly would then affect the long-run sustainable rate of output or unemployment) and shocks that affected short-run demand. This distinction is critical to stabilization policy. Governments should not try to offset supply side shocks that affect the natural rate of unemployment. If shocks occur that mean that unemployment can now safely be 2% rather than 4% without inflation accelerating, governments should not try to tighten policy and reduce the level of demand in the economy when unemployment falls beneath 4%. But if a temporary demand shock (for example, stock prices are bid up irrationally, consumers start spending in a wave of optimism) drives unemployment beneath its natural rate of 4%, governments might want to head off incipient inflation by reducing demand. The dilemma faced by Alan Greenspan in the late 1990s was to identify which of these scenarios is most important.

16.5 Credibility—The Good News about Shifting Expectations

Friedman's analysis suggests governments should not try and exploit the Phillips curve in a regular manner and implies that demand side policies cannot affect the level of unemployment. The reason for this pessimism is the fact that inflation expectations change with observed inflation. However, the importance of shifting inflation expectations also brings good news for monetary policymakers. Shifting expectations may lead to the ability to lower inflation without large increases in unemployment.

From the Phillips curve we have that every 1% increase in unemployment produces an A% decline in inflation. Therefore, to reduce inflation by 1% we need to increase unemployment by (1/A)%—this is called the **sacrifice ratio**, how much unemployment needs to be generated to lower inflation by 1%. If, however, the government can persuade the private sector that inflation will be reduced, then inflation expectations will fall and so will inflation *without any need for higher unemployment*. Therefore, the more that inflation expectations change, the less disinflationary work unemployment has to perform.

To see how this argument works, consider Figure 16.10. Suppose that the private sector—either through inertia and myopia, or through scepticism about what government policy can actually achieve—believes that the current inflation rate is likely to stay the same. Suppose also that inflation is higher than the government wants it to be. To be specific, suppose that the inflation rate is 6% and everyone thinks that it will stay there. Suppose now that the government tries to reduce inflation. We can use the Phillips curve to work out how the economy might evolve. We start at point A in Figure 16.10. The government now tightens policy—by having the central bank increase interest rates, by cutting government spending, or by increasing taxes—and by doing so lowers inflation to, say, 4%. But because people still expect that inflation will stay at 6%,

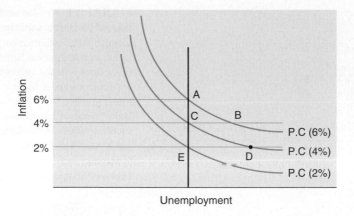

FIGURE 16.10 **Disinflation when expectations are slow to change.** The central bank can lower inflation either by moving along a Phillips curve by achieving higher than expected inflation (i.e., A to C) or by lowering inflation expectations (A to C) and shifting the Phillips curve down.

they do *not* respond to this tougher policy by lowering their anticipation of future price rises, and wage settlements continue to run at a level that reflects expectations of a 6% rises in general prices. This means wages are set too high relative to inflation, the real wage is high, and unemployment increases and we move to point B.

If the economy remains at B for long enough, then eventually the private sector will adjust its inflation expectations. It will realize that the government is serious about producing low inflation and is even prepared to accept high unemployment in order to do so. If people now believe that inflation will stay at 4% the Phillips curve shifts down and we move toward point C. But suppose the government really wants to cut inflation to 2%, but with actual inflation at 4%. It has to again announce a tough policy of relatively high interest rates and/or relatively tight fiscal policy. If people continue to believe that inflation will stay at its current rate (4%), we have to endure the pain of higher unemployment again to drive the inflation rate down. Given expectations of 4% inflation, unemployment must rise to point D for actual inflation to be 2%. Only after another spell of unemployment do we eventually drive expectations of inflation down to 2%. Then we can return to the original level of unemployment, but with inflation at 2% rather than 6%. The government has achieved its planned disinflation but only at the cost of a prolonged period with unemployment above its natural rate. The longer that inflation expectations take to fall, the more prolonged is this period.

But now suppose that the private sector was rational, forward-looking, *and*, crucially, believes that the government will ultimately bring the inflation rate down to 2%. Then as soon as the government announces its intentions, expectations of inflation move down from 6% to 2%. The unemployment rate does not have to increase at all. Instead, wage bargains immediately reflect expectations of 2% rather than 6% inflation. So we move directly from point A to point E in Figure 16.10. The credibility of the government's policy, and the forward-looking nature of price setting in labor and goods markets, means that the sacrifice ratio is zero! Therefore, the more that disinflation can be achieved by lowering expectations, shifting the Phillips curve down, rather than raising unemployment, moving *along* a given Phillips curve, the lower the sacrifice ratio.

However, whether inflation expectations shift downwards depends on the credibility of the government's announced disinflation plan. Governments cannot just announce a policy of being tough on inflation and expect that inflation will immediately

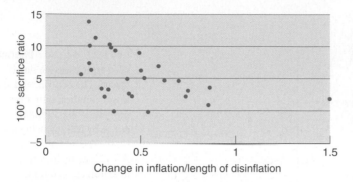

FIGURE 16.11 The sacrifice ratio and the speed of disinflation. Countries that achieve sharp reductions in inflation benefit more from reduced inflation expectations and achieve a lower sacrifice ratio. *Source*: Ball, "What determines the sacrifice ratio?" in G. Mankiw (ed.), *Monetary Policy*, (Chicago: Univ. of Chicago Press, 1994) pp. 240–281.

fall at zero cost. The private sector may have good reason *not* to believe the government. If this is the same government that started out with low inflation, but through its misguided attempts to lower unemployment raised inflation to 6%, the private sector will be extremely skeptical if the government announces a plan to reduce inflation to 2%. That was after all where inflation started out! In order to gain credibility governments have to earn it—either by making tough decisions, for instance demonstrating the need to accept high unemployment in order to lower inflation, or by having a track record of always achieving low inflation. As we saw in Chapter 12, the Bundesbank has achieved low inflation by international standards over the last 40 years and as a result enjoyed substantial credibility. The Bank of Italy and the Bank of England have less impressive inflation records and their attempts at lowering inflation have been hampered by credibility problems (at least in the 1970s and 1980s).

Figure 16.11 shows the sacrifice ratio for OECD countries when they reduced inflation in the 1980s. It shows that those countries that reduced inflation the fastest (what is known as the "cold turkey" approach to disinflation) achieved the lowest sacrifice ratios, i.e., the smallest increases in unemployment. When countries implement a sharp tightening of monetary policy, unemployment will rise substantially. However, this signals to the private sector the determination of the government to lower inflation regardless of the unemployment cost. As a result, inflation expectations adjust swiftly, the Phillips curve moves down, and inflation falls. By contrast, if disinflation occurs slowly, expectations do not adjust quickly and the government comes under prolonged political pressure in the wake of a slow and long-lasting increase in unemployment.

16.6 Time Inconsistency

A feature of our analysis in this chapter is the importance of expectations in determining the success of policy. In particular we have found that the success of government actions *today* depends on the private sector's beliefs about what the government will do *tomorrow*. For instance, the success of an anti-inflation policy depends on whether the private sector believes inflation will be low in the future. This dependence of the current situation on expectations of the future raises the problem of **time inconsistency**; that is, when the future arrives it may no longer be optimal to carry out your plan. If people are aware of this problem then they have no reason to believe your predictions.

The problem of time inconsistency arises in many settings—monetary policy, threatening punishments to children if they don't carry out chores, or more seriously, governments dealing with terrorists. Every government would like every potential hostage taker to think that it will never negotiate. If that really were credible, terrorists would never hijack airplanes because they would know, in advance, that governments would not give way. But after the hijack, when the plane is stuck at the airport with bombs onboard and 80 million people watching on TV, the government has a strong incentive to negotiate. This is an example of time inconsistency. A time inconsistent policy is one in which a rule that seemed optimal at one time (e.g., we do not negotiate with terrorists) subsequently becomes undesirable. When the government announces its nonnegotiating stance it genuinely believes it will follow this strategy. However, talk is cheap and unless other actions are taken to make this a credible strategy the stance will be ignored.

Time inconsistency is a major problem for governments when they wish to achieve low inflation. Consider again Figure 16.10 and a government that finds itself at A, with 6% inflation. If it successfully persuades the private sector that inflation will be 2%, then the economy will shift to E. However, if inflation expectations have fallen to 2%, why not generate inflation of 4%? This will produce a fall in inflation (from 6% to 4%) as well as a fall in unemployment as real wages are pushed down by unanticipated inflation. If the private sector realize that if it expects inflation will be 2%, then inflation will actually be 4%, then it won't adjust its expectations and inflation will not fall. If the government cannot credibly commit to producing low inflation, inflation will remain high.

MONETARY POLICY AS A GAME

We can show this more formally in the context of a very simple game between the private sector and the government. Consider the case in which the government can produce either low or high inflation. Table 16.1 shows the various possibilities for unemployment in this game, depending on whether inflation is greater than, less than, or equal to inflation expectations.

Before we can analyze what choices the government and private sector will make we have to know their preferences. We assume that the government likes low unemployment

TABLE 16.1   Possible Outcomes in Monetary Policy Game

Scenario	Inflation	Inflation Expectations	Unemployment
A	Low	Low	Natural Rate
B	Low	High	Above Natural Rate
C	High	Low	Below Natural Rate
D	High	High	Natural Rate

The level of unemployment depends on whether inflation expectations hold or not.

TABLE 16.2 Payoffs to Government and Private Sector

Governments		Private Sector Inflation Expectations	
		High	Low
Inflation Choice	High	−3,0	3,−3
	Low	−5,−3	0,0

The first number in each cell is the return to the government; the second is the return to the private sector.

Governments will always choose high inflation, regardless of inflation expectations of the private sector.

and low inflation, but has a stronger preference for low unemployment. Its most preferred outcome is scenario C (inflation higher than expectations and unemployment below the natural rate). Its next best outcome is A (low inflation and unemployment at the natural rate), followed by D (high inflation and natural rate unemployment), and its least preferred is B (low inflation, high expectations, and unemployment above the natural rate). In Table 16.2 we show these preferences and we attach numerical values to each outcome, reflecting the value government places on each. The first number in each cell is the payoff to the government and the second that to the private sector. We assume that the private sector dislikes having its expectations turn out to be wrong, in other words, it finds only unexpected inflation costly. Therefore it is indifferent between low or high inflation so long as expectations are in line with outcomes (this could be modified to have a preference for low inflation without altering our conclusions). The private sector does not value unemployment below the natural rate because this is only achieved by real wages being low as a result of false expectations.

We can now examine the equilibrium of this game between the private sector and the government. The structure of the game is as follows: first, the private sector negotiates wages on the basis of its inflation expectations, and then the government decides the level of inflation. It is crucial that the private sector has to decide first—time inconsistency only arises because agents' expectations of the future influence the success of events today.

Consider first the actions of the government. If the private sector has high inflation expectations, then the best course of action for the government is to produce high inflation. With this outcome, unemployment equals the natural rate. If instead the government produces low inflation, then real wages will be too high (as they have been set assuming high inflation) and unemployment will be above the natural rate. Because the government places a higher weight on unemployment, the low inflation in this scenario does not compensate for the higher unemployment. Therefore if the private sector has high inflation expectations, in this model the government will deliver high inflation. If instead, inflation expectations are low, the government will still find it optimal to produce high inflation. With low inflation expectations, high inflation leads to a low real wage and lower unemployment. The government preference for low unemployment means this outweighs the high inflation. The other alternative would be to have low

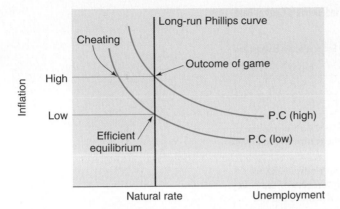

FIGURE 16.12 **Inflation bias.** Because the government has a preference for low unemployment it cannot achieve a low inflation equilibrium; inflation is too high.

inflation, but this would lead unemployment to be equal to its natural rate which is not optimal for the government. **Therefore, regardless of the private sector's inflation expectations, the government will choose high inflation**. Knowing this, the private sector sets its expectations for high inflation.

The situation is illustrated in Figure 16.12. However, the outcome of the game is inefficient—society prefers the low inflation, natural rate unemployment outcome (A in Table 16.1) to the high inflation, natural rate unemployment outcome (D). However, it is not possible to be at A because even if the government claims it will produce low inflation, as soon as the private sector lowers its expectations the government has an incentive to cheat, produce high inflation and lower unemployment. Sticking to a low inflation policy is a time inconsistent promise by the government and so the economy stays at a high inflation outcome. The mere fact that a Phillips curve exists and may be exploited by governments creates an inflationary bias in the economy.

If governments could remove the option to use discretionary policy, and abandon the opportunity to exploit the Phillips curve, this inflationary bias would disappear. But so long as governments have a preference for lower unemployment they will be tempted to use this option. Notice that this preference for low unemployment is futile— in equilibrium unemployment is at its natural rate so the government never benefits from low unemployment. In other words, it might as well just focus on low inflation.

CENTRAL BANK INDEPENDENCE

How can governments overcome this problem of time inconsistency? As our analysis suggests, the answer is to give up the option of discretion and instead follow certain rules. One way this can be achieved is to hand control of inflation policy over to an independent central bank and give it the goal of controlling inflation *with no reference to unemployment*. By setting up incentives that penalize the central bank when inflation exceeds its target, by not making its prestige depend upon unemployment, the government effectively changes the preferences of the policymaker. Table 16.3 shows how we can incorporate this change into our game theoretic analysis. Assume that the central banker has no preference over unemployment but simply prefers low to high inflation.

TABLE 16.3 Payoffs to Independent Central Bank and Private Sector

Central Bank		Private Sector Inflation Expectations	
		High	Low
Inflation Choice	High	−3,0	−3,−3
	Low	0,−3	0,0

The first number in each cell is the return to the central bank; the second is the return to the private sector.

By appointing an independent central bank to control only inflation, the preferences of the policy authority change and now can achieve the low inflation outcome.

The central bank is then indifferent between scenario A and B (low inflation, natural rate unemployment and low inflation, unemployment above the natural rate, respectively) but prefers these to C and D (high inflation, below natural rate unemployment; high inflation, natural rate unemployment, respectively). Repeating our earlier analysis, we find that with these preferences **the central banker will always choose low inflation regardless of the private sector's expectations**. Given this, the private sector will set their expectations for low inflation. As a result, the inflationary bias disappears and the economy will be in a low inflation equilibrium.

This result is obviously a paradox—by setting monetary policy without worrying about unemployment the outcome is better than if you are allowed discretion. However, there are many examples in which denying yourself certain options in the future actually generates better outcomes. The classical reference here is to Homer's *The Odyssey*. Odysseus knew that if he allowed himself to hear the Sirens' songs while he was still in command of his ship, the sound and sight of the Sirens would lure him toward them where he would meet a horrible death. So he had his crew stop up their ears with wax and tie him to the mast, so that he could neither persuade the crew to change direction nor steer the ship himself. As a result, he could hear the beautiful singing of the Sirens without losing his ship or his soul. This classic example illustrates the advantages of "tying ones hands"—by denying yourself short-term flexibility, a better outcome is achieved.

The ability of independent central banks to overcome the inflationary bias of monetary policy is given substantial support in Figure 16.13. Countries with strong, independent central banks achieve substantially lower inflation. Some economists argue that all Figure 16.13 shows is that countries which have a strong dislike of inflation achieve low inflation and have independent central banks. It is the dislike of inflation that matters rather than whether the central bank is independent. It is argued that if society does not strongly dislike inflation then an unelected central bank that pursues severe anti-inflationary policies will not exist for long. However, the logic of the time inconsistency argument and the evidence of Figure 16.13 has been extremely influential over the last decade with many governments granting substantial independence to central banks. It may seem strange for governments to pass

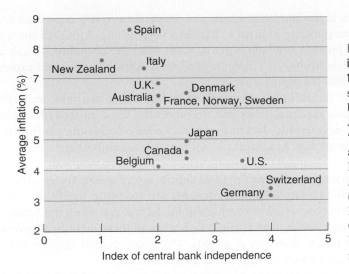

FIGURE 16.13 **Central bank independence and inflation, 1955–1988.** Countries with strongly independent central banks achieve lower inflation. *Source*: Alesina and Summers, "Central Bank Independence and Macroeconomic Performance," *Journal of Money, Credit and Banking*, (May 1993), pp. 151–162. Reprinted by permission © Copyright 1993 by Ohio State University Press. All rights reserved.

such an important policy instrument over to an unelected group of officials and to ask them to target only inflation. However, our analysis shows that the fact the central bankers are unelected and do not have a policy goal of achieving low unemployment is crucial in achieving a better outcome for society.

16.7 Rules versus Discretion

We have outlined three broad sets of arguments which suggest that governments may find it preferable to follow fixed rules in operating monetary and fiscal policy rather than discretionary policies.

(a) Pragmatic concerns regarding whether the authorities have enough up-to-date and reliable information about the state of the economy and whether inevitable lags in the system will make stabilization policy actually destabilizing.

(b) Concerns over whether the government really has the ability to control the level of demand. The impact of fiscal deficits will, at least in part, be offset by the actions of the private sector as we saw with crowding out and Ricardian equivalence. Further, the central bank can only set the short-term nominal interest rate. The important long-term real interest rate is not under its control.

(b) Time inconsistency arguments suggest that denying themselves discretion and following fixed rules can achieve better outcomes.

In combination these three arguments have been so persuasive that most governments no longer try to use fiscal and monetary policy to fine-tune the economy. Monetary policy is now based on achieving announced targets for inflation and is operated mostly by independent central banks whose overriding aim is the control of inflation. We will examine the structure of monetary policy in more detail in the next chapter. Similarly, fiscal policy is rarely used in a conscious way to influence the business cycle (the exception is Japan in the late 1990s where as a result of a severely depressed economy the authorities are pursuing policies to handle a depression). Although the automatic fiscal stabilizers operate and help inject demand when the economy is weak and remove it when growth is strong, governments now rarely adjust tax rates and expenditure in an effort to control the business cycle.

However, whereas the rules for operating monetary policy are now well established, this is not the case for fiscal policy and we expect this to be an area of considerable research over the next decade. Just like monetary policy, fiscal policy suffers from problems of time inconsistency. In Chapter 11 we saw that tax smoothing was an optimal policy. Tax smoothing implies that governments only need to worry about balancing their budget over a long run. Therefore fiscal deficits are allowable today so long as they are followed by future surpluses. Governments can therefore justify not raising taxes today because of expected higher revenues in the future. But when the future occurs, the government may decide that it would rather spend these additional revenues or even reduce taxes rather than run a surplus. The result is that deficits are not matched by surpluses and government debt increases continually.

The perception that governments may face incentives to spend more than they raise in taxes lies behind the various balanced budget amendments to constitutions that have been advocated in some countries (most notably the United States). The logic behind these amendments is similar to the arguments for central bank independence: governments (or politicians) left to themselves face too many temptations to cut interest rates or taxes, or to boost expenditure, in order to gain electoral popularity.

There are a variety of ways in which the discretion of governments in setting fiscal policy could be reduced. A particularly draconian form would be a requirement that government expenditure (or planned expenditure) could never exceed taxation in any year. In practice, to avoid the penalties of breaching this requirement, governments would generate surpluses almost every period so as to avoid even the smallest chance of not covering spending out of current taxation. A more modest balanced budget requirement would require the government to balance its budget over a longer planning horizon (maybe five or seven years, or some period reflecting the average duration of the economic cycle). The UK government takes this approach with its Code for Fiscal Stability. Alternatively, restrictions could be placed on the size of fiscal deficit that a country can run—this is the approach of countries in the European Monetary Union with the Growth and Stability Pact.

Although there are analogies between balanced budget amendments and governments handing over control of monetary policies to central banks, we should not take these too far. As we shall see in Chapter 17, granting control over monetary policy to even the most independent central bank does *not* mean that monetary policy should be set to preclude stabilization. In fact, any central bank that was pursuing a target for inflation would almost certainly be loosening policy when unemployment was rising above, and output falling beneath, its equilibrium level and tightening monetary policy when the opposite was happening. The same would *not* be true, however, with a tightly specified balanced budget amendment. If governments could never run a budget deficit, they would have to cut spending in a recession, when tax revenues tend to fall, and would have to cut taxes or increase spending in a boom (when revenues tend to rise). So a tightly specified balanced budget requirement is almost certainly *inconsistent* with a stabilizing role for fiscal policy.

SUMMARY

Output and inflation fluctuate substantially over the business cycle. If this volatility is undesirable governments can try and manage the level of demand in the economy using fiscal and monetary policy. This is stabilization policy.

However, achieving successful stabilization policy is fraught with problems—knowledge about the economy and how it operates is imperfect and macroeconomic data is only available with a delay of several months. Further, the instruments of stabilization policy operate with long and uncertain lags. There exists uncertainty over the impact of these policy instruments on the economy, as the efforts of the government can be offset by the actions of the private sector. The delays and uncertainty over impact are particularly problematic for fiscal policy.

The Phillips curve is a negative relationship between inflation and unemployment. In the 1950s and 1960s it was believed this offered governments a tradeoff between inflation and unemployment. However, recognizing the importance of inflation expectations and how they change over time led to a belief that the long-run Phillips curve was vertical. This also raised awareness of the importance of inflation expectations in achieving low inflation outcomes.

Because expectations of the future influence events today, monetary policy suffers from a problem of time inconsistency. Governments may not find it optimal to deliver the low inflation that they promise. We showed how this leads to an inflation bias in the economy which can be removed if the government follows rules rather than a discretionary approach to policy. Handing control of monetary policy to an independent central bank is a way of overcoming this bias and has been widely adopted.

The preference for rules rather than discretion is now firmly based among macroeconomic policymakers. Whereas the rules and operating procedures are well developed for monetary policy, governments are only just beginning to investigate the fiscal rules they should follow.

CONCEPTUAL QUESTIONS

1. Think of how lower prices (or lower inflation) may generate greater overall demand within the economy. Could these mechanisms be more powerful than forces that reduce overall demand when prices (or inflation) rise?

2. Fiscal and monetary policy in small open economies with fixed exchange rates are not likely to significantly influence the level of demand for the output of domestic producers. Why are things different in a country like the United States, which is not very open and has a floating exchange rate?

3. How might a big hike in oil prices affect the natural rate of unemployment in a country that relies heavily on imported fuel and where oil is an essential input into the production of many goods? How might things be different for an oil producer?

4. The natural rate of employment depends on the stock of capital, which in turn obviously depends on investment expenditure. The natural rate also depends on technical progress which is also likely to depend on levels of investment and research and development spending.

Suppose that governments can affect investment in the short term by demand management policies. Does it follow that demand management must have long-term impacts on the level of employment?

5. In the 1990s as output fell and unemployment rose in Japan the level of interest rates was cut to zero and the government ran large deficits; output remained depressed. Does this show that stabilization policy is ineffective?

ANALYTICAL QUESTIONS

1. Consider the monetary policy game between the government and the private sector but this time assume that the private sector dislikes high inflation, even if it is expected, and also values low unemployment. The payoff matrix is now

Governments		Private Sector Inflation Expectations	
		High	Low
Inflation Choice	High	−3,−1	3,−2
	Low	−5,−3	0.1

   (a) How does this alter your analysis?
   (b) How would you construct the payoff matrix for the case in which the government, rather than make the central bank independent, appoints a central bank chairman with a pathological hatred of inflation?
   (c) What about if the government appoints a trade union leader as chairman?

2. Imagine the Phillips curve is

   inflation = inflation expectations + 0.5 × (natural rate of unemployment
            − unemployment)

   Over the next 10 years the data is as follows

Year	1	2	3	4	5	6	7	8	9	10
Inflation Expectations	3	3	4	4	4	4	3	3	3	3
Natural Rate	5	5	5	5	5	6	6	6	7	7
Unemployment	5	3	4	5	5.2	5.7	6.1	6.4	6.8	7.2

   (a) Calculate inflation in each year.
   (b) Draw a chart showing inflation and unemployment over these periods. What evidence do you have for a Phillips curve?
   (c) Can you explain your answer to (b)? Can you rescue the Phillips curve?

3. Consider the following two specifications for the Phillips curve:

    inflation = 5 − 0.3 × natural logarithm of unemployment rate

and

    inflation = 5 − 0.3 × unemployment rate

(a) Graph each of these Phillips curves over the range of unemployment from 1 to 10.
(b) What is the difference between the two curves? Which do you think is more plausible?
(c) How does the sacrifice ratio differ in each case?

4. The economy responds to changes in interest rates with a lag. Suppose that aggregate demand for goods is given by the equation

$$Y_t = A + bY_{t-1} - cr_{t-2} + e_t$$

Where Y_t is demand in year t; r_{t-2} is the interest rate in year $t - 2$; and e_t is a shock to demand in period t. A = 200; b = 0.7; and c = 10.

(a) Suppose that the economy goes through many years in which interest rates are steady at 6 and there are no shocks. What is the equilibrium level of demand?
(b) Now there is a sudden, one-time shock to demand in period t of − 30 ($e_t = -30$). Show what happens to demand over the next five years if there is no monetary policy response. (Assume that e returns to zero after the first year.)
(c) Now assume the government immediately reduces interest rates from 6% to 3% to offset the shock. Show how the economy responds over the five years after the shock when interest rates stay at 3%.
(d) Can you devise a better response to the shock than cutting interest rates to 3% and leaving them there?

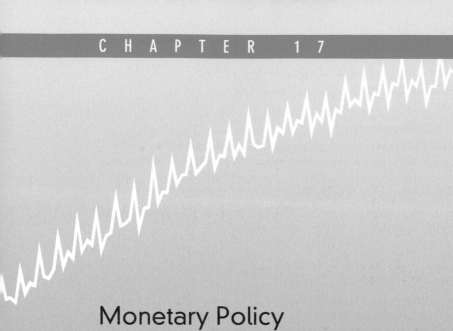

Monetary Policy

Overview

By the end of the twentieth century, monetary policy was, almost always and almost everywhere, aimed at controlling inflationary pressures. By the 1990s most governments in the industrial world had ceased using fiscal and monetary policy to fine-tune the economy; that is, adjust both fiscal and monetary policy to try and keep output close to a target path. Governments no longer saw fiscal policy as an effective tool for manipulating short-term demand. Instead they saw monetary policy—and specifically short-term interest rates—as an instrument they could use to try and dampen inflation. How this situation came to exist and whether it will last are important questions we address in this chapter. We also consider how governments operate monetary policy, what they try to target, how they seek to achieve this, and how monetary policy affects the economy. Finally, we consider how this impact may change with developments in the banking sector.

17.1 The Influence of Central Banks

The number and power of central banks have never been greater than they are today. Before the twentieth century, the United States did not even have a central bank to implement monetary policy. Figure 17.1 shows that the number of central banks has increased dramatically since 1870. Now most countries have a central bank that

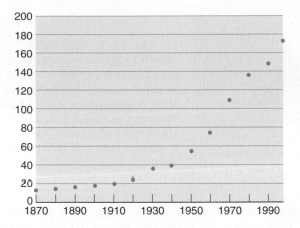

FIGURE 17.1 **Number of central banks, 1870–1999.** In the twentieth century the shift away from commodity money has increased the importance and number of central banks. *Source*: Mervyn King, "Challenges for Monetary Policy: New and Old," paper presented at New Challenges for Monetary Policy conference at Jackson Hole, Wyoming, 1999.

implements a form of monetary policy. Many more of these central banks are now independent of government than was the case even 10 or 15 years ago.[1] The Bundesbank in Germany and the Federal Reserve in the United States have had considerable independence over monetary policy for decades. But until recently, that was the exception rather than the rule. Within the last 20 years, several major central banks—the Bank of England, the Reserve Banks of Australia and New Zealand, the European Central Bank (responsible for setting monetary policy in the euro area)—have gained substantial autonomy to set monetary policy. Furthermore, most of these central banks set policy explicitly to control inflation.

Why have central banks become influential in setting monetary policy and why has monetary policy become so focused on controlling inflation? Until the breakdown of the gold standard because of the First World War, the operation of monetary policy was of limited significance because in most countries money had always been commodity money, and the central banks that then existed had little discretion and few policy choices open to them. (This, of course, was why so few central banks existed, as Figure 17.1 shows.) The breakdown of the gold standard marked the end of the long centuries of commodity moneys. For the first time, central banks, usually under the control and instruction of governments, could influence monetary conditions and faced real choices.

But as Figure 17.2 illustrates, for much of the twentieth century, inflation in the world has been far from insignificant. The monetary history of the twentieth century is a long process of learning the appropriate institutional and operational structure for monetary policy.

---

[1]"Independent" is a somewhat slippery concept. What we mean here is that the central bank does not merely implement monetary policy decisions that have been made by the government. Full central bank independence means that the bank sets its own targets and chooses monetary policy accordingly. However, in some cases the target is set by government, and the central bank is independent in its choice of monetary policy to meet that target.

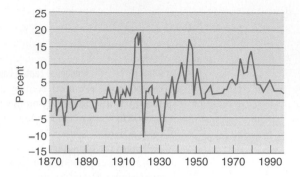

FIGURE 17.2 **Global inflation,** **1870–1999.** High levels of inflation have been a recurring global problem in the twentieth century. *Source*: Mervyn King, "Challenges for Monetary Policy: New and Old," paper presented at New Challenges for Monetary Policy conference at Jackson Hole, Wyoming, 1999.

To understand monetary policy we have to distinguish among three different elements, as shown in Figure 17.3. The first is the *target* that the central bank wishes to achieve, whether this be inflation, output growth, or employment. However, monetary policy does not impact on the economy immediately but with a lag. Therefore, in order to achieve their ultimate target, central banks have to try and achieve an *intermediate target*, a variable that if it can be controlled by the central bank will enable it to achieve its ultimate target. Central banks have used numerous different intermediate targets, with money supply growth and exchange rates being popular options. If the ultimate target of the central bank is to control inflation, then we can think of these intermediate targets as a nominal anchor—if the bank successfully meets its intermediate target then it will keep the price level under control. Finally, there is the *operational instrument*— what the central bank uses to implement monetary policy. For most countries this is the level of short-term interest rates.

17.2 What Does Monetary Policy Target?

In the 1950s and 1960s, most governments passed legislation that stated they would use monetary and fiscal policy to achieve low inflation, high employment, and fast output growth, and to avoid balance of payments problems. The setting of interest rates was a key component of this strategy. However, as our analysis of stabilization policy in Chapter 16 showed, this approach to policy broke down with the high inflation and un-

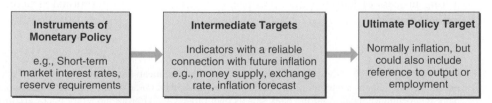

FIGURE 17.3 **The three aspects of monetary policy.** The central bank uses instruments of monetary policy to achieve an outcome for an intermediate target and in that way control its ultimate target, usually inflation.

employment of the 1970s. The idea that there was only a short-run tradeoff between inflation and unemployment and that in the long run the Phillips curve was vertical became widely accepted. A vertical Phillips curve means that when the government or central bank chooses a target inflation rate it should not worry about output or employment. In the long run output and employment are not influenced by monetary policy. Therefore the central bank should just target an optimal inflation rate.

By announcing that it only worries about inflation and no other target, the central bank also can achieve the reputational and credibility gains that we outlined at the end of Chapter 16. We showed there, in the context of a very simple game, that if agents can be made to believe that the central bank only worries about inflation, then the outcome will be a lower level of inflation. As a result of this logic[2] many governments, in the course of the 1980s and 1990s, accepted the benefits of having a formal target for monetary policy, one which was clearly stated in advance and one for which the monetary authorities would be held accountable. The most popular form of these formal targets is currently an explicit inflation target. The Reserve Bank of New Zealand, for example, in 2000 had an inflation target range of 0 to 3%. The Bank of England's inflation target was 2.5% per year, while the European Central Bank sought to limit inflation to no more than 2%.

As these examples show, most governments currently target inflation of around 2% per annum. As we saw in Chapter 12 inflation is costly, so achieving a low level of inflation is desirable. But why do governments aim at 2% inflation—if inflation is costly, why not aim for price stability and inflation of 0%?

One reason is because we mismeasure prices. As discussed in Chapter 12, official price indexes do not adequately abstract from quality improvements. Therefore, some of the increases in prices reflect an improvement in quality rather than exactly the same good selling at a higher price. The extent of this bias varies across countries, depending on how price indexes are constructed, but it is believed to be typically worth somewhere between 0.5% and 2%. Therefore, aiming for an inflation rate of 2% may in effect be the same as aiming for price stability if there is a 2% overstatement of inflation due to measurement problems.

Another reason why aiming for zero inflation may be undesirable has to do with the labor market. Individuals are very reluctant to accept wage cuts, although they will sometimes accept a wage freeze, that is, 0% increase in nominal salaries. Evidence for this can be seen from wage bargaining data which reveals a cluster of wage settlements near 0%. If employees will not accept wage cuts, then the only way that real wages can fall is if inflation is positive. If the central bank targets 0% inflation, then even this channel is not feasible and real wages may remain too high in a recession, leading to increases in unemployment. By allowing for a modest amount of inflation, the central bank can achieve some variation in real wages even if nominal wages are sticky.

Further support for not attempting to target price stability comes from the experience of Japan in the 1990s. As shown in Figure 17.4 the Japanese economy remained in recession for most of the 1990s even though the Bank of Japan reduced interest rates to

---

[2]As well as the more pragmatic reason that attempts to fine-tune the economy failed to work.

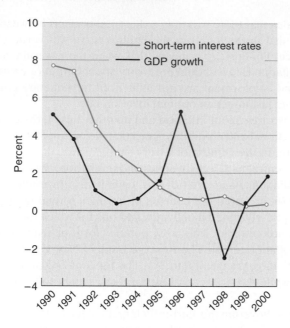

FIGURE 17.4   **Japanese interest rates and GDP growth, 1990–2000.** Low Japanese interest rates failed to stimulate the economy in the 1990s. *Source*: OECD, *Economic Outlook* (June 2000). Copyright OECD.

virtually zero. As we saw in our analysis of consumption and investment, low interest rates should stimulate output growth, but this did not happen in Japan. Because interest rates cannot go below zero, and if the rate of inflation is less than, say, 1%, then real interest rates cannot be below a certain level (in this case −1%). The optimal level of real interest rates for an economy in a slump may be substantially negative. This implies that monetary policy cannot be set optimally unless inflation is substantially positive because there is a floor of zero on the nominal interest rate.

How serious a problem is this? With an inflation target of 0%, the zero lower bound for nominal interest rates can only be a problem for monetary policy if the real interest rate should be negative. Figures 17.5*a* and *b* show estimates of the real interest rate in the United States and the UK.[3] In only a few isolated quarters do we observe negative real interest rates and even then barely so. Figure 17.5 shows that the average U.S. real interest rate is around 3%, which with an inflation target of 2% suggests nominal interest rates around 5%. This gives the central bank plenty of scope to stimulate the economy by reducing interest rates to as low as 0%. This would give a −2% real interest rate which Figure 17.5 suggests is enough to deal with most eventualities. The experience of Japan in the 1990s suggests that rare events do happen and the lower bound on interest rates may prevent monetary policy from assisting output growth in some circumstances. But the consensus is that such events are sufficiently rare that they should not unduly influence the inflation target. Every day there is a remote possibility that my office will be struck by a meteorite, but the chance is so unlikely that it does not disrupt my working patterns.

[3]These estimates are constructed using indexed bonds issued by the government—see Chapter 22 for a fuller discussion.

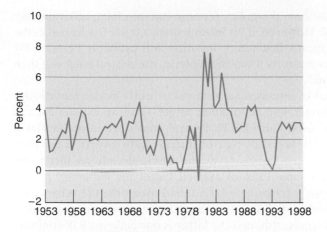

FIGURE 17.5a   Estimates of U.S. real interest rate, 1953–1998.

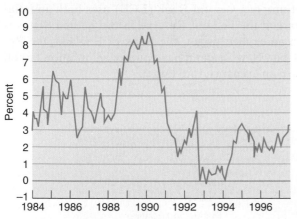

FIGURE 17.5b   Estimates of U.K. real interest rate, 1984–1997. Real interest rates are volatile but average around 3% and rarely go negative. *Source*: Mervyn King, "Challenges for Monetary Policy: New and Old," paper presented at New Challenges for Monetary Policy conference at Jackson Hole, Wyoming, 1999.

Therefore, because inflation is costly, central banks wish to achieve a low inflation rate. However, for measurement reasons and in order to provide them with some flexibility in how they use monetary policy, central banks do not target a zero inflation rate but somewhere between 2% and 3%. Such low rates achieve what Federal Reserve Chairman Alan Greenspan calls "price stability"—*"price levels sufficiently stable . . . that expectations of change do not become major factors in key economic decisions."*

17.3   What Intermediate Target Should Central Banks Use?

In trying to achieve a given inflation target the central bank has to use an intermediate target. An intermediate target is a variable which reliably tracks future inflation and which the central bank can control. The need for the intermediate target to track *future* inflation is because of the lags involved between changing monetary policy and its effect on inflation. If the central bank only responds when it sees actual inflation increasing, then by the time the policy reponse has an effect, inflation may be even further out of control. However, if an intermediate target, for instance, the money supply, increases this means that future inflation will probably be high. By tightening monetary policy preemptively today in response, the central bank can then avoid the higher future inflation.

There are three main forms of intermediate targets currently in use: money supply targets, an exchange rate target, and an inflation target—and we explain each in detail below. As well as being used individually, central banks can also consider a combination of them. Figure 17.6 shows the type of intermediate targets in use over the 1990s for a sample of 91 central banks. Over the whole decade an increasing number of banks have adopted some form of explicit target for monetary policy. Several banks use more than one intermediate target, and over time the reliance on using just monetary targets has declined. Inflation targeting is growing in popularity, as is the use of exchange rate targets, although the latter is normally used in conjunction with another indicator. The European Central Bank (ECB) uses both an inflation target and a money supply target; the Federal Reserve in the United States is one of the few central banks with no explicit target; the Bank of England, the Reserve Banks of Australia, Canada, and New Zealand have purely an inflation target, and Argentina and Hong Kong have an exchange rate target.

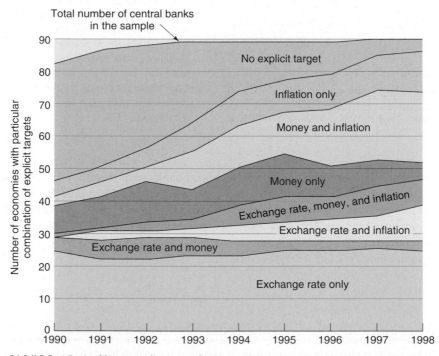

FIGURE 17.6 **Monetary policy targets for 91 countries.** The use of explicit monetary targets has increased over time, with inflation and exchange rate targets becoming more popular and money supply targets less so. *Source*: Sterne, "The Use of Explicit Targets for Monetary Policy: Practical Experience of 91 Countries," *Bank of England Quarterly Bulletin* (August 1999) vol. 39, no. 3. Reprinted with permission from the Bank of England.

17.4 Money Supply Targeting

Chapter 12 outlined in detail the quantity theory of money, which states that by definition

percentage change in the money supply + percentage change in velocity of circulation = inflation + percentage change in real output

If we add the assumption that the velocity of money is constant (or at least predictable) and that the growth of output is given by the real factors considered in Chapters 4 to 9, then we have a simple relationship between money supply growth and inflation. If velocity is constant and real output grows at a trend rate of 2.5%, then money supply growth of 4.5% will produce inflation of 2%. Therefore, using a money supply growth rate of 4.5% as an intermediate target should mean we hit a target of 2% inflation.

In the 1980s such monetarist policies were implemented in many advanced economies. While inflation did decline (see Figure 17.2), the reliance solely on monetary targets was not seen as successful. In Chapter 12 we showed how the quantity theory was excellent at explaining long-run inflation but not very successful in explaining short-run inflation. Purely relying on money supply targets to control short-run inflation proved difficult for five reasons.

(I) WHICH MONEY SUPPLY?

If all monetary aggregates behave similarly, then it does not matter which monetary aggregate the central bank targets. However, in practice different monetary aggregates behave in different ways. Figure 17.7 shows the behavior of U.S. M1 and M3 growth. Until the late 1970s M1 and M3 showed fairly similar behavior, but not afterwards. Frequently while one aggregate is showing rapid growth, the other is

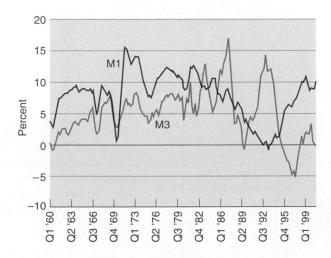

FIGURE 17.7 U.S. money supply growth, 1960–2000. Different money supply measures show very different behavior. *Source*: Federal Reserve Board, http://www.federalreserve.gov/releases/H6

slowing down. In 1992 should the Fed have been relaxed about inflation because M3 growth was falling to zero or deeply alarmed that M1 growth was over 15%? Heated debate occurred during these years as to the relative merits of each monetary aggregate and often central banks would switch from one intermediate target to another. However, in the end, none of them proved reliable and *Goodhart's Law* was established—this states that any observed regularity between a monetary aggregate and inflation will break down when central bankers try and exploit it for policy purposes.

(II) THE VELOCITY OF MONEY IS NOT PREDICTABLE

One reason why the monetary aggregates behaved differently was because of large changes in the velocity of circulation. Figure 17.8 shows the velocity for a narrow and a broad measure of money for the UK. During this period the introduction of ATMs (automatic telling machines) led to a large increase in velocity for narrow money. Because it was easier to get hold of cash, people reduced the amount they withdrew from their bank on each trip and held less cash in their wallet. As a result, the velocity of narrow money increased substantially. At the same time, however, the velocity of broad money fell. Changes in legislation meant that more financial institutions could make loans and the result was intense competition and an increase in credit and broad money, which lowered the velocity of broad money. If these trends were predictable, then allowance could be made for them when setting the money supply target, but they were not predicted. No one knew when these changes would come to an end nor what would happen in the year ahead. The result was to weaken considerably the link between the money supply and inflation.

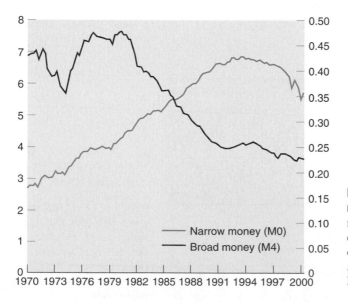

FIGURE 17.8 **UK velocity of money, 1970–2000.** Velocity of money has shown large changes that have been difficult to predict. *Source*: Author's calculations using Bank of England data.

(III) CAN THE CENTRAL BANK CONTROL THE MONEY SUPPLY?

In Chapter 12 we outlined the credit multiplier which implies that the great majority of broad money is the creation of commercial banks through their credit policies, rather than something which is under the direct control of the central bank. As we shall see later, using interest rates a central bank can only influence the cost at which a commercial bank can borrow. Whether this cost increase is passed on to a bank's loan customers and whether this increase in lending rates will affect demand for loans is not something the central bank can be certain of. Without a predictable link between changes in interest rates and changes in the money supply it is problematic to use monetary aggregates as a reliable intermediate target.

(IV) IS THE SUPPLY CURVE VERTICAL?

Our example of a 4.5% money supply target producing a 2% inflation rate was based on stable output growth of 2.5% per annum. In Chapter 12 we explained the idea of a vertical long-run supply curve which shifts out over time because of technological progress and capital accumulation. With a vertical supply curve, any increase in the money supply will raise aggregate demand but lead only to higher prices and no extra output, as shown in Figure 17.9. However, we also saw in Chapter 15 that in reponse to an increase in demand firms do not immediately increase prices. Either because of real or nominal rigidities, firms choose to keep prices fixed initially and increase output. While this policy is not sustainable, in the short run, while it lasts, the supply curve will not be vertical but have a flatter slope. The result is, as shown in Figure 17.9, that increases in the money supply lead to higher output and inflationary pressure in the short run. Therefore, any attempt at controlling inflation via money supply targeting must make an assumption about the current slope of the supply curve and how long it will take for the inflationary pressures to emerge. To achieve a 2%

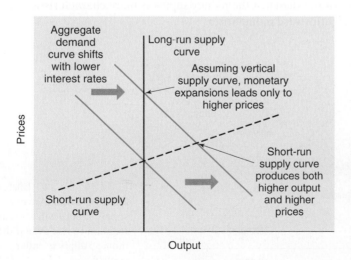

FIGURE 17.9 **Effects of monetary expansion on prices and output.** Assuming a long-run vertical supply curve, monetary expansions produce only inflation. With a short-run supply curve, output and prices both increase.

inflation target will take different money supply growth depending on whether output is growing at 1% or 4% this year.

(V) SUPPLY SHOCKS

Even if the velocity of money is constant and the money supply is under control, this does not mean that inflation will be on target. Figure 17.10 shows the case of an adverse supply shock, such as an oil price increase. Even if the money supply is controlled so the demand curve remains fixed, the oil price increase will produce higher inflation and lower output. If these effects are only temporary, then it is less important. But if the supply shocks occur over a long period of time (for instance, a sustained improvement in technology), then the effects on inflation will be long lasting and must be taken into account.

While the long-run performance of the quantity theory in explaining inflation is impressive, each of these five factors meant that simple reliance on monetary aggregates was insufficient to control inflation in the short run. As an ex-governor of the Bank of Canada said, "We didn't abandon the monetary aggregates, they abandoned us." As a consequence, very few countries still maintain such a pure version of money supply targeting. This does not mean that the money supply numbers are uninformative for inflation. It simply means that central banks have to monitor other variables and use additional or alternative intermediate targets.

One country that does profess faith in money supply targeting is Germany. The German enthusiasm for monetary targeting was important in establishing the "twin pillar" approach of the ECB to monetary policy—to use both inflation targeting and monetary indicators in setting interest rates. However, even in Germany the use of money supply targeting is not as simple as the approach outlined above. The Bundesbank would only set its money supply target after it had considered in detail the likely behaviour of velocity and gross domestic product (GDP) growth over the next year. Changes in these forecasts would lead them to revise their money supply targets. This focus on a wide range of variables rather than just the money supply is more characteristic of inflation targeting than straightforward monetarism.

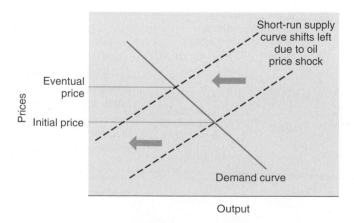

FIGURE 17.10 **Inflation and supply shocks.** Adverse supply shocks will also cause inflation to rise even if the money supply is under control.

17.5 Exchange Rate Targets

An alternative nominal anchor to money supply targets is to set monetary policy in order to achieve a target exchange rate. In Chapters 18 and 19 we examine in detail the behavior of exchange rates and the links between inflation and interest rates and the relative merits of fixed exchange rates. For now we take a more informal approach and note that if the central bank achieves a fixed exchange rate then it is likely that over the medium term it will achieve the same inflation rate as the country with which it has a fixed rate of exchange (see the detailed discussion of *purchasing power parity* in Chapter 18).[4] In order to achieve its exchange rate target, a central bank can raise interest rates if it wants the currency to appreciate or lower them if it wishes the currency to fall (see the discussion of *uncovered interest parity* in Chapter 19). By dedicating monetary policy to fixing the exchange rate the hope is to achieve inflation control.

As Figure 17.6 shows, many countries use exchange rates as a guide to operating monetary policy. However, exchange rate targets can also be costly. The main cost is that in using monetary policy to fix the exchange rate it cannot also be used to influence the domestic economy. This lack of an independent monetary policy was at the heart of the UK and Italian exit from the European Exchange Rate Mechanism in 1992. With the Bundesbank raising interest rates to control German inflation, other countries had to follow in order to maintain a fixed exchange rate. However, with other countries in recession, this increase in interest rates was unwelcome, and as a result of these tensions the pound sterling and the lira were forced to leave the fixed exchange rate system. For small open economies whose economy is closely tied to that of the country whose exchange rate they are targeting, fixed exchange rates seem to work well. For larger economies they are more problematic.

17.6 Inflation Targeting

The problem that many central banks encountered with money supply or exchange rate targets is their inflexibility. This is ironic as the very reason they were adopted was the belief that by following a fixed rule, central banks would achieve a reputation for being tough on inflation, which would in turn help them produce lower inflation. As discussed in Chapter 16, the adoption of rules rather than discretion is crucial if policymakers are to gain credibility. But money supply or exchange rate rules are too inflexible—policymakers only focus on one statistic, be it the money supply or the exchange rate, in order to control inflation. Any other information cannot be used to override the rule. Consider again the case of the UK and the Exchange Rate Mechanism. While Germany was expanding rapidly and seeing inflation increase, the

---

[4]The intuition is as follows: If one country has a higher inflation rate than another, then its currency will buy fewer items in that country. Therefore people will sell the high inflation currency, leading it to depreciate. If the exchange rate is fixed, it must be because individuals are indifferent as to which currency they hold—they both buy the same amount. This means inflation must be equal in the two countries.

UK was in recession and faced no inflationary pressures. If the Bank of England could give weight to a wide range of evidence, then it might conclude that even if sterling depreciated against the deutsche mark this would not threaten higher UK inflation. As a result it might be able to leave interest rates unchanged. By contrast, under a fixed exchange rate the central bank does not have this discretion—regardless of what the data for output or inflation says, the central bank would have to respond to a devaluation in sterling by increasing interest rates to maintain the exchange rate target.

This example suggests the desirability of adopting a monetary policy rule that utilizes a wide range of information and that is flexible enough for policymakers to respond differently to different circumstances. However, no rule could be written down that describes how policy would be set in all possible outcomes. This leaves two alternatives. First, choose a simple rule—such as a money supply or exchange rate target—and face the occasional risk of having to abandon the rule in certain circumstances, with all the adverse credibility consequences this implies. Alternatively, develop a framework that offers the central bank some discretion in how it responds to the data but also provides a clear objective to which policy is directed and against which the performance of monetary policy can be assessed. This latter option is referred to as "constrained discretion."

Inflation targeting is an attempt to achieve this constrained discretion. Inflation targeting involves the central bank stating explicit quantitative targets (or ranges) for inflation for a specific time horizon. The central bank also dedicates monetary policy to achieving a low inflation rate and no other purpose. The intermediate target in this framework becomes the central bank's own inflation forecast. If the forecast is for inflation to exceed its target, the central bank has to raise interest rates accordingly. By using the forecast rate of inflation as an intermediate target variable the central bank can take into consideration a huge range of information. Any variable that influences inflation should be considered, including the exchange rate and the money supply. However, under inflation targeting no one variable is dominant and the net effect of all of them is considered.

This obviously provides the central bank with a large amount of discretion, so in order to preserve credibility, inflation targeting is characterized by vigorous efforts at communicating with the public. Through publications and speeches the central bank reveals the logic behind its deliberations and actions, and publishes its forecasts and its analysis of how it thinks the economy and monetary policy operate. After decades of acting with the utmost secrecy, the adoption of inflation targeting has brought about a dramatic change in the behavior of central bankers.

The belief is that by explaining in a consistent and logical manner the reason behind monetary policy decisions, the public will appreciate that inflation targeting is desirable, should be supported, and will be consistently followed. Further, if this is understood the public will not fear the central bank using its discretion to risk high inflation but instead use it to set monetary policy in a flexible manner. Indeed, some advocates of inflation targeting argue that it should increase credibility. Simple inflexible rules will inevitably be abandoned in certain circumstances but not flexible approaches like inflation targeting.

In short, inflation targeting is a *framework* for monetary policy, not a rule—it occupies a midpoint on the rules versus discretion spectrum. It provides a forward-looking discipline that should enhance credibility but allows flexible responses to events (such as shocks to the demand for money). Inflation targeting does not provide mechanical instructions to the central bank but allows it to use its discretion in the short run.

Inflation targeting has been enthusiastically adopted by central banks. Starting with New Zealand in 1990 and subsequently Canada, the UK, Finland, Sweden, Australia, Israel, Chile, Mexico, and Brazil, inflation targeting has become a common *modus operandi*. The European Central Bank also operates a form of inflation targeting, although it places a special reference on the money supply figures.

In adopting inflation targeting numerous operational issues have to be determined — What measure of inflation should be used? What inflation rate to target? Should a range be targeted or a specific value? What horizon should the central bank focus on? Most countries focus on increases in consumer prices (sometimes extracting volatile components) and a target of around 2%. Some countries specify that inflation should be below a certain limit (the ECB sets a target of 2% or less), while others allow deviations from the target rate within a narrow band (the Bank of England targets 2.5% inflation around a band of 1% either side, New Zealand, a range of 0–3%).

17.7   The Operational Instruments of Monetary Policy

As well as the ultimate and intermediate targets, the other key component of monetary policy is the instruments the central bank has at its disposal. Currently the key tool of monetary policy is the short-term interest rate.

How can central banks, with limited resources, control almost exactly the level of short-term interest rates? The answer is that, at least in the current state of monetary arrangements and transactions technologies, money remains essential, and the central bank is the monopoly supplier of so-called *base money*; that is, the cash plus reserves that the commercial banking system holds.

The monetary system in most developed economies is, ultimately, similar. At its center stand commercial banks, which take deposits from the private sector, make loans, and, crucially, help facilitate transactions by honoring checks and other payment instructions from their customers. If the customers of a bank write more checks in a working day than they receive in payment, that bank may have to make a net transfer of funds to another bank. For example, suppose that the customers of Deutschebank write checks that customers of Dresdnerbank pay in and that compensating flows in the other direction do not match them. Suppose that at the end of the day Deutschebank needs to transfer 50 million euro to Dresdnerbank. Both banks will typically have accounts with the central bank; the central bank will hold accounts for the major commercial banks that allow them to settle transactions with each other. Central banks severely limit the ability of private banks to overdraw these accounts or take their reserves below a critical threshold (the reserve requirement). This means that if toward the end of a working day Deutschebank has insufficient funds to transfer the necessary amount to the Dresdnerbank account, Deutschebank will need to do something.

The interbank market allows Deutschebank to borrow money overnight, so that it does not go into deficit at the central bank. But suppose that most major banks are going to be overdrawn at the end of the day and that the system does not have enough funds to allow individual banks to borrow from others that had a surplus at the central bank. Suppose, for example, that a large corporation pays its tax bill on a particular day. When it pays its tax bill, it transfers a large quantity of funds from its account at a commercial bank to a government account. Government accounts are normally held with the central bank, so that clearing the check will result in a net drain of funds from the pool of money available to private banks. If the central bank did nothing to alleviate this shortage, private banks would be bidding for funds on the interbank market and would begin to drive interest rates up. If the central bank did not allow individual banks to go into significant deficit without incurring enormous penalties, interest rates on the interbank market would be bid up to high levels as individual banks sought desperately to borrow money to prevent being overdrawn at the central bank.

In this system, central banks operate by providing reserves, mainly through so called **open market operations** or through lending at the discount window. During a working day, a central bank may realize that the money market will run short of funds unless it acts. The central bank will then signal that the system is likely to run short of funds that day and that it will buy short-term securities in exchange for cash[5] **at a specified interest rate**. Every time the central bank buys a security from a private bank, that bank's reserves with the central bank are credited with the sale proceeds. So by buying securities (that is, engaging in open market operations), the central bank can help regulate the quantity of reserves in the system. Central banks can also control reserves by directly lending funds to the private banks that require funds. In the U.S. system, such loans are called *discount window lending.*

The key thing to remember about all this is that the central bank has rules about how much funds the private sector banks have to hold with it. The private sector banks will, in certain circumstances, find that there is a shortage (or sometimes a glut) of reserves. If the central bank were to do nothing, the level of money market interest rates would move. The central bank can prevent significant movement in these money market rates by buying or selling securities or by lending money at the discount window. The central bank has enormous influence over the level of money market interest rates because it can supply almost unlimited quantities of funds to the market or, by selling securities, it can drain enormous quantities of reserves from the market. *Central banks decide the terms at which they will purchase or sell securities and lend them at the discount window.*

Note that if commercial banks were not required to hold reserves at the central banks, the central banks would not have the power to alter interest rates. The precise nature of the reserve requirements the central bank requires differs from system to system. In the United States, commercial banks that hold accounts at the Fed for settlement of flows are required not to be in deficit, on average, over a two-week period. Other systems require that individual banks not be overdrawn on a daily basis. Regard-

---

[5]Short-term securities are certificates which represent ownership of loans to government (treasury bills) or companies (commercial paper) where the loans are less than 6 months.

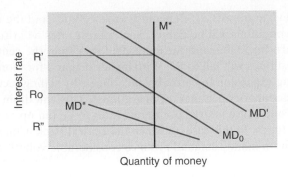

FIGURE 17.11 **Monetary policy when targeting the money supply.** Money supply targets imply volatile interest rates if money demand is unstable.

less of the specific detail, the key point is that failure to meet these reserve requirements is penalized by the central bank and only the central bank can supply reserves to the banking system. This is the reason behind the central bank's influence over short-term interest rates.

17.8 | Controlling the Money Supply or Interest Rates?

Earlier in this chapter, we reviewed how central banks have tended to move away from trying to control the money supply to a framework of inflation targeting. In order to better understand how a central bank implements monetary policy we shall consider each of these cases. Figures 17.11 and 17.12 illustrate the difference between these two systems.

Figure 17.11 illustrates a situation in which the central bank has a target for some measure of the money supply. We assume a negative relation between the level of the short-term nominal interest rate and the stock of money. The higher the interest rate, the more expensive it is to hold cash, so narrow money demand falls; and the more expensive it is to borrow, so credit and broad money declines. M* is the target level, and MD_0 illustrates the expected position of the money demand curve. If demand for money turns out to be what the central bank anticipated, then interest rates will be R_0. But if the demand for money is either higher or lower than the central bank

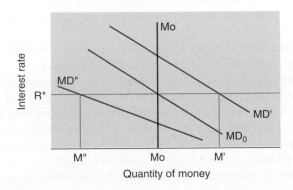

FIGURE 17.12 **Monetary policy when central bank sets interest rates.** When the central bank sets interest rates, volatility occurs in the money supply.

anticipates, interest rates will deviate from R_0. If demand is at level MD' and the target does not change, monetary conditions will be tighter, and interest rates will rise to R' to reflect the scarcity of funds. But if demand for money is lower than the central bank anticipates, at MD", interest rates will fall to R". With higher demand for money, the central bank will be offsetting expansion in banks balance sheets by selling securities (that is, entering into contractionary open market operations). This will drain reserves from the banking system and cause interbank interest rates to be bid up as the commercial banks vie to attract funds. In this case, in which the central bank is targeting the money supply, fluctuations in money demand produce considerable volatility in interest rates.

Under inflation targeting, the central bank sets interest rates to achieve a particular inflation target. This case is shown in Figure 17.12. Again, MD_0 denotes the level of demand for money that the central bank anticipates. If the central bank aims to keep interest rates at R^* *and* if demand turns out to be MD_0, the money supply will be at M_0. But if demand deviates from MD_0 and interest rates are kept at level R*, the supply of money will deviate from M_0. So, for example, if the money demand schedule is to the right of MD_0, the quantity of money will exceed M_0. And if the demand for money balances is substantially lower than MD_0, then so will be the stock of money.

If the demand for money schedule is predictable, there is no substantive difference between interest rate targeting and money supply targeting. The central bank could choose to specify a money supply target or a particular level of interest rate, and the two would be equivalent because each interest rate corresponds to a particular (known) level of money demand. As we discussed earlier, it was unpredictable shifts in money demand, due to technological developments and financial innovation, that contributed to central banks looking for alternatives to targeting the money supply.

17.9 How Monetary Policy Affects the Economy— The Transmission Mechanism

We have outlined the aims of a central bank and how it adjusts the instruments of monetary policy to achieve them, but we have not yet outlined how changes in interest rates affect inflation and output. This is called the **transmission mechanism of monetary policy**—the link among changes in interest rates, changes in components of demand within the economy, and how such changes in demand can affect inflation pressures.

Figure 17.13 outlines the main links through which the transmission mechanism works. When the central bank increases official interest rates, this will begin to have an effect on interest rates of all maturities and will influence asset prices. Assuming inflation in the short term is relatively unchanged, short-term *real* interest rates will be higher. If the markets believe the higher interest rates are not purely transitory, this will also increase longer-term bond yields. These increases in interest rates will have a direct effect in lowering demand. As we saw in Chapter 13, increases in interest rates lead to reductions in consumption. In addition, higher interest rates will affect the cost of borrowing and the real rate of return that needs to be earned on investments projects

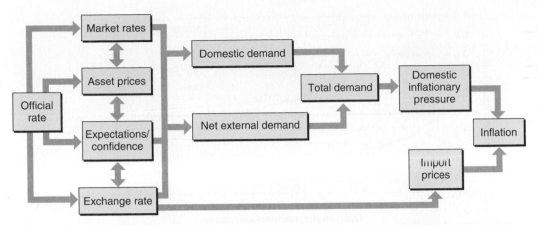

FIGURE 17.13 **The transmission mechanism of monetary policy.** Interest rates affect output and inflation through numerous channels. *Source*: Monetary Policy Committee, Bank of England, *The Transmission Mechanism of Monetary Policy* (1999). Reprinted with permission from the Bank of England.

leading to a fall in investment spending. The higher interest rates will also lead to a fall in asset prices (see Chapters 21 and 22) and further reductions in consumption and investment through wealth effects and the Q theory of investment (see Chapter 14). If higher interest rates are expected to lead to a future slowdown in the economy, consumer and producer confidence will also fall, which in turn will lead to retrenchment of consumption and investment plans.

The increase in interest rates will also affect external demand in the economy. As we noted earlier, higher interest rates lead to an increase in the exchange rate. The higher exchange rate makes imports cheaper, which may place downward pressure on domestic inflation. Further, the higher exchange rate makes exports more expensive and so reduces demand in the economy. The overall impact of the increase in interest rates is therefore to reduce demand in the economy.

Figure 17.13 focuses on how increases in the price of money, the interest rate, affect the economy. However, in some cases monetary policy operates less as a result of changes in the price of money and more through the *quantity* of lending banks undertake. This is known as the **credit channel** of monetary policy. Increases in interest rates can produce declines in real estate and equity prices, which reduce the collateral firms can offer banks. As a consequence, banks reduce their loans to the corporate sector, which has a direct effect on consumption and investment. It has been argued that the credit channel rather than inappropriate levels of interest rates was responsible for the severity of the Great Depression. The credit channel occurred through the failure of the Federal Reserve to offset the dramatic decline in the stock of money by providing banks with cash that they could lend.[6] The Fed could have done this by buying securities from the banking sector and providing it with loanable funds.

[6]Friedman, M. and Schwartz, A.(1963) "A Monetary History of the United States 1867–1960," Princeton University Press.

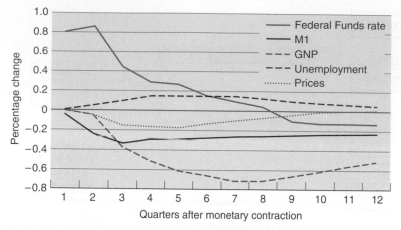

FIGURE 17.14   **The impact of a 1% increase in interest rates on the U.S. economy.** Higher interest rates lead to declines in prices, output, and the money supply and to higher unemployment. Their effect on prices peaks after a year, and on output after two. *Source*: Christiano, Eichenbaum, and Evans, "The effects of Monetary Policy Shocks: Evidence from the Flow of Funds," *Review of Economics and Statistics* (1996) vol. 78, pp. 16–34. © by the President and Fellows of Harvard College and the Massachusetts Institute of Technology.

Figure 17.13 only outlines the channels through which interest rates effect output and inflation, not the magnitude of the effects nor how long the impact takes. Figure 17.14 shows empirical estimates of how the U.S. economy is affected by a 1% increase in the main Federal Funds interest rate. As our analysis predicts, the higher interest rates lead to a fall in the money supply, increases in unemployment, and lower prices and output. At its peak, output falls by around 0.7% after around two years. Prices are lower by around 0.2%, with the effect peaking after a year. These long lags in the transmission mechanism show the importance of using a forward-looking intermediate target when setting interest rates.

The magnitude of interest rate effects and how quickly they impact the economy depends on the economy's financial structure. Monetary policy will be particularly effective if many domestic firms and households rely strongly on banks for credit, as the interest rate on bank loans varies closely with changes in the short-rates under the control of the central bank. In contrast, the cost to companies of issuing equity is likely to be less affected than the cost of borrowing on a loan from a bank. If some firms and households find it difficult to substitute other forms of finance (for example, issues of equities or long-dated bonds) for bank loans, shifts in monetary policy are likely to hit them hard. The degree of substitutability between bank finance and other forms of finance will also be an important influence on the scale of the credit channel. Because financial structure varies across countries, so does the monetary policy transmission mechanism. Figure 17.15 shows how the impact of higher interest rates varies across countries. The overall shape of all the responses is the same, but when the peak impact occurs and how substantial the impact is varies.[7]

[7]Figures 17.14 and 17.15 are taken from different studies covering different time periods. As a result, the results for the United States are not identical.

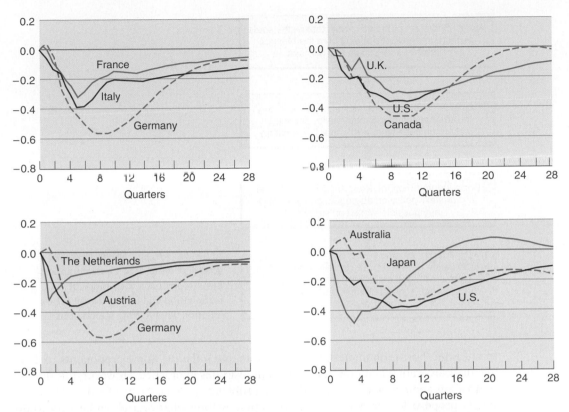

FIGURE 17.15 **Impact of 1% higher interest rates on GDP**. *Source*: Mihov, "Monetary Policy Implementation and Transmission in the European Monetary Union," INSEAD mimeo (2000).

17.10 Monetary Policy in Practice

Let's assume, as is the case in most developed countries, that the central bank sets monetary policy. In general terms how central banks set policy is uncontroversial. The central bank will first analyze the economy and then consider how best to set the policy instruments that it has, usually short-term money market interest rates. Central banks act in light of the current economic situation and, crucially, based on their assessments of how the policy instrument will affect the overall level of demand in the economy and on how demand is linked to the ultimate policy target. A stylized description of this process is shown in Figure 17.16.

As this discussion and our earlier one regarding inflation targeting reveal, setting interest rates to control inflation is a complex activity. A useful way of summarizing the way interest rates are set are "Taylor rules."[8] Taylor rules specify a link between the

---

[8] After the Stanford economist, John Taylor. See his "Discretion versus Policy Rules in Practice," Carnegie-Rochester Conference Series on Public Policy (November 1993) vol. 39, pp. 195–214.

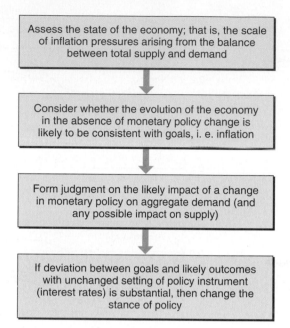

Assess the state of the economy; that is, the scale of inflation pressures arising from the balance between total supply and demand

Consider whether the evolution of the economy in the absence of monetary policy change is likely to be consistent with goals, i. e. inflation

Form judgment on the likely impact of a change in monetary policy on aggregate demand (and any possible impact on supply)

If deviation between goals and likely outcomes with unchanged setting of policy instrument (interest rates) is substantial, then change the stance of policy

FIGURE 17.16   Stylized description of behavior of central bank. Central bankers have to process a wide range of information and form views of future inflation when setting interest rates.

level of the short-term interest rate and output and inflation. Some proponents of Taylor rules advocate them for use in setting interest rates in practice. However, our discussion of inflation targeting outlined some problems with using fixed rules. Here we simply propose Taylor rules as a way of approximating what central bankers try to do when setting rates. A number of studies have found such rules provide a reasonably good explanation of actual central bank behavior.

The following equation gives the typical structure for a Taylor rule:

$$\text{nominal interest rate} = \text{equilibrium nominal interest rate} + \lambda \times \text{output gap} + \alpha \times (\text{inflation} - \text{inflation target})$$

where the equilibrium nominal interest rate is the real interest rate plus the inflation target and λ and α are positive numbers. The Taylor rule says that if the output gap is positive (GDP is above its trend value), then the central bank should raise interest rates. Similarly, if inflation is above its target, then interest rates also should be increased. A variety of versions of the Taylor rule exist. Some use the gap between expected future inflation and the inflation target, rather than current inflation. Also, interest rates from the last period are often included in order to smooth the changes in interest rates, something that central banks appear to do.

The positive coefficients λ and α reflect an assessment of sensitivity of inflation and output to shifts in monetary policy *and* to the chosen tradeoff between inflation volatility and output volatility. If inflation is very sensitive to changes in interest rates, then other things being equal, α will be small, similarly for λ. If the central bank will not tolerate much volatility in inflation, then α will be large, similarly for λ and output volatility. For the United States, the values of λ and α that best account for the behavior of interest rates are about 0.5 and 1.5, respectively. This says that in response to a 1% increase in the output gap the Fed tends to raise interest rates by 0.5%. In response to inflation being 1% above its target, the Fed raises interest rates by 1.5%. It cuts them by 1.5% when inflation is 1% below target. Broadly similar values are obtained for other countries, although differences in attitudes toward inflation mean there are some variations.

If α equals 1, then nominal interest rates would only rise in line with inflation and the real interest rate would not alter. When α exceeds 1, then the central bank responds to higher inflation by increasing the real interest rate—it is the increase in real interest rates that makes the policy contractionary. The Taylor rule, and its ability to track actual changes in interest rates, suggests that central bankers translate the various messages that a wide range of macroeconomic variables convey into movements in the output gap and inflation relative to the target. Then, having formed these views, they adjust interest rates accordingly.

17.11 The Future of Central Banks

In 1999 Mervyn King, deputy governor of the Bank of England, noted:

The future of central banks is not entirely secure. Their numbers may decline over the next century. The enthusiasm of governments for national currencies has waned as capital flows have become liberalized and exchange rates more volatile. Following the example of the European Central Bank, more regional monetary unions could emerge. Short of this the creation of currency boards, or even complete currency substitution, might also reduce the number of independent national monetary authorities.[9]

Fewer central banks does not imply a reduction in the power of monetary policy. But the forces that King describes—liberalization of capital flows in particular—may undermine the influence of the few remaining central banks. We noted above that central banks get their power to set short-term nominal interest rates because commercial banks need to hold funds at the central bank to settle transactions among themselves and central banks are the only institution that can provide settlement balances. But for how long will this remain true? The Internet and other types of electronic transfer of information may allow companies and individuals to settle transactions instantaneously and without using what we normally think of as money.

Suppose, for example, that an efficient and highly liquid market exists for a range of securities in which prices are known second by second across the globe. For some assets we are almost in that situation already. The prices of bonds and equities that large companies and governments in developed economies issue are known instantaneously and more or less 24 hours a day across the world. Suppose it were also known, and could be verified, what the value was of the portfolio of such assets that individuals or corporations held. We could then imagine that buyers could purchase commodities and services by immediately transferring claims to such assets to the accounts of sellers.

[9]"Challenges for Monetary Policy: New and Old," a paper prepared for the Symposium on "New Challenges for Monetary Policy," Jackson Hole, Wyoming, August 27, 1999.

We might go further and imagine that the ultimate means of settlement was not the monetary unit of account of one country but rather a universal unit of account that could be some sort of commodity money in which the underlying commodity, rather than being gold or silver, was a collection of financial assets. Suppose, for example, our unit of account was a composite equity. Imagine that the world currency, call it the Global, is equal to one share in IBM, one long-dated U.S. government bond, one share in Microsoft, one share in Shell, and one share in Deutschebank. One Global is that collection of assets. The prices of all commodities could then be quoted in terms of Globals.

Suppose I want to purchase music over the Internet. Its price is one-hundredth of a Global and my Internet account publicly reveals that I have 3,000 Globals. The seller of the music is happy to accept marketable securities whose value is the equivalent of one-hundredth of a Global, and by pressing a button, securities of that value are immediately transferred to the seller's account. There are no reserve balances of money with central banks, and as a result, central banks do not set interest rates because there are no open market operations. This brave new world would also not have generalized price inflation, unless the supply of the equities and bonds that make up the Global were to increase.

Under such a scenario, we would have returned to a sort of gold standard, one based on the value of corporations and bonds. Further, this system need not operate in just a few developed countries, it could be a truly global system and one in which monetary policy would play no role.

SUMMARY

The twentieth century has experienced a large increase in the number of central banks as the move away from commodity-based money has given governments more discretion over monetary policy.

Monetary policy consists of three main components: the target the central bank wishes to achieve; an intermediate target the central bank tries to control in order to meet its ultimate target; and the instruments of policy the central bank has at its disposal.

A belief in a vertical long-run supply curve, pessimism over the ability to fine-tune the economy, and a belief that following rules will improve credibility and achieve lower inflation have all combined to persuade many central banks to try to keep inflation at around 2%.

Countries have experimented with a range of intermediate targets, with money supply, fixed exchange rates, and inflation targeting the most common. In the 1980s a number of countries attempted to control inflation via controlling the money supply. However, this proved unsatisfactory in practice so that now inflation targeting exchange rate targets are the most common policies. Inflation targeting is attractive to central banks because it provides discretion as to how to respond to economic events while still providing a rules based framework to help promote credibility.

In implementing monetary policy, central banks invariably use short-term market interest rates. The central bank has control over these because it is the only supplier of reserves to the banking system. Some commentators believe that technological developments may remove this monopoly position and undermine central banks' role in monetary policy.

Monetary policy affects demand directly by changing interest rates, asset prices, exchange rates, and affecting consumption, investment, and exports. Additional effects work through changes in producer and consumer confidence. Further, a credit channel is believed to sometimes affect the economy. This operates through changes in the supply and demand for credit that are not directly related to interest rates. Empirical estimates suggest that the effect of changing interest rates accumulates over time and takes between 18 months and 2 years to have its peak impact.

In setting interest rates central bankers monitor a wide range of statistics. Taylor rules are a useful way of conceptualizing this process. Interest rates increase when the output gap is large and when inflation exceeds its target.

CONCEPTUAL QUESTIONS

1. Should something that has such a large impact on the economy as monetary policy be handed over to a central bank rather than decided by elected politicians?

2. Why not specify a goal for the monetary authorities that included both a price level and an unemployment target?

3. Should measures of inflation include asset prices (e.g., stock prices and house prices), so that inflation targeting would require the monetary authorities to act when asset prices rise dramatically?

4. Central banks control short-term interest rates because they control the supply of base money, which is the ultimate, final form of settlement for transactions. Are central banks abusing this power by using it to determine interest rates?

5. In a world in which electronic transfer of funds is becoming easier and the value of more and more people's assets is easier to ascertain, is the power of central banks doomed to decline? Is this worrying?

6. At Christmas and Easter the public withdraws large amounts of cash from their accounts. What should central banks do during these periods to stabilize interest rates?

ANALYTICAL QUESTIONS

1. The Federal Reserve Bank of Albion operates a Taylor rule of

interest rate = inflation target + equilibrium real interest rate + 0.5* (output gap)
+ 1.5*(inflation − inflation target)

It has an inflation target of 2% and believes the equilibrium real rate to be 3%. Currently the output gap is zero and trend output growth is 2% per annum.

   (a) If output growth is predicted to be 4% this year and inflation 3%, what level should interest rates move to?

   (b) How does your answer change if the central bank changes its inflation target to 3%?

   (c) Consider again the economy in (a). What should the central bank do if it thinks that trend output growth may have increased to 3.5%? What would happen if it was wrong?

2. The Community of Pacific States (CPS) operates a Taylor rule of the form

interest rates = 5% + A × output gap + B × (inflation − inflation target)

Inflation is determined by a Phillips curve so that

inflation = inflation target + 0.5 × output gap last year

And interest rates impact on the output gap so that

*output gap = −0.5 * (interest rates last period − 5%)*

The output gap is currently 2% and inflation is 3% with a target of 2%. The central bank of the CPS is considering two alternative policy rules. One sets A = 0.75 and B = 1, whereas the other sets A = 0.25 and B = 2.

   (a) Compare the behavior of interest rates, inflation, and output over the next five years for both rules.
   (b) How does the volatility of inflation and output vary in each case?
   (c) Examine how your answers change when the slope of the Phillips curve and the sensitivity of interest rates change.
   (d) How would your answers change if

inflation = last year's inflation + 0.5 × output gap last year

3. The League of Big States (LBS) has inflation expectations of 5% and an estimated natural rate of unemployment of 5%. A 2% rise (fall) in unemployment leads to a 1% fall (increase) in inflation.

   (a) What is inflation when unemployment equals 5%?
   (b) What is inflation when unemployment falls to 3%?
   (c) If unemployment falls to 3% but the Central Bank of LBS thinks that the natural rate has also fallen to 3%, what will happen to inflation?
   (d) How will the behavior of interest rates differ in your answers to (b) and (c) if the Central Bank uses higher interest rates to keep inflation at 5%?
   (e) The Central Bank is not sure whether or not the natural rate of unemployment has changed. How will its behavior vary depending upon whether its goal is (1) to achieve inflation of 5% or less; (2) try and maintain stable inflation and unemployment; or (3) inflation should be in the range of 4.5–5.5%?
   (f) Let inflation expectations be equal to last period's inflation. Unemployment is currently 5%, the natural rate is 5%, and last year inflation was 5%. The Central Bank wants to lower inflation from 5% to 2%. Compare how unemployment and inflation vary over the next four years when (1) the government wants to achieve 2% inflation next year, (2) the government wants to achieve 2% inflation by lowering inflation by 1% each year.

Exchange Rate Determination I: Prices and the Real Exchange Rate

Overview

The nominal exchange rate is the rate at which the currencies of two countries can be exchanged, whereas the real exchange rate is the ratio of what a specified amount of domestic currency will buy in one country compared with what it can buy in another. This chapter focuses on why the real exchange rate is so volatile. We first consider the law of one price, which says that in the absence of trade restrictions the same commodity should have the same price wherever it is sold. We then discuss purchasing power parity (PPP), which says that identical bundles of goods should cost the same in different countries. This implies that the real exchange rate should be constant and equal to one. Next we discuss why the real exchange rate changes and focus on the current and capital accounts of a country. The current account reflects trade in the goods and services of a country, and the capital account reflects the trade in assets. Finally, we review the factors that influence the capital and current accounts and their impact on the real exchange rate.

18.1 Definitions

BILATERAL AND EFFECTIVE ROLES

Exchange rates are confusing. Pick up any financial paper and you will see various exchange rates quoted. Part of the confusion is that there are many countries and different exchange rates, but there are also spot and forward rates, bilateral and effective exchange rates, and real and nominal rates. In this section we clarify these terms.

We start with bilateral exchange rates. Different countries often have different currencies. A **bilateral exchange rate** is the rate at which you can swap the money of one country for that of another. For instance, if one euro can be swapped for one U.S. dollar, then the exchange rate is 1:1 or simply 1. If the euro *appreciates*, then it rises in value—it becomes more expensive to buy euros if you are holding dollars. For instance, if it takes $1.10 to buy a euro, then the euro has appreciated by 10%; you need 10% more dollars to buy the same number of euros. By contrast, if the exchange rate falls to 0.90, then you only need 90 cents to buy a euro, which has *devalued* by 10%.

We now need to deal with yet another source of confusion about exchange rates—how should you express the exchange rate? For most currencies, including the U.S. dollar, the exchange rate is written as the amount of domestic currency that buys one unit of foreign currency. In other words, if $1 buys ¥100, the exchange rate is 0.01. However, for some currencies, notably the British pound sterling, the exchange rate is quoted as the amount of foreign currency you can buy with one unit of the domestic currency. In other words, if £1 buys $1.65, the exchange rate is 1.65 as opposed to 1/1.65 = 0.66 (it takes 66 pence to buy $1). To work out whether a currency is appreciating or depreciating, you have to know how the currency is expressed. If it is expressed in terms of how much domestic currency you need to buy one unit of foreign currency, then an appreciation means that the quoted exchange rate gets *smaller*—you need to spend less domestic currency to get one unit of foreign currency. However, expressed British style, if a currency appreciates, then the quoted exchange rate *rises*—you get more foreign currency for one unit of domestic currency.

Bilateral exchange rates are particularly important for foreign trade. For instance, if a German firm sells goods to Canada, then the bilateral euro—Canadian dollar rate is what matters. However, over any particular period, a currency will move in different directions against other currencies. For instance, the euro may rise against the U.S. dollar and the pound but depreciate against the Canadian dollar and the Japanese yen. Has the euro appreciated or depreciated? To answer this question, we need a measure of how the currency has done on average against *all* countries rather than just against one other currency. The **effective exchange rate** is a measure of this average performance. However, certain currencies are more important than others. For instance, in assessing the performance of the euro, it is more important to know how the euro has done against the U.S. dollar rather than the Thai baht because Europe trades far more with the United States than with Thailand. We can measure a currency's performance by calculating the *effective exchange rate on a trade-weighted basis*. If a country's trade (the sum of imports and exports) with the United States is ten times more than with Thailand, the dollar will get a weight 10 times higher. Therefore, if the euro appreciates against the dollar by 1% but depreciates euro by 1% against the Thai baht, while remaining unchanged against all other currencies, the effective exchange rate will rise.

The weights reflect trade in a particular year, and as trading patterns change over time, these weights are revised. Because the Euro effective exchange rate represents an average across a variety of currencies, it has no natural units (what do you get when you cross a dollar with a euro, a yen, and British sterling?). Therefore, we always express the effective exchange rate in an index form, so that in one particular year (usually the year that the trade weights refer to), it has a value of 100. Therefore, if the effective exchange rate appreciates on average by 10% from that date, the index will be 110, whereas if it depreciates, it will be 90.

FIGURE 18.1 **Effective exchange rates, 1975–2000.** Nominal exchange rates are very volatile. *Source*: IMF, *International Financial Statistics* (September 2000). Courtesy of IMF.

Figure 18.1 plots the effective exchange rate since 1970 for the United States, Japan, and Germany. The main trend is for a substantial appreciation of the yen, except for the last few years, when the Japanese recession has caused the yen to depreciate. The U.S. and German currencies have, on the whole, been less volatile. But between 1979 and 1986, the dollar appreciated by 50% before declining back to its original level.

REAL VERSUS NOMINAL EXCHANGE RATES

Throughout this book we have distinguished between *real* and *nominal* variables—real variables reflect quantities or volume measures, while nominal variables reflect money values. The **nominal exchange rate** is the rate at which you can swap two different currencies—this is the exchange rate we have just been discussing. If at an airport you wish to swap Australian for Canadian dollars, you can do so at the nominal exchange rate. The **real exchange rate** tells you how expensive commodities arc in different countries and reflects the competitiveness of a country's exports.

Consider the following simple example. A cup of coffee costs 200 yen in Japan and $1 in the United States, and the nominal exchange rate is ¥100 to $1. Imagine that you are about to leave New Orleans for a holiday in Tokyo and want to buy a cup of coffee. In New Orleans coffee costs $1, but how many cups of coffee could you buy if you converted your money into yen and went to Japan? The current nominal exchange rate means that $1 can be swapped for ¥100, but in Tokyo ¥100 only buys half a cup of coffee. The real exchange rate is therefore 0.5—one American cup of coffee costs the equivalent of 50% of a cup of coffee in Japan. While the nominal exchange rate tells you how much you can swap money for, the real exchange rate tells you what you can purchase for your money. A New Yorker returning from a vacation who says that Tokyo was expensive is essentially saying that the yen-U.S. dollar real exchange rate is low—goods in the United States are cheap by comparison.

However, the real exchange rate is not just about *one* commodity; it reflects all the goods you purchase in a foreign country. In other words, it is about the overall price level in a country and not just the cost of a cup of coffee. The real exchange rate is the ratio of what you can buy in one country compared to what your money buys elsewhere. We define it as

real exchange rate = nominal exchange rate × domestic price level/overseas price level

Consider the case of the U.S.–French real exchange rate in which what costs $1 in the United States costs 5Fr in France and the nominal exchange rate is 0.2 (20 cents buys one franc). In this case we have

$$\text{real exchange rate} = \frac{0.2 \times 5}{1} = 1$$

which means that expressed in a common currency, goods cost the same in France as they do in the United States—the real exchange rate is 1, and you can buy exactly the same amount for your money in either country. If, instead, everything that costs $1 in the United States costs 10Fr in France, then we have

$$\text{real exchange rate} = \frac{0.2 \times 10}{1} = 2$$

so that you can buy twice as much with your money in the United States as in France (the real exchange rate for the franc is 2).

As with the nominal exchange rate, we can express the real exchange rate either in a bilateral form or as an effective index. Figure 18.2 shows the behavior of the effective real exchange rate for the dollar, the DM (deutsch mark, or German mark), and the yen.

Comparing Figures 18.1 and 18.2, we can see how closely fluctuations in the real exchange rate track movements in the nominal exchange rate. Explaining this similarity in the behavior of real and nominal exchange rates is a substantial challenge for exchange rate economists. One argument says that real and nominal exchange rates behave so similarly because the real exchange rate is just the nominal exchange rate multiplied by

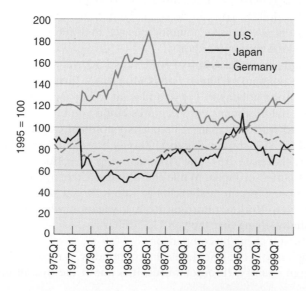

FIGURE 18.2 **Real effective exchange rates, 1975–2000.** Real exchange rates are also volatile and display a similar pattern to nominal exchange rates. *Source*: IMF, *International Financial Statistics* (September 2000). Courtesy of IMF.

the ratio of overseas to domestic prices. Every minute of the day, the nominal exchange rate changes, often substantially, because of currency transactions—quoted exchange rates are volatile. However, prices in a country change only slowly—as we showed in Chapter 15, prices are sticky. If prices hardly change, then movements in the nominal exchange rate will generate fluctuations in real exchange rates. A different argument is that because the factors that determine the real exchange rate are volatile, changes in the real exchange rate drive the substantial volatility in the nominal exchange rate. In the following sections we will try to outline both of these arguments.

18.2 Law of One Price

The **law of one price** states that identical commodities should sell at the same price wherever they are sold. In other words, the same model of television set should cost the same whether it is sold in Madrid or Barcelona. The basis of the law of one price is arbitrage. If the television is cheaper in Barcelona, a firm can buy televisions in Barcelona, sell them in Madrid, and pocket the difference. This would increase the demand for television sets in Barcelona and their supply in Madrid. It would thus push up the price of televisions in Barcelona and lower them in Madrid, and so reduce the price discrepancy between the two cities. Arbitrage will continue until the price of the television is exactly the same in each city—one price prevails. Note that this result of only one price depends on there being no travel costs. If it costs 1000 pesetas to shift a television from Barcelona to Madrid, arbitrage will stop when the price differential is 1000 peseta.

The law of one price refers not just to similar commodities in the same country but also across different economies. Ignoring transportation costs, once prices are expressed in a common currency, identical commodities should sell in different economies at the same price. Let the U.S. dollar be worth 150 pesetas and imagine that the television set retails in Barcelona for 15,000 pesetas. Arbitrage should ensure that in America the television set costs $100 (15,000/150 = 100). In other words, the law of one price says

dollar price of television in United States = dollar/peseta exchange rate × peseta price of television in Barcelona

Does the law of one price hold? The answer is basically no—except for a few commodities, little evidence supports the law of one price. The exceptions tend to be goods

TABLE 18.1   Price of Gold

Country	$ Price One Troy Ounce
Hong Kong (late)	270.65
London (late)	270.10
Paris (afternoon)	270.23
Zurich (late afternoon)	269.95
New York	270.20

Source: Associated Press, December 18, 2000. Reprinted with permission of The Associated Press.

that are similar or homogenous. For instance, Table 18.1 shows the price of gold in various international markets. The gold market is international—you can find prices in the markets in many countries and buy gold for much the same price—the law of one price seems to hold for gold. However, even for gold the law of one price is less convincing than it first appears. The prices in Table 18.1 for the purchase of gold do not include delivery charges. If you live in the Netherlands and wish to receive gold from either the London or New York market you will end up paying different amounts. In other words, gold in New York is a different commodity from gold in London. This rather obvious point is important. The law of one price says that identical commodities should sell for identical prices. But if transport costs matter, then location is an important feature of a commodity. If transport costs are high and the distance between markets is great, the same commodity will sell for different prices in different locations.

HOW BIG ARE TRANSPORT COSTS?

How large are these transport costs and can they account for much of the deviations from the law of one price that we observe? We can measure transport costs by comparing the prices of goods when they leave a country as exports to their cost when they arrive at their destination as imports. Customs authorities collect vast amounts of trade data, including two sets of prices: exports f.o.b. (free on board) and imports c.i.f.. (cost of insurance and freight). Exports f.o.b. refers to the value of commodities when they are loaded on board the ship. Imports c.i.f. refers to the value of imports when they arrive, including the cost of insurance and freight. To see the magnitude of these costs, consider aircraft engines traded between two countries, e.g., Japan and Germany. If we compare the value of the aircraft engines exported f.o.b. from Germany to Japan with the value of the aircraft engines imported c.i.f. into Japan from Germany, we can estimate these transport costs. Figure 18.3 shows that the estimated transport costs using this method vary from around 2% for tobacco and transport equipment to around 9% for oil and stone. Whereas Figure 18.3 focuses on a few highly aggregated industries

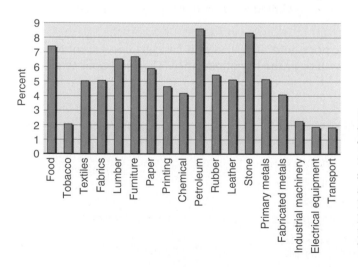

FIGURE 18.3 **Estimated transport costs for global trade.** The transport costs of tradeable commodities are significant. *Source*: Ravn and Mazzenga, "Frictions in International Trade and Relative Price Movements," London Business School Working Paper (1999).

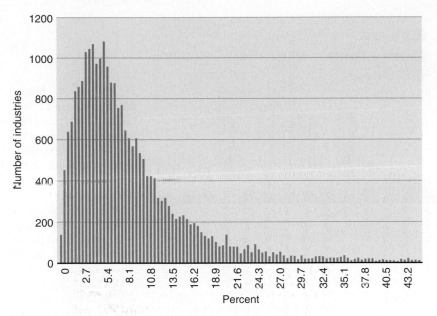

FIGURE 18.4   **Estimated transport costs for U.S. manufacturing imports.** Some industries have very large transport costs, which partly explains why the law of one price does not hold. *Source*: Ravn and Mazzenga, "Frictions in International Trade and Relative Price Movements, "London Business School Working Paper (1999).

covering all global trade, Figure 18.4 shows the distribution of transport costs for imports to the United States from over 25,000 manufacturing industries.

For most industries transport costs are under 10%. However, for a minority of industries, transport costs are over 25% of value. With transport costs of this magnitude, identical commodities sell for very different prices in different locations.

THE BORDER EFFECT

But transportation costs matter both between and within countries. San Francisco is a long way from Boston, so we can expect that the prices of televisions will be different in these cities just as they are between New York and Barcelona. However, close examination suggests that differences in prices between cities in the *same* country for the same commodity are small compared to the huge differences in price for the same commodity in *different* countries. This suggests that border effects are another reason why the law of one price fails to hold. The difference in prices for the same commodity increases not just with distance and transport costs but also when the commodity crosses a national border.

To see how important this border effect is, consider Figure 18.5, which measures the volatility or dispersion of prices across cities in the United States and Canada between 1978 and 1994. If prices were exactly the same in each city, volatility would be zero. The higher the measure, the greater the discrepancy between prices in different

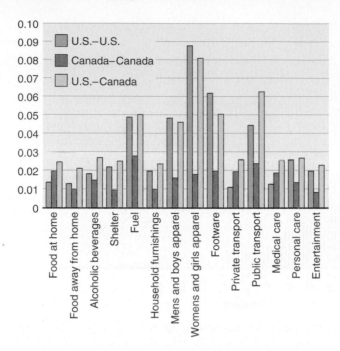

FIGURE 18.5 **Price differences between U.S. and Canadian cities.** Price differences between cities cannot be explain just by transport costs— differences in prices between U.S. and Canadian cities are greater than differences within countries regardless of distance apart. *Source*: Engel and Rogers , "How Wide Is the Border?" *American Economic Review* (1996) vol. 86, pp. 1112–1125. Reprinted with permission from American Economic Association.

cities. Figure 18.5 shows that except for three categories, the discrepancies between prices in Canadian and U.S. cities are larger than those between U.S. cities or between Canadian cities. The data in Figure 18.5 show that crossing a national border substantially increases price differences—it is equivalent to adding an additional 1800 miles of transport costs over and above the actual distance between a U.S. and Canadian city.

Why does the border matter so much? One reason is tariffs. Table 18.2 shows the average tariffs for several countries. Tariffs prevent arbitrage and are one reason why the law of one price fails to hold. There are other reasons—technical requirements (U.S. and Spanish television sets work on different electrical voltages, cars in the UK and Japan need to be right-hand drive but are left-hand drive in the United States and Continental Europe) or attempts by firms to obtain regional monopoly power (if a European buys a camera in the United States, for example, warranties are only valid in the United States). These factors reduce the role of arbitrage in establishing the law of one price.

More fundamental is that not all commodities are tradeable. If you live in Sydney, how can you take advantage of the cheaper haircuts in Delhi? Most goods have a substantial nontraded component. Consider a pineapple on sale in a supermarket. Its cost contains substantial amounts of nontraded input—the real estate cost of the supermarket, marketing and advertising, transport from wholesale to retailer, and so forth. All of these factors explain why the law of one price does not hold and why prices in different countries can be so different.

But we have not discussed the most important reason why prices differ so much between countries: prices in Spain are quoted in pesetas and prices in the United States in

TABLE 18.2 **Average Tariffs**

Region	Average Tariff (%)
Developed Countries	3.9
Canada	4.8
European Union	3.6
Japan	1.7
United States	3.0
Developing Countries	12.3
Economies in Transition	6.0

Source: Schott, *The Uruguay Round—An Assessment* (Institute for International Economics, 1994). Reprinted with permission.

TABLE 18.3 **Relative Price Volatility between and across European Cities**

	Variance of Change in Relative Prices		
	1 Month	1 Year	4 Years
Intranational	0.17	0.96	2.83
International	2.76	52.3	159.8
	Variance of Change In Exchange Rates		
International	2.62	53.1	159

Source. Engel and Rogers, "Donations from Purchasing Power Parts: Causes and Welfare Costs," Reprinted from Journal of International Economics (2001) Vol. 51, no. 1, with permission from Elsevier Science.

dollars. The peseta–dollar exchange rate changes daily, but the price of television sets in Barcelona and New York changes only occasionally. Therefore, the same commodity is not consistently sold for the same price (expressed in one currency) around the world. This combination of sticky retail prices and volatile nominal exchange rates not only helps explain why prices differ across countries, but also why the relative price of a commodity in different countries is so volatile.

Table 18.3, which focuses on 65 European cities between 1981 and 1997, shows evidence for this volatility for particular commodities (e.g., the ratio of Munich car prices to Paris car prices) both for cities within a country (*intranational*) and for cities in different countries (*international*) for one month, one year, and four years.

Table 18.3 shows that relative prices *between different* countries are far more volatile (by around 20 to 50 times) than relative prices *within* a country. The last row of the table shows why—the volatility in relative prices between countries is almost exactly the same as the volatility in exchange rates. What does this mean?

The law of one price says that an identical commodity should be priced the same in the United States and Spain. But this implies that *any* changes in the dollar–peseta exchange rate should also change U.S. dollar or Spanish peseta prices. Consider a television set that costs 15,000 pesetas in Spain and assume that there are 150 pesetas to the dollar. The law of one price says that the television should retail for $100 in the United States. If instead the exchange rate is 100 pesetas to the dollar, the U.S. price should be $150. But what happens when the currency changes, but the U.S. price remains $100? At the new exchange rate of 100 pesetas to the dollar, the cost of the television in the United States translates into 10,000 pesetas—much cheaper than the price in Spain. The law of one price fails to hold. In this case, the fall of a third in the exchange rate brings about a fall of a third in the relative price of the U.S. television set. The volatility in the exchange rate seems to match closely the volatility of relative prices across countries. Therefore, the main reason that the law of one price fails to hold is that while prices tend to be sticky in each country, nominal exchange rates tend to be volatile.

PRICING TO MARKET

Let's consider this result in more detail. Consider the case of a Spanish television manufacturer who sells to the United States. When the exchange rate is 150 pesetas to the dollar, its television set retails at $100. However, when the exchange rate goes to 100 pesetas, the firm should charge $150 to preserve the same peseta price. But this is a huge increase in price, which will undermine the competitiveness of Spanish products. Therefore, the Spanish producer may keep the U.S. retail price at $100 and sell the product for the equivalent of 10,000 pesetas in the United States but 15,000 in Spain. The Spanish producer is **pricing to market**—the price is set in dollars when selling to the U.S. market, taking into consideration U.S. circumstances rather than the domestic costs of production and the domestic selling price of the Spanish producer. Transport costs and tariffs mean that the Spanish firm can charge a different price for its product in New York and Barcelona, although if the exchange rate changes too much, the gap between the U.S. and Spanish price may get so wide that arbitrage occurs.

With pricing to market, the Spanish producer incurs production costs in pesetas but sets the U.S. sale price in dollars. Fluctuations in the exchange rate therefore do not change the dollar price at which Spanish televisions are sold. However, they do affect the peseta value that these U.S. sales generate. Therefore, with pricing to market, the Spanish firm's profit margin varies with changes in the exchange rate. This is why exchange rate fluctuations matter to exporters—a low exchange rate and a pricing to market strategy mean high profit margins, but when the exchange rate is high, the firm may even lose money if it keeps its foreign currency–denominated export prices fixed.

Pricing to market also opens up another issue—exchange rate pass-through. When the exchange rate depreciates, imports become more expensive when converted into domestic prices. The 15,000 peseta television rises in retail value from $100 to $150 in the U.S. if the law of one price holds. Therefore, a depreciating exchange rate may lead to higher import prices and thus put upward pressure on wages and inflation. Central banks are always concerned about this "pass-through" effect on inflation. However, if pricing to market occurs, then exchange rate changes need not lead to higher inflation—if the Spanish producer is pricing to the U.S. market, it charges $100 no matter what happens to the exchange rate.

The precise amount of pass-through obviously depends on different countries and different industries. If no U.S. television producers rival the Spanish firm, then pass-through of exchange rate changes will be higher, and dollar prices will rise as the dollar appreciates. But more competitive industries may have no pass through. Studies suggest that pass-through is never complete. For instance, one study finds that only around 50% of exchange rate volatility is passed through in changed prices of imports in the U.S.[1] For Germany, the estimate is 60% pass-through; for Japan, 70%. For Canada and Belgium, smaller economies and smaller markets, the pass-through is about 90%.

---

[1] Kreinin, "The Effect of Exchange Rate Changes on the Prices and Volume of Foreign Trade," *International Monetary Fund Staff Papers* (July 1977) vol. 24 no. 2., pp. 297–329.

18.3 Purchasing Power Parity

The law of one price is a crucial part of our first theory of real exchange rate determination: **purchasing power parity** (PPP). The law of one price refers to particular commodities. PPP applies the law of one price to *all* commodities—whether they are tradeables or not. Imagine going shopping in Germany and buying commodities that cost DM100. If in Japan the same purchases cost ¥5000, then according to PPP, the yen–DM exchange rate should be 5000/100 = 50. At this exchange rate, the yen price of the shopping equals the deutsche mark cost in Germany. Therefore PPP says

PPP nominal exchange rate = Japanese price / German price

If the German price increases to DM110 and the Japanese cost to ¥6000, then PPP implies that the exchange rate should adjust to 54.54 (=6000/110). It is worth going back to our definition of the real exchange rate to grasp the implications of PPP. We have

real ¥-DM exchange rate = nominal ¥-DM exchange rate × German prices / Japanese prices

But according to PPP, the nominal ¥-DM exchange rate equals Japanese prices divided by German prices, and putting this into our definition of the real exchange rate results in the value 1—things cost the same in each country. In other words, PPP implies that all countries are equally competitive, that commodity baskets cost the same the world over, and that the real exchange rate is forever equal to 1.

PPP further implies that because

PPP nominal exchange rate = Japanese price / German price

then

changes in ¥-DM exchange rate = Japanese inflation − German inflation

In other words, PPP implies that currencies depreciate if they have higher inflation and appreciate if they have lower inflation. We showed above that when the shopping cost is DM100 in Germany and ¥5000 in Japan, PPP implies an exchange rate of 50. If German inflation is 10%, so that costs increase to DM110, but Japanese inflation is 20%, so the price rises to ¥6000, PPP implies an exchange rate of 54.54.[2] This is an appreciation in the deutsche mark of around 10%—or the difference between German and Japanese inflation.

How well does PPP agree with historical evidence? We have already shown evidence that suggests that PPP will perform poorly—we saw that the real exchange rate is volatile and that the law of one price (the basis for PPP) holds for only a few commodities. However, PPP does have some successes—in particular, PPP appears to be a useful model for explaining long-run data.

---

[2]Although Japanese inflation is 10% higher than German inflation, the exchange rate does not depreciate by exactly 10% but by the factor $100\left(\dfrac{1.10}{1.20} - 1\right)$%—this is approximately −10%.

We can see the relative successes and failures of PPP in Figure 18.6*a, b, c, d,* which compares several countries' exchange rates and inflation rates relative to the United States over various time horizons. If PPP holds, the relationship should be one for one—for every 1% higher inflation a country has compared to the United States, its exchange rate should devalue by 1% against the dollar. In Figure 18.6*a,* which shows inflation and exchange rate depreciations for the last quarter of 2000, we see no evidence in favor of PPP. Over this period exchange rate fluctuations appeared to have nothing to do with inflation differences. Figure 18.6*b,* which looks at data for the whole of 2000, tells a similar story. In Figure 18.6*c,* which shows changes in the exchange rate over 1995–2000, the negative correlation of Figures 18.6*a* and 18.6*b* disappears, but no strong relationship between inflation and changes in the exchange rate emerges. However, Figure 18.6*d,* which shows averages over the last 20 years,

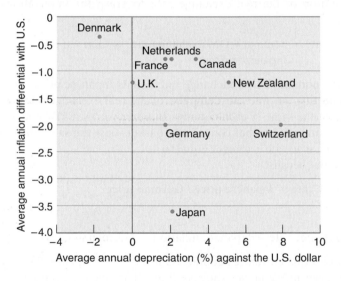

FIGURE 18.6a **Inflation and the quarterly change in exchange rates, 2000q4.** *Source*: IMF, *International Financial Statistics* (2000).

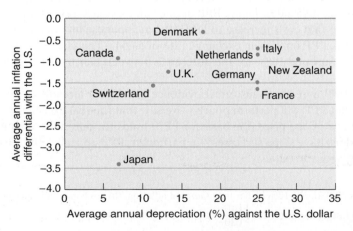

FIGURE 18.6b **Annual inflation and annual change in exchange rates, 1999q4–2000q4.** *Source*: IMF, *International Financial Statistics* (2000). Courtesy of IMF.

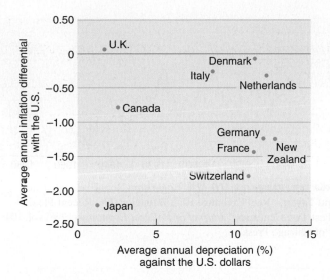

FIGURE 18.6c **Average inflation differential and depreciation, 1995q4–2000q4.** *Source*: IMF, *International Financial Statistics* (2000). Courtesy of IMF.

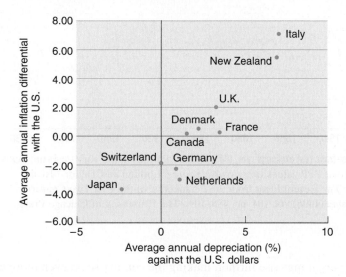

FIGURE 18.6d **Average inflation differential and depreciation, 1980q4–2000q4.** Over short periods of time PPP is a poor explanation of exchange rates, but over 20-year periods it performs extremely well. *Source*: IMF, *International Financial Statistics* (2000). Courtesy of IMF.

finally supports PPP. Over long periods the currency of high inflation countries does seem to depreciate.

Figures 18.7*a* and 18.7*b*, which plot the real exchange rate between the UK and the United States from 1791 and for the UK and France since 1805 offer further support for the long-run validity of PPP. Figure 18.7 supports the weakest implications of PPP—there is some average value to which the real exchange rate eventually returns (the zero line). The exchange rate may not return to this long-run average value for decades, but eventually it does—a country does not stay forever overpriced. However, the correction in the real exchange rate overvaluation is not immediate, and before the

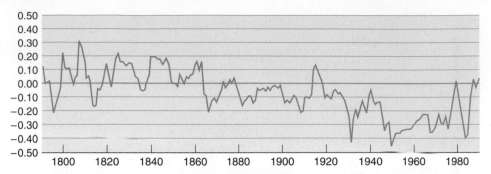

FIGURE 18.7a   **Sterling–dollar real exchange rate, 1791–1990.** Logarithm Real Exchange Rate (ppp = 0) *Source*: Lothian and Taylor, "Real Exchange Rate Behavior: The Recent Float from the Perspective of the Past Two Centuries," *Journal of Political Economy* (1996) vol. 104, pp. 488–509. The University of Chicago Press.

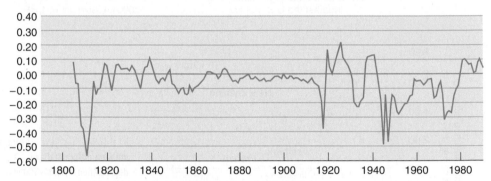

FIGURE 18.7b   **Sterling–franc real exchange rate, 1805–1990.** PPP holds in the very long run, but real exchange rates return to their PPP values very slowly. *Source*: Lothian and Taylor, "Real Exchange Rate Behavior: The Recent Float from the Perspective of the Past Two Centuries," *Journal of Political Economy* (1996) vol. 104, pp. 488–509. The University of Chicago Press.

real exchange rate declines, it may rise further, making the country seem even more expensive. The forces that bring about equality of prices are weak and take a long time to work.

Therefore, we should not discard PPP completely—over decades depreciations of nominal currencies are related to inflation differentials. However, PPP does not offer a reliable guide to the short-run volatility of real and nominal exchange rates.

PPP is a more reliable guide to short-term exchange rate fluctuations for countries that have very high inflation rates. Figure 18.8, where we plot the quarterly percentage Brazilian inflation rate and the quarterly depreciation of the currency against the U.S. dollar, shows this. Although the link is not exact, inflation and depreciation are much more closely connected in the short run for hyperinflation countries than for the OECD countries in Figure 18.6.

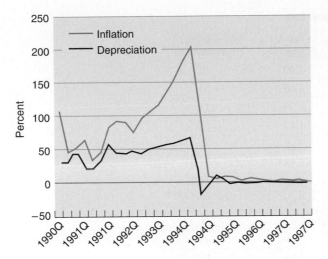

THE BIG MAC INDEX

The *Economist* magazine popularizes a version of PPP with its Big Mac index. Under PPP identical commodities should sell for the same price wherever they are sold. The *Economist* uses the domestic price of Big Macs to estimate PPP exchange rates. The Big Mac PPP estimate is the ratio of the price of Big Macs in each country. For instance, if a Big Mac costs $1 in the U.S. and 10Fr in France, the implied Big Mac exchange rate is 10Fr:$1. If the actual exchange rate is 7Fr:$1, then the French currency is overvalued—French Big Macs are more expensive than American ones.

Table 18.4 shows actual exchange rates and the Big Mac PPP exchange rates in April 2000 and the implied over- or undervaluation. If we use the Big Mac rates as a guide to PPP, the currencies in China, Indonesia, and Hungary are undervalued. The Danish krona and the British pound were overvalued and restoration of PPP would involve their depreciation. Unfortunately a trading strategy based on the Big Mac index is unlikely to make you rich. As we have stressed, PPP is a long-run influence on exchange rates, and PPP rates exert only a weak attraction for exchange rates. In the short term, an undervalued currency can become even more undervalued relative to PPP measures, and it may take decades to return to its PPP level. While the currency becomes more undervalued, the Big Mac inspired trade will be losing money.

The Big Mac index has other problems over and above failures of PPP. First, the Big Mac has more to do with the law of one price than with PPP—it refers to one commodity rather than a basket of goods. Second, the Big Mac may be identical across countries, but it is not tradeable—a freshly cooked Big Mac in London is a different commodity from a reheated one imported from China. Third, Big Macs are not identical—a Big Mac consumed in Tokyo reflects the cost of rent for a retail outlet in Tokyo

TABLE 18.4   **Big Mac Exchange Rates**

	Big Mac Exchange Rate	Actual Exchange Rate	Over(+)/Under(−) Valuation
Argentina	1.00	1.00	0
Australia	1.03	1.68	−38
Brazil	1.18	1.79	−34
Canada	1.14	1.47	−23
Chile	502	514	−2
China	3.87	8.28	−53
Czech Republic	21.7	39.1	−45
Denmark	9.28	7.62	32
France	7.37	7.07	4
Germany	1.99	2.11	−6
Hong Kong	4.06	7.79	−48
Hungary	135	279	−52
Indonesia	5777	7945	−27
Japan	117	106	11
Malaysia	1.80	3.80	−53
Russia	15.7	28.5	−45
Sweden	9.56	8.84	8
United Kingdom	1.32	1.58	20

Source: *The Economist* (April 27, 2000). © The Economist
Newspaper Limited, London (1951).

plus various local labor and indirect taxes. This makes it a different commodity from a Big Mac sold in Manila. Finally, transport costs are high relative to the price of a Big Mac. For this reason the Russian price of a Big Mac may always be lower than that of one in Copenhagen without affecting the rouble–krona exchange rate.

WHY DO RICH COUNTRIES HAVE HIGHER PRICES?

One systematic deviation from PPP is that prices tend to be higher in industrial economies than in emerging nations—as Figure 18.9 shows. This is known as the **Balassa-Samuelson effect**. The Balassa-Samuelson explanation assumes that productivity growth in the service sector (which is substantially nontradeable) is lower than in the tradeable sector. In other words, it is harder to boost the productivity of hairdressers than manufacturing firms. How does this explain price differences across countries? With rising productivity in the tradeable sector, producer real wages (wages divided by output prices) will be increasing in these industries (see Chapter 8). If the nontradeable

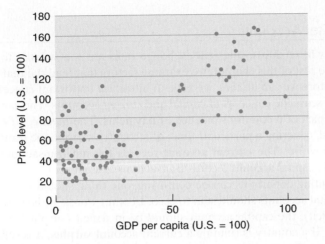

FIGURE 18.9 **Wealthy countries have high prices.** Prices in OECD countries are higher than in the developing world. *Source*: Summers and Heston dataset, http://cansim.chass.utoronto.ca:5680/pwt/

sector is to continue to hire workers, then wages in the nontradeable sector will also have to rise in line with those in the tradeable sector. However, the nontradeable sector does not have the productivity improvements that boost wages in the tradeable sector, so the only way to finance higher wages is to charge a higher price for services. This can be done because there is no threat of foreign competition. The result is higher prices (originating from the nontradeable sector) in countries with high levels of productivity in the tradeable sector.

Figure 18.10, which shows, for a group of 13 OECD countries, the relationship between nontradeable inflation and the gap between productivity in the tradeable and nontradeable sector, offers further support for the Balassa-Samuelson effect. According to the Balassa-Samuelson theory, countries with higher productivity in tradeable sectors will have to have higher nontradeable wages and thus higher nontradeable inflation—this is exactly what Figure 18.10 shows.

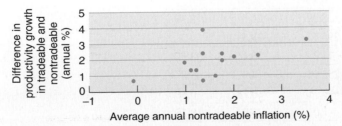

FIGURE 18.10 **The Balassa-Samuelson effect, OECD, 1960–1998.** High productivity in the tradeable sector leads to high inflation in the nontradeable sector as wages rise across the economy. *Source*: Authors' calculations from OECD data.

18.4   Current and Capital Accounts

The previous sections have shown that real exchange rates are too volatile to be consistent with PPP. In the rest of this chapter, we examine factors that lead the real exchange rate to change. Before we can do that, we have to introduce important concepts. In particular we have to discuss the concepts of *capital* and *current* accounts. The capital and current accounts are part of a country's balance of payments. The *balance of payments* is a statistical record, covering a particular time, of a country's economic transactions with the rest of the world. The **current account** records the net transactions in goods and services, and the **capital account** records transactions in assets between countries. Although the accounting definitions can be confusing, one thing should be made clear: the current and capital accounts should sum to zero. In other words, if the current account is in surplus (deficit), the capital account should be in deficit (surplus) by an equivalent amount. Why? If a country is running a current account surplus, it is selling more goods and services overseas than it is purchasing and thus has a surplus of foreign currency. This foreign currency has to go somewhere, and the financial system will recycle it to buy overseas assets. Buying overseas assets leads to a capital account deficit because foreign currency is used to finance the purchases. That is why the current and capital accounts must sum to zero.

THE CURRENT ACCOUNT

The current account measures the net flow of goods and services between a country and the rest of the world. It consists of records of four main types of trade: in goods, services, income, and transfers. Let's start with trade in goods. Countries both

TABLE 18.5   Capital and Current Account Flows, 1997 ($bn)

	United States	United Kingdom	Thailand
Balance Goods, Services, and Income	−115.53	17.85	−3.5
Net Current Transfers	−39.85	−7.81	0.48
Current Account	−155.35	10.04	−3.02
Capital Account	0.16	1.37	−
Net Direct Investment	−28.39	−26.5	3.35
Net Portfolio Investment	295.53	−38.5	4.3
Net Other Investment	−11.2	50.4	−23.5
Financial Account	255.94	−14.6	−15.8
Net Errors and Omissions	−99.71	−0.74	0.58
Overall Balance	1.01	−3.9	−18.25
Reserve Assets	−1.01	3.9	18.25

Source: IMF, *International Financial Statistics* (March 1999).
Courtesy of IMF.

export and import goods (automobiles, wheat, oil, etc). For instance, in 1997 the UK exported to the rest of the world $281.3 billion worth of goods and imported $300.8 billion. Therefore, its net exports of goods were −$19.5 billion—what economists term a *balance of trade* deficit. However, trade in services is also important. Services account for a broad collection of activities—such as transport services, telecommunications, legal and financial services—and in 1997, UK exports of services were $93.8 billion against imports of $74.3 billion providing a surplus on services of $19.5 billion. Therefore, the surplus on services offset the deficit on goods, so that the UK had a balance on its trade in goods and services of zero (subject to rounding error).

There are two other aspects of the current account: income and transfers. As we shall see when we study the capital account, the UK owns assets overseas, and foreign companies own assets in the UK. For instance, UK pension funds and insurance companies have invested in the United States and Japanese stock markets, and firms such as Nissan and Merrill Lynch own factories and offices in the UK. The UK funds invested overseas earn interest and dividends that are paid to UK investors. Similarly, Nissan, UK, sends profits and dividends back to Nissan, Japan. The current account records these income flows (but *not* the investment flows). We can think of the money invested in Nissan, UK, as Nissan lending machinery to the UK—in other words, providing productive services. In return for these services, a dividend is paid, but it represents payment for an economic service provided (the provision of machinery). The current account represents a measure of all the transactions in goods and services between a country and the rest of the world and so should contain this income measure. However, as we shall see below, when Nissan makes its investment in the UK, it is acquiring an asset and not providing a productive service. So that investment will appear in the capital account; any future income flows arising from the transaction will feature in the current account. In 1997 the UK received $176.6 billion in income on its current account and paid out $158.7 billion leaving a credit of $17.9 billion. Therefore, the UK's balance of payments on goods, services, and income was $17.9 billion, as shown in Table 18.5.

The current account has one final component, which reflects transfer payments. Transfer payments occur when no asset or good is provided in return for money paid. For instance, if the UK donates resources to Venezuela for flood relief, this is a transfer payment because either goods or money flows in one direction only. In 1997 the UK paid out $7.8 billion in net transfers. If we add this to the balance on goods, services, and income, we have the current account—for the UK in 1997, a $10 billion surplus. The UK earned $10 billion more from its exports of goods and services, and from income received, than it paid out on total imports, income on foreign assets based in the UK, and transfers.

current account = balance of trade (exports goods—imports goods)

+ balance on services (exports services—imports services)

+ investment income and dividends

+ Net Transfers

CAPITAL ACCOUNT

The current account records transactions in goods and services between a country and the rest of the world. The capital account records transactions in assets—both financial and nonfinancial. Strictly speaking, we should refer to the *capital and financial account*, where the *capital account* refers to capital transfers (such as debt forgiveness) as well as the acquisition or disposal of nonproduced, nonfinancial assets (like copyright ownership and patents), and the *financial account* refers to the acquisition and disposal of financial assets.[3] However, this distinction is rare, and we normally refer to the whole of the capital and financial account as just the *capital account*. We shall follow this practice throughout this chapter, except in the next few paragraphs, where we distinguish between the capital and financial accounts.

Table 18.5 shows that in 1997 the United States had a small surplus on its capital account of $0.16 billion. A surplus means that the United States was a net recipient of funds, which could have arisen either from a government transfer or more likely the United States selling a nonproduced, nonfinancial asset, for example, royalty rights on a record label or movie or the sale of a chemical patent. However, the size of the financial account dominates these sorts of asset flows. The following gives the financial account:

$$\text{financial account} = \text{net direct investment} + \text{net portfolio flows} + \text{net other investment}$$

Each of the these terms on the right-hand side reflects how the United States is transacting with the rest of the world over various asset classes. *Direct investment* is when an individual or firm in one country acquires a lasting interest in an enterprise resident in another economy. Direct investment implies a long-term relationship between the investor and the recipient firm in which the investor has significant influence over the enterprise.[4] For instance, if Coca-Cola, U.S., opens a bottling factory in the Philippines, it would count as U.S. foreign direct investment abroad. If Toshiba opens a production factory in California, it would count as Japanese foreign direct investment abroad. Here we need to be careful about what signs we use when we measure the financial account. When Coca-Cola opens its Philippines bottling plant, it is in effect purchasing an overseas asset. Therefore, U.S. investment overseas counts as a negative for the U.S. financial account. Just as the U.S. purchase of cars made in the Philippines would count as a current account import, so the U.S. purchase of a bottling factory in the Philippines counts as a capital account import. Table 18.5 shows that in 1997, the United States had a deficit of $28.4 billion on direct investment (consisting of $121.84 billion of foreign investment compared to investment in the United States by foreign firms of $93.45 billion).

The portfolio assets section of the financial account refers to various assets, but mainly equities and bonds. In 1997 for the United States, this part of the financial

---

[3]For those of you who wish to speak strictly on balance of payments accounting issues there is no better place to learn than the IMF's *Balance of Payments Textbook*, which is updated occasionally. This offers a complete overview of the structure of balance of payments accounting as well as detailed definitions of various terms.

[4]The investor does not, however, have to have majority control—a 10% stake or more is normally enough. See IMF, *Balance of Payments Textbook*, p. 107.

account saw a surplus of $295.5 billion—the United States sold this many more equities and bonds than it bought from overseas. This is an unusually high financial inflow and reflects the extraordinary events of 1997 (we discuss the Asian crisis in detail in Chapter 19). As Table 18.5 shows, this large inflow of money into U.S. bonds and equities occurred at the same time as outflows from the Thai markets, as U.S. investors fled from volatile emerging market funds, and Thai investors sought to invest in dollar assets before their own currencies depreciated.

Another part of the financial account is investment in other assets. As its name suggests, it reflects a range of different transactions (such as trade credit), but its most important category is bank deposits and bank loans. When a U.S. investor places funds on deposit in a London account, the funds will appear in the "other investment" category (with a negative sign for the United States—the United States is acquiring an asset in the UK). When a Korean firm borrows from a New York–based bank, the loan will also show up in this category (as a positive term—the Korean economy has increased its liabilities to the rest of the world). In 1997 the United States had a deficit of $11.2 billion in this other investment category.

The final part of the capital account is the *reserve asset* category. This reflects mainly the government's financial interactions with the rest of the world, and in particular, with other governments. More specifically, reserve assets are the means governments use to avoid financing problems and balance of payments problems. But what do we mean by balance of payments problems?

Consider the case of Thailand in 1997 (see Table 18.5), which had a current account deficit of $3.02 billion. This means that counting trade in goods and services, and allowing for income and transfers, the Thai economy purchased $3.02 billion more commodities from abroad than it sold to foreign countries. Somehow it had to finance this $3 billion deficit (find $3 billion of foreign currency) and this is reflected in the capital and financial account (remember that the capital and current accounts have to sum to zero). However, the financial account shows a deficit of $15.8 billion—in 1997 domestic and foreign investors withdrew their money from Thai banks and financial markets and sent it to the United States and elsewhere. Far from providing the necessary foreign currency to settle current account flows, the financial account created the need for an additional $15.8 billion of foreign currency. The Thai economy had to find $18.25 billion of foreign currency to fund the financial account.[5] This is what we call a **balance of payments problem**—the capital and financial account are not providing the foreign currency needed to fund the current account deficit.

Governments have various means to try to solve such a balance of payments problem. The central bank can sell any foreign currency reserves it possesses. In 1997 Thailand had a desperate shortage of foreign currency, and as a result, the domestic currency was falling. If the Thai central bank had stocks of dollars and yen, it could intervene in the market and sell them (thus providing the desired foreign currency) and buy baht to try to increase the value of the baht. However, if the central bank has sold all its reserves, then it has to finance the balance of payments crisis in other ways. This

---

[5] Note that the current account and financial account deficit do not add to the total financing number we quote. This is because of a term called "errors and omissions"—more of which later.

is where the International Monetary Fund (IMF) and other international institutions play a role. By transferring funds to Thailand and arranging exceptional financing (which allow Thailand to borrow foreign currency from other central banks), they can use reserve assets to finance the balance of payments crisis. In fact in 1997, the official financing of $18.25 billion in Thailand was made up by $9.9 billion of reserve sales by the Thai central bank, a $2.4 billion loan from the IMF, and exceptional financing of $5.9 billion (mainly loans from other central banks).

The financial account is the sum of all these four categories (direct investment, portfolio investment, other investment, and reserve changes in assets). For the United States in 1997 the financial account was

$28.4bn (net direct investment) + $295.5 bn (net portfolio investment)

− $11.2bn (net other investment)

= a surplus of $254.9bn

Add to this the capital account surplus of $0.16 billion and the change in reserve assets and the United States was the net recipient of just over $255 billion in 1997 through its capital and financial transactions.

However, in 1997 the U.S. current account deficit was $155.4 billion. In other words, the U.S. economy only required an inflow of about $155 billion to finance its current account deficit but instead took in $255 billion—around $100 billion too much. This brings us to the last term in our exhaustive discussion of capital and current accounts: *errors and omissions*. Logging all the financial transactions between a country and the rest of the world is a Herculean task. First, some transactions just do not want to be registered—money laundering— so these transactions will be excluded from the balance of payments. Second, even legitimate transactions will not always come to the attention of statisticians. For these reasons, the capital and financial account will not always exactly offset the current accounts, and the size of the discrepancy is a measure of the magnitude of the errors and omissions made in the calculations. Thus for the United States in 1997, the errors and omissions are calculated as an enormous $99.7 billion—around two-thirds of the current account itself. By definition these errors and omissions are unmeasured—they are recorded as $99.7 billion only because that is the value that ensures that the current and capital accounts offset each other.

18.5 Who Is Rich and Who Is Poor?

The capital account records disposals and acquisitions of assets within a particular period, it is therefore a flow concept. If a country is running a capital account deficit (buying overseas assets every year), then its *stock* of overseas assets is rising. Further, if this stock of wealth is invested in assets that earn a positive rate of return, then the wealth is increasing *even if there is no further capital account deficits/overseas investment*. The net *international investment position* (IIP) measures this stock of external wealth. If this is a positive number, then a country has more foreign assets than it has liabilities; if it is negative, then the country owes the rest of the world money.

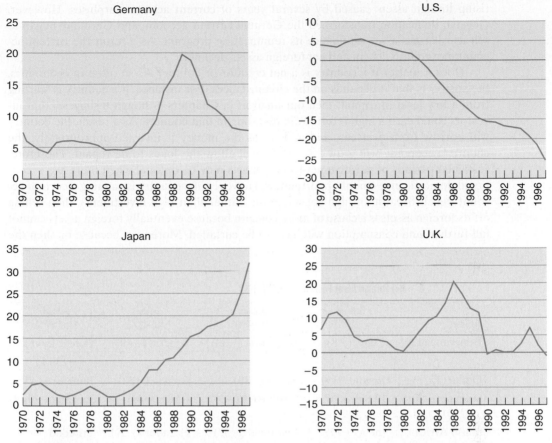

FIGURE 18.11 **Net foreign assets (% GDP).** Germany and Japan are important global creditors; the United States is a debtor. *Source:* Lane and Milessi-Ferretti, "The External Wealth of Nations," CEPR Discussion Paper 2231 (1999).

Figure 18.11 shows the net IIP (expressed as a percentage of GDP) for the United States, Japan, Germany, and the UK between 1970 and 1997. Throughout this period Germany and Japan had net overseas assets, whereas the United States and the UK had switched from being creditor nations to debtor nations. The slow deterioration of the U.S. position from a positive stock of around 10% of GDP to a net debt of 15% reflects the years of persistent current account deficits. Capital account surpluses have to offset current account deficits, which means selling U.S. assets or overseas investors gaining claims over U.S. assets, hence the deterioration in the U.S. stock of net overseas assets. By contrast, the Japanese graph shows a continual increase in overseas assets from a stock of around 3% of GDP in 1970 to over 30% by 1997. The ability of the Japanese economy to generate current account surpluses means that Japan continually had capital account deficits. Capital account deficits mean that a country is buying more assets overseas than it is selling domestic assets to foreign investors. As a result, its stock of foreign wealth rises. Until 1989 Germany experienced a similar pattern of rising foreign assets caused by several years of current account surpluses. However, German unification transformed the German current account, and Germany began to sell its overseas assets to finance its reunification program. As a result the current account moved into deficit, and net foreign assets declined.

Does it matter if a country is a net creditor or debtor? As so often in economics, the answer is that it depends on the circumstances. For instance, if a country is starting from a low level of capital, then our analysis in Chapters 4 though 6 suggests that investors could earn a high return from investing in that country. As a result, the country will borrow from overseas, and as long as the money is invested appropriately, the country's economy will grow fast, which will allow the loans to be repaid. Therefore, sustained periods of negative net foreign assets may be optimal when there are exceptional domestic investment opportunities. However, if a country is running a current account deficit because of high consumption (rather than high investment), then selling off its foreign assets is a cause of more concern because eventually foreign assets cannot fall further, and consumption will have to be curtailed. Moreover, because by then the

TABLE 18.6 **Net Foreign Asset Position (% GDP), 1997**

Creditors	Debtors (0–20%)	Debtors (20–40%)	Debtors (40–60%)	Debtors (over 60%)
Botswana (120)	China (−8)	Argentina (−33)	Algeria (−49)	Cote d'Ivoire (−139.1)
Oman (15)	Egypt (−19)	Brazil (−30)	Bolivia (−52)	Jamaica (−79)
Singapore (210)	El Salvador (−9)	Costa Rica (−37)	Chile (−48)	Jordan (−70)
South Africa (16)	India (−17)	Colombia (−32)	Ecuador (−57)	Trinidad (−80)
Taiwan (49)	Israel (−12)	Dominican Republic (−36)	Indonesia (−54)	
Uruguay (11)	Korea (−5)	Guatemala (−28)	Malaysia (−45)	
Venezuela (16)	Austria (−10)	Mauritius (−33)	Mexico (−43)	
Netherlands (27)	Belgium (−9)	Paraguay (−21)	Morocco (−41)	
Norway (19)	Spain (−18)	Philippines (−32)	Pakistan (−50)	
Switzerland (48)		Sri Lanka (−38)	Peru (−47)	
France (3)		Syria (−22)	Thailand (−47)	
		Turkey (−30)	Tunisia (−43)	
		Finland (−21)	Zimbabwe (−55)	
		Greece (−40)	Australia (−55)	
		Canada (−24)		

Source: Lane and Milesi-Ferretti, "The External Wealth of Nations: Measures of Foreign Assets and Liabilities for Industrial and Developing Countries," CEPR Discussion Paper 2231(1999).

country has fewer foreign assets, it will be earning less overseas interest and so will have to lower consumption even more. In the next chapter, we shall consider currency crashes and see that an undue reliance on foreign loans (negative foreign assets), particularly short-term foreign currency loans, can be particularly problematic for a country.

Note also that a stock of overseas assets enables a country to potentially run a continual current account deficit. A country can always maintain a current account deficit if it also has a capital account surplus. A capital account surplus means that a country is selling its assets to overseas investors. If the Netherlands has a stock of overseas assets, then these will be increasing every year either through interest and dividends or because of capital gains. If the Netherlands every year sells foreign assets equal to these gains, then it will create a capital account surplus (it is selling Dutch assets) while maintaining a constant level of foreign assets (it only sells the gains it realizes from the assets, not the capital itself). It can thus maintain a continuous current account deficit if desired. Table 18.6 shows the debtor and creditor status of several countries in 1997.

18.6 A BIG Equation

One reason for outlining in such detail the current and capital accounts was that these concepts help us understand why the real exchange rate is volatile. To grasp this, we need to consider the following crucial equation:

net savings (savings − investment) = net exports (exports − imports)

We have already come across this formula—it says that the capital account deficit (surplus) must equal the current account surplus (deficit). Net exports are total exports less total imports, which is the current account surplus. But why does net savings—or the surplus of savings over investment—equal the capital account deficit? Consider the case in which net savings is positive—savings within a country exceed investment. The banking system can therefore finance all the domestic investment needs of a country and still have surplus deposit funds left over. But banks want to make a profit and will not simply sit on these surplus funds. Instead they will lend them overseas and earn a profit on them. But lending money overseas means that a country gains a claim over agents in another country—this is the same as running a capital account deficit. If the surplus savings are invested in overseas equity markets, then the portfolio asset part of the financial account will show a deficit. If instead the bank lends the money to an overseas firm, then the other investment category of the capital account will show a deficit. Either way the level of net savings is equal to the capital account deficit; that net savings equals net exports is just another way of saying that the capital and the current accounts sum to zero.

But why does net savings equal net exports? To show this, we need to return to the national accounts—the way of recording how output is used that we studied in Chapter 2. There we showed that GDP (Y) is used in one of four ways—as consumption (C), investment in physical machinery or buildings (I), as government expenditure on goods and services (G), or as net exports (X−M). Therefore,

$$Y = C + I + G + (X - M)$$

Or alternatively, if we subtract from GDP the amount of consumption, we are left with the sum of investment, government expenditure, and net exports

$$(X - M) + I + G = Y - C \tag{1}$$

However, as we also discussed in Chapter 2, GDP is a measure of income, not just of output. The income that the economy earns is used in one of three ways: it is spent as consumption (C); it is used to pay taxes (T); or it is saved in the financial system (S). Therefore

$$Y = C + T + S$$

Or if we take away from income the amount of consumption, what is left is the amount of savings and taxes the economy pays

$$T + S = Y - C \tag{2}$$

Comparing (1) and (2) we can see that they both equal the same amount: $Y - C$. Therefore $I + G + (X - M)$ must have the same value as $T + S$. Therefore

$$I + G + (X - M) = T + S$$

We can rewrite this as

$$X - M = T - G + S - I$$

The term $X - M$ is just net exports—the current account surplus. The other side of the equation refers to savings in the economy. The term $T - G$ is the government's fiscal surplus and is the amount of savings by the government. The term $S - I$ is the private sector's net savings—their total savings less their total investment. Thus $T - G + S - I$ denotes total savings in the economy; this equals the capital account deficit.

We can use the fact that net savings equals net exports to consider some of the factors that alter the current account. Consider the case of an economy that starts to run a large fiscal deficit. If net savings by the private sector do not increase, the larger fiscal deficit means a lower level of net national savings. This in turn means that the capital account deficit will fall and may even become a surplus as the government's financial needs mean that less funds are available for overseas investment. A falling capital account deficit (e.g., a move into surplus) means a deteriorating current account deficit, so that a fiscal expansion leading to a larger public sector deficit will *worsen* the current

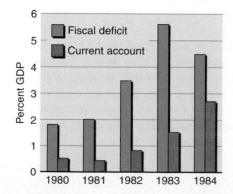

FIGURE 18.12   **U.S. fiscal expansion leads to current account deficit.** Fiscal deficits lead to worsening of the current account. *Source*: IMF, *International Financial Statistics* (September 2000). Courtesy of IMF.

account. Figure 18.12 shows this is what happened in the United States in the early 1980s. In the early years of the Reagan administration the fiscal deficit widened because of tax cuts and increased military expenditure and the current account simultaneously deteriorated.

THE ROLE OF THE REAL EXCHANGE RATE

What mechanism assures that net savings equals net exports? After all, the people who are deciding whether to save and invest are different from those considering whether to export or import, so the two need not be equal. We will now outline a model that gives a key role for the real exchange rate in achieving balance between net savings and net investment and use this to explain the volatility of the real exchange rate.

Our key assumption is that the real exchange rate does not influence the level of net savings but does affect net exports. As outlined at the beginning of this chapter, the real exchange rate reflects a country's competitiveness—the higher its real exchange rate, the more expensive its commodities are to overseas residents. With a high real exchange rate, a country's exports will be low and imports high because foreign goods are cheap. Therefore, the higher the real exchange rate, the lower the level of net exports and the higher the current account deficit. Figure 18.13 shows this negative relationship between the real exchange rate and net exports.

Figure 18.13 suggests that when countries experience a real depreciation their current account should ultimately improve. We stress two features of this statement. First, it is the *real* exchange rate that matters. If the nominal exchange rate falls but is offset by higher domestic inflation, so that the real exchange rate is unaltered, then there is no effect on net exports. Second, the beneficial effect of the depreciation may not be immediately felt. In fact in the short term, the current account may worsen. When the real exchange rate depreciates, the cost of imports rises in domestic currency terms. Eventually this higher cost of imports will lead to a lower demand for them, and net exports will improve. However, in the short run, firms and individuals may be contracted to purchase, at specified *foreign currency* prices, goods from overseas. While these contracts are in force, the costs of imports will rise without offsetting benefits from reduced demand. Of course, as contracts come up for renewal, the extra cost means that many will be cancelled, and net exports will improve. Therefore the depreciation of the real exchange rate may lead the current account to deteriorate at first before an

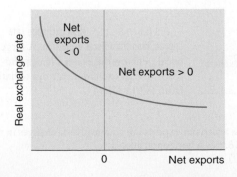

FIGURE 18.13 **Real exchange rate and net exports.**
Net exports rise when the real exchange rate falls.

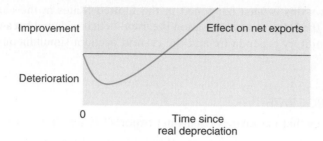

FIGURE 18.14 J curve. The current account initially worsens before improving after real depreciation.

improvement occurs. It may take six months or more before the improvement manifests itself. Economists call this delayed beneficial effect on the current account the J-curve effect for reasons that should be obvious from Figure 18.14.

We can now complete our model and show how the real exchange rate will alter in response to changes in the economy. Consider again the case of the Reagan fiscal expansion, which through a larger fiscal deficit produced a lower level of net savings (larger capital account surplus), which in turn required a lower level of net exports (larger current account deficit). To produce this larger current account deficit, the real exchange rate has to rise. A higher real exchange rate makes U.S. goods more expensive and overseas goods cheaper, which leads the current account to deteriorate. Therefore, the real exchange rate has to change to equate net savings and net exports; clearly this is not in line with the implications of purchasing power parity.[6] Figure 18.15 models the effect of this fiscal expansion on the real exchange rate.

This helps explain what happened in the United States in the early 1980s—a large fiscal deficit leading to a substantial real appreciation (Figure 18.16). Figure 18.17 shows that the same phenomenon occurred in Germany during the early 1990s after the large fiscal deficit that unification caused.

However, it is not just changes in net savings (driven by changes in fiscal policy, private sector savings, or investment) that cause the real exchange rate to fluctuate. Anything that shifts the net export schedule will also change the real exchange rate. Consider what happens when Mediterranean goods suddenly become fashionable. At

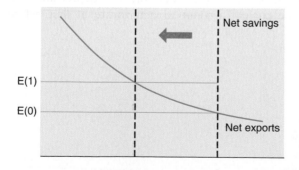

FIGURE 18.15 Real exchange rate appreciation from fiscal expansion. A large fiscal deficit reduces net savings and leads to real exchange rate appreciation from E(0) to E(1).

[6]In fact PPP is a special cases of our model in which net exports are so sensitive to changes in relative prices that the net export schedule in Figure 18.15 is a horizontal line.

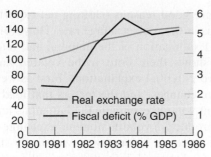

FIGURE 18.16 U S fiscal expansion and dollar appreciation. Reagan-era deficits led to the dollar rising. *Source*: IMF, *International Financial Statistics* (September 2000).

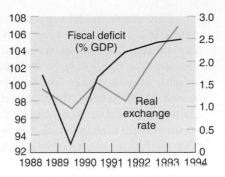

FIGURE 18.17 Real appreciation after German unification. The deutsche mark appreciated in the wake of large deficits caused by unification. *Source*: IMF, *International Financial Statistics* (September 2000). Courtesy of IMF.

any particular real exchange rate, exports from Italy and Spain will be higher than before—the net export schedule shifts to the right, as in Figure 18.18. However, net savings have not altered, so as a result neither can net exports—the capital and current accounts must sum to zero. But, at the existing exchange rate, Italian net exports have increased and will be greater than net savings. Because this cannot happen, the real exchange rate will have to increase to choke off the demand for Italian goods. Figure 18.18 shows this case—in which the increased demand for Italian goods leads to an appreciation of the exchange rate from E(0) to E(1).

Note that we can use the same diagram to examine import controls. If a government introduces import controls, then for a given real exchange rate, the level of imports is reduced, but exports are unchanged, so that net exports increase *for a particular exchange rate*. But import controls can only influence the current account if they also affect net savings or the capital account. In our analysis the introduction of import controls does not affect the level of net savings and thus cannot affect the current account deficit. As a result, the real exchange rate has to rise to reduce exports in line with the reduction in imports that import controls caused.

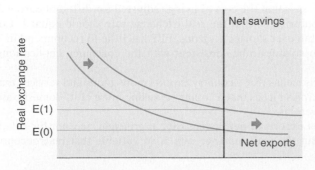

FIGURE 18.18 Shift in export demand and real appreciation. An increase in demand for a country's net exports leads to appreciation.

This simple model suggests that there are good reasons (shifting net export and net savings curves) for expecting fluctuations in the real exchange rate. However, the key question here is one we posed earlier. Examination of the nominal and real exchange rate (e.g., Figures 18.1 and 18.2) shows them both to be volatile and to roughly move together. These facts have two potential explanations. First as we suggested in this section, the real exchange rate changes, and the factors that lead it to change are volatile. According to this account volatile economic fundamentals lead to a volatile real exchange rate, which in turn produces a volatile nominal exchange rate. The alternative explanation is that because prices in a country are relatively sticky, then changes in the nominal exchange rate feed through into changes in the real exchange rate. According to that analysis, we need to focus on the nominal exchange rate, and in particular monetary models, to understand the volatility of the real exchange rate.

Which of these two explanations is correct? While opinions differ, the general consensus is that real exchange rates are far too volatile to be explained by changes in the macroeconomic fundamentals that underpin the net exports and net savings curve. As our analysis of the Reagan years and German unification show, we can use changes in macroeconomic fundamentals to explain some of the fluctuations in the real exchange rate. However, the real exchange rate is too volatile for changes in fundamentals to explain fluctuations. For that reason, in Chapter 19 we will discuss changes in the nominal exchange rate.

SUMMARY

The nominal exchange rate reflects the rate at which you can swap different currencies, whereas the real exchange rate represents the relative cheapness of one country compared to another.

The law of one price implies that the same good should sell for the same price, making allowance for different currencies, wherever it is sold. However, transport costs, tariffs, monopoly practices, and transaction costs mean that similar commodities sold in different places are effectively different commodities and can sell for different prices. Differences in prices are far more marked than trade restrictions and transport costs alone would merit.

Purchasing power parity says that the cost of living (adjusted for different currencies) should be the same in all countries, so that the real exchange rate should equal 1. Long-run evidence supports PPP, but over shorter horizons, PPP has little to recommend it. The real exchange rate is far too volatile to be consistent with the constancy implications of PPP.

A current account surplus means that a country exports more goods and services than it imports. A capital account surplus means that a country is selling more of its domestic assets than it is purchasing assets overseas.

Fluctuations in either net exports or net savings can, in principle, account for volatility in the real exchange rate. But the real exchange rate is so variable that macroeconomic fundamentals cannot explain it. Instead, the consensus view is that fluctuations in the real exchange rate reflect variations in the nominal exchange rate.

CONCEPTUAL QUESTIONS

1. Did the last foreign country you visited seem expensive to you? What does this imply about the real exchange rate?
2. If you can swap one Eurasian dollar for four Oceanean dollars or six Kingdom dollars, what does this imply about the relative cost of goods in Eurasia, Oceania, and Kingdom?
3. Examine the different foreign currency prices of an issue of the *Economist* and see whether the law of one price holds. Which would be a better guide to the law of one price—the price of Big Macs or the price of an issue of the *Economist*?
4. What does the Internet imply about purchasing power parity?
5. A multinational has asked you for a 30-year forecast of various African exchange rates against the U.S. dollar. The firm will give you any macroeconomic forecasts you need. What data would you ask for?
6. Microsoft takes a stake in a software firm in Bombay. How does that affect the U.S. capital account?
7. A German investor places some funds with an emerging economy stock market fund and intends to leave them there for five years and have all dividends paid into a Munich bank account. How will this affect the German current and capital account over the next five years?
8. The Hong Kong dollar depreciates by 5% against the United States dollar, but Hong Kong inflation also rises by 5%. What will happen to the Hong Kong current account? How would your answer differ if the authorities managed to prevent inflation from increasing?

ANALYTICAL QUESTIONS

1. The United States of Albion does 30% of its total trade with the Republic of Oz, 25% with the Federation of Tropical States (FTS), and 45% with the Banana Republic. Over the last three years the exchange rate changes against the United States dollar have been

	Republic of Oz	FTS	Banana Republic
Year 0	−4%	−3%	+8%
Year 1	+2%	−1%	+4%
Year2	+2%	−1%	+5%

Calculate the effective exchange rate for the United States dollar.

2. Calculate the purchasing power parity exchange rate between the following countries

Commodity	United States of Albion	Republic of Oz
Gasoline	120	180
Meat	80	140
Books	20	33
Fruit Juice	40	40
Coffee	15	10
Clothes	70	160

3. Use the model of real exchange rate determination in Section 18.6
   (a) to analyze the impact on the euro of a surge in European investment
   (b) to analyze the impact of import controls where the net savings line depends positively on the real exchange rate

4. What slope does the net export schedule in Question 3(a) have to have in order to account for purchasing power parity? What is the economic justification of assuming this slope?

Exchange Rate Determination II: Nominal Exchange Rates and Currency Crises

Overview

In this chapter we consider the link between asset markets and exchange rates, focusing on the relation between nominal exchange rates and interest rates. We outline the theory of uncovered interest parity (UIP) which implies that the current exchange rate should reflect the expected future path of interest rates. Through its dependence on expectations of the future this theory can account for the volatility observed in exchange rates. The core of UIP is the notion that exchange rates are driven by macroeconomic factors. We assess the validity of this claim and consider the dynamics of the market and the views of market participants regarding what drives the short-run behavior of exchange rates.

One of the most marked features of exchange rate markets are the periodic large and abrupt devaluations of currencies—or currency crises. We outline a number of alternative theories of currency crises and use these to consider historical episodes in Latin America, Europe, and Asia. We focus in particular on the issue of whether speculators or governments cause currency crises.

19.1 The Importance of Asset Markets

Figure 19.1 shows daily turnover in foreign exchange markets between 1989 and 1998. Both *spot* transactions (for immediate delivery of one currency in exchange for another) and *forward* transactions (in which exchange rates are fixed today but delivery

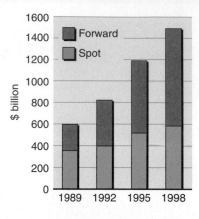

FIGURE 19.1 **Average daily turnover ($bn) in foreign exchange markets.** Foreign exchange markets grew rapidly in this period. *Source*: Bank for International Settlements, "Central Bank Survey of Foreign Exchange and Derivatives Market Activity in April 1998" (October 1998).

and payment is in the future) increased, so that by 1998 their combined level of *daily* turnover approximately equaled the *annual* GDP of Germany.

Figure 19.2 indicates which currencies are most heavily traded by showing the percentage shares of daily turnover.[1] Not surprisingly the three largest economies (the United States, Japan, and Germany) have the three most heavily traded currencies. Table 19.1 shows the twelve most common currency transactions with dollar–deutsch mark trades dominating. Table 19.2 shows where these currency trades occur. Foreign exchange markets are global—even though the British pound accounts for only around

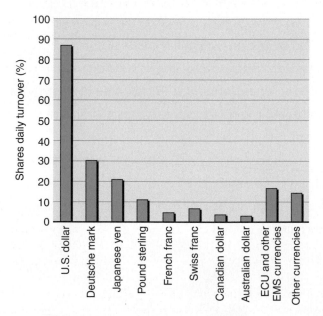

FIGURE 19.2 **Currency distribution of foreign exchange market activity.** The dollar dominates foreign exchange markets. *Source*: Bank for International Settlements, "Central Bank Survey of Foreign Exchange and Derivatives Market Activity in April 1998" (October 1998).

[1]These percentage shares add to 200% because a dollar–yen trade is recorded as both a dollar and a yen trade.

TABLE 19.1   Foreign Exchange Market Turnover by Currency Pair

Currency Pair	Daily Average Trade ($bn)
U.S. Dollar/Deutsche Mark	290.5
U.S. Dollar/Yen	266.6
U.S. Dollar/Other European Monetary System	175.8
U.S. Dollar/Pound Sterling	117.7
U.S. Dollar/Swiss Franc	78.6
U.S. Dollar/French Franc	57.9
U.S. Dollar/Canadian Dollar	50.0
U.S. Dollar/Australian Dollar	42.2
Deutsche Mark/Other European Monetary System	35.1
Deutsche Mark/Pound Sterling	30.7
Deutsche Mark/Yen	24.2

A high proportion of foreign exchange rate transactions involve the U.S. dollar.

Source: Bank for International Settlements, "Central Bank Survey of Foreign Exchange and Derivatives Market Activity in April 1998" (October 1998).

TABLE 19.2
Geographical Distribution of Foreign Exchange Market Activity

United Kingdom	32.3
United States	17.8
Japan	7.5
Singapore	7.1
Germany	4.8
Switzerland	4.2
Hong Kong	4.0
France	3.7

London is the main foreign exchange market.

Source: Bank for International Settlements, "Central Bank Survey of Foreign Exchange and Derivatives Market Activity in April 1998" (October 1998).

5% of total trade in foreign exchange, London accounts for a third of all turnover. An awful lot of dollar trades occur in London even if they are not sterling transactions.

In this chapter we explain how international asset markets, particularly the difference in interest rates across countries, influence the nominal exchange rate. Just as we did with the law of one price and purchasing power parity (PPP) in Chapter 18, we consider what arbitrage implies for exchange rate fluctuations. However, whereas with PPP we focused on arbitrage in goods and services, we now focus on arbitrage between investment opportunities in different economies.

19.2   Covered Interest Parity

We examine first the simplest case in which the investor faces no uncertainty. This is the case of **covered interest parity**, or CIP. If a Japanese investor can earn a higher rate of return for sure by investing in the United States rather than in Japan, she will shift her portfolio abroad. Equilibrium will only occur when the return from investing in each country is the same.

Consider the Japanese investor deciding whether to invest 100,000 yen in a yen or a dollar bank account. The yen account pays an interest of 1%, the dollar account 4%. What the investor does depends on what she expects the yen–dollar exchange rate to be. For the Japanese investor, the return on the yen account is straightforward—it is simply the interest rate of 1%. However, the return on the dollar account consists of

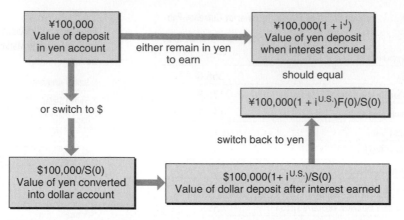

FIGURE 19.3 **Covered interest parity.** Covered interest parity implies that the difference between forward and spot exchange rates compensates for any interest rate differential.

two factors: the dollar interest rate (4%) and any change in the value of the dollar relative to the yen. If the current exchange rate is ¥100:$1, but the one-year forward rate (the rate at which you can purchase currencies a year ahead but at a price, or exchange rate, that is fixed today) is ¥110, then $1000, which currently equals ¥100,000, will be worth ¥110,000 in a year. This is in addition to any interest received on the account.

The Japanese investor therefore has to compare two different investments (as outlined in Figure 19.3). The first is investing ¥100,000 for one year in a yen account and earning interest i^J, which in our example is 1%, or 0.01. The alternative is to invest in a dollar bank account. Assume the current exchange rate is $S(0)$. (The notation $S(0)$ reminds us that we are talking about today's *spot* rate. In our example, $S(0)$ is ¥100:$1.) So the Japanese investor would deposit $100,000/S(0)$ in the dollar account. This pays interest at the rate i^{US} (4% or 0.04), so that at the end of the year the account is worth $100,000(1 + i^{US})/S(0)$.

However, this is a dollar amount, and to compare it with the yen bank account, we need to convert the dollars we would have in the future back into yen. With CIP we do this by using the current forward rate. At any point in time, you can swap one currency for another, and the rate at which this transaction occurs is the spot rate—the transaction actually occurs today.[2] However, you can also arrange to swap currencies at some point in the future, but at a rate that is decided today. Our Japanese investor wishes to know the future yen value of $100,000(1 + i^{US})/S(0)$. If the current one-year-ahead forward rate is $F(0)$, this dollar bank account will be worth ¥100,000$(1 + i^{US})F(0)/S(0)$ one year ahead if we agree today to switch future dollars into yen at the currently announced forward rate. Note there is no uncertainty here because all transactions are

[2]Technically this is not accurate. Foreign exchange rates are actually the rate at which bank accounts denominated in different currencies are swapped (e.g., if a $1.65 million dollar account is swapped for a £1 million sterling account, the dollar–sterling exchange rate is $1.65:£1). However, bank account transactions cannot be immediately processed, so that there is actually a delay of 24 to 48 hours before the currency transaction is concluded, although these are still called "spot" transactions.

made today—the investor converts yen for dollars today at the rate S(0) and agrees to convert dollars back into yen one year ahead at the rate F(0), a rate that she knows. Therefore, *whether the investor chooses a yen or a dollar account, she faces no exchange rate risk if she uses forward contracts*.

If $¥100,000(1 + i^{US})F(0)/S(0)$ exceeds $¥100,000(1 + i^J)$, the Japanese investor will sell yen in the spot market (to open a dollar account) but will be buying yen in the forward market (to convert the dollar account back into yen). But as the investor sells yen today, it will drive up the spot value of the dollar and increase S(0). As the investor buys yen forward, it will tend to push up the price of yen in the forward market and lower F(0). As this happens, the advantage of investing in the dollar account diminishes as $¥100,000(1 + i^{U3})F(0)/S(0)$ falls. Eventually the decrease in F(0)/S(0) means that the returns to investing in the dollar and yen account are identical. Investors, therefore, have no incentive to shift funds, and the spot and forward rates stabilize when

$$¥100,000(1 + i^{US})F(0)/S(0) = ¥100,000(1 + i^J)$$

or equivalently

$$F(0)/S(0) = (1 + i^J)/(1 + i^{US})$$

The right-hand side of the equation is the ratio of Japanese to U.S. interest rates. If U.S. rates are greater than Japanese rates, this number is less than 1. This equation therefore says that in equilibrium, if Japanese interest rates are less than U.S. rates, the forward rate is less than the current spot rate and the market expects the dollar to depreciate (F(0) is less than S(0)). If instead U.S. rates are less than Japanese interest rates, the market expects the dollar to rise. In fact, we can write this equation even more clearly as

expected market appreciation of dollar = $(F(0) − S(0))/S(0)$
= Japanese interest rate less U.S. interest rate

The term $F(0) − S(0)$ is called the forward premium. The CIP condition is simply that the forward premium reflects interest rate differences. If this were not true, investors could make money while being covered against exchange rate risk by selling currencies forward.

What does CIP really say? For a Japanese investor the return on a U.S. account consists of interest earned any appreciation of the dollar. In equilibrium the return on the yen account must equal the return on a dollar account. This means that the *Japanese interest rate must equal the U.S. interest rate plus an appreciation of the dollar*. In our example, U.S. interest rates were 4% and Japanese rates were 1%. This means that covered interest rate parity implies there is a forward dollar discount of 3%—the forward rate is 3% lower than the current yen–dollar rate, and the market is pricing the dollar to *depreciate* by 3%. Any Japanese investor who invests in a dollar account to get higher interest rates and sells the dollars forward will find she loses 3% over a year due to forward dollars trading at a discount to the current spot exchange rate. As a result, she is indifferent between the two investment strategies.

Does CIP hold? The answer is a resounding "yes." If it did not hold, investors could make infinite amounts of money at no risk by switching funds between currencies. There is, however, one caveat. CIP only holds exactly if there is absolutely no risk to either the yen or dollar side of the transactions. Imagine a Japanese investor comparing a yen deposit account in Tokyo with the Bank of Sashimi or a dollar account based in Moscow with the Russian Samovarbank. Because the accounts are based in different countries and with different banks, their risk characteristics may not be identical. For instance, one country might impose capital controls or one of the banks might become insolvent in which case the investor will lose his money. In this case the investor may place his funds in the account that offers a lower return because it is less risky. However, if we consider deposits in the same country with the same bank, these risk differences do not exist and CIP holds exactly. Empirical evidence is entirely consistent with this.

19.3 Uncovered Interest Parity

The key aspect of CIP was that the investor faced no uncertainty when comparing yen and dollar accounts. By contrast, with **uncovered interest parity** (UIP), the investor does not buy forward but waits before converting dollars back into yen at the future spot rate. In other words, instead of comparing ¥100,000$(1 + i^J)$ with ¥100,000$(1 + i^{US})$ $F(0)/S(0)$, the investor compares it with ¥100,000$(1 + i^{US})S^e(1)/S(0)$, where $S^e(1)$ is what the investor *expects* the spot exchange rate to be one period in the future. Of course, the investor could be wrong—$S^e(1)$ may not equal $S(1)$: the outcome may be different from the investor's forecast. In this case, the investor will not earn the return he expected on his U.S. investment. But this is the risk the investor takes because he does not cover his position by a forward transaction.

Under UIP investors who are not troubled by exchange rate risk will rearrange their portfolio until the return on the yen account is equal to the expected return on the dollar account (the same logic as Figure 19.3). In the case of UIP, we have

expected appreciation of dollar $(S^e(1) - S(0))/S(0)$
= Japanese interest rate less U.S. interest rate

In other words, if U.S. interest rates are higher than Japanese interest rates, investors must be expecting a depreciation (or negative appreciation) of the dollar. This expected depreciation of the dollar offsets any interest rate advantage to investing in dollars.

THE RISKS OF INVESTING IN HIGH YIELDING COUNTRIES

UIP helps explain why investors do not place all their funds in countries offering high interest rates or why a foreign currency mortgage in a currency that offers low interest rates may not be beneficial. In Figure 19.4 we show Russian and U.S. interest rates in 1998. On the basis solely of interest rates, putting funds in Russian bank accounts was the best move. For instance, in January 1998 Russian accounts were offering about 24% against the U.S. rate of around 5%, while in September Russian interest rates were 140% compared to 4.7% in the United States. Why shouldn't U.S. investors take advantage of this huge difference and invest in rubles? The reason is that U.S. investors placing funds in a ruble bank account need to worry about the future ruble–dollar exchange rate. Figure 19.5 shows the annual depreciation of the ruble against the dollar

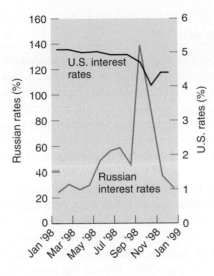

FIGURE 19.4 **Russian and U.S. interest rates.**
Throughout 1998 Russian interest rates were much
higher than those in the United States. *Source*: IMF,
International Financial Statistics (September 2000).
Courtesy of IMF.

(using official exchange rates) for each month of 1998. In every single month the ruble
depreciated against the dollar, partly offsetting the higher Russian interest rates.

Early in 1998 the ruble was depreciating by around 6% annually, so even allowing for
ruble depreciation, the Russian investment paid a higher return because of higher interest
rates. The ruble maintained this rate of depreciation until the middle of the year, so that
the increase in Russian interest rates in Figure 19.4 translated into an even higher rate of
return for U.S. investors (see Figure 19.5). However, by the second half of 1998, the ruble
collapsed (from 6.2 rubles to the dollar in July to 20.65 in December). This sharp depreciation more than offset the higher Russian interest rates, so that U.S. investors were experiencing heavy losses (of around 50% a month) by the end of the year. Potential
fluctuations in the exchange rate are an important component of investors' returns.

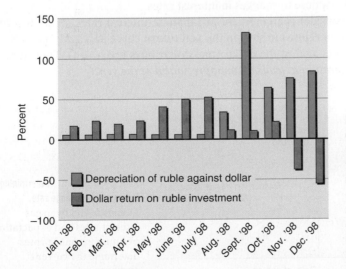

FIGURE 19.5 **Ruble
depreciation and dollar return on
ruble investment.** Higher Russian
interest rates reflected the high
risk of devaluation—high rates
did not produce a high dollar
return. *Source*: IMF,
*International Financial
Statistics* (September 2000).
Courtesy of IMF.

19.4 Pinning Down the Exchange Rate with UIP

UIP is a relationship between the expected change in the nominal exchange rate and interest rate differentials. But usually we are interested in what determines the level of the current exchange rate rather than how it is expected to change. We can use the UIP condition to help understand the current exchange rate, but we need to take what may appear to be an unusual approach. This approach is characteristic of any attempt at modeling asset markets, and we will also use it again later in this book when we focus on equity markets and property. The key feature of this approach is to work out today's exchange rate *taking as fixed expectations of where the exchange rate will be tomorrow*. In other words, we reverse the flow of time. Rather than try to work out expectations of where the exchange rate will be tomorrow by reference to the current exchange and interest rates, we do the opposite—*we calculate the current exchange rate by reference to interest rates and where we expect the exchange rate to be in the future.*

Consider again the comparison of a U.S. and Japanese investment. The return on the yen account for the Japanese investor is i^J, and the expected return on the dollar account is $i^{US} + [S^e(1) - S(0)]/S(0)$. As we change $S(0)$, nothing happens to Japanese interest rates, so the return on the yen account is given by a vertical line in Figure 19.6. However, for a fixed forecast of the future exchange rate [$S^e(1)$ constant], the higher is the current spot rate [$S(0)$], the *lower* the return expected on the dollar investment. The reason is simple—by keeping fixed the forecast of the future exchange rate but increasing the current strength of the dollar, there is less dollar appreciation (or more depreciation) and as a result a lower return on dollars. Therefore, the return in yen on the dollar account depends *negatively* on the current exchange rate $S(0)$ in Figure 19.6. Note that the expected return on the dollar account depends on $S^e(1)$—expectations of the future exchange rate. Changing expectations will shift this line. UIP says that in equilibrium the return on the yen account must equal the expected return on the dollar account. This occurs at the point at which the two lines in Figure 19.6 intersect, and this determines the current exchange rate—shown as $S^*(0)$. We now use this analysis to consider how the current exchange rate changes in response to changes in interest rates.

The first case we consider is an increase in Japanese interest rates, i^J. As shown in Figure 19.7, this leads to a rightward shift in the yen return curve and a *decline* in $S^*(0)$, so that the yen *appreciates* against the dollar (one dollar buys fewer yen). Therefore, *an increase in Japanese interest rates leads to an appreciation of the yen.*

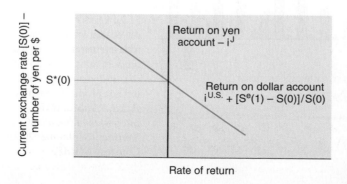

FIGURE 19.6 **Determining the nominal exchange rate.** Domestic and overseas interest rates and expectation of future exchange rates determine the current exchange rate.

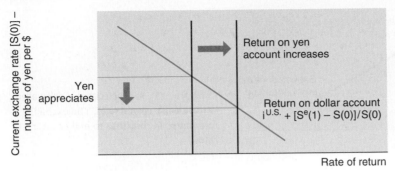

FIGURE 19.7
Increase in domestic interest rates leads to appreciation. Higher domestic interest rates mean currency appreciates.

Figure 19.8 shows the impact on the yen-dollar exchange rate of an increase in U.S. interest rates. For a given current exchange rate an increase in U.S. rates leads to an increase in the return on dollar investments, and the dollar line shifts to the right, as in Figure 19.8. As a result the yen-dollar rate increases—the dollar strengthens and can be used to buy more yen per dollar. Therefore, while an increase in Japanese rates strengthens the yen, a rise in U.S. rates leads to a yen depreciation/dollar appreciation.

But how can we reconcile this result that higher U.S. interest rates lead to a dollar appreciation with our previous statement, also implied by UIP, that high U.S. interest rates relative to Japan lead to an expected dollar depreciation? The trick in reconciling these viewpoints is our forward looking approach to exchange rates. UIP implies that higher U.S. interest rates means an even larger depreciation of the dollar is expected. With a fixed forecast for $S(1)$, this can only hold if the dollar appreciates *now*. Therefore, an increase in U.S. interest rates leads to an immediate rise in the dollar in order to produce a greater future depreciation.

Consider the case in which U.S. interest rates are 4%, Japanese rates 1%, and investors expect the yen–dollar rate to be 97 in a year's time. Because U.S. interest rates are 3% higher, UIP implies an expected dollar devaluation of 3%, which gives a current exchange rate very close to 100 (3% higher than the expected future value of 97). If U.S. interest rates increase to 5%, UIP implies an expected 4% devaluation of the dollar, so the current exchange rate should be approximately 101. Therefore, in response to the 1% increase in U.S. interest rates, the dollar *strengthens* from 100 to 101. At an unchanged exchange rate of 100, an expected yen appreciation of 3%, and U.S. interest

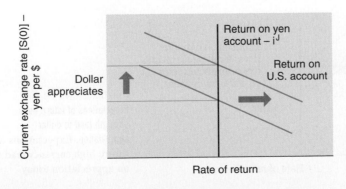

FIGURE 19.8 Rising U.S. rates lead to rising dollar. Higher overseas rates lead to the exchange rate depreciating.

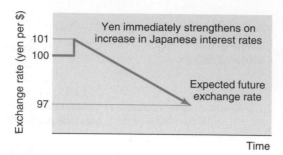

FIGURE 19.9 **Appreciation of dollar after increase in U.S. interest rates.** The exchange rate jumps in response to higher interest rates.

rates of 5%, the return on a dollar investment (2%) exceeds that on yen investments (1%). Investors will therefore switch into dollar assets by selling yen and buying dollars, causing the dollar to strengthen. When the dollar has risen to 101, its strength persuades investors to stop purchasing dollar assets, and the market is once more in equilibrium. Therefore, UIP says that an increase in current interest rates leads to a strengthening of the currency today *to provide scope for the future devaluation that UIP implies*. Figure 19.9 shows this situation.

We can also use our analysis to consider the impact of an increase in U.S. interest rates. For a given current yen–dollar exchange rate, this leads to an increase in the return on dollar investments, and the dollar return line shifts to the right, as in Figure 19.9. As a result, the yen–dollar rate increases—the dollar strengthens and can be used to buy more yen per dollar. Therefore, while an increase in Japanese rates strengthens the yen, a rise in U.S. rates leads to a yen depreciation.

THE IMPORTANCE OF THE FUTURE

We have so far concentrated on how interest rates influence the current exchange rate. However, expectations of future exchange rates are also important as they influence the expected return on overseas investment.

Figure 19.10 shows the case in which the market revises upwards its expectation of future dollar strength—this increases the expected return from the dollar investment and shifts the return schedule on the U.S. investment to the right. Investors now expect a larger capital gain from holding dollars. The result is an increase in the current value of dollars—*market expectations of future dollar strength lead to an immediate appreciation of the dollar.*

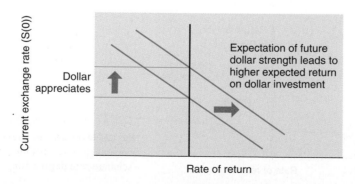

FIGURE 19.10
Expectations of future dollar strength lead to dollar appreciation. Expectations of future high currency lead to an appreciation today.

This makes sense—if an investor thinks the dollar will be strong in the future, he will wish to buy dollars now to benefit from this, which will lead to an appreciation today.

But what determines expectations of future exchange rates, $S^e(1)$? Without knowing this we have not really arrived at a model that explains the current exchange rate. However, modeling $S^e(1)$ is easy—we can just use UIP again! We have shown how to determine the current exchange rate, $S(0)$, based on current interest rates and a forecast of the future exchange rate, $S^e(1)$. However, this analysis should hold for all periods, not just today. In other words, we could use the same analysis to deduce the expected exchange rate tomorrow, $S^e(1)$, given expectations of interest rates tomorrow and of the exchange rate two periods from now, $S^e(2)$. Because $S(0)$ depends on current interest rates and $S^e(1)$, this in turn implies that today's spot rate ($S(0)$) depends on interest rates this year and the year after as well as on expectations of $S(2)$ (the spot rate in two years' time).

However, we still have not completed our model of exchange rate determination. What determines $S^e(2)$? Again, however, we can use UIP and derive $S^e(2)$ as depending on interest rates three periods from now as well as on expectations of the exchange rate in three periods time, $S^e(3)$. We can keep performing this trick until we have expressed the current exchange rate in terms of the expectation of some long-run equilibrium exchange rate ($S^e(LR)$) that will exist at some distant future point and *the whole intervening course of domestic and foreign interest rates*. Figure 19.11 illustrates the idea.

Therefore, repeated use of UIP implies that the whole future path of monetary policy, or more specifically, interest rates between two economies, and an expected long-run exchange rate, $S^e(LR)$, determine the current exchange rate. How can we pin down this long-run equilibrium exchange rate? In Chapter 12 we showed that over several decades purchasing power parity seemed a reasonable guide to how nominal exchange rates behaved. This suggests we can use PPP to pin down $S^e(LR)$. For instance, if over

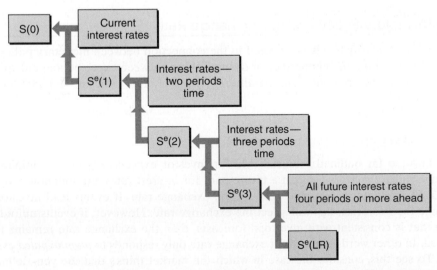

FIGURE 19.11 **Dependence of current exchange rate on all future interest rates.** Because the exchange rate depends on interest rates and the exchange rate forecast, the current exchange rate depends on all future interest rates.

the next 20 years U.S. inflation is expected to be 40% higher cumulatively than Japanese inflation, then PPP would suggest that over the next 20 years the dollar will depreciate against the yen by 40%—this pins down $S^e(LR)$. However, the dollar will not experience a straight-line depreciation over this 20-year period: differences between U.S. and Japanese interest rates will add additional exchange rate dynamics.

This dependence on the whole future path of interest rates can potentially account for substantial volatility in exchange rates. Consider the case in which the market expects only a temporary increase in U.S. interest rates over the next year. This does not affect $S^e(LR)$ (a temporary increase in interest rates is unlikely to affect long-run U.S. inflation) or even $S^e(1)$ (unless it influences interest rates more than one period from now). Therefore, the effect on the current exchange rate is relatively small—the dollar appreciates by the amount of the interest rate increase.

Compare this with the case in which the United States increases interest rates and the market expects them to stay permanently higher. In this case the dollar will appreciate substantially. First, the permanently higher interest rates should lower long-run U.S. inflation. As a result $S^e(LR)$ will increase because PPP implies that the dollar should be higher in the long run in response to the sustained lower U.S. inflation rate. Second, the whole future path of U.S. interest rates is now expected to be higher, so that according to UIP, the dollar now has to *depreciate* by more over the coming years. This faster depreciation is not just in the next year but in every subsequent year. To provide room for this depreciation, the dollar has to appreciate immediately and substantially relative to $S^e(LR)$, which has itself increased anyway. As a result, a permanent change in monetary policy will exert a substantial impact on the current exchange rate. Therefore, UIP implies that rational, forward-looking investors can generate a highly volatile exchange rate if changes in monetary policy are highly persistent.

19.5   Monetary Policy and the Exchange Rate

We now clarify two issues related to the connection between monetary policy and the exchange rate: the importance of distinguishing between expected and unexpected changes in monetary policy and the different impacts of increases in real and nominal interest rates.

EXPECTED/UNEXPECTED INTEREST RATE CHANGES

We have so far outlined a crucial role for investor expectations in determining exchange rates. Investors forecast a future path for interest rates and inflation and then use it to calculate an expected path for the exchange rate. If events lead investors to change their forecast, this will affect the exchange rate. However, if events unfold in a way that is consistent with investors' forecasts, then the exchange rate remains unaffected. In other words, the current exchange rate only responds to *unanticipated* events.

To see this, consider the case in which the market thinks that the yen–dollar exchange rate will be 100 next period, $S^e(1) = 100$, and U.S. interest rates are 4% and Japanese rates 1%. The market is expecting that today's meeting of the Federal Reserve Board will raise U.S. rates to 6%. On the basis of this 6% expectation for U.S. interest rates, the current exchange rate is 105—at 6% interest rates UIP predicts a 5% decline of the dollar against the yen to a level of 100 in a year's time. Suppose the Federal Reserve only increases interest rates from 4% to 5%. With a 5% U.S. interest rate, UIP predicts only a 4% devaluation, so that the dollar falls to 104. Even though U.S. interest rates have increased, the currency has immediately depreciated. However, this does not contradict our previous analysis—the key point is that U.S. interest rates are lower than the market expected, which is why the dollar falls.

IMPACT OF INCREASES IN REAL AND NOMINAL INTEREST RATES

When central banks change the interest rate, it can reflect one of two events: either rising inflation means that nominal interest rates have to increase to keep real interest rates constant, or nominal interest rates have risen faster than inflation, so that the real interest rate has increased. Whether real or nominal, interest rates change has important implications for exchange rates.

In Figure 19.7 we showed the impact on the yen–dollar rate of an increase in Japanese interest rates. This analysis is valid for an increase in the nominal interest rate that is more than the rate of inflation—in other words, an increase in the real interest rate. If instead, the increase in nominal interest rates just reflects higher inflation, then we need a different analysis. Consider the case in which Japanese inflation rises from 0% to 1%, and in response the Bank of Japan raises interest rates from 1% to 2%. In this case the real interest rate remains unchanged at 1% and the yen–dollar exchange rate should not change. The reason is there are two different and offsetting effects on the exchange rate. The first is that higher nominal interest rates lead to a stronger yen, via UIP. However, interest rates only increase because inflation increases. This higher level of Japanese inflation will, via PPP, weaken the long-run level of the yen ($S^e(LR)$), which, via expectations, will weaken the current value of the yen. If the long-run PPP impact fully affects the current exchange rate, it will weaken the yen by 1%, the increase in Japanese inflation. Therefore, the net effect is for no change in the exchange rate—the weakening of the yen due to higher inflation and PPP directly offsets the upward pressure on the yen from higher nominal interest rates via UIP.

When the increase in nominal interest rates is purely an increase in real interest rates, $S^e(LR)$ does not change because the inflation rate has not changed. So PPP does not weaken the currency. The only effect is that the higher Japanese interest rates cause the yen to rise. Therefore, we can expect the exchange rate to respond differently to interest rate increases depending on whether they are perceived as real or nominal increases.

19.6 Does UIP Hold?

We have spent a lot of time outlining UIP, but we have not yet assessed the empirical validity of the model. Does UIP predict exchange rate changes?

Figure 19.12 shows the U.S.–Japanese interest rate differential between January 1996 and November 2000 as well as the monthly depreciation of the dollar against the

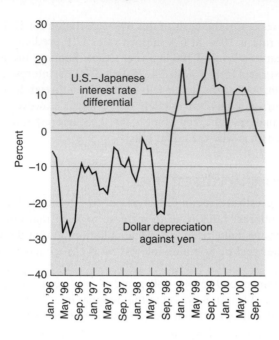

FIGURE 19.12   **Do interest rate differentials predict exchange rate depreciations?** Evidence for UIP is weak; countries with high interest rates often experience an appreciation. *Source*: Federal Reserve Board website http://www.federalreserve.gov/releases/

yen. If UIP is to be a useful guide, on average the dollar should depreciate when U.S. interest rates are higher than those in Japan.

Throughout this period, U.S. interest rates were higher than Japanese rates and by an average of 4.9%. UIP would therefore predict a depreciation of the dollar over the entire period. But between January 1996 and November 2000, the dollar actually *appreciated* by 3%—from 106 to 109.

Figure 19.12 shows just one exchange rate for one particular time period. But a more systematic analysis of the data also suggests that UIP performs poorly. Table 19.3 shows the results of one study which examined the variability in several exchange

TABLE 19.3   **Exchange Rate Predictability and Interest Rate Differentials**

Exchange Rate	Actual Average Absolute Change	Change Predicted by Interest Rate	Unpredictable Component
Yen–Dollar	5.15	0.26	5.12
DM–Dollar	5.75	0.29	5.84
Franc–DM	1.12	0.45	1.18
Schilling–DM	0.4	0.08	0.43

UIP frequently predicts the wrong direction for the exchange rate.

Source: Isard, *Exchange Rate Economics* (*London*: *Cambridge University Press*, *1995*). Reprinted with the permission of Cambridge University Press.

rates from 1980 to 1994 and whether interest rate differentials could explain them. Interest rates only account for a small amount of the variability in exchange rates—interest rates do not change very much. Not only do interest rate differentials fail to account for the magnitude of exchange rate fluctuations, they also tend to predict incorrectly the *direction* of the exchange rate. In Table 19.3 the focus is on the absolute value of exchange rate changes—in other words, whether the currency appreciates or depreciates by 5%, the value 5 is recorded. If interest rate differentials predict a 1% *depreciation* of the currency, but the outcome is an *increase* of 3%, then the forecast error is 4%, and the table would read 3,1,4. Therefore, the sum of the predictable component of exchange rate changes (predictable by the interest rate differential) and the error term (1 + 4) can add to more than the actual exchange rate change (3) if interest rates consistently forecast the exchange rate moving in the wrong direction. Table 19.3 shows that for every exchange rate, UIP fails both to explain the volatility of exchange rates and *to predict whether a currency is going to appreciate or depreciate.*

Another way to see this failure of UIP is to consider what happens when an econometrician runs the regression

% depreciation of currency = constant + β × (domestic interest rate-overseas rate)

If UIP is correct, the interest rate differential should have a coefficient of 1 ($\beta = 1$). However, one survey of 75 published estimates of this regression found the average value was -0.88.[3] In other words, contrary to the implications of UIP, the currency of countries with high interest rates tends to *appreciate*.

These results suggest, at best, that even though interest rate differentials influence exchange rates, they also fluctuate for many other reasons. We now consider two explanations for these fluctuations. The first introduces risk aversion to try to remedy the defects of UIP and aims to explain exchange rate changes by variations in macroeconomic risk. The second moves away from trying to relate exchange rate changes to macroeconomic events and instead focuses on the market structure and what those who participate in markets believe.

19.7 Introducing Risk-Averse Investors

In this section we modify one of the assumptions of UIP—that investors ignore risk. When we moved from CIP to UIP, we stressed that the investor no longer covered the future exchange rate risk by buying forward. As a result, the exchange rate risk clearly makes the U.S. investment more risky for a Japanese investor than the yen investment. If Japanese investors are *risk* neutral, the extra risk involved in the dollar investment does not influence their decisions, and the UIP condition assumes that this is the case. The investor only compares the expected return on the yen investment to the expected return on the dollar investment.

[3]Froot, "Short Rates and Expected Asset Returns," NBER Working Paper 3247 (1990).

However, if Japanese investors are *risk averse*, then when given the choice between two assets with the same expected return, but in which one is more risky, they will choose the less risky one. This means that to be indifferent between the yen and dollar investments, the Japanese investor will require a higher expected return on the U.S. asset. This additional average return, which is required to compensate for higher risk, is the *risk premium*. In this case we have to modify the UIP equation to read

$$\text{Japanese interest rate} + \text{risk premium} = \text{U.S. interest rate}$$
$$+ \text{expected dollar appreciation}$$

Imagine that Japanese investors require a risk premium of 2% on U.S. investments. Then if the Japanese interest rate is 1% and the U.S. interest rate is 4%, this equation tells us that the market is expecting a 1% fall in the dollar. However, so far we have only been considering the case of a Japanese investor. Investing in yen assets is much riskier for a U.S. investor than investing in a dollar account. Therefore, U.S. investors will require a positive risk premium if they are to invest in yen accounts. Obviously both U.S. and Japanese investors cannot simultaneously achieve a positive risk premium, so the sign and size of the risk premium will depend on the relative risk aversion of each group of investors and the perceived risk in each country.

Figure 19.13 shows the implications of introducing a risk premium into our UIP analysis. Consider the case in which the risk premiums that Japanese investors demand from overseas investments decline—in this case the United States becomes like a "safe haven." For a given current exchange rate and unchanged U.S. interest rates, this is equivalent to boosting the risk adjusted return from investing in dollar accounts, so the overseas return schedule shifts to the right. This immediately strengthens the dollar. Therefore, the perception that a currency is now less risky, or has become a safe haven, will lead the currency to appreciate even if interest rates have not altered.

A risk premium adds an additional source of exchange rate volatility and can *potentially* explain some of the problems with UIP. If the risk premium increases when U.S. interest rates increase, then the U.S.–Japanese interest rate differential will not equal the depreciation of the dollar. However, we noted that countries with higher interest rates tend to experience an appreciating currency ($\beta < 0$). To explain this through

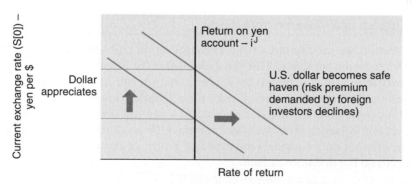

FIGURE 19.13   **Risk premiums and exchange rate fluctuations.** Introducing risk premiums produces a more volatile exchange rate.

the risk premium term, we need the increase in the risk premium to be *greater* than the increase in U.S. rates. Therefore, *to explain exchange rate fluctuations via a risk premium–augmented UIP model, we must have a risk premium that is large, volatile, and sensitive to the macroeconomic variables that drive interest rates*.

However, empirical studies suggest that these conditions are unlikely to explain the data. The first problem is that studies based on interest rate data and market expectations of future exchange rates reveal that although a risk premium exists, and varies over time, it is neither large enough to account for the magnitude of exchange rate volatility nor correlated with interest rate differentials in the way UIP requires. The second problem is that exchange rate changes appear to be uncorrelated with macroeconomic developments, which rules out any role for risk premiums based on macroeconomic developments. As one recent study concludes, "*the exchange rates of low-inflation countries are almost unrelated to macroeconomic phenomena.*"[4] This suggests that macroeconomic variables cannot predict much of the fluctuation in exchange rates. Indeed, a seminal study in 1983 (whose results have remained essentially unchallenged) concluded that a wide variety of economic models of the exchange rate were unable to outperform the simple forecasting rule that the future exchange rate over the next year would remain unchanged.[5] Despite an exhaustive hunt, researchers have struggled to overcome this result. As a result, exchange rate economists are pursuing new avenues. One of the most promising is to concentrate on the microstructure of exchange rate markets, that is, to examine how traders in the foreign exchange market coordinate their activities, what the structure of costs are, and what foreign exchange dealers believe.

19.8   What Are Exchange Rate Markets Really Like?

We use a recent survey of market participants in the London FX (Foreign Exchange) market to understand how the market works and to evaluate the appropriateness of the various models we have outlined.[6]

The first revealing feature is how quickly the market responds to economic information (see Table 19.4). Two-thirds of respondents believe that the market assimilates new information about interest rates within 10 seconds, and the overwhelming view is that markets have incorporated all macroeconomic developments within one minute.

The survey also tells us which economic variables FX dealers think most influence exchange rates. Figure 19.14 shows that the most significant variable is the interest rate, which offers some support for UIP. Also important are unemployment and inflation, which are key determinants of monetary policy. Output and trade deficits have little impact.

---

[4]Flood and Rose, "Understanding Exchange Rate Volatility without the Contrivance of Macroeconomics," *The Economic Journal* (1999) vol. 109, pp. F660–F672.

[5]Meese and Rogoff, "Empirical Exchange Rate Models of the Seventies: Do They Fit Out of Sample?" *Journal of International Economics* (1983) vol. 14, pp. 3–24.

[6]Cheung, Chinn, and Marsh, "How Do UK-Based Foreign Exchange Dealers Think Their Market Operates?" NBER Working Paper 7524 (February 2000).

TABLE 19.4   **Responsiveness of Exchange Rates to Marcoeconomic Information**

	<10 seconds	<1 minute	<10 minutes	<30 minutes	>30 minutes
Unemployment Rate	51	44	10	1	1
Trade Deficit	45	46	13	1	2
Inflation	49	40	14	2	2
GDP	29	50	23	1	3
Interest Rates	65	30	9	0	3
Money Supply	22	61	20	2	2

Proportion of respondents answering the question, "How fast do you believe the market can assimilate the new information when the following economic announcements from the major developed countries differ from their market expectations?"

Exchange rates respond swiftly to macroeconomic data.

Source: Cheung, Chinn, and Marsh, "How do UK-Based Foreign Exchange Dealers Think Their Market Operates?" NBER Working Paper 7524 (2000).

Figure 19.14 shows that interest rates and inflation have an important impact on exchange rates, but how much support does this survey offer to PPP and UIP? It offers little support for PPP. When asked the following question:

In your opinion the purchasing power parity condition
(a) can be used to compute the fair spot exchange rate
(b) proposes national price levels, once converted to the same currency via the appropriate exchange rate, should be the same
(c) is only an academic jargon and has no practical relevance to the FX market
(d) other

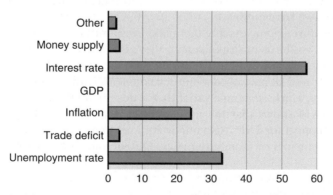

FIGURE 19.14   **Impact of economic data on exchange rates.** Proportion of respondents answering question, "In your opinion which one of the following economics announcement from the major developed countries has the biggest impact on the FX market?"

Interest rates are the most important macroeconomic variable for the markets. Source: Cheung, Chinn, and Marsh, "How Do UK-Based Foreign Exchange Dealers Think Their Market Operates?" NBER Working Paper 7524 (February 2000).

TABLE 19.5 What Drives Exchange Rates?

	Intraday	Medium Run (up to 6 months)	Long Run (over 6 months)
Bandwagon Effects	51	13	1
Overreaction to News	57	1	0
Speculative Forces	44	42	3
Economic Fundamentals	1	43	80
Technical Trading	18	36	11
Other	3	2	2

In the short run, macroeconomics has little influence on market participants.

Proportion of respondents answering the question, "Select the *single* most important factor that determines exchange rate movements in each of the three horizons listed."

Source: Cheung, Chinn, and Marsh, "How do UK-Based Foreign Exchange Dealers Think Their Market Operates?" NBER Working Paper 7524 (February 2000).

Sixty percent of respondents chose (c). The survey also reveals that 70% of respondents would take no trading action when PPP calculations indicate the dollar is overvalued and only 29% would sell the dollar are further evidence of the lack of faith in PPP as a useful guide to exchange rate developments.

The most informative part of the survey asks dealers what factors they think drive exchange rates at different horizons. Table 19.5 shows the results. Hardly anyone gives much of a role to economic fundamentals in the short run. This is consistent with our conclusion at the end of the last section. The short-run behavior of exchange rates appears to have nothing to do with macroeconomic forces. Instead, the momentum of the market and the beliefs of dealers dominate (bandwagon effects, speculative forces, and overreaction to news). Over the medium run (up to 6 months), economic fundamentals play a bigger role, and bandwagon effects and overreaction cease to matter. But even at this horizon, speculative forces are just as important as macroeconomics. Macroeconomic fundamentals exert the main influence only in the long run (over 6 months).

That noneconomic factors may influence exchange rates in the short run has encouraged researchers to look at how the FX markets operate to try to see if exchange rates are predictable—economists call this the "**microstructure**" approach. A key variable in all microstructure models (whether it be equity markets, housing markets, or exchange rates) is order flow, which is used as a measure of buying and selling pressure. **Order flow** is the difference between buyer-initiated orders and seller-initiated orders. For instance, if an exchange rate dealer quotes an exchange rate of ¥100:$1 and receives 10 orders purchasing $100 dollars and 2 selling $100 dollars, the order flow would be +800.

Figure 19.15 shows how order flows and exchange rates move closely together over time. Using order flow dynamics, the exchange rate becomes predictable over short time horizons, and the forecast produced dominates simply using the current exchange rate as the future forecast (a no-change forecast). Although macroeconomic factors (in

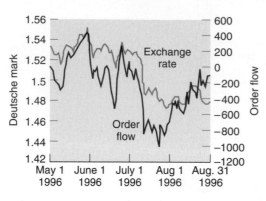
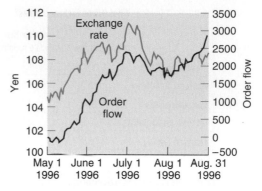

FIGURE 19.15 **Exchange rates and order flows.** Buying and selling pressure closely mimics exchange rate fluctuations. *Source*: Evans and Lyons, "Order Flows and Exchange Rate Dynamics," Journal of Political Economy (forthcoming) © The University of Chicago. All rights reserved.

particular the interest rate) still play a role, it is small compared with the impact of order flow. Econometric estimates suggest that $1 billion of net dollar purchases increases the DM/$ exchange rate by about 1 pfennig.

Although these results are striking, they are simply a statistical fact and raise the question why order flows matter so much for exchange rates. If only macroeconomic factors determine exchange rates, and if this information is fully available, then exchange rates would change even without order flows. As soon as data are released, everyone would be aware of it, and the exchange rate should adjust immediately. For order flows to matter, some information must not be publicly available and only be revealed through trading. For instance, as more investors buy dollars, the market gets information that the dollar is underpriced and starts to increase its demand for dollars. The apparent significance of order flows in predicting exchange rates suggests that these effects are important. It does not tell us what mechanism is behind these informational flows.

19.9   Currency Crashes

The most dramatic form of exchange rate volatility is a currency crisis—when an exchange rate depreciates substantially in a short period. Such events push macroeconomics to the top of news summaries and on to the front pages of newspapers. They can have huge political and commercial implications. In the remainder of this chapter, we will examine the frequency of currency crashes and outline theories to explain them.

Before proceeding, we need to be more precise about what we mean by a "**currency crisis**." A currency crisis must have two features: the exchange rate depreciation must be large relative to recent experience, and the nominal exchange rate depreciation must also affect the real exchange rate. In other words, the depreciation must not just reflect inflation and the operation of PPP. As we saw in Chapter 12, PPP tends to hold in the short run for countries with high inflation, and such countries will experience a continual substantial nominal exchange rate depreciation without the real exchange

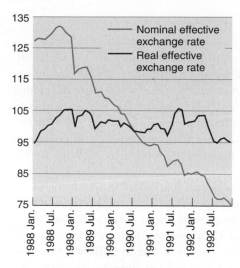

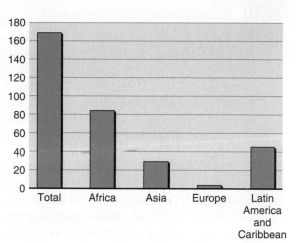

FIGURE 19.16 **Israeli nominal and real exchange rate, 1988–1992.** Some countries experience continual nominal depreciation and a constant real exchange rate—this is not a case of a currency crash. *Source*: IMF, *International Financial Statistics*. Courtesy of IMF.

FIGURE 19.17 **Currency crises, 1970–1996.** Emerging markets are the scene of most currency crises. *Source*: Glick and Rose, "Contagion and Trade: Why are Currency Crises Regional?" *Journal of International Money and Finance* (1999) vol. 18, no. 4, pp. 603–617. Copyright 1999, with permission from Elsevier Science.

rate necessarily changing. Figure 19.16, which plots the nominal and real exchange rate for Israel from 1988 to 1992, shows an example of this. The nominal exchange rate declined around 15% per year throughout the period, but the real exchange rate hardly changed—the nominal depreciation simply reflects relatively high Israeli inflation. Such cases are not currency crises.

Even when we restrict our attention in this way, we still find that currency crashes are frequent. Figure 19.17 shows that between 1970 and 1996 over 160 currency crashes occurred, and Figure 19.18 suggests that they have become more common (especially if the numbers were updated to include the events of 1997). Currency crises are therefore a frequent economic phenomena and they may be amenable to theoretical analysis. It is this analysis we consider next.

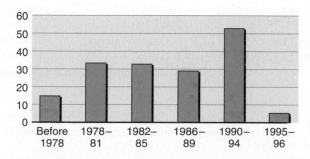

FIGURE 19.18 **Time distribution of currency crashes.** There are some signs that currency crises are becoming more common. *Source*: Glick and Rose, "Contagion and Trade: Why are Currency Crises Regional?" *Journal of International Money and Finance* (1999) vol. 18, no. 4, pp. 603–617. Copyright 1999, with permission from Elsevier Science.

19.10 First-Generation Models

Because currency crises tend to have enormous political, economic, and social implications, economists devote a lot of attention trying to determine who is responsible for them. In so-called first-generation models of currency crises, which were developed in the late 1970s and early 1980s, the answer is straightforward: the government is to blame for pursuing inconsistent domestic and external policies. However, when the crisis occurs, speculators and global capital markets are the main actors, and politicians blame them. But, speculators are merely the messengers—and their message is that governments have to change their policy.

Let's consider the most straightforward first-generation model in which a government announces a fixed exchange rate target but also wishes to pursue an expansionary fiscal policy.[7] To finance the fiscal deficit, the government has in part to print money; it has to resort to the inflation tax (see Chapters 10–12 of this book). However, such an expansionary monetary policy leads to low interest rates and capital outflows. Investors withdraw funds to place them abroad, and to do so, they sell the domestic currency. This puts downward pressure on the exchange rate; but the government is committed to a fixed exchange rate target. To try and maintain the exchange rate, the government sells foreign currency reserves and buys the domestic currency. In this scenario the country is experiencing a large and continual fiscal deficit, high money supply growth, rapid inflation, and a fixed nominal exchange rate; this implies an appreciating real exchange rate (because inflation is high). Further, government foreign exchange reserves are falling. This situation will continue as long as the government maintains its policy of fixing the exchange rate *and* simultaneously running a large fiscal deficit. If it dropped its commitment to a fixed exchange rate, it would no longer have to sell foreign exchange reserves to support the currency, and the exchange rate could depreciate. Alternatively, if it reduced its fiscal deficit, interest rates could be higher, and less capital would flow out, and the exchange rate would not be under pressure. However, if the government does not change its policies, foreign exchange reserves will continue to fall, as shown in Figure 19.19.

These circumstances cannot continue indefinitely—eventually the central bank will run out of foreign exchange reserves and the currency will depreciate sharply. However, the currency crash will occur *before* the central bank runs out of reserves. In particular, at a critical level of reserves (R_c in Figure 19.19), a speculative attack will occur, and the currency will drop. Why does this happen? Investors will not want to wait until the foreign exchange reserves of the central bank are zero. At this point the currency will depreciate sharply, and anyone holding it will lose money. Therefore, the investor will want to sell the domestic currency *before* reserves run out and will try and sell the domestic currency before a crisis. When the central bank has high levels of foreign currency reserves, it can withstand the pressure of a speculative attack—investors selling the domestic currency. But when reserves reach the critical level, they are too low to offset the sell orders for the domestic currency. Investors know that in a few months

---

[7]This model is based on Krugman, "A Model of Balance of Payments Crises," *Journal of Money, Credit and Banking* (1978), vol. 11, pp. 311–325. Subsequent work has extended the relevence of the model, but the basic insights remain the same.

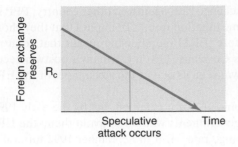

FIGURE 19.19 **First-generation models of currency crises.** Fiscal deficits cause foreign exchange reserves to fall and attack comes in advance of reserve depletion.

reserves will be exhausted, and the currency will crash. At this point they sell the domestic currency in large amounts, and the government either wastes what little reserves it has left or immediately devalues the currency.

When all this occurs, the government will blame investors. They will argue that it was committed to defending the exchange rate and that it still had several months of foreign exchange reserves left. However, according to first-generation models, this is beside the point. Domestic and external policy are inconsistent and a sharp depreciation of the currency is inevitable. By simultaneously pursuing two inconsistent aims, the government has caused the currency crisis.

These first-generation models cannot account for all currency crashes. However, they do explain the volatile exchange rates of Latin America in the 1970s when many governments tried to target the exchange rate to stabilize high inflation rates while still running large fiscal deficits. In empirical attempts to develop "early warning indicators" of currency crises, all the variables that play an important role in first-generation models were found to be important: declining foreign exchange reserves, large fiscal deficits, capital outflows, high rates of seignorage and inflation.

First-generation models of exchange rate crises and the role of inconsistent government policy in triggering currency crashes have considerable empirical support. However, another set of theories offers a very different perspective on the causes of currency crises. In these theories global capital markets and speculators are not so blameless.

19.11 Second-Generation Models and the ERM Crisis

Although first-generation models can account for many features of the Latin American crises in the 1970s and 1980s, they cannot shed any light on the currency crisis that hit the European Exchange Rate Mechanism (ERM) in 1992. The ERM was a system of fixed exchange rates among European countries. Each currency had a central exchange rate around which the currency could vary within specified bands. Governments could either buy and sell foreign exchange reserves to keep exchange rates within these bands or change interest rates. If these policies did not work, the central parity (the midpoint of the bands) would have to be altered. In practice the key country in the ERM was Germany, with countries effectively linking their currency to the

Deutsche mark. For a country to fix its exchange rate against another country, PPP implies that both countries must have the same inflation rate. UIP implies that they should also share the same interest rates. Therefore, ERM membership meant that countries had to adopt the same monetary policy as Germany. Given Germany's postwar record in achieving low and stable inflation, this was seen as one of the advantages of the ERM for participating countries.

In the early years of the ERM, realignments were common, but by the early 1990s, devaluations were increasingly rare, and governments wanted to avoid them; the ERM had become a stable system of fixed exchange rates. But in September 1992 turmoil hit the European foreign exchange markets. Events first developed on September 8 when Finland devalued its currency by 13%, and Sweden was forced to raise interest rates from 24% to 75%. By September 10, pressure had moved onto the Italian lira, which fell by around 7% (although it still remained within the ERM). On September 16 and 17, the system came under enormous pressure. The pound sterling came under attack, and despite enormous sales of foreign exchange reserves by the Bank of England, and British interest rates increasing from 10% to 15%, the pound was eventually devalued by around 15%. British membership in the ERM was suspended. The Italian lira also came under renewed attack, and Italy also left the ERM system with a similar size devaluation. Pressure continued. The Spanish peseta fell by around 5%, and Swedish and Irish official interest rates reached 500% and 300%, respectively. Market focus then switched to the French franc, and France raised interest rates by 2.5%. However, the French managed to remain in the ERM, at the previous central exchange rate, and by the end of September, the crisis was abating. The three-week crisis had seen Italy and the UK leave the system, substantial devaluations of central rates for other countries, high interest rates, and huge depletions of central bank foreign exchange reserves.

What caused the crisis? Table 19.6 suggests that first-generation models cannot account for the events. Although the countries had different experiences, there were no

TABLE 19.6   European Inflation and Fiscal Deficits, 1990–1992

	Fiscal Deficit (% GDP)			Inflation		
	1990	1991	1992	1990	1991	1992
United Kingdom	1.5	2.8	6.5	8.0	4.7	3.5
Spain	4.3	4.5	4.1	6.5	6.4	6.4
Finland	5.4	1.1	5.5	5.8	5.6	4.1
Ireland	2.3	2.4	2.5	2.1	8.5	5.5
Sweden	−4.2	1.1	7.8	9.9	10.3	2.2
German	2.1	3.3	2.6	2.7	3.7	4.7
France	1.5	2.0	3.9	2.8	3.2	2.4
Italy	11.2	10.2	9.6	6.3	6.9	5.6

Before the ERM crash of 1992, there was no sign that European economies were running large fiscal deficits or had high inflation—this is not a first-generation example.

Source: IMF, *International Financial Statistics* (September 2000). Courtesy of IMF.

sharp differences between those that had to leave the ERM system, or devalue, and those that remained. To account for the ERM crisis, economists developed a new set of currency crisis models (called, rather unimaginatively, second-generation (SG) models). In SG models a fixed exchange rate can survive indefinitely as long as the currency is not attacked. However, if the currency comes under selling pressure, the fixed exchange rate peg will go. SG models therefore possess multiple equilibria—the fixed exchange rate may not survive. SG models are also characterized by "*self-fulfilling equilibria*." If investors think the fixed exchange rate is stable, they will not attack, and the fixed exchange rate will survive. However, if they believe the exchange rate is vulnerable, they sell the currency, and the exchange rate target will fail—investor beliefs are self-fulfilling. Such a model can explain the ERM crisis—there is no need to appeal to poor policies before the currency crash, and it can explain why some countries with greater credibility (notably Germany and France) survived the crisis, while other countries (Italy, the UK) were forced to leave the ERM.

SG models are based on three key assumptions:

(a) Governments want to maintain the fixed exchange rate because it yields benefits, e.g., lower and stable inflation.
(b) Governments perceive advantages in abandoning the fixed exchange rate, i.e., they can loosen monetary policy and stimulate the economy.
(c) The perceived advantages to dropping the fixed exchange rate increase the more investors think that the exchange rate will depreciate.

In Figure 19.20 we have drawn the benefits from maintaining the fixed exchange rate as being constant regardless of investors' beliefs. However, the benefits from leaving the system increase as investor confidence in the exchange rate target falls. As more investors believe that the exchange rate is going to be devalued, interest rates have to increase to prevent capital outflow. The less confidence investors have in the fixed exchange rate, the greater the required increase in interest rates. However, the higher are interest rates, the greater the incentive for the government to abandon the peg by devaluing and choosing a looser monetary policy.

As long as lack of confidence in the exchange rate does not exceed C, it will not crash. Below C the benefits to the government of staying in the system exceed the costs, and the central bank will defend the currency. However, if investor confidence in the

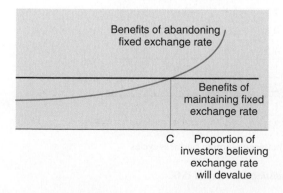

FIGURE 19.20 **Second-generation models of currency crises.** With second-generation models, the government no longer defends the exchange rate target when a large number of investors think a devaluation is imminent.

fixed exchange rate deteriorates to a position above C, then the system is no longer stable. If investors start to sell the currency, the government will abandon the exchange rate target because the costs of holding the line exceed the benefits. Hence the self-fulfilling nature of attacks—if investors think the currency is stable, the fixed exchange rate holds, but if confidence is weak, the government no longer wants to stay in the system, and the currency depreciates. This model helps to make sense of the lament of ERM-country finance ministers that capital markets forced them to leave the system—without an attack and if investor confidence remains to the left of C, the government is happy to stay in the system. Only when this confidence deteriorates are governments no longer prepared to pay the price of membership in the fixed exchange rate system.

Although SG models allow for self-fulfilling equilibria, fundamental economic factors still play a role. Fundamentals have three relevant ranges. One range occurs when the fundamentals of the economy and policy are so strong that the fixed exchange rate is secure, no matter what investors believe. Another range occurs when a currency crash is inevitable because the fundamentals are so poor. Finally, over an intermediate range, the self-fulfilling equilibria of SG models apply and a currency crisis depends on investor behavior.

How do these SG models account for the ERM crisis? The essence of the ERM was that member countries had to adopt the same monetary policy as Germany. However, because of German unification, the appropriate monetary policy for Germany was different from that best suited for the rest of Europe. By 1992 the investment boom and large fiscal deficit that German unification had triggered *within Germany* was beginning to lead to higher German inflation and the Bundesbank (the German central bank) sought to reduce inflationary pressures by increasing interest rates. This meant that other countries in the ERM also had to increase their interest rates to keep to their exchange rate target. However, outside Germany inflationary pressures were weak—as Table 19.7 shows. For instance, the UK was stuck in a recession, and the government's performance in the opinion polls was declining. As the UK raised interest rates in line with the Bundesbank, the opinion polls worsened—making it more attractive to leave the ERM.

TABLE 19.7   **Gross Domestic Product Growth and Inflation in the ERM**

	1990		1991		1992	
	GDP Growth	Inflation	GDP Growth	Inflation	GDP Growth	Inflation
Finland	0.0	6	−7.1	4.3	−3.6	3.0
France	2.5	3.4	0.8	3.2	1.2	2.4
Germany	5.7	2.7	4.5	3.6	2.1	5.1
Italy	2.1	6.0	1.1	6.5	0.6	5.3
Spain	3.7	6.7	2.3	5.9	0.7	5.9
Sweden	1.3	10.4	−1.1	9.7	−1.4	2.6
United Kingdom	0.4	9.5	−2.0	5.9	−0.5	3.6

The ERM crisis was due to asymmetry between German business cycles and the rest of Europe.

Source: IMF, *International Financial Statistics*. Courtesy of IMF.

Financial markets were aware of this tension and became concerned that sterling might be devalued. This placed more upward pressure on UK interest rates, which further worsened the state of the economy and government popularity. Eventually investor confidence deteriorated so much that the UK government was no longer prepared to preserve the exchange rate target—once interest rates hit 15%, the government decided to devalue the pound. By contrast, France managed to avoid devaluation. The French had been in the ERM much longer than the UK and had already established a reputation for wanting to keep inflation low, even in the face of high unemployment. The financial markets did not believe that the French government would devalue the franc. So investors had more confidence in the security of the franc exchange rate target, which meant, using the analysis of Figure 19.20, that the net benefits from staying in the system were higher for the French than the British.

19.12 The Asian Crisis

In 1997 many of the fast-growing economies of Southeast Asia experienced a currency crisis. The problems began in Thailand, but soon spread to Indonesia, Malaysia, South Korea, and the Philippines. Taiwan, Singapore, and Hong Kong also felt the pressure. During this period the behavior of capital markets was so volatile that the Asian currency crises spilled over into other emerging markets as far away as Russia, South Africa, and Brazil.

In the early 1990s, many Asian economies liberalized their capital accounts to allow for the free flow of capital in and out of the economy. After several decades of fast growth, and with seemingly robust fundamentals, these economies received large amounts of capital inflow. For instance, in 1996 the five largest ASEAN (Association of Southeast Asian Nations) economies had a capital account surplus of $55 billion. But by 1998 confidence in these economies was reduced, and they now had a capital account *deficit* of $59 billion. Instead of receiving an additional $55 billion a year to fund

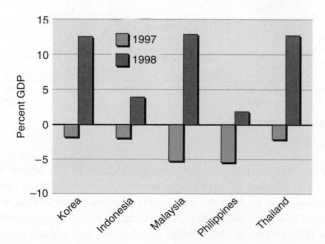

FIGURE 19.21a **Asian current account positions, 1997–1998.**

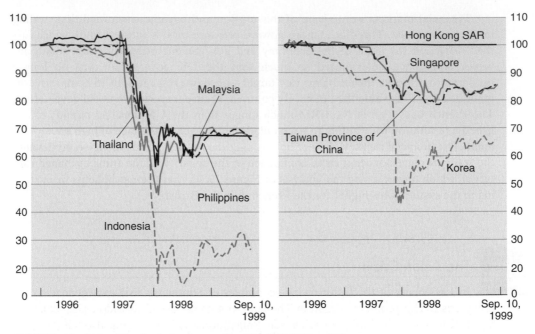

FIGURE 19.21b   Asian nominal exchange rates, 1996–1999, (1996 = 100).

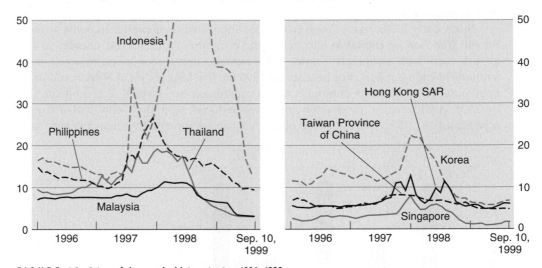

FIGURE 19.21c   Asian nominal interest rates, 1996–1999.

investment, these economies had to pay out $59 billion. Figure 19.21*a* shows this dramatic reversal. As we saw in Chapter 18, such large capital account deficits put downward pressure on the currency, and in Asia the currencies plummeted, breaking what had been a reasonably stable link with the dollar. As currencies fell, foreign investors became worried about the falling value of their Asian investments and started to withdraw funds. This led to a larger capital account deficit and further selling pressure on the

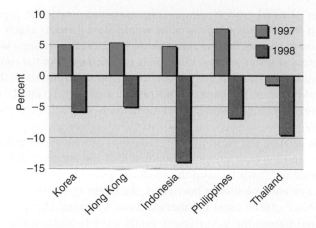

FIGURE 19.21d   **Asian GDP growth, 1997–1998.** The Asian crisis saw dramatic falls in exchange rates, large increases in interest rates, and sharp recessions. *Source*: IMF, *International Financial Statistics.* Courtesy of IMF.

Asian currencies. Figure 19.21*b* shows that currencies fell by around 50% and even more in the case of Indonesia.

To try to prevent these currencies collapsing, Asian banks sold foreign exchange reserves and bought their own currencies (selling well over $50 billion of reserves); they also borrowed extensively from the International Monetary Fund (IMF) and other international institutions (over $100 billion of loans were arranged) and they aggressively raised interest rates (see Figure 19.21*c*). Eventually the pressure on the currency subsided, but the large increase in interest rates and the dramatic outflow of capital from the banking system left economies in a severe recession (see Figure 19.21*d*).

First-generation models appear at first to be unhelpful in explaining these events because nearly all the Asian economies were operating sound fiscal policy—in 1996, Indonesia, Malaysia, the Philippines, and Thailand recorded fiscal surpluses, and although South Korea had a deficit, it was only 0.1% of gross domestic product (GDP). Neither do second-generation models help because all these economies had fast growth, stable inflation, and no unemployment problems. Governments appeared committed to stable exchange rates and had no other inconsistent policy aims.

So why did Asia crash? The first view argues that a combination of poor fundamentals and inconsistent fiscal and monetary policy caused the currency crash.[8] The argument goes like this. Having grown fast for decades, through high levels of investment and capital accumulation, Asian policymakers wished to maintain this growth. Capital account liberalization enabled them to borrow substantial funds to boost investment. It also enabled Asian banks and firms to borrow foreign currency at lower interest rates than prevailed domestically. According to UIP, depreciation of the Asian currencies should have offset this interest rate differential. But the authorities committed themselves to a fixed exchange rate against the dollar, apparently removing this currency risk.

However, this is only half the story—a crucial part of the argument concerns the level of investment in Asia. Critics argue that East Asian levels of investment were too

[8]This argument is associated with Krugman, "What Happened to Asia?" *www.wws.princeton.edu/pkrugman* and Corsetti, Presenti, and Roubini, "Paper Tigers," *European Economic Review* (1999), vol. 43, no. 7, pp. 1211–1236.

high; and that after decades of rapid growth, diminishing marginal product of capital was beginning to set in. But lower levels of investment would slow growth, which the authorities were not prepared to accept. To stimulate investment, banks and firms were encouraged to borrow overseas at lower interest rates. This exposed them to the risk of a currency crash. If Asian banks borrowed in dollars but lent in domestic currency, then a currency depreciation would increase the banks' debts (as the dollar appreciated), but their assets (the domestic currency loans) would not change. Such a depreciation could cause banks and firms to fail.

Some have argued that in Asia the close interrelationships among policymakers, corporations, and banks meant that most people thought that if the currency did fall, the government would provide the funds to keep the banking system stable. The more foreign currency that the Asian banking system borrowed, the larger this potential government liability became. While official fiscal numbers showed a surplus, these figures could not reflect the potential payout the government would have to make if the currency depreciated. At some point the potential payout becomes so large that markets are aware that only inflationary monetary policy can finance it. But inflation will, via PPP, lead to a depreciating currency, so the exchange rate comes under pressure. As the exchange rate falls, the liability of the government is no longer potential but has to be paid, and the further the exchange rate falls, the larger the bailout, and the greater the expected inflation.

Figure 19.22 supports this argument by showing that in 1997 depreciation on the South Korean capital stock was essentially wiping out corporate profits, so that the capital stock was no longer contributing to consumption. This suggests that the Asian economies, which were already saving around 30% of GDP, did not need the additional investment of around 5–7% of GDP that a capital account surplus provided. A further relevant factor was that to rebuild bank balance sheets after a banking crisis is extremely expensive for a government. Estimates suggest that the fiscal cost of improving the balance sheets of South Korean banks was around 14% of GDP; for Thailand it was around 25%. (Even the U.S. Savings and Loan (S&L) disaster in the early 1990s only cost around 2–5% of U.S. GDP; but the Chilean crisis of the early 1980s cost a staggering 32–41% of GDP). This view of the Asian crisis therefore blames government policy mistakes: overaccumulation of capital, fixed exchange rates, and implicit government subsidies to the banking sector.

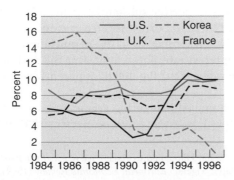

FIGURE 19.22 **Korean overaccumulation of capital (net contribution of capital to GDP—profits less depreciation).** Prior to the Asian crisis, Korea saw a sharp fall in the profitability of its investment. *Source*: OECD, *National Accounts*, vol. II. Copyright OECD.

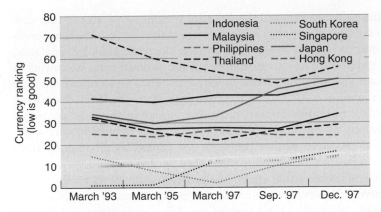

FIGURE 19.23 **Euromoney country risk ratings.** There was no evidence from credit rating agencies before the crash of an impending crisis. *Source*: Radelet and Sachs, "The East Asian Financial Crisis: Diagnosis, Remedies, Prospects," *Brookings Papers on Economic Activities*, 1:1998. http:www.hiid.harvard.edu/pub/other/asiacrisis.html

However, an alternative view places more blame on the behavior of financial markets.[9] It argues that either financial markets lent too much money to Asia before the crisis, or they withdrew funds too rapidly during the crisis. Either way it is hard to argue that the fundamentals of the Asian economies deteriorated so rapidly in just a few months to merit the capital account crisis. There was certainly little sign before the crisis that markets suspected that things were either bad or worsening in Asia. Every year *Euromoney* surveys investors' rankings of the stability of different economies—the lower the number, the more stable and robust the economy is perceived to be. As Figure 19.23 shows, investors' perceptions of problems in the Asian economies before 1997 had not increased. If there were problems, then investors were unaware of them.

With no perceptions of problems before the crisis, this line of thought suggests that the crisis itself must have provoked the problems—that investor overreaction and panic led to the currency crash. Asia's financial system was exposed for two reasons: Asian banks had borrowed in foreign currency but had lent to domestic firms in domestic currency, and like many financial institutions, Asian banks had borrowed short term but lent longer term. For instance, many South Korean banks had borrowed money on 90-day terms but had then lent it to fund longer-term investment. In these circumstances, if investors start to panic and withdraw funds from a country, then a banking crisis can occur (see Chapter 24 for a full analysis of bank runs). If U.S. banks or investors are no longer prepared to lend funds to Asian firms, there will be a shortage of dollars, and the Asian currencies will depreciate. This will lead to losses for Asian banks and a worsening of their balance sheets. This in turn will increase concerns among overseas investors about the health of Asian banks and make them reluctant to lend money. This will only exacerbate the dollar shortage and put further downward pressure on the Asian currencies.

The banks will also face domestic problems. Denied overseas funding, they will have to reduce their lending, leading to a fall in long-term investment plans and real estate projects. Real estate prices will fall, which will reduce the value of collateral that banks hold (see Chapter 23), further worsening their balance sheets and extending the crisis. According to this viewpoint, a $100 billion turnaround on the capital account can

[9]Radelet and Sachs, "The Onset of the East Asian Financial Crisis" (1998), http://www.hiid.harvard.edu/pub/other/asiacrisis.html

trigger a collapse in the exchange rate and the financial system. Advocates of this view of the Asian crisis do not deny that policy mistakes were made nor that the fundamentals of the economy may have been weak. They criticize domestic banking regulation that did not monitor and prevent an excessive dependence on short-term borrowing in foreign currency to fund long-term real estate investments. They also criticize the role of the IMF. To restore investor confidence in the financial system, the IMF advocated a tightening of fiscal policy, increasing interest rates, and closing of the most obviously bankrupt financial institutions. However, critics argue the fiscal tightening only worsened the recession and produced further problems for banks; higher interest rates meant that banks had to pay out more money when they needed to build up their own reserves; and the closing of certain banks created panic because investors were not sure which banks would survive. However, while noting that policy mistakes were made and fundamentals were weak, advocates of this view of the Asian crisis argue that the collapse of currencies and the dramatic withdrawal of funds were out of all proportion to the initial problems.

This view of the Asian crisis raises many issues that we will examine in Chapter 20: What is the appropriate institutional structure for international economic organizations? Should we allow the free flow of capital across countries, or are capital controls necessary?

What can we learn from these two competing views of the Asian crisis? The first is to qualify our analysis from Chapter 4 where we stated that the higher a country's investment rate, the higher its steady state output level. This holds true if we compare countries with similar quality financial intermediaries. However, in the late 1990s, Asian financial institutions had to deal in a short space of time with domestic deregulation and the removal of credit controls. They were experiencing a huge inflow of funds, but were relatively inexperienced at making loans in a competitive and deregulated financial system. As a result, much of this investment was inefficient. Second, large capital account imbalances (substantial gaps between domestic savings and investment) make a country and its currency vulnerable to changes in investor opinion. The substantial capital inflows that can finance investment levels above domestic savings can rapidly become outflows and lead to a shortage of foreign currency and a collapsing domestic currency. This is particularly so if much of these capital inflows is short-term loans, as was the case for many of the Asian economies. Third, cross-border lending is both less regulated and more volatile than domestic finance. This suggests that currency volatility like that in Asia in 1997 may be a feature of a world with large capital flows between different currency areas.

SUMMARY

Foreign exchange markets are enormous. Daily turnover exceeds the annual GDP of Germany. Capital rather than current account transactions motivate these flows. Covered interest parity states that because of arbitrage the interest rate differential between two countries is equal to the difference between the forward and spot rate. The evidence supports CIP because it involves riskless transactions. By contrast, with uncovered interest parity, the investor does not use a forward contract to buy the currency but instead estimates the future spot rate and then holds the currency in the hope of trading at that rate in the future. UIP implies that the interest rate differential between two countries equals the percentage difference between the expected spot rate in the future and the current spot rate. This implies that the exchange rate could be volatile because it depends on the whole expected future path of interest rates in the two economies.

However, while UIP has some empirical successes, it predicts a negative relationship between interest rate differentials and future exchange rate changes, whereas in practice the relationship is positive. Allowing for risk aversion among investors helps explain this, but only if the riskiness of investing in a currency increases substantially when interest rates rise. Although this introduces additional volatility into interest rates, the empirical evidence suggests that it cannot account for the observed positive relationship between exchange rate changes and interest rate differentials.

Recently focus has been placed on analyzing the microstructure of foreign exchange markets. The evidence supports the theory that order flows drive exchange rates in the short run and that market transactions reveal information. This can lead to bandwagon effects and market momentum that may be very different from the forces that macroeconomic fundamentals generate. One of the most notable forms of exchange rate volatility are currency crashes—where the nominal exchange rate falls dramatically in a short time. There are a variety of reasons that explain currency crashes. In first-generation models, the government pursues an inconsistent domestic and external policy, so that eventually the exchange rate will have to depreciate as speculators attack. By contrast, second-generation models suggest that the markets are more responsible for currency crashes and that investor beliefs are crucial. If the market does not expect the currency to depreciate, investors do not attack, and the currency remains stable. But, if investors believe that the currency is about to fall, policymakers are more likely to devalue.

CONCEPTUAL QUESTIONS

1. If the chairperson of the U.S Federal Reserve Board warns of an overheating economy, what will happen to the dollar? Why?

2. What has happened to the yen–dollar or yen–euro rate over the last month? What factors help explain it?

3. In the run up to the formation of the euro, the pound sterling appreciated and the Deutsche mark depreciated. Can changing risk premia explain this given that the UK announced it would not be entering the euro?

4. A government has poor opinion poll ratings in a recession but is attempting to maintain a fixed exchange rate. To defend the currency, it raises interest rates from 5% to 10%. How do you think the markets will respond?

5. Imagine you are a central banker who feels that an exchange rate appreciation would reduce inflationary pressures, but you wish to avoid raising interest rates today. What can you say in public to make the currency rise? What difficulties might this strategy cause?

6. You are aware of all public macroeconomic information but note that many dealers are buying the dollar even though you think the dollar is overvalued. How would you respond? Why do you think order flows appear to predict future exchange rates?

7. Is exchange rate volatility an obvious sign of a poorly operating market?

8. Imagine that U.S. interest rates are 5% and Japanese interest rates are 0.5% and you are buying a house in New York. Should you take out a yen-denominated mortgage?

9. Are speculators or governments most to blame for currency crashes?

ANALYTICAL QUESTIONS

1. What is the dollar rate of return on a $10,000 investment in Tokyo if the annual Japanese interest rate is 1% and the yen–dollar exchange rate moves from 100 to 110 over the next year?

2. The spot euro/£ is 1.5 and the one year forward euro/£ exchange rate is 1.6 per £. What is the forward premium for sterling? If covered interest parity holds, what is the euro–sterling interest rate differential?

3. This morning the exchange rate between the USA (United States of Albion) dollar and the Republic of Oz dollar was 1.50:1 and interest rates in both countries were 6%.
   (a) If the market thinks that later today the Republic of Oz will raise interest rates to 8%, what will happen to the exchange rate?
   (b) If instead interest rates in Oz are increased to only 7%, what will happen to the exchange rate?
   (c) What is the relationship between exchange rates and interest rates in your example? Does this contradict UIP?

4. Interest rates between the United States of Albion and the Republic of Oz are currently equal. However, you now think there is a 50% chance that the Oz dollar will depreciate by 30% over the next week. What has to happen to interest rates in Oz to keep a fixed exchange rate with the USA?

5. The exchange rate between the United States of Albion and the Republic of Oz is now 1:1, with inflation in both countries expected to be 2% and interest rates 4%.
   (a) What does PPP imply about the exchange rate in 20 years time?
   (b) If inflation in the USA increases to 3%, how does your answer change?
   (c) What happens to the current exchange rate if USA interest rates rise to 5% with inflation increasing to 3%?

Exchange Rate Systems and Global Capital Markets

Overview

In this chapter we consider the relative merits of fixed and flexible exchange rates. Fixed exchange rates have proved useful for some developing economies but have caused problems when economies become more integrated into global capital markets—as the currency crises of Mexico in 1994 and Southeast Asia in 1998 demonstrate. As a result, interest in either freely floating exchange rates or more rigid versions of fixed exchange rates has increased. We discuss two such rigid systems—currency boards and single currencies—and examine the establishment of the single European currency as well as the merits of dollarization.

We then consider the large flow of financial funds between countries from both a contemporary and historical perspective. We discuss in particular whether a global capital market truly exists. We also discuss whether the free flow of capital between countries should be restricted, and review the history of capital controls examining how their removal affects economies.

20.1 Fixed or Flexible Exchange Rates?

With a floating exchange rate the value of a country's currency can vary freely and will be influenced by the forces we analyzed in Chapters 18 and 19. By contrast, with a fixed exchange rate, the government will either change interest rates or sell/buy foreign

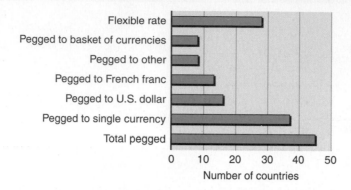

FIGURE 20.1 **Exchange rate regimes among small economies.** There is a wide variety of exchange rate regimes across countries. *Source*: IMF, *Exchange Rate Regimes in an Increasingly Integrated World Economy* (April 2000). Courtesy of IMF.

currency to maintain a fixed value for the currency. Fixed exchange rates come in many varieties: from a pure peg, in which the exchange rate is fixed at a single numerical value, to a crawling peg, in which the government keeps the exchange rate within a certain band but the band itself moves over time in a scheduled way.

Throughout the nineteenth century (and up until 1914), and again for some time in the 1920s and 1930s, a fixed exchange rate system (the gold standard) operated. Under this system a country fixed its currency to be worth a certain amount of gold, which defined a system of fixed exchange rates between different currencies. Between 1945 and 1971, under the Bretton Woods system, only the dollar was pegged against gold, and all other currencies were pegged to the dollar. Since 1971 the world has experimented with flexible exchange rates, although many countries still prefer fixed exchange rate systems.

Whether fixed or flexible exchange rates are better depends on the country and its circumstances—there are no universal laws. Figure 20.1 shows how exchange rate regimes vary considerably across 71 small economies (with nominal gross domestic product (GDP) of less than $5 billion in 1998.)

To understand the advantages and disadvantages of a fixed exchange rate, we begin with the **impossible trilogy**, which says that a government can choose at most **two** of the following **three** options:

- independent monetary policy
- fixed exchange rate
- absence of capital controls

In other words, if a country chooses a fixed exchange rate, it must either abandon an independent monetary policy or impose capital controls, that is, impose constraints on the free flow of money into and out of a country.

To understand the impossible trilogy, consider again the case of uncovered interest parity (UIP) (see Chapter 19), which is based on an arbitrage relation in which investors reallocate funds to the country that offers the highest expected return. This reallocation can only happen in the absence of capital controls. According to the impossible trilogy, UIP implies that the government cannot operate both a fixed exchange rate and an independent monetary policy. The key result for UIP was that interest rate differentials equal expected exchange rate depreciations. However, under a fixed exchange rate the expected devaluation is zero. Therefore, UIP implies that interest rates should be the same between countries with fixed exchange rates—the countries cannot run independent monetary policies. If the fixed exchange rate regime allows for small fluctuations around a central rate, then interest rates can differ between countries in the expectation of small depreciations. Adding a risk premium to UIP allows for more interest rate differentials. However, assuming a narrow exchange rate band and a stable risk premium, then even if interest rates do not have to be *identical* there will be strong linkages. In particular, countries that participate in a fixed exchange rate system will tend to raise interest rates together even if not by exactly the same amount.

However, with capital controls it is possible to have a fixed exchange rate and choose an independent monetary policy. Consider the case of a country with a fixed exchange rate which unilaterally lowers its interest rate. Without capital controls investors would move funds out of the country to overseas where a higher return can be earned. This would put downward pressure on the currency and threaten the exchange rate target. However, if capital controls are in place, this outflow can be restricted and so pressures on the exchange rate can be avoided; with capital controls, the government can have an independent monetary policy *and* an exchange rate target. Without capital controls the impossible trilogy tells us that the cost of a fixed exchange rate is the inability to choose a monetary policy to suit the country's specific circumstances.

This inability to set your own monetary policy is, paradoxically, often one of the main attractions of a fixed exchange rate, particularly for countries with a history of poor monetary policy and high inflation. By fixing the exchange rate against the currency of a country with a good inflation record, such a country can benefit from losing monetary independence. This is what led Italy and the UK to join the European Exchange Rate Mechanism and fix their exchange rates against the German Deutsche mark. However, a country can lose by giving up an independent monetary policy if the other countries in the fixed exchange rate system have different economies and experience different shocks. Under these circumstances a country will often wish to choose different interest rates.

However, adopting a fixed exchange rate to try to lower inflation is not a trivial task. Inflation changes only slowly. Therefore, after having fixed its exchange rate, a country may find its inflation higher than the country its currency is pegged against, which causes the real exchange rate to increase. If the country has flexible labor markets, then wages can adjust, so that even though the real exchange rate is high, the country retains its export competitiveness. In the absence of labor market flexibility, decreased competitiveness will reduce output growth as the export sector suffers. The growth slowdown due to real exchange rate appreciation will raise concern among investors that the currency might depreciate, making it vulnerable to speculative attack. To prevent a currency attack, the government can increase interest rates, but while this helps preserve the fixed exchange rate, it places further downward pressure on growth. This is the impossible trilogy at work—with no capital controls, fixed exchange rates can lead to clashes between the internal (growth) and external (exchange rate) targets of monetary policy.

SO WHO SHOULD FIX THEIR EXCHANGE RATE?

The more of the following six characteristics a country has, the more advantageous fixed exchange rates are:

* poor reputation for controlling inflation
* significant levels of trade with a country whose exchange rate is being targeted
* similar macroeconomic shocks as the country whose exchange rate is being targeted
* relatively little involvement in global capital markets
* flexible labor markets
* high levels of foreign exchange reserves

Table 20.1 lists developing economies that operate a fixed exchange rate. Our six characteristics tell us why the Carribean states target the dollar and Lesotho, Namibia, and Swaziland the South African rand. Their economic well-being is so closely tied to these larger and richer nations that the loss of an independent monetary policy arising from a fixed exchange rate is minimal.

However, for larger, more complex economies that interact extensively with global capital markets things are different. The currency turmoil that hit Mexico, Southeast Asia, Russia, and Brazil in the late 1990s have brought the advantages of a fixed exchange rate into question. The combination of real exchange rate overvaluation and

TABLE 20.1   Fixed Exchange Rate Arrangements for Small Economies

Pegged to U.S. Dollar	Pegged to French Franc	Pegged to Other Currency
Antigua and Barbuda	Benin	Bhutan
Bahamas	Burkina Faso	Brunei Darussalam
Barbados	Central African Republic	Cape Verde
Belize	Chad	Kiribati
Djibouti	Comoros	Lesotho
Dominica	Republic of Congo	Namibia
Grenada	Equatorial Guineau	San Marino
Liberia	Gabon	Swaziland
Maldives	Guinea-Bissau	
Marshall Islands	Mali	
Micronesia	Niger	
Netherlands Antilles	Senegal	
St. Kitts and Nevis	Togo	
St. Lucia		
St. Vincent and Grenadines		
Suriname		

Source: IMF, *Exchange Rate Regimes in an Increasingly Integrated World Economy* (April 2000). Courtesy of IMF.

large volatile capital flows led to forced devaluations and extreme volatility in interest rates. The impact of these currency crises on the real economy led to declines in gross domestic product (GDP), frequently of more than 10% in a year. In response to these events, economists have suggested two different policy responses: to advocate flexible exchange rates and a move away from fixed targets, or to seek more extreme forms of exchange rate stability than an exchange rate target, e.g., currency boards and single currencies. We will now discuss these more extreme forms of exchange rate stability.

20.2 Currency Boards

Under a **currency board**, the central bank of a country is committed to exchanging its monetary liabilities at a fixed exchange rate. The monetary liabilities of a central bank are essentially the currency that it has issued. Therefore, the central bank can only issue as much domestic currency as it has holdings of foreign currency given the fixed exchange rate. For instance, the Hong Kong Monetary Authority (HKMA) operates a currency board that in 2001 was based on an exchange rate of HK$7.80:U.S.$1. If the HKMA has U.S. dollar reserves of U.S.$80 billion, it can issue domestic currency worth 7.80 × $80 billion = HK$624 billion. The domestic central bank can only expand the money supply by obtaining more foreign exchange. If instead its foreign exchange reserves fall, then so will the domestic money supply.

In 2001, there were 14 currency boards—10 countries have linked themselves to the U.S. dollar (Argentina, Antigua, Djibouti, Dominica, Grenada, St. Kitts and Nevis, St. Lucia, St. Vincent, Hong Kong, and Lithuania), 3 to the deutsche mark (now the euro—Bosnia, Bulgaria, and Estonia), and 1 to the Singapore dollar (Brunei-Darussalam). In Djibouti the currency board has been in place for nearly 50 years; for the eastern Carribean countries, more than 30 years; in Hong Kong, since 1985; and in Argentina, since 1991.

Under a currency board, the central bank has only one role: exchanging foreign currency for domestic currency at a specific rate. Unless foreign exchange reserves exceed the current stock of monetary liabilities, the central bank cannot increase the money supply, and it can *never* produce *fiat* money.[1]

Under a currency board system legislation has to be passed to restrict the role of the central bank. Compared to standard fixed exchange rate systems, this makes it more difficult and politically expensive to abandon a currency board. Paradoxically, the additional costs of leaving a currency board (compared to a fixed exchange rate target) help make them effective at reducing inflation. A difficulty in achieving low inflation is persuading agents in the economy that inflation will actually be lowered. If inflation expectations can be reduced, wage claims and price increases will be more moderate, which will help produce low inflation (see Chapter 16 for a full analysis). The greater political

---

[1]Fiat money is money worth its value by government decree—a $1 bill is worth $1 because the U.S. government declares it so, not because you can exchange it for gold worth $1. See Chapter 12 for full details.

TABLE 20.2   Inflation Stablizations from Currency Boards

Country	Beginning Date	Inflation at Start	Inflation after 3 Years	Inflation in 1998
Argentina	4/1991	267	4.3	0.7
Estonia	6/1992	1086	29.2	4.4
Lithuania	4/1994	189	8.4	2.4
Bulgaria	7/1997	1472	—	3.2

Source: IMF, *Exchange Rate Regimes in an Increasingly Integrated World Economy* April 2000. Courtesy of IMF.

and institutional costs of leaving a currency board compared to a standard fixed exchange rate should therefore help lower inflation. Table 20.2 shows that the adoption of a currency board has lowered and stabilized inflation in several countries.

But currency boards achieve more than just lower inflation. As Figure 20.2 shows, currency boards can improve overall economic performance—inflation, inflation volatility, the fiscal deficit, and growth all improve under a currency board compared to alternative regimes. Remember, however, when interpreting Figure 20.2, that currency boards tend to be adopted as part of an *overall* package to reduce high inflation. In Chapter 12 we discussed how large fiscal deficits financed by printing money (seignorage) ultimately caused hyperinflation. Under a currency board, countries cannot print money, so the central bank can no longer finance the government's fiscal deficit. But a currency board without fiscal reform is unworkable—the pressure for the central bank to print money and abandon the currency board will become overwhelming. Currency boards appear so successful in Figure 20.2 because they have been implemented as one part of an overall program that includes fiscal reform.

Although currency boards have reduced inflation, they also suffer from real exchange rate appreciation. For instance, between 1992 and 1996, Estonia's real exchange rate appreciated by 70%, and its competitiveness was so affected that its current account

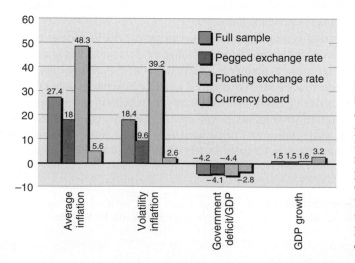

FIGURE 20.2 **Economic performance under currency boards.** Currency boards combined with fiscal reform produce substantial improvements in macroeconomic performance. *Source*: Ghosh, Gulde, and Wolf, "Currency Boards: The ultimate fix?" IMF Working Paper 98/8 (1998). Courtesy of IMF.

moved from a surplus of 3.4% of GDP to a deficit of 6.8%. The inertia in inflation makes this a problem that affects all fixed exchange rate systems (see our earlier discussion), but the difficulties in adjusting the exchange rate make it particularly serious for currency boards. The more flexible labor markets are, the easier it is for wages to offset the increase in the real exchange rate and preserve competitiveness. However, the required flexibility can be substantial. In 1997 labor costs in Argentinian manufacturing fell by nearly 13%, but unemployment still remained above 15%. Achieving exchange rate stability through a currency board can create substantial volatility for the real economy.

Currency boards can also induce substantial volatility in interest rates. For instance, during the 1998 Asian crisis, investors were concerned that Hong Kong might abandon its currency board and devalue the Hong Kong dollar. As a result, the Hong Kong Monetary Authority had to swap their reserves of U.S. dollars and buy Hong Kong dollars. Because of this, the HKMA's holdings of U.S. dollars fell, meaning that the supply of Hong Kong dollars also fell, which put pressure on interest rates. Interest rate volatility strains a country's financial system. High interest rates cause problems for debtors and can precipitate bankruptcy, followed by fire sales of assets that depress asset prices and lower the value of collateral that banks hold. Banks respond by calling in loans or not granting credit extensions, which can trigger another wave of bankruptcies, and more fire sales and asset price declines (this is the credit crunch mechanism we outline in Chapter 24).

This strain on the banking system is a particular problem for currency boards because the central bank cannot act as a "lender of last resort." The lender of last resort in an economy is an institution that can provide unlimited liquidity to the banking sector. When a bank has temporary liquidity problems, a lender of last resort can provide funds that the bank can repay when the problem has passed. However, the lender of last resort must be able to provide unlimited funds to rescue the bank. Under a currency board, this is impossible—the central bank cannot create fiat money and can only supply domestic currency if it has enough foreign currency to back it. Given that the shortage of foreign currency reserves has increased interest rates in the first place, this is of little use. Countries adopting a currency board need to ensure that their prudential supervision of the banking sector is of a high quality. This helps minimize the risk that banks face from high interest rates and a credit crunch.

20.3 Single Currencies

Although currency boards have worked well for some countries, they have drawbacks. They are still vulnerable to speculative attack, which leads to periods of high and volatile interest rates. Further, if we use the risk-adjusted UIP model, then even though no one *expects* the currency board to end and the exchange rate to be devalued, the *possibility* that it might can cause investors to demand a risk premium. This leads to higher interest rates, lower investment, and a lower capital stock and standard of living. To overcome these problems, a country can institute the ultimate fixed exchange rate: adopt the same currency as another country. With no distinction between domestic and foreign currency, devaluation is impossible, which should reduce the risk premium and lower interest rates. The absence of exchange rate uncertainty and the fact that goods in different countries are now priced in a common currency may also boost trade and investment links between countries. Of course, a single currency also involves disadvantages: loss of monetary policy independence, the need for labor market flexibility, and the inability of the central bank to act as a lender of last resort. However, these disadvantages also exist with a currency board, so some countries (at the time of writing, Argentina and Ecuador) are planning "dollarization"—replacing their domestic currency with the U.S. dollar.

20.4 Optimal Currency Areas

The theory of **optimal currency areas** argues that there are four criteria that are relevant when considering adopting a common currency:

- the degree of trade between countries who adopt a common currency
- the extent to which different countries experience similar shocks
- the degree of labor market mobility in each region
- the amount of fiscal transfers between regions

If countries trade extensively with each other, then their economies are closely linked, and the greater the exchange rate stability between them, the stronger are these links. The need for regions to experience similar shocks (and to respond similarly to these shocks) is linked to the impossible trilogy. A single currency requires a "one size fits all" monetary policy. If the loss of an independent monetary policy is not to be costly, countries must experience similar shocks.

High labor mobility between the countries helps overcome the problem with a one size fits all monetary policy. Imagine that one economy is expanding and another contracting, but both have the same interest rates. If labor is mobile and markets flexible, the unemployed in the depressed economy will seek employment in the one that is booming. However, even if labor markets are not flexible, income differences can be reduced as long as there are fiscal transfers between economies—the expanding areas can pay higher taxes that are transferred to the contracting areas. The United States obviously meets these criteria well—states trade extensively with each other, labor migrates across states, and the federal tax system redistributes funds.

20.5 The Euro

On January 1, 1999, 11 European nations permanently fixed their exchange rate against each other and launched the euro.[2] National currencies were initially still used within each country, but by January 1, 2002,[3] euro notes and coins became legal tender

---

[2]The 11 countries were Austria, Belgium, Finland, France, Germany, Ireland, Italy, Luxembourg, Netherlands, Portugal, and Spain.

[3]Greece joined the system by this date.

in all countries, and by July 1, 2002, all national currencies will disappear. Do the euro-land economies constitute an optimal currency area?

LEVELS OF EUROLAND TRADE

Figure 20.3 shows the percentage of intra–European Union (EU) trade for each EU country (Denmark, Sweden, and the UK are in the EU but not (in 2001) participating in the euro project). Clearly the countries are closely interlinked. On this criteria the EU countries do seem to constitute an optimal currency area.

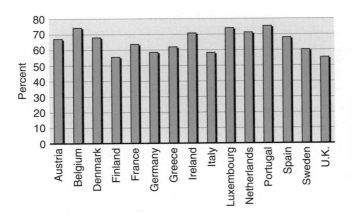

FIGURE 20.3 **Importance of EU trade for EU countries, 1998.** High levels of trade between EU countries make a single currency more feasible *Source*: OECD, *International Trade by Commodity Statistic* (2000). Copyright OECD.

SIMILARITY OF SHOCKS

Figure 20.4 shows the extent to which GDP growth in each EU country is correlated with the EU average. A strong correlation suggests that countries experience similar business cycles to the rest of the EU and so have no need to run a separate monetary policy.

Figure 20.4 shows that the degree of similarity in GDP fluctuations varies across countries in the EU. A central core of countries (France, Germany, Belgium, the Netherlands) has a very strong correlation with EU average output growth. This suggests that these economies will find the transition to a single currency relatively easy. By way of comparison, Figure 20.5 shows the correlation coefficient among numerous U.S. states. Comparing Figures 20.4 and 20.5 suggests that the degree of business cycle synchronization is strong for Europe. However, there is also a group of European countries for whom the correlation coefficient is low, suggesting greater need for country-specific setting of monetary policy.

LABOR MOBILITY

Even if different shocks hit EU countries, this can be offset if labor is mobile among them. However, as we saw in Chapter 8, European labor markets tend to be much less fluid than those in the United States, with regional migration three or four times higher in the United States.

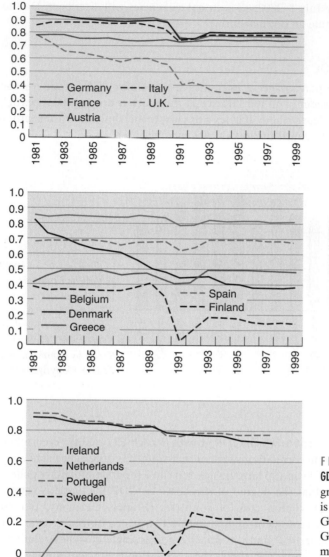

FIGURE 20.4 **Correlation of GDP in EU countries.** There is a core group of countries whose GDP is strongly correlated with EU GDP, e.g., France and Germany. Monetary union is more suitable for these regions. *Source*: Author's calculations from IMF, *International Financial Statistics* (September 2000). Courtesy of IMF.

FISCAL TRANSFERS

Another way of alleviating differences in economic performance among European countries would be through cross-country fiscal transfers. Such transfers are important in the United States where the federal tax and expenditure system transfers income from the richer to the poorer states on both a temporary and permanent basis. By contrast, in the EU redistribution among economies is currently minimal.

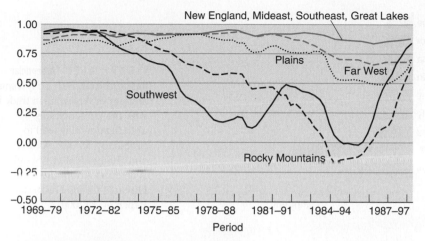

FIGURE 20.5 **Correlation of output among U.S. regions.** There is very little correlation across U.S. regions but still a single currency operates. *Source*: Mihov, "Monetary Polity Implementation and Transmission in the European Monetary Union," Insead, Paris mimeo (2000).

THE EURO—A SUMMARY

The EU countries therefore do not satisfy all the criteria for an optimal currency area. All of them show a high degree of trade with each other, and France, Germany, and the Benelux countries also experience similar shocks. This suggests that they will cope best with the single European interest rate that the euro implies. The lack of labor mobility and fiscal transfers suggests that other nations will find that the loss of an independent monetary policy results in larger business cycle fluctuations than before the euro was introduced.

This analysis helps explain the mixed enthusiasm across EU countries for the euro—from the skepticism of Denmark and the UK to the enthusiasm of France and Italy—as different countries will meet the four criteria to differing extents. Countries heavily involved in EU trade (Benelux), that experience similar shocks as other European nations (France and Germany), or for which a common European monetary policy may bring lower inflation than an independently operated monetary policy (Greece, Italy), will display the most enthusiasm. Those countries that experience different shocks from the rest of Europe (UK?) or for which a common monetary policy may worsen inflation (Germany?) will be less enthusiastic.

20.6 Dollarization

Argentina has operated a currency board since 1991 but is considering dollarization—the adoption of the U.S. dollar as its national currency. Several countries operate a bi-monetary system based on a domestic and a foreign currency, but few have adopted the currency of a foreign country. Panama (which dollarized in 1904) is one of the few exceptions. Compared to a currency board, dollarization can lower interest rate

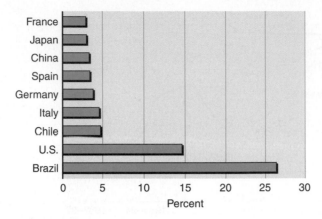

FIGURE 20.6 **Argentinian trading partners, 1997.** Only a small amount of Argentinian trade is with the United States—dollarization may lead to problems. *Source*: Anthony and Hughes Hallet, "Should Argentina Adopt the U.S. Dollar?" CEPR Discussion Paper 2412 (2000).

volatility and reduce interest rates (the risk premium declines because there is no risk of devaluation) and allow a country to integrate its asset and good markets with those of the country whose currency it has adopted.

We can apply our four criteria for a single currency to assess whether dollarization makes sense for Argentina. Figure 20.6, which indicates how much trade Argentina does with its major trading partners, shows that the United States is only Argentina's second most important trading country. The level of trade between Argentina and the United States is substantially below that among European nations. Argentinian GDP also shows little correlation with U.S. GDP—between 1983 and 1998, it was −0.19. Argentinian GDP tends to be high when U.S. GDP is low.

This suggests that the U.S. dollar might not be the optimal currency for Argentina—the loss of an independent monetary policy could be a significant cost. Whether dollarization is beneficial overall for Argentina depends on whether the gains from lower interest rates and the possible dynamic gains from closer integration with the United States will offset the loss of an independent monetary policy.

 20.7 Global Capital Markets

RECENT DEVELOPMENTS

Capital flows, flows of finance between countries, have recently been increasing dramatically. The size of these flows has produced the policy dilemmas we examined in the first half of this chapter. There are three reasons for this dramatic increase:

1. Advances in communications and large cost reductions. International telephone calls are less than 1% of their cost 30 years ago, and improvements in information technology will lower them further.

2. Removal of capital account controls. Starting with the more developed economies, and now in many emerging markets, capital account liberalization—the removal of restrictions on the inflows and outflows of capital between countries—has grown.
3. Deregulation of the domestic financial system. Over the last 20 years, many countries have deregulated their domestic markets and removed the monopoly power that domestic providers of financial services enjoyed. This enables overseas banks to enter and compete for market share.

Figure 20.7 shows evidence of this huge increase in capital flows. Figure 20.7 plots the amount of gross investment flows leaving industrialized nations from 1970 onwards and distinguishes between foreign direct investment (FDI) and portfolio flows (e.g., equity, bonds, or bank loans—see Chapter 18 for a detailed discussion). Comparing 1997 with 1990, FDI flows almost doubled and portfolio flows tripled.

As Figure 20.8 shows in this period substantial funds have flowed into developing countries (but note the outflow of bank loans in 1998 after the Asian crisis), although Figure 20.9 reveals that not all countries have benefited equally.

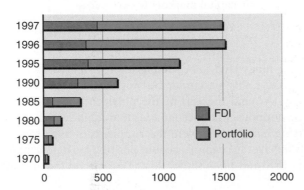

FIGURE 20.7 **Gross investment flows from major industrialized nations ($bn).** Capital flows are increasing substantially each year. *Source*: IMF, *International Capital Markets* (2000).

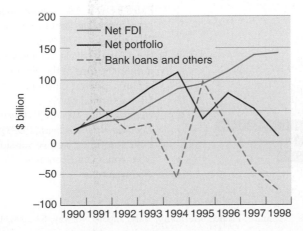

FIGURE 20.8 **Capital flows by asset type to emerging markets, 1990–1999.** Foreign direct investment flows are more stable than bank loans or bonds and equity purchases. *Source*: IMF, *International Capital Markets* (2000). Courtesy of IMF.

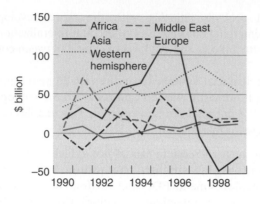

FIGURE 20.9   **Total capital inflows to emerging market regions, 1990–1999.** Africa receives only small capital inflows. Large inflows into Asia reversed in the late 1990s. *Source*: IMF, *International Capital Markets* (2000). Courtesy of IMF.

20.8   Are Capital Markets Really Global?

This enormous growth in capital flows has increased awareness of global capital markets and their influence. But how global are these markets? Do they really perform at a global level what we expect domestic capital markets to do?

HISTORICAL PRECEDENT

The huge capital flows we observe today tend to be seen as unprecedented. In terms of their absolute size in billions of dollars, this is accurate, but not when they are measured as a proportion of the economy. Around the end of the nineteenth century, capital flows between economies were enormous. Many economies that are now rich and part of the OECD were then emerging markets and were the recipients of huge capital inflows. Figure 20.10, which plots the average capital account position (as a percentage of GDP) for 12 countries between 1870 and 1996, shows this.[4] To focus on the magnitude

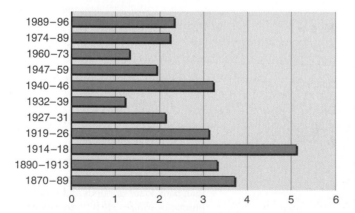

FIGURE 20.10   **Average absolute capital account surpluses (%GDP) for 12 OECD economics, 1870–1996.** The peak years for global capital flows were around the turn of the nineteenth century. *Source*: Obstfeld, "The Global Capital Market: Benefactor or Menace?" *Journal Economic Perspectives* (1999) pp. 1–30. Reprinted with permission from American Economic Assoiciation.

[4]Argentina, Australia, Canada, Denmark, France, Germany, Italy, Japan, Norway, Sweden, UK, and the United States.

FIGURE 20.11 **Capital account flows to emerging markets as percentage of investment.** Compared to the past only relatively small amounts of investment are financed through global capital markets. *Source*: Obstfeld, "The Global Capital Market: Benefactor or Menance?" *Journal of Economic Perspectives* (1999) pp. 1–30. Reprinted with permission from American Economic Assoiciation.

of the flows between countries, we show only the *absolute* value of the capital account—whether a country has a capital account surplus of 5% of GDP or a deficit of 5% of GDP, it appears as 5% in Figure 20.10.

Figure 20.11 shows evidence that capital flows today are not historically unprecedented. It indicates the amount of investment in a country that the capital account financed. Even after the surge in capital flows to developing economies in the 1990s, overseas capital financed proportionately less investment than 100 years ago.

IS THERE A GLOBAL INTEREST RATE?

A simple way to assess whether a single global market is in place is to determine whether a common interest rate at which countries can lend and borrow exists. In the absence of a global capital market, firms have to borrow at the rate prevailing in their national market. But if borrowing from abroad is not restricted and, if borrowing rates are lower in another country, then the firm will borrow from there. Competition among banks in different countries to attract lenders and borrowers will result in a single, common interest rate.

We can establish this result of a single real interest rate more formally by combining purchasing power parity (PPP) and uncovered interest parity (UIP). UIP implies

> U.S. nominal interest rate = Japanese nominal interest rate
> + expected depreciation of dollar against yen

As the nominal interest rate equals the real interest rate plus the expected inflation rate (the so-called Fisher equation), we can write this as

> U.S. real interest rate + expected U.S. inflation = Japanese real interest rate
> + expected Japanese inflation + expected depreciation of dollar against yen

However, PPP states that

$$\text{expected depreciation of dollar} = \text{expected U.S. inflation} \\ - \text{expected Japanese inflation}$$

Substituting this into our expanded UIP equation, we arrive at

$$\text{U.S. real interest rate} = \text{Japanese real interest rate}$$

In other words, in the absence of capital controls that restrict the flow of funds between economies, the real interest rate should be identical between countries. If no global capital market exists, the real interest rate will differ across economies.

Figure 20.12 shows estimates of the real interest rate for five economies. Even though there are some signs of convergence (especially among the United States, Canada, and Australia), at the end of the 1990s, no common global interest rate existed.

Why no single global real interest rate exists remains controversial. Our derivation required the use of PPP, which we argued in Chapter 18 was only useful as a long-run theory—therefore, perhaps a common real interest exists only as a long-run phenomenon. Further, our discussion of UIP in Chapter 19 suggested that we should add a risk premium because of exchange rate volatility and inflation and interest rate uncertainty, which implies that Figure 20.12 measures real interest rates *plus* a risk premium.

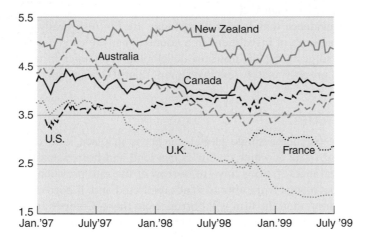

FIGURE 20.12 **Real interest rates.** Countries face important differences in real interest rates. *Source*: Breedon, Henry, and Williams, "Long-Term Real Interest Rates," *Oxford Review of Economic Policy* (1999) vol. 15, no. 2, pp. 128–142. Reproduced by permission of Oxford University Press.

SAVINGS AND INVESTMENT CORRELATION

Capital markets use funds from savers and lend them to individuals/firms/countries that can invest them profitably. This means that countries that do the investment do not have to be the same as those who do the saving so that, for instance, Africa can undertake large levels of investment even if African savings are low. Although investment is high and saving low, Africa will experience a capital account surplus (it will be selling domestic assets/claims to overseas banks and investors). Once the investment starts to yield a return, a country can start to repay the loans, its savings will be higher than investment, and it will run a capital account deficit.

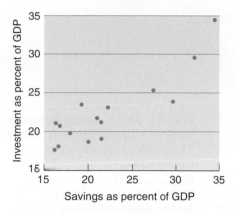

FIGURE 20.13 OECD cross-country savings–investment correlations, 1980–1998. High saving economics also have high investment. *Source*: Authors' calculations from OECD, *Economic Outlook* (June 2000).

This argument suggests that we should not expect to find any cross-country correlation between savings and investment—countries with high investments do not also have to have high savings. However, Figure 20.13 shows that among OECD countries savings are strongly correlated with investment.

A high correlation between savings and investment also exists within a country over time. Global capital markets should mean that if in one year a country has low savings it need not affect investment—the country can just borrow temporarily from abroad by running a capital account surplus. Similarly, if savings are unusually high, investment does not need to rise because the country can invest abroad generating a capital account deficit. So with a truly global capital market, there should be no correlation over time within a country between periods of high savings and high investment.

Figure 20.14 shows the correlation over time between savings and investment rate for a variety of OECD economies. The majority of countries have a strong correlation over time between their savings and investment—in years in which their savings are low, so too is their investment. Repeating these calculations for regions within a country leads to different results. For instance, in the UK, Canada, and Japan, there is essentially a

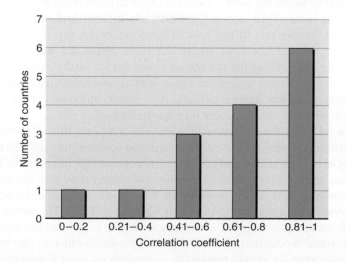

FIGURE 20.14 Correlation of savings and investment over time in OECD economies. There is a strong correlation within a country between saving and investment—when a country's saving falls, so too does its investment. *Source*: Authors' calculations using data from OECD Economic Outlook.

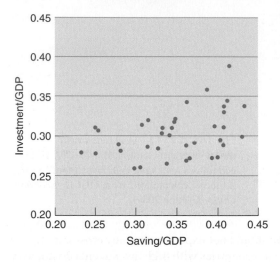

FIGURE 20.15   **Savings and investment correlation in Japanese prefectures, 1985–1990.** There is no correlation within Japanese regions between savings and investment— the market works well. *Source*: van Wincoop "Intranational versus International Saving–Investment Comovements," Federal Reserve Bank of New York mimeo (1999).

zero correlation between savings and investment within a region. In the United States, the correlation is negative. Figure 20.15 shows the correlation between savings and investment across the 48 prefectures of Japan. In contrast to Figure 20.14 there is little correlation. This suggests that within a country the domestic banking system allocates funds from savers to investors on a much larger scale than occurs between countries. Even though flows between countries are large and growing, they do not lead to the kind of separation between savings and investment that we observe *within* a country.

A CONSUMPTION PUZZLE

Financial markets also finance people through bad times. Consider a Canadian construction worker whose income is seasonal—low in the first and fourth quarter of the year, but high in the second and third quarter. To maintain consumption, the worker should borrow from the bank during the low income quarters (see Chapter 13 for a full analysis). For this example to work, the bank must have funds to lend, but it will if there exists a retail worker who works hard during the Christmas quarter and in the New Year sales period but not for the rest of the time. Therefore, in the first and fourth quarter, the retail worker, through the bank where she saves, lends the construction worker money to maintain him during his periods of low income. In the second and third quarter, the construction worker repays the retail worker and helps her to maintain her consumption during her low income periods. As a result, individual consumption shows no correlation with individual income on a quarterly basis.

The above system works only for idiosyncratic income fluctuations, that is, changes that not everyone experiences. Consider the case in which the economy moves into recession and the incomes of both the retail *and* construction workers fall. Because the incomes of both have fallen, the banking system cannot borrow money from one and lend to the other—both of them wish to keep consumption high in the recession, so both want to borrow. As a result, the consumption of both workers will fall. The financial system can help smooth consumption against idiosyncratic shocks to income but not in response to aggregate income shocks that affect everyone. So with an efficient financial system, every person's consumption should rise or fall depending on what is happening

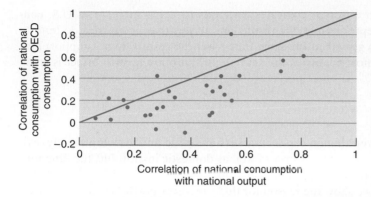

FIGURE 20.16 **Risk sharing among OECD nations, 1960–1999.** For OECD countries, output is more closely correlated than consumption over the business cycle. *Source*: Authors' calculations using IMF, *International Financial Statistics* (September 2000).

to aggregate income, but individual consumption should not show any response to purely idiosyncratic fluctuations in income.

Applying this logic to countries suggests that national and world consumption should be strongly correlated and that this should be higher than the correlation between national consumption and national GDP. If, for instance, German GDP is weak today while French GDP is high, then France can temporarily lend money to Germany (Germany has a capital account surplus), which is then reversed when German GDP is stronger than French GDP in the future.

Figure 20.16 shows that for only 4 out of 28 countries is the correlation between national and OECD consumption greater than the correlation between national consumption and national GDP. In other words, evidence suggests that global capital markets achieve only limited consumption smoothing with respect to country-specific output fluctuations.

If risk sharing among nations were perfect, we would expect to see a perfect positive correlation between different countries' consumption. To gauge the extent to which this occurs, consider Table 20.3, which reports the extent to which

TABLE 20.3 **Consumption Risk Sharing with United States, 1980–98**

Country	Impact on Consumption Growth of 1% Increase in U.S. Consumption Growth
Australia	0.168
Canada	0.474
France	0.144
Italy	−0.047
Japan	0.413
Switzerland	0.088
United Kingdom	0.297

Only weak evidence of global consumption smoothing.

Source: Ravn, "*Consumption Risk Sharing*," London Business School mimeo (1999).

consumption growth in different countries responds to a 1% increase in U.S. consumption growth. Except for Italy, the results are all positive—countries do tend to have high consumption growth at the same time—but the results do not support perfect risk sharing. For most countries the shared consumption growth effect is small and weak.

A HOME BIAS PUZZLE

We have shown that even though capital markets are large and growing rapidly, evidence suggests that they do not perform as well as domestic institutions the functions we expect of capital markets (e.g., capital smoothing, converting savings into investments). In this section we show the reason for this—investor portfolios are heavily biased toward their home economy. In other words, holdings of overseas assets are small, so domestic saving has to finance much domestic investment. Savings and investment track each other closely over the business cycle; and each country's consumption relies heavily on its output because portfolios are not sufficiently diversified.

Table 20.4 shows estimates of the equity portfolio allocation for the United States, Japan, and the UK in 1989. It shows little evidence of portfolio diversification: all three countries invested most of their funds in their domestic market.

TABLE 20.4   International Diversification of Equity Portfolios, December 1989

	U.S. Portfolios	Japanese Portfolios	UK Portfolios
United States	93.8%	1.3%	5.9%
Japan	3.1%	98.1%	4.8%
United Kingdom	1.1%	0.2%	82.0%
France	0.5%	0.1%	3.2%
Germany	0.5%	0.1%	3.5%
Canada	1%	0.1%	0.6%

Source: French and Poterba, "Investor Diversification and International Equity Markets," *American Economic Review Papers and Proceedings* (May 1991) vol. 81, pp. 222–226.

The increasing capital account flows of the 1990s have increased these portfolio shares, but as Figure 20.17 shows, although portfolios are now more diversified, they are still biased toward domestic assets.

Why are investment portfolios so undiversified internationally? The answer has significant implications for the future of capital markets—can we expect global capital markets to continue to grow until they perform their role as well as domestic markets, or will international diversification always be constrained?

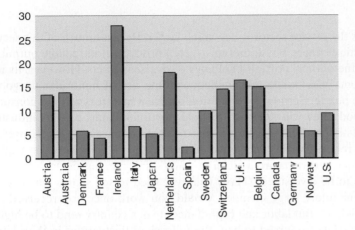

FIGURE 20.17 Overseas assets as percentage of private sector total financial wealth, 1998. Private sector portfolios are strongly biased toward domestic assets. *Source*: Data collected and kindly made available by Intersec, London.

EXPLAINING THE HOME BIAS PUZZLE

Each of the following four factors helps explain the lack of portfolio diversification we observe:

- capital market restrictions
- measurement issues
- nontraded goods
- asymmetric information

CAPITAL MARKET RESTRICTIONS

Many OECD economies did not substantially remove capital controls until the 1980s, and only in the 1990s did several emerging markets follow this policy. Restrictions on capital account flows will dramatically reduce holdings of overseas equity and can account for the home bias in portfolios. The reduction in capital controls over the last decade also helps explain the observed increase in portfolio diversification. However, capital controls cannot fully account for the magnitude of the home bias. For instance, there are few capital controls between France and Germany, but equity cross-holdings between these nations are still low.

MEASUREMENT PROBLEMS

Table 20.4 and Figure 20.17 might overstate the lack of international diversification in portfolios. Consider a Finnish investor holding a large portfolio of Finnish equity. This may appear to be an instance of home bias, but closer inspection reveals that Nokia, the telecommunications company, accounts for more than 80% of the Finnish equity market. Nokia is an international firm and earns its profits around the world. Therefore, by buying shares in Nokia on the Finnish exchange, the investor is diversifying her portfolio away from the Finnish economy. Such international diversification through holding domestic equity somewhat (but not completely) alleviates the home bias problem.

NONTRADED GOODS

In OECD economies the service sector is becoming larger. Because much of this sector (hairdressing, domestic cleaners, physiotherapists, etc,) produces nontradable output, it has implications for the optimal portfolio holdings of overseas assets. However, its implications for the home bias puzzle are ambiguous. One use of nontradeable goods helps account for the puzzle. Because by definition overseas investors will not consume the nontradeable good, they will not wish to hold portfolio claims on this industry. Therefore, the domestic portfolio will be weighted toward domestic assets. However, this argument is not robust. For instance, income in a country is split between capital and labor income. Equity markets are a claim on capital income, but no such markets enable labor income to be diversified. (Have you ever tried to sell shares whose dividends depend on your future wage income? Would you work once you received the money for the share issue?) But labor and capital income in a country tend to be highly correlated, so if individuals are forced to bear the full risk of fluctuations in their labor income, they will not want to be exposed to additional risk by holding domestic equity. They would prefer to hold large amounts of foreign assets and low levels of domestic equity. Therefore, nontraded goods may only exacerbate the home bias puzzle.

ASYMMETRIC INFORMATION

If you are a U.S.-based investor, you can easily gain information about U.S. firms and economic developments—trading screens, newspapers, television advertisements, and even conversations with taxi drivers are all potential sources of information. Getting this information is much more costly for non-U.S.-based investors. Therefore, U.S. equity will be cheaper for U.S. investors, and they will have a much greater U.S. portfolio holding than non-U.S. investors. A close examination of OECD cross-border equity flows between 1989 and 1996 supports informational asymmetries as an explanation of the home bias puzzle. Table 20.5 shows the results of an econometric study of equity investment from country i into country j. The larger the equity markets in country i and country j, the greater the equity investment from i into country j. Further, the more sophisticated the financial markets of country i, the more outward investment it performs.

TABLE 20.5 **Determinants of Cross-Border Equity Flows**

Variable	Effect
Market Capitalization in Investing Country	+
Market Capitalization in Recipient Economy	+
Distance between Two Economies	−
Telephone Calls between Two Economies	+
Sophistication of Investing Countries' Financial Markets	+
Number of Bank Branches of Investing Country in Recipient Economy	+
Absence of Insider Trading in Recipient Economy	+

Source: Summary of results of Portes and Rey, "The Determinants of Cross-Border Equity Flows," NBER Working Paper 7336 (1999).

Three key variables that reflect information flows between nations also affect overseas equity investment. The evidence suggests that the further apart two countries are geographically, the less equity flows between them. However, equity flows increase with the number of telephone calls between the two countries and the number of bank branches the investing country has in the recipient country. The more telephone calls and the more overseas bank branches there are, the easier it is for overseas investors to gain information, so the more equity they are prepared to invest overseas.

20.9 Should We Impose Capital Controls?

Should we try to encourage capital account flows and eliminate restrictions (a process called "capital account liberalization"), or should we consider completely free flows of capital a potential problem for the macroeconomy that needs to be controlled and restricted?

That capital account flows can improve the economy is beyond dispute. They can enable poor economies with low levels of domestic savings but profitable investment opportunities to accumulate capital rapidly and increase their standard of living. They can also help share consumption risk, so that country-specific fluctuations in output do not affect consumption. Global capital flows also impose discipline on policymakers. If domestic and foreign investors can withdraw funds from a country that pursues poor policies, then it will be forced to adopt better economic policies.

Table 20.6 compares the behavior of macroeconomic variables five years before capital account liberalization and five years after for several emerging markets. Many other things will have altered in these countries other than just capital account liberalization, and we need to interpret the table with care. However, after capital account

TABLE 20.6 **Macroeconomic Performance before and after Capital Account Liberalization**

	5 Years Before	5 Years After
Dividend Yield	3.86	2.65
Correlation with World Equity Markets	0.09	0.18
Stock Market Volatility	44.4	36.9
Exchange Rate Volatility	0.16	0.11
Real GDP Growth	2.73	2.98
Average Trade Surplus/GDP	1.43	2.76
Average Inflation	21.6	18.8
Interest Rates	28.2	25.3
Real Exchange Rate	104.2	99.0

Source: Bekaert and Harvey, "Capital Flows and the Behavior of Emerging Market Equity Returns," NBER Working Paper W6669, July 1998.

liberalization, the dividend yield fell, which suggests that the cost of capital to the corporate sector declined and GDP growth increased. Evidence also suggests that capital account liberalization increases the depth and sophistication of a country's financial system, an important prerequisite for growth. Both the scale of capital inflows and the arrival of overseas banks improve the domestic financial system. These advantages help understand why the International Monetary Fund (IMF) advocates capital account liberalization and why many developing economies embarked on it during the 1990s.

However, capital account liberalization also has its critics. For instance, Paul Krugman writes, "*sooner or later we will have to turn the clock at least part of the way back: to limit capital flows for countries that are unsuitable for either currency unions or free floating.*"[5] One concern is that volatile capital flows can interact with asymmetric information and lead to excessive risk taking and financial crisis. In this case, capital controls, rather than capital account liberalization, would be the sensible policy. The Asian crisis of 1998 lent support for this view. From the measured tones of U.S. Federal Reserve Board Chairman Alan Greenspan ("*In retrospect it is clear that more investment monies flowed into these* [Asian] *economies than could profitably be employed at reasonable risk*") to the more forthright comments of Malaysian Prime Minister Mahatir Mohammed (describing the global capital markets as "*a jungle of ferocious beasts*"), the behavior of global capital markets inspired increasing concern.

Three main criticisms are made of high levels of capital mobility:

- They create dilemmas for monetary policy.
- They lead to equalization of factor prices and declining capital taxes.
- Volatility of capital flows creates substantial fragility in domestic banking systems.

MONETARY POLICY DILEMMAS

Many emerging markets face a substantial real exchange rate appreciation in response to capital inflows. If a country has good policies and is seen as a profitable investment, large capital inflows will occur. This will push up the real exchange rate and put pressure on exports, and in particular, manufacturing—normally sectors that are key to growth. Lowering interest rates may offset this high exchange rate, but this might conflict with domestic objectives. As we shall see, in response to such developments, countries sometimes restrict capital inflows (e.g., Chile 1991–1998) to reduce the real exchange rate appreciation and allow monetary policy to be set to meet domestic objectives.

FACTOR PRICE EQUALIZATION

In Chapter 9 we showed how free trade in goods and services would lead to factors of production being paid the same amount across countries. The same outcome also occurs when financial capital is mobile between countries. If wages are higher (adjusting

[5]"Saving Asia: It's Time to Get Radical," *Fortune*, September 7, 1998.

for productivity) in one country than another, firms will relocate production to the cheaper country. This reduces the capital stock, the marginal product of labor, and the real wage in the high-wage economy and increases them in the recipient country. The process will continue until wages are equalized.

This process can be painful, and generates fear and opposition, especially among organized labor. Allied to this fear of factor price equalization is the concern that capital mobility between countries will reduce capital taxes. If capital is mobile between countries, it will move to where it is taxed most lightly. As capital taxes can go negative (if governments offer subsidies), this suggests that countries will compete with one another to offer more generous tax and subsidy packages to attract mobile capital. If governments are to remain solvent, this must result in either reduced government expenditure on noncapital-related items (e.g., social security systems) or higher labor taxes. Whether this is good or bad depends on your view of the role of the state. If the state is seen as responsible for providing an excessively large welfare system and causing low levels of economic efficiency, then capital mobility will produce a smaller state and a better economy. But if the state is viewed as the necessary provider of certain services that the market cannot provide (see Chapter 10), capital mobility will bring problems. With average EU corporate tax rates falling by 6% during the 1980s, and with the reduction of corporate taxes to 10% partly responsible for the success of the Irish economy, tax competition provokes genuine concern.

Consider a U.S. firm that has decided that it must have a European-based operation. Every European nation will offer the firm tax inducements. The U.S. firm will then choose the location with the lowest taxes/highest subsidies. If all countries eventually offer the same package, the U.S. firm will locate wherever the other economic advantages are greatest. However, as a result of the tax competition the host country gets little tax benefit from having the U.S. firm within its borders. Therefore, noncooperative behavior between the various national tax authorities leads to a poor outcome. If instead the EU can prevent countries from offering subsidies and special tax deals, then at least one country will gain the tax benefits of having a U.S. firm locate in Europe. The EU cannot control the subsidies that non-EU economies offer, but as long as firms have a reason to locate within the EU (for instance, there are no trade restrictions for intra-EU trade), this may not matter.[6]

20.10 Capital Controls

To avoid these problems associated with capital account flows, three types of restrictions have been proposed: taxes on capital account transactions, quantitative restrictions on either inflows or outflows, and prudential supervision of domestic banks and their overseas borrowings.

---

[6]Evidence that this is the case can be found in Devereux and Griffith, "Taxes and the Location of Production: Evidence from a Panel of U.S. Multinationals," *Journal of Public Economics* (1998) vol. 68, pp. 335–355.

TAXES

The most famous proponent of taxes on capital flows is Nobel Laureate James Tobin who advocates *"throwing sand in the wheels of international finance."* The Asian crisis illustrates the problem that Tobin's tax suggestion seeks to remedy. The real economy—investment, production, and employment decisions and the level of wages and prices moves much more slowly than capital flows from one country to another. This difference in speed causes problems for the real economy (for example, those stemming from high interest rates, the dramatic change in exchange rates, and fluctuations in output and unemployment). To slow down capital movements, Tobin suggests levying a small tax on each foreign exchange transaction. Such a tax would reduce the volatility of foreign exchange transactions and reduce the magnitude of speculative positions.

Although the Tobin tax has its advocates, it has not generated much official enthusiasm. The main problem is enforcement. To work, all countries must simultaneously implement the Tobin tax. Even if one small country decides not to implement it, the proposal will not work because this nation could act as an offshore tax haven for all foreign exchange transactions.

QUANTITATIVE RESTRICTIONS

To minimize a country's exposure to capital flows, the amount of capital that can flow into or out of a country can be restricted. These restrictions often aim to reduce particular types of capital flows, such as short-term bank loans.

Capital inflows are restricted to prevent a *future* currency crisis (they limit the size of the potential outflow) and limit the size of real exchange rate appreciations (which was relevant in Chile in 1991). Governments often restrict capital outflows during a currency crisis to prevent further capital flows and exchange rate depreciation and to lower interest rates to help their economy (i.e., Malaysia in 1998).

But do such quantitative restrictions work? Firms may be able to circumvent restrictions on borrowing short-term funds from overseas. An exporting firm only needs to overinvoice for goods sold and then repay at a later date—a transaction that mimics a short-term loan. For this reason governments need to monitor capital controls vigilantly and change their structure frequently to close loopholes. Overseas investors have a strong incentive to overcome such controls. Capital controls mean that domestic firms have to pay a higher interest rate on their loans than firms in other countries. This gives foreign banks an incentive to overcome the controls and earn greater profits than they could elsewhere. In such an environment, making capital controls work is extremely difficult.

A much cited example of the successful use of capital controls is Chile, which in 1991 introduced an unrenumerated reserve requirement (URR): a deposit of 20% of any capital inflow, which did not earn any interest, had to be placed at the central bank for the duration of any investment. In 1992 the reserve requirement became 30% and had to be deposited at the central bank for one year regardless of the duration of the investment. Such a URR penalizes short-term capital flows more than long-term flows. Table 20.7 shows that the policy seemed to work because the proportion of external borrowing in Chile that was on a short-term basis fell substantially. Capital controls enabled Chile to increase interest rates to control inflation in a rapidly growing economy

TABLE 20.7   Short-Term Loans as Proportion of Chilean External Debt

1990	1991	1992	1993	1994	1995	1996	1997	1998
19.4	13.4	19.0	18.2	18.0	15.8	11.5	4.8	5.4

Source: de Gregorio, Edwards, and Valdes, "Controls on Capital Inflows: Do They Work?" NBER Working Paper 7645 (1999).

without encouraging substantial short-term capital inflows or a large appreciation of the real exchange rate.

An alternative to controls on capital inflows is the emergency introduction of capital controls to stop outflows during a currency crisis. The most recent example of such policy is Malaysia during the 1998 Asian crisis. The international investment community attacked this policy. With the Malaysian exchange rate and stock market plummeting and the economy in recession, investors wished to withdraw funds, but emergency measures prevented them from doing so. This emergency action quickly led to costs—credit-rating agencies reduced their sovereign rating of Malaysian debt, and a higher risk premium increased the cost of foreign exchange borrowing. Further, when the capital controls are removed investors will probably be reluctant to commit funds for fear that Malaysia may reimpose controls. However, these emergency capital controls also had some benefits in Malaysia. The suspension of capital mobility meant that monetary policy could be aimed at the domestic economy rather than stabilizing capital outflows. It also offered a breathing space during which the government could make reforms to aid recovery from the crisis.

PRUDENTIAL RESTRICTIONS

This is the least controversial of the four recommendations arising from the Asian crisis. Many of the criticisms of global capital markets (that they suffer from asymmetric information, moral hazard, herd behavior, asset/liability mismatch, volatility of inflows and outflows) are valid for all financial markets—domestic or global. Domestically these problems are resolved by ensuring the central bank operates prudential regulations that prevent banks from being exposed to capital outflows or from concentrating their assets too heavily in a particular region or area. Some problems are specific to global capital markets (e.g., greater volatility risks because of their size, the absence of a lender of last resort to underpin investor confidence), but many of these problems can be solved the same way they are domestically—by prudential regulations.

Prudential requirements have two aspects. First, the domestic central bank can supervise and impose restrictions, for example on the maximum proportion of short-term foreign currency borrowing. Second, a global capital market must require appropriate global institutions or global arrangements to share information between national central banks. An intense debate is occurring regarding the appropriate international infrastructure for modern global capital markets. The role of the IMF raises many questions. Can it prevent currency crises, reduce asymmetric information, help coordinate the orderly withdrawal of investors? By lending large amounts of foreign currency to countries in difficulties, does it only encourage international investors to take excessive risks?

CAPITAL ACCOUNT LIBERALIZATION AND CAPITAL CONTROLS—A SUMMARY

Capital account mobility has both advantages and disadvantages. While capital controls are unlikely to work on a permanent basis and may not work at all, they can sometimes be useful.

The Asian crisis of the late 1990s shows that capital account liberalization on its own may not benefit an economy. Liberalization should be part of an overall package of reform. Only if sequenced appropriately will it yield benefits—capital account liberalization *alone* cannot boost long-term growth. Capital account liberalization if enacted too early in a country's reform process will either have no impact or be harmful. As a result the sequencing of economic reform is important and should begin with *current* account liberalization—the unrestricted use of currency for the purchase of goods and services. Next should be deregulation of the domestic banking system and the development of a strong system of financial supervision. Finally, once these stages are complete and sound macroeconomic policies are in place, capital account liberalization can occur. One of the mistakes that was made before the Asian crisis was the simultaneous deregulation of domestic banking and capital account liberalization. The result was a substantial inflow of money that the banking system invested inefficiently and which the banking authorities did not adequately monitor. This increased the risk of a systemic financial crisis, which triggered the events of 1997 and 1998.

# SUMMARY

Fixed exchange rates can help stabilize inflation but are vulnerable to speculative attack and rule out the use of an independent monetary policy. In response to these disadvantages, interest is growing in more extreme forms of fixed exchange rates: currency boards and single currencies.

Currency boards have succeeded when implemented along with fiscal reform in countries with high inflation rates. However, currency boards are still vulnerable to speculative pressure, which makes a single currency more attractive.

If countries have high levels of trade with each other; experience similar economic shocks; have high levels of labor market mobility; and there are cross-regional fiscal transfers, then single currencies may work. Absent these conditions the hope is that lower interest rates associated with the reduced risk of a currency crash will generate enough gains to offset the loss of independent monetary policy.

Removing restrictions on capital account transactions offers benefits for an economy—the ability to finance investment even in the absence of savings and to smooth out temporary income fluctuations, and the imposition of discipline on policymakers. However, it also brings potential problems—the loss of freedom to set monetary policy for domestic purposes; lowering of capital taxes; pressure on social security; and greater risk of financial crisis. Capital controls may overcome these problems, but the most popular option is improved prudential supervision of international transactions. Capital account liberalization brings advantages although not without good macroeconomic policies.

CONCEPTUAL QUESTIONS

1. What exchange rate system does your country operate? Is there concern about the value of the currency?

2. Would regions in your country benefit from a separate currency? Why?

3. Using a newspaper or the Web, examine the current tensions among countries that have adopted the euro. Are these tensions diminishing?

4. Should the world move to a system of only three exchange rates: dollar, euro, and yen?

5. How hard is it for you to find information about companies listed on foreign equity markets? Does this explain the home bias puzzle?

6. "Governments criticize global capital markets only because they exert a constant discipline that prevents them following politically expedient but economically inefficient policies." Discuss.

7. "Capital account liberalization is like a medicine that is usually beneficial but often produces horrific side effects. Such a medicine cannot be left unregulated." Discuss.

8. Do you use bank borrowing to smooth your own consumption? Does your answer shed any light on the behavior of a country's capital account and the close link between savings and investment?

9. Are the problems of global capital markets different from those of domestic financial markets?

10. Are global capital markets undermining the role of national governments?

ANALYTICAL QUESTION

1. Total national income in three countries over a recent, and typical, 10-year period is shown below.

Year	1	2	3	4	5	6	7	8	9	10
Country A	10	8	7	9	10	14	12	16	18	8
Country B	11	12	11	13	15	8	7	16	18	10
Country C	10	12	13	11	11	7	9	5	4	10

    (a) Is there scope for risk sharing between countries? Describe exactly how this might work.

    (b) With which country should country A look to share risk?

    (c) If country A is prevented from trading risk with country C but can trade with country B, can this help? Assume that B can itself trade risk with C.

    (d) Suppose country A was 100 times larger than either B or C (so we multiply all the numbers in the first row by 100). How does this affect your answers to (a), (b), and (c)?

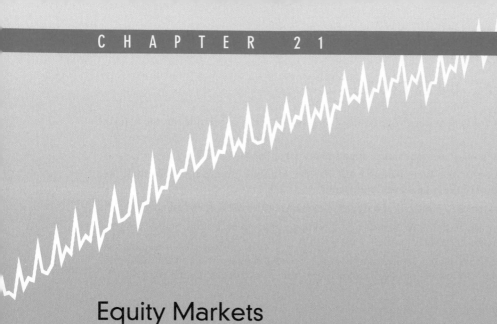

Equity Markets

Overview

How stock prices are determined and why they move are issues of major economic importance. Shifts in equity prices affect the value of wealth, influence the new investment decisions of firms, and can trigger restructuring of companies if they lead to takeovers. We first develop a way of valuing equities based on the earnings potential of a firm's assets—these assets can be machines, buildings, the experience of the workforce and management, the value of brand names, or the future advantages of market dominance. But whether such a valuation model that bases itself on these fundamentals can explain the observed volatility of equity prices is controversial. Therefore, we will also consider the role of speculative bubbles, irrational herd-like behavior by investors, and myopia in forecasting the future in making stock price volatile. We will also consider whether equities in general may become mispriced for long periods relative to other assets.

21.1 What Are Equities?

A company consists of assets that include physical capital as well as less tangible things that, for many firms, may have more value, such as brands, monopoly power, patents, or a good reputation. Equities, or shares, are claims to own these assets; in effect they are claims on the future stream of profits that these assets may generate. Trade in shares enables sellers to swap a claim on a flow of future (and uncertain) income from corporate assets in exchange for immediate funds; buyers acquire a claim on a future flow of income in return for cash. In essence, equity markets are where a significant part of the value of the physical assets of the world's largest economies are continually put up for sale.

In most developed economies, the aggregate flow of corporate profits is huge. Figure 21.1 shows the share of the total value added of the corporate sectors of the main industrialized countries that accrues to owners of the firms. On average, about two-thirds of the value of the flow of output goes to labor as wages; the rest goes to providers of equity and debt capital. Because equities are claims on much of this flow, the total value of such claims is large. Table 21.1 shows the total market value of the equities traded in the major economies at the end of 1998. In the United States, equities were worth well over 150% of one year's gross domestic product (GDP). In the UK, the market value of equities was closer to two years' annual GDP. In the 1980s and early 1990s, the value of Japanese equities was sometimes in excess of annual GDP—though not by the end of 1990s. Annual turnover in equity markets is also enormous. Table 21.1 shows that transactions in the major stock markets in the world in 1998 typically added up to around 50% of the value of the outstanding stock; in other words, shares changed hands on average about once every two years. In the United States—by far the largest market in the world—turnover was higher in 1998, and shares changed hands about once a year.

Share prices themselves fluctuate widely. Even if we look at averages of the share prices of many companies, which smoothes out a lot of volatility, variability is substantial. Figures 21.2 through 21.4 show the history of the main national stock price indexes for the three largest stock markets in the world over the last few decades. In the UK and the United States, stock prices over this period show an upward trend, reflecting the strong returns stocks in those countries generated. In Japan, prices rose and fell on either side of the peak in the market at the end of the 1980s. In all countries short-term volatility was considerable: in the United States, the market fell over 20% in one day in 1987!

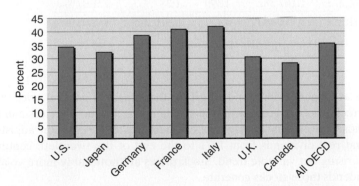

FIGURE 21.1 **Share of capital income in business sector (%) in 1999.** Profits—which accrue to suppliers of capital—average around one-third of corporate sector value added in the developed world. *Source*: OECD, *Economic Outlook* 2000. Copyright OECD.

TABLE 21.1   Stock Markets around the World (1998 data; values are $mn)

Country	Market Capitalization	Trading Volume	Number of Companies	GDP	Market Capital/ GDP Ratio
Australia	874,283	407,420	1,162	363,677	240.40%
Austria	34,106	16,566	139	212,923	16.02%
Belgium	245,657	55,360	146	254,632	96.48%
Canada	543,394	355,585	1,384	599,663	90.62%
Czech Republic	12,046	4,741	261	55,077	21.87%
Denmark	98,881	64,954	242	173,824	56.89%
Finland	154,518	60,321	129	126,437	122.21%
France	991,484	572,151	711	1,436,226	69.03%
Germany	1,093,962	1,390,798	741	2,138,358	51.16%
Greece	79,992	46,999	244	106,800	74.90%
Hungary	14,028	16,135	55	51,249	27.37%
Ireland	29,956	22,126	79	78,825	38.00%
Italy	569,731	475,791	320	1,024,105	55.63%
Japan	2,495,757	948,522	2,387	3,962,614	62.98%
Mexico	91,746	33,841	194	417,219	21.99%
Netherlands	603,182	379,166	212	377,409	159.82%
Norway	56,285	42,638	236	147,169	38.25%
Poland	20,461	8,921	198	149,428	13.69%
Portugal	62,955	47,577	135	115,463	54.52%
South Korea	114,593	137,859	748	449,517	25.49%
Spain	114,593	699,034	484	578,557	19.81%
Sweden	278,707	203,690	258	227,257	122.64%
Switzerland	689,199	637,344	232	263,859	261.20%
United Kingdom	2,374,273	1,167,382	2,399	1,387,933	171.07%
United States	13,451,352	13,148,480	8,450	8,510,975	158.05%

Source: Global Financial Data at btaylor; @globalfindata.com

Even if we look at longer periods, and adjust for the impact of general price inflation by measuring stock prices in real terms, the strong upward trend in prices and the high volatility of those prices remain. Figure 21.5 measures real (inflation adjusted) U.S. stock prices and real dividends from 1871 to the end of the twentieth century.[1] Both series are on a rising but variable trend. Stock prices are noticeably more volatile than the flow of dividends those stocks generate.

---

[1]Robert Shiller of Yale University compiled the series. It has been the basis for much work on long-run stock price trends; it is based on the values of the standard and Poor's stock price index.

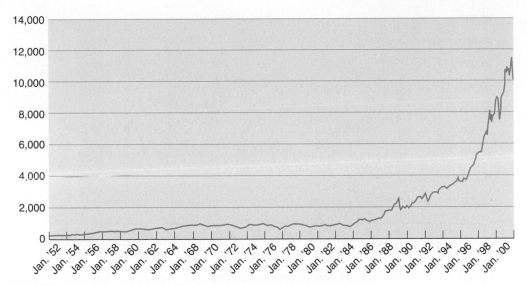

FIGURE 21.2 **Dow Jones industrials stock index.** *Source*: Datastream.

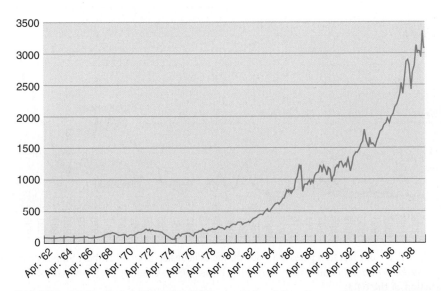

FIGURE 21.3 **Financial Times Stock Exchange all share index.** *Source*: Datastream. Copyright Global Financial Data.

The pattern of stock prices revealed in the figures and the data on the overall value of the stock markets across different countries raise several questions: Why do share prices move? Are the substantial fluctuations we observe in the stock market related to economic fundamentals or the whims of speculators? How important are equities in the portfolios of the private sectors across different countries? Why have

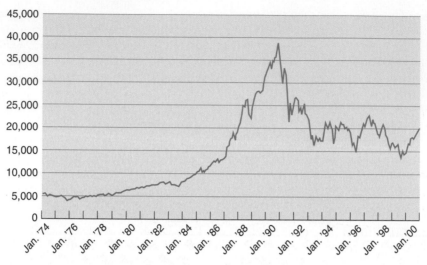

FIGURE 21.4   **Nikkei 225 stock index.** *Source*: Datastream.

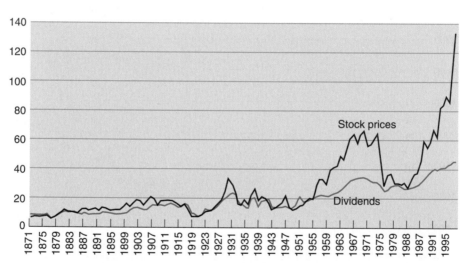

FIGURE 21.5   **U.S. real stock prices and dividends: The Shiller data.** *Source*: Robert Shiller data; see Shiller, *Market Volatility* (Cambridge, MA: MIT Press, 1989), Chapter 26, for details of the construction of the data.

equities in the past tended to yield greater returns than those earned on most other assets? Can we expect this excess return on equities to continue into the future? The range of questions is wide, and their economic significance is great; we will address each of them.

Economists have thought a lot about these questions. Equity markets fascinate them, partly because these markets seem to meet many of the strong assumptions that standard economic theory often makes: they are markets with many participants, none of whom has much monopoly power, all of whom have access to a lot of information, and most of whom want to make money. Does such a market really function well—do prices reflect a sensible judgment on the future earnings power of the underlying assets of corporations? Because stock markets are so important, this is not just an academic question. We saw in Chapter 14 that investment expenditure should depend on stock prices. Table 21.1 shows that in many of the major economies total stock market values are large relative to the size of the economy. For both these reasons, how equity markets work has great economic significance.

As well as trying to answer some of these fundamental questions about how equity markets work, we also hope to help you make sense of the massive amount of commentary on stock markets in the media. This commentary often addresses another set of issues, usually why the market went down or up yesterday. For example, a recent report we read on the day's trading in the U.S. stock market said, "On a wave of buying, U.S. stocks rallied 220 points in early trading on Wall Street today."

However, because every transaction involves a seller as well as a buyer, this statement makes about as much sense as, "On a wave of selling U.S. stocks rallied 220 points."[2] The financial pages also often contain quotes from celebrated market gurus who will make comments such as, "If the market moves below 6500 it will break a key resistance point and will then fall to 6000." Such a statement seems to imply that stock prices are subject to external pressures like the unknowable forces of nature, but what are they, and what economic factors lie behind them?

Our own favorite piece of misleading "analysis" is the almost universal tendency of media commentators to want to identify a single piece of news as responsible for the movement in a stock price index. Remember that an index is an average of prices based on companies in completely different sectors of the economy and often (effectively) in different countries. We are routinely told things such as, "News of the latest comments from the chairman of the U.S. Federal Reserve sent stocks tumbling in Europe, but was already discounted in Wall Street prices." This confident type of assertion about a causal link between two events that happened at about the same time cannot be proved or refuted. These assertions are unverifiable stories, not economic analysis.

Therefore this chapter will provide a more formal analysis to help you understand how equity markets operate. This is worth doing because how these markets work is important. It matters greatly whether stock price movements are the result of rational and reasoned responses by investors to information on the long-term economic prospects of firms or whether they are the result of a whim or of herd-like behavior that is triggered by sports results, the weather, or blind panic. The investment decisions of firms are likely to depend to some extent on movements in financial asset prices, so it would be worrying if those financial market valuations were dissociated from fundamental determinants of corporate profitability. When markets work well, they reward those who are most efficient at producing what society wants and punish those who are not. The price of buying a company's equity is the cost of acquiring the right to take over the management of a collection of corporate assets. To put resources to their most productive use, the equity price should be highest when the best managers are in

---

[2]Although the market can fall by 220 points without any trades.

charge. So it would be worrying if the price at which firms can be taken over—possibly changing how they are run—bears little relation to their earnings prospects. If there was only a weak link between the efficiency with which a company was run and its stock price, good managers would be as likely to lose their jobs after a hostile takeover deal as bad ones. And if stock price movements bear little relation to underlying economic conditions in the corporate sector, it would be folly for former centrally planned economies to be reshaped to give the stock market a key role in allocating resources.

21.2 International Comparisons of Equity Markets

The importance of equity markets varies greatly across countries. For instance, in continental Europe stock markets have played a smaller role in funding companies than in the United States or the UK and the aggregate value of equities has constituted a smaller part of the total stock of financial assets. Where companies rely heavily on banks and bond issues to finance investment, and less on new equity issues and retained profits, the value of the equity market relative to GDP will tend to be smaller. And where private firms that are not quoted on a stock market account for a substantial part of economic activity, the importance of publicly traded stock is correspondingly lower. Figure 21.6 shows the proportion of the total financial assets of the private sectors in the major economies that is equities.

Clearly the relative importance of equity in the total stock of financial assets has varied greatly across countries; and the variability does not just reflect differences between advanced, capitalist countries and less developed, or centrally planned, economies. Ireland, the UK, and the United States are countries where at the end of

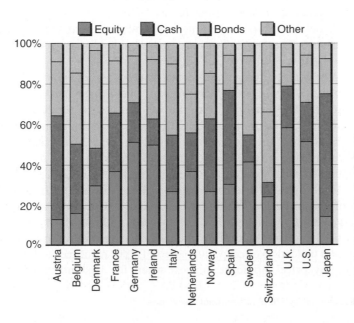

FIGURE 21.6 **Portfolio allocation of the private sector, 1998.** The importance of equity investments varies greatly across the developed world. *Source*: Author calculations based on Intersec data derived from national sources. Thanks to Intersec Research Corp. London for permission to use their data.

the 1990s equities represented over 50% of the total stock of financial assets; that proportion has been substantially lower in most of the advanced, free market economies of continental Europe. Why?

One reason why stock markets have been more important in the UK, the United States, Ireland, and (to a lesser extent) the Netherlands is because a substantial part of the incomes going to the retired come from funded pensions in these countries. In most continental European countries, unfunded state pensions, financed by taxes on current workers, have generated a much higher proportion of income for the elderly. This matters because pension funds are long-term investors, and over the long term, equities in the biggest stock markets have substantially outperformed other asset classes. Figure 21.7 shows the real returns on U.S. stocks, bonds, bills, gold, and cash since 1800. A dollar bill held since 1800 would have been worth about 7 cents, in real terms, by the end of the twentieth century; inflation has eroded more than 90% of its value. Gold—often thought to be a safe long-term investment—would have done better and been worth about 84 cents by the end of the period—still a decline of 16%. Bills and bonds would have done better still; $1 invested in the bond market in 1800 would have been worth about $800 200 years later. But look at the equity line. Despite big falls in 1929 and in the early 1970s, the equity line consistently rises faster than any of the others. Note how even big shocks—like the 1987 stock market crash—have been washed away by the overwhelming tendency over the longer term for stock prices to rise faster than the prices of bonds, bills, and gold. That same $1 invested in 1800 would have been worth over $550,000 by the end of the period if put into U.S. stocks. Furthermore, in almost none of the 20-year intervals from 1800 do cash (dollar bills), gold, or U.S. bonds or bills outperform U.S. stocks.[3]

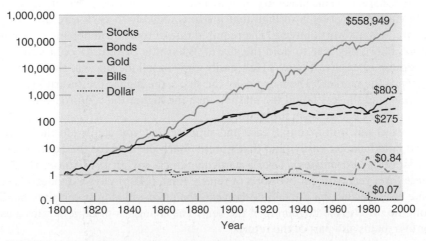

FIGURE 21.7 **The value of $1 invested in 1800.** Equities have massively outperformed other investments in the United States over the past 200 years. *Source*: Siegel, *Stocks for the Long Run*, 2nd edition (New York: McGraw-Hill, 1999). Reproduced with kind permission of The McGraw-Hill Companies.

[3]The exception is the 20 years starting just before the Wall Street crash of 1929.

The average time lag between when a pension fund receives money to invest on behalf of a worker and when it pays that money back to the worker might be 30 years. Therefore, pension funds will be particularly attracted to the exceptional long-run performance of equities, and pension funds in the United States and the UK have typically held between 60% and 80% of their overall portfolios in equities.

As we saw in Chapter 10 the aging population of OECD countries could put intolerable strains on state pensions systems within Europe because, for Europe as a whole, the ratio of those of retirement age to those of working age will roughly double by 2040. This may force governments to reduce the value of the state pension, which might encourage rapid growth of private, funded pensions, stimulating the demand for equities. Whether that would be beneficial depends on whether the signals that stock prices give are an appropriate means to direct resources. So how equity prices and rates of return are determined will be critical. But how are those prices determined?

21.3   The Determination of Stock Prices

Our analysis of what determines share prices starts with a model in which fundamentals pin down equity prices—that is, expectations of the future profitability of the companies whose stocks are being valued. Later we will consider additional factors, including market psychology.

When someone buys a share, she has in mind a required rate of return—that is, a percentage overall yield that is partly made up of a return in the form of income (that is, dividends) and partly as a return in the form of capital gain. If, at the current market price of the share, it seems likely to generate a return at or above the required level, it is worth buying; if the price is so high that it seems unlikely to earn a return at the required rate, it is not worth buying. The required rate of return will depend on a number of factors. How risky is it to hold the share? What rate of return could you earn on other, perhaps safer, investments? How easily can you sell the share at short notice, i.e., how liquid is the market? The more risky the share, the higher the return available on other assets, and the less liquid the market, then the higher the required rate of return the investor will demand from the share.

Let's start out with a simple case and suppose that you can trade the share in a deep and liquid market easily (and that's pretty much the case for the equities of large firms in developed countries). Take a particular stock, say an IBM share. If you hold this share for a year, you get two sorts of return. First, if IBM pays a dividend, you will get some cash. Second, by the end of the year, the price will almost certainly be different from the price at the beginning of the year. The change in price generates a capital gain or loss that is also part of the return.

If the stock market is working efficiently, the rate of return (or yield) people *expect* to get from an asset should just equal the required rate of return that they demand. Consider the case in which the typical (or representative) investor would hold the share if it was expected to deliver a return of 15% over the next year, but that currently, at the existing market price, she thinks that the share is likely to yield 18%. In these circumstances the share is a good buy and remains so while the expected return is above the required return. However, as the typical investor buys more and more of the share, its current price will tend to rise. Assuming that expectations of next period's price do not change, then a rise in the current price reduces expectations of future capital gains. In other words, the expected return on the share declines. Eventually the current price will rise until the expected and required rates of return are equal. At this point the investor will stop purchasing shares, and the price will stop rising. By contrast, consider the case in which the expected return is 12%—below the required return of 15%. In this case, the investor will start to sell her share holding. This will tend to lower the share price. As the share price falls, the investor increases her expectation of future capital gains. This leads to a higher expected rate of return until eventually the share price falls to a level at which the expected and required rates of return are equal.

The expected rate of return from holding a share is equal to the expected capital gain plus any dividend payments (all expressed as a percentage of the original share price). For simplicity, assume that investors' required return is the same from period to period and is equal to r. We need the expected return (capital gain plus dividend) to be equal to r. Let's write today's share price as $P(0)$ and the expected share price one period (say a year) ahead as $P(1)$. Let the expected value of dividends paid this year be $D(1)$. We require that

expected capital gains + dividend yield = required rate of return

$$[P(1) - P(0)]/P(0) + D(1)/P(0) \qquad = r \qquad\qquad\qquad (1)$$

Figure 21.8 shows the relation among $P(0)$, $P(1)$, $D(1)$, and r. On the horizontal axis, we measure the expected return from holding a share given the price at which we can buy it. That price is $P(0)$ and is measured on the vertical axis.

The left-hand side of equation (1) gives the return. For a given set of expectations about the price one year ahead and about the dividends to be paid, then the higher is the current price the lower is the expected return. Keeping expectations of the future constant, a higher current price means lower capital gains and a smaller dividend yield. Therefore, there is a negative relationship between the expected rate of return and the current price which the downward-sloping line in Figure 21.8 shows. The required rate of return does not depend on the current price, so we draw it as the vertical line at r. Equilibrium in the market requires that the expected rate of return equals the required rate of return. This occurs when the downward-sloping expected returns schedule intersects the

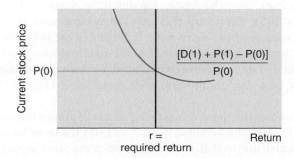

FIGURE 21.8 **Share prices and expectations.** $D(1)$ is the anticipated per share dividend at the end of the year; $P(1)$ is the expected share price one year ahead; r is the required expected return over a year.

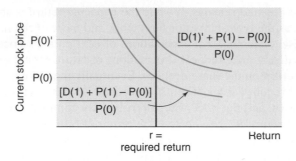

FIGURE 21.9   **An increase in expected dividends.** $D(1)$ is the initial value of the expected dividend per share for the year ahead; $D(1)'$ is the revised, and more optimistic, expectation for the dividend.

vertical required rate of return line. This therefore determines the current share price for given expectations about equity prices next period and for given expectations of dividends and a particular required rate of return.

Anything that changes expectations of capital gains, dividends, or the required rate of return will affect the current price. For instance, imagine that the investor revised upwards her expectation of next period's stock price, $P(1)$. For a given level of current prices, this would lead to a rightward shift of the expected return line (as in Figure 21.9) and so to a higher level of current prices. Investors would buy the stock today in expectation of a higher price tomorrow. This leads to a higher price today until the expected return on the stock is again equal to the required rate of return.

Consider the implications of some good news that raises people's expectations of the dividend to be paid this year—$D(1)$ increases. If this does not change people's expectations of *next* period's price, the current share price must rise. Figure 21.9 illustrates why. The sloping line shifts up if $D(1)$ rises, so the equilibrium share price today must increase from $P(0)$ to $P(0)'$. Before the increase in forecast dividends, investors were happy to hold the share because it offered a rate of return equal to r. Assuming the current market price did not change, then the increase in dividends will lead to a rate of return in excess of r. As a result, the investor will buy more of the share, which will push prices up. Eventually prices will rise until the expected return is no longer in excess of the required rate of return. This is why good news about future corporate profits and dividends leads to an increase in current share prices.

What if the required rate of return were to increase? Suppose, for instance, that the central bank raises interest rates, so that investors can now get a higher return on relatively safe investments such as bank deposits. Again, for simplicity, suppose that this rise in interest rates is expected to be temporary and only last for one year. It might then be reasonable to expect no change in the share price at the end of the year. The increase in current interest rates leads to a rightward shift in the required rate of return line. (Remember, this is the required rate of return over one year.) Assuming that both $P(1)$ and $D(1)$ were unchanged, then the current share price must fall—as Figure 21.10 shows.

Before the interest rate increase, the share was offering a rate of return just equal to the desired rate of return. However, the increase in interest rates led to an increase in the required rate of return, which means that at its current price the stock would fail

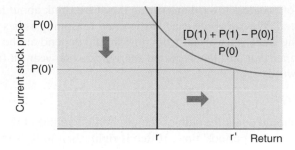

FIGURE 21.10 **An increase in interest rates leads to lower share prices.** Point r is the initial value of the required rate of return; r' is the new, higher required rate of return.

to meet the investor's target. The investor would no longer wish to hold the share and would sell it. This pushes the share price down until eventually the expectation of increased capital gains (because the share price has fallen) and the higher dividend yield, i.e., $(D(1)/P(0)$ means that the expected return on the stock has risen to a level consistent with the investor's new required rate of return. This model therefore implies that when governments increase interest rates (or when economic data are released that suggest that the government will have to raise interest rates) then, all else being equal, the share price will have to fall.

It should be obvious from all this that stock prices are forward-looking variables. The value of the share now should depend on your judgment about the dividend that will be paid this year and on what you think the share might be worth at the end of the year. To see this, we can simply rearrange equation (1). First, we know that the expected amount of money earned on holding the share is the rate of return times the purchase price of the share—that is, $rP(0)$. This must equal the anticipated capital gains from holding the stock plus the dividends earned: $P(1) - P(0) + D(1)$. Therefore

$$rP(0) = P(1) - P(0) + D(1)$$

which can also be written as

$$(1 + r)P(0) - P(1) + D(1)$$

or

$$P(0) = [P(1) + D(1)]/(1 + r)$$

This shows us that the current share price is equal to the expectation of next period's stock price plus the expected dividend all divided by (or more accurately *discounted* by) 1 plus the required rate of return.

This may not appear too helpful; after all, it simply says that today's price should depend on what people expect the price will be tomorrow, and that hardly seems to be a theory that ties down where prices should be. The message seems to be that if people expect a share price to be fantastically high in a year's time, then it should be fantastically high today. And that theory seems to allow share prices to be pretty much anywhere at all. To make this more useful we need to work out what people's expectations of next period's price will be.

In fact, we can make a lot of progress toward answering this if we think about how prices will be valued a year ahead. We can apply exactly the same reasoning as lies behind Figure 21.8 to argue that the share price a year from now should depend on the anticipated dividend in the year *after that* plus the expected share price one year on (i.e., two years from now). In other words

$$P(1) = [P(2) + D(2)]/(1 + r)$$

So the stock price *next* period should equal the sum of the discounted values of the expected stock price and dividend in *two* periods' time. If that is right, then today's share price should depend positively on expected dividends over the next *two* years plus the expected value of the share price two years ahead. Imagine investors increasing their forecast of dividends two years hence, that is, an increase in $D(2)$. This will therefore lead to an increase in $P(1)$ in Figure 21.9. But Figure 21.9 also implies that if next period's stock price increases, a rise in $P(1)$, then so does the *current* price, $P(0)$.

We can use the same argument again and think of the share price two years from now as reflecting what people expect the dividend to be the year after *that* and their expectations of what the price will be *three* years from now. If we apply this argument over and over, we can write the share price as being equal to the discounted value of the stream of dividends up to some point far in the future *plus* the discounted value of the price at that point in the future.[4] In other words, the current share price reflects *all* future information about *all* future dividends. Any news regarding *future* dividends should influence today's stock price.

However, note that while the current stock price reflects information about all future dividends, all dividends are not equally important. Because of discounting, current dividends influence the current stock price more than dividends in the far future. The discounting works as follows. The current stock price depends on the discounted expected price and dividends next period, $P(0) = [P(1) + D(1)]/(1 + r)$. We also know that next period's price equals the discounted value of expected prices and dividends in period 2. Therefore, in influencing today's stock price, current dividends are discounted only once, $D(1)/(1 + r)$, but dividends expected in period 2 are discounted twice. That is because we have to discount $P(1)$ when considering its influence on $P(0)$ and because $P(1)$ itself depends on discounted dividends in period 2. Therefore, the influence of period 2 dividends on the current stock price is twice discounted, $D(2)/(1 + r)^2$. Because $(1 + r)^2$ is greater than $(1 + r)$, future dividends drive the current stock price *less* than current dividends do. In fact, the further ahead we look, the less influence dividends have on current prices.

We have therefore shown that the current share price depends on the discounted sum of future dividends. This is why we called this approach a means of valuing shares that depends on fundamentals. How much you are prepared to pay for the stock depends on the underlying profitability of the company and the dividends it pays. It does

---

[4]We have that $P(1) = [P(2) + D(2)]/(1 + r)$ and that $P(0) = [P(1) + D(1)]/(1 + r)$. Therefore, we can write $P(0) = [[P(2) + D(2)]/(1 + r) + D(1)]/(1 + r) = P(2)/(1 + r)^2 + D(2)/(1 + r)^2 + D(1)/(1 + r)$. However, we also have that $P(2) = [P(3) + D(3)]/(1 + r)$, so we can use this to write $P(0) = P(3)/(1 + r)^3 + D(3)/(1 + r)^3 + D(2)/(1 + r)^2 + D(1)/(1 + r)$. If we continue in this manner, we would arrive at $P(0) = P(40)/(1 + r)^{40} + D(40)/(1 + r)^{40} + \ldots + D(2)/(1 + r)^2 + D(1)/(1 + r)$. We could, of course, carry on like this indefinitely and arrive at an expression $P(0) = P(N)/(1 + r)^N + D(N)/(1 + r)^N + \ldots + D(2)/(1 + r)^2 + D(1)/(1 + r)$, where N is any large integer you want to specify.

not depend on whether the Dow Jones has fallen below 6000 on the third Tuesday of a month with an R in its name—the price you should pay depends only on the profitability of the underlying asset. However, we still need to tie up a loose end here. We have shown that the current share price depends on the discounted stream of dividends **and the discounted expected stock price several periods in the future**. In other words, the current share price, P(0), depends on all discounted dividends over the next, say, 40 years, $D(1)/(1 + r) + D(2)/(1 + r)^2 + \ldots$ all the way to $D(40)/(1 + r)^{40}$, but it also depends on the discounted value of the share price in 40 years' time: $P(40)/(1 + r)^{40}$. We still have to solve the problem that if stock prices are forward-looking then the current stock price must depend on both future dividends and how much investors think the stock will be worth in the future. Unless we can somehow get round this dependence on future prices, we will have a circularity that we cannot solve.

However, we can probably ignore this discounted future price term—that is, we can expect that $P(40)/(1 + r)^{40}$ is small. So long as the average annual growth in share prices over the next 40 years is less than r, then P(40) is less than $(1 + r)^{40}$ times its value today; if that is true over any long horizon, $P(n)/(1 + r)^n$ eventually goes to zero.

But would the share price in the distant future be small relative to the discount factor? The answer is basically—yes. The reason is straightforward. The real rate of return on relatively safe assets (like inflation-proof government bonds) has been around 3–4% over the past 20-odd years (the only period when bonds guaranteeing a real rate of return have existed). This means that a typical share (which is riskier than these safe assets) is likely to have a required real rate of return in excess of 3–4%. In other words, the value of r in equation (1) is likely to be greater than .03, and probably significantly greater (note that we are talking in *real* terms). The sustainable, or long-run, rate of growth of real GDP in nearly all developed economies is under 3%. So now consider what would happen if the price of an IBM share were expected to consistently rise in real terms by more than r, when r itself is in excess of the growth of GDP. This would mean that the value of one share in IBM would, eventually, be larger than the whole GDP that the advanced economies produced. This seems implausible, so it seems sensible to assume that share prices ultimately grow at a slower rate than r. If this is the case, then the discounted share price eventually tends to zero, and we can write the current share price as depending *only* on the discounted sum of future dividends.

So we can think of the price of a share as equal to the expected discounted value of the flow of all future dividends. This implies that share prices can, indeed should, move in response to anything that changes the expected value of dividends at any point in the future (such as new products or inventions, changes in regulatory rules, increases in corporate taxes) *or* anything that causes people to change their required rates of return over any period in the future (changes in interest rates, changes in how investors assess risk). Anything that causes the expectation of the dividend to be paid in the future to rise will cause stock prices to rise *now*. And anything that causes investors to require a higher rate of return causes share prices to fall *now*. Therefore, we can begin to see why stocks might be so volatile and dependent on rumor and information.

The idea that the value of a share should equal the discounted value of expected future dividends has a powerful logic behind it. But is it right? After all, some companies pay no dividends, show no inclination to do so, and yet have high share prices. Microsoft was one of the star performers in the U.S. stock market in the 1990s, yet over that period it did not pay one cent in dividends. More dramatically, many internet stocks when initially launched saw their stock market values soar.[5] Not only have these companies generally not paid dividends, many have not even earned profits from which dividends could be paid (unlike the highly profitable Microsoft). By the end of the 1990s such companies dominated the NASDAQ index of U.S. stocks, which in the 1990s outperformed the Dow Jones index of industrial stocks by a large margin. Between January 1990 and January 2000, the average annual rate of price increase in the high-tech-dominated NASDAQ index was over 25%, compared with about 15% for the Dow (see Figure 21.11).

But the dividend/discount account of stock prices is not, at least in principle, inconsistent with the value of a Microsoft or an Internet stock. The dividend discount model says that the expectation of a dividend being paid *at some point in the future* generates value today. That point could be 20 years off; as long as the eventual payoff is big, so is the stock price today. In fact, the payoff need not actually come as a dividend. Share repurchases by the company, or purchases of stock by another company that launches a successful takeover bid, are other means of distributing cash to shareholders. (We can think of these as forms of dividend payment; in a takeover the purchase of stock is really a final dividend payment to the holders of shares in the company that is taken over.)

So in principle the massive valuations of some dot.com (Internet) companies that were seen at the end of the 1990s and the notion that stock values reflect the present discounted value of future cash distributions by the company are not inconsistent. But in

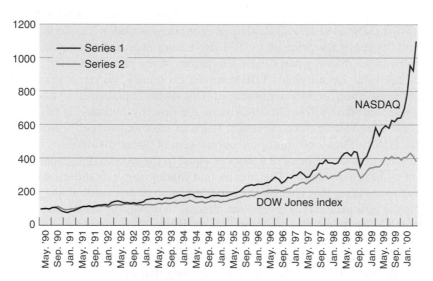

FIGURE 21.11   **U.S. stock price indexes, January 1990 = 100.** In the United States, high-tech stocks, which dominate the NASDAQ index, outperformed industrials by a large margin in the 1990s. Subsequent performance was dramatically worse. *Source*: Thomson Financial Datastream.

[5]A majority also saw their values subsequently slump!

practice most stock valuations in the Internet frenzy at the end of the 1990s were hard to reconcile with rational valuation. Consider what happened to the Internet stock At Home:

> *At Home went public at $17 per share, and its stock valuation went through the roof. At the time of its IPO* (initial public offering of shares) *in July 1997, At Home's revenue was only $750,000 but its market capitalization was $2.6 billion. By the summer of 1998 its market capitalization was up to $5.6 billion, even though in the previous 12 months its revenue was only $12 million. And by the time At Home announced the acquisition of Excite in January 1999, At Home capitalization was all the way up to $12.4 billion, even though in its most recent quarter the company posted a loss of $7.6 million. "You'd think you'd do forward earnings estimates based on the year 2000," quips one venture capitalist. "I guess I was wrong—it's actually based on the year 3000."[6]*

Start-up companies certainly do have uneven profiles for dividends. This is less true for mature companies or for the market as a whole. Figure 21.5 showed that an index of real dividends paid on all industrial stocks since 1871 is fairly steady; certainly it appears less volatile than the index of stock prices themselves. If dividends—either on an individual stock or the aggregate of all companies—grow at a roughly constant rate, we can use simple algebra to come up with a useful way of expressing share prices.

First recall what the dividend discount model predicts for the price today of a stock, denoted $P(0)$

$$P(0) = D(1)/(1 + r) + D(2)/(1 + r)^2 + D(3)/(1 + r)^3 + \ldots + D(N)/(1 + r)^N$$

where for any value of j, $D(j)$ is the expected dividend to be paid in period j. We assume here that the required rate of return does not change from period to period.

Suppose dividends grow at a constant rate g, so that

$$D(2) = (1 + g)D(1)$$
$$D(3) = (1 + g)D(2) = (1 + g)^2 D(1)$$
$$D(4) = (1 + g)D(3) = (1 + g)^3 D(1) \text{ etc.}$$

We can then write the stock price

$$P(0) = [D(1)/(1 + r)] * \{1 + (1 + g)/(1 + r) + [(1 + g)/(1 + r)]^2$$
$$+ [(1 + g)/(1 + r)]^3 \ldots + [(1 + g)/(1 + r)]^N\}$$

This messy looking formula is just an infinite geometric progression. Each term in the final set of braces is a constant multiple of $(1 + g)/(1 + r)$ times the previous term, and there are an infinite number of such terms to be added. As long as g is less than r (and we argued above that this is plausible), such a sum has a finite limit of $(1 + r)/(r - g)$, which gives a value for $P(0)$ of

$$P(0) = D(1)/(r - g)$$

If we rearrange this equation we get

$$D(1)/P(0) = r - g$$

[6]Perkins and Perkins, *The Internet Bubble* (New York: Harper Collins, 1999) p. 169.

This equation says that the ratio of the next dividend paid to the current stock price, which is called the (prospective) dividend yield, is the difference between the required rate of return and the long-run growth of dividends. Because we can measure the dividend yield on a stock, or on an index of the stocks of many companies, accurately, we now have a way of judging what the gap between the required rate of return and the anticipated growth of dividends is. We just take the latest stock price and dividends, and by forming the dividend yield, we can measure the implied expected excess return over and above the anticipated growth of dividends. This simple and useful relation says that if the dividend yield is low either the required rate of return on equities is itself low or the anticipated growth of dividends is high.

Figure 21.12 shows the dividend yield on the Shiller index of U.S. stock prices from 1870 to the end of the twentieth century. In 1929, on the eve of the massive fall in U.S. stock prices, the dividend yield on U.S. stocks was around 4%. This was significantly below the average from the previous 50 years. At that time short-term nominal interest rates were about 4%, and inflation had been low. So real interest rates might have been just under 4%. If we add an equity risk premium of about 3% to a real interest rate of just under 4%, we generate a required real return on stocks of about 7%. Now if we suppose that people expected dividends to grow in real terms by about 3%, we can explain a dividend yield of around 4%. This just equals the required rate of return on equities—a 4% real rate on relatively safe assets plus a 3% risk premium—minus the anticipated growth of dividends of 3%. Because the U.S. economy had been growing steadily for much of the 1920s an expectation of 3% real growth of dividends might not have seemed unreasonable. Certainly the great U.S. economist Irving Fisher believed on the eve of the stock market crash that U.S. equity prices were sustainable. In fact, U.S. real GDP has not grown by 3% a year over the long term since the 1920s, and because dividends tend to grow in line with output, at least over the long term, the belief

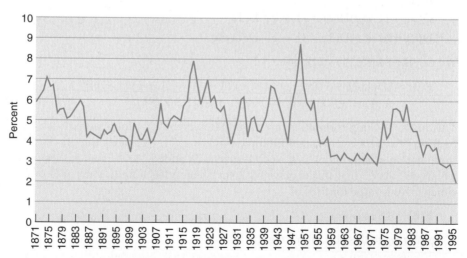

FIGURE 21.12 **Dividend yield on U.S. stocks (Shiller estimates).** *Source*: Data kindly provided by Robert Shiller; see Shiller, *Market Volatility* (Cambridge, MA: MIT Press, 1989), Chapter 26, for details.

that dividends would grow 3% over the long term was, *in retrospect*, too optimistic. In 1929 prices fell, the dividend yield rose sharply, and the implied anticipated growth of dividends (given stock prices) probably moved down sharply.

Note from Figure 21.12 how low the U.S. dividend yield fell during the 1990s. One interpretation of this fall is that people became more optimistic about long-run economic growth and the growth of dividends. Another explanation, which is not inconsistent with the first, is that people came to see equities as less risky, so their required rate of return fell. Either of these forces could account for a decline in the dividend yield. We will consider the risk premium issues in more detail shortly.

21.4 On the Unpredictability of Share Prices

We have offered a theory of what determines share prices based on fundamentals—the anticipated value of future corporate dividends. But can we use this theory to make money? That depends on how predictable stock price movements might be, which, in turn, depends on what drives share values. Our examples so far have focused on changes in stock prices that are driven by news about economic fundamentals. But rational expectations of current and future economic conditions are not the only determinants of stock prices.[7] Expectations do not have to be formed in a scientific, logical, coherent, consistent way. Indeed many puzzles about stock market prices and movements in returns on equities are hard to square with the view that prices are the discounted value of expected future earnings *and* that people form rational and coherent expectations. We will look at some of that evidence shortly. But our theory of rational investors evaluating the fundamentals before purchasing a stock is not inconsistent with volatile and unpredictable movements in share prices. In fact, it is certainly *not* a puzzle that movements in stock prices might appear to be random. Indeed, we shall now show that if the world is peopled by rational, calculating individuals, movements in stock prices over short periods should appear to be random and unforecastable; and if that is so, even smart people won't be able to make money by predicting movements in stock market prices.

But why should movements in stock prices appear random? Assume that stock prices are equal to the discounted values of the sum of future expected dividends. We could then think of the *change* in the price of an equity over a short period of time as simply being equal to the *change* in the expectation of the (discounted) stream of future dividend payments—assuming that the required rate of return does not change. If this is the case, then rational behavior makes those changes unforecastable. In other words, share prices should be unpredictable. We should dwell on this point for a moment and illustrate it with an example. Suppose I asked you now what your best guess was for the temperature at noon in New York City on Christmas Day, 2050. Let's say your answer

---

[7]We have in mind a technical definition here of rational expectations—that agents use all the information at their disposal and the appropriate model of the economy and of share prices in forming their guesses of what the future holds. This does not mean that agents do not make mistakes—it just means that they cannot forecast their own mistakes.

is 30 degrees Fahrenheit. Now suppose I ask you a different question: "What do you expect your answer will be if I ask this same question again a year from now?" Any answer other than 30 degrees Fahrenheit would be illogical. It would make no sense to say that your best guess now about the temperature in New York City at Christmas in 2050 is 30 degrees but that you also expected that your best guess about the answer to the *same* question a year from now would be different. That is not to say that when I ask you *in a year's time* that you must still answer 30 degrees. In the meantime you may have all kinds of news about global warming and how it will affect New York, and if so you would be perfectly reasonable to change your answer. But the key point is that you cannot *now* expect your best guess to be different in the future. Any change in expectations must itself be unforecastable if you are using information sensibly. In other words, while you will quite likely change your forecast of the temperature in New York at Christmas in 2050 over the coming years, you cannot predict how you will revise your forecast. Therefore, you should not be able to forecast changes in your own forecast.

The same logic applies to your best guess about future dividends. We have shown that the current stock price depends on your current forecast of all future dividends. Similarly the stock price in a year will reflect your forecast in a year of all future dividends. Therefore, the difference in the share price today and next period will reflect how your forecasts of future dividends have altered. If you revise up your forecasts of future dividends, the share price will rise: if you revise your forecast downwards, the share price will fall. However, *you cannot today forecast how you will change your forecast—just as with the New York temperature example, this would be irrational.* Therefore, your current best guess of the next instant's stock price must be today's price—changes in stock prices should be unpredictable. Technically this means that stock prices should follow what is called a "random walk": whatever the past path of the price, the next move is as likely to be up as down. So random fluctuations in stock prices rather than necessarily being the result of chaos, irrational behavior, indecision, inconsistency, bubbles, or other hiccups in the market are more or less an implication of rational and efficient behavior. In fact, stock price changes do look random. Figure 21.13 shows the annual percentage change in U.S. stock prices from 1870. The year to year fluctuations in prices have no obvious pattern. This is at least consistent with the notion of a rational and efficient market. (But apparent unpredictability does not *imply* that the market is rational and efficient—it is a necessary but not sufficient condition. If a flip of a coin governed stock price changes, they would look random, but such changes have nothing to do with revisions to future forecasts of company earnings.)

This combination of rationality and the forward-looking nature of stock prices also explains other features of stock prices that might appear puzzling. When the central bank cuts interest rates or a firm announces an increase in dividends, the share price often falls. How can this be?—we have just shown at great length that lower interest rates or higher dividends should *boost* the current stock price. However, the market expectation of future events affects share prices. Imagine that the market expects the central bank to cut interest rates by 0.5% or expects a firm to announce a 10% increase in dividends. The market will therefore price stocks based on these assumptions. If the government only cuts interest rates by 0.25%, or the firm announces only a 5% rise in

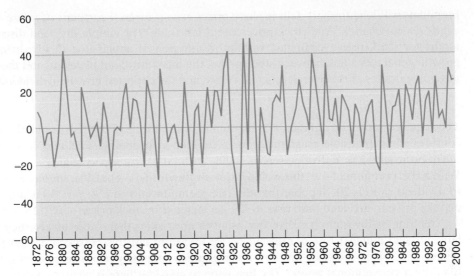

FIGURE 21.13   **Percent stock price change (Shiller data on U.S. market).** *Source:* Authors' calculations on data kindly provided by Robert Shiller; see Shiller, *Market Volatility* (Cambridge, MA: MIT Press, 1989), Chapter 26, for details.

dividends, the market will have to change its forecast. The market now sees that interest rates will not be as low as it thought or that dividends will be lower than forecast, so the price of shares will fall. Similarly, if the government cut rates by 1%, or the firm announced dividend growth of 20%, the stock price would rise. Finally, if the interest rate cut was 0.5% or dividend growth was 10%, nothing would happen—the market had already forecast this, so these announcements contain no information, and the market has no reason to change its forecast. As a result, the stock price does not alter.

21.5   Risk, Equity Prices, and Excess Return

We noted above that, at least in the UK and the United States, the rate of return on equities over the last 100 years had, on average, substantially exceeded the rate of return available on government bonds. This makes perfect sense as long as the risk on equities substantially exceeds the risk of those other investments. But what do we mean by risk here and how might we measure it? The answer to these questions matters a lot because movements in the risk premium can dramatically affect stock prices. If people come to think of equities as a lot more risky, they might require that, on average, they yield 10% more than government bonds, rather than, say, 5% more. Discounting future dividends at a rate that is higher by 5% could easily generate 40% or 50% falls in the price of equities. We can see, in principle, why this is so if we look again at Figure 21.8. Anything that causes the required rate of return to increase will decrease share prices unless there are compensating shifts in future dividends. Therefore, increases in risk premiums will lead to sharp falls in share prices *even if investor forecasts of future dividends do not change*. And stock prices could fall a lot. The simple dividend discount model for stock prices, combined with an assumption of anticipated steady dividend growth, generates a link between stock prices, the latest dividend payment, and the relative magnitudes of the overall required return and the expected growth in dividends

$$P = D/(r - g)$$

The required return on equities, r, is the sum of a safe rate and the risk premium. Let's consider some plausible magnitudes for a developed economy. The safe (real) rate might be around 3%. If dividends grow in line with GDP, 2% a year might be plausible. With a risk premium of 4%, this would imply a value for $(r - g)$ of 5%, so that the price to dividend ratio is 20. Suppose that the risk premium falls to 2%; $(r - g)$ is now 3% and the price to dividend ratio rises to 33—an increase in stock prices of 65%!

As long as investors perceive that equities are riskier than other assets, they will have to yield a higher rate of return. Can we therefore use this perspective to explain Figure 21.7, which shows by just how much equities have outperformed rates of return than other conventional assets? The first issue to consider here is whether equities really are riskier than most other investment categories.

It may seem obvious that equities are riskier than bank deposits or government bonds. But that is a hasty conclusion. What matters are *real* rates of returns; that is, the proportionate increase in the money value of the asset less the rise in the general cost of living. Most government bonds guarantee a nominal rate of return, and even then, that return is only guaranteed if you hold the debt until maturity and if the government has a zero probability of default. Holders of U.S., Italian, and UK government bonds found that those assets generated substantial negative real returns through much of the 1970s because inflation was higher than expected. Holders of Russian government bonds had a much nastier shock in 1998; their market value fell by about 80% during the year. Nor do bank deposits generate predictable real rates of return; inflation is unpredictable even over a five-month horizon, let alone over five or ten years. These facts should make us think harder about the relative riskiness of equities and other assets.

To gauge whether the extra 6% or so a year over the return on bonds or bank deposits that investors in U.S. or UK equities have got (on average) over the last century is a fair compensation for risk, we need to use a more formal apparatus. In 1985 Raj Mehra and Ed Prescott published an influential paper on the "equity premium"; that is, the extra return that equities yield over risk-free assets.[9] Using past data, Mehra and Prescott estimated that the U.S. risk premium was about 6%. This is in line with the long data series Robert Shiller put together and which Table 21.2 summarizes. The Shiller data generate an average excess return on equities from 1870 to the end of the twentieth century of just over 5.8%.

Mehra and Prescott's paper suggests that the equity premium has been too high. In other words, investors have been overcompensated for the higher risk that equities involve. Mehra and Prescott call this the "equity premium puzzle"—the puzzle is, why do equities yield such a high rate of return?

[9]Mehra and Prescott "The Equity Premium: A Puzzle," *Journal of Monetary Economics* (1985), vol. 15, pp. 145–161.

TABLE 21.2   The Equity Premium in the United States

Time Period	Percent Return on "Riskless" Asset (commercial paper rate)	Percent Return on S&P Stocks	Risk Premium
1871–1998	4.87%	10.69%	5.82%

Source: Authors' calculations based on data kindly supplied by
Robert Shiller; see Shiller, *Market Volatility* (Cambridge, MA: MIT
Press, 1989), Chapter 26, for details.

Of course, whether this is a puzzle depends on whether investors—you and me ultimately—are averse to taking risks.[10] The measure of risk aversion economists most frequently use is the coefficient of relative risk aversion (CRRA). Mehra and Prescott argued that unless for the typical investor this measure is well above 2 (and probably nearer 10), standard economic theory cannot account for the observed magnitude of the equity premium.

But what does a CRRA of 5 or 10 mean, and are people this averse to uncertainty? Suppose you have been offered a job that is potentially lucrative but risky. If the job goes well, you will get an average annual income over the next 20 years (in present value terms) of $80,000. The value of your human capital (the present value of future labor income) would then be $1.6 million (20 × $80,000). We will assume that this is your only source of wealth. But there is a 50% chance that the risky job will go badly—there are spells of unemployment, you have to change firms, your reputation and your resumé gets to look shaky. In this case your average income over the next 20 years would be only $20,000 (in present value), so that the overall value of human capital would be $400,000 (20 × $20,000).

We can work out how risk averse you are by knowing what certain level of income in a completely safe job gives you the same utility level as accepting this risky job. If you would consider a safe job earning an average salary of $50,000 a year as giving you the same welfare as the risky job, you have no aversion to risk; your CRRA is 0. This is because the expected value of the average annual salary in the risky job is $50,000—halfway between the good outcome ($80,000) and the bad outcome ($20,000)—which is exactly the same as the guaranteed income in the safe job. A CRRA of 0 therefore indicates that individuals are indifferent between certain outcomes and risky outcomes with the same average value.

However, if an investor has a CRRA of greater than zero, she would rather take the certain salary than its equivalent fair bet. This also implies that she would prefer a slightly lower salary if it was guaranteed to a higher but riskier salary. The degree of risk aversion determines exactly how much lower the guaranteed salary can be for the person to be indifferent. For instance, if you think a job that guarantees you an annual salary of $48,000 gives you the same utility as the risky job in our example, your level of CRRA is 0.21—this is close to being indifferent to risk. A person with this level of CRRA is

---

[10]As well as depending on risk aversion, the magnitude of the equity premium should also depend on how much risk there is in the world. Focusing on aggregate consumption changes, Mehra and Prescott argue that measured in this way risk is fairly small—consumption changes fluctuate between −2 and +4% per year. Therefore, we can only account for the equity premium if agents are highly risk averse because measured risk is too small to play a substantial role.

indifferent between a guaranteed income of $48,000 or a risky bet with expected outcome of $50,000. Clearly this person is not very risk averse. However, as we increase the level of risk aversion, the guaranteed income the person requires falls—for instance, with a CRRA of 0.4, the fixed income falls to $46,000, while a CRRA of 1 means that people are sufficiently risk averse that they are indifferent between a safe job paying $40,000 or the riskier employment opportunity. When risk aversion rises to 2.4, the safe job need pay only $30,000, while a CRRA of 4 implies a safe salary of $25,000.

Remember that Mehra and Prescott concluded that unless CRRA was greater than 5, standard economic theory could not account for the observed historical equity premium. As our example shows, this implies that investors are incredibly risk averse. As a result, Mehra and Precott conclude that U.S. equities have yielded far too much for the excess returns just to reflect a risk premium.

If Mehra and Prescott are right, the market has mispriced equities in the largest stock market in the world for over 100 years and by a huge magnitude. The scale of that mispricing is staggering. Suppose that equities, on average, should not yield any more than "safe" government debt—perhaps around 2% per year in real terms. In that case $1000 invested in 1870 in the stock market should have generated a value by 2000 of about $(1.02)^{130}$, which is about $13,122. In fact, the rate of return was more like 8% a year, so that the real value of $1000 invested in equity by the end of the period was about $22,135,000. This is 1686 times its assumed fair value, which by any criteria would imply colossal market error and overcompensation for risk bearing.

Since Mehra and Prescott published their article, a huge academic debate has occurred about whether the equity premium really poses a puzzle. Perhaps the most interesting counter to the Mehra and Prescott argument is to question whether the *ex post* (or actual) average excess rates of return in the UK and the United States over the last century really do measure the equity premium. In assessing the equity premium, the *ex ante* (or expected) return on equities, not the *ex post excess* return, is important. In other words, what is relevant is the excess return investors expected they were going to earn rather than what they actually did obtain. The problem may be that the United States is not a representative economy, so that returns on equity may have been much higher than elsewhere. After all, the United States is the most successful capitalist nation and emerged relatively unscathed from two major world wars. But would an investor have predicted this in 1870 when the United States was still in its economic adolescence? Was it really so clear to U.S, investors in 1932 that the stock market would rise strongly over the coming decades? Or on the morning after Pearl Harbor? And what about investors in Tsarist Russia in 1870—would they feel that equity investors have been overcompensated for the risk they have borne? They lost everything with the Russian Revolution in 1917. In other words, focusing on the United States may make it look like the market has overcompensated equity investors, but this is misleading—equities really are risky, and examining other countries and other periods of time suggests that not all investors have benefited from an equity premium. History offers many examples of investors who have lost fortunes by buying bonds and equities issued by companies operating in countries where returns looked to be fabulous, but where the economy subsequently performed dreadfully—as a result of war or catastrophic mismanagement. One needs to remember just how much more successful than other countries U.S. economic performance has been over the past 150

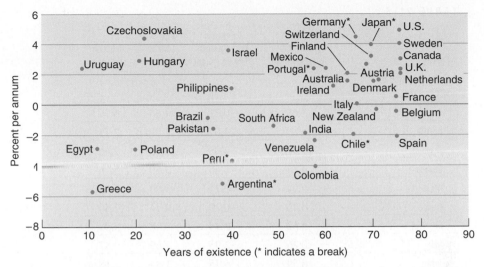

FIGURE 21.14   Real returns on global stock markets sorted by years of existence. *Source*: Goetzmann and Jorion, "Global Stock Markets in the 20th Century," *The Journal of Finance* (1999), vol. 54, no. 3, pp. 953–980. Copyright American Finance Association.

years before assuming that the equity premium on U.S. equity indicates the average outcome for equity investments.

Figure 21.14 and the data in Table 21.3 indicate that this focus on the United States might be misleading. They show rates of return across many economies for various time intervals over the last century. If one includes countries that were defeated in world wars (Germany, Japan, and those countries that were occupied), the overall rate of return on equity looks to be substantially lower than the UK/U.S. average. Figure 21.14 brings this point out clearly. It shows a positive relation between the amount of time a stock market has traded more or less continuously and the average return over that period. So in countries where there was discontinuity in the stock market (generally because of economic disintegration, often as the result of war), average rates of return tend to have been lower. This implies that focusing on those stock markets that have traded continuously for the longest period may introduce a systematic upward bias to rates of return. This is a problem of survivorship bias. If you take the excess rate of return of equities over debt including all the countries in Table 21.3, the figure is not as high as the 6% that puzzled Mehra and Prescott.

Sample selection for countries also affects how we interpret the investment performance of individuals. The financial pages of newspapers love stories about star investors who have outperformed the market over the past 1, 5, 10, or even 20 years. Should these stars impress us? Probably not. Newspapers focus on winners and tend to ignore the average performers or those who did even less well than that. Some investor will always have the best record over the past 10 years, and their return will be much higher than the average if they are the best performers out of a sample of 10,000 investors. But there would be a "best investor," with an apparently fantastic ability to

TABLE 21.3

Country	Compound Return with Dividend (% pa)	Compound Return without Dividend (% pa)	Difference due to Dividend	Inflation (% pa)
Markets covered by MSCIP, 1970–95				
Australia	3.65	−0.71	4.36	6.79
Austria	4.89	2.07	2.82	2.75
Belgium	12.97	4.05	8.92	2.46
Canada	4.34	0.65	3.69	5.78
Denmark	6.54	2.71	3.83	5.62
France	4.45	−0.29	4.74	7.40
Germany	5.52	1.44	4.08	3.09
Italy	−0.26	−2.95	2.69	9.87
Japan	8.59	6.75	1.84	2.18
Netherlands	8.84	3.09	5.74	3.41
Norway	6.03	2.78	3.26	5.90
Spain	2.30	−4.00	6.31	8.40
Sweden	8.79	5.03	3.76	7.42
Switzerland	5.72	3.06	2.66	2.54
United Kingdom	6.39	1.23	5.16	8.35
United States	6.15	2.01	4.14	4.89
Average	5.93	1.68	4.25	5.43
Long-Term Markets				
Denmark 1923–95	4.88	0.64	4.24	3.72
Sweden 1926–95	7.13	3.30	3.83	3.64
Germany 1924–95	4.83	1.21	3.63	2.47
Switzerland 1921–95	5.57	2.12	3.45	2.49
United Kingdom 1921–95	8.16	2.99	5.17	3.75
United States 1921–95	8.22	3.38	4.84	2.69

Note: For the Morgan Stanley Capital International Perspective (MSCIP) indexes, the compound real returns are measured by deflating by the Wholesale Price Index. The other long-term series are obtained from various sources, which all report the Consumer Price Index, except for Denmark, for which the WPI is used.

Source: Goetzmann and Jorion, "Global Stock Markets in the 20th Century," *The Journal of Finance* (1999) vol. 54, No. 3, pp. 953–980. Copyright American Finance Association.

pick winners, even if every investor chose stocks by throwing a dart at a dartboard. Our advice is not to be too impressed by fantastic past performance.

Sample selection is important and may explain the Mehra and Prescott puzzle. So maybe the equity premium puzzle is not a puzzle after all. This may reassure academics, but it is sobering if you are thinking about rates of return that you might earn in stock markets in the future. The sample selection story suggests that measuring the average rate of return over the last century by focusing on the UK and the United States (which looks sensible given that they are big markets that have existed for a long time) inflates the estimate of the likely rates of return in the future.

21.6 Are Stock Prices Forecastable?

Other important characteristics of stock prices have concerned economists and have put a question mark on basic economic theories of asset markets which assume rational forecasts of fundamental factors. If stock market values do not reflect a rational assessment of future profits and dividends of companies, the life of investors becomes tricky, and companies cannot rely on the signals stock markets give to guide their investment. This second point is of prime importance. The Q theory of investment, which we discussed in Chapter 14, links the amount of new investment undertaken to stock market valuations of existing assets. If the stock market valuations are substantially different from a rational assessment of the true worth of the assets (based on their ability to generate future profits), new investment based on stock prices will misallocate funds. So whether stock prices really do reflect fundamental profitability matters. If they do not, economists would say that the market displays a form of inefficiency.

Belief in efficient (or rational) stock market pricing has taken big blows over the last 20 years. Robert Shiller led the intellectual assault on belief in stock market efficiency in a series of papers written more than 20 years ago.[11] In 1981 Shiller argued that stock prices in the U.S. over the 100-year period starting in 1870 were far too volatile to be consistent with a rational evaluation of the fundamental value of the corporate sector.[12] In making this point, Shiller used essentially the following argument. Suppose that you had known in 1870 what dividends U.S. companies would pay over the next 100 years. Then using the logic of Figure 21.8, you could work out what the price of equities should have been over this period on the basis of this perfect foresight. (Of course, this depends on choosing a discount factor r.) Shiller wanted to compare the volatility of stock prices observed in practice with the volatility of share prices if they are based on rational forecasts of future dividends. However, we cannot recreate *now* what rational forecasts of future dividends were in 1870. Therefore, instead Shiller focused on the volatility of share prices assuming that the investor had perfect foresight about future

[11]For an excellent review of this work, see Shiller's book, *Market Volatility* (Cambridge, MA: MIT Press, 1989).

[12]Shiller, "Do Stock Prices Move Too Much to Be Justified by Subsequent Changes in Dividends?" *American Economic Review* (1981), vol. 71, pp. 421–436.

dividends. Shiller argued that the actual path of dividends that companies paid over that 100-year period should have been *more* volatile than the path that it was rational to expect in 1870. In other words, if actual share prices are more volatile than Shiller's perfect foresight share price then they must also be more volatile than share prices based on forecasts of fundamentals.

Crucial to Shiller's argument was the claim that the share price based on perfect foresight should be more volatile than the share price based on rational forecasts. The argument was subtle, some would say intellectually dangerous. An analogy might be helpful in understanding it.

Suppose I asked you what you expected to be the average outcome of tossing an unbiased coin 100 times. You would probably say that you would expect 50 heads and 50 tails. Suppose now I actually tossed a coin 100 times. The outcome is unlikely to be exactly 50 heads and 50 tails. I could repeat the same question to you over and over again, and toss a coin 100 times after each answer. We would find significant variability from one occasion to the next in the actual outcome of tossing a coin 100 times, but no variability in your expectation of what the result would be (you keep saying 50 heads and 50 tails). Shiller argued analogously that the expectation of future dividends should be less variable than actual future dividends. This implied that the price calculated by discounting the actual future course of dividends (the perfect foresight price) should be more volatile than the share price that would result from people forming rational expectations of the present value of future dividends. This meant that Shiller expected the perfect foresight share price to be more volatile than the actual history of share prices. Figure 21.15 shows what he saw.

The p line is actual share prices, and the line marked p* is the perfect foresight path. Remember, the perfect foresight line should be *more* volatile than the smooth line. Clearly it is not! Shiller concluded that a sensible reaction to news about future economic fundamentals was not driving variability in stock prices; if it was, we could expect the perfect foresight path to be much more variable relative to the actual path for prices.

If Shiller is right, things are rather worrying. Big swings in prices either up or down might have much more to do with irrational sentiment than with changing expectations

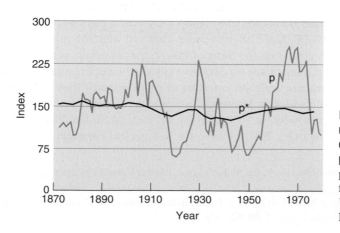

FIGURE 21.15 **Share prices more volatile compared to those constructed using actual dividends paid.** Reproduced with permission from MIT Press from Robert Shiller, *Market Volatility* (Cambridge, MA: MIT Press, 1989) Chapter 5.

of future profits. But is he right? The jury is still out on this one. The statistical issues are subtle and still not resolved. Furthermore, sample selection bias that we argued was relevant to the equity premium puzzle is also relevant to the Shiller story. In a sense, the 100-year period between 1870 and 1970 that Shiller used for his original work was not a large sample of observations. It was one run of history for one country. And one observation is a small sample on which to base a devastating hypothesis.

In defense of Shiller, you could argue that dramatic volatility in stock prices is not confined to the U.S. Huge swings in prices occur in stock markets in most countries: in the UK, share prices dropped by 35% in 1973 and by 55% in 1974. In Russia, the stock market index fell by over 80% between January and September 1998. Between 1990 and 1992, the Japanese stock market fell by 50%.

But stock price volatility, and more specifically big drops in prices in short periods, are not inconsistent with an efficient market. If news arrives that causes a substantial change in expected future profits (on which dividends are based), prices should move a lot. Smart economists can construct stories around the events in Russia, Japan, and the UK at the time of big market falls that are consistent with efficient markets. Despite this, the work of Robert Shiller began to undermine faith in efficient markets. A key insight of his was to note that although efficient markets might imply near random behavior in asset prices (under certain circumstances), such randomness did not imply efficiency; it was a necessary but not sufficient condition for efficiency.

21.7 Speculation or Fundamentals?

But the efficient market view that movement in stock prices are unpredictable has also been assaulted. Many respectable academic papers argue that asset price movements are predictable in ways that are difficult to square with an efficient market. Jim Poterba and Lawrence Summers, for example, have presented evidence of *mean reversion* in stock prices.[13] Mean reversion is a statistical concept that implies that a variable tends to return to some long-term value. For instance, the average temperature in New York City in January may be 30 degrees Fahrenheit, although in any one year it may be colder or hotter. For several consecutive years the weather may be warmer in January. However, if the temperature is mean reverting, eventually the temperature in January in New York will revert back to around 30 degrees Fahrenheit.

If mean reversion exists in share prices, it implies that when prices have moved up substantially, relative to some underlining trend, they are more likely to fall; and

[13]See Poterba and Summers "Mean Reversion in Stock Prices: Evidence and Implications," *Journal of Financial Economics* (1988), vol. 22, pp. 27–60; Summers, "Does the Stock Market Really Reflect Fundamental Value?" *Journal of Finance*, (1986), vol. 41, pp. 591–601; Cutler, Poterba, and Summers, "Speculative Dynamics," *Review of Economic Studies*, (1991a), vol. 58, pp. 529–546; Cutler, Poterba and Summers "Speculative Dynamics and the Role of Feedback Traders," *American Economic Review* (1991b), vol. 80, pp. 63–68.

when asset prices have moved down sharply relative to some longer-run trend, they are more likely to rise. It might seem like common sense that asset prices would behave in this way, but if they consistently did, smart traders could consistently make big profits. If there is mean reversion, then as the price of an asset falls further below some underlying path, it becomes increasingly likely that it will return toward it, thus generating capital gains. But if that were so, wouldn't the buying and selling decisions of smart speculators prevent the price moving far from the underlying equilibrium? They would be bidding the price up when it was below equilibrium and driving it down (by selling) when it was above. So how can any significant mean reversion persist?

It has been argued that while arbitrage arguments like this might remove mispricing of assets relative to others that were close substitutes (what is called pure arbitrage), they were not relevant for equities in general. The idea that a small group of smart investors could, by their seeking to take advantage of mispricing, drive prices back to "fundamental value" depends on an infinitely elastic demand (e.g., investors undertake unlimited purchases when they see a price discrepancy). This is plausible (just!) for pure arbitrage, when no risk is involved in the trade, but not when risky speculative positions have to be taken. Some researchers have argued that there is no equivalent arbitrage argument applicable to equities in general—to bet against the level of the market means taking big risks.

Summers and Shleifer have argued that the amount of capital that could be gambled against general, and potentially persistent, mispricing of assets (e.g., equities) is small.[14] Regular monitoring of fund managers by their clients may make it risky for the funds to follow a strategy of betting against the market—**relative** underperformance in the period before their bet comes good may cost them their job/mandate. After all, clients can really only judge ability from relative performance. Because some asset managers out there are lousy, clients with funds to manage may be unwilling to take the gamble that you are a good one. And lots of other people want to handle the assets. All this means that taking a stand against the market—which is how overshooting would tend to be eradicated—can be costly.

Shiller, Shleifer, Summers, and others have also argued that fads, rumors, and group pressures that can make deviations from fundamental values substantial and prolonged. Evidence from psychological experiments shows a tendency to extrapolate from recent trends even when no link to the future exists. Experiments also show strong tendencies for groups to influence each other and make common mistakes (peer group errors) or display *herding behavior*.

The many historical examples of massive price rises followed by sharp falls provide the strongest evidence that these factors are sometimes at work. Two that have received considerable attention from economists are the tulip mania of the seventeenth century and the South Sea bubble of the eighteenth century. Early in the seven-

[14]Shleifer and Summers, "The Noise Trader Approach to Finance," *Journal of Economic Perspectives* (1990), vol. 4, no. 2, p. 19–33.

teenth century, the price of tulips in the Netherlands rose dramatically before collapsing. Garber reports that a single Semper Augustus bulb sold for 2000 guilders in 1625.[15] In late 1637 prices surged again and continued rising fast until February 1639. But then they collapsed, and bulbs could not be sold at even 10% of their values of a few weeks earlier. Equity prices have seen equally dramatic price rises and falls. Shares in the now infamous South Sea Company (which aimed to buy British government debt in the 1720s and fund the purchases by issuing equity) were dramatically volatile. Between February and July 1720, its share price increased about eightfold. But by the end of September, the price was back at its original level. Both these cases that of tulip mania and the South Sea bubble—saw a dramatic clamor for assets once prices had begun to rise fast. Investors trying to calculate potential future returns seem to have attached much more weight to recent high returns than to the future earnings power of the underlying assets. If speculators do that, their actions can clearly be destabilizing—falls in price generate more selling, while rises in price only generate higher demand.

Of course, all arguments that prices can deviate in systematic (i.e., partly predictable) ways from their longer-term trend are open to the counterargument that smart gamblers will start trading, taking prices back to fundamental value. But if the length of deviations from fundamentals is uncertain, and potentially long, gambling against those who have driven prices away from fundamentals is risky; any investor who sold Japanese stocks in 1985 when the market-price-to-earnings ratio was 30 would have lost his or her shirt in 1986 when price-to-earnings ratios went to 60.[16] Smart speculators might do better to try to "ride" deviations from fundamental value, and time their exit from the bubble, rather than just trade against deviations from fundamental value. Of course, if speculators do that, their activities may not help bring prices back to fundamental value.

But none of these observations would have had much force without the apparently dramatic empirical evidence against efficiency. Summers and his coauthors show evidence of mean reversion across a range of markets, which suggests persistent and predictable deviations from fundamentals. They find positive correlation in excess returns at short horizons and negative correlations at long horizons. This is consistent with people following trading rules based on extrapolation so that deviations from fundamentals are exacerbated rather than eradicated quickly.

This leaves the efficient market enthusiasts with awkward facts to explain. Nonetheless, the proponents of the efficient markets view have cast doubt on the validity of much of the "evidence" against efficient markets. Many events that matter hugely for stock prices are unique, or at least have not happened often—wars, monetary unions, the invention of cheap computing, and the Internet. Forming expectations about how these things affect corporate profits and dividends is hard, so it is tough to be sure that some market movement is inconsistent with investors behaving sensibly.

---

[15]Garber, "Famous First Bubbles," *Journal of Economic Perspectives* (1990), vol. 4, no. 2, pp. 35–54.

[16]That is the average ratio of company stock prices to latest annual corporate earnings.

21.8 Bubbles

A form of market inefficiency that has interested economists is asset market bubbles. A bubble occurs when an asset price is different from its fundamentals, and this difference does not disappear even if investors know the price is above its fundamental value.[17]

With bubbles, if the deviation in the asset price is to be sustainable, the deviation from fundamentals must become even more pronounced. We can demonstrate this with an example. Suppose prices start out 20% above "fundamentals" with a 1 in 10 chance of dropping back to their equilibrium level. To generate an annual average return of, say, 15%, the following equation must hold

$$15\% = x\%(0.9) - 20\%(0.1)$$

Where x is the proportionate rate of price increase *if* the bubble does not burst—which is 90% probable. There is a 1 in 10 chance that the price will fall back to its fundamental value, which is 20% lower, hence the final term in the equation. The solution to this equation is $x = 18.9\%$. Therefore, even though the price starts off 20% overvalued in a bubble, we can expect to see it rise by almost 19%. This means that prices are even further above fundamentals if the bubble persists; and next period's value of x needs to be even higher because if prices crash, they fall further.

In provocative research Peter Garber has argued that when you look at events that people have universally accepted as asset price bubbles, a bubble may not really have existed.[18] Indeed, we have already mentioned the events he looks at—the tulip mania of the 1630s, the South Sea bubble of the 1720s. In each case he cannot rule out nonbubble explanations for the massive price movements.

21.9 Market Efficiency—What Should We Think?

We have seen that from the perspective of standard economic theory equity markets have several puzzles. So what! Does it matter if stock market prices sometimes are substantially above, and sometimes substantially below, valuations that would more accurately reflect the fundamental economic value of corporations?

We think that these things do matter. Prices are supposed to guide the allocation of resources. So in principle, substantial and prolonged asset price deviations from fundamental values are significant. Of course, people who actually allocate resources are generally not economists, do not believe the efficient markets theory, and probably would not look to the stock market to help them decide whether to build a new factory or open a new shop. Companies probably do not base investment decisions on the current level of their stock price, a proposition consistent with the failure of Q theories to ex-

[17]By the "fundamental value," we mean the value based on the discounted sum of expected future earnings that the underlying productive asset generates.

[18]Garber, "Famous First Bubbles," *Journal of Economic Perspectives* (1990) vol. 4, no. 2, pp. 35–54.

plain actual movements in physical investment. Here is the founder of the Internet company Yahoo, billionaire Jerry Yang, on how stock market valuations of his company affect his business decisions:

> *We're on the field, we're playing the game, and it's probably the bottom of the third inning. I have no idea what the spectators are doing. They could be selling tickets for this game, even at the scalper's prices. I have no control over that. We've just got to win this game.*[19]

But if the prices of financial assets do not much influence resource allocation within a capitalist economy, this is hardly comforting. After all, market prices are *supposed* to guide the allocation of resources. And evidence on how companies actually make investment decisions is worrying: they often use payback periods as an investment criterion (which is anathema to economists), and they often seem to confuse nominal and real discount rates.

Even if it did not affect new investment, excess price volatility in equity markets, or sustained persistence of price deviations from fundamentals, can be costly for other reasons. Asset price movements shift the distribution of wealth. They makes saving over a person's lifetime more difficult (although paradoxically they may actually increase saving). Volatile asset market prices may put people off funded pensions. They can generate risk premiums that are too high in terms of fundamentals. Asset price volatility may cause unnecessary takeovers and make it more difficult to monitor company management because investors cannot confidently assess the true worth of the company by reference to market values. Volatility unrelated to fundamentals can makes portfolio allocation more difficult.

So it matters that asset prices might move much more than fundamentals would justify—it certainly matters if you have to sell most of your portfolio of equities and the market drops 30%! In a world in which most people are risk averse, it also matters if diversifiable sources of risk are not diversified away. And all this will matter even more if equity markets become a more important source of funds for corporations in the world and account for an increasing share of portfolios of wealth.

So what should we think? The idea that stock market prices—or indeed prices in any asset market—become *permanently* dissociated from fundamental values strikes us as implausible. If stock prices were several times greater than a plausible assessment of their worth based on likely future corporate earnings, eventually even the most slow-witted, or most irrationally optimistic, investors would cotton on. But that process can take a long time, so mispricing of a large margin can last for several years. And this sort of mispricing is likely to be larger and persist longer if many investors base their judgment on future returns not directly on an assessment of corporate incomes but rather on share price movements themselves. Robert Shiller has collected valuable information on the tendency of investors to do just this. He sent out about 2000 questionnaires after the October 1987 stock market crash in the United States to try to find out what investors were thinking on the day of one of the largest price changes in history. On October 19 the Dow Jones industrial average fell 508 points, a drop of 22.6%. Shiller's sur-

---

[19]Quoted in Perkins and Perkins, *The Internet Bubble* (New York: Harper Collins, 1999), p. 163.

vey results suggest that rather than being a response to news about fundamentals, investors' reactions to the most recent price changes drove changes in sentiment about prices. In summarizing the survey results Shiller observed:

> *Since no news story or any other recognizable event outside the market appears to be immediately responsible for the crash, we will . . . turn to considerations of a theory of the crash as being determined endogenously by investors: that the . . . crash was related to some internal dynamics of investor thinking, investors reactions to price and to each other. . . . There were two channels by which price declines could feed back into further price declines: first a price-to-price channel—investors on October 19 were reacting to price changes; second, a social-psychological channel—investors were directly reacting to each other. From the information collected on the frequency with which investors checked prices and talked with each other on October 19, both feedbacks were happening.[20]*

We think that prices in stock markets often reflect a tendency of investors to infer something about true value by looking at prices themselves rather than the fundamentals and that, as a result, prices can move away from fundamental value. It can also make sharp price falls or rises self-reinforcing. But if investors only gauged fair value by reference to actual price, prices could rise or fall without limit—we certainly could not expect to see mean reversion in asset prices. In practice, mean reversion in stock (and other asset) prices does seem to exist. This suggests that the pull of fundamental value—that is, of assessments based on expectations of the future path of the earnings of the underlying assets being valued—is powerful in the longer term. Jeff Bezos, founder of Amazon.com, sums this view up succinctly:

> *I subscribe to . . . the view that there is no correlation between great companies and short-term stock prices. But in the long term there is 100% correlation.[21]*

SUMMARY

Stock prices are important because they give an indication of the value of firms and help guide investment decisions. Fluctuations in prices also generate big movements in the wealth of the private sector and are likely to cause movements in spending. The value of a company's equity should reflect the expected value of the earnings that it will generate into the future, earnings out of which dividends can be paid. If this is how stock prices are determined we should not be surprised by the fact that changes in stock market values appear random. Shifts in expectations and movements in required returns will drive shifts in stock prices. But while volatility of stock prices, per se, is not inconsistent with the efficient functioning of the market, the degree to which prices fluctuate may be. Stock price gyrations do often appear hard to reconcile with the notion that cool-headed investors make rational assessments of future earnings of companies and discount those earnings appropriately.

[20]Shiller, *Market Volatility* (Cambridge, MA: MIT Press, 1989), Chapter 23.

[21]Quoted in Perkins and Perkins, *The Internet Bubble* (New York: Harper Collins, 1999), p. 159.

Stock returns in the United States have exceeded returns on bonds and most other assets by a large margin over the last 200 years. This creates another puzzle: the excess return puzzle. In part this may reflect a systematic sample selection problem—history records the deeds of the winners. If that is so the past returns in the world's most successful large capitalist country give an exaggerated estimate of the likely returns on equities in the future.

CONCEPTUAL QUESTIONS:

1. Suppose a company cuts its dividend today to finance more investment from retained current profit. Under what circumstances would this increase, decrease, and leave unchanged the share price?

2. "Share price changes are volatile and unpredictable, therefore the stock market is unrelated to what happens in the rest of the economy; it's just a casino."

   "Share price changes are volatile and unpredictable; therefore the stock market is efficient and helps allocate resources effectively."

   What is wrong with each of these propositions?

3. Firms tend to use retained earnings rather than issue new shares to finance a higher proportion of new investment. Does this mean the stock market is largely irrelevant for companies?

4. Suppose stock prices are more variable than efficiency implies, in the sense that stock prices vary more than do rational expectations of discounted future dividends. What implications does this have about the efficiency of the takeover mechanism as a means to discipline the managers of companies?

5. Suppose you know that some other people know some things that are relevant for predicting future corporate earnings. You do not know what these things are nor who knows them. How does this affect your response to a rise in demand for stocks and big price increases? Is it rational to follow the herd?

6. How would you judge what the equity risk premium is today? How would you assess whether it was adequate?

ANALYTICAL QUESTIONS

1. Investors expect that a company will pay dividends per share of $1.50 for each year over the next five years. The next dividend is due a year from now. They also anticipate that the share price at the end of five years will be $17. They require an expected rate of return of 9%.
   (a) What is the current share price?
   (b) What happens to the share price if anticipated dividends over the next five years rise to $2.00 but this is viewed as temporary so there is no change in the anticipated share price five years ahead?
   (c) What happens if the required rate of return falls to 8%, and as a result, the five-year ahead anticipated share price rises to $18.75?

2. In an economy, aggregate dividends paid by companies are expected to grow in line with GDP. The trend rate of growth of GDP is 2.5% per annum. The required rate of return on equities equals a safe rate plus a risk premium. The safe (real) rate is 3%, and the risk premium is 5%. What would you expect the dividend price ratio (or the dividend yield) to be? By how much would stock market prices change if the risk premium increased to 6%?

3. Suppose you are risk neutral, so that your coefficient of risk aversion is 0. You are on a game show where you have already won $500,000. You can quit now with the $500,000 or take a chance by answering a question you are not sure of. If you guess right, your winnings go to $1,000,000, and you walk away a millionaire. If you guess wrong, you get to keep a miserable $50,000. You assess that there is a 50:50 chance of guessing right. Should you gamble? What would the odds need to be on a correct guess to make you indifferent between gambling and quitting? Suppose the fall-back prize if you guess wrong is $250,000. How does this change your answers to the first two questions?

4. Suppose that the price of a share always either goes up by 20% or falls by 30% over the next year whatever its current level. The chances of an up move are 0.75 and the chances of a down move are 0.25. The stock pays no dividends. Suppose you know nothing about the recent performance of the stock. What is the expected rate of return on the stock? Suppose you now discover that over the past five years the returns on the stock have been: +20%, +20%, −30%, −30%, −30%. What do now think the expected return for the next year is?

5. A stock is expected to pay a dividend of $3.00 each year forever. You assess that the expected return is 10% and from this you conclude that the fair price should be $30. But you know that stock prices sometimes deviate from fair value by significant amounts. When those deviations occur you estimate that prices do revert back to fair value, but not immediately. You believe that one quarter the discrepancy between the current price and the fundamental price is closed each year. If the current price is $22, what do you calculate the expected return on the stock will be over each of the next five years?

6. Suppose your weight fluctuates randomly from month to month; it is as likely to go up as down. Your current weight is 161 pounds. Looking back at your records of your weight over the past year the pattern is:

Jan.	Feb.	Mar.	Apr.	May	June	July	Aug.	Sep.	Oct.	Nov.	Dec.
150	145	148	153	157	155	158	160	161	159	159	161

What is your best guess on the profile of monthly weights over the next 12 months? How volatile is the path of actual monthly weights over the next year likely to be relative to your estimated profile?

The Bond Market

Overview

Companies and governments borrow to finance investment and cover current expenditure—households, ultimately, provide the funds. The household sector's stocks of financial assets are—either directly or indirectly—claims on future revenues of corporations and governments. Those claims come in many forms. Broadly speaking, they are of two sorts: debt and equity. In this chapter, we focus on a particular type of debt: bonds. The bond market is important because it is where interest rates on medium- and long-term debt are determined. We will discuss how bonds are used, how they are priced, what their risks are, and how shifts in bond values affect the wider economy. The links among monetary policy, the cost of borrowing, and the value of bonds are significant; we will see how governments and central banks through their influence on the bond market can affect the wider economy. These effects can be positive, but often they are negative, sometimes disastrously so.

Key to understanding the significance of the bond market is the relation among bond prices, rates of return (or yields), and expectations of future short-term interest rates. Central banks implement monetary policy by controlling short-term interest rates. But longer-term interest rates, that is, the rates of return required on investments over 5- 10- or 20-year horizons—rather than the interest rates on 1-month bank loans or deposits that central banks directly influence—are probably the most important for private sector saving and investing decisions. But short-term rates and longer-term rates are linked, and one of the aims of this chapter is to explain and then assess this link.

22.1   What Is a Bond?

A bond is basically an IOU (an "I owe you"). When a company or a government is-sues a bond, it promises to repay certain amounts of money at specific dates in the fu-ture. Most bonds specify the precise cash values of the repayments, and their timing, in advance.[1] These IOUs often have long lives; many governments want to borrow money for 20 or 30 years, and debt issued today may not finally be repaid until 2020 or 2030. Indeed, the UK government issued bonds to help finance the First World War (1914–1918) that have an indefinite life—they are merely promises to pay a certain amount of cash to the holder each year until the end of time (or until the end of the UK!). Like equities, bonds are traded in a secondary market—holders of bonds can sell their claims to third parties and liquidate their holding without recourse to the issuer. For this reason a 30-year bond—one that the issuer will not finally repay for three decades—can nonetheless be a highly liquid asset.

Bonds are traded in securities markets (the bond market); this distinguishes bonds from bank debt—claims held by banks cannot, in general, be sold to a third party. And the debts banks issue directly to the public—that is, deposits—are also not traded in a secondary market. When you want the cash you have lent a bank, you get it from the bank rather than by selling your deposit to someone else. In this sense, bonds have more in common with equities than with bank debt because both bonds and equities are traded securities that you can cash in by selling to other investors; the original issuer is not involved.

Bond prices are set, on a minute-by-minute basis, by market makers who typically work for large financial institutions like Morgan Stanley, Merrill Lynch, or Goldman Sachs. They quote prices at which they will buy and sell bonds. These prices reflect the flow of buy and sell orders they receive. As always, the forces underlying demand and supply generate prices. Expectations about whether bondholders will really receive the money bond issuers have promised them are crucial, as are the ways in which people value money that will only be paid 5, 10, or 20 years ahead. As people's views on these factors change, demand and supply curves shift, which generates changes in prices. The prices reflect the cost of borrowing money for various time periods and are a major fac-tor behind corporate investment decisions.

The big distinction between bonds and equities is that the repayment schedule for bonds is specified in great detail, whereas equities merely represent a claim on some unspecified fraction of whatever corporate profits (after tax and interest payments) happen to exist in the future. As a result, bonds have different risk characteristics.

Bond markets are certainly big news. Table 22.1 indicates the size of the global market. At the end of 1999, bonds that governments and companies in the major devel-oped countries had issued had a market value of over $31 trillion. The U.S. bond

---

[1]The cash (or nominal) values are usually known, though the *real* value of those payments is not because inflation is uncertain. Some bonds pay future amounts that are linked to inflation outturns and generate cash flows with known real values.

TABLE 22.1   Size and Structure of the World Bond Market at End of 1999 (nominal value in billions of U.S. dollars)

Country	Total Out-standing	Percent World Bond Market	Government U.S. $bn	Percent of Government	Corporate U.S. $bn	Percent of Corporate	Foreign U.S. $bn	Percent of Foreign	Eurobond U.S. $bn	Percent of Eurobond
United States	14595	47.0	7723	45.2	4129	50.03	422	38.0	2320	49.6
Euroland	7121	23.0	3139	18.8	2110	25.8	401	35.9	1416	30.2
Japan	5668	18.2	4075	23.9	1096	13.4	82	7.4	415	8.9
United Kingdom	939	3.0	466	2.7	40	0.5	90	8.1	342	7.3
Canada	539	1.7	396	2.3	86	1.1	0	0.0	56	1.2
Switzerland	269	0.9	49	0.3	87	1.1	107	9.6	25	0.5
Denmark	263	0.8	82	0.5	169	2.1	0	0.0	11	0.2
Australia	197	0.6	82	0.5	70	0.9	5	0.5	38	0.8
Sweden	188	0.6	94	0.6	84	1.0	4	0.4	4	0.1
Norway	51	0.2	22	0.1	25	0.3	0	0.0	3	0.1
New Zealand	23	0.1	12	0.1	0	0.0	0	0.0	10	0.2
Subtotal	29857	96.1	16198	94.9	7901	96.4	1113	100.0	4644	99.2
Emerging/ Converging Markets										
Asia	722	2.3	410	2.4	292	3.6	na	na	19	0.4
Latin America	252	0.8	250	1.5	na	na	na	na	1	0.0
Eastern Europe, Middle East, and Africa	222	0.7	211	1.2	3	0.0	na	na	16	0.3
World Total	31054	100.0	17071	100.0	8196	100.0	1113	100.0	4681	100.0

Source: Compiled by Karim Basta and published by Merrill Lynch.

All data is for a calendar year-end. Foreign bonds are bonds issued by firms or governments outside of the issuer's home country. Euro bonds are bonds issued and sold outside the country of the currency in which they are denominated.

In the United States, agency debt is included in the government category. In Euroland, Pfandbriefe are included in the corporate category (that is because the underlying loans remain on the balance sheet of banks).

market rivals the size of the U.S. stock market. At the end of 1999, the total value of bonds that the U.S. government and big U.S. corporations had issued was almost $15 trillion; at that time U.S. equity market capitalization was about $16 trillion. The U.S. bond market is also far larger than any other market (Figure 22.1).

In many countries, as Table 22.1 shows, the government dominates the bond market. In 2000, governments issued about 55% of all bonds in the world (down from about 62% in 1990). The importance of government debt reflects two factors: First, governments often need to borrow on a large scale because they cannot cover

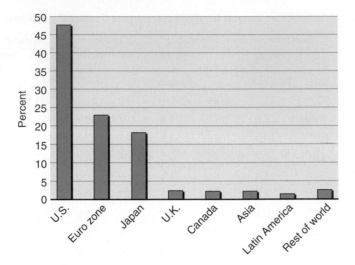

FIGURE 22.1 **Shares of the world bond market, 1999.** Shares in total world stock of bonds by currency of issuance. *Source*: Merrill Lynch "Size and Structure of the World Bond Market" (2000).

their expenditure out of tax revenue—sometimes by choice and sometimes of necessity. This is particularly true during war. The stock of government debt outstanding has often increased massively because of long and expensive conflicts. Second, governments issue bonds because they cannot issue equities. Corporations have a wide choice of financing techniques; governments do not. If you think about the difference between bonds and equities, this makes sense. The returns that shareholders get from holding equities depend on the profits that companies earn, and these, in turn, reflect a company's efficiency and skill in producing things that people want. Governments, in contrast, do not aim to make profits. If they did, life would be strange. After all, governments can (in most developed countries at least) raise taxes further and thus can (within limits) generate a surplus of revenue over spending. If governments really decided to maximize the excess of their revenues over their expenditure, they could generate huge "profits." If governments considered it their duty to maximize profits to generate returns to shareholders, taxpayers would suffer. Furthermore, shareholders might only be willing to buy equity in governments if, in exchange, they had a say in how government was run. This is hard to square with "one man one vote" democracy!

So when governments want to borrow, they typically look to the bond market. Table 22.1 shows that among the developed countries the government remains the major issuer of bonds, often by a huge margin. But corporations are also big players in the bond market; this has long been true in the United States, and in the 1990s, European companies also became significant issuers of bonds. When companies issue bonds, they are, like governments, issuing IOUs that give the holder of the bond the right to some portion of future corporate revenues.

The prices at which companies and governments can issue bonds are crucial because they reflect the rate of return that investors demand to hand over cash now in exchange for the promise of repayment in the future. This is a key determinant of the level of corporate investment. The price at which governments can issue bonds determines the cost of the national debt. The cost of debt to companies and governments is, of course, the mirror image of the return savers earn. Bond prices reflect the balance of supply and demand for debt. The flow of new bonds coming on to the market depends on the level of investment that companies wish to undertake and the needs of government to borrow. The demand for new bonds reflects the desired level of saving of households and companies. Both demand and supply in the bond market depend on returns on other financial assets—for example, equities and bank deposits. To understand how these factors affect bond prices and the volumes of debt issued, we need to understand the link between returns, or yields, and bond prices.

22.2   Prices, Yields, and Interest Rates

If you buy a bond, you hold a piece of paper that gives you the right to receive cash flows at specified dates in the future. The expectation of receiving those cash flows gives your piece of paper some value today. Because there are alternatives to holding bonds—for example, putting the money in a bank where it will earn a particular rate of interest—bonds have to generate a positive expected return to make them worth holding. We can think of the price of a bond as simply reflecting the value today of all the streams of cash that it will generate in the future. However, because we value the cash paid to us tomorrow less than the cash that is in our pocket today, we will discount those future receipts of cash that a bond entitles us to. So the *price* of a bond is the appropriately discounted value of all the repayments on the bond until it is finally redeemed. Those repayments come in two forms: regular *coupon* payments, plus a final payment of the *face value* of the bond at the *redemption date* (when the bond matures). The *yield* on a bond is simply the rate of return that, when used to discount future cash receipts, makes its total value equal to its current market price.

We need to be more precise about these relations. If we denote the yield on a bond by y and its price by P, then the relationship between the price and the yield on a bond with n periods to maturity is given by:

$$P = \frac{C}{1 + y} + \frac{C}{(1 + y)^2} + \cdots\cdots + \frac{C}{(1 + y)^n} + \frac{F}{(1 + y)^n} \tag{1}$$

where C is the regular annual coupon payment on the bond, and F is the final payment in the last period of the bond's life (sometimes called its "face value"). Here we assume that coupon payments come at 12-month intervals, and the first coupon is paid exactly a year from today. (In practice, some bonds pay coupons more than once a year, while others only make a final repayment.) The bond *matures* (or is redeemed) n years from now. Such a bond has a *residual maturity* of n years; obviously as time passes, n falls. So a bond issued in 1985 with an original maturity of 30 years, and a face value of $100, will guarantee to its holder in 2015 a final payment of $100. By 2002 the bond's residual maturity is 13 years.

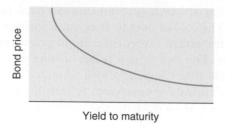

FIGURE 22.2 **Bond price/yield to maturity relationship.** There is a negative, nonlinear relation between the yield on a bond and its price.

You can see from the relation in equation (1) that the prices of bonds and their yields have an inverse relationship. The higher is the yield to maturity y, the lower is price. Figure 22.2 shows that relationship.

The yield to maturity is a measure of the average rate of return a buyer will earn on a bond if the buyer holds it to maturity. If you buy a bond at a low price, then given that it will make regular payments each year of $$C$ and also will generate a final payout of $$F$ when it matures in n periods' time, the bond will generate a high return over its entire life. The higher the price you have to pay for the bond today, the less, *on average*, you will earn on it, year by year, over its life. The key point is that the amount of money you get back from holding the bond is fixed in advance. This is why bonds are sometimes described as *fixed income securities*.[2] By paying more now to get the right to those fixed future amounts, you are getting a worse deal, i.e., a lower yield.

Let's take a concrete example of bond pricing: a bond with a face value of $100 , a maturity of four years, and a coupon rate of 8%. The issuer promises to pay $8 (the coupon rate times the face value) each year and to make a final (or redemption) payment of the full face value ($100). Suppose the next coupon payment is due a year from now, and the final coupon payment is made at the time of redemption exactly four years from now. Finally, suppose that the required yield on the bond is 6%. This means that the rate of return needed over a four-year horizon, expressed as an annual rate, is 6%.

The value of the bond will be the sum of the present values of each of the cash flows using a 6% discount rate to calculate those present values.

The first coupon is worth today: $8/(1.06)
The subsequent coupons are worth: $8/(1.06)^2; $8/(1.06)^3; $8/(1.06)^4
The final repayment of the face value is worth today: $100/(1.06)^4

Evaluating each of these terms and summing them give us the bond price today:

$$P = \$7.55 + \$7.12 + \$6.72 + \$6.34 + \$79.21 = \$106.94$$

---

[2]Not all bonds pay amounts fixed in advance. For example, inflation-protected bonds (sometimes called index-linked bonds) pay coupons and have a final redemption payment which depend on what happens to inflation between the time the bond is bought and its maturity. Such bonds have guaranteed real repayments but uncertain nominal repayments. Other bonds have cash flows that vary in line with movements in interest rates (floating rate bonds).

Note here that because the yield on the bond (6%) is less than the coupon rate (8%), the price exceeds the face value. If you paid the face value of $100 (this is sometimes called the "par value"), you would be earning 8% a year because that is what the coupon rate is. But the required return is only 6%. So you are willing to pay more than $100 to buy the bond. The price will be driven up from a face value of $100 to $106.94 to generate a return of 6%. If the yield (or required return) were to coincide with the coupon rate, the annual coupons would generate a return equal to the yield as long as the price stayed at $100. If the yield were in excess of the coupon, the price would be below the face value. When governments and companies issue bonds, they typically set the coupon rate at close to what they expect the yield on the bond to be, so that bond prices are usually around face values near to the issue date; such bonds are said to be trading at par.

Figure 22.2 reveals an important fact about bonds: not only is the relation between price and yield *inverse*, it is also nonlinear. An increase in yields of a given amount has a smaller negative impact on price at high yields than at low yields. We will also see below that a given shift in yields also has different impacts on the prices of bonds of different maturities.

So far we have just defined what we mean by the yield on the bond—it is simply the average return you will earn from holding the bond *until the time at which the debt is finally repaid.* This is why we sometimes call yields "yields to maturity" or "redemption yields." We do not really know yet what will determine those yields and tie down bond prices. This is a crucial and difficult question, but expectations of future short-term interest rates, which central banks largely control, should be a key part of the story. To see the link more clearly, suppose you wanted to invest some money for 10 years. You could buy a 10-year bond. For simplicity, let's assume that this bond will make no payments until the end of the 10 years when the issuer—a government or a company—will send you a check for $100 for every bond that you own. (In other words, the coupon rate is zero; such bonds are sometimes called "zeros.") Buying and holding such a bond would clearly be one way to invest money for 10 years. You could also put the money in a bank savings account in which interest was reset every month in line with money market interest rates. Those money market interest rates will be closely linked to the rates of interest that the central bank will fix (see Chapter 17).

We now have two options:

(a) to buy now, at its current market price, a government bond that has 10 years still to run until maturity; or
(b) to put your money in a bank and leave it there for 10 years, accruing interest each month at a rate that will be reset at the beginning of each month in line with whatever short-term interest rates then rule.

Suppose that we do not care too much about the uncertainty of future short-term interest rates. In this case, if we are going to be indifferent between these two investment strategies, the yield on the 10-year government bond, a number that we know for sure today, had better be close to the average interest rate we think we are going to earn on those bank deposits if we hold them for a decade. If that was not true, then one or other of the two strategies would clearly be dominant, and if enough people agreed that one of these strategies was better than the other, there would be either massive movements of funds out of bank deposits and into bonds or huge selling of government bonds and a massive inflow of funds into banks. Of course, such large movements would generate price changes. So suppose that 10-year bond yields were substantially higher—given current bond prices—than people's expectations of what the average interest rate would be on bank deposits over the next 10 years. People would have an incentive to buy bonds and write checks on their banks to pay for them. The massive increase in demand for bonds would boost their price—and by equation (1) above would obviously reduce their yields—and the big outflows of money from banks would encourage banks to increase their deposit rates. This process would continue until the 10-year bond yield was close to the average expected interest rate on bank deposits over the next 10 years.

Let's take a concrete example. Suppose the U.S. Federal Reserve funds rate was 3%, and the rate on Treasury bills with one month to maturity was at the same level—reflecting an expectation that over a one-month horizon, at least, the Federal Reserve was likely to hold rates steady. Now 3% is an unusually low rate for the United States, and if the Fed had engineered short rates down to that level, investors would not expect them to keep them there for long. Let's assume that investors thought that rates on one-month Treasury bills would have moved up to 4% by 12 months ahead because the Fed was set to increase rates. Suppose further that the Fed was expected to raise rates gradually to 5% by two years ahead and to 6% by three years ahead. After that the consensus view was that the Fed would leave rates at 6%. Figure 22.4 shows the path along which the one-month Treasury bill rate is expected to evolve. Now consider what the yield on a bond with one year to maturity should be. If one-month Treasury bill rates are now 3% and are expected to gradually move up to 4% by a year from now, then the average of one-month rates over the next 12

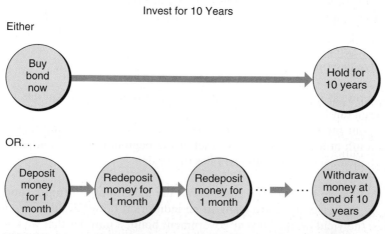

FIGURE 22.3   Alternative strategies for an investor with a 10-year horizon.

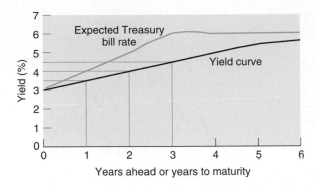

FIGURE 22.4 **Expected Treasury bill rate against yield curve.** The anticipation of rising short-term interest rates generates an upward-sloping yield curve.

months is 3.5%. This is approximately where the yield on one-year bonds should be. If you kept investing in one-month Treasury bills and as each bill matured you bought another, the average interest rate you would earn, over the year, is 3.5%. The one-year bond yield is, by definition, the return you get from holding a one-year bond to maturity, so this should be close to the 3.5% you expect to earn from buying a series of one-month bills.

What about two-year bonds? The average Treasury bill rate over the first year is expected to be 3.5%, and the average over the second year is expected to be 4.5% [(4 + 5)/2)]. The simple average of short rates over the whole two years is expected to be 4%, which is about where two-year bond yields should be. A similar argument shows that the average of one month rates over the next three years is expected to be 4.5%. As we consider bonds with longer and longer maturities, the average of expected one-month Treasury bill rates over the time to their redemption gets closer and closer to 6% (though it always remains below 6%). The yield curve, which shows the relation between yields to maturity and time to maturity, would be upward sloping toward 6%, as Figure 22.4 shows. The yield curve shows the average return that is expected to be earned holding bonds of different maturities.

Now consider what would happen if the chairperson of the Federal Reserve announced that in the view of the Fed inflationary pressures in the U.S. economy were likely to remain low over the foreseeable future and that there was no reason to expect that the Fed would significantly increase interest rates. Assuming that the chairperson had at least some credibility, expectations of future short-term interest rates would come down. If the chairperson had complete credibility, expected future one-month rates would fall to 3%, the current Fed rate. As long as future expected short rates fall, so do longer-dated bond yields; in the extreme case of complete credibility, all bond yields would fall immediately to 3%.

So one would expect that bond yields will be sensitive to expectations of where short-term interest rates will be moving in the future. Bond yields thus tend to move around a good deal over time. Figure 22.5 shows the yield on long-dated U.S. government bonds between 1926 and the end of 1999. Over that period yields have varied dramatically. In the mid-1970s, when inflation and short-term interest rates were high,

FIGURE 22.5 **U.S. long-term bond yield.** Yields rose sharply in the 1970s as inflation in the United States increased to high levels. *Source*: Thomson Financial Datastream.

bond yields were frequently in double figures. By the mid 1990s, government bond yields had moved down substantially. Yields were almost 9% in January 1990; they fell to 7% by early 1993 and to under 6% by early 1998. By early 2000 yields were still close to 6%. In Europe, yields in the 1990s declined even more. Italian government bond yields moved down sharply as expectations rose that Italy would be among the first countries to join a monetary union and that its short-term interest rates would move down to the much lower German levels.

Note that for a given change in yields the movement in price tends to be greater for longer-dated bonds. We can illustrate this with zero-coupon (or *pure discount*) bonds. Suppose initially that the yield curve is flat at 5%. Column 1 in Table 22.2 shows the prices of bonds of various maturities, all with face values of $100. Column 2 shows how

TABLE 22.2 **The Relation between Prices and Yields**

	Price at 5% Yield	Price at 5.1% Yield	Percent Change in Price
1-year bond	95.24	95.15	−0.1
2-year bond	90.70	90.53	−0.19
5-year bond	78.35	77.98	−0.48
10-year bond	61.39	60.81	−0.96
15-year bond	48.10	47.42	−1.44
20-year bond	37.69	36.98	−1.92
30-year bond	23.14	22.49	−2.90

prices would move if yields rose by 10 basis points, to 5.1%. Column 3 shows the percentage change in the price. Note that the percentage impact on price is greater the longer the maturity of the bonds. In fact, the percent change is roughly proportional to maturity. This is a special feature of zero-coupon bonds. More generally, how a yield change affects the price depends on both coupon and maturity. To be more specific, the relation between price change and yield change depends on the *duration* of a bond, which is a measure of the average time that your money is tied up in a bond if you hold it to maturity. For coupon-paying bonds, duration is less than maturity because you get cash back before the redemption date. For zero-coupon bonds, duration and maturity coincide, which is why the link between the percentage price changes in Table 22.2 and the maturity of the bonds is so close. The general point is that prices and yields are inversely related and that prices are more sensitive to yield the longer you lend your money to the issuer of the bond.

22.3 The Bond Market in April 2000

The concept of the yield curve that we introduced in the last section is straightforward—it is the relation at a point in time between the yields to maturity on bonds and time to maturity. But in practice no *single* yield curve exists because a huge number of companies and governments issue bonds. Bonds differ by type of issuer (government and corporations), by currency of issue, and by maturity. The market is global—bonds are issued in all major currencies (and many minor ones); corporations from all developed countries and governments from both developed and less developed countries issue them. Well-established, large corporations that are household names around the world issue them, but so do largely unknown start-up companies that may not survive for five years.

Prices of bonds with the same coupon rate and maturity can differ if they are issued in different currencies because people expect currencies to shift in value. Bonds denominated in the same currency can have different prices (or yields) because people do not consider all promises to pay coupons and make final redemption equally good. Both governments and corporations can default on the promises implicit in those IOUs. People who held bonds issued by the Tsarist regime that ruled in Russia until 1917 would testify to this. For developed countries at least, governments are usually considered better risks than corporations. This does not mean that the market thinks that governments are better run than companies! It reflects governments' ability to raise taxes to generate more revenue. Companies cannot do that, and if their debt is large relative to their assets, they may be unable to generate enough revenue in competitive product markets to pay bondholders. Because of the higher risk of default, corporate bonds generally need to offer a higher rate of return than government debt. In the major economies, the difference between the return promised on a company's bonds and the yield on government debt is a common measure of a company's credit-worthiness. As we shall see, there are huge differences in credit-worthiness. Spreads over government bonds—that is, the amount by which corporate bond yields exceed those on government debt of similar maturity—can be as low as 10 basis points (one-tenth of one full percentage point); with this tight a spread, if a government bond is paying a return of 9%, a corporate bond would need to offer an average return over the bond's life of 9.10%. Spreads can also be many thousands of basis points. In early 1999 Russian government bonds yielded 38%, while U.S. Treasuries yielded around 5%; this is a spread of 3300 basis points!

For bonds of a given currency, the yield on domestic government bonds is generally the benchmark against which other issuers are compared. Table 22.3 shows the yield to maturity in April 2000 on medium-dated bonds that various governments had issued in their domestic currency. These are 10-year bond yields; that is, (roughly speaking) the average annual rate of return that could be earned from buying a 10-year IOU from the government and holding it until repayment in early 2010. The second column in the table shows how the yield of the bond (in the currency of the issuing government) differs from the yield on euro bonds that the German government issued. The

TABLE 22.3   10-Year Benchmark Spreads In April 2000 (%)

	Bid Yield	Spread vs. Euros	Spread vs. T-Bonds
Australia	6.32	+1.13	+0.29
Austria	5.46	+0.27	−0.57
Belgium	5.45	+0.26	−0.58
Canada	5.94	+0.75	−0.09
Denmark	5.54	+0.35	−0.49
Finland	5.40	+0.21	−0.63
France	5.29	+0.10	−0.74
Germany	5.19	—	−0.84
Greece	6.08	+0.89	+0.05
Ireland	5.43	+0.24	−0.60
Italy	5.49	+0.30	−0.54
Japan	1.78	−3.41	−4.25
Netherlands	5.33	+0.14	−0.70
New Zealand	6.86	+1.67	+0.84
Norway	6.03	+0.84	—
Portugal	5.47	+0.28	−0.56
Spain	5.42	+0.23	−0.61
Sweden	5.36	+0.17	−0.67
Switzerland	3.76	−1.43	−2.27
United Kingdom	5.21	+0.02	−0.82
United States	6.03	+0.84	—

Source: Financial Times (April 12, 2000).
Annualized yield basis.

third column shows the yield relative to the dollar yield on 10-year U.S. government bonds (which are known as Treasuries or T-bonds). Table 22.3 shows that yields on different government bonds vary a lot—even when we focus only on bonds that governments in developed and relatively stable (politically and economically) countries issue. Ten-year Swiss government bonds in April 2000 were yielding around 3.75%; Japanese government bonds were yielding about half this (1.78%); in contrast, U.S. Treasuries offered just over 6%, but in a different currency.

When we look at yields on bonds that emerging countries issue, the spread in rates of return becomes much more dramatic. Table 22.4 shows that the Brazilian government bonds, denominated in U.S. dollars, were yielding over 13%—well over double the yield on U.S. Treasuries. A few months earlier, Russian government bonds (again denominated in dollars) yielded almost 40%—reflecting great uncertainty over whether the Russian government would be able to repay the debt in full. Clearly yield differences of this magnitude affect the incentives to borrow, the levels of expenditure that government and firms finance by issuing debt and their willingness to default.

Tables 22.5 through 22.7 further illustrate the diversity of issuers and the types of bonds that they issue—in terms of currency and for how long money is borrowed. Table

TABLE 22.4   Emerging Market Bonds (April 12, 2000)

	Redemption Date	S & P Rating	Price	Yield	Spread vs U.S. Dollar
EUROPE (EUROS)					
Croatia	03/06	BBB−	99.67	7.44	+1.27
Slovenia	03/09	A	92.39	6.00	+0.01
Hungary	02/09	BBB+	86.99	6.34	+0.35
LATIN AMERICA DOLLAR					
Argentina	02/20	BB	98.50	12.20	+6.32
Brazil	01/20	B+	96.00	13.32	+7.44
Mexico	02/10	BB+	104.00	9.24	+3.30
ASIA DOLLAR					
China	12/08	BBB	97.73	7.66	+1.61
Phillipines	01/19	BB+	90.02	11.15	+5.26
South Korea	04/08	BBB	104.06	8.17	+2.12
AFRICA/MIDDLE EAST DOLLARS					
Lebanon	10/09	BB−	101.07	10.07	+4.08
South Africa	10/06	BBB−	95.50	9.31	+3.14
Turkey	09/07	B	96.87	10.62	+4.51

S & P ratings reflect perceived credit quality.

London closing. Prices in U.S. dollars. Standard & Poor's ratings.

S & P ratings range from AAA (highest quality) to D (bonds in default).

Source: Financial Times (April 12, 2000).

TABLE 22.5   U.S. Corporate Bonds (April 12, 2000)

	Redemption Date	Coupon	S & P Rating	Moody's Rating	Price	Yield	Spread vs. Governments
UTILITIES							
Pac Bell	07/02	7.25	AA−	Aa3	99.99	7.24	+0.85
NY Telecom	08/25	7.00	A+	A2	86.23	8.30	+2.46
CWE	05/08	8.00	BBB+	Baa1	103.15	7.47	+1.50
FINANCIALS							
GEEC	05/07	8.75	AAA	Aaa	107.51	7.36	+1.39
Bank One	08/02	7.25	A−	A1	99.73	7.37	+0.98
CNA Fin	01/18	6.95	BBB	Baa1	81.00	9.12	+3.28
INDUSTRIALS							
Lucent	03/29	6.45	A	A2	87.23	7.53	+1.69
News Corp	10/08	7.38	BBB−	Baa3	96.01	8.03	+2.06
TCI Comm	05/03	6.38	Aa−	A2	97.31	7.37	+0.98

Source: *Financial Times* (April 12, 2000).

22.5 shows details of bonds that large U.S. corporations issued in U.S. dollars. The spread of maturity dates in the first column is large; in April 2000 New York Telecom had issued bonds that had over 25 years more to run until final repayment. The second to last column of the table shows the yields on the bonds at the close of business on April 12, and the final column shows the difference in yield from U.S. government bonds. In April 2000, 25-year New York Telecom bonds were offering yields close to 2.5% above U.S. government bonds of long maturity.

Tables 22.6 and 22.7 show prices and yields on bonds that corporations throughout the world issued in various currencies. Table 22.6 shows details of bonds denominated in U.S., Canadian, and Australian dollars, UK pounds, Swiss francs, and Japanese yen. Table 22.7 shows details of bonds denominated in euros. Again, the range of maturities and the spread of yields are large.

22.4   Inflation and the Bond Market

By now, you should understand why people who hold conventional (fixed rate) bonds are hit hard when inflation rises unexpectedly. An inflationary environment erodes the real value of fixed income securities, and persistent and unanticipated inflation can inflict enormous damage to returns on bonds. The inflation rate in the 10 years from January 1970 to January 1980 was, in almost every developed country, higher than the 10-year bond yield at the start of the decade. Investors in government bonds who bought in the early 1970s invariably earned negative real returns. But the losses on bonds that the developed countries issued in the 1970s pale alongside the much greater

TABLE 22.6   International Bonds (April 2000)

	Redemption Date	Coupon	S & P Rating	Moody's Rating	Price	Yield	Spread vs. Governments
$							
EIB	1/09	5.250	AAA	Aaa	87.68	7.19	+1.20
ABN Amro	06/07	7.125	AA−	Aa3	97.04	7.67	+1.56
Quebec	02/09	5.750	A+	A2	90.07	7.29	+1.30
Citicorp FRN	02/04	6.173	AA−	Aa3	99.54	6.48	+0.20
C$							
Bayer L-Bk	08/04	9.500	AAA	Aaa	110.96	6.49	+0.34
Toronto (M of)	05/04	8.500	AA+	Aa2	107.46	6.37	+0.22
Bell Canada	10/04	10.875	A+	A2	116.21	6.56	+0.41
Deutsche B FRN	09/02	5.875	AA	Aa3	99.32	6.45	+0.42
£							
EIB	12/09	5.500	AAA	Aaa	95.01	6.20	+0.80
Boots	07/08	8.875	A	A2	112.27	6.86	+1.27
British Gas	07/08	8.875	A	A2	112.27	6.86	+1.27
Halifax	04/08	6.375	AA	Aa1	98.85	6.56	+0.97
SFR							
EIB	01/08	3.750	AAA	Aaa	98.22	4.02	+0.33
Brit Columbia	02/02	3.250	AA−	Aa2	99.00	3.81	+0.39
Hydro-Quebec	05/01	6.750	A+	A2	102.62	4.24	+1.22
General Electric	09/01	2.400	AAA	Aaa	99.78	3.34	+0.32
YEN							
IBRD (World Bk)	03/02	5.250	AAA	Aaa	109.27	0.40	10.03
Spain (Kingdom)	03/02	5.750	AA+	Aa2	110.16	0.46	+0.09
KFW Int	12/04	1.000	AAA	Aaa	99.62	1.08	+0.19
Eurofima	06/05	0.292	AAA	Aaa	99.86	1.17	+0.01
A$							
IBRD (World Bk)	02/08	6.000	AAA	Aaa	96.45	6.59	+0.32
Nw Sth Wales Tr	05/06	6.500	n/a	n/a	99.35	6.63	+0.33
S. Aus Gov Fin	06/03	7.750	AA+	Aa2	102.51	6.84	+0.55
GMAC Aust	05/01	9.000	A	A2	102.24	6.79	+0.74

Source: *Financial Times* (April 12, 2000).

London closing. Standard & Poor's ratings. Yields: Local market standard/Annualized basis.

TABLE 22.7   Euro-Zone Bonds (April 12, 2000)

	Redemption Date	Coupon	S&P Rating	Moody's Rating	Price	Yield	Spread vs. Governments
UTILITIES							
EDF	01/09	5.000	AA+	Aaa	95.91	5.60	+0.46
TEPCO	05/09	4.375	AA	Aa2	90.26	5.78	+0.64
Hydro-Quebec	03/08	5.375	A+	A2	96.91	5.87	+0.79
Powergen (UK)	07/09	5.000	A	A2	91.32	6.26	+1.12
FINANCIALS							
Bad Wurtt	02/10	5.375	AAA	Aaa	96.90	5.79	+0.60
OKB	04/08	5.250	AAA	Aaa	98.09	5.55	+0.47
Credit Local	04/09	4.750	n/a	Aa1	93.00	5.77	+0.63
Abbey Natl	01/09	5.000	AA−	Aa3	92.56	6.12	+0.98
INDUSTRIALS							
Unilever	05/04	6.500	AAA	Aaa	104.00	5.37	+0.60
McDonalds	03/08	5.125	AA	Aa2	96.49	5.68	+0.60
Philip Morris	06/08	5.625	A	A2	89.67	7.34	+2.26
BAT Int Fin	07/06	5.375	A	A2	91.57	7.07	+2.14
HIGH YIELD							
Jazztel	12/09	13.250	CCC+	Caa1	101.04	13.05	+7.91
Kpnqwest	06/09	7.125	BB	Ba1	97.47	7.51	+2.37
Kappa Baheer	07/09	10.625	B	B2	105.97	9.63	+4.49
Utd Pan-Europe	08/09	10.875	B	B2	97.05	11.39	+6.25

Source: *Financial Times* (April 12, 2000).

losses on the debt of emerging countries that occurred in the 1980s and 1990s. Russia is a case in point. Yields on ruble bonds moved up sharply during the 1990s as inflation in Russia reached hundreds of percent a year. Faced with hyperinflation, the government pushed up ruble short-term interest rates sharply, generating massive increases in bond yields and causing huge falls in bond prices that all but wiped out the value of investments.

The inverse relation between yields and prices makes inflation, which nearly always brings higher short-term interest rates, the enemy of the bond holder. That inverse relation also explains what might otherwise appear puzzling. You often hear descriptions of activity in the bond market that sound something like this, "Yesterday was a good day for the U.S. bond market as yields on long-dated Treasuries fell 20 basis points on expectations of further Fed easing." Now bonds are debt, and people that hold bonds own IOUs. So why are bondholders laughing when interest rates come down, which is normally thought to be bad for people who hold debt? The reason is that bonds, as we noted above, are typically *fixed income securities*. In other words, the amount of cash that you are going to get in the future from holding a bond does not change when interest rates and yields move, *but the present value of that cash does*. In other words, bond prices rise leading to capital gains for bondholders.

All this is in marked contrast to the situation in which holders of bank debt (or bank deposits) find themselves. Depositors with banks are, other things equal, better off when central banks push up interest rates because most bank deposits are earning interest at rates that typically move closely in line with shifts in central bank rates. Note the contrast here with conventional bonds, which are fixed income securities, and where the coupon payments are usually fixed in nominal terms in advance. The fixity of the nominal repayment schedule on bonds means that bond prices have to move when required rates of return shift. With bank deposits the interest stream (analogous to coupons on bonds) is generally not fixed, and as the general level of interest rates moves, the steam of interest income that the deposit generates also moves, so that the value of the underlying deposit does not change. The absence of sharp changes in capital values distinguishes bonds from bank deposits and makes the return on fixed income assets more volatile. It also means that the link between changes in monetary policy, both actual and anticipated, and the price of bonds is important. We discuss this link next.

22.5 Government Policy and the Yield Curve

We argued above that yields on long-dated bonds are likely to reflect expectations of future short-term interest rates. This is the essence of the so-called expectations theory of the yield curve. In this section we discuss in more detail the link between what governments and central banks do, particularly in setting short-term interest rates through monetary policy decisions, and the longer-term interest rates that are likely to be important for private sector saving and investment decisions.

Figure 22.6 shows the yield curve on U.S. government bonds in mid-February 1999. (Note that we always have to give a particular date to the yield curve; hence it only

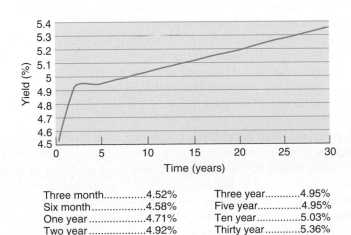

Three month	4.52%	Three year	4.95%
Six month	4.58%	Five year	4.95%
One year	4.71%	Ten year	5.03%
Two year	4.92%	Thirty year	5.36%

FIGURE 22.6 **U.S. yield curve.** With short-term interest rates in early 1999 at unusually low levels there was a widespread perception that the next movements in short rates would be up. *Source*: Curve constructed from data reported in the *Financial Times*, February 16, 1999.

makes sense to talk about "the U.S. government bond yield curve" on a specific day.) The figure shows that U.S. government bonds that only had a year or so still to run were yielding about 4.7%. Bonds with about five years still to run were yielding about 5%, and bonds that had 20 or 30 years still to run were yielding 5.35%. Yield curves can slope up sharply, slope down sharply, or be flat. Again, the main factor is expectations about future short-term interest rates. At this time it was widely believed that the U.S. Fed would need to increase interest rates—the Fed funds rate was under 5% but was expected to rise over the course of the next few years.

Suppose, for example, that short-term (say three-month) interest rates were currently high but were expected to fall gradually over the next 5 to 10 years. (This happened for many European countries before the monetary union at the start of 1999.) If you expect short-term interest rates to decline gradually, then the average of the interest rates over the next year will be greater than the average of the interest rates over the next three years, which, in turn, will be greater than the average of short-term interest rates over the next five years. Because the yield on one-year bonds should be linked to average short-term interest rates over a year, and the yield on five-year bonds should be linked to the average of short-term interest rate over five years, one would expect that five-year bond yields would be substantially lower than one year bond yields. In other words, the yield curve would be sloping downwards. Clearly if you expected short-term interest rates to rise over the next five years, then five-year bonds would tend to have much higher yields than one-year bonds. In that case the yield curve would slope up.

Is this expectations theory consistent with the evidence? If it is, and assuming that expectations of future short-term interest rates and inflation are rational, the shape of the yield curve should help predict changes in inflation and short-term interest rates. The evidence supports this view. Figure 22.7 estimates what you would have predicted the change in interest rates to be, given the yield curve (forward spread), and what subsequently happened to (one-year) interest rates over the next year (spot change). There is some correlation between these lines for the four countries. But clearly one would only have predicted the general shape of changes, and even then only been right on average, rather than have an accurate measure of the future course of short-term interest rates. The predictive ability of the forward spread is modest.

The yield curve appears to be slightly more informative in predicting inflation. When two-year bond yields exceed (fall short of) one-year yields, evidence shows that inflation is higher (lower) two years ahead than one year ahead. Figure 22.8 shows the actual change in inflation against the predicted change, based on the slope of the yield curve (as measured by the term spread between two-year and one-year bonds). Clearly the two are significantly correlated.

Therefore, the slope of the yield curve tends to change over the business cycle. When an economy emerges from a recession, short-term nominal interest rates are generally low; but central banks should be expected to increase rates gradually as growth picks up and the economy moves back to full capacity. With low current interest rates and the expectation of higher rates to come, the yield curve will tend to slope upwards. During a boom, in contrast, the central bank may have raised short-term interest rates to levels substantially above the long-term average. If tightening monetary policy is effective, the market will anticipate slower growth and falling inflation, which would

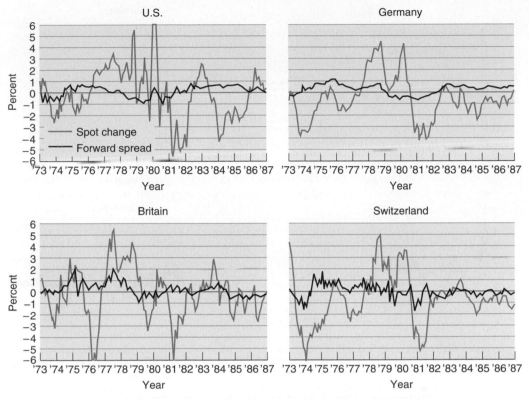

F I G U R E 22.7 **Some evidence in support of expectations theory of term structure.** The broad pattern of movements in short-term interest rates is explained moderately well by looking at the slope of the yield curve. *Source*: Jourion and Mishkin, "A Multicountry Comparison of Term Structure Forecasts at Long Horizons," *Journal of Financial Economics* (1991) vol. 29, no. 1, pp. 59–80. Reprinted with permission from Elsevier Science.

allow the central bank to reduce interest rates in the future. In this environment longer-dated bonds will tend to have yields *below* short-term interest rates, and the yield curve will slope down. Inversions of the yield curve—that is, downward-sloping curves—are common, though over the long run, yields on long-maturity bonds tend to be higher than yields on short-dated bonds and Treasury bills.

Because yields on bonds reflect expectations over future monetary policy, they give us useful information about the future of the economy. This information has at least three elements. First, we might focus on the *absolute levels* of government bond yields of different maturities. This tells us something about the level of short-term interest rates that we can expect in the future, and those levels are likely to reflect demand pressures in the economy, the strength of output growth, and inflation pressures. So, for example, if 10-year bond yields are at 15%, this is likely to reflect a strong belief that inflation is going to be so consistently high that the central bank will need to set short-term nominal rates at double digit levels. Second, as noted above, the *slope* of the yield curve is likely to reveal something about how monetary policy will be *changing*, and

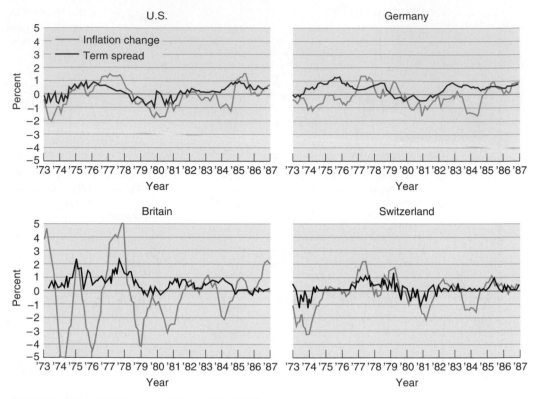

FIGURE 22.8 **Yield spread useful in predicting inflation.** The shape of the yield curve also gives some information about changes in future inflation—when the yield curve slopes up more than usual, inflation tends to be on the increase. *Source*: Jourion and Mishkin, *Journal of Financial Economics* (1991) vol. 29, pp. 59–80. Reprinted with permission from Elsevier Science.

that, in turn, should reflect whether the economy is slowing down or accelerating. Third, we can learn something about shifts in perceptions of bankruptcy risk from movements in the average *spreads* between government and corporate bonds. After the major sell-off in emerging market bonds (particularly in Russian government bonds) in mid-1998, spreads between corporate and government bond yields in the United States widened as fears about default risks for highly geared companies increased.

Evidence shows that bond prices, specifically the shape of the yield curve, do provide useful information for predicting movements in output. For example, economists have found that when the yield curve has a shallow slope (or slopes down), recession is more likely. Under the expectations theory, a downward-sloping yield curve suggests that short-term interest rates are falling, which is likely if the economy goes into a recession.

The sensitivity of bond prices to expectations of what the central bank will do in the future gives monetary policy real teeth. Even in countries in which individuals and companies do not borrow money at short-term variable rates of interest, the central bank can still significantly affect the cost of borrowing. Remember, central banks only have *direct* influence over short-term interest rates. If individuals borrow at long-term fixed rates of interest (e.g., by taking out mortgages), or if companies issue long-dated bonds to finance investment, governments and central banks might not seem to have much influence on the relevant cost of borrowing. Not so! Long-dated bond yields depend on expectations of short-term interest rates into the future. So by influencing expectations about their *future* actions when setting short-term interest rates, central banks can *today* influence the cost of borrowing money for long periods ahead. They can also generate big swings in bond prices. The expectation that a central bank might have to increase short-term interest rates sharply in the future can cause bond prices to decline. Given the value of the total stock of debt outstanding (Table 22.1) big percentage changes in bond prices can significantly change the total wealth of the private sector, which, in turn, can cause major changes in consumption. In the United States the value of bonds in 2000 was about twice annual GDP. Therefore an important element in the transmission mechanism of monetary policy is the induced impact on bond yields and bond prices of current central bank actions.

22.6 Deficits and Bond Prices

In all financial markets, prices reflect the interaction of demand and supply. In focusing on expectations of future interest rates as the key determinant of bond prices, we have implicitly assumed that these are the driving forces between movements in demand and supply curves, and that seems sensible. Why would a company issue 10-year bonds at a yield of 9% if it expected over the next decade to be able to borrow from a bank at an interest rate that varied around an average of 6%? And why should a pension fund buy five-year bonds with yields of 4% if three-month interest rates on large deposits are 6% and are not expected to fall? So both the supply and demand for bonds are sensitive to expectations of future interest rates. However, governments may have to issue large quantities of debt from time to time, even though yields may be temporarily high. Governments have been issuing bonds for centuries. The UK government, for example, started issuing bonds just over 300 years ago to help finance a war. (Figure 22.9 shows what has happened to yields on long-dated UK government bonds over those three centuries.)

Because most governments now have large stocks of debt outstanding, and because a good chunk of that debt matures in any one year, they are constantly rolling forward the debt by issuing new bonds. We have mentioned wars already: Figure 22.10 shows the outstanding stock of UK government debt over a 300-year period. (The UK is one of the few countries that has an uninterrupted history of trading in a large stock of government bonds; other countries' financial markets collapsed often because of hyperinflation, revolution, invasion, or civil war—sometimes all four!) The stock of debt here is measured relative to GDP. The Napoleonic Wars of the early nineteenth century and the World Wars of the twentieth century increased the stock of UK government debt enormously.

To finance these expensive struggles, the UK government could not rely on tax revenues. It would not have been feasible to finance such massive increases in military

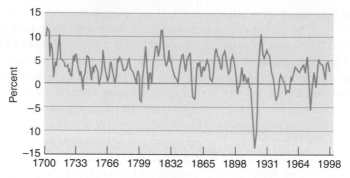

FIGURE 22.9   **UK long-term real interest rate, 1700–1998 (yield on medium-dated government bonds minus moving average of inflation).** Real interest rates on UK government bonds have moved around a great deal—but much of the fluctuation has been due to unanticipated inflation rather than shifts in expected real returns on bonds. *Source*: Miles, "Interest Rate from the 17th to the 21st Century," Merrill Lynch Report (June 1998).

expenditure by increasing tax revenues in a short period. Indeed, any temporary increase in government expenditure is probably best met by increasing government debt rather than increasing taxes only to reduce them again in a year or two. Sharp fluctuations in tax rates are likely to disrupt the economy more than sudden increases or decreases in the amount of new government debt that is to be sold. A sudden increase in the corporation tax rate that was expected to be followed by future reductions might give companies major incentives to push receipts of revenue into future periods. Big increases in

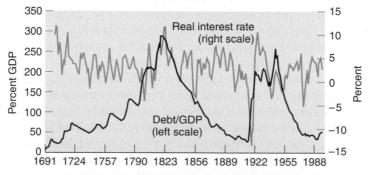

FIGURE 22.10   **Stock of UK government debt/GDP (1691–1998) and real interest rate (medium-dated bond yield minus five-year moving average of inflation).** In the UK over a 300-year period there has been little relation between movements in real interest rates and shifts in the stock of government debt. *Source*: Miles, "Interest Rates from the 17th to the 21st Century," Merrill Lynch Report (June 1998).

TABLE 22.8 Stock of Government Debt
Relative to Annual GDP (%)

	1981	1991	2000
United States	36.2	59.6	57.1
Japan	54.2	59.3	114.1
Germany	35.0	44.4	61.7
France	30.1	41.0	64.6
Italy	60.3	108.4	115.2
Spain	24,0	51.5	70.6
United Kingdom	54.5	40.6	51.2

Source: OECD Economic Outlook 2001.
Copyright OECD.

income tax that people expect to be reversed would encourage them to work less today, and more in the future. These kinds of tax arbitrage cause costly revisions to plans. Therefore, governments should use bond issues as a safety valve to smooth out temporary differences between revenues and expenditures. But does issuing more bonds affect yields?

In most countries the level of government borrowing in the bond market varies from year to year. Over the long-term, at least in Europe, the stock of government debt has increased. Government debt outstanding at the end of the 1990s in Europe was substantially higher than it was 20 years earlier. Table 22.8 shows the sharp rise in outstanding government bonds. But the effect of this on yields is unclear. We have already discussed Ricardian equivalence in Chapter 11—the argument that the private sector perceives government debt as simply deferred taxation. If people themselves (or their children or their children's children or . . .) have to repay government debt in the future by paying higher taxes, they will want to save more now to generate enough income for that future tax. This suggests that the demand for financial wealth from the private sector goes up exactly in line with increases in the supply of government bonds. After all, the value of the government bonds sold equals the present value of the future tax that governments will need to levy to buy those bonds back in the future.

If this consideration is relevant, we might not expect to see a strong relation between the stock of government debt outstanding and the price of that debt. In effect, both the supply and demand curves will shift by precisely the same amount in response to higher government deficits. Indeed, economists have had difficulty finding a significant and consistent relation between bond prices and the stock of government debt. Figure 22.10 showed the stock of UK government debt (relative to GDP) outstanding since the end of the seventeenth century and a simple measure of the *real* yield on that debt. That yield measure simply subtracts the 10-year moving average of actual inflation from the nominal bond yield. The figure shows no clear relation between these series, and formal statistical tests also show little link.

But government debt issuance involves more than simply deciding how many bonds to issue. Governments have at least three dimensions of choice even after

TABLE 22.9   Composition (%) Government Debt, 1995

	T-Bill	Variable	Indexed	Fix-Bond	Foreign	Loan	Saving
Australia	13.3	3.5	3.0	76.4	3.1	0.7	
Austria	1.6	6.4		45.7	22.0	24.3	
Belgium	17.4	2.0		60.3	11.4		0.9
Canada	35.4		1.2	52.5	3.5	0.7	6.6
Denmark	7.6	2.7		73.9	15.6		0.2
Finland	10.2			38.3	46.4	5.1	
France	8.9	2.7		70.3	3.7	2.1	11.9
Germany	0.4	0.8		49.2		40.5	3.9
Greece	26.5	35.3			22.8	15.4	
Ireland	2.9	4.7		44.9	35.1		10
Italy	18.1	22.8		36.9	7.4	5.6	9.0
Japan	12.9	1.5		64.5		21.1	
Netherlands	3.1			78		18.1	
Portugal	12.7	26.9		20.9	17.4	0.9	21.3
Spain	32.3			54.4	8.7	3.1	
Sweden	14.4		1.2	47.3	27.9		8.9
United Kingdom	3.2	1.7	13.6	59.6	5.0		15.4
United States	11.8			39.8		45.6	2.9

Governments achieve some fiscal insurance by issuing mixed portfolio of bonds.

Source: Missale, *Public Debt Management* (London: Oxford Univ. Press, 1999), by permission of Oxford University Press.

deciding what the overall level of bond issuance will be. Government bonds differ by maturity, by currency, and by whether payments are fixed in nominal terms (conventional bonds) or real terms (index-linked bonds). Historically, governments have issued by far the largest part of their stock of debt in nominal bonds in the domestic currency. This is surprising. You would expect that savers would find index-linked debt attractive, especially since 1945 when inflation has been higher, more variable, and more persistent than before. And governments can offer indexed debt because the source of revenue from which future payments on bonds will be made—that is tax revenue—tends to naturally move in line with the level of prices. So on risk grounds, both governments and investors might be better off if most government bonds were inflation-proof. Yet as Table 22.9 reveals, most government debt is nominal (or fixed rate) bonds issued in domestic currency. Short-dated government debt—Treasury bills—makes up a significant part of the stock of debt in only a few countries; governments have usually preferred to issue longer-term paper. Indexed bonds remain relatively unimportant.

22.7 Bond Yields and Equity Yields

We have focused on the level of bond yields and how they vary both by maturity and over time. But how bond yields compare with returns on equity is also important because it may affect how companies finance their investment and how households structure their portfolios. One might expect that over the long term bonds tend to generate lower returns than equities. Equities represent a claim on the *residual* profits of companies after interest and capital repayments on debt have been made. The money that equity holders put into a firm helps prevent bad outcomes from eroding the value of bonds. This tends to make the flow of returns to shareholders more volatile than the flow of returns to bondholders. Empirical evidence backs up this simple point. Government bond yields over the long term have typically been well beneath the rates of return that equities have generated. Of course, government bonds tend to be the least risky type of bonds, so it is interesting to compare corporate bond yields with equity returns. In the United States, most large companies can borrow at yields that are somewhere between 0.05% and 3% above yields on government debt. If one added 2% to the average return on U.S. government bonds over the last 100 years one would have a very crude estimate of the type of return one could have got on a portfolio of corporate bonds issued by large companies. In the United States, over the last 100 years, equities have yielded about 6% more a year than government bonds; so the excess return on corporate equity over corporate bonds might be about 2% lower, leaving a still hefty 4% risk premium on equity.

If we look at even longer horizons, the yield differences are no less dramatic. Jeremy Siegel estimates that $1 invested in U.S. equities in 1802 would have been worth about $560,000 by 1997 (if dividends were re-invested). One dollar put into bonds in 1802 would have been worth a paltry $803 in comparison. Over that period equities generated an average annual real return of about 7%, while bonds generated a return of about 3.5%. How much of this yield difference is due to a rational reaction by investors to differences in risk and how much to misperceptions of inflation is moot. The whole of the yield gap probably does not reflect risk premiums; remember, these bonds were not inflation proof, so their real return would have been diminished if inflation turned out higher than people had expected when they bought bonds. For much of the period since 1945 in the United States, inflation has been significantly higher than it was between 1845 and 1945, so on average, inflation has probably exceeded expectations.

Table 22.10 shows how the recent value of the U.S. equity premium over bonds squares up against the type of excess returns earned in other countries. Clearly equities typically yield more than bonds elsewhere, too. But the size of the yield gap between debt and equity is not the same across countries. This is not surprising. First, unexpected inflation has probably been different across countries since the 1940s. Second, companies and governments typically have different levels of debt in different countries. The higher the level of debt a company has, the more it is unlikely to be able to repay all its debt in a downturn—it will default. The greater the default risk, the lower will be the price of bonds, and the higher will be their yield. So in countries in which corporate debt is high and in which corporate revenues vary greatly from year to year,

TABLE 22.10   Average Annual MSCI* Return and Long-Term
Government Bond Return from September 1970 to December 1999 (%)

	Average Annual MSCI Return (1)	Average Annual Long-Term Government Bond Return (2)	(1) − (2)
Germany	10.90	7.92	2.98
Italy	14.19	12.97	1.22
Japan	9.96	7.16	2.80
France	15.60	10.33	5.27
United States	13.30	9.17	4.13
United Kingdom	16.29	12.23	4.06

Source: Thomson Financial Datastream.

*denotes percent change in Morgan Stanley Capital Index; this is
a measure of returns on national equities.

we would expect corporate bonds to yield more, and perhaps the gap between corporate debt and the return on equity to be lower.

Another factor could explain differences in return across countries: global bond markets (and equity markets for that matter) may not be well integrated. We hear a lot of talk about globalization, which implies that financial markets are almost fully integrated everywhere. In fact, investors in most countries tend to have dramatically nondiversified (geographically) portfolios. Figure 22.11 breaks down the portfolios of private sector assets in the world's 29 major economies at the end of the 1990s.

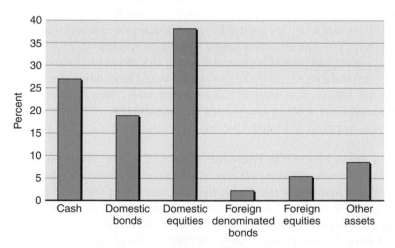

FIGURE 22.11   **World portfolio allocation: start 1999.** Proportions of total financial wealth held in various categories. World totals are the sum of assets held in 29 economies with the largest stocks of wealth. *Source*: Author calculations based on data collected and supplied by InterSec Research Corp., London.

Bonds make up about 20% of total financial assets. Equities account for about 40%. Cash, largely bank deposits, accounts for about 25%. More than 90% of total financial wealth held in the major economies is debt or equities that the domestic government, domestic nonfinancial corporations, or domestic banks issued. Of all the bonds held across the major economies, about 90% is domestic. This suggests that in fact financial markets have been much more segregated than is usually assumed. We would not therefore expect rates of return to be equalized across countries.

Exchange rate variability helps explain the lack of integration. A U.S. investor will generally be concerned with returns in U.S. dollars, so buying a German government bond exposes that investor to variability in the euro–dollar exchange rate. If exchange rate variability does partly explain the lack of integration in financial markets we would expect asset prices and rates of return to move more closely together when that variability is removed. This happened to government bond yields in Europe in the run up to the creation of monetary union at the start of 1999. Figure 22.12 shows yields to maturity on 10-year bonds issued by the major European countries. The yields are shown from 1990 up to the eve of the creation of the European Monetary Union (the end of 1998). Yields on 10-year government bonds were much closer together by the middle of 1998 than they had been in 1990. As it became clearer that many countries would join the monetary union from the outset, the yields on European government bonds that matured well after the creation of the currency union moved closely together. This fits in neatly with our observation that the yields on longer-term debt should be highly sensitive to expectations of future interest rates. All countries in the European Monetary Union face the same set of central bank interest rates. There is only one European central bank and one set of interest rates that it determines in the wholesale money markets. Bonds European governments issued prior to monetary union were redenominated into euros from January 1999. Once the European Monetary Union was formed, the only difference among a

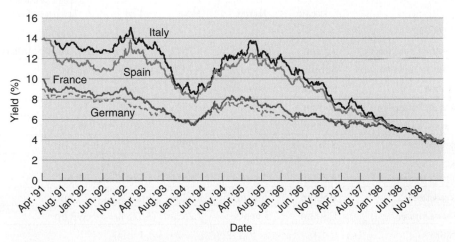

FIGURE 22.12   **Yield to maturity on 10-year government bonds in France, Germany, Italy, and Spain, 1991–1998.** In the lead up to the launch of the European Monetary Union yields on government bonds issued by countries thought likely to be initial members converged. *Source*: Thomson Financial Datastream.

French government bond, a German government bond, and an Italian government bond was due to differences in probabilities of default of those governments and a residual possibility that the monetary union would fracture and that the lire, the deutsch mark, and the French franc would again become three separate currencies. Figure 22.12 implies that by the middle of 1998 people thought monetary union was a certainty *and* that it would prove sustainable.

22.8   Corporate Bonds and Leverage

We noted above that the link between the stock of government debt outstanding (relative to GDP) and the yield on government bonds did not appear to be strong. At the corporate level, we would, however, expect to find a substantial relation between bond prices and outstanding debt (or leverage); but this is not because any one company can dramatically affect the overall stock of debt outstanding in the world—no company is that big (although governments certainly are—the Japanese and U.S. government stock of debt is huge relative to the overall world stock). A company's decision to issue more debt will affect the price of its existing bonds to the extent that it influences the perceived probability that it may default.

There are, in fact, dramatic differences in the market's view of default risks. So-called credit spreads—differences in the yields on bonds that share a common currency and maturity but are issued by different entities—can be enormous. Table 22.11 lists the

TABLE 22.11   New International Bond Issues (February 1999)

	Amount	Maturity	Coupon	Yield	Launch Spread over Government Bonds
U.S. DOLLARS					
Sun America Global Funding	$150m	10 years	5.75%	5.94%	+87 basis points (bp)
Ford Motor Credit Corporation	$2billion	5 years	5.75%	5.76%	+83 bp
JP Morgan	$1billion	5 years	5.75%	5.86%	+93 bp
British Sky Broadcasting	$600m	10 years	6.875%	6.948%	+198 bp
Lebanese Republic	$200m	5 years	8.5%	8.626%	+355 bp
Argentina	$1billion	20 years	12.125%	12.17%	+678 bp
EUROS					
Vattenfall Treasury	E250m	12 years	4.5%	4.758%	+67 bp
Abbey National	E500m	5 years	3.62%	3.681%	+25 bp
Lebanese Republic	E300m	5 years	7.25%	7.321%	+393 bp
STERLING					
LCR Finance	£1 billion	11 years	4.75%	4.81%	+37.5 bp
Hyder	£60m	21 years	7.0%	6.98%	+210 bp

Source: *Financial Times* (February 1999).

details of bonds that both corporate and sovereigns (i.e., governments) had newly issued in international bond markets in February 1999. It reveals important facts about the global bond market. First, different entities face *very* different costs of borrowing. The Ford motor company (more specifically a part of the Ford group called Ford Motor credit) issued $2 billion worth of 10-year U.S. dollar bonds yielding close to 5.75%. At that time, U.S. government bonds with 10 years to maturity yielded just under 5%; the Ford spread over Treasuries was 83 basis points. British Sky Broadcasting was not considered as good a bet as Ford and the spread on its dollar-denominated bonds over U.S. government bonds was a fraction under 2 full percentage points (198 basis points). The Republic of Argentina was considered much more risky; the yield on its 20-year U.S. dollar bonds was almost 7% above yields on U.S. Treasury bonds (a spread of 678 basis points).

Table 22.11 illustrates how international the bond market is. The government of Lebanon, for example, issued 300 million euros worth of 5-year bonds at a yield of 7.25%—a yield of close to 4% (393 basis points) higher than the yield on German government 20-year euro bonds. Lebanon also issued $200 million 5-year U.S. dollar bonds at a spread over 5-year U.S. Treasury yields of 355 basis points.

Table 22.11 also shows how the bond market offers investors many choices—about the maturity of bonds, about the currency of the bonds, and about the creditworthiness of the borrower. In part, borrowers can control their creditworthiness. The more debt a company has, the lower, other things being equal, its credit rating will be, and the higher the yield on its bonds will be. A large issue of debt could cause an issuer's perceived credit rating to slide and its bond prices to fall.

Of course, we would not expect a switch from one *form* of debt to another to have this impact. So, for example, if a company issued bonds to repay bank debt, we would not expect this to substantially affect the default premium on its bonds. Indeed, assuming that the corporation did this to reduce its overall cost of borrowing, we might expect its perceived chances of default to be reduced. So there is a big difference between companies switching from one form of debt to another and increasing their overall indebtedness.

Switching from bank to bond debt has been increasingly important in the United States for several decades and could become more important in Europe. The process whereby debt that had not been traded becomes traded is sometimes called *securitization*. Think of a move by a company away from relying on bank debt (which is not tradeable in a market) to greater reliance on bond finance (in which the debt securities are traded in liquid markets) as a form of securitization. Until recently corporations in Europe have not relied much on issuing bonds to finance investment. Nonfinancial companies have relied almost exclusively on the banking system to fund debt. But times change, and monetary union in Europe brought with it a deeper, more liquid, and more integrated market in corporate bonds.

Let's suppose that companies increasingly use corporate bonds instead of bank debt and perhaps also equity. Would that have wider economic significance, beyond its influence on the relative job prospects of bank managers and bond traders? The theory of corporate finance as it has developed over the past 40 years says that if markets work in an efficient and frictionless way, and the tax system does not distort investing and borrowing decisions, whether firms finance investment from issuing bonds, borrowing from banks, or selling equities should not matter. The celebrated Modigilani-Miller theorem states that the structure of corporate financial liabilities does not matter; firms cannot be better off (nor can they do any harm) by switching from one form of debt to another or from changing the ratio of debt to equity. This is not the place to prove that result, but the intuition is clear: if a firm switches its debt to equity ratio or alters the type of debt it issues, it will be allocating its future revenue stream to different kinds of investors and in different ways. But unless it simultaneously changes its capital stock of productive machines and buildings, or changes how much research and development it does, or alters its pricing or employment, the value of those future company revenues will not change. As long as the revenues do not change, the fundamental factor behind the overall value of the company has not altered. So neither should the way the market values the whole firm.

This is a powerful and intuitive result. But it relies on smooth and efficient markets in which all the players involved—investors and those that run companies—know and understand what each other is doing. And, of course, that is unrealistic. The people who run companies sometimes have incentives to conceal things from shareholders, banks, and bondholders. They may want debtors to believe that the firm is acting one way, while the firm is actually doing something different to benefit shareholders. Both shareholders and bondholders can often legitimately fear what is being done with their money. And then the differences among equities, bonds, and bank debt matter a lot. With equity funds the company—once it has issued shares—has no obligation to give the money back; shareholders can try to sell their shares to other investors, but they cannot ask the company for their own money back—companies do not have to buy back their own shares. By contrast, the bondholder lends funds for a finite period. This may keep those who run companies "honest" because they know that even if they do not need *net* new funds they will have to keep returning to the bond market to sell more bonds as old debt matures.

With bank debt, a company owes the money it raises to one institution that will have its own techniques for assessing risk and monitoring the performance of the company. Bond markets do their monitoring in different ways, often relying on the influence of bond rating agencies (e.g., Moody's and Standard and Poor's) whose judgments profoundly and immediately affect the yield that companies have to pay on bonds.

SUMMARY

Bond markets are where borrowers (governments and companies) meet savers (ultimately households). The prices that match supply and demand in this market reflect the required rates of return for lending money in different currencies, for different time periods, and to borrowers of different credit quality. These prices significantly affect the investment decisions of firms and the cost for government of running fiscal deficits. Shifts in prices reflect changing expectations about monetary policy and inflation. Those changes in price can generate big gains or losses to bondholders and the movements in wealth cause further shifts in spending and saving.

It is in the bond market that much of the impact of changes in monetary policy is transmitted to the wider economy. Bond prices are strongly influenced by the interest rate set by the central bank. Where short-term interest rates are, and how they are expected to move, are the key determinants of longer-term yields. Central banks only control very short-term interest rates. Spending and borrowing decisions by the private sector are likely to depend on longer-term rates that are only indirectly influenced by monetary policy. But the expectations theory of the yield curve suggests that this indirect influence is likely to be very strong.

CONCEPTUAL QUESTIONS

1. How would you expect a rise in inflation to affect the yields and prices of nominal, fixed rate bonds? Distinguish between an anticipated and unanticipated shock to inflation and between one that was expected to persist and one that was temporary.

2. Consider the kind of inflation shocks described in Question 1 and analyze how they would affect yields for inflation-proof (indexed) bonds.

3. What do you expect to happen to short-term interest rates when the yield curve is unusually steep? Would you expect an inverted yield curve, where longer rates are below shorter rates, to be sustainable?

4. Suppose yields on one-year bonds are at 6%, on two-year bonds are at 7%, and on three-year bonds are at 6.5%. What does this imply about future short-term interest rates if the expectations theory of the yield curve is valid?

5. "Ricardian equivalence implies that the supply and demand curves for government debt move by the same amount." What does this statement mean? Is it likely to be true?

6. On risk grounds should governments continue to issue fixed-rate, nominal debt when their sources of revenue are, largely, linked to inflation? Would they not be better off issuing inflation-proof debt?

7. Suppose that two-year bonds the U.S. government issues yield 1% *less* than bonds the UK government issues but that yields on 10-year U.S. debt are 2% *more* than 10-year UK debt. What might this tell you about what direction people think the dollar–pound exchange rate is going?

ANALYTICAL QUESTIONS

1. Using a spreadsheet calculate the price of the following bonds on the assumption that yields to maturity are 7% for all maturity dates:
   (a) a bond with exactly 10 years to maturity that pays no coupon and has a face value of $100
   (b) a bond that pays an annual coupon worth 5% of face value and will pay a coupon every year for 10 years and then be redeemed for $100

(c) a bond that pays an annual coupon worth 7% of face value and will pay a coupon every year for 10 years and then be redeemed for $100

(d) a bond that pays an annual coupon worth 9% of face value and will pay a coupon every year for 10 years and then be redeemed for $100

What is the percentage change in the price of each bond if yields move up from 7% to 7.5%?

2. Consider each of the bonds you priced in Question 1. Calculate the percentage change in the price of each bond between the start of one year and the start of the following year. Assume yields to maturity remain at a constant level of 7% throughout. Now add the coupon yield (the ratio of coupon to price) to the percentage change in price. What do the one-year returns on each bond look like? (The one-year returns are the percentage change in price plus the coupon yield.)

3. The central bank in a country has set the short-term interest rate at 6%. It is widely expected that the short-term rate will stay at this level for a year and then rise to 7% for a year before moving back to an equilibrium level of 6.5%, where it is expected to remain from two years ahead indefinitely. Assuming that the expectations theory is true, what would you expect the yield to be on government bonds of maturities from 1 year up to 10 years?

4. Suppose it is believed that the U.S. dollar will steadily depreciate against the euro at a rate of 2% a year over the next three years. After that people expect the dollar–euro rate to be steady. Ten-year U.S. government dollar bonds yield 8%. What would you expect the yield to be on 10-year euro government bonds? Assume risk neutral behavior.

5. Suppose that short-term interest rates in an economy fluctuate as the central bank tries to keep inflation stable in the face of various types of shocks. People anticipate that short-term interest rates will fluctuate around 6%, but that deviations from that level will be persistent. Specifically, they expect the three-month interest rate will follow the process:

$$R_{3t} = R_{3t-1} + 0.2(6 - R_{3t-1})$$

Where R_{3t} is the three-month rate in quarter t and R_{3t-1} is the three-month rate one quarter earlier. If three-month rates are initially at 11%, calculate the expected path of three-month rates over the next 40 quarters. (Use a spreadsheet for this.) Calculate the yield on zero-coupon 10-year bonds assuming the pure expectations theory is correct. What happens if the three-month interest rate suddenly drops to 9%?

6. Assume short-term interest rates are set in the way outlined in Question 5. Investment expenditure is sensitive to yields on five-year bonds. For every 1% (100 basis points) rise in yields, investment expenditure falls by 0.5%. Consumption expenditure is also sensitive to yields. For every 1% rise in yields on five-year bonds, consumption falls by 0.25%. Government expenditure is unaffected by changes in yields. Initially investment spending and government spending are each 20% of GDP; consumption is 60% of GDP. There is no trade. Calculate the impact on aggregate spending if the central bank raises interest rates from 8% to 10%.

Real Estate

Overview

If we look at the portfolio of assets that the private sectors in developed countries hold, financial assets—bank deposits, bonds, and equities—make up a large proportion of total wealth. But households also own tangible, or physical, assets. By far the most important is residential property. Corporations also hold stocks of financial and tangible assets. For companies (certainly nonfinancial ones) physical assets are typically a much larger proportion of overall assets than are financial assets; as with households, property (land and buildings) usually makes up most of those physical assets. In this chapter we focus on property (or real estate) markets, analyzing both the residential and the commercial (that is, factories, warehouses, shops, offices, and such) markets. By property, we mean structures—where we live and work.

The total value of structures in modern economies is larger relative to total annual output. Fluctuations in the market value of those structures can significantly affect consumption and investment expenditure, levels of employment, and the flow of output. Because property is durable, its value depends on expectations of its usefulness that stretch decades into the future. As we will see, property prices have fluctuated greatly in most developed countries. We will discuss the source of such fluctuations and their impact. How government policy affects property values, and therefore macroeconomic conditions, is of prime importance. Governments can affect the value of property, the amount of new construction, and the pattern of ownership of buildings and houses in many ways. Shifts in taxation, planning controls, and movements in interest rates by central banks can profoundly affect property prices and new investment in structures.

23.1 Why Is Property Distinctive?

Property, or real estate, is a source of wealth and also a factor of production. A factory is a tangible asset that has value precisely because it helps generate revenue for its owners over a sustained period of time. So too, though perhaps less obviously, does residential property. A house has a value ultimately because it generates a flow of benefits to its occupier over many years. One can think of the income a house generates to an owner-occupier as the rent that that occupier would need to pay each year to enjoy the benefits of living in his or her own house.[1] In this sense, commercial and residential property are similar.

For households, that part of their wealth held in financial assets (bank deposits, bonds, equities, claims on insurance companies, etc.) is different from their ownership of physical assets, of which residential property is by far the most important part. The financial assets generate returns in the form of capital gains and interest and dividend income. Ultimately, physical assets usually underlie the financial assets that a household holds. Equities that an individual holds represent a claim (albeit a rather vague one) on profits that the assets that corporations hold generate; a high proportion of these corporate assets are tangible. But equities themselves are paper assets. Residential property, in contrast, generates an implicit income (at least to an owner-occupier), and its market value is much less easily measured than the value of a bond or an equity. This is largely because properties, unlike most financial assets and indeed many other physical assets, are unique. No two buildings are identical. Even if their physical structure were the same, their location, by the laws of physics, cannot be. Unlike a bank deposit, a computer, a CD, or a copy of a book, no two examples of commercial or residential property are identical. This is one reason why it is more difficult to value property than equities or bonds. Because each building is unique, if only due to its physical location, but usually because of many other factors, we can only accurately ascertain its value when it is sold.

Although the values of individual buildings are often difficult to ascertain, the aggregate value of all property in all developed economies is clearly huge, relative both to the total assets of a country and to the flow of total output produced each year (GDP).

Let's start by looking at data on the value of commercial structures and residential property. Figure 23.1 shows for many countries the ratio between the total value of residential buildings and other structures that companies and governments use relative to total physical assets in the economy. The figures indicate the proportion of the total stock of physical assets, that is, structures as opposed to machines, vehicles, computers, furniture, and so forth. Across all the countries in the figure, structures average close to

---

[1] Owner-occupiers obviously do not pay rent to themselves! But the value of the services owner-occupied housing generates is as much a part of annual aggregate income as are the incomes owners of rental property receive from tenants. For this reason measures of gross domestic product (GDP) should—and often do—include an estimate of (imputed) income from owner occupation.

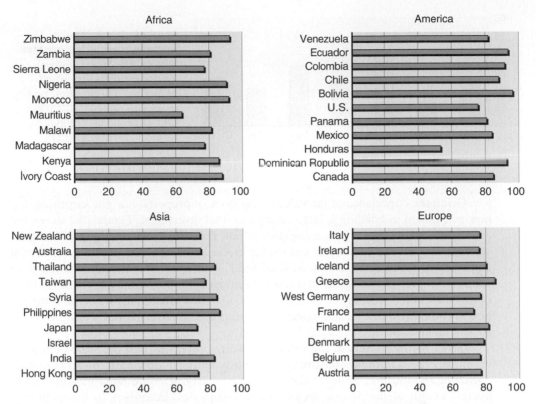

FIGURE 23.1   **Residential and nonresidential structures as a percentage of total physical assets.** Property makes up by far the largest part of the stock of physical capital in most countries. *Source*: Penn World Tables, data collected by Heston and Summers; figures refer to mid-1990s. http://pwt.econ.upenn.edu/

80% of the total value of the productive capital stock. In developing countries, buildings represent a slightly higher proportion of total physical capital than in developed countries. The average across the African countries is around 85%, and across developed countries is around 75%.

In aggregate, the value of residential property in many advanced countries is larger than the total value of commercial property (or commercial structures). For example, in the United States in 1997, the total value of residential property was $8,526 billion; the total value of private nonresidential structures (commercial property, farm buildings, and infrastructure) was $5,468 billion, and the total value of all privately held tangible assets was $17,316 billion.[2]

---

[2]All data are from the January 1999 Survey of Current Business.

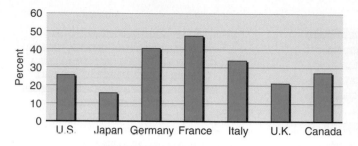

FIGURE 23.2 **Housing investment as percent total investment (average 1995–2000).** Housing investment makes up a high proportion of total investment in developed economies. *Source*: OECD Economic Outlook (2001). Copyright OECD.

Given the importance of the value of the stock of property, it is not surprising that new investment in building is large relative to total investment. Figure 23.2 shows the ratio between investment in housing (that is, new residential construction) and total investment for several developed economies in the late 1990s. On average, residential construction represented about 30% of total investment. If we add investment in commercial property to residential property investment, they jointly account for most of total investment in many economies. Figure 23.3 shows that in the UK total construction spending (residential and commercial property investment) has averaged about 60% of all investment in the period since 1965.

Given the magnitude of the value of existing properties, and the scale of new investment expenditure on construction, property markets are clearly of great macroeconomic significance. Shifts in the value of property generate large changes in the overall wealth of the private sector and in companies' incentives to invest in new property. Construction investment is one of the most cyclical elements of aggregate expenditure in most developed economies. Figure 23.4 shows one example—construction spending in the Netherlands from 1988 to 1999 was dramatically more volatile than GDP.

Movements in house prices and in the value of commercial property are likely to significantly affect investment and consumption expenditure. It is the volatility in these values that is one factor behind the volatility in construction expenditure. But what determines those prices?

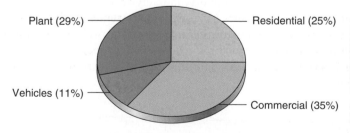

FIGURE 23.3 **UK investment by category, average for the period.** Total real estate investment for the majority of investments (UK). *Source*: Thomson Financial Datastream.

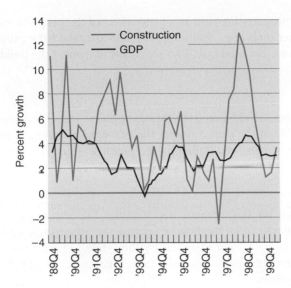

(Annual percentage changes in real values.) In most economies, construction spending is procyclical but much more volatile than GDP: the Netherlands is a case in point. *Source*: Thomson Financial Datastream.

23.2 Property Value

To value a specific property ask yourself the following question: *What price am I prepared to pay to own this piece of property for a particular period, given the benefits that will accrue from ownership?*

Let's think about the benefits side first. Suppose we are talking about an office block and that the relevant time horizon is one year. The money value of the income the office block produces will simply be the rental stream it generates over the year. Against this, we need to measure the overall net costs of owning the office block. These costs are made up of several different elements. Suppose we borrow the money to buy the building; then a major element of cost will be the annual interest rate multiplied by the purchase price of the office block at the start of the year.[3] There will also be costs of repairs and maintenance to the building and insurance and property taxes. At the end of the year, the value of the office block is unlikely to be the same as it was at the start of the year. So we should also take account of the capital gain (or loss) on the building; this is a deduction from the cost of ownership and can, effectively, be netted off the interest cost of the loan.

We can put together the various elements of the cost of ownership in a simple formula. Suppose the (nominal) cost of borrowing is r; let the cost of repairs (which we could think of as the depreciation rate) be δP, where δ is the percent of the purchase price of the building (P) which has to be spent annually to prevent the building from

[3]Even if we did not borrow to finance the purchase, an interest rate is an appropriate measure of the cost of the funds tied up in a building. If funds used to buy the office block could have been sitting in a bank account, the appropriate rate to use is the bank deposit rate.

deteriorating. We will measure property tax paid as a proportion of the property value and denote the tax rate by *t*; other costs (e.g., insurance) are also assumed to be proportional to the property value and are denoted by *c*. The *gross* cost of owning the building is then:

$$P(r + t + \delta + c)$$

We should deduct from these costs the net gain from capital appreciation. If this capital gain is not taxed, the money value of the gain is simply the percentage change in price over the year (which we denote by *pdot*) multiplied by the purchase price (*P*). So now the net cost of owning the building is

$$P(r + t + \delta + c - pdot)$$

In equilibrium, and ignoring for the moment tricky things like uncertainty and transaction costs, this net cost should equal the flow of income the property generates. We can think of the income as being a yield (denoted by the symbol *y*) multiplied by the price. In this case the yield times the price is just the rent. We denote this rent by *R*. So the equilibrium condition becomes

$$R = yP = P(r + t + \delta + c - pdot) \tag{1}$$

The right-hand side of this equation is usually referred to as the "*user cost of property.*" It measures the net cost of owning a building over a year. We can apply this simple relation to any kind of property and certainly to residential property. For residential property the right-hand side of the equation would depend on the cost of mortgage finance, repairs and renovations, property taxes, and, crucially, expectations of house price changes. The left-hand side of the equation would represent the real value of the benefits from living in the house for a year. If we were talking about a rented property this benefit is easy to measure; it is simply the rent that we would need to pay to give us occupation rights for one year. For an owner-occupied house, *y* is the implicit rental yield on the property.

This simple equilibrium condition is a useful starting point for thinking about the determinants of property values. Let's rearrange equation (1) slightly to give us a relation between the price of a property and the other factors.

Now think of the income the property provides as a number of dollars. Again, we denote this by *R*. Using *R* in place of *yP* and rearranging (1) we now have

$$P = R/(r + t + \delta + c - pdot) \tag{2}$$

Equation (2) is an equation for the equilibrium value of a property that ensures that the net cost of owning a property for a year is just equal to the income (either explicit or implicit) derived from ownership. Figure 23.5 shows that the equilibrium price is one that ensures that equation (2) holds. In Figure 23.5 we measure the rent divided by the net user cost on the vertical axis. If we hold the expected price one period ahead constant, then the higher is the current price the smaller is *pdot* and the greater is the ratio of rent to net user cost.

If interest rates go up, (2) says that house values should fall, other things being equal. If property taxes are increased, or if the cost of repairs goes up, then property values also

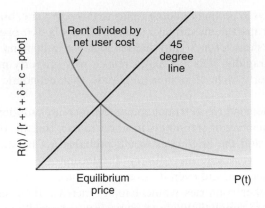

FIGURE 23.5 **Equilibrium in the property market.** When the user cost of property equals the rent, the market is in equilibrium. At this point price equals rent divided by a discount factor which reflects interest rates, other property costs, and the expected rise in prices. For a given forecast of future prices, a higher current price means lower capital gains and a lower value of rent dividend by net user cost.

fall. Figure 23.6 illustrates this. If people suddenly expect that property prices will rise sharply, *pdot* will become more positive; equation (2) then predicts that *current* market values should also move up sharply (Figure 23.7). This is not surprising. If enough people think that house prices or the value of office buildings are going to move up sharply over the next year, we would expect demand for property to increase *now* and for prices to rise.

Of course, the same set of factors that determine today's price should determine next period's price. Equation (2) implies that the price of a property next period depends on rents in the next period and on interest rates, taxes, and depreciation in that period. It also depends on how people think prices will be changing between the next period and the period after that. But then prices in the period after the next period depend on rents, taxes, interest rates, and so on two periods from now. The pattern is familiar—as with foreign exchange, bonds, and equities, expectations of the fundamental determinants of value far into the future determine today's value.

The price of property is so sensitive to expectations of future price increases—driven by shifts in future incomes, taxes, interest rates, and so on—because the supply of property is, pretty much, fixed in the short run. It takes time to build new houses, office

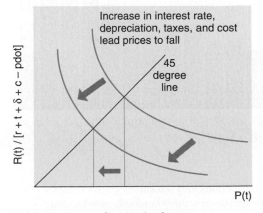

FIGURE 23.6 **Current price decreases.**

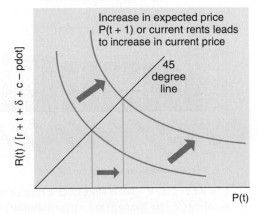

FIGURE 23.7 **Current price increases.**

blocks and shops. Even without delays in getting building rights to develop a site, building a large office block or residential apartments can take years. The supply of property is almost completely inelastic in the short term. So any sudden increase in demand for property is likely to increase prices rapidly. This is a major reason why property markets are more volatile, and the property cycle of greater amplitude, than economic cycles in general.

Think what happens when the demand for personal computers increases suddenly. We might expect, for a short time, the price of computers in stores to rise. But this phenomenon would only be temporary and the price rises would probably not be sharp. Computers are in fairly elastic supply in any one country. Producers of computers within that country can step up production; and even if domestic production is limited, computer manufacturers in many other countries would happily increase their shipments to meet extra demand. So extra supply is likely to come forward rapidly in response to increased demand for PCs. This stops the price from gyrating wildly. But that mechanism does not work in the same way in the property market because the value of a structure can largely depend on its position. The position of a building, literally its location in three-dimensional space, is a commodity in absolutely fixed supply. It is easy to produce another PC, which is more or less identical to the one you have on your desk now; it is more or less impossible to produce another property with the same characteristics as the house in which you live or the place where you work.

Figure 23.8 illustrates the low degree of substitutability of buildings that differ in location. It measures the cost of office space in major cities. Per-square-meter costs are three times as high in London as in Madrid. Moreover, in January 1999 office space in Moscow—according to the estimates—was more expensive than in New York.

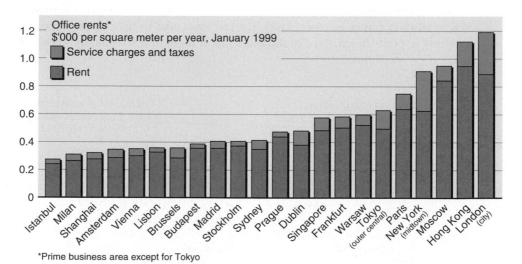

*Prime business area except for Tokyo

FIGURE 23.8   Cost of office space in major cities. Office rents vary enormously across cities—buildings in one location are a poor substitute for similar structures hundreds of miles away. *Source*: *The Economist* (13 March, 1999) p. 162.

Let's put some semirealistic numbers into equation (2). Suppose we are looking at an apartment in a major city and that the going rental rate is $800 a month. This gives an annual income of $9,600. Assume that the mortgage rate (r) is 8%, the property tax rate (t) is 1% a year, repairs and renovations (δ) come to about 2% of the value of the property over the year, and insurance and other costs (c) come to a further 1%. Finally, assume that property prices will go up by 4% a year. Plugging these numbers into equation (2) above gives

$$\$9,600 = P\,(\,8\% + 1\% + 2\% + 1\% - 4\%\,)$$
$$\$9,600 = P \times 8\%$$
$$P = \$9,600 \,/\, .08 = \$120,000$$

With current prices at that level, and with expectations of a 4% rise in house prices, people are anticipating that by the end of the year the apartment would be worth $124,800 (1.04 x 120,000). Suppose, instead, that due to some wonderful piece of economic news people thought that the value of this apartment, by the end of the year, would be $140,000.[4] What should the price of the apartment be today? To answer this, we need to rearrange equation (2), but when we have done that, we can place a value on today's apartment that is substantially higher than $120,000.

In fact, the price will need to move up by almost $9,000 to $133,570. At that price, and if we expect a year-ahead price of $140,000, we would be anticipating a capital gain of 4.814%. If we use this figure in equation (2), we find

$$133,570 \approx 9600 \,/\, (.08 + .01 + .02 + .01 - .04814)$$

So $133,570 is indeed about the equilibrium price.

This is like our discussion about valuing equities where we said that the price of a share depends on what we expect its price to be one period ahead. The same story applies to property and indeed to any asset. But just as we weren't happy to leave the story there for equities, we should not be happy simply to say that the value of some piece of property should depend on what we expect its value to be in a year. We need a theory of what determines that value in a year. But now the same argument that would apply to equities applies to property. We argued that equities' value today should reflect what income we expect them to generate into the far distant future, discounted by a rate equal to the required return on stocks. The same holds good for property. The value of a piece of property today should equal the expected discounted value of the income it will generate into the far distant future. We can think of this income as the rental value of the structure. What about the discount factor? Actually, we have pretty much worked this one out already. The appropriate discount factor to use should depend positively on the cost of borrowing (r) and on the other costs of property ownership—depreciation (δ), taxes (t), and insurance and other charges (c). The discount factor may be different for different periods: if interest rates or property taxes are going to come down in the future, a lower discount

---

[4]For example, a cut in interest rates. Of course, this would not be wonderful news to someone who did not have a mortgage but had squirreled away their life savings in a bank.

should be applied to the flow of benefits accruing in the future, which will increase property prices today.

Because most properties are highly durable assets, expectations about their use value into the far distant future help determine their value today. But note the other factors that influence that value. The user cost of housing depends on interest rates, on the tax treatment of property, the rate of decay (or depreciation) of buildings, and other costs such as property insurance and any transaction costs arising from sale. Changes in any of these factors, *or the anticipation of future changes in them*, will influence property prices now just as shifts in expectations of future rental incomes (either implicit or explicit) will drive today's valuations.[5]

Of course, we have not mentioned the supply of new property. As we noted above, in the short term, supply is virtually inelastic; what we have are current finished buildings, and it takes time to increase this stock. But, in the longer term, new properties are built. In principle, the anticipation of the supply of new property should help prevent such large fluctuations in the price of existing property. One would expect more investment in new property the higher the price of properties becomes. The anticipation that massive increases in prices will bring forth lots of new buildings should itself cap price appreciation. Remember, as with all durable assets, today's price depends on the anticipation of prices in future periods, and if high prices today will bring forth lots of new buildings in two, three, or five years the market price of buildings should reflect that in some way down the line; and that, of course, will help dampen price rises *today*. So in principle the construction sector helps prevent such large fluctuations in prices. But the price we pay for having the amount of new construction act as a safety valve for pressure building up in property markets is that the level of construction itself varies highly over time. (Look again at Figure 23.4.)

This suggests that both property prices and new construction will tend to vary, probably by much more than fluctuations in aggregate GDP. And the evidence bears this out. Table 23.1 shows movements in real house prices in European countries between the mid-1980s and mid-1990s. Note how volatile real prices are from year to year. The standard deviation of real house prices over this 11-year period was close to 10% in many countries—most notably in the UK, Finland, Sweden, Spain, and France (Figure 23.9a). The volatility in the prices of industrial properties is even more marked. Figure 23.9b shows the standard deviation of the annual change in real prices of industrial property between 1987 and 1997. The average standard deviation across countries is about 25%—this means that periods when prices went up by more than a quarter, or fell by as much, are fairly common. This is dramatically higher than the standard deviation in the annual rate of change of GDP. At the regional level, fluctuations in property values are even more dramatic. Take the state of Texas in the United States, for example. Fluctuations in the fortunes of a few industries (notably oil) hit Texas particularly hard. You cannot lift office and apartment blocks and move them from one part of the country to another when demand tails off in one region. Supply is fixed, so price must do all the adjusting. This is exactly what happened with property prices in Texas in the 1980s.

---

[5]See Miles, *Housing, Financial Markets and the Wider Economy* (New York: John Wiley, 1994) for a detailed discussion of the determinants of residential property values.

TABLE 23.1 Movements in Real House Prices in European Union Countries (Percentage)

	Belgium	Denmark	Germany	Greece	Spain	France	Ireland	Italy	Luxembourg	Netherlands	Austria	Portugal	Finland	Sweden	United Kingdom
1986	5.0	11.0	2.0	0.0	−2.0	1.0	0.0	—	4.0	5.0	—	−1.0	5.2	1.3	10.0
1987	2.9	−1.8	1.0	3.0	17.3	1.0	3.0	A— B 1.0	3.8	4.8	—	−2.0	8.1	8.6	11.8
1988	*4.8	*−1.7	1.0	2.9	−20.2	−6.9	*7.5	A6.9 B—	0.9	*3.7	—	0.0	*29.8	*11.0	*20.5
1989	8.9	−4.8	1.0	1.9	17.5	10.5	7.2	A16.7 B24.6	2.8	5.4	—	−1.0	18.3	11.6	13.6
1990	4.1	−10.9	3.7	0.9	8.2	*13.3	9.0	A12.7 B18.9	*1.5	−0.4	—	*−0.4	−11.9	0.7	−10.1
1991	2.8	−1.4	0.9	0.9	8.1	−3.6	−1.2	A4.2 B5.6	1.7	−0.1	5.0	−0.5	−18.3	10.3	−8.7
1992	6.1	−8.0	0.9	−5.6	−6.7	−8.1	−0.1	A6.8 B0.8	3.7	4.6	5.7	5.1	−20.3	−15.9	−7.8
1993	4.2	−5.1	1.2	−3.9	−5.5	−0.4	−0.5	A−3.2 B−3.4	−2.2	7.3	6.3	5.7	−6.2	−7.6	−6.2
1994	4.9	4.9	−0.9	—	−3.8	1.1	2.3	A— B−7.2	−1.0	4.6	5.1	5.9	5.1	−1.4	1.0
1995	3.0	−2.1	−0.8	—	−1.2	−6.1	3.8	A— B−3.7	−0.1	1.9	3.2	1.7	3.3	−0.8	−2.9
1996	2.2	*7.2	−1.5	—	−1.0	−9.0	10.3	A— B−3.9	−0.5	8.3	1.6	8.3	5.5	−1.2	1.2
1997**	−0.2	6.3	−2.6	—	−1.2	−3.2	15.2	A— B—	0.1	5.8	3.1	4.6	15.9	6.0	6.3
Standard Deviation	2.2	6.6	1.8	3.1	9.4	7.0	5.1	A7.7 B11.6	2.0	2.6	1.7	3.5	15.0	8.2	10.0

Source: Maclennan, D, Muellbauer, J, and Stephens, M (2000) "Asymmetries in Housing and Financial Market Institutions and EMU," chapter 5 in T.J. Jenkinson (ed) "Readings in Macroeconomics," Oxford, Oxford University Press.

* Possible discontinuity in series.

** Estimated for part of year.

For Italy, series A and B are alternative estimates.

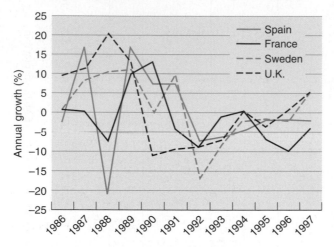

FIGURE 23.9a **Annual growth in residential house prices.**

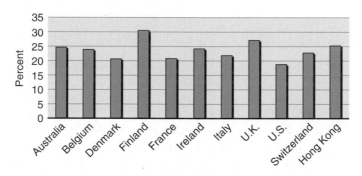

FIGURE 23.9b **Volatility of prices of industrial property, 1987–1997.**
Prices of residential and commercial property are highly volatile.
The chart shows the standard deviation of the annual change in
the price of industrial property in real terms. Data are translated
into U.S. values and real returns calculated using U.S. consumer
price index. *Source:* Case, Goetzmann, and Rouwenhorst,
"Global Real Estate Markets—Cycles and Fundamentals,"
NBER Discussion Paper 7566 (February 2000).

Figure 23.10 shows an index of average residential property prices in the
United States between 1975 and 1995. It also shows prices of housing in Houston,
Texas. Both series are normalized to 100 in 1987. Between the end of 1975 and the
middle of 1983, house prices in Houston rose by 122%; prices nationally over that
period were up by 80%. But over the next four years, while prices for the United
States as a whole grew by a further 33%, Houston prices *fell* by almost a quarter.
The slump in commercial property prices—particularly in office buildings—was
even greater.

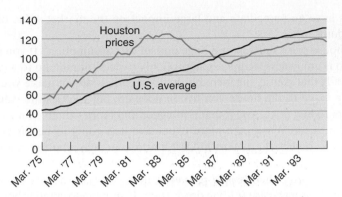

FIGURE 23.10 **Houston residential prices and U.S. average prices (Freddie Mac/Fannie Mae series).** The Texas boom and bust in property saw prices rise much faster there than in the rest of the United States in the early 1980s but fall sharply in the second half of the 1980s. *Source*: Thomson Financial Datastream.

23.3 Property Price Changes and the Wider Economy

We have seen why in theory property prices tend to be volatile; and empirical evidence indicates that volatility is significant. How property price movements affect the economy depends, to a large extent, on how the private sector reacts to shifts in the market value of its wealth. The first point to note is that shifts in property prices can have a large impact on individual households. Figure 23.11 shows owner occupation rates across the major economies. On average across the developed countries, about 60% of households are owner-occupiers. The value of an owner-occupied home is typically a substantial multiple of annual income—often three or four times as high.[6] So big

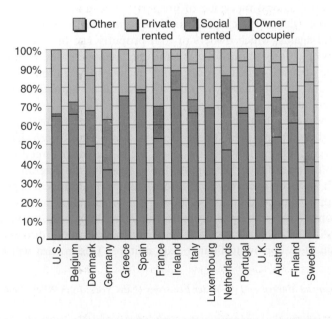

FIGURE 23.11 **Tenure in housing.** (Figures show ownership structure in the mid-1990s.) Owner occupation rates vary greatly across countries. *Source*: Maclennan, Muellbauer, and Stephens, "Asymmetries in Housing and Financial Market Institutions and EMU," CEPR Discussion Paper 2062 (1999).

[6]See Kennedy and Anderson, "Household Saving and Real House Prices, an International Perspective," BIS Discussion Paper 20 (January 1994).

shifts in house prices have an immediate and large impact on the market value of the assets of most households.

But why should house price shifts have a huge impact on consumption? If you are a young household who is an owner-occupier, you probably expect to trade up to a larger property in the future. If that is true, big increases in house prices do not make you better off. Of course, the value of the house you live in goes up; but so does the value of the house that you aim to buy next. And if that is a bigger and more valuable house, the greater the price of houses increases, the more expensive it is going to be for you to trade up. Of course, the reverse argument holds for those people who are about to trade down; they are better off when house prices rise. Given that the supply of houses is roughly fixed in the short run, then people who are trading up (i.e., moving to bigger houses) tend to balance those who are trading down (people moving to smaller houses). So does the whole process balance out and is the net impact on real wealth and consumption shifts in house prices close to zero?[7] In practice this is unlikely. First, people have different propensities to consume, so the "winners" from house price shifts may spend a different fraction of their gain than the losers. But property price movements can be expected to substantially affect consumption and investment for a more powerful reason: credit cycles and the value of collateral.

CREDIT CYCLES AND COLLATERAL

Properties are good collateral; they can't walk away in the night, so people who lend money are usually happier to do so against the value of property than against cars, computers, or the promise of the value of a good idea in someone's head. Most of the lending households do is secured against the value of property. And much borrowing by companies is secured on the value of their buildings.[8] When the value of property rises, the value of the collateral against which owners of that property can borrow also increases. This can be a powerful force, indeed it can reinforce price increases. It can also be a powerful force in the opposite direction; prices may decline so much that they decrease the value of collateral, and the inability to borrow curtails consumption and investment expenditure even further.

Figure 23.12 illustrates the mechanisms we have in mind. It shows factors that come into play during so-called credit crunches. These are self-reinforcing forces that can either drive lending and expenditure down to low levels or, in the other direction, encourage further increases in expenditure. We can use the simple stylistic diagram to explain how a credit crunch, or its opposite (a credit boom), may work. Suppose a region suffers an adverse economic shock—think about how a sharp reduction in oil prices affected the Texas economy. This is likely to decrease the value of corporate and residential property. This will reduce the value of collateral and make it more difficult for corporations and individuals to borrow to finance expenditure. This in turn will feed

---

[7]See Miles, *Housing, Financial Markets and the Wider Economy* (New York: John Wiley, 1994) for an elaboration of this point.

[8]This is obviously true of construction companies whose only asset is usually a half-built piece of real estate; but it is also true of service sector companies, such as advertising agencies, supermarkets, or theater companies.

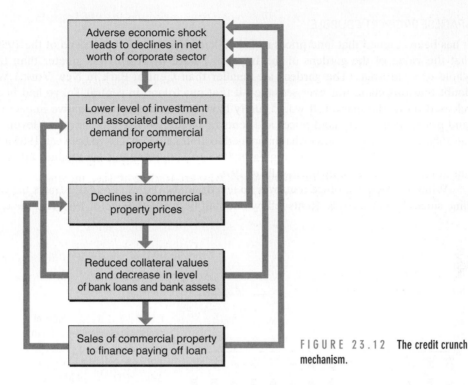

FIGURE 23.12 **The credit crunch mechanism.**

back on demand in the local economy, causing further declines in incomes and property prices. This further reduces collateral values, as well as the real estate assets owned by banks, limiting the potential to borrow, and forcing some corporations and households to sell their property to finance necessary expenditure. This further depresses property prices.

The story can also work in the other direction. Consider a concrete example based on residential property. Suppose I am a first-time buyer and I can scrape together the $10,000 deposit that I need for my dream apartment, which costs $80,000. I borrow the remaining $70,000, buy the apartment, and live there in domestic bliss for a year. Then prices start to move up in my neighborhood. Suppose that by the end of the second year prices are about 25% higher than when I bought. I now own a property worth close to $100,000, but my mortgage is likely to be a shade below $70,000. I am now sitting on home equity worth $30,000.[9] Assume I can still borrow up to 90% of the value of a new house. With the $30,000 clear that I will realize if I sell my existing apartment and pay off the mortgage, I can now buy a property worth $300,000. And if I think that prices are going to go on rising at the rate they have been, I should trade up fast! The point of the example is that price rises, by generating the deposit for my next property and increasing collateral, have a geared impact on new expenditure, and this can feed price bubbles. Again, this process can work in reverse. Consider what happened to property markets in Japan in the 1980s.

[9]The difference between the market value of the property and the mortgage debt.

THE JAPANESE PROPERTY BUBBLE

It has been claimed that land prices in Tokyo had risen so high by the end of the 1980s that the value of the gardens of the Imperial Palace in Tokyo was greater than the whole of California. (The gardens are smaller than Central Park in New York.) We doubt that this claim was ever sensible—if that much land in central Tokyo had been released on to the market, it would surely have had a substantial negative impact on land prices. But clearly land prices and rents in Japan had risen to enormous levels in the 1980s. Figure 23.13 shows what happened to land values in Tokyo between 1985 and the end of 1998. Prices tripled from early 1985 to late 1990. But land values fell to a third of their 1990 value by the middle of 1998.

What happened to office rents was no less dramatic. Figure 23.14 illustrates the decline since the early 1990s. Rents fell by one-half between the end of 1992 and the end

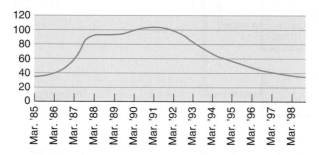

FIGURE 23.13   **Index of commercial land values in Tokyo.** Commercial land prices in Tokyo fell by half in the early 1990s. *Source*: Thomson Financial Datastream.

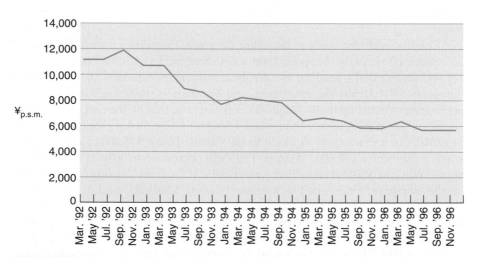

FIGURE 23.14   **Tokyo office rental (yen per square meter).** Office rents in Tokyo also plummeted in the early 1990s and had not recovered by the turn of the century. *Source*: Thomson Financial Datastream.

of 1996. And prices continued to slide further. The impact of the falls in values was starkly spelled out in the *Financial Times* of March 1999:

Japanese Property Price Fall Quickens

Japanese real estate prices declined last year for the eighth straight year, raising concerns about the prospects for economic recovery amid the gathering pace of deflation. Commercial real estate prices in the three large urban areas fell an average 10.2% last year, compared with 7.5% in 1997. Residential property prices in the same areas dropped 5.7%, compared with 2.2% previously. The decline in real estate prices has taken commercial property prices in Tokyo 75% below their peak in 1991.

Private spending is depressed in large part because corporations and households which invested in real estate during the bubble years have huge volumes of shrinking assets, said Seiichiro Saitow, professor at Rikkyo University. At the same time, although real estate prices have fallen sharply, investment in the market has been hampered by high taxes and a reluctance by banks to lend for property investment, Mr Yasouka said.

Financial Times, March 26, 1999

The fall in prices and the knock-on effects on the wider economy were so severe that the *Financial Times* chose to devote an editorial to the subject:

Down in Japan

Pity the economic policymakers of Japan. No sooner do they plug one hold in the dam than it springs a leak elsewhere. The latest case in point concerns the property market, where the rate at which prices are falling has started to accelerate again.

Given the extraordinary amount of wealth that has already been destroyed in property since the bubble economy period in the 1980s, this is a particularly vicious turn of the screw for the heavily indebted Japanese. And it has the potential to exacerbate deflationary pressures because of the impact on savings behavior. The problem is chiefly one of negative equity in housing. The outstanding amount of many home loans is well above the value of the related housing. Borrowers then save more in an attempt to close the gap. This acts as an offset to efforts to stimulate domestic demand because it tends to weaken consumer spending when incomes from employment are already under pressure. In an economy where the level of savings already far exceeds the scope for profitable domestic investment, it also puts further upward pressure on the structural trade surplus. The second difficulty relates to Japan's troubled banks. Property provides collateral for the banking system, so further falls in the value of both residential and commercial property cause the capital of the banks to shrink further. While the government has belatedly moved to recapitalize bank balance sheets, the property phenomenon is an offsetting factor that acts as a constraint on credit creation.

Financial Times, March 16, 1999

23.4   Portfolio Allocation and Property

One simple message from portfolio theory is that diversification is good; people should spread their wealth across a wide range of assets to insure themselves against sharp movements in the price of individual stocks or shares. But when it comes to property, most people hold *undiversified* portfolios. Many people own a single property (the one in which they live), and its value often makes up a very high proportion of their total wealth. This may be pretty dumb on portfolio allocation grounds, but is hard to avoid if you want to own the house in which you live. People often borrow heavily to buy their house and find that their asset can fluctuate rapidly in value, but their debt is stubbornly fixed. Figures 23.15 through 23.18 illustrate what this can imply by showing key features of the U.S. housing market.

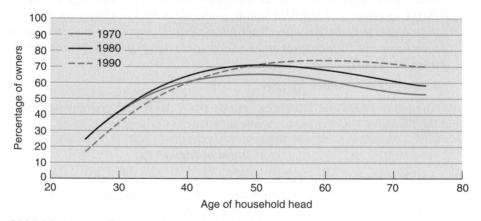

FIGURE 23.15   **Home ownership rates in the United States.** Ownership rates rise sharply among 30-year-olds in the United States. *Source*: Reproduced from Caplin, Chan, Freeman, and Tracy, *Housing Partnerships* (Cambridge, MA: MIT Press, 1997).

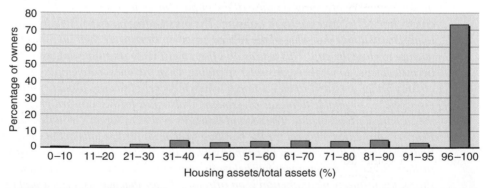

FIGURE 23.16   **Distribution of housing assets as a proportion of total nonpension assets for owners over 60 (mean proportion = 88.7%).** For a great many homeowners their property is by far the largest element of their total wealth. *Source*: Reproduced from Caplin et al. (1997) based on data from the U.S. Consumer Expenditure Survey (1990).

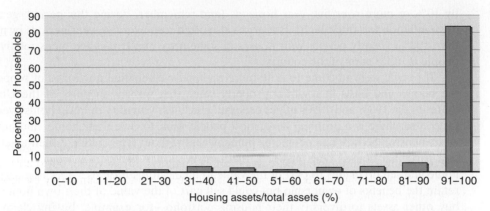

FIGURE 23.17 **Distribution of housing assets as a proportion of total nonpension assets for younger homeowners.** Among young homeowners property dominates the portfolio of assets. *Source*: Reproduced from Caplin et al. (1997) based on data from the U.S. Consumer Expenditure Survey (1990).

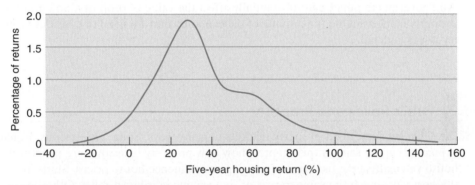

FIGURE 23.18 **Smoothed distribution of housing returns: Freddie Mac repeat sales house price indices from 42 regions: distribution of 5-year percentage changes.** Residential house prices in the United States have been very volatile and quite different in different regions. *Source*: Reproduced form Caplin et al. (1997) based on data from U.S. Consumer Expenditure Survey (1990).

Figure 23.15 shows that Americans tend to buy houses at a relatively young age—in 1990 about 50% of people were homeowners by the age of 32. Figures 23.16 and 23.17 show the proportion of total household assets (excluding pension assets) that the value of their home represents for people who are owner-occupiers. Most homeowners aged 60 or more, have houses worth between 95% and 100% of all assets (Figure 23.16). For young homeowners, the dominance of housing wealth in total assets is even more marked (Figure 23.17).

Houses not only comprise a high proportion of household assets, but their values fluctuate a lot. Figure 23.18 shows the distribution of house price rises over five-year horizons using U.S. price data from 42 large metropolitan areas over the period 1975 to 1994. Note how wide the dispersion is: in a substantial number of cases prices declined by 10% or more over five-year horizons (and remember, during this period, general price inflation was often high). But prices also often rose over five-year periods by more than 100%. Clearly people with houses in some areas made massive gains relative to people in other parts of the country.

If people were to come to hold more regionally diversified portfolios of property, the booms and busts in regional property value that we saw in parts of the United States in the 1980s and 1990s might generate much less volatility in households' wealth. Of course, there is a problem here: most people want to own their home, and houses are expensive. So how can people be homeowners without tying much of their assets up in a particular house? One answer is that people should own part shares in their own home and sell off claims to part of the value to financial institutions.[10] Occupiers would retain the benefits of ownership but could sell part of the value of their own home and buy other assets to diversify their housing portfolio—for example, buying claims on houses in other parts of the country. Such schemes may become popular, but they face problems: for example, part ownership changes people's incentives to properly repair and maintain a house.

Even if people gradually come to hold more diversified portfolios of residential property the aggregate impact of changes in property prices would remain substantial. And government policy can substantially affect the value of property. So important are property markets in the functioning of the economy that we need to consider those policy issues in detail.

23.5 Public Policy and Property

Governments affect property markets in many ways. Some are obvious. Equations (1) and (2) at the start of this chapter show how property taxes that are proportional to house value affect the user cost of housing and influence house prices. Shifts in taxes of this sort have much the same impact as movements in interest rates. Other taxes work in different ways. If governments tax capital gains on property, then we need to reduce the inflation term in the user cost and house price value formulas (i.e., the *pdot* term in equations (1) and (2)) by a factor of (1 − capital gains tax rate). This reduces house values. Transaction taxes, which are levied at the time of purchase and are usually part of the purchase price, increase the cost of home-ownership—thereby reducing house values—but in a way that depends on turnover in the market. As a tax on transactions, they discourage buying a house, which may discourage labor mobility. Table 23.2 shows that transaction costs are high in most countries, and transaction taxes often comprise the largest element of cost. (But note from Table 23.2 that a measure of interregional mobility is not closely linked to overall transaction costs.)

The tax treatment of rental income from property and of the implicit income from occupation can affect patterns of property ownership. For tax purposes most countries

---

[10]Persuasively advocated by Caplin, Chan, Freeman, and Tracy in *Housing Partnerships* (Cambridge: MIT Press, 1997)

TABLE 23.2   Transaction Costs and Labor Mobility

Country	Total Transaction Cost as Percent Price[1]	Taxation Tax as Percent Price[a]	Interregional Mobility (% population)[b] 1993
Spain	10.4	6.4	0.56
France	13.8	10.0	1.07
Germany	7.1	2.0	1.23
Italy	7.4	4.2	0.50
United Kingdom	2.0	1.0	1.58
United States	9.0	1.5	2.8

Source: Maclennan, D, Muellbauer, J, and Stephens, M (2000)
"Asymmetries in Housing and Financial Market Institutions and
EMU," Chapter 5 in T.J. Jenkinson (ed) "Readings in
Macroeconomic's," Oxford, Oxford University Press.
[a]On £80,000 property.
[b]1993, except United States, 1987.

treat rental income accruing to landlords of property much the way they treat other sources of income. But the implicit income to owner-occupiers from their property is often not taxed. This gives a tax advantage to owner-occupation and tends to make renting less common. It also means that people tend to have undiversified portfolios of property, as we noted in Section 23.4.

Public policy on land development has obvious and profound impacts on the value and location of property. Desire to preserve the quality of life for existing residents often prompts local and central governments to restrict the uses to which green spaces can be put. The externalities—or knock-on effects—of my building a new development of 500 houses on an open space next to your quiet and secluded semirural home are obvious. Given the growth in populations of nearly all developed countries over the past 50 years, conflicts of interest among existing residents, property developers, and new (as yet unhoused!) households have been common and intense. How governments should trade off the interests of existing homeowners against those of new households and also of companies that want to develop sites close to established homes is a problem. The legal system often cannot resolve conflicts because property rights are unclear. I do not own the view out of my window on to the secluded wood opposite; I can only guarantee that the view is not spoiled by owning the wood. If I don't own the wood, can I expect the government to stop others from building on it when that could be both commercially profitable and provide needed new homes? Do I have a right *not* to have my nice view ruined?

Such conflicts are inevitable where valuable commodities (e.g., nice views) are in limited supply and property rights are not well established in law. Two trends in developed countries may help alleviate the seriousness of such conflicts. First, population growth in most developed countries has been slowing for years and will probably continue to decline; projections show that the aggregate populations of some advanced European countries will be lower in 30 years than now. (The United Nations produces regular projections of populations by country up to 100 years ahead. In Germany, for example, the population is expected to be lower in 2030 than it is today; in Japan it could be very much lower.)

Second, technology changes how we live and work. Computers may diminish the need for most of us to work in a common place with other employees often far from our homes. And even if most of us do still have to travel to work, technical advances may reduce journey times. Both these developments may make it feasible to live further from where we are employed and from other people. So although the size of the countries in which we live may be fixed, the proportion of it that it is feasible for us to have homes in most certainly can grow?

SUMMARY

Commercial and residential property is important: around 80% of the tangible assets of most economies are in the form of buildings and houses. The prices of these assets are volatile, as is the level of new investment. Fluctuations in the total value of property are therefore large relative to the wealth of the private sector and large relative to GDP. Because property is good collateral, shifts in its value can cause fluctuations in borrowing and in expenditure financed by loans. This mechanism can exacerbate fluctuations in the property market and in the wider economy.

Prices fluctuate because expectations are very important in determining values and because supply is fixed in the short term. Fixed supply means that fluctuations in demand, at least in the short run, generate price movements. Those price movements are likely to influence expectations of future prices and this has an impact on the user cost of property—effectively its price. As well as expectations of future property values, taxes, costs of repairs, depreciation, insurance costs, and interest rates affect the user cost of property. The influence of these factors—and anticipation of future changes in any of them—can be very great.

CONCEPTUAL QUESTIONS

1. Suppose a government announced that it would increase the purchase tax on residential homes from 2% to 10% of house value. The tax rise would not come into effect for one year. What do you think would happen to house prices and transactions in the short and longer run?

2. Would house prices be less volatile if more people rented property? Why?

3. What has happened to house prices in your region over the past few years? Does it differ significantly from trends in other parts of the country? Can fundamental economic factors explain the regional house price differences you observe?

4. Does it make sense to levy taxes on ownership of residential and commercial property? If so, should taxes be proportional to the value of the property?

5. When property prices in a country increase, is the country wealthier? Who gains from property price inflation?

6. Consider the impact on the prices of residential and commercial property of information technology developments that make it much easier to work effectively away from the office or to buy goods without going to stores.

7. What relative risks does a company face if it rents premises rather than buys them?

ANALYTICAL QUESTIONS

1. The annual user cost of property (UC) is given by:

$$UC = P(r + t + \delta + c - pdot)$$

where P is the price of property,
r is the opportunity cost of funds (which we think of as the annual interest rate),
t is the annual tax rate on property,
δ is the annual depreciation rate (or cost of repairs),
c are insurance and other costs, and
$pdot$ is the anticipated the rate of change of property prices over the coming year.

Calculate the user cost of a property with the following characteristics:

$P = \$500,000$
$r = 0.09$
$t = 0.025$
expected price one year ahead: $520,000
$\delta = 0.03$
$c = 0.025$

What happens to the user cost if annual interest rates rise to 12% but are expected to be back down to their original level 12 months ahead? How would your answer differ if the interest rate rise from 9% to 12% was expected to be more persistent?

2. Consider the original situation in Question 1 in which interest rates are at a 9% level. What level of annual rent would you anticipate the owner of the property could charge in a competitive market? How will this rent change if the tax on the owner of a property increased from 0.025 of the property value a year to 0.05 a year. What would happen if the tax rate increased from 0.025 of the property value a year to 0.05 but the tax was shifted from the owner to the renter?

3. A poll tax is one in which the amount levied is the same for each person and does not depend upon wealth or income. Consider the implications of a switch in property taxes on residential property away from a system in which the annual tax paid is 5% of the property value to a poll tax system in which the tax is $1000 a year for each adult living in a property. What would you expect to happen to the differential between properties in smart and run-down neighborhoods?

4. A young homeowner has just bought a property worth $120,000. She borrowed 80% of the value and raised the remaining 20% by saving while she rented. Eighty percent is the largest loan to value ratio available. The homeowner would have preferred to borrow more and buy

a bigger property but her patience with renting ran out once she had saved $24,000. The homeowner still wants to borrow more and live in a bigger, better (and more expensive!) apartment. Show what happens to this homeowner's ability to buy if the price of her home:

  (a) Rises 20%
  (b) Rises 15%
  (c) Rises 10%
  (d) Rises 5%
  (e) Falls 10%

Assume in each case she can sell without cost and borrow again up to 80% of the value of a new home. Which way does the demand curve slope?

5. Suppose people go through four phases of their life. Phase 1 is early adulthood when people rent. Phase 2 is the childrearing period when the demand for housing is high but money is short—in this phase people are typically looking for three-bedroom houses in modest neighborhoods. Phase 3 is the affluent period when people look to trade up to a bigger (four-bedroom) house in a better area. Phase 4 is winding down toward death—the demand for housing falls and a two-bedroom house or apartment is fine. Who gains when all house prices unexpectedly rise by 35% in a year? Who is better off if prices fall by 35%? Does it matter in answering these questions how the elderly analyze their decisions on bequeathing wealth?

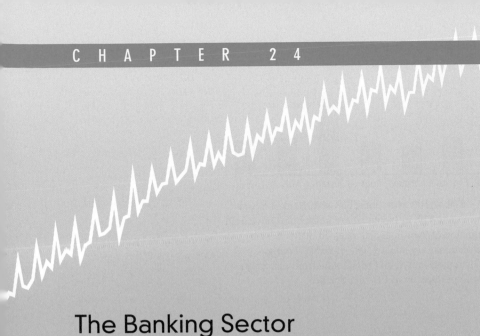

CHAPTER 24

The Banking Sector

Overview

Banks play a critical role in the economy. Their liabilities are largely made up of deposits, which represent much of the financial assets of the household sector and most of the money supply. Bank assets—loans of various sorts—represent much of the debt finance of companies and most of the credit extended to households. When banks work well, they channel funds from those who wish to save to those who wish to spend more than their current income. In performing this function, banks create financial assets and liabilities, which form the balance sheets of the banking sector. The size of those balance sheets is enormous and reflects banks' role in helping finance expenditure and allowing households to smooth consumption over time by accumulating liquid assets (that is, bank deposits). Therefore, banking market failures can have major macroeconomic significance.

In this chapter we discuss how banks affect the economy. We look at the services that banks perform and their role in the transmission mechanism of monetary policy. Banking crises have influenced the evolution of many economies. In this chapter we discuss the theory and the practice of what can go wrong, focusing on recent problems in Southeast Asia and Japan. Finally, we consider the future of banking, focusing on regulation and technological change.

24.1 The Role of Banks

Banks are financial intermediaries. They intermediate (or channel) funds from savers to those who need to borrow to finance investment or consumption. The scale of this intermediation both *within* and *between* countries is great. Figure 24.1 shows that

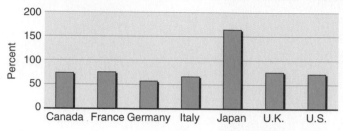

FIGURE 24.1   **Bank deposits as percent of GDP, 1998.** Bank deposits are large in relation to GDP; in Japan, where households have held a very high proportion of their financial assets in deposits with banks, savings with banks are about 150% of GDP. *Source*: Author's own calculations based on OECD data from national balance sheets with permission of Elsevier Science.

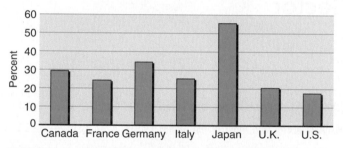

FIGURE 24.2   **Bank deposits as percent of total financial wealth, 1999.** On average about one-third of financial wealth in developed countries is in the form of savings with banks—it is lower in the United States and the UK where securities markets (in which bonds and equities are traded) are more important. *Source*: Data collected and kindly made available by Intersec Corporation, London.

total bank deposits vary between about 50% and 150% of annual GDP among developed countries. On average, bank deposits make up about 30% of the total financial wealth of developed economies (Figure 24.2). Table 24.1 indicates the importance of banks as a source of finance to borrowers and as a home for lenders' saving. It shows the number of banks (or more accurately deposit-taking institutions) in the major economies in 1996. The United States had over 23,000 deposit-taking institutions. The second column of the table shows that the United States had about 100,000 bank branches in the mid-1990s. In fact, that number is relatively small given the United States population of about 270,000,000. The third column of the table shows that there was, on average, about one branch for every 1500 of the population across the developed economies, but only one per 2800 citizens in the United States.

Even though the United States has relatively few bank branches, banks are far from unimportant to the U.S. economy. Table 24.2 shows that U.S. commercial banks and savings institutions account for about 30% of all the assets that U.S. financial intermediaries

TABLE 24.1   Depository Institutions and Offices in the Group of Eleven Countries, 1996

	Number of Institutions	Number of Offices	Number of Inhabitants per Office
Belgium	143	9,464	1,075
Canada	2,497	16,209	1,857
France	547	47,263	1,238
Germany	3,509	70,118	1,169
Italy	939	40,030	1,436
Japan	4,635	77,013	1,634
Netherlands	126	6,820	2,277
Sweden	125	3,859	2,291
Switzerland	372	7,512	946
United Kingdom	561	36,507	1,611
United States	23,123	95,777	2,772

Statistics on Payment Systems in the Group of Eleven Countries, Bank for International Settlements, December 1997. The number of offices for the United States includes commercial banks, thrifts, and credit unions.

Source: Reproduced from Berger, Demsetz, and Strahan, "The Consolidation of the Financial Services Industry: Cases, Consequences and Implications for the Future," *Journal of Banking and Finance* (1999) vol. 23, pp. 135–194.

TABLE 24.2   Financial Institutions in the United States

	Assets (U.S.$bn) 1998	Percent of Total Assets of Intermediaries				
		1960	1970	1980	1990	1998
Mutual Funds						
Money Market	1154	0.0	0.0	1.8	4.4	5.0
Others	3456	2.9	3.5	1.6	5.7	14.8
Insurance Companies						
Life	2693	19.4	14.8	11.0	12.1	11.6
Casualty	889	4.4	3.7	4.3	4.7	3.8
Pension Funds						
Private	3982	6.3	8.1	12.0	14.4	17.1
Public	2285	3.3	4.4	4.7	6.5	9.8
Depository Institutions						
Commercial Banks	5782	39.3	38.6	37.2	31.2	24.8
Savings Institutions	1047	18.8	18.8	18.8	12.1	4.5
Government	1190	1.0	3.4	4.2	3.7	5.1
Others (Finance Company)	796	4.7	4.7	4.9	5.4	3.4
Total	23,300					

Source: Board of Governors of the Federal Reserve System.

hold. But 60% this proportion has been falling since the early 1970s when banks accounted for almost of all assets channeled through intermediaries.

In developed economies, most households have at least one bank deposit. Those deposits are rechanneled to domestic and overseas borrowers. The scale of bank lending to emerging markets indicates the degree of international intermediation of funds.

Figure 24.3 shows how large and volatile those flows of bank lending between countries can be. At times in the early and mid-1990s, over $50 billion of new bank loans were made to emerging markets in Asia, Latin America, and Eastern Europe—nearly all of these flows represented the savings of individuals and companies in developed economies to finance expenditure in emerging markets. But in 1997, 1998, and 1999, the net flow of lending was dramatically negative (e.g., money was repatriated). The magnitudes indicate both the significance of bank lending in financing investment and the enormous variability in cross-border flows.

Why are banks so important, both within a country and between countries, in helping to finance expenditure? After all, you could imagine a situation in which companies and individuals that wanted to borrow money did so directly by approaching savers themselves, rather than by going through the intermediate step of borrowing from banks. Why have banks become middle men? The answer to this profound question tells us a lot about the benefits, but also the potential problems, of banks.

First, intermediation through banks allows portfolio diversification to small lenders at low cost. When I take $5,000 to the bank, the money, effectively, is used to finance loans to a large and diverse pool of borrowers. The bank may lend some of that money to individuals who live near me who have borrowed on mortgage. Some of it may be channeled to companies at the other end of the country that are investing in high-tech ventures. Some of it may be channeled to an emerging market to help finance an office block. I acquire a diversified portfolio of loans by simply depositing my money in a large bank. And this diminishes risk. It would be prohibitively costly for me to allocate part of that $5,000 to a loan to help finance a house purchase by one of my neighbors, a loan to the high-tech computer company a thousand miles away, and part to a construction company in Southeast Asia. The bank, by accumulating small deposits from many individuals, can spread the cost of allocating those funds across thousands of people, thereby reducing the transaction costs of channeling funds.

There is a second major benefit from having banks intermediate funds. If I were to lend money to many different enterprises and individuals, I would need to spend a lot of

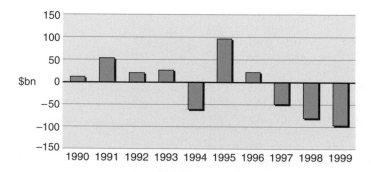

FIGURE 24.3 **Bank lending to emerging markets (U.S. $bn).** The net supply of bank loans to emerging economies went dramatically into reverse at the end of the 1990s. *Source*: International Monetary Fund, International Capital Markets (2000). Courtesy IMF.

time monitoring whether they were using my money sensibly. Suppose, instead, that a million people like me put their deposits in a bank. Instead of one million people each having to monitor, say, 100 different borrowers, the bank does the monitoring for them. This saves an enormous amount of monitoring, and after all, monitoring is boring and time consuming, at least for people who have to make their living from doing something else.

Third, when I put my $5,000 in the bank, I am probably not sure when I will need it again. I benefit from being able to get access to it at short notice. In contrast, the person who borrows money from a bank often needs it for a long time. If I am borrowing money to buy a house, I may not be able to repay most of it for 10 or even 20 years. And it may take 10 or 15 years for the flow of rents to pay off the money used to finance the construction of an office building. *People who borrow typically want the money for much longer than the people who deposit the money are prepared to give up access to their funds.* This would be a major problem if all the money lent to someone who was buying a house came from one or two depositors, because at some point one or both of those lenders would probably want their money back at short notice. But suppose that the money that helps finance my house purchase comes not from one or two savers but from a million savers. While it may be hard to predict whether an individual saver will want her money back this month or next month, the proportion of the deposits that one million savers want back at short notice is much more predictable. Banks can use the law of large numbers to get round the maturity mismatch problem. They can be confident, *at least in normal times*, that only a small proportion of their deposits will be withdrawn within any particular month. In fact, money going out the door basically balances money coming in the door, so that the total amount of deposits with a bank only tends to change by a relatively small amount from month to month. This means that banks can confidently lend money long term without being afraid that they will need to recall loans at short notice to pay depositors.

So channeling a substantial portion of savings through banks yields real economic benefits. By channeling funds banks play a critical role in the transmission mechanism of monetary policy. In the balance sheet of a large bank, different types of deposit on which the bank pays various types of interest (depending on the maturity and liquidity of the deposit and on whether depositors can write checks on the account) dominate the liabilities side. Table 24.3 shows the balance sheet of Citibank, the U.S. giant, on

TABLE 24.3 Citibank Accounts, March 31, 1999

$ billions Assets		Liabilities	
Cash	20.2	Equity Capital	20.2
Securities	36.1	Fed Funds Borrowed	7
Fixed Assets and Other Real Estate	4.3	Deposits	241.0
Trading Assets	31.2	Other Borrowing	36.0
Loans	194.0	Other Borrowing	0.1
Other Assets	18.5		
Total	304.3	Total	304.3

TABLE 24.4   U.S. Commercial Banks in November 2000

Assets (uses of funds)		Liabilities (sources of funds)	
Reserves, Cash	5.0%	Checkable Deposits	13.0%
Securities	21.7%	Nontransaction Deposits	50.0%
Loans	68.0%	Borrowings	19.8%
Commercial	18.0%	Miscellaneous	9.7%
Mortgage	27.3%		
Consumer	8.9%		
Interbank	4.1%	Net Worth	7.5%
Others	9.7%		
Miscellaneous	5.3%		

Source: Federal Reserve Board of the United States.

Note: Net worth is bank capital.

March 31, 1999. Various types of loans make up most of the assets side of the bank's balance sheet; as with deposits, the bank charges different interest rates on these loans depending on the size and maturity of the loan and the credit worthiness of the borrower. Table 24.4 shows the balance sheets of all commercial banks in the United States in 2000. What was true of Citibank goes for banks in general: most of their assets are in the form of loans, and most of their funds come from deposits.

Banks set key prices: the interest rates that are paid on deposits and that are charged on loans affect the allocation of resources in an economy. The monetary authorities (central banks) influence those prices in an important and direct way. We saw in Chapter 17 that central banks control the level of short-term, nominal interest rates in the wholesale money markets. Those short-term money market interest rates, in turn, directly affect the pattern of interest rates banks set. This is the case because the rates of interest that banks are prepared to offer on deposits from small savers or large companies are linked to the rate of interest that banks themselves can receive from lending money to other banks in the wholesale money markets. If the rate of interest that one bank can earn by lending large amounts of money to another bank in the wholesale money market increases sharply, the bank will start paying higher interest on its deposits because it then has an incentive to take in more deposits that it can lend at a good margin. Competition among banks to pull in deposits tends to bid deposit rates up. We can use a similar argument to show a close link between the rates of interest that the central bank directly influences and the interest rates the commercial banks set for loans or mortgages.

The *margin* between the average interest rate paid on bank deposits and the average rate charged on bank loans tends to be relatively stable over time. The overall *level* of nominal interest rates, in contrast, fluctuates sharply. We have seen in earlier chapters that nominal interest rates in many developed countries were in double figures for much of the 1970s and again at the end of the 1980s. But they had fallen sharply by the end of the 1990s. The margin between bank lending and borrowing rates does not fluctuate by anything like the same magnitude. This means that when central banks move nominal interest rates they can be pretty sure that the overall level of interest rates paid on deposits, and the overall level of interest rates charged on loans bank, will tend to move roughly in line, though often with a time lag. By setting interest rates on loans and deposits bank, banks are playing an important role in the transmission mechanism of monetary policy.

All this is fine and wonderful and makes banks sound like important institutions that play an essential role in the efficient allocation of resources. And indeed they do. But many of the factors that have made banks important can also create problems.

24.2 | Problems in Banking Markets

Banks help overcome two problems that would exist if savings were to be channeled directly to lenders. The first is the maturity mismatch issue—I want to have access to my savings at fairly short notice, while the person who wants to build a factory needs the money for 10 years or more. The second problem is that I do not want to spend my life checking to see that the 30 people I have lent money to really are using it for what they said they would. Banks help overcome these problems. But in doing so, they face other severe problems. First, if I, as a depositor, have delegated to the bank the responsibility for monitoring loans made with my savings, then inevitably I will not know a lot about the real value of those loans. Most of the time, this does not matter much, because I can probably be confident that at least most of the loans that the bank make are good, that I am going to get my money back, and that the bank will not become insolvent. And most of the time, it also does not matter very much that my deposit is highly liquid (that is, I can go in and get my money back at short notice), whereas the assets backing my deposit are loans that have a long maturity, which implies that the bank cannot get its hands on the cash at short notice.

But suppose that many people start to worry about the solvency, or health, of the bank where they have deposits. Anyone worried about the health of his or her bank would want to get their money out quickly. Sometimes, you have to pay a small penalty for accessing your money at short notice; in fact, with most current accounts, you can get your money back with no penalty. Suppose my worry turns out to be pointless, and in fact the bank is perfectly solvent. The only cost I will have incurred by taking my money out and then putting it back again a few weeks later is the (probably small) amount of interest I will have lost in the interim. In contrast, if I do not pull my money out and the bank *does* become insolvent, I may only get back 50 cents on every dollar that I deposited. Given the two possibilities—the bank is insolvent, the bank is solvent—I only need to attach a small probability to the insolvency outcome to make it rational to take my money out now. You can see the problem here. If enough people start to worry and go to the bank to withdraw their funds, the bank is going to be in trouble. It may find that it has to try to pull in loans at short notice to pay off depositors. But trying to pull in loans at short notice itself causes problems. If companies have borrowed from a bank on overdraft, fully expecting to be able to roll the overdraft forward and not have to repay the money at short notice, they can get

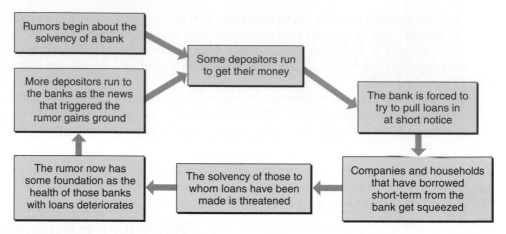

FIGURE 24.4   Self-fulfilling bank panic.

into trouble if the bank suddenly stops the line of credit. The company, in turn, may need to try to pull money in from its trade creditors who will themselves be squeezed. You can image a situation in which the very fact that banks try to pull in loans at short notice undermines the economic health of people they have lent money to and thereby reduces the real value of those loans. *Banking panics can become self-fulfilling* (Figure 24.4).

If enough people believe that a bank may have solvency problems and decide to try to get their money out, then that run on the bank could become self-justifying. The history of banking is littered with such bank runs. The most famous were in the United States in the 1930s during the Great Depression when, to prevent runs on the banks, the Roosevelt administration closed all banks by presidential decree and euphemistically called this a "bank holiday." This was an attempt to break the vicious circle of self-fulfilling panic, which had caused many banks to go under as depositors— rationally—tried to get their money out.

Bank runs show that the maturity mismatch between banks' assets and their liabilities have caused severe problems. Most developed countries have banking regulations and deposit insurance to try to counter the problem of bank runs. In most developed economies, if my bank goes bankrupt, the government guarantees that I will receive most of my funds back.[1] This helps prevent bank panic; if I know that ultimately the government will pay up for each dollar of my deposit, I have much less incentive to run to the bank because of a rumor that it has got into trouble. But, of course, the very fact that depositors may not care much about the lending practices can cause a problem. Generous deposit insurance may make banks more likely to undertake risky loans. This is a potentially big problem because banks are highly geared (or leveraged); that is, their debts are high relative to their overall assets. It is important to understand why this can cause a problem.

---

[1]These guarantees usually only cover deposits up to a certain limit—$100,000 in the United States.

GEARING, MORAL HAZARD, AND RISKY BORROWING

Banks are highly geared. This means that a relatively small amount of equity capital and a relatively large amount of debt help to finance the loans that banks make. Look again at the balance sheet of one of the largest banks in the world, Citibank (Table 24.3). About two-thirds of Citibank's assets were loans—most of which are relatively illiquid. Around 80% of its liabilities were in the form of bank deposits—most of which were payable at short notice. Adding in other types of debt—loans from the money market and bonds—generates an overall ratio of debt to total assets of about 93%. Few companies besides banks have such high gearing.

High gearing and highly insured deposits can generate unwelcome incentives for banks. Let's suppose that a bank's depositors are not concerned about insolvency risks, either because the government explicitly guarantees their deposits or else because they believe that the government will not let a big bank go under. In that case the bank may be able to take in deposits at relatively low interest rates, even though it may be lending on highly risky projects. But why would a bank take on very risky loans? The answer has to do with the limited liability of shareholders.

Shareholders in banks typically have limited liability, which means that the most they can lose is the money they put in to buy shares. If the bank becomes insolvent—that is, its assets are worth less than the debt—the shareholders do not have to contribute more money to ensure that the debtors are paid in full. This generates an asymmetry in payoffs. Let's take a simple example. Suppose that a bank has virtually no equity capital and finances nearly all its loans by deposits. Suppose also that the bank could undertake two types of loans: safe loans that pay 8% interest for certain, and risky loans that might pay back $1.20 for every dollar loaned (a 20% return), but which could go badly wrong, in which case each dollar loaned could only be worth 80 cents (a −20% return). For risky loans, suppose that the bank has an equal chance of good returns (+20%) and of bad returns (−20%). You might think that a sensible bank would prefer to loan at a guaranteed rate of 8%. A guaranteed rate of 8% is, on average, much better than a 50% chance of earning 20% and a 50% chance of *losing* 20%. After all, the average rate of return on the risky loan is zero, so even someone who didn't care about risk would prefer a guaranteed 8%. And if a person is risk averse, surely then there is no contest here.

However, we should look at these options from the point of view of the bank's owners. *They aren't the depositors, they are the shareholders*. From their point of view, the risky loans could go two ways: Number one, they could make a high profit by getting a 20% rate of return on the funds loaned and paying only a small fraction of that as interest on the deposits that finance the loan. If the cost of deposits is 4%, by making risky loans the bank has a 50% chance of earning a net +16% on each dollar loaned. Number two, if the risky loan fails and the bank is insolvent, its owners get nothing. So they face a 50% chance of nothing and a 50% chance of earning 16% on every dollar loaned. This is an average rate of return of 8% on each dollar Now suppose that instead the bank makes the riskless loans. These generate 8% for sure, which gives a net profit to the shareholders of 4% on every dollar loaned. That 4% is a lot less than an average return of 8%, and since the risk really resides with the government—who we assume insures the deposits—the bank has every incentive to play roulette. Note that the crucial

650 CHAPTER 24 The Banking Sector

incentive to play the risky option is that the potential losses do not fall on the shareholders. We assumed there was virtually no equity funding, so the shareholders only stood to gain if things went well. It is because the incentives to gamble become large when the equity capital of banks is small that banking regulations in most countries set a minimum on the amount of equity banks have. We describe this system of capital-adequacy rules later in this chapter.

This potential for banks to take too much risk is not just theoretical. Many banks have done just that. In the United States, savings and loan associations in the 1980s undertook massive risky and speculative lending that ultimately went wrong when property prices declined. The cost of the insolvency of savings and loans ultimately fell on the U.S. government, that is, U.S. taxpayers. These losses were staggering. Over 1100 savings and loan institutions and almost 1400 banks were closed in the United States in the 1980s.

Table 24.5 shows that what happened in the United States in the savings and loan crisis of the 1980s was by no means the most dramatic example of bank failures in recent years. In both developed and less developed economies, governments have incurred enormous costs from large-scale banking problems. Some of these banking problems were truly immense. In the Czech Republic at the end of the 1990s, for example, almost 40% of the total loans banks had made were nonperforming (which is a euphemism for "worth little"). To bail out these banks cost the government about 12% of gross domestic product (GDP). In the early 1980s in Uruguay about 60% of bank loans were close to worthless, and the cost to the government was about 30% of annual GDP. The problems in the Japanese banking system at the end of the 1990s—which we will consider in more detail in a moment—were much larger than the savings and loan crisis in the United States.

But the cost to the government of bailing out insolvent banks to prevent depositors losing money is only the most immediate and direct impact of banking problems. Bank problems also disrupt the flow of lending to companies and households that rely on bank finance. In many countries small firms rely heavily on banks and find it difficult to find alternative sources of finance if bank credit dries up. Even if the banks themselves remain solvent, and the direct cost to taxpayers of bailing out banks is zero, the impact on investment expenditure and employment in the corporate sector can be enormous if banking problems cause the flow of lending to suddenly dry up. How large the impact is depends on whether borrowers have other sources of finance available besides bank loans.

If borrowers can simply issue equities, or sell bonds, to finance expenditure when banks do not want to lend, consumption and investment may not be much affected. In this case what really matters to borrowers is the *price* of funds in general, rather than the *quantity* that actually comes from the banking system. But suppose that some borrowers cannot easily issue equity or bonds—either because of scale (they are too small to warrant an issue of equity or incur the costs of trying to sell their own bonds) or because of information problems, which can be severe. Suppose a small company has a longstanding relation with a bank that has come to know its business and feels confident about lending it money. Because the company has a good relationship with the bank, it may have felt no need to tap bond and equity markets to raise funds. But now suppose that the bank will not lend it any more money. The company may find it hard to persuade the capital markets that they should invest in it quickly. That the company might be prepared to pay a high coupon on its bonds, or promise a high rate of return on its

TABLE 24.5   Review of Selected Countries Banking Problems, 1980–1996

Country	Period	Non-performing Loans[a]	Fiscal Cost	Comments[b]
Argentina	1980–82	9%	4%	
	1989–90	27%	N/A	37% of state-owned banks were nonperforming. Failed banks held 40% of financial system assets.
	1995	N/A	N/A	45 of 205 institutions were closed or merged.
Australia	1989–92	6%	1.9%	
Brazil	1994–96			
Chile	1981–87	16%	19%	8 banks intervened in 1981 (33% of outstanding loans); 11 in 1982–83 (45% of outstanding loans).
Colombia	1982–85	15%	5%	
Czech Republic	1991–Present	38%	12%	
Finland	1991–94	13%	8%	Liquidity crisis in 1991.
France	1991–95	9%	1%	
Indonesia	1992–95	25%	2%	Nonperforming loans concentrated in state-owned banks.
Italy	1990–95	10%	N/A	
South Korea	Mid–1980s	7%	N/A	
Malaysia	1985–88	32%	5%	Loans' loss equivalent to 1.4% of GDP.
Mexico	1982	N/A	N/A	Banking system nationalized.
	1994–Present	12%	6%	
Niger	1983–Present	50%	N/A	
Norway	1987–93	6%	3%	
Philippines	1981–87	30%	13%	
Sweden	1990–93	18%	4%	
United States	1980–92	4%	2%	1,142 S&L institutions and 1,395 banks were closed.
Uruguay	1981–85	59%	31%	
Venezuela	1994–Present	N/A	17%	

Source: Reproduced from Hoshi and Kashyap, "The Japanese Banking Crisis: Where Did It Come From and How Will It End?" National Bureau of Economic Research *Macroeconomics Annual* (1999) vol. 14, pp. 129–212.
Notes: [a]Estimated at peak of the crisis, in percentage of total loans. [b]Estimated in percentage of annual GDP during the restructuring period.

equity, may cut no ice. In fact, the more generous the returns that a company promises to potential buyers of its equity and bonds, the more wary potential investors might become. If you don't know much about someone who wants to borrow from you, you may become more suspicious if he promises to pay higher and higher rates of return in exchange for your cash.

If these sorts of information problems affect many borrowers, then many will have no easy alternative to bank finance. And if this is the case, then not only the price of raising money matters, so does the quantity offered. If I cannot raise money from the equity or bond markets at *any* price, then the quantity of money that the bank will lend me really matters. As a borrower I may be insensitive to changes in bank interest rates, but highly sensitive to the amount of money that the bank is prepared to lend me. This has important implications for the transmission mechanism of monetary policy. In thinking about how monetary policy works, we have focused on the effect the central bank has on the economy when it changes short-term nominal interest rates. But the crucial variable for many types of borrower may be the *quantity* of lending that banks undertake (the so-called "credit channel"). If that is so, then one important way in which monetary policy works is by influencing the quantity, rather than just the price, of bank lending.

Consider a specific example. Suppose that the central bank engages in open market operations—by selling Treasury bills it drains reserves from the banking system. Suppose too that some banks have difficulty borrowing from others on the interbank market and have to curtail their lending when their reserves with the central bank begin to dip beneath a critical level. All this may have occurred without any significant change in Treasury bill prices, so that interest rates hardly move. Nonetheless, some banks may need to curtail their borrowing sharply, and if a substantial proportion of people who rely on borrowing money from them cannot gain access to other sources of finance, it could affect the overall level of investment and consumption spending in the economy. (Figure 24.4)

How important this credit mechanism has been is a matter of debate. In the United States evidence suggests that the so-called credit channel is important. Bernanke and Blinder showed that a decline in the volume of total bank lending tends to follow a tightening in monetary policy.[2] This is at least consistent with the notion of a credit channel operating as part of the monetary policy transmission mechanism. But it is difficult to distinguish between a reduction in demand for loans and a reduction in supply.

Bernanke and Lown also suggest another mechanism whereby bank loan availability affects expenditure. They present evidence that shifts in the amount of equity capital that banks have can influence their willingness to lend *at given rates of interest*.[3] The argument goes like this: Banking regulation typically limits how much equity capital banks must have. So, for example, a bank that had loans worth $1 billion might have to have equity capital of at least $80 million or 8%. Suppose that a bank loses some of its asset value, perhaps because a loan turned bad. This could reduce the value of its capital beneath the critical level set by the banking regulators. Suppose also that the bank cannot replenish its capital easily. For example, it may take years of profitability for a bank to replenish its capital substantially. Issuing new equity might be problematic when the bank is under pressure. No matter why raising

[2]"The Federal Funds Rate and the Channels of Monetary Transmission," *American Economic Review* (1992) vol. 82, no. 4, pp. 901–921.

[3]"The Credit Crunch," *Brookings Papers on Economic Activity* (1991) vol. 2, pp. 220–271.

new capital is difficult, the result is the same: to meet the capital requirement, the bank has to curtail its lending; thereby reducing its stock of assets and allowing the capital ratio to rise back toward 8%. Bernanke and Lown find that banks that had relatively small amounts of capital (relative to levels set by regulators) tended to reduce their lending substantially more than banks that were in an otherwise similar economic environment.

24.3 Bank Lending and Instability

Several of the mechanisms that we have described can make the economy unstable. Consider Bernanke and Lown's capital crunch argument. Suppose that an important local company to which a bank has lent money becomes insolvent. This will diminish the bank's capital and possibly reduce the amount of lending that it is willing or able to undertake. Suppose too that this has a negative impact on local firms. Some of the firms that have borrowed money from the bank are property developers. The bank may now call in some of its loans to them. They are likely to find it difficult to liquidate their assets at short notice—perhaps because many of these assets are unfinished buildings. They can probably sell at least some of their assets. But as a result of trying to sell a large stock of properties quickly, prices are likely to fall. This will have a negative impact on other property firms and will also reduce the collateral of not just property companies but other corporations as well. As the value of the tangible assets of corporations in the region begins to fall, so does the value of the collateral against which they can borrow. This is likely to cause banks to reduce their lending. This, in turn, can depress economic activity and drive the prices of properties and factories down yet further.

This has the potential for a vicious downward spiral as illustrated in Figure 24.5. But, of course, the mechanism could go into reverse. Suppose banks have lent money to property companies, and those companies prosper as prices move up. This increases the creditworthiness and collateral of existing and potential property companies, which find it easier to raise money. This can have a knock on effect on the value of the collateral of the local corporate sector in general and can help engender a borrowing and investing boom that can drive asset prices up even further.

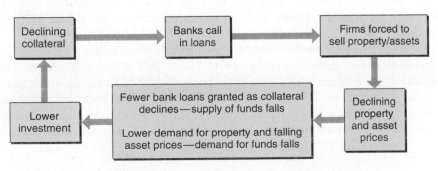

FIGURE 24.5 **Credit crunch.**

These mechanisms are not just theoretical possibilities. What happened in Southeast Asia and Japan in the 1990s illustrates the power of these forces. Even the U.S. economy, which in recent decades has not suffered the kind of instability that hit Southeast Asia, shows evidence of cycles of excess and then insufficient bank lending. Recent research suggests that banks typically change their lending standards—from tightness to laxness—systematically over the business cycle, thereby exacerbating volatility in the economy.[4] The authors of one study conclude:

> *We have demonstrated that the market for bank loans experiences systematic cycles of over and under lending. In addition, we have shown that the cycles in bank lending exert considerable influence on aggregate fluctuations. The lending pattern suggests that loans extended on "easier" quotes during expansions return to haunt banks as problem loans during contraction. As a consequence, credit market imperfections may have a more profound effect on aggregate economic activity during expansions when the seeds of future recessions are sown than during contractions.*

The experience of Japan and Southeast Asia in the 1990s dramatically illustrates the tendency for banks to exacerbate economic cycles.

24.4 The Southeast Asia Problem

The Southeast Asian economies—particularly Thailand, Singapore, Malaysia, South Korea, and Indonesia—grew phenomenally through most of the 1990s. Indeed, their performance was described as almost miraculous. This went dramatically into reverse in 1998 when exchange rates tumbled, output collapsed, and investment all but dried up.

The banking sector in these countries played a key role in this turmoil. Banks had extended credit to companies in these Southeast Asian economies on an enormous scale in the mid-1990s, and much of the funds ultimately came from banks in the developed world. Between 1990 and the end of 1996, bank loans from the rest of the world to Indonesia, Malaysia, South Korea, and Thailand totaled more than $140 billion. Once lenders suspected that the value of assets purchased with these bank loans was inflated and set to fall sharply, bank lending unraveled with dramatic speed. Between the end of 1997 and the end of 1998, the stock of loans from Bank for International Settlements (BIS) banks to domestic banks in these countries declined by almost $170 billion (Table 24.6).

Essentially, Western banks decided in 1998 that they had to get their money out of the Southeast Asian banking system because loans that domestic banks had made, using funds from Western banks, were going badly wrong. Asset prices, which had been bid up hugely in the mid-1990s, collapsed as loans were pulled back and investment in new developments halted. Figure 24.5 illustrates the mechanism. Figure 24.6 shows stock prices, office prices, and house prices in the major Southeast Asian economies.

[4]Asea and Blomberg, "Lending Cycles," NBER Working Paper 5951 (1997).

TABLE 24.6   Cross-Border Claims of BIS Banks
on Domestic Banking Sector (in billions of U.S. dollars)

Asia	End 1996	End 1997	End 1998
China	22.8	26.8	21.5
Hong Kong SAR	135.3	126.4	64.8
Indonesia	11.8	11.5	5.2
Korea	65.9	55.6	34.5
Malaysia	6.5	9.6	5.7
Singapore	156.9	155.5	93.3
Thailand	25.9	17.5	8.8
Total	424.9	402.9	233.8

Bank lending to South East Asia collapsed in 1998.

Sources: Bank for International Settlements,
Consolidated International Banking Statistics,
May 31, 1999; International Monetary Fund,
International Financial Statistics, 2000. Courtesy
IMF.

During 1998 prices of all these assets plummeted, reducing the net worth of companies that had borrowed enormously in the previous five years. As a result, much of the banking systems of these countries became insolvent almost overnight.

How did this happen? One could say that this was another example of banks being irrationally optimistic and then becoming irrationally pessimistic in a short time. In fact, what happened is more explicable in terms of economic agents responding rationally to perceptions of their environment. It seemed sensible for banks, both in the wider world and within Southeast Asia, to assume that *if* the asset price boom was reversed and the value of domestic bank assets declined, that governments would—somehow—bail out insolvent domestic institutions. If you believed that this would happen, you would continue to lend because you assumed that if things did not go badly, good times would roll on and profits keep coming in; but if things did go wrong, then you would not lose your money. Taxpayers would end up financing deficits. For banks it was a case of heads I win, tails you lose. With those odds, you might as well go on gambling.

Paul Krugman has argued that this sort of problem is worse if banking markets are globalized.[5] If domestic banks can finance loans to domestic companies by borrowing from international banks on a world capital market, then essentially they face a highly elastic supply of money—at the current interest rate, they can borrow almost as much as they want and keep fueling the domestic boom. In contrast, if domestic banks have to keep dragging in more and more deposits from domestic savers to finance ever more extravagant investment projects by domestic companies, they would soon encounter limits. They would have to increase interest rates to encourage more savings from the

[5]"What Happened to Asia?" available online at Paul Krugman's Website: http://web.mit.edu/krugman

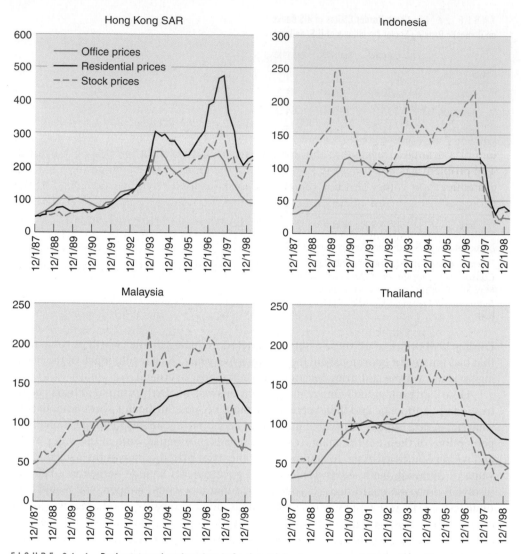

FIGURE 24.6   **Real estate and equity prices in Southeast Asia.** Asset prices followed a roller-coaster ride in the 1990s in the Southeast Asian economies. *Source*: "International Capital Markets," Inc., September 1999.

domestic population, which would limit the amount of new lending that they could profitably undertake. Because these countries could borrow enormously from overseas banks, it exacerbated the asset price boom.

Of course, all this can hurt the real economy. A drought is likely to follow a glut of borrowing, and companies that had found it easy to get funds from domestic banks would not have built up relations in capital markets. As a result, they will find it hard to issue equity directly when bank loans dry up.

24.5   The Japanese Problem

Many of the problems that arose dramatically in Southeast Asia in 1998 built up more slowly in Japan. The problems of the Japanese banking system that emerged in the 1990s and continued into the new century were in some ways rather similar to what happened in Southeast Asia; but in important respects were very different. Unlike in Southeast Asia, bank lending in Japan has not ultimately been financed by bank deposits coming from outside the country. The problem in Japan has not been one of a dramatic reversal in the flow of capital coming from the rest of the world. The problem has been that the assets backing the loans made by domestic banks fell dramatically in value. This has generated enormous losses to domestic banks. At the end of 1999 estimates of bad loans in Japan were running at almost 10% of GDP. The crisis included the first significant bank failure since the end of the U.S. occupation of Japan. The Japanese banking crisis was very much larger than the U.S. savings and loan crisis. And all this came at a time when the government was already running a large fiscal deficit. The budget deficit in 2000 was estimated to be in excess of 6% of GDP.

Two major banks were nationalized in late 1998, and most remaining major banks were recapitalized with public funds in March 1999. The Long Term Credit Bank was nationalized in October of 1998, at a time when the bank was estimated to have negative net worth of yen 340 billion. By March of 1999 it was estimated that the bank had negative net worth that actually was dramatically higher at yen 2.7 trillion. Each month that went by in 1998 and 1999, the scale of the problem was estimated to be even larger. At the end of 1998 a second major bank—the Nippon Credit Bank—was taken under state control. Even in 2001 it was too early to work out how much all this will eventually cost Japanese taxpayers, but it seems likely that the figure will be in excess of 10% of GDP.

But as we noted at the start of this chapter, the real cost to the Japanese may be far in excess of the direct burden on government financing of bailing out some large banks. Japanese companies have relied on bank debt to a greater extent than in many other countries. Table 24.7 shows a comparison between the level of bank debt held by large U.S. and Japanese manufacturing firms. In 1998 Japanese manufacturing firms had debt which was about twice as great, relative to their total assets, as was the case in the United States. But the large companies were probably in a much better position than small companies to ride out a period of lower bank lending. Loans to small enterprises had grown strongly in Japan in the 1980s and had taken up a significantly increasing proportion of the total loans made by banks. Evidence from most developed countries suggest that it is small companies that are most affected by a decline in the availability of bank finance. And the decline in bank lending in Japan certainly was dramatic during the 1990s, as Figure 24.7 illustrates.

The problems in the Japanese banking sector have had a substantial knock-on impact on economic activity. The International Monetary Fund and the Organization for Economic Cooperation and Development have both pointed to banking problems as key factors behind the significant slowdown in growth in the late 1990s and the sluggishness in activity in 1999 and 2000 (see Figure 24.8). The Japanese government itself

TABLE 24.7   Industry-Level Comparisons of Bank
Debt to Total Assets Ratio for Large U.S. and Japanese
Manufacturing Firms

Industry	United States 1998	Japan 1998
Food	0.12	0.13
Textile	0.20	0.24
Pulp and Paper	0.11	0.35
Printing and Publishing	0.08	0.08
Chemical	0.07	0.16
Petroleum and Coal	0.02	0.41
Stone, Glass, and Clay	0.15	0.19
Iron and Steel	0.11	0.26
Nonferrous Metals	0.07	0.35
Metal Products	0.17	0.17
Machinery	0.07	0.15
Electronic Machinery	0.04	0.09
Transportation Durable	0.03	0.10
Precision Machinery	0.15	0.10
Average	0.10	0.20

Source: Kashyap and Hoshi, "The Japanese Banking
Crisis: Where Did It Come From and How Will It
End?" NBER *Macroeconomics Annual* (2000) vol.
14, pp. 129–212.

Note: Large U.S. firms are defined as having assets
over $25 million.

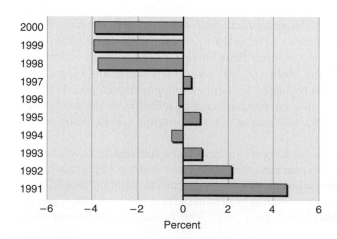

FIGURE 24.7   **Japanese bank lending.**
With banking problems emerging in
the late 1990s the flow of new lending
went sharply into reverse. Percent
change in the stock of loans
outstanding held by Japanese banks
(includes city banks, long-term credit
banks, trust banks, and regional
banks). *Source:* "International Capital
Markets," IMF.

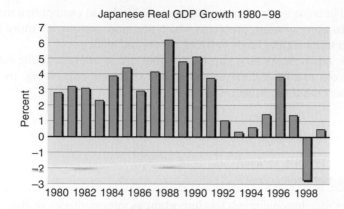

Japanese Real GDP Growth 1980–98

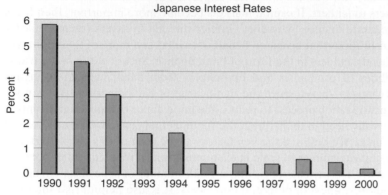

Japanese Interest Rates

FIGURE 24.8 **The Japanese slump in the 1990s.** Interest rates have been cut aggressively in order to support demand *Source*: Thomson Financial Datastream.

identified problems in the financial sector as a major factor behind the length and severity of the recession. Recent research finds that shifts in asset prices played a significant role in the Japanese business cycle and that the impact that movement in asset prices had was largely transmitted through bank lending.[6] He finds that if there had not been associated changes in bank lending, then asset price fluctuations would not have had such a large impact on the real economy.

So how did all this come about? Many of the forces that we have described earlier in this chapter have clearly been relevant. Movements in asset prices first increased the value of collateral of the Japanese corporate sector—encouraging further bank lending which ramped prices up further—and the subsequent declines in asset prices in the 1990s dramatically reduced the ability of banks to lend while also generating insolvencies. Perceptions that banks were too big to fail, that depositors would not lose money because the government would bail out insolvent institutions, have largely been justified by subsequent events. The Japanese government nationalized some of the largest insolvent institutions and injected vast amounts of money to prop up the banking system and prevent depositors sustaining serious losses. So if depositors with Japanese banks did not pay too much attention to the quality of loans of those banks, then they

[6]Bayoumi, "The Morning After: Explaining the Slowdown in Japanese Growth in the 1990s," IMF Working Paper (1998).

were perfectly rational in doing so. In short, what happened in Japan exemplified many of the problems with banking systems, problems which are more serious the more important banks are for intermediating funds between savers and lenders.

What happened in Japan shows how important banks are in intermediating funds and how regulation needs to curb excessive lending and excessive risk taking. In the final section we consider both these issues.

24.6   Regulation and Securitization: An End to Banking Problems?

In the future banks *may* become much less important as intermediaries in channeling funds from savers to lenders. If capital markets become more important, then firms will increasingly generate finance by issuing equities directly to savers (or more accurately, directly to institutions that invest on behalf of savers) and more of their debt will be in the form of bonds and less in the form of bank finance. Securitization—the transformation of liabilities of companies and households from bank loans to securities traded on stock exchanges—may reduce the significance of banking crises. But can we really expect this securitization process to reduce the importance of banks significantly? To answer that we really need to think about the fundamental economic factors behind intermediation of funds. We outlined the key factors at the start of this chapter. Banks are useful in generating economies of scale in channeling funds from lenders to borrowers. Most important are the benefits of having a small number of specialists engage in monitoring the creditworthiness of potential borrowers. It is also helpful that intermediaries allow the maturity mismatch problem to be solved and also allow diversification benefits to be gained with low transaction costs.

Increasingly, securities markets are able to generate the benefits of these scale economies in much the same way as banks have historically. For example, specialist credit rating agencies— Standard and Poor's and Moody's—can perform the credit rating services of banks and provide the information to securities markets. We saw in Chapter 22 that corporate bonds are given credit rankings and their prices are highly sensitive to this. The benefits of having specialists assess the creditworthiness of potential borrowers does not require that funds be intermediated through banks. And portfolio diversification and maturity mismatch issues can, to a large extent, be handled perfectly well in the securities markets. Individuals who contribute to pension funds or put money in unit trusts have their savings invested on their behalf in pooled investment funds. These allow benefits of diversification at relatively low cost to small savers. Maturity mismatch problems can, in may ways, be handled at least as well in securities markets as in banking markets. When a company issues equity it is under no obligation at all to buy back that equity at short notice if the holders of stocks need to liquidate their investment. A well-developed securities market allows holders of bonds and equities to cash in their chips—liquidate their investments—at short notice without any recourse to the original issuer of the debt.

So when we think about the factors that have been important in making banks significant players in the economy it is far from obvious that their impact will continue to make banks so central to the allocation of resources. It is plausible that, slowly, securities markets will become increasingly important in economies in which in the past banks have intermediated most funds from savers to lenders. But that process will be slow and banks will continue to be hugely important for the foreseeable future. This means that the impact of banking problems will continue to be great and that regulations designed to minimize the chances of banking disruption are important.

BANK REGULATION

How bank regulation is undertaken continues to change. Perhaps the most important type of regulations are so-called capital adequacy requirements. What stands between a decline in the value of the assets of a bank and its insolvency is the capital the bank has. If a bank has assets worth $1000 million and capital worth $80 million, then at least 8% of the value of the assets could be wiped out without depositors losing any money and without the bank becoming insolvent. The more capital a bank has, the less likely it is that it will become insolvent. But we noted above that if banks are highly geared they face incentives to undertake risky investment which, with limited liability, can generate higher average returns for their shareholders. In an environment in which owners have limited liability banks may have incentives to gear up. Because of these perverse incentives, capital adequacy requirements have been established.

The Bank for International Settlements has established a system of capital adequacy requirements that has been adopted in most developed economies. The way the system works is straightforward. Every time a bank acquires an extra million dollars of a particular sort of asset, it has to increase its amount of capital by a certain amount. The more risky the asset is judged to be (by the regulators), the greater is the extra capital that the bank has to acquire. At the moment (in 2001), banks that lend money to governments of OECD countries need set aside no capital at all for this sort of lending. Loans to banks within the OECD area only require 1.6% of capital. Residential mortgages require 4% of capital, and most other types of loans require 8% of capital. Clearly there are substantial differences in these capital requirements for different types of bank asset. Getting these risk weightings wrong can have a substantial impact on banks' incentive to undertake different types of lending and can have significant impacts on bank risk. As George Graham, banking analyst at the *Financial Times*, put it:

> *. . . all this matters because the Basle rules are not merely in the abstract formula humming away in the background, but the parameter in which banks make real life decisions on their loan books and counter trading parties. If lending to a particular emerging market suddenly starts to attract a higher regulatory capital charge, other banks will start to demand higher returns to compensate them.*

At the time of writing the regulators are proposing rather significant changes to the risk weights attached for bank lending to selected governments. Table 24.8 shows the existing risk weights and the proposed risk weights. A weight of 100 means that the loan is treated in the same way as lending to most private sector companies and requires an amount of capital equal to 8% of the loan. What regulators are trying to do is bring the capital requirements more into line with the perceived risks of different types of assets. To some extent regulators are inevitably reacting to yesterday's crisis when they

TABLE 24.8   Current versus Proposed Risk Weights for Selected Governments

	Rating	OECD	Risk Current	Weight (%) Proposed
Argentina	BB	No	100	100
Brazil	B+	No	100	100
Chile	A−	No	100	20
China	BBB	No	100	50
Colombia	BBB−	No	100	50
Czech Republic	A−	Yes	0	20
Greece	BBB	Yes	0	50
Hungary	BBB−	Yes	0	50
Indonesia	CCC+	No	100	150
Israel	A	No	100	20
South Korea	BBB	Yes	0	50
Malaysia	BBB−	No	100	50
Mexico	BB	Yes	0	100
Poland	BBB−	Yes	0	50
Russia	CC−	No	100	150
Singapore	AAA	No	100	0
South Africa	BB+	No	100	100
Thailand	BBB−	No	100	50
Turkey	B	Yes	0	100

Source used in compiling table: Standard & Poor's, BIS.
Ratings are as of September 1999.

The 100% risk weighting implies a capital charge of 8%.

establish new risk weights. The risk weight on South Korean sovereign debt in 1999 was zero, but it was proposed that it increase to 50%. The risk weight of Mexico was also proposed to increase from zero to 100%. What regulators really need to do is to think about where the *next* banking problem may be rather than where the last one was. No one really expected Southeast Asia to be the source of so many problems in the late 1990s. This was where economic miracles had, apparently, taken place. But miracles more frequently exist in the eyes of the beholder than in the real world.

The importance of banking regulation—and more specifically of capital requirements on various types of loan—reflects both the harm that banking problems can cause and the significance of banks in intermediating funds. Banks matter because they do some things that are not done well by other means. In the past, banks, rather than pension funds, insurance companies, or mutual funds, have been the key link between companies wanting to raise funds and savers. But the preeminence of banks in playing this role has already declined substantially in the United States, where bond and equity markets have become increasingly important. One indication of this is the declining ratio between the total U.S. bank deposits of the private sector and total financial wealth. In 1983, about 25% of total financial assets were deposits in banks. By 1999 this fraction had fallen by one-half.

Whether this trend will continue and be followed in other developed countries has profound implications for the conduct of monetary policy. Central banks have a more direct impact on the cost of borrowing when a larger part of corporate and household liabilities are in the form of bank debt in which interest charges are sensitive to the level of short-term money market rates. Central banks in the future may have less leverage on the economy but may also be less concerned about the damage done by problems in the baking sector. Whether this will come about is hard to judge; if it does it may represent a position with which central banks and governments are content.

SUMMARY

Banks are important financial intermediaries. They help channel funds from savers to borrowers. The scale of intermediation done by banks is immense—a large proportion of corporate and personal investment is financed with bank credit. Banks are also important because it is through their pricing—setting rates to charge on loans and rates paid on deposits—that the actions of central banks in fixing short-term rates are transmitted to a large number of borrowers and lenders.

For hundreds of years banks have been at the center of resource allocation by directing savings. Banking crises have occurred at regular intervals, and they still occur. Bank runs occur when depositors fear that they will not receive all their funds back. Asset pricing bubbles, fueled by too easy availability of bank credit, are often followed by crashes in which the erosion of collateral curtails bank lending and drives spending and asset prices down further. Because of their central role, banking regulations exist to try to prevent problems in banking markets spreading to the wider economy and to stop depositors from losing money.

CONCEPTUAL QUESTIONS

1. "Governments that support failing banks are encouraging inappropriate behavior from both savers and banks—bank bailouts represent a huge waste of resources."

   "Banks are so important that governments simply cannot let them fail—that is what the banking panics and bank failures in the United States in the 1930s show."

   Which position is more defensible? Does it matter which country we are focusing on and when in its history we are considering?

2. Consider the links you have with banks. Could you imagine all the services that banks provide to you being provided by nonbanks?

3. One proposal to alleviate banking problems is to insist that banks match their deposits with highly marketable securities that can be liquidated at short notice (e.g., Treasury bills). Consider the economic implications of this proposal.

4. If information about the risks of investing in companies improves and is more readily available to small investors, would you expect more savings from households to be channeled directly to companies looking for funds and less to go via banks?

5. In some markets governments follow the dictum *caveat emptor* (let the buyer beware) and do not impose many restrictions on suppliers of goods. With banks, however, there are now a lot of special restrictions (for example, capital adequacy requirements). Why is this? Do you think there is something special about banks which justifies this?

6. Would you expect the Internet to mean that banks become less important in the economy as people can invest in stocks and bonds more easily and do not need to visit branches to pay bills and check on accounts?

ANALYTICAL QUESTIONS

1. To loan money successfully requires monitoring those to whom money has been loaned. Assume that the annual monitoring costs are $300 a year for each loan regardless of the size of the loan. Suppose that the typical saver has $30,000 to lend and would not want to lend to less than 10 different borrowers so as to diversify risk. Compare a situation in which each saver directly lends money to 10 borrowers and a situation in which each saver joins a 1000 others to form a bank that lends to 10 (very large) borrowers. What is the saving in monitoring costs?

2. A bank has deposits that are instantly redeemable at no penalty. It makes loans which are repaid gradually over a period of several years. It cannot call the loans in at short notice. It also holds some of its assets in the form of cash balances which it can use immediately to pay out those who want to withdraw funds. Assume loans earn a rate of return of 9% a year and that cash balances earn nothing. Explain exactly how the bank should think about the optimal split in its assets between loans and cash balances. Assume the penalty for running out of cash (not being able to pay depositors) is very large. How does your analysis depend upon the availability and cost of loans in an interbank market in which a bank can borrow money at short term from other banks?

3. A bank is near insolvency—its assets are worth $1000 million, only a fraction more than its debt liabilities of $999.5 million. As a result, the true value of its equity is small. The bank is able to take $100 million more deposits from the public in return for a promise to pay a 6% return. The bank considers two possible uses to which the new deposits can be put. The safe option is to lend at a rate of 8%. There is a 95% chance that such a loan will be repaid in full. There is a 5% chance that for each dollar loaned the bank will simply get its money back (but receive no interest). The alternative loan is very risky. There is a 60% chance that the bank can make the risky loan at an interest rate of 40% and be paid in full (receiving $1.40 for each $1). There is a 40% chance that it will be repaid nothing. Which loan has the higher expected return? Which loan would shareholders, who have limited liability, prefer the bank to make?

4. Explain why a bank run is a Nash equilibrium and why not running to the bank is also a Nash equilibrium. Because one of these equilibria is less desirable than the other, it would be useful to devise arrangements which made bank runs unlikely. Describe some possible arrangements that would achieve this.

5. Assume that the annual cost to commercial banks of taking in deposits and lending them out again is 2.5% of the amount of money intermediated. This cost reflects paying wages to staff, advertising, upkeep and rent on buildings, etc. It also reflects the profit margin that banks need to earn to satisfy equity investors. Banks can attract deposits if they pay no less than 1% below the rate that the central bank fixes in the wholesale money market. If the central bank sets the short-term rate at 7.5%, what is the rate banks charge on loans? Now assume that productivity gains reduce the size of the costs of intermediating in half. Keener competition between banks also means that they cannot pay less than 0.5% below the central bank rate on their deposits. By how much must the central bank change its rate to keep the cost of loans to those who borrow from banks constant?

Adverse selection A problem of asymmetric information in which, because it is not possible to know the characteristics of agents, a disproportionate number are less desirable, e.g., banks may not know whether loan applicants are good or bad credit risks and get a substantial number of the latter.

Aggregate demand curve The negative relation between the overall price level and the aggregate quantity of output demanded.

Aggregate supply curve The relation between the overall price level and the aggregate quantity of output firms produce.

Appreciation An increase in the value of a currency against other currencies in the market for foreign exchange. (Opposite of depreciation.)

Arbitrage The scope to buy in one market at a lower price than is available for the same good in another market.

Asymmetric information A situation in which economic agents have different information which cannot be pooled.

Asymmetric shocks Shocks that affect different countries/regions/industries differently.

Automatic stabilizer The impact of policies that automatically tend to boost demand in a slump and reduce demand in a boom. For example, taxes on incomes tend to rise in a boom and fall in a slump; government spending on unemployment benefits has a similar impact.

Average propensity to consume (APC) The ratio of consumption to income (C/Y).

Balance sheet A record of the assets and liabilities of a company, an individual, or a nation.

Balance of payments Record of a country's international transactions.

Balanced budget A situation in which receipts equal expenditures.

Balassa-Samuelson effect The phenomenon in which prices (especially of nontradables) are higher in richer, more productive countries.

Bank for International Settlements (BIS) An international organization that fosters cooperation among central banks and other agencies in pursuit of monetary and financial stability.

Bank run A situation in which depositors withdraw funds from a bank for fear that it may go bankrupt and not honor its liabilities.

Bond A financial instrument that promises to pay flows of money at specific intervals. Bonds are a form of debt issued by corporations and governments.

Borrowing constraint A restriction on the amount a person can borrow. Individuals unable to borrow against the prospect of high future labor income may be constrained if current income is low.

Bubble Nonsustainable behavior of asset prices in which values are bid up in a way that is not linked to underlying fundamentals.

Budget constraint The requirement that over the relevant horizon the value of spending must equal the value of receipts.

Budget deficit A situation in which receipts are less than expenditure.

Budget surplus A situation in which receipts exceed expenditure.

Business cycle Regular, medium-term aggregate fluctuations in output, incomes, and employment.

Business fixed investment Expenditure on equipment and structures that businesses use in production.

Capacity utilization A measure of the extent to which physical capital and employment are being fully utilized in production.

Capital stock The stock of physical equipment and structures used in production.

Capital account Record of a country's financial transactions with the rest of the world. Sales of a country's assets increase the capital account; purchases of overseas assets reduce the capital account.

Capital accumulation Process whereby the stock of physical capital increases when gross investment exceeds depreciation.

Capital adequacy rules Rules that restrict the amount and type of lending that banks can make depending upon their equity capital.

Capital gain The rise in the price of an asset.

Catch-up (*see also* convergence) When rich countries grow more slowly than poor ones.

Central bank The institution that implements monetary policy, such as the Federal Reserve in the United States and the European Central Bank in Europe.

Closed economy A country that neither borrows nor invests overseas and does not trade goods and services with other countries.

Cobb-Douglas production function A production function in which output is given by $F(K,L) = AK^\beta L^{1-\beta}$, where K is capital, L is labor, and A and β are parameters. If capital and labor receive their marginal product, β is the share of capital income in total output and $1-\beta$ is the share of labor.

Commodity money Money that has a value in itself even if it were to become unacceptable as money (e.g., gold, silver).

Comparative advantage A situation in which a country has a lower opportunity cost of producing a certain commodity or the industry in which a country has greatest productivity advantage (or smallest disadvantage) compared to other nations.

Competitiveness Productivity in a country compared to other nations (often used with reference to high value added industries).

Constant prices   The use of the same prices across several years when calculating real GDP in order to focus on output changes.

Constant returns to scale   A situation in which the same percentage increase in all factors of production generates an equal percentage change in output.

Consumer price index (CPI)   A measure of the general level of prices that consumers have to pay for goods.

Consumption   Goods and services bought and used by consumers.

Consumption function   The relationship between consumption and its determinants. The simplest consumption function has spending depending just on current income.

Contractionary policy   Government actions that reduce demand in the economy and cause employment to fall. (Opposite of expansionary policy.)

Convergence   Process whereby poor countries grow faster than rich ones.

Cost of capital   The overall amount of resources that has to be sacrificed to acquire the use of a unit of capital for one period. The cost reflects interest, depreciation, and the gain or loss from the change in the price of the capital.

Countercyclical   Tending to move in the opposite direction to aggregate output and employment over the business cycle. (Opposite of procyclical.)

Coupon   Regular (normally fixed) payment made to bond holders.

Covered interest parity   Prediction that the gap between two countries' interest rates should be the same as that between their current spot exchange rate and the current forward exchange rate.

Credit constraint   An inability to borrow against future income.

Credit crunch   Negative interrelationship among bank lending, property prices, and bank assets.

Crowding out   The tendency of extra government spending to cause reductions in private spending through induced changes in interest rates.

Currency   Coins and paper (fiat) money issued by the authorities of a country.

Currency board   An arrangement whereby a country can only issue domestic currency if it is backed up by central bank holdings of a specific foreign currency.

Current account   Record of trade between countries in goods and services. Selling more goods and services overseas than are purchased generates a current account surplus and buying more overseas goods and services than are sold produces a current account deficit.

Current prices   Use of current year prices when measuring the value of output in each year generates a measure of nominal GDP. Changes in nominal GDP reflect both output and price changes.

Deflation   A fall in the general level of prices. (Opposite of inflation.)

Deflator   A price index which converts a nominal series to a real one.

Demand deposits   Bank deposits that are available on demand and that can be used to settle transactions, e.g., checking accounts.

Depreciation   Wear and tear on physical capital that reduces its effective quantity over time. Depreciation also refers to a fall in the value of a currency relative to other (foreign) currencies.

Depression   A protracted slump; an unusually severe and long-lasting recession.

Devaluation   A policy of reducing the foreign exchange value of a currency implemented by a central bank.

Diminishing marginal product   A situation in which the addition to output from increasing the use of a single factor declines the more of the factor is added, holding other factors constant.

Discount rate   The interest rate set by the central bank when it makes loans to banks.

Discounting   Scaling back the value of future receipts (or payments) to convert them to current equivalent values so as to reflect the interest rate over the relevant interval.

Discretionary policy   Policy that is not fixed by preset rules but that can respond to different events.

Disinflation   A reduction in the rate of inflation.

Disposable income   Income available after deducting taxes.

Distortions   Deviations from the efficient market outcome caused, for example, by taxes.

Divergence   When poor countries do not catch up with rich ones through faster growth.

Dividend yield   Dividend payments on a share expressed as a percentage of the share price.

Efficient stock market hypothesis   Prediction that equity prices reflect all available information about future share prices and dividends.

Efficiency wages   Wages that maximize efficiency and profits for the firm.

Elasticity   The percent change in one variable caused by a 1% change in another variable.

Employment protection legislation (EPL)   Government regulations aimed at increasing the cost or reducing the speed with which firms can reduce employment.

Endogenous growth   Model in which long-run growth of the economy is modeled directly by the theory.

Endogenous variable   A variable whose value is driven by other variables in a model of the economy. (Opposite of an exogenous variable.)

Equilibrium   A situation of balance between various forces, e.g., the balance of supply against demand in a market.

Equities   (also shares or stocks) Paper asset reflecting part ownership of company and the future stream of income it earns.

Equity premium puzzle   The finding that returns on equities have in many countries far exceeded that on other assets even after allowing for the riskier nature of equity.

European Union (EU)   The free trade area and (limited) political union among a group of European countries. In 2001 the countries of the European Union were: Austria, Belgium, Denmark, Finland, France, Germany, Greece, Ireland, Italy, Luxembourg, Netherlands, Portugal, Spain, Sweden, and the United Kingdom.

Ex ante real interest rate   The nominal interest rate less expected inflation over a specific time horizon. Contrast this with the *ex post* real interest rate, which is the interest rate minus actual inflation.

Ex post real interest rate   The interest rate minus actual, as opposed to expected, inflation.

Exchange rate   The rate at which one currency exchanges for another on the foreign exchange market.

Exogenous variable   A variable that is not determined within a model but is taken as a given. (Opposite of endogenous variable.)

Expansionary policy Government policy that raises aggregate demand and increases employment and incomes.

Exports Goods and services sold to other countries.

Externality When the behavior of an agent affects the return of others in a way that is not reflected in market prices.

Factor intensity Extent to which a country or industry uses a particular factor of production.

Factor of production A resource used as an input into the productive process, e.g., capital or labor.

Factor price The price of one unit of a factor of production.

Factor price equalization Process whereby the return paid to factors of production for producing output are equalized across countries.

Factor share The share of total output (or income) going to a factor of production.

Federal Reserve (the Fed) The central bank of the United States.

Fiat money Money that is not valuable in itself and that would have no use were it to become unacceptable in exchange.

Financial intermediation The channelling of funds from savers to ultimate users of funds via financial institutions (e.g., banks, pension funds, mutual funds, unit trusts, insurance companies).

Fiscal policy Government policy relating to levels of spending and taxation.

Fisher effect The one-for-one link between the nominal interest rate and expected inflation.

Fisher equation The relation that makes the nominal interest rate the sum of the real interest rate and expected inflation.

Fixed exchange rate A rate of exchange for currencies determined by the central bank rather than fluctuating day by day to clear the foreign exchange market.

Flexible prices Prices that move rapidly when supply or demand conditions alter to keep the market in equilibrium.

Floating exchange rate A rate of exchange for currencies moving day by day to balance private sector flows of money across the foreign exchange market.

Flow A variable that is measured per unit of time and that only exists during that time period.

Foreign direct investment (FDI) Purchase of a substantial ownership in, or construction of, a factory/operation in a country by an overseas agent.

Foreign exchange reserves Holdings of foreign currency by a central bank.

Forward rate Price paid today for delivery of a currency at some future point.

Frisch-Slutsky paradigm View of business cycles as being triggered by random shocks that are propagated through mechanisms to influence the economy over time to create business cycles.

Fundamentals The real forces of supply and demand that determine the evolution of output, asset prices, and other real economic variables

G7 Seven largest industrial nations (in order): United States, Japan, Germany, France, United Kingdom, Italy, and Canada.

GDP *See* gross domestic product.

GDP deflator The ratio of nominal (or current price) GDP to real (or constant price) GDP; as a ratio of current to constant prices the deflator is a measure of the prices in one year relative to a base year.

General Agreement on Trades and Tariffs (GATT) Precursor to the World Trade Organization which arranged a sequence of trade negotiations leading to lower tariffs

GNP *See* Gross national product.

Gold standard A system in which gold is used in exchange either directly or indirectly (because currencies can be converted to gold).

Golden Rule Investment criteria that maximizes consumption in the steady state.

Government purchases Goods and services bought by the government. Government spending can include government purchases and transfer payments (e.g., social security spending).

Gross domestic product (GDP) The total value of output produced in a country without any adjustment for depreciation of capital. GDP also equals the sum of income earned domestically by both nationals and foreign citizens working in the country.

Gross domestic fixed capital formation (GDFCF) Total amount of output used within a period to augment the capital stock *including* repairs and maintenance.

Gross national product (GNP) The total output (or income) of all residents of a nation wherever they produce or earn income. It includes income from abroad paid to national citizens owning factors used overseas.

Growth accounting Attempt to attribute observed growth in GDP to increases in various factors of production.

Hecksher-Ohlin model Prediction that countries export goods and services that require the intensive use of a factor of production that the country possesses in abundance.

Human capital Skills and knowledge possessed by individuals.

Hyperinflation Explosively high inflation.

Idiosyncratic risk Uncertainty or income variability that is specific to an individual.

Imports Goods and services bought from other countries.

Imputed value The value of the services provided by ownership of an asset but not actually received as income in a market exchange.

Income effect The change in demand or supply for a good when income is different but the price of the good is held constant.

Indifference curves Sets of points that show combinations of goods that yield the same level of enjoyment or welfare.

Inflation An increase in the overall level of prices. (Opposite of deflation.)

Inflation tax Revenue raised by a government through printing money (equals inflation multiplied by stock of non-interest-bearing money).

Infrastructure Part of the capital stock that is basic to the operation of an economy, e.g., roads, railways, etc.

Interest rate The return from lending money or the cost of borrowing money; the price of moving spending from one period to another.

Intermediate target Variable that a government tries to control/influence not because it is of direct policy interest but because it is closely linked with a variable that is.

Intermediation Process whereby financial markets and institutions pass the funds provided by savers to those who wish to invest.

International Monetary Fund (IMF) The IMF, founded in 1946, is an international organization of 183 member countries, established to promote international monetary cooperation, exchange stability, and orderly exchange arrangements; to foster economic growth and high levels of employment; and to provide temporary financial assistance to countries to help ease balance of payments adjustment.

Intertemporal budget constraint   The constraint that makes the total values of all outgoings over time equal to the total value of all receipts where both outflows and inflows are expressed in current values.

Inventory investment   The change in the stocks of finished and intermediate goods held by companies.

Investment   Goods purchased by individuals, companies, or governments that increase their stock of physical or financial capital.

Invisible hand   Adam Smith's result that individuals pursuing their own self-interest will be guided by market prices to an outcome that is efficient for society.

Keynesian policies   Use of fiscal and monetary policy to boost demand in a recession and reduce demand in an expansion.

Labor force   Those in the population who either work or are seeking work.

Labor-force participation rate   The proportion of the adult population in the labor force.

Labor productivity   Output divided by employment (either persons or hours worked).

Labor supply curve   Relationship between wages and hours of work supplied.

Laffer curve   Relationship between tax rates and tax revenue in which revenue is maximized at tax rates below 100%.

Laissez-faire   The free operation of markets without government intervention.

Law of one price   Notion that identical goods will sell for identical prices.

Leverage   Amount of borrowing (normally expressed as a proportion of income or of revenue or of total assets).

Life-cycle hypothesis   A theory of consumption in which individuals plan a path of consumption over their lives that is smooth and that balances the present value of spending against the sum of current wealth and the future values of earnings.

Liquid   Easily converted into a form that allows transactions to be completed.

Long-run supply curve   The long-run link between output that is produced in an economy and the level of prices. Because sustained variations in capital, labor input, and technology are unlikely to be driven by changes in nominal magnitudes, the long-run supply curve is vertical.

M1, M2, M3   Different measures of the aggregate stock of money in the economy. Higher numbers encompass wider definitions of what counts as money and are therefore larger in value.

Marginal produce of capital (MPK)   The extra output produced when the amount of capital used in production is increased by one unit holding fixed the labor force and technology.

Marginal product of labor (MPL)   The extra output produced when the amount of labor used in production is increased by one unit holding fixed the capital stock and technology.

Marginal propensity to consume (MPC)   The increase in consumption following a rise in income.

Market failure   Situations in which the free operations of market forces will not produce an efficient (or optimal) outcome.

Mean reversion   Process whereby a variable eventually returns to its long-run average.

Medium of exchange   That which is accepted as a means of paying for goods; one of the roles of money.

Menu costs   The resources used in changing prices.

Modigliani-Miller theorem   Prediction that the financial structure of an institution's liabilities does not influence its value, i.e., a firm's overall value does not depend on whether it is financed by bonds or equity.

Monetarism   The theory that inflation results from changes in the money supply and that control of the money supply is a necessary and sufficient means to control inflation.

Monetary policy   The central bank's decisions on the terms at which it will lend money and buy securities.

Monetary transmission mechanism   The mechanisms by which changes in monetary policy affect the economy.

Money   The stock of assets used for transactions.

Money illusion   When individuals confuse nominal and relative prices.

Money multiplier   The eventual increase in a measure of the money supply resulting from an increase in central bank (high powered) money.

Monopoly power   Ability of an agent or firm to set market prices.

Moral hazard   The tendency of people to shirk or not try hard when their behavior is not monitored perfectly and when effort is costly.

Nash equilibrium   A situation in which each agent is following an optimal strategy given the actions of other agents.

National income accounting   The system used for measuring overall output and its constituent parts.

National income accounts identity   Output can be used for either consumption, government expenditure, investment or net exports ($Y = C + I + G + X - M$).

National saving   A nation's income minus private and public consumption.

Natural rate of unemployment   The rate of unemployment at which inflation can be steady and to which the economy will move so that inflation is neither rising nor falling.

Net exports   Exports minus imports.

Net foreign investment   The net flow of funds being invested overseas which equals domestic saving minus domestic investment.

Net investment   Total investment expenditure less depreciation of the existing stock of capital.

Neutrality   Result that nominal variables (money supply, prices, etc.) cannot influence real variables (output, unemployment, etc.).

Nominal   Measured in current prices.

Nominal exchange rate   The terms of exchange between a unit of one currency and a unit of another.

Nominal interest rate   Interest rate paid/received without making allowance for the fact that the price of goods is changing.

OPEC (Organization of Oil Producing and Exporting Countries)   A group of major oil-producing countries who meet to discuss, and try to control, oil output and prices.

Open economy   An economy in which people can freely engage in international trade in goods and capital.

Open-market operations   Purchase or sale of assets by the central bank in order to increase or decrease the money supply.

Opportunity cost   Activities or revenue foregone through pursuing an activity.

Optimal currency area Region over which it is optimal to have just one currency.

Organization for Economic Cooperation and Development (OECD) The OECD is a group of 30 member countries (Australia, Austria, Belgium, Canada, Czech Republic, Denmark, Finland, France, Germany, Greece, Hungary, Iceland, Ireland, Italy, Japan, Korea, Luxembourg, Mexico, Netherlands, New Zealand, Norway, Poland, Portugal, Slovak Republic, Spain, Sweden, Switzerland, Turkey, United Kingdom, United States) in an organization that provides governments a setting in which to discuss and develop economic and social policy.

Output gap Difference between GDP and its trend level.

Pareto efficiency Situation in which it is impossible to make anyone better off without making someone worse off.

Participation rate Proportion of the population (sometimes noninstitutional population) who wish to have a job.

Per capita Amount per person.

Perfect competition Situation in which each agent/firm is small compared to the marketplace and has to accept prices as beyond its control.

Permanent income The level of income that someone can reasonably expect to be sustained into the future.

Permanent-income hypothesis The theory that consumption is proportional to the anticipated value of future average labor income (plus a share of current wealth) as opposed to the idea that current income is the prime determinant of spending.

Phillips curve The relationship between unemployment and inflation, claimed by A.W. Phillips to be negative.

Physical capital Stock of machines and buildings.

Poverty trap Situation in which a country cannot grow because it is so poor.

Precautionary saving Saving that reflects the impact of uncertainty about the future and is done as a form of insurance.

Present value The amount today that has the same value as an amount to be paid or received in the future having adjusted for the interest that could be earned (or must be paid) in the intervening period.

Price index Measure of the price of a basket of goods.

Primary balance Government tax revenue less expenditure *excluding* interest payments.

Private saving Disposable income less private consumption expenditure.

Procyclical Tending to move in a similar direction to aggregate output and employment. (Opposite of countercyclical.)

Production function The form of the relation between inputs to the production process and outputs.

Productivity *See* labor productivity.

Profits Firm's revenue less costs.

Public good Commodity that it is impossible to exclude individuals from consuming.

Public saving Government receipts less spending on consumption and transfers.

Purchasing-power parity (PPP) The theory that exchange rates will move so that the price of goods that are tradable are the same in all countries.

Q theory of investment The theory that investment depends upon the ratio of the stock market value of a firm's assets to the cost of buying those assets.

Quantity equation $MV = PY$ where M is the money supply, V the velocity of circulation, P prices, and Y output.

Quantity theory of money Theory that assumes that the velocity of money is predictable and that money is neutral for output so that increases in the money supply lead directly to inflation.

Random walk An unpredictable path where at each point upward and downward movements are equally likely.

Rate of return Income and capital gains on an asset expressed as a percentage of its price.

Rational expectations A situation in which forecast errors are unpredictable and agents' expectations, on average, equal outturns.

Real Measured in constant prices having allowed for inflation.

Real-Business-Cycle theory Theory that variations in total factor productivity cause business cycle fluctuations.

Real exchange rate The rate at which one country's goods exchange for another country's goods.

Real interest rate The cost of borrowing (or the return to saving) in real terms, i.e., after adjusting for inflation.

Real money balances The amount of money measured in terms of the quantity of goods it could buy; the nominal stock of money relative to an index of prices.

Real wages Wages divided by prices.

Recession A period of falling aggregate output in the economy. Often used to refer to the situation in which output declines for two or more consecutive quarters.

Rental price of capital *See* user cost of capital.

Replacement rate Benefits (especially pensions or unemployment benefits) expressed as a percentage of average or previous earnings.

Research and development (R & D) Resources spent on fostering invention or innovation.

Reserve requirement Rules governing minimum levels of reserves to be held with the central bank.

Residential investment Investment in new houses.

Ricardian equivalence Prediction that fiscal deficits or surpluses do not influence GDP.

Risk aversion When consumers prefer risk-free assets even if the return on riskier assets is higher.

Risk premium Additional return required by investors if they are to invest in riskier assets.

Sacrifice ratio The amount (percentage) of lost output per year to reduce inflation by a full percentage.

Saving *See* national saving, private saving, and public saving.

Saving rate Savings expressed as a percentage of income or output.

Seasonal fluctuations Fluctuations in economic variables that repeat themselves but that complete their cycle within a year.

Seigniorage Revenue raised by a central bank through printing money due to the difference between the face value of money and the costs of production.

Shock An exogenous and unpredictable change in an economic variable that generates changes in endogenous variables.

Shoeleather cost The cost of inflation from people holding fewer real money balances and having to incur more costs in financing transactions.

Small open economy An open economy that is small enough that its actions do not influence interest rates or other prices set in global markets.

Solow growth model Model of growth based around capital accumulation and diminishing marginal product of capital that culminates in a country reaching its steady state.

Solow residual The growth in total factor productivity, i.e., that part of a rise in output not explained by the increase in factor inputs.

Spillovers Events or actions in one industry or market that affect other industries as well.

Stabilization policy Government policy aimed at keeping output and employment on steady trend paths.

Stagflation A situation of falling output and high inflation.

Steady state A situation in which key variables are not changing. In the Solow growth model this is where gross investment equals depreciation.

Sticky prices Prices that are slow to adjust when demand or supply conditions change.

Stock The outstanding amount of a variable at a point in time. Also used to denote a share issued by a firm and traded in the stock market.

Stock market The market in which corporate stocks (or equities) are bought and sold.

Stolper-Samuelson effect Result showing that a factor of production that is in relatively scarce supply sees a fall in its real income as a result of more trade.

Substitution effect The change in demand or supply for a good due to a change in the relative price holding income constant.

Tariff A tax on imported goods.

Tax wedge Gap between the price paid by consumers and received by producers because of taxes.

Taylor rule Relationship among interest rates, the output gap and inflation.

Technical progress Improvements in knowledge that enable more output to be produced from given inputs.

Terms of trade Price of a country's exports divided by the price of its imports.

Time inconsistency Problem in which future plans are only optimal when announced but not when they have to be implemented.

Tobin's q The ratio of the market value of a company's existing capital to its replacement cost.

Total factor productivity Efficiency with which factors of production are utilized. Reflects a huge range of influences, both economic and sociocultural.

Transactions costs Costs incurred in trading assets or goods and services. Includes taxes and brokers charges as well as transport costs, where relevant.

Transfer payments Payments from the government to people that are not in payment for goods and services, e.g., unemployment benefits; old-age pensions.

Transitory income A current shock to income that people do not expect to persist into the future.

Uncovered interest parity Prediction that the interest rate differential between countries will be exactly offset by future depreciation.

Underground economy Economic activity not reported in official statistics which reflects the aim to avoid taxation.

Unemployment rate The percentage of those in the labor force who are not working.

Unit of account Unit used to measure the value of economic activity.

User cost of capital Cost of using a unit of capital during a period of time, including rental and depreciation charges and any capital gains.

Value added The value of a firm's output minus the value of the intermediate goods the firm purchased.

Velocity of circulation The ratio of aggregate nominal spending to the money supply which reflects the average rate at which money changes hands.

Wage The amount paid for one unit of labor.

Wealth Assets less liabilities

Wealth effect Influence of changes in the value of wealth on consumption and investment decisions.

World Bank The World Bank uses its financial resources and staff to help developing countries achieve long-run sustainable growth and alleviate poverty.

World Trade Organization (WTO) The WTO deals with the rules of trade between nations. At its heart are the WTO agreements, negotiated and signed by the bulk of the world's trading nations and ratified in their parliaments.

Yield Discount rate that makes current bond price equal to the net present value of the future income stream generated by the bond.

Yield curve Relationship showing how yields on bonds vary with the maturity of bonds.

"Sources of Economic Growth," *Carnegie Rochester Conference Series on Public Policy*, 1994. Reprinted with permission from Elsevier Science. *Table 7.6:* Easterly and Levine, "Africa's Growth Tragedy: Policies and Ethnic Divisions" (November 1997), vol. 112, pp. 1203–1250. Yale University Press. *Tables 7.7* and *7.8:* Bloom and Sachs, "Geography, Demography, and Economic Growth in Africa," presented at the Brookings Panel on Economic Activity, September 1998. *Table 7.9: World Economic Outlook*, May 2000. Courtesy of IMF.

Chapter 8   *Figs. 8.1, 8.3, 8.14, 8.15, 8.19, 8.20, 8.21* and *Tables 8.1, 8.2, 8.5: Employment Outlook* (June 1999). Copyright OECD.   *Fig. 8.2:* U.S. Bureau of Labor Statistics, April 2000.   *Table 8.3:* OECD Fiscal Dataset.   *Fig. 8.12: Jobs Study: Evidence and Explanations* (1994). Copyright OECD.   *Figs. 8.13, 8.16, 8.17: Assessing Performance and Policy* (1999). Copyright OECD.   *Table 8.4:* Clamfors and Driffill, "Centralization of Wage Bargaining and Macroeconomic Performance," *Economic Policy* (1988), vol. 6, pp. 15–61. Blackwell Publishers.   *Table 8.6:* Nickell and Van Ours, "The Netherlands and the UK: European Unemployment Miracle," *Economic Policy* (2000), vol. 30, pp. 135–180. Blackwell Publishers.   *Table 8.7:* Dang, Fore, "Index of Income Distribution and Poverty in Selected OECD Countries," OECD Working Paper 189 (March 1998).   *Figs. 8.22, 8.23* and *Table 8.9:* Autor, Katz, Krueger, "Computing Inequality: Have Computers Changed the Labor Market?" NBER Working Paper 5956 (March 1997). *Table 8.8:* Nickell and Layard, "Labor Market Institutions and Economic Performance," in *Handbook of Labor Economics, Vol. 3*, 1999. Reprinted with permission from Elsevier Science.

Chapter 9   *Fig. 9.1:* Taken from material contained in *Southeast Asian Exports since the 14th Century: Cloves, Pepper, Coffee and Sugar* compiled by David Bulbeck, Anthony Reid, Lay Cheng Tan, and Yiqi Wu. Reproduced here with the kind permission of the publisher, Institute of Southeast Asian Studies, Singapore, *www.iseas.edu.sg/pub.html*.   *Fig. 9.2:* Harley, C. Knick, "Ocean Freight Rates and Productivity, 1740–1913: The Primacy of Mechanical Invention Reaffirmed," *Journal of Economic History*, vol. 48 (1988): 851–876. Reprinted with the permission of Cambridge University Press.   *Figs. 9.3, 9.4: Monitoring the World Economy, 1820–1992* (1995). Copyright OECD. Updated using WTO Annual Report (2000).   *Table 9.1:* Maddison, *Dynamic Forces in Capitalistic Development: A Long run Comparative View*, 1991. By permission of Oxford University Press.   *Fig. 9.5: The Economist*, July 20, 1991. © The Economist Newspaper Limited, London (1991).   *Fig. 9.6* and *Table 9.10:* Yarbrough and Yarbrough, *The World Economy* (1997). The Dryden Press.   *Figs. 9.7, 9.8* and *Table 9.2:* WTO Annual Report (1999 and 2000).   *Fig. 9.11:* G.D.A. MacDougall, "British and American Exports," *The Economic Journal*, 1951, 61, 703–707.   *Figs. 9.12, 9.13, 9.14: International Financial Statistics*, CD-ROM, December 2000, Courtesy of the IMF.   *Table 9.4:* Sachs and Shatz, "Trade and Jobs in US Manufacturing," *Brookings Papers on Economic Activity*, I: 1994.   *Fig. 9.15:* U.S. Bureau of Economic Analysis (*www.bea.doc.gov*).   *Table 9.5:* Reprinted with permission from *The Uruguay Round—An Assessment*. Jeffrey J. Schott, assisted by Johanna W. Buurmann. © 1994 by the Institute for International Economics. *Table 9.6:* Bowen, Leamer, Svelkauskas, "Multicountry, Multifactor Test of the Factor Abundance Theory," *American Economic Review* (1987), 77, 791–809.   *Fig. 9.16:* Grimiracle, *International Trade: New Patterns of Trade, Production, and Investment*, 1989. Reprinted with permission of Routeledge.   *Fig. 9.17:* U.S. Bureau of Labor Statistics (*www.bls.gov/flshome.htm*).   *Fig. 9.18:* Trefler, "International Factor Price Differences: Leontief Was Right!" *Journal of Political Economy* (1993), vol. 101, pp. 961–987.

Chapter 10   *Figs. 10.1, 10.2, 10.3: Economic Outlook* (2000). Copyright OECD.   *Table 10.1:* Tanzi and Schuknecht, "The Growth of Government and the Reform of the State in Industrial Countries," IMF Working Paper (1995); updated with OECD data for 1998.   *Fig. 10.4 a–h: IMF Government Finance Statistics Yearbooks 1995, 1996, 1997*. Courtesy of IMF.   *Table 10.3:* Robert B. Barsky, F. Thomas Juster, Miles S. Kimball, and Matthew D. Shapiro, "Preference Parameters and Behavioral Heterogeneity: An Experimental Approach to the Health and Retire Survey," *Quarterly Journal of Economics* (May 1997), 112: 537–579. © 1997 by the President and Fellows of Harvard College and the Massachusetts Institute of Technology.   *Figs. 10.9, 10.10: The Tax/Benefit Position of Employees—1997*. Copyright 1998 OECD.   *Fig. 10.11: OECD Historical Statistics, 1999*. Copyright OECD.   *Table 10.4:* Kopits, "Are Europe's Social Security Finances Compatible with EMU?" IMF Fiscal Affairs Department Working Paper (IMF, 1997); Chang and Jaeger, "Aging Populations and Public Pension Schemes," IMF Occasional Paper no. 147 (IMF, 1996); Leibfritz, Fore, and Wurzel, "Ageing Populations, Pension Systems and Government Budget Simulations for 20 OECD Countries," Economics Department Working Paper no. 168 (OECD, 1996).   *Fig. 10.12:* United Nations Population Projections.   *Fig. 10.13:* Roseveare, Leibfritz, Fore, and Wurzel, "Ageing Populations, Pension Systems and Government Budget Simulations for 20 OECD Countries," Economics Department Working Paper no. 168 (OECD, 1996).

Chapter 11   *Fig. 11.1:* Elmdorf and Mankiw, "Government Debt," in J. Taylor and M. Woodford (eds.) *The Handbook of Macroeconomics*, Vol. 1, p. 1618. Reprinted by permission from Elsevier Science.   *Fig. 11.2* and *Tables 11.1, 11.2: OECD Economic Outlook* (various issues). Copyright OECD.   *Fig. 11.3: OECD Economic Outlook* (CD-ROM). Copyright OECD.   *Figs. 11.4, 11.5, 11.6:* Kotikoff and Leibfritz, "An International Comparison of Generational Accounts," NBER Working Paper W6447 (March 1998).   *Figs. 11.8, 11.9:* Alesina and Perotti, "The Political Economy of Budget Deficits," IMF Staff Paper (March 1995) Vol. 42, pp. 1–31. Courtesy of IMF.

Chapter 12   *Figs. 12.1, 12.2, 12.12:* B. R. Mitchell, *British Historical Statistics*, 1988 (data from Chapters 12 and 17). © 1998 Cambridge University Press. Updated using Office of National Statistics data.   *Fig. 12.3: www.nber.org/macrohistory/m04NNN.db*.   *Figs. 12.4, 12.5, 12.6, 12.7, 12.10, 12.13, 12.14* and *Tables 12.7, 12.8: IMF International Financial Statistics* (various issues). Courtesy of IMF.   *Fig. 12.8* and *Tables 12.1, 12.2, 12.3:* Shiller, "Why Do People Dislike Inflation?" in Romer & Romer (eds), *Reducing Inflation: Motivation and Strategy*. University of Chicago Press, 1997.   *Fig. 12.9:* Barro, "Inflation and Economic Growth," NBER Discussion Paper 5326 (1995).   *Table 12.4: www.federalreserve.gov/rnd.htm*.   *Table 12.5: www.ecb.int*.   *Fig. 12.11:* Authors' calculations and T. Sargent, *Rational Expectations* (tables 3.3, 3.10, 3.15, and 3.18). © 1985, 1993 by Addison Wesley Longman, Inc. Reprinted by permission of Addison Wesley Longman.

Chapter 13 *Table 13.1:* U.S. Bureau of Labor Statistics (http://www.bls.gov/csxhome.htm). *Figs. 13.1* and *13.2:* U.S. Bureau of Economic Analysis (http://www.bea.doc.gov/). *Table 13.2* and *Fig. 13.3 a & b: IMF International Financial Statistics* (2000). Courtesy of IMF. *Figs. 13.4, 13.5, 13.13: OECD Economic Outlook* (various issues). Copyright OECD. *Fig. 13.16:* Peach and Steindal, "A Nation of Spendthrifts?" *Current Issues in Economic and Finance* (September 2000), vol. 6, no. 10, pp. 1–30. *Fig. 13.17* and *Tables 13.3, 13.4: Consumer Expenditure Survey,* U.S. Bureau of Labor Statistics (*http://www.bls.gov/csxhome.htm*).

Chapter 14 *Figs. 14.1, 14.2, 14.7:* Summers and Heston dataset, Penn World Tables 5.5, *http://www.nber.org.* *Figs. 14.3, 14.4, 14.5, 14.6 a & b, 14.8, 14.9, 14.10 a–c: OECD Economic Outlook* (various issues). Copyright OECD. *Table 14.1:* Corbett and Jenkinson, "How Is Investment Financed? *The Manchester School* (1996), vol. LXV, pp. 69–94. *Fig. 14.15:* Thomson Financial Datastream. *Table 14.5:* Rajan and Zingales, "What Do We Know about Capital Structure: Some Evidence from International Data," *Journal of Finance* (1995), vol. 50, pp. 1421–1460. Reprinted by permission of Blackwell Publishers. *Fig. 14.16:* Cooper, Haltiwanger, and Power, "Machine Replacement and the Business Cycle: Lumps and Bumps," *American Economic Review* (September 1999), vol. 89, no. 4, pp. 921–946. Reprinted with the permission of the American Economic Association. *Figs. 14.17* and *14.18:* Philip Lane and Gian Maria Milesi-Ferretti, "The External Wealth of Nations," IMF Working Paper WP/95/115 (August 1999). Courtesy of the IMF. *Fig. 14.19 a–c:* OECD Calculations (Gordon and Tchilinguirian, "Marginal Effective Tax Rates on Physical, Human, and R&D Capital," OECD Discussion Paper 199 (1999). Copyright OECD.

Chapter 15 *Figs. 15.1, 15.2, 15.8, 15.9: OECD Economic Outlook* (various issues). Copyright OECD. *Table 15.1: Monitoring the World Economy, 1820–1992* (1995). Copyright OECD. *Fig. 15.3a:* Basu and Taylor, "Business Cycles in International Historical Perspectives," *Journal of Economic Perspectives* (1999), pp. 45–48. Reprinted by permission of the American Economics Association. *Figs. 15.3b, 15.6, 15.7, 15.27* and *Table 15.7: IMF International Financial Statistics* (September 2000). Courtesy of the IMF. *Figs. 15.4* and *15.5:* Artis, Kontolemis and Osborn, "Classical Business Cycles for G7 and European Countries," CEPR Discussion Paper No. 1137, 1995. *Fig. 15.10: Economic Trends,* UK Office for National Statistics, various issues. *Table 15.2:* Authors' calculations from data from U.S. Bureau of Economic Analysis, *www.bea.doc.gov.* *Table 15.3* and *Fig. 15.12:* Authors' calculations from datasets used in Basu and Taylor, "Business Cycles in International Historical Perspectives," *Journal of Economic Perspectives* (1999), pp. 45–48; and updated from IMF *International Financial Statistics* (September 2000). *Table 15.4:* Romer, "The Cyclical Behavior of Industrial Production Series 1889–1984, *Quarterly Journal of Economics* (February 1991), pp. 1–31. *Figs. 15.14, 15.15* and *Table 15.6:* Clark, Leslie, and Symons, "The Cost of Recessions," *Economic Journal,* 1994, vol. 104, pp. 10–37. Reprinted with permission from Blackwell Publishers. *Fig. 15.16:* Summers and Heston dataset, *http://cansim.chass.utoronto.ca:5680/pwt/.* *Figs. 15.22, 15.23, 15.24:* Hall, Walsh, and Yates, "How Do UK Companies Set Prices?" Bank of England Working Paper 67 (1997). Reprinted with permission of the Bank of England. *Table 15.8:* Canova and Nicolo, "On the Sources of Business Cycles in the G7," Uriversitat Pompeu Fabra mimeo (2000).

Chapter 16 *Fig. 16.1 a & b: IMF World Economic Outlook* (October 2000). Courtesy of IMF. *Figs. 16.5, 16.8:* Haldane and Quah, "The UK Philips Curve and Monetary Policy," *Journal of Monetary Economics,* vol. 44, 1999, pp. 259–278. Reprinted with permission of Elsevier Science. *Fig. 16.7 a–c: OECD Economic Outlook* (June 2000). Copyright OECD. *Fig. 16.11:* Ball, "What Determines the Sacrifice Ratio?" in *Monetary Policy,* G. Mankiw (ed.). University of Chicago Press, 1994, pp. 240–281. *Fig. 16.13:* "Central Bank Independence and Macroeconomic Performance: Some Comparative Evidence," by Alberto Alesina and Lawrence H. Summers, *Journal of Money, Credit, and Banking,* Volume 25, Number 2 (May 1993). Reprinted by permission. Copyright 1993 by Ohio State University Press. All rights reserved.

Chapter 17 *Figs. 17.1, 17.2, 17.5 a & b:* Mervyn King, "Challenges for Monetary Policy, New and Old," paper presented at New Challenges for Monetary Policy conference at Jackson Hole, Wyoming, 1999. *Fig. 17.4: OECD Economic Outlook* (June 2000). Copyright OECD. *Fig. 17.6:* Sterne, "The Use of Explicit Targets for Monetary Policy: Practical Experience of 91 Countries," *Bank of England Quarterly Bulletin* (August 1999), vol. 39, no. 3. Reprinted with permission from the Bank of England. *Fig. 17.7:* U.S. Federal Reserve Board (http://www.federalreserve.gov/releases/H6). *Fig. 17.8:* Authors' calculations using Bank of England data. *Fig. 17.13: The Transmission Mechanism of Monetary Policy.* Monetary Policy Committee, Bank of England. Reprinted with permission from the Bank of England. *Fig. 17.14:* Lawrence J. Christiano, Martin Eichenbaum, and Charles Evans, "The Effects of Monetary Policy Shocks: Evidence from the Flow of Funds," *The Review of Economics and Statistics,* 78:1 (February, 1996), pp. 16–34. © by the President and Fellows of Harvard College and the Massachusetts Institute of Technology. *Fig. 17.15:* I. Mihov, "Monetary Policy Implementation and Transmission in the European Monetary Union," INSEAD mimeo (2000).

Chapter 18 *Figs. 18.1, 18.2, 18.6 a–d, 18.8, 18.12, 18.16, 18.17* and *Table 18.3: IMF International Financial Statistics* (various issues). Courtesy of IMF. *Table 18.1:* Associated Press, December 18, 2000. Reprinted with permission of The Associated Press. *Figs. 18.3* and *18.4:* Ravn and Mazzenga, "Frictions in International Trade and Relative Price Movements," London Business School Working Paper (1999). *Fig. 18.5:* Engel and Rogers, "How Wide Is the Border?" *American Economic Review* (1996), vol. 86, pp. 1112–1125. Reprinted with permission from American Economic Association. *Table 18.2:* Reprinted with permission from *The Uruguay Round—An Assessment.* Jeffrey J. Schott, assisted by Johanna W. Buurmann. © 1994 by the Institute for International Economics. *Table 18.3:* Reprinted from *Journal of International Economics,* vol. 51, no. 1. Engel and Rogers, "Deviations from Purchasing Power Parity: Causes and Welfare Costs." Copyright 2001, with permission from Elsevier Science. *Fig. 18.7 a & b:* Lothian and Taylor, "Real Exchange Rate Behavior, *Journal of Political Economy,* vol. 104, pp. 488–509. The University of Chicago Press. *Table 18.4: The Economist,* April 27, 2000 © The Economist Newspaper Limited, London (1991). *Fig. 18.9:* Summers and Heston dataset, *http://cansim.chass.utoronto.ca:5680/pwt/.* *Fig. 18.10:* Authors' calculations from OECD data. *Fig. 18.11* and *Table 18.6:* Lane and Milessi-Ferretti, "The External Wealth of Nations," CPER Discussion Paper no. 2231, 1999.

Chapter 19 *Figs. 19.1, 19.2* and *Tables 19.1, 19.2:* Bank for International Settlements, *Central Bank Survey of Foreign Exchange and Derivatives Market Activity in April 1998* (October 1998). *Figs. 19.3, 19.4, 19.16, 19.21 a–d* and *Tables 19.6, 19.7: IMF International Financial Statistics* (various issues). Courtesy of IMF. *Fig. 19.12:* U.S. Federal Reserve Board website (*http://www.federalreserve.gov/release*). *Table 19.3:* Isard, *Exchange Rate Economics*, Cambridge University Press, 1995. Reprinted by permission of Cambridge University Press. *Fig. 19.14* and *Tables 19.4, 19.5:* Cheung, Chinn, and Marsh, "How Do UK-based Foreign Exchange Dealers Think Their Market Operates?" NBER Working Paper 7524. *Fig. 19.15:* Evans & Lyons, "Order Flow & Exchange Rate Dynamics," *Journal of Political Economy* (forthcoming from the University of Chicago Press). *Figs. 19.17* and *19.18:* Glick and Rose, "Contagious Trade: Why Are Currency Crises Regional?" *Journal of International Money and Finance*, 1999. Reprinted with permission from Elsevier Science. *Fig. 19.22: National Account, Vol. II.* Copyright OECD. *Fig. 19.23:* Radelet and Sachs, "The East Asian Financial Crisis: Diagnosis, Remedies, Prospects," *Brookings Papers on Economic Activities*, I: 1998. (http://www.hiid.harvard.edu/pub/other/asiacrisis.html)

Chapter 20 *Fig. 20.1* and *Tables 20.1, 20.2:* IMF *Exchange Rate Regimes in an Increasingly Integrated World Economy* (April 2000). Courtesy of IMF. *Fig. 20.2:* Ghosh, Gulde, and Wolf, "Currency Boards: The Ultimate Fix?" IMF Working Paper 89/8 (1998). Courtesy of IMF. *Fig. 20.3: International Trade By Commodity Statistic* (2000), Copyright OECD. *Figs. 20.4, 20.14, 20.16: IMF International Financial Statistics* (September 2000). Courtesy of IMF. *Fig. 20.5:* I. Mihov, "Monetary Policy Implementation and Transmission in the European Monetary Union," INSEAD mimeo (2000). *Fig. 20.6:* Anthony and Hughes Hallett, "Should Argentina Adopt the US Dollar?" CEPR Discussion Paper No. 2412. *Figs. 20.7, 20.8, 20.9: IMF International Capital Markets* (2000). Courtesy of IMF. *Figs. 20.10, 20.11:* Obstfeld, "The Global Capital Market: Benefactor or Menance?" *Journal of Economic Perspectives* (1999), pp. 1–30. Reprinted with permission from American Economic Association. *Fig. 20.12:* Breedon, Henry and Williams, "Long Term Real Interest Rates," *Oxford Review of Economic Policy*, 1999, vol. 15, no. 2, pp. 128–142. Reproduced with the permission of Oxford University Press. *Fig. 20.13:* Authors' calculations from OECD, *Economic Outlook* (June 2000). *Fig. 20.15:* van Wincoop, "International versus International Saving Investment Comovements," Federal Reserve Bank of New York mimeo (1999). *Table 20.3:* Ravn, "Consumption Risk Sharing," London Business School mimeo (1999). *Table 20.4:* French and Poterba, "Investor Diversification and International Equity Markets," *American Economic Review Papers and Proceedings*, May 1991, vol. 81, pp. 222–226. *Fig. 20.17:* InterSec Research Corp., London. *Table 20.6:* Geert Bekaert and Campbell R. Harvey, "Capital Flows and the Behavior of Emerging Market Equity Returns," NBER Working Paper No. W6669, July 1998. *Table 20.7:* de Gregorio, Edwards, and Valdes, Controls on Capital Inflows: Do They Work?" *Journal of Development Economics*, vol. 63, no. 1, 2000, pp. 59–83. Reprinted with permission from Elsevier Science.

Chapter 21 *Fig. 21.1: OECD Economic Outlook 2000.* Copyright OECD. *Table 21.1:* © Global Financial Data at *btaylor@globalfinddata.com*. *Figs. 21.2, 21.3, 21.4, 21.11:* Thomson Financial Datastream. *Figs. 21.5, 21.12, 21.13, 21.15* and *Table 21.2:* Robert Shiller data in *Market Volatility* (MIT Press, 1989). *Fig. 21.6:* collected by InterSec Research Corp., London. *Fig. 21.7:* J. Siegel, *Stocks for the Long Run* (1994, McGraw-Hill). Reprinted with permission of The McGraw-Hill Companies. *Fig. 21.14* and *Table 21.3:* Jorion and Goetzmann, "Global Stock Markets in the 20th Century," *Journal of Finance*, vol. 54 (1999). Copyright American Finance Association. Reprinted with permission of Blackwell Publishers.

Chapter 22 *Table 22.1:* Compiled by Karim Basta and published by Merrill Lynch in "The Size and Structure of World Bond Markets," April 2000. *Fig. 22.1* and *22.11:* InterSec Research Corp., London. *Figs. 22.5, 22.12* and *Table 22.10:* Thomson Financial Datastream. *Tables 22.3, 22.4, 22.5, 22.6, 22.7, 22.11* and *Fig. 22.6: Financial Times* (26 March 1999). *Figs. 22.7* and *22.8:* Jourion and Miskin, "A Multicountry Comparison of Term Structure Forecasts at Long Horizons," *Journal of Financial Economics* (1991), vol. 29, no. 1, pp. 59–80. Reprinted with permission from Elsevier Science. *Table 22.8: OECD Economic Outlook 2001.* Copyright OECD. *Table 22.9:* Missale, *Public Debt Management.* 1999 Oxford University Press. Reprinted by permission of Oxford University Press.

Chapter 23 *Fig. 23.1:* Summers and Heston dataset, Penn World Tables 5.5, *http://www.nber.org*. *Fig. 23.2: OECD World Economic Outlook 2001.* Copyright OECD. *Figs. 23.3, 23.4, 23.10, 23.13, 23.14:* Thomson Financial Datastream. *Fig. 23.8: The Economist*, 13 March 1999, p. 162. © The Economist Newspaper Limited, London (1999). *Fig. 23.11* and *Tables 23.1, 23.2:* Maclennan, Muelbauer, and Stephens, "Asymmetries in Housing and Financial Market Institutions and EMU," CEPR Discussion Paper 2962 (1999). *Fig. 23.9 a & b:* © Brad Case, William N. Goetzmann, K. Geert Rouwenhorst, "Global Real Estate Markets: Cycles and Fundamentals," NBER Discussion Paper 7566 (February 2000). *Figs. 23.15, 23.16, 23.17, 23.18:* Caplin, Andrew, S. Chan & C. Freeman, *Housing Partnerships.* Copyright 1997 by MIT Press.

Chapter 24 *Fig. 24.1:* Authors' calculations based on OECD data. *Fig. 24.2:* InterSec Research Corp., London. *Table 24.1:* Reprinted from *Journal of Banking and Finance*, vol. 23, Berger et al., "The Consolidation of the Financial Services Industry," pp. 135–194 (1999), with permission from Elsevier Science. *Tables 24.2* and *24.4:* Federal Reserve Board of the U.S. *Figs. 24.3* and *24.6:* Data from International Monetary Fund. Courtesy of IMF. *Tables 24.5* and *24.7:* Takeo Hoshi and Anil Kashyap, "The Japanese Banking Crisis: Where Did It Come from and How Will It End?" *NBER Macroeconomics Annual*, 14 (1999), pp. 129–212. © 1999 by the National Bureau of Economic Research and the Massachusetts Institute of Technology. *Table 24.6:* Bank for International Settlements, *Consolidated International Banking Statistics*, May 31, 1999; and International Monetary Fund, *International Financial Statistics, 2000.* *Figs. 24.7* and *24.8:* Thomson Financial Datastream.

Note: *n* = footnotes or source notes, *t* = tabular information and *f* = illustrations.